"Our Father"
The Lord's Prayer for Our Persecutors

The most popular prayer in the world could be our strongest conflict management tool when used to pray for our persecutors

Charles L. Manto
www.LordsPrayer.world

Westphalia Press
An Imprint of the Policy Studies Organization
Washington, DC

Our Father

All Rights Reserved © 2021 by Policy Studies Organization

Westphalia Press
An imprint of Policy Studies Organization
1527 New Hampshire Ave., NW
Washington, D.C. 20036
info@ipsonet.org

ISBN: 978-1-63391-924-2

Daniel Gutierrez-Sandoval, Executive Director
PSO and Westphalia Press

Updated material and comments on this edition
can be found at the Westphalia Press website:
www.westphaliapress.org

"Chuck Manto has brought together new insights about the Sermon on the Mount. He points out that one of the most important is how Christ looks at relationships. He emphasizes how the Sermon on the Mount highlights the way we should treat one another. As a pastoral counselor I realize the importance of loving communities and relationships. Too often people are divided. Chuck Manto shows how Jesus' emphasis on peace is important for us all. By highlighting the importance of the Lord's Prayer, Chuck shows how the Lord's Prayer is a very good way to begin pastoral counseling sessions. Too often, people neglect the meaning of the prayer and merely repeat it without acknowledging what it really means. Unfortunately, people too often engage in debate and disregard the needs of the other person. We often do not listen. Chuck Manto's practical scholarship shows the importance of listening to the needs of others. In short, I highly recommend this book to you. It left me with important insights that I can use in my own life and with my clients."

> **John Belcher, Ph.D.**, Professor, pastoral counselor, University of Maryland School of Social Work. MDiv, Lexington Theological Seminary, MSW, University of Kentucky, Ph.D., Ohio State University

"This book had its origins in the exegetical insight that the Lord's prayer in Matthew is set in the context of Jesus' teaching about loving enemies. As sometimes happens, this new perception of the prayer opens a window of new possibilities. Breathing this fresh air of Jesus' approach to peace-making is an invitation to new ways of prayer and of action in relation to personal and corporate conflicts. It is a discovery of hidden treasure."

> **Thomas E. Boomershine, Ph.D.** Founder of Network of Biblical Storytellers International, Founder and Past Chair of the SBL Bible in Ancient and Modern Media Seminar/Section, and Professor Emeritus of New Testament and of Christianity and Communications at United Theological Seminary in Dayton, Ohio. His recent books include: The Messiah of Peace.

"I believe Charles Manto's work on Christ's Sermon on the Mount will quickly become a seminal teaching tool. Chuck's pastoral and counseling background, the use of primary materials and his language skills, makes this manual an important and effective instructional resource for scholars and teachers. I am confident that religious scholars and pastors of all backgrounds and traditions working in conflict resolution and mediation will welcome this significant and new instructional manual."

> **David E. Cassens, MA, MLIS**, Dean of Libraries, Pius XII Memorial Library, Saint Louis University

"There are sometimes lakes in the high mountains, it is said, whose water is so pure that the lakes become super cooled without freezing until someone throws a rock and the lake turns to crystal. Having read and appreciated the Sermon on the Mount and the Lord's Prayer thousands of times, I thought that I knew the pure waters of those words. Reading Chuck Manto's new book on the Sermon on the Mount, however, crystalized a thought pattern for me. And the stone thrown in was the word "our." "Who is 'our' in the sentence beginning 'Our father'?" Chuck asks. And the answer, which entails breaking the artificial bounds of chapter breaks inserted into the original texts of the gospels is simply fascinating. Chuck's book is mind-altering and ministers to those of us who struggle with our histories and our rage and seek some solace, maybe a paradigm shift will work."

> **William H. (Bill) Dannenmaier, CEO**, BlackBox Partners, US Navy Vet, MA, MBA, PMP

"Charles Manto has produced here a rich resource book for peace-making on a very practical level. A central theme of Manto's book is that the Lord's Prayer, examined through solid scholarly analysis in the context of the Sermon on the Mount in Matthew, can discern Jesus' peace-teaching and open up modern people of faith to interactive engagement and reconciliation with enemies. On the scholarly side, and with convincing originality, Manto studies patterns in the Sermon on the Mount that show how love of enemies is linked rhetorically with the Lord's Prayer; as well, the Sermon is addressed to the crowds to convey Jesus' intent to make all disciples devoted to peace. On the practical side, the book offers guiding questions and practical examples from workshops that demonstrate how modern prayer practice based upon understanding the Lord's Prayer as a reconciliation prayer can achieve constructive responses and results. Following the lead of Matthew's Jesus, Manto advocates an interactive prayer-process to learn peace-making and to create peacemakers, wherein prayer linked with love for enemies overcomes enmity and brings genuine reconciliation. This book offers a unique slant on the meaning of the Great Commission of Matthew 28, to teach peace to all the nations.

> **Douglas E. Oakman, Ph.D.** is Professor of New Testament at Pacific Lutheran University in Tacoma Washington. He is author of Palestine in the Time of Jesus (2008), Jesus and the Peasants (2008), The Political Aims of Jesus (2012), Jesus, Debt, and the Lord's Prayer (2014), and The Radical Jesus, the Bible, and the Great Transformation (2021). Oakman was a founding member of the Context Group and has been Chair of Religion and Dean of Humanities. He is an ordained pastor in the Evangelical Lutheran Church.

"Every now and then one comes across a contemporary Christian who takes a deeper dive than the average bear into the heart of Jesus' teaching. Chuck Manto has taken his early inspiration from the Sermon on the Mount and turned it into a lifetime of study and reflection on the Lord's Prayer as a prayer for peacemakers. I have found his reflections inspiring and helpful in my own pastoral work, both in teaching about the prayer from this perspective, and utilizing the prayer in pastoral care and counseling. May the voice of the Prince of Peace continue to be heard as we wrestle with his call to live in peace in our own time and at peace with our own enemies."

> **The Reverend Doctor Stephen P. Verkouw** is senior pastor at Grace Lutheran Church in Lancaster, Pennsylvania.

"Our Father" The Lord's Prayer for Our Persecutors
Linking Jesus' Prayer Request to the Crowds with the "Our Father"
A Resource Book for the Lord's Prayer in Matthew

In Partial Fulfillment of B-302/B-302-B New Testament Exegesis: The Gospel of Matthew

Bethany Theological Seminary

By Charles L. Manto

(Email: chuckLmanto@gmail.com)

410-991-1469

Intended audience: This collaborative resource book is intended for a broad range of those interested in studying the Lord's Prayer as it appears in Matthew Chapter 6 in its context of Matthew 5-7. Classes I taught, such as those transcribed in the appendix, have always had a mix of adults ranging from little biblical background to doctoral degrees. Those with extensive backgrounds in anthropological, biblical, economic, historical, legal, linguistic, performance, political, project management and quality management, rhetoric, psychological, legal, or sociological studies and the arts have participated bringing their interests, life experience and expertise to these texts and related study groups. I continue to learn much from them and my friends who discuss and reach each other's works. Much of the material here provides examples of interactive discussions and studies, whether community Bible studies or models for skits that can be modified by readers as conflict resolution simulations for their own purposes. This approach to the Lord's Prayer, as in a related treatment on the "beatitudes" in Matthew 5, provides a step-by-step approach to anger and conflict management designed to assist in "disciple-making." Participants are encouraged to share experiences with each other and interact through websites such as www.LordsPrayer.world.

Matthew 5:1-2 Seeing the **crowds**, he went up on the mountain, and when he sat down his **disciples** came to him. And he opened his mouth and **taught them** saying…

Matthew 5:44-45 But I say to you, love your enemies and **pray for those who persecute you**, so that you may be sons of your Father who is in heaven; for he makes his sun rise on the evil and on the good, and sends rain on the just and the unjust.

Matthew 6:9-15 Pray then like this: Our Father who art in heaven, Hallowed be thy name, Thy kingdom come, Thy will be done, On earth as it is in heaven. Give us this day our daily bread, and forgive us our debts, As we have forgiven our debtors; And lead us not into temptation, But deliver us from evil. For if you forgive men their trespasses, your heavenly Father also will forgive you; but if you do not forgive men their trespasses, neither will your Father forgive your trespasses.

Matthew 7:28-29 And when Jesus finished these sayings, **the crowds were astonished** at his teaching, for he taught them as one who had authority, and not as their scribes.

(From the Revised Standard Version, Oxford University Press, New York, London, 1965)

Permission for citations and photos as cited within include:

American Bible Society: *Contemporary English Version (Into the Light)* (CEV) American Bible Society (Contact Details as for *Good News Bible*); *Acknowledgement*: From the *Contemporary English Version* New Testament © American Bible Society 1991, 1992, 1995. Used with permission/Anglicizations © British & Foreign Bible Society 1996.; Good News Bible (GNB)*Acknowledgement*: From the *Good News Bible* published by the Bible Societies and HarperCollins Publishers, © American Bible Society 1994, used with permission. Good News Translation ® (Today's English Version, Second Edition) © 1992 American Bible Society. All rights reserved.

Bible text from the Good News Translation (GNT) is not to be reproduced in copies or otherwise by any means except as permitted in writing by American Bible Society, 101 North Independence Mall East, FL 8, Philadelphia, PA 19106 (www.americanbible.org).

British Library Board: Photo of the page of Matthew 6:4 and following from Codex Sinaiticus © and licensed by The British Library Board (Codex Sinaiticus, http://www.bl.uk/manuscripts/Viewer.aspx?ref=add_ms_43725_f202v) licensed for reprinting to Charles Manto as in "Drivers" section and cover.

Confraternity of Christian Doctrine: Scripture texts in this work are taken from the *New American Bible with Revised New Testament and Revised Psalms* © 1991, 1986, 1970 Confraternity of Christian Doctrine, Washington, D.C. and are used by permission of the copyright owner. All Rights Reserved. No part of the *New American Bible* may be reproduced in any form without permission in writing from the copyright owner.

Darton, Longman &Todd Ltd *Acknowledgement*: Taken from *The Jerusalem Bible,* published and copyright 1966,1967 and 1968 by Darton, Longman &Todd Ltd and Doubleday and Co. Inc, and used by permission of the publishers. Taken from *The New Jerusalem Bible*, published and copyright 1985 by Darton, Longman & Todd Ltd and *Les Editions du Cerf*, and used by permission of the publishers.

German Bible Society, Deutsche Bibelgesellschaft: The Greek New Testament, Fifth Revised Edition, edited by Barbara Aland, Kurt Aland, Johannes Karavidopoulos, Carlo M. Martini, and Bruce M. Metzger in cooperation with the Institute for New Testament Textual Research, Münster/Westphalia, © 2014 Deutsche Bibelgesellschaft, Stuttgart. Used by permission.

Nestle-Aland, Novum Testamentum Graece, 28th Revised Edition, edited by Barbara and Kurt Aland, Johannes Karavidopoulos, Carlo M. Martini, and Bruce M. Metzger in cooperation with the Institute for New Testament Textual Research, Münster/Westphalia, © 2012 Deutsche Bibelgesellschaft, Stuttgart. Used by permission

International Bible Society: *New International Version (NIV)*. The NIV text may be quoted in any form (written, visual, electronic or audio), up to and inclusive of five hundred (500) verses, without express written permission of the Publisher, providing the verses quoted do not amount to a complete book of the Bible nor do the verses quoted account for 25 percent or more of the total text of the work in which they are quoted. *Acknowledgement*: Scripture quotations taken from the HOLY BIBLE, NEW INTERNATIONAL VERSION. Copyright © 1973, 1978, 1984 by International Bible Society. Used by permission of Hodder & Stoughton, a member of the Hodder Headline Group. All rights reserved. 'NIV' is a trademark of the International Bible Society. UK trademark number 1448790.

Laura James: Artwork of *Sermon on the Mount, Love One Another* ©Laura James, 2002 Licensed and used with permission. See https://www.laurajamesart.com

Andrew Kelly/ USNW: Photo of ancient clay tablet by permission of owner, Andrew Kelly/UNSW.

ScienceAlert: Article from ScienceAlert printed with permission: https://www.sciencealert.com/scientists-just-solved-a-maths-problem-on-this-3-700-year-old-clay-tablet.

Lockman Foundation: "Scripture quotations taken from the (NASB®) New American Standard Bible®, Copyright © 1960, 1971, 1977, 1995, 2020 by The Lockman Foundation. Used by permission. All rights reserved. www.lockman.org"

National Council of Churches in the USA, Division of Christian Education [Scripture quotations are] from *The Revised Standard Version of the Bible* copyright © 1946, 1952 and 1971 by the Division of Christian Education of the National Council of Churches in the USA. Used by permission. All Rights Reserved. [Scripture quotations are] from *The New Revised Standard Version of the Bible* copyright © 1989 by the Division of Christian Education of the National Council of Churches in the USA. Used by permission. All Rights Reserved.

OakTree Software, Inc.: Maps are from OakTree software from Accordance 13 © April 2021, licensed to Charles Manto and used with permission.

Table of Contents

Foreword from Brussels, Rwanda and Dallas, TX	p. ix
Preface: A Personal Note on Beating Up God in the Playground	p. xi

Section 1: Introduction:

Resource Book Roadmap and Class Outline	p. xiii
My Changing Attitude towards the Audience of the Prayer	p. 1
Reframing Matthew 6's Lord's Prayer in Light of Matthew 5	p. 5
Core Text Needing Exploration	p. 7
Benefits of Reframing & Sample User Comments	p. 10
Orientation: Approach, Background, Context, Drivers	p. 19
Approach	p. 19
Background (Author, Date, Locale, Social, Religious, Political)	p. 24
Context	p. 31
Drivers	p. 37
Context of the Lord's Prayer Text (with conflict matrix and map)	p. 40

Section 2: Commentary

Outline of Brief Commentary of 4:17-6:15	p. 45
Exegesis of Preceding Context 4:17-6:4	p. 47
Beatitudes	
4:17-25 Setting for the Lord's Prayer	p. 49
5:1-2 Who were the crowds?	p. 51
5:3-16 A Pair of Blessing Bookends, 3 Blessing Pairs between	p. 54
Antitheses	
5:17-32 Law Fulfilled with 2 Ancient Sayings & 3 Conflicts Each	p. 64
5:33-37 Significance of Oaths & Tie to Damages	p. 69
5:38-42 Connecting Conflicts and Chiasmus	p. 70
Prayer Request and the Connection to the Lord's Prayer	
5:43-48 Prayer Request for Persecutors	p. 75
6:1-4 Fastening the Lord's Prayer to Request & Beatitudes	p. 78
Exegesis of Microtext of Matthew 6:5-15	p. 82
6:5-8 Resuming prayer in the primary position	p. 82
6:9-10 Who is "Our," "Father." "Kingdom"?	p. 87
6:11 Give who? Give what?	p. 89
6:12-15 Two-variable agile prayer formula	p. 91
6:16-7:29 Complimentary material through 7:29	p. 98
Conclusion of the Lord's Prayer and 3 Conflict Prayers	p. 106

Ancient Use of Columns and Rows	p. 111
Overview of Interpretive Methods and Genre Analysis of Matthew	p. 112
Partially Annotated Bibliography	p. 118
Review of Three Commentaries: Betz, Davies and Allison, Luz	p. 154
Epilogue and Final Application Note	p. 160

Section 3: Appendix — p. 163

Limited Distribution Papers by Manto and Colleagues

Most of the following documents are examples of interactions regarding the Lord's Prayer in Matthew 5-7 showing how the material in Matthew 5-7 lends itself to interactive discussions. (Note that a Kindle version of this book can used as a search tool and index.)

- Summary of Audience and Mnemonics of the Sermon on the Mount, August 2014 presented to the Scholars Forum of the Network of Biblical Studies and discussed within the group—p. 163
- Draft publication for CC, "Who is the 'our' in the Our Father?" 2020 accepted for publication by *Christian Century* magazine—p.166
- Use of the Lord's Prayer for Persecutors by Dr. Verkouw in his Lenten series for his congregation in March 2020 and his email introduction of the material—p. 169
- Lord's Prayer Sermon by Dr. Laura Truax, Pastor, LaSalle Street Church, Chicago—p. 177
- Interactive Bible Study, Video Link & Transcript, Matthew 5; June 28, 2019 with commentary by Pastor Stahlberg on July 27, 2019—p. 182
- Interactive Bible Study, Video Link & Transcript, Matthew 6; June 29, 2019—p. 216
- Interactive Lord's Prayer Tandem-Preached Sermon, Video Link & Transcript, Dillon, CO; June 30, 2019—p. 249
- Interactive Discussion on Lord's Prayer for Enemies with Atlanta Lyft Driver from Nigeria, Video Link and Transcript; June 22, 2019—p. 259
- Lord's Prayer as Preparation for Meditation—p. 262
- "The Joke," Lord's Prayer Skit. Manto, 2017—p. 266
- Quick Overview of My Stake in Conflict Resolution *(response to request for author's background in conflicts)*—p. 280
- Discussion Questions Used in Body of Text—p. 287
- Letter Regarding Anger and Conflict Resolution from Reader—p. 291
- "Relationships Come First—Maslow's Hierarchy of Needs Contradicts the Facts of Human Existence"—p. 295
- Script without Spacing Exercise—p. 299
- Status of Global Christianity Charts—p. 301
- Bible Manuscript and Greek language resources—p. 302

Volume II	Study Guide (forthcoming)
Volume III	Alternative Texts (forthcoming)
Volume IV	Prayer Journal (forthcoming)

Foreword from Brussels, Dallas and Rwanda

From Brussels: As former Provost and Chair of the Biblical and Systematic Theology department at Trinity Evangelical Divinity School, I have worked with leading New Testament scholars and theologians. You might think there is not much new to be said about the Lord's Prayer and the Sermon on the Mount. So much has been written! But as the famous Mayflower pilgrim John Robinson said so marvelously, "I am verily persuaded the Lord hath more truth yet to break forth out of His Holy Word."

So, I'm delighted to see how Chuck Manto has brought insights from his research in the use of rhetoric in the Sermon on the Mount to reveal the primary conflict management role of the Lord's Prayer for the crowds - and not just the disciples. This is a major contribution to our understanding of the very first word of the prayer, "our" as the Father of "me and the one with whom I am in conflict". It's a path to revisit the use of the prayer in our lives, including the teaching of the Sermon on the Mount as a whole. Mr. Manto also proposes that the Matthean community advocated this use of conflict management to attract new disciples which starts with listening to the needs of others rather than debating. In a time when civil discourse and religion can be exceedingly divisive, it is so timely that this approach has been brought to our attention. Read the so-familiar words of the Lord's Prayer afresh. Let them bring peace into the relationships and conflicts we engage every day. Here's a rich resource book that will richly repay our study.

> **Nigel M. de S. Cameron, PhD, BA, MA,** Emmanuel College, University of Cambridge, BD, PhD, University of Edinburgh. In the 1990s, he served as Distinguished Professor of Theology and Culture at Trinity Evangelical Divinity School and was first Provost of Trinity International University. His most recent books are *Will Robots Take Your Job? A Plea for Consensus* (Polity/Wiley, 2017), and *The Robots are Coming*. He represented the United States on delegations to the United Nations General Assembly and UNESCO and been a participant in the U.S./EU dialogue Perspectives on the Future of Science and Technology.

From Rwanda and Dallas, TX: Before my interactions with Chuck Manto on the topic of forgiveness from the perspective of the Lord's Prayer, I had not realized this powerful tool for forgiveness and reconciliation of enmities that Christ has given to his disciples for meaningful and fruitful daily living in the midst of suffering persecutions of all kinds. Christ teaches us that only daily forgiveness can sustain our daily communal life in our crooked and cruel society with those who hate, persecute, and malign us, just like our daily bread will sustain our physical bodies. For Christ, our daily healthy relationships are sustained by the daily practice of granting and receiving forgiveness. Through this incredible practical study of the Lord's Prayer for our persecutors and tormentors, Mr. Manto brings out the best of Christian witness and Christian living that has been ignored over years. The Lord's Prayer is not meant just for reciting, it is meant for empowering anyone how to love not only their neighbors as themselves but to love those neighbors even when those neighbors are the persecutors or murderers of one's family or friends. This is my prayer and commitment: "Oh merciful, compassionate, and forgiving God, teach me how to forgive so I can sincerely and humbly come into your presence and dare say to you: 'Forgive me my sins as I forgive those who sin against me.' Give me the strength to let go of grudges, bitterness, anger and vengeful thoughts and actions. Help me to love genuinely and speak kindly to those who have been cruel and rude to me. And when I have means, help me to feed their families, husbands, wives, and children. Amen."

> **Rev. Celestin Musekura, Ph.D.**, President & CEO, ALARM USA, Founder & Global Ambassador, ALARM Africa, Co-author of *FORGIVING As We've Been FORGIVEN, Community Practices for Making Peace* Website: www.alarm-inc.org

Preface

Beating Up God on the Playground—The Problem of Bullies

My first interest in loving enemies arose from a richly imagined event when I was twelve years old: beating up God on the playground. Although raised in Chicago as a secular child, from time to time, if I wanted to play with a childhood friend on a Sunday, his parents might give permission as long as I went to Sunday School first. That is where I first learned stories of Jesus speaking the Sermon on the Mount.

Between 5th and 6th grade, another neighborhood church was holding Vacation Bible School (VBS). We learned how to operate wood working equipment for part of the time and were taught Bible lessons the rest of the time. A woman in our Northside apartment building heard me being invited to VBS and asked if I had a Bible. I said "no," so she offered me hers. I accepted her Bible—with the words of Jesus in red. I knew the Bible was an important book. It looked like a lot of reading, but now I could just read the red words, get the basic ideas and save time.

Many of the teachings impressed me. Why gain the whole world if you lose your own soul? Better to go cut off a hand or pluck out an eye if they cause you to sin and go wounded into heaven than go whole into hell. I understood the idea of priorities but was a little concerned that I might run out of body parts. The teaching that impressed me most was the idea of turning the other cheek. Experiencing the nuisance of a group of bullies from an early age, I learned quickly that you either had to take out the leader, talk your way out of it, or cut and run. I wasn't fast enough to run. Was it possible to be both loving enough and tough enough to look the bully in the eye and turn the other cheek? No one, in my experience, did that.

By 7th and 8th grade, some friends in school asked me to join them in winter softball games. They explained that a church had a gym where we could play for free. However, we were required to listen to Bible stories and learn Bible verses. That seemed a bit odd but, in view of my prior experiences at Sunday School and VBS, it was probably safe. So, I went. There we learned the verses that talked about how much God loved us and sent his son to die for us. He loved us when we could care less and even went to the cross on our behalf.

I went home and started to think about what all these different teachings might mean. I imagined being a playground bully at my northside elementary school, Louisa May Alcott. I approached a boy and began to push him around, knock him down, slap him around, make him cry and about the time I was raising my fist to smack him in the face, he kindly looked me straight in the eye and turned his cheek. At that moment, I realized the kid I was bullying was God sneaking into the world as a little boy and I was in big trouble. God could obviously beat me up, and everyone else in the playground, the city or the planet for that matter. In fact, the infinite One could snap his fingers and restart the multiverse if he chose to do so. The infinite One was allowing me, the infinitesimal one to hit him; and what little power I had was given by him. To make matters worse, the one with all the power was 100% in the right and I was 100% in the wrong.

In that moment, I felt that I stumbled across the largest love model possible. No one could be more powerful than the infinite God and no one smaller than a dependent infinitesimal me. No one could be more right than 100% or more wrong than 100%. I was immediately impressed because not only did we face the nuisance of bullies in 1964-1965, but we also faced the threat of nuclear war. We watched science movies about nuclear weapons and were taught to look for fallout shelters on the walk home. There might not be time to get home once we heard the air raid sirens. I thought that if everyone could take this idea of love seriously, it might keep us from destroying each other.

Might there be a more compelling model? The only thing more powerful would be if the model were true. But how would I find proof? No amount of time and education would produce enough data and analysis. Empirical research seemed hopeless. Then, I thought more about it and realized the people who wrote these stories were pretty smart and that God was smarter and kinder. And at that moment it dawned on me that it would be just like God to love so completely. It would not surprise me at all that God would come into the world as a little boy and turn his cheek for me, even on a cross. That was when I prayed and asked the Father to forgive and accept me—not because I deserved it, was better or smarter than anyone else but only because Jesus turned his cheek for me on the cross. Since then, I have been captivated by this conflict-resolution model and continue to learn more as I contemplate these chapters in Matthew. This is what drove me to write this guide and encourage readers to find ways to interact with each other on these texts in the near future.

The *"Our Father"* Resource Book Roadmap

This resource book provides material in three sections: An Introduction, a Commentary, and an Appendix.

The Introduction provides an orientation to the approach used to study Matthew 5-7 (the Sermon on the Mount) with a focus on the Lord's Prayer. It helps to review this section to see how strong the links are between the request to love enemies and pray for persecutors in Matthew 5:44 and the Lord's Prayer in Matthew 6:5-15, highlighting the embedded use of ancient persuasion and memory techniques in predominantly oral communication methods in its historical context.

The Commentary section begins with the background of the Sermon on the Mount at Matthew 4:12. But, the material is arranged so that a student can begin at any point whether there or at Matthew 5:1 the beginning of the Sermon on the Mount passage; or the request to pray in Matthew 5:44; or Matthew 6:1 where the linkage to the Lord's Prayer is made; or, in Matthew 6:5 where discussion on prayer is picked up again. The conclusion includes a short integration with the rest of Matthew 6-7 in the context of Matthew that could be continued in a later study of the Sermon on the Mount as a whole. The text is provided in columns including the oldest Greek texts, two different English versions with some notes by the author and what might be added by the reader. The Greek text will make it easier for those wanting to become familiar with Greek and the patterns that appear there.

The Commentary section includes an annotated bibliography and a couple of short essays that round out the combined material of the introduction commenting on its "genre" and the commentary including perspectives on three commentaries.

The Appendix section provides additional material such as a transcript of an interactive Bible study of the author with a group of about 25, a template for a skit that students might use to write their own conflict skit involving the Lord's Prayer, and other interactive sources including conversations, sermons, and writings. It also mentions that the electronic Kindle version of this work is being offered in lieu of an index so that the text and its hyperlinks can be interactive.

The following outline using this material can be adapted for a five or ten-session class linking some of the introductory and appendix material with specific texts in the commentary of Matthew.

Suggested Class Outline for the *"Our Father"*—*Lord's Prayer for Our Persecutors*
In 5-10 Sessions
In the Context of Matthew 4:12-8:1

Discussion Introduction: This is an overview of each of the five sessions covering the Lord's Prayer in Matthew 6 showing "how" one would "pray for persecutors" as requested in Matthew 5:44. This is designed either to be an online or blended online and in-person group. While no preparation is needed, each session has an overview with recommended readings within the core commentary section of the resource book, *Our Father -- The Lord's Prayer for Our Persecutors,* by Charles Manto. There is additional material in the introduction and in the appendix that will allow a participant to go into as little or as much detail as desired. Additional material is planned to be placed at www.LordsPrayer.world. Groups can choose to do this in a set of five sessions where each is done in one sitting (likely an hour or an hour and a half), or each session can be split up into two or more segments to allow for more discussion. It is recommended that each section of Matthew be read aloud at the beginning of each discussion to replicate the experience of the initial audience.

Additional resources: See the fill-in-the-blank prayer-template and other resources at www.LordsPrayer.world .

First session overview: The first session will provide an overview of the audience of the Lord's Prayer and its role in the Sermon on the Mount and in the Gospel of Matthew as a whole. This material will explore an alternative way to engage those suffering, in conflict and anxious or angry about something through a concept of "fishing lessons" promised in Matthew 4:19. The session will explore the persuasive rhetorical role of these methods embodied in the written material of Matthew 5-7 as scripts to be memorized then shared orally with others. (The typical debate or recruiting method often comes across as judgmental, opposite of advice in Matthew 7:1-6.)

1) **Reading material:** This will cover the audience and stated purpose of the material:

    a) **Matthew 4:12-5:2, 7:1-6, 28-8:1** and commentary section of 4:12-5:2.
    b) **Introduction**: Read "Reframing Matthew 6's Lord's Prayer in Light of Matthew 5". It is recommended to scan the entirety of Matthew 5-8:1 and the resource book. If possible, read the title page, table of contents, preface, and introduction through Orientation through the background section.
    c) **Appendix:** Read the essay, "Overview of Interpretive Methods and Genre Analysis of Matthew" just prior to the appendix. See also the transcripts of interactive Bible study in CO and notes about the author in the biographical section.

Second session overview: The primary focus will be the beatitude section that includes the salt and light declarations. Evidence will be presented for the organization of the beatitudes as four pairs instead of two groups of four and how they relate to those not yet disciples.

2) **Reading material**: for the beatitude pairs and connection to salt:

    a) **Matthew 5:3-16** and commentary section of 5:3-16.
    b) **Introduction**: Read Orientation and its sections on Conflicts and Drivers.
    c) **Appendix:** Read "Summary and Audience and Mnemonics" oral presentation to Scholars Forum, NBTSI, Dec. 2014; "Letter regarding anger and conflict resolution".

Third Session Overview: This covers the claim that entry to the kingdom of heaven requires exceeding the justice of the scribes and Pharisees. This section covers legal issues and conflicts showing rhetorical drivers to the goal of loving enemies and praying for persecutors. See the role of anger in chapter 5, both within the listener and one taking the listener to court. How might the "out of court settlement" in chapter 5 set the stage for forgiveness later in chapter 6? Compare that to the request to not resist evil but to turn the other cheek, etc. Note the phrase "justice must exceed that of …" and the use of "justice" in the previous section of 5:6 and 5:10, and the following "Antitheses" section "You heard it was said, but I say…" Note the contrasts of you "heard" "but I say". See also the range of conflicts covered in 5:39-42, setting up the significance of the prayer for persecutors.

3) **Reading material:** The Lord's Prayer for persecutors:

    a) **Matthew 5:17-49** and its commentary section of 5:17-49.
    b) **Introduction:** Read the introduction section on the "Core Text Needing Exploration"
    c) **Appendix:** Read the transcribed Bible study in CO in 2019 for an interactive discussion about audience and beatitudes.

Fourth Session Overview: Note the connections between the request to love and pray for enemies in 5:44 and the prayer section in 6:5-15. Note the connections in reverse order as a chiasmus between the turn the other cheek section in 5:39-42 and the "we" petitions of the Lord's Prayer in 6:11-13. See the emotional anger and conflict management escalation between the elements of the Lord's Prayer and how it mirrors the same in the beatitude pairs. See how the two variables within the prayer can be applied to each of the conflicts of the turn-the-other-cheek section. Discuss prayer scenarios from various conflicts outlined in Matthew 5:38-42 which link to the "we-petitions" of Matthew 6:11-13. Consider the chiasmus between the two sections and the data compression method used to maximize the flexible application of the prayer to various conflicts. The discussion can cover examples of how the prayer might be used for different conflicts throughout the day that can be used to construct personal prayer journals or prepare for meditation.

4) **Reading Material:** The transition and the pattern showing "how" to pray for persecutors.
   a) **Matthew 6:1-34.** Note ties between "pray for persecutors" in **Matthew 5:43-48** and "Lord's Prayer in **Matthew 6:5-15**. See commentary section from Matthew 6:1- conclusion.
   b) **Introduction:** Read "Context of the Lord's Prayer as Script" and accompanying tables.
   c) **Appendix:** Read the *Christian Century* article, letters from readers, use of prayer three times a day and for meditation.

Fifth Session Overview and Review: This session will compare three conflict prayers in Matthew, review the material and cover additional questions and possible next steps and interactions after these sessions. Compare the Lord's Prayer in Matthew 6:5-15; the "ask, seek, and knock" prayer in Matthew 7:7-12; and the reconciliation prayer in Matthew 18:15-20. Note the reciprocity elements in each of the prayers of Matthew 6, 7 and 18 along with the story of the unforgiving servant in Matthew 18:23-35. What might be the connections between the prayers in Matthew 6 & 7 along with the request to not judge and not try to win people through debate? As time permits, class participants can offer examples of how the prayer might be used for different conflicts throughout the day. Discuss how these might be used to reduce anger, anxiety, and grief. Discuss any questions from all sessions.

5) **Reading Material:** Comparing the three prayers and their roles in defining forgiveness.

   a) **Matthew 7:1-8:1 and 18:1-35.**
   b) **Introduction:** Read "Benefits" section and letters in the introduction section and the "Unforgiving and Half-forgiving Servant" section at the end of the conclusion section.
   c) **Appendix:** Read the Lord's Prayer as Preparation for Meditation, "The Joke", Lord's Prayer Skit Kit and peruse the annotated bibliography.

Section 1: Introduction

The Railroad to Personal Discovery

In 2004, I was doing a daily commute from Annapolis to DC where I drove halfway to the end of the Metro line at New Carrolton and took the train the rest of the way to an office in the Navy Yard neighborhood. While driving in, I was trying to think of a way to make good use of the time on the train when I heard a challenge on National Public Radio by a guest claiming that those learning languages and music improved their aging brains. So, I thought of the passages in Matthew chapters 5-7 that dared us to turn the other cheek and love enemies and thought that is what I could do on the train ride. I could memorize all of Matthew 5-7 in the ancient Greek I learned in college and set it to music.

As I looked at this passage beginning with eight to ten blessings, I felt that I could memorize three or four of them, but eight seemed a bit too much. And they were only the first third of the first of three chapters. Suddenly, I remembered how awful my rote memory was and how little patience I had for it. So, instead of trying to memorize them, I looked first for patterns that might make it easier to remember. That was actually more interesting.

I got lucky since the first thing I noticed while glancing over the passage was that only two of the blessings had the phrase, "theirs is the kingdom of heaven". And they were the first and the eighth with six blessings in between. If I could figure out what made those bookends a pair, then, maybe the six in between might be three pairs. Three pairs of something in common would be easier to remember then six without something in common. Then I wondered whether those pairs were arranged in some meaningful order that would make the sequence easier to remember. Once I discovered the pairs and the purpose behind their sequencing, then the whole section would be easier to remember.

Discovering this made it easier to see why these words and phrases were chosen in that order. It not only made it easier to make sense of the material but made it easier to follow and made it easier to memorize without mechanical repetition. When combined with the unusual claims Jesus made, that the good news was that the people on the bottom were really at the top, these blessings showed what Jesus did to command attention and foster retention. Then it made sense to see why listeners were able to follow what he said, comprehend his message and declare at the end of Matthew chapter 7 that they never heard someone speak with such "authority". The crowds could not forget what he said, even if they wanted to. Later, this made it easier for those who may have been literate 2,000 years ago, but too poor to take the scrolls home, to read or hear someone read the material written by Matthew where the scrolls were held, intentionally memorize it without a lot of difficulty, then recall to study them at home later and recite or explain it to others.

Only after paying attention to how to memorize these texts without mechanical repetition[1] and asking why certain words were used and why one phrase was next to another, did I then begin to notice *patterns* that I overlooked previously. Then, I began to notice more about the audience within the text as I joined them in trying to hear, memorize and recite even just portions of the text. In turn, I started paying more attention to how these texts would impact listeners of that day, in particular the listeners within the "crowds."

Asking how these passages affected the crowds led to a series of related questions. How could it be that the crowds, not just the disciples, were already blessed, declared to be salt and light and encouraged to pray for their persecutors in Chapter 5?[2]

---

[1] Throughout this work, I often use the word "memorize" as the end result and not the repetitive rote process assumed by many. See the quote of Kelber by Baukham on p. 283, *Jesus and the Eye Witnesses*, distinguishing between mnemonics and memorization and Baukham's comment, on p. 281: "memorization would not always entail completely verbatim learning by rote, but some degree of memorization was indispensable to any deliberate attempt to learn and transmit tradition faithfully."

[2] See Ben Witherington's *Matthew*, p. 123 describing "salt and light, the character of the disciples". Craig Keener in The Gospel of Matthew,

While noticing how these passages were put together to be memorized and repeated orally, I discovered *connections* that I overlooked previously. One of the most interesting was the request by Jesus to love enemies and pray for persecutors in Matthew 5:44 followed by the details of the Lord's Prayer in Matthew 6:5-15. The only thing separating those two sections was a memory device that weaved them together in 6:1-4. These connections are described in detail later. The consequences were unexpected for me.

For starters, this changed the way I could interpret the contextual definition of "our" and "Father" in the first two words of the Lord's Prayer. If I were a person in the crowd who was asked to pray alone, as the instructions explicitly require before the Lord's Prayer begins in 6:9, then why would Jesus ask me to say, "our Father" instead of "my Father"? I often assumed that "our" made sense in that context because I usually recited the prayer in a group leading me to assume it was the Father of me and the others praying with me. But, in the context of 6:6 where Jesus asked the crowds to pray alone, I had to consider that it meant something else to those listeners. On further reflection, I could have thought that "our" referred to the Father "of me and all other believers whether they were praying with me or not. Or, I might have thought "our" Father could refer to "me and all of creation." Perhaps, the Father "of me and Jesus." There are only so many possible ways to interpret that word "our" and any one of them may be reasonable for the Lord's Prayer outside the context of Matthew.

Only after seeing the reinforced connection of the prayer in chapter 6 with the request to pray for the persecutors in 5:44 —"*but I tell you, love your enemies and pray for those who persecute you…*" — did I finally consider that the one definition of "our" that I had missed was the one explicitly mentioned in the text. (See the discussion in the commentary section and papers included as exhibits for more details.) That was the option where I, a member of the crowd (in 5:1 and 7:28), was asked to pray for my persecutor (in 5:44) and do it alone (in 6:6) starting with the words "our Father" (in 6:9). In other words, "our Father" was defined by the context as "the Father of 'me and my persecutor.'" That in turn helped me understand all the other plurals such as "our necessary bread" which became the necessity that I and the persecutor(s) were fighting over. It also helped me see that forgiveness had something to do with that conflict. This opened an entirely different perspective on each of the elements of the Lord's Prayer and all that led to it from the beginning of the Sermon on the Mount.

These insights caused me to reconsider the purpose of the Lord's Prayer in Matthew and its similarity to the other conflict prayers of Matthew 7 and Matthew 18. The purpose includes its intended use as a conflict management, anxiety, or anger management prayer, along with its role in the recruitment and development of new disciples promised in 4:19 and at the end of the Gospel in 28:18-20.

But, not needing those memory devices now, commentators typically don't see that link between the request to pray for persecutors through the end of chapter 5 and the Lord's Prayer section beginning in 6:5. Instead, commentators apparently assume that Jesus changed the topic in 6:1 when talking about almsgiving and public displays of righteousness or justice. Once I noticed that link between the prayer request in 5:44 and the prayer in 6:9-13, it appeared that the most popular prayer in the world might just be the strongest conflict management tool as the prayer for persecutors. Perhaps, by reconsidering these texts through the pages that follow and how they were presented to their original audiences, you might draw similar conclusions. If you agree, perhaps you might be able to work with friends and colleagues to see how the Lord's Prayer could be used in the conflicts that you face.

Resource and Relationship Resilience

Forgiving or releasing a debt assumes there is a loss or anticipated loss. Matthew's description of Jesus asking the crowd to love their enemies and pray for the worst-case persecutors speaks to these losses. Listeners who pray the Lord's Prayer for their worst-case opponents see their heavenly Father's release of their debts[3] as something that

---

p. 165, shows how several scholars look at the crowds who were there as "potential disciples" quoting Daniel Patte, but not with a message crafted to them as crowd members prior to being disciples. Dale Allison views the crowds as a substantial part of the audience. See his *The Sermon on the Mount*, p. 9.

3   The detail that follows explores ancient economies and the role of debt and conflict, especially in the works of Douglas Oakman referenced

would motivate the listeners' release of their debtors. As the book of Matthew develops in Chapters 24 and 25, it becomes clear that this concept of love is encouraged even in the worst of times when manmade and natural disasters cause the love of most to grow cold. Loss and debts will only grow as resources such as food, water, clothing, shelter diminish and many will be blamed for it and as a result will be persecuted, imprisoned, and executed—betrayed even by family and fellow church members (Matthew 10:21-22; 24:9-11).

My professional life in the last couple of decades has been focused on emergency and disaster planning for even the most extreme cases when these resources become scarce.[4] In a world where we have maximized efficiency by minimizing resiliency, we have become increasingly dependent on the remote resources of highly efficient centralized systems such as power and communications that are fragile and dependent on each other. As a result, we have minimized our ability to help ourselves and our neighbors in widespread long-term losses of these essential services such as power, communications, water, food, healthcare and so on. Most are not yet aware that we could lose these resources for months due to causes ranging from climate change, extreme space weather, cyber-attack, coordinated physical attacks, or high-altitude nuclear explosions causing land based infrastructure failure due to its electromagnetic pulse.[5] However, when communities can plan for worst-case scenarios of infrastructure and resource loss, they can become more resilient for lesser case scenarios and problems they might not have anticipated.[6] Those who examine worst-case disaster planning scenarios realize the importance of building greater ability for local communities and families to become more resilient even if it costs more to do so.

In the same way, being able to love and pray for the worst-case opponents in the worst of times will make it easier to love and pray in less difficult times. If we can find the supernatural love that will compel us to love others when the world around us looks like it is coming to an end and the love of most will grow cold, then we may also find the love to keep us strong when misunderstandings or disappointments cause others to "fall out of love" with us and we face the end of a relationship, or, the loss of a job. Either way, resource and relationship resilience arise from the joy and cost of persistent love.

Matthew shows a link between paying the price of forgiving a debt as our heavenly Father does for us and our own work of forgiving our debtors. That is the work of God as a peacemaker in our lives and the subsequent work of a peacemaker that we are encouraged to do. This works whether we are reacting to a loss someone caused us or a loss we willingly take on to provide the resources someone else needs at our cost, whether those resources are food, water, clothing, shelter, or support while in prison. The inclusion of visiting someone in prison may seem like an odd thing to include in this list for modern readers. But it represented the worst-case scenario for most two thousand years ago who faced the loss of all these things as they fell into debt they could not pay and were sent to prison to come up with the funds or be sold into slavery[7]. Debtors were not sent to prison to be warehoused but to dispose of their debts step by step until the entire debt was met or the debtor and family were sold into slavery.

This study also made me reconsider whether I have personally been applying these concepts of forgiveness and rec-

---

throughout and in the annotated bibliography.

4   See *Resilient Hospitals Handbook* by Manto, Dr. Terbush and Dr. Motzer. Westphalia Press, 2017. https://asprtracie.hhs.gov/technical-resources/resource/5609/resilient-hospitals-handbook-strhening-healthcare-and-public-health-resilience-in-advance-of-a-prolonged-and-widespread-power-outage . See the patents by Manto for mitigation measures listed in the bibliography under Manto and Soysal. For additional information see the LinkedIn profile for Charles Manto.

5   See leading experts from government and industry speak on these topics at annual conferences co-sponsored by the Policy Studies Organization and the FBI led by the InfraGard National Disaster Resilience Council in five of the conference proceedings under the title, *High Impact Threats to Critical Infrastructure*. Each conference proceedings, edited by Manto and Lokmer, have bibliography that include weblinks to the conferences and many of the bibliographical references. See also the articles in the bibliography by Manto in the INCOSE journal *Insight*, and *DomPrep Journal* of DomesticPreparedness.com on various mega-disaster mitigation and planning scenarios from engineering and emergency planning perspectives.

6   See examples of community resilience dividends in *The Resilience Dividend* by Judith Rodin.

7   See examples of selling off children or mothers to cover debt and examples of debt forgiveness in Michael Hudson's work, *... and forgive them their debts*, by ISLET-Verlag, Dresden, 2018. P.59 shows the role of interest in debt attested as early as 6,000 BC and noteworthy debt forgiveness restoring families in 2400 BC on p. 77.

onciliation in my personal relationships. Given my tendencies to avoid conflict and either agree to or rush to premature solutions, I have fallen short of a full restoration of a relationship. Items in the texts of Matthew provide objective measures that can help us calibrate how complete our communication and reconciliation efforts are and provide basic suggestions about how to go about it. The prayers of Matthew and their embedded concepts of forgiveness and restoration influenced me to reflect on how my desire for God's love and restoration can be replicated in my own relationships. This became the bottom line for me as I wrote the conclusion section to the reflections on the Lord's Prayer in Matthew 6. I trust that readers who take the time to work through this material will come to their own conclusions and work with trusted friends and their study groups to do the same.

Using This Resource Material in a Study Group

This material is organized so that someone might go directly to the section on the Lord's Prayer in Matthew 6:5-15. But, since the link to the request to pray is so strong and strengthened in what appears to many as a break between the request beginning in 5:44 and the prayer material in 6:5-15, it may help to start either in Matthew 6:1, or the section beginning in Matthew 5:44 where the section on prayer begins. However, those same links tie back to what should be done in the presence of people versus what should not be done before people all the way back to the beatitudes in 5:1. For that reason, it is recommended to begin with the context just prior to 5:1 and work through the related elements to the Lord's Prayer if time permits.

The conclusion portion of the commentary will also offer suggested links to the rest of Matthew and suggested questions for discussion that may set the stage for further study. The inclusion of suggested discussion questions and contemporary applications throughout this resource book hopefully will encourage deeper interactions, study, and consideration of this text of Matthew. For additional background, see comments and notes on each verse throughout the commentary text along with related comments in the introduction and appendix by searching for the same verses there. Searching might be aided by using the electronic version of this work, also.

Section 1: Introduction

Reframing Matthew 6's Lord's Prayer in Light of Matthew 5

The Link between the Prayer Request in 5:44-48 and the Prayer in 6:5-15—Summary of Differences in Interpretation and Approach to the Lord's Prayer: The following material is a simple but admittedly radically different approach to the Lord's Prayer. By seeing that the material that follows the prayer request starting in Matthew 5:44-48 is connected to the prayer in Matthew 6:5-15 by the material in 6:1-4[8] rather than disconnected, then a series of other things fall into place, including defining who the "our" is in "our Father". It results in acknowledging that Jesus was asking that the crowds, not just the disciples, pray this prayer for their persecutors; therefore, this approach to the Lord's Prayer in Matthew:

1) **Reveals Contextual Connections:** Shows the verses of Matthew 6:1-4 as linking the request of the crowd members to pray for their persecutors in 5:44-48 to the Lord's Prayer in 6:5-15 using strong connective rhetorical devices instead of separating the two sections.

    a. **Shows Prior Connections:** Reveals connections between the Lord's Prayer and what comes before it in the range of conflicts in the "turn the other cheek" passage in 5:38-43; the antitheses in 5:21-32; the emphasis on law in 5:17-20; and the beatitudes and related salt and light section in 5:1-16.

    b. **Demonstrates Parallels between Lord's Prayer and Beatitudes:** Shows the parallel use of conflict management in the beatitudes and the Lord's Prayer when the beatitude bookends using "theirs is the kingdom of heaven" are seen as a pair and the six blessings in between them are shown as three distinct pairs that escalate in emotion like the sections of the Lord's Prayer when prayed for persecutors.

    c. **Reveals Connections to Prayer after Lord's Prayer:** Reveals the connections between the Lord's Prayer in the passages that immediately follow including the "ask, seek, knock" prayer in Matthew 7:7 and the prayer of 2-3 people resolving conflict in Matthew 18:19-20.

    d. **Shows Connections by Use of Rhetorical Devices:** Shows the use of rhetorical devices (such as weaving, sound mapping and pivotal plays on words, use of the central position in phrasing, word chains, chiasmus, inversions, and inclusions[9]) in the overall attempt to persuade, the core concept of rhetoric developed by ancient cultures for at least four centuries prior to Christ. This will include the beatitudes arranged in pairs as suggested by the bookends, possible linkages between sets of items across the first couple of Chapters leading through the Lord's Prayer, including a matrix of various conflicts using data compression techniques for easier memorization and maximally flexible applications, and at least two sets of *chiasmi*. (A key *chiasmus* is one between the conflicts described in 5:39-41 and the "we-petitions" of 6:11-13.)

    e. **Connects to Rhetoric Used in Historical Context:** Reflects Hellenized Jewish influence such as this use of rhetoric especially prevalent throughout the Gospel of Matthew originally written in Greek. This would be especially useful for Greek-speaking Jewish Christians dispersed after Jerusalem's demise in 70 C.E.[10]

---

8   I am almost tempted to label Matthew 6:1-4 as the "missing link" between the prayer request and the prayer.

9   See John D. Harvey, *Listening to the Text, Oral Patterning in Paul's Letters*, Baker Books, 1998. This is a helpful introduction to oral and literary patterns in the first century (his Chapter 2) and "Categories and Controls" (Chapter 5). There he discusses jargon used by literary scholars with the example of "chiasmus" that sometimes may cause confusion since different words are sometimes used to describe similar techniques. He compares chiasmus that inverts a series of words ("identical, synonymous, or antonymous words or phrases" at the "sentence level"), whereas inversion is the term used where "a word or phrase on one side of the construction is developed in a sentence or paragraph on the other" (pp. 99, 100). I see these used in various sections of the Sermon on the Mount, though he does not cite usage in Matthew.

10 See more information in the background section. Also, see the YouTube video on the destruction of Jerusalem at: https://www.youtube.com/watch?v=y741QbT1YEo .

2) **Defines "our Father":** Defines the "our" in "*our* Father" as the "Father" of "me", the one praying alone and "the one opposing me," and defines "*our* necessary bread" as the necessity we are contesting (Matthew 5:44). Defines "Father" as the one who gives sunshine and rain to the just and unjust (Matthew 5:45).
    a. Creates solidarity between the one praying, the persecutors, and the Father.
    b. Provides detail on how to pray for persecutors as requested in Matthew 5:44 in a step-by-step progression providing peace, forgiveness, and the way to become a peace maker.
    c. Provides the purpose of the Lord's Prayer in Matthew 6:9-13.
    d. Provides specific criteria for complete interpersonal communications including mutual feedback needed for reconciliation.
    e. Shows expectations for relationship restoration in Lord's Prayer 6:5-15 and Matthew 18.
3) **Demonstrates "fishing lessons":** Shows how the disciples could use the Lord's Prayer as a flexible persuasion tool fulfilling the promise of "fishing lessons" to the disciples in 4:19 to be used as they make new disciples among the nations (28:18-20) and how not to fish and the role of "false prophets."
    a. Shows key role of receiving forgiveness and its quality as indicative of how the forgiven forgives others.
    b. Shows forgiveness as the key to entrance into the Kingdom of Heaven.

Section 1: Introduction

Core Text Needing Exploration[11] & The Role of the Lord's Prayer in the Sermon on the Mount

The entire Sermon on the Mount in Matthew Chapters 5-7 is focused on the message of Jesus and his good news announcement of the kingdom for the audience through their own perceived priorities of suffering and conflict. So, it would not be surprising to discover that the Lord's Prayer in the center of the Sermon turns out to be a conflict management prayer. Seeing its position and connections to the context, especially when looking at the context to define[12] the words of the Lord's Prayer, will be the key to unlocking some of the remaining mysteries of the prayer, such as its purpose and relationship to the prayer request of Jesus in Matthew 5:44-48 just moments before the listener hears the Lord's Prayer discussion in 6:5-15.

Discovering the "Our" in the "Our Father" through the Linking Section of 6:1-4?[13]

"But I say to you, love your enemies and pray for those who persecute you." Those words of Jesus from Matthew 5:44 are likely among the most well-known quotes of the entire Bible. Those who write on this passage mentioned how wonderful it is that Jesus asked us to love and pray for enemies and persecutors rather than pray against them and possibly notice similar themes in the writing of the New Testament and early church literature. However, they tend to comment far more on the part of the text asking listeners to love enemies than on the part asking them to pray for persecutors. They usually don't go into detail on the portion on prayer.

This is understandable because of the significance of that first clause, "love your enemies." It is also understandable since they sometimes admit that they don't seem to find much detail on praying right there. R.T. France is explicitly honest when he says Jesus asks "disciples" to pray for "persecutors," "without specifying its content."[14] By the time Jesus makes the prayer request at the end of Matthew 5, he appears, in the opinion of many, to change the topic and begins talking about something else in Matthew Chapter 6, namely not doing acts of justice and mercy before people, apparently discontinuing the discussion on praying for persecutors.[15] When noted scholar Hans Dieter Betz arrives

---

11 My goal is to help the reader to explore this approach to the Lord's Prayer in Matthew. The references and some of the detail on various methods of interpretation in general are provided for those who would like to go into greater detail and possibly consider the work of others but laid out so that it can be skipped by those who would prefer to do that at another time. My hope is that it will be easier to use this as supplemental material for classes or workshops that may range from a couple of hours to several months, depending on time available and goals of the classes.

12 Other definitions of the words as well as the interpretations of the Lord's Prayer are perfectly reasonable alternatives when the prayer is taken out of its context of Matthew. However, much value can be overlooked when other definitions are read into the text rather than derived from its context.

13 See the draft article by that name written by Manto in the appendix and accepted for publication by the *Christian Century*.

14 R.T. France, *The Gospel of Matthew*, William B. Eerdmans, 2007, p. 226. See his footnote on John Piper's work on loving enemies who does make the connection though France does not elaborate on what Piper discovered.

15 By the time Chrysostom and Augustine, contemporary church fathers in 400 A.D., write sermons on the Gospel of Matthew, they take many weeks to cover in a sermon series what would have taken twenty minutes to hear in one sitting if listening to Matthew 5-7 spoken without comment. (See and listen to the oral production of Matthew 5-7 in just 20 minutes and eleven seconds at this website: https://www.youtube.com/watch?v=D7Q69QJkYLM (Note that many of the oral clues are lost in contemporary translations that remove repetitive use of words to avoid "redundant" style elements that were purposeful in the original ancient Greek material worded to be more easily memorized and recited; or, broken into interconnected segments for discussion.) As a result of these early sermon series, they don't cover some of the connections that might be apparent to those listening to the material in one sitting. (See Augustine on the *Sermon on the Mount* in volume VI of the Nicene and Post-Nicene Fathers by T&T Clark, and Chrysostom's *Homilies on Matthew* in volume X.) Pastor Sarah Wilson presented her entire Sermon on the Mount poetic translation in a presentation to the Center for Catholic and Evangelical Theology annual conference on June 7, 2021. In her presentation she discussed the insights that are gained when one listens to the entire sermon at one time. She explained that to hear the entire sermon now in sermons limited by the scripture verses covered by the lectionary, that most of the verses would require 17 years to cover the material and even then, not all the verses would be covered. It was ironic since at the moment of her presentation, Brood X cicadas swarms just emerged after 17 years of life underground and was making an extremely loud mating call sound just outside the conference auditorium of Loyola University in Baltimore, Maryland. For lectionary cycles, see: https://lectionary.library.vanderbilt.edu/citationindex.php

Some commentators, such as John Calvin (1509-1564), do not see links between the sections within Matthew 5-7 as shown by his com-at the Lord's Prayer in 6:9-15, he asks, "What did Jesus intend by the creation of this prayer? One can only speculate about this question because none of the sources is explicit about this."[16] Betz does not connect the request to pray for persecutors with the passage of the Lord's Prayer in 6:5-15 and thereby misses an opportunity to notice the "explicit" intention of the prayer.

By way of contrast, I will attempt to show how to find what Betz, Luz and others[17] admittedly missed when they did not see the crowds as the explicit primary audience in Matthew 5-7, but which is clearly shown in Matthew 4:19; 5:1-2 and 7:28-29 and 8:1. **As a result of connecting the audience with the links between the two texts, the "missing content" of Matthew 5:44 is provided by the Lord's Prayer beginning in 6:9, and the "missing purpose" of the Lord's Prayer is the requirement and way to pray for persecutors requested in 5:44.**

How Matthew 6:1-4 Connects instead of Disconnects the Prayer Request from the Prayer: The key reason this seems to be missed is that the block of text at Matthew 6:1-4 appears to many as a change of topic from prayer ending in Matthew 5 to almsgiving at the beginning of Matthew 6. Instead of being a block of texts that transitions from prayer, this resource book will show various rhetorical elements, such as weaving, and a sound-alike play on words makes Matthew 6:1-4 a strong connective tissue that enhances the link between the request to of crowd members to pray for persecutors in 5:44 with the Lord's Prayer in 6:5-15.

Connecting the "crowds" to the Lord's Prayer: By discovering the complete audience of the Lord's Prayer, in 6:5-15 as the crowd members in 5:44-48, it becomes possible to see the solutions to these and other unanswered questions, perceived tensions or contradictions in the Lord's Prayer and its place in Matthew's Sermon on the Mount. That audience is the "crowds" (5:1-2 and 7:28-29 & 8:1) being recruited (or "fished" as in 4:19) by Jesus in the presence of his disciples (5:1-2) who were promised recruitment or "fishing" lessons (4:19). Once the audience is comprehended, it is easier to perceive the links that show that Jesus' request of the crowds to pray for their persecutors (5:44-48) was connected to the Lord's Prayer (6:5-15). It can also show how Matthew 7 shows how not to go fishing, the role of false prophets and the consequences of failing to fish from love and forgiveness compared to how others will fish from hate, anger, and lack of forgiveness.

Connecting to fishing for people: In this way, it can be seen how the Lord's Prayer was primarily intended in three ways. First, it was used by Matthew who claimed that Jesus spoke this to his disciples to show them how to "fish for people" prior to the "crowds" becoming disciples to bring them peace and become children of their Father, evidenced by empathy with and forgiveness for their persecutors. Then they could ultimately lead them to the place where they

---

ments on 5:1 "For the design of both Evangelists was, to collect into one place the leading points of the doctrine of Christ, which related to a devout and holy life…. It is probable, that this discourse was not delivered until Christ had chosen the twelve: but in attending to the order of time, which I saw that the Spirit of God had disregarded, I did not wish to be too precise. Pious and modest readers ought to be satisfied with having a brief summary of the doctrine of Christ placed before their eyes, collected out of his many and various discourses, the first of which was that in which he spoke to his disciples about true happiness." See: the online version of Calvin's Commentary at https://www.studylight.org/commentaries/cal/matthew-5.html .

"Others such as Davies see a number of connections in a well-organized block of material. See: Davies, W.D.; *The Sermon on the Mount*, Cambridge University Press, London, 1966,1969. This 165-page book covers the setting with section on the "Setting in Matthew," the "Jewish Messianic Expectation," "Contemporary Judaism," "the Early Church," and the "Ministry of Jesus." He reviews the disciplines of "source, form and liturgical criticism: (p. 4) as providing unnecessary bias for considering the material as a haphazard collection." His view is expressed on p. 5 where he says, "This emphasis is that we should think of Matthew, as of the other composers of the Gospels, not as mere editors, manipulating sources with scissors and paste, so to speak, to produce a mosaic of snippets, but as themselves in a real sense 'authors.' Dependent on a tradition there were, but they were not passive transmitters of it. By what they preserved, by the way they changed it and, above all, arranged it, they left their impress on it. This is particularly true of Matthew…. And in light of this we must insist that Matthew, the final author of the Gospel (note we write 'author' not 'editor'), did himself regard v-vii as a unit. the concluding formula in vii.28-9 makes this clear. The section finishes with these words: 'and it came to pass when Jesus had ended these sayings the people were astonished at his doctrine, for he taught them as one having authority and not as the scribes.'… So that v-vii do constitute for him (Matthew) an essential unity." Davies also emphasizes the significant role of the beginning and ending sections of the gospel encouraging readers to consider it as tightly connected sections.

16   Betz, Hans Dieter; *The Sermon on the Mount*, Fortress Press, 1995. See p. 373, column 2.

17   See Enrst Lohmeyer on p. 59 of *Our Father* and comments on Matthew 6:9, and Luz, *Mathew 1-7*, p.314, "petitions of the Lord's Prayer are so short that it is hard to establish their meaning unambiguously".

would become the new peacemaking disciples. Secondly, it was also used by Matthew for his communities after Jesus's time who would also be able to embrace this prayer to bring peace to them and to those they were discipling. Thirdly, the claims throughout Matthew ending in the "Great Commission" shows the intention of Matthew that this approach to the good news and disciple-making would be relevant to "the end of the age."

In the treatment that follows, I intend to show how the entire Sermon on the Mount of Matthew 5-7 works as a highly integrated and elaborated collection of scenarios like formal handbooks of Greek and Roman rhetoric (persuasion methods) and Jewish methods[18] such as the work of Nathan the prophet with King David. In the exegesis section of the texts below, I will link these examples to the explicit recruiting or "fishing lessons" promised to the disciples. In fact, it appears that Jesus is showing the disciples how to persuade those in the crowd to become disciples by showing the crowd how to persuade those they conflict with to reconcile.

In effect, all in the audience are being persuaded "how to persuade" or, as in the material in Chapter 7, how **not** to persuade or be persuaded. I will also attempt to show: 1) The Lord's Prayer (6:9-13) is not only our effort at persuading God through our supplication, it is also the ultimately flexible example of a recruitment and persuasion method which can cause change within us as we pray the prayer; 2) The Lord's Prayer is situated in the strategic center of the Sermon on the Mount of Matthew 5-7; 3) The Lord's Prayer is integral to the Sermon on the Mount serving as the primary discourse in Matthew laying the groundwork for the purpose of the entire Gospel enabling the disciples to make disciples among all the nations. (Matthew 28:19-20.)

Connecting to ancient rhetoric: These persuasion or "fishing" lessons in Matthew 5-7 are similar to formal rhetoric lessons developed through ancient Greece from 400 B.C.E. named *technai* that included elaboration or integration methods (similar to specific Jewish biblical methods) for training advanced students of persuasion such as lawyers. By 100 B.C.E., formal handbooks and teaching methods were extended for larger groups of beginning students and organized in *progymnasmata*.[19] Even today lawyers are trained to practice switching from the prosecutor to the defense attorney and are expected to be able to argue for either side. Those trained in law and persuasion in the four centuries leading up to the time of this teaching in a Hellenistic world including Judaism were taught and experienced a broad range of tools for persuasion that were intended to be highly adaptable into multiple scenarios. This made it possible for them to adjust quickly in a debate and in effect argue extemporaneously to fit the circumstances at hand.

Though the method presented in here is the opposite of debate and confrontation that is considered "throwing pearls before swine" in Matthew 7:6, it is similar in that the Lord's Prayer is a maximally adaptable persuasion technique. The Lord's Prayer in its context of Matthew 5 can be applicable to any subject of any conflict represented by the "our"; and to the object of any conflict represented by the "necessary bread." In the case of the Lord's Prayer for persecutors, the" our" is the combination of any person from the crowd praying alone and the one or ones persecuting them. This may include anyone who may unintentionally hurt us or block us from something important. It could also include those intending to help us so much that they over-promise something they might not be able to deliver as indicated by Jesus' discussion of oath taking moments before. Together the parties within the conflict comprise the "*our*" in "*our* Father", "*our* necessary bread," "*our* debts", and "*our* debtors." Together they comprise the "*us*" in "give *us*," "release *us*," "lead *us*," and "deliver *us*." This ultimately can guide the one praying through a process[20] to become a new peace-making disciple. Together, these elements show how this written material was arranged to grab attention, be memorable, be easily memorized and orally taught. In the same way that ancient Greeks had generic persuasion

---

18 See the later discussion on rhetoric and the works listed in the bibliography that focus on rhetoric, memory, pedagogy, and performance criticism by Allen, Bauckham, Boomershine, Burke, Estes, Gerhandsson, Green, Harvey, Hogan, Kelber, Kennedy, Lee & Scott, McIver, Mack; Robbins, Bruehler & von Thaden; and the works of the Biblical Performance Criticism series that include volumes by Hearon, Phil-Ruge-Jones, Dewey and Boomershine.

19 See Burton Mack on p. 33 of *Patterns of Persuasion in the Gospels* and his distinction between *technai* and *progymnasmata*, especially the further development of the *technai* as formally presented for a broader audience of younger students. See also, Parsons and Martin's *Ancient Rhetoric and the New Testament*, pp. 9-27.

20 That peacemaking process is described further in the exegesis section, the article on the "our in Our Father" and the similar treatments of the beatitudes in the context section and the paper presented to the NBS Scholars Forum, "Mnemonics and Audience..." in the appendix.

handbooks, these Greek-speaking Jewish Christians were given a handbook on how to persuade people to become new disciples.

Elsewhere the prayer in Matthew will be distinguished from the version in Luke where the audience is a disciple that creates a different assumption about the one praying forgiving the offender. The Matthew prayer is most similar to its use in the Didache which asks the one learning how to love and pray for enemies to pray this prayer three times a day, obviously not in a group worship session but where they lived.[21]

Benefits of This Unique Approach to the Lord's Prayer

If this approach to the Lord's Prayer (LP) in Matthew makes sense in its context, then it can add to the work of others who have done extensive work on the material in Matthew especially where they have admitted having some difficulties in interpreting these passages on prayer in Matthew 5:44 and 6:9-13. One such highly acknowledged Bible scholar is Hans Dieter Betz[22] who writes on the prayer for 90 pages in his commentary on Matthew 5-7 and provides a bibliography of over 120 and 600 references, many of which would have just as many references or more of their own. Many of the references in the bibliography at the end of this resource book have bibliographies of their own that make it possible to cover much of the most important work on the topic. It is not surprising that scholars such as Douglas Oakman say, "Much has been written about the Lord's Prayer during the modern era. It may seem as if everything has been said that could have been said."[23]

Hopefully, application of this approach to the Lord's Prayer and its context in Matthew would provide the following benefits:

1) Offers engagement and intervention opportunities:

    a. Facilitates approaches to listening and productive discussions as opposed to divisive debating.

    b. Provides opportunity for greater use of the LP for anger management.

    c. Reduces the abusive and harmful interactions of those in conflict.

    d. Encourages greater listening, dialog, forgiveness, reconciliation, and restoration with specific steps.

    e. Links the concepts of entry into the "kingdom of heaven" with the forgiveness and restoration of the Father and its resulting evidence in the lives of those who embrace it.

    f. Breaks the cycle of abuse and oppression so that those whose peace has been broken can receive peace and become new peacemakers instead of peace breakers or peace fakers.

    g. Provides contexts for cross-cultural interactions and conflict resolution as demonstrated in the texts of Matthew.

    h. Welcomes the expertise and experience of those with backgrounds other than biblical scholarship.

---

21 See *Ante-Nicene Fathers* such as the one edited by Roberts and Donaldson in Volume 7 for the *Teaching of the Twelve (Didache)* and the *Apostolic Constitutions*. In Chapter I of the *Didache*, the very first paragraph teaches the way of life following the two great commands to love God and neighbor with an immediate appeal to the Sermon on the Mount of Matthew: "And of these sayings, the teaching is this: Bless them that curse you, and pray for your enemies, and fast for them that persecute you." Then later in section VIII, it speaks of praying and fasting quoting the Lord's Prayer of MT 6 with the words, "Thrice in the day pray thus." To hear one of the oldest known chants of the Lord's Prayer, hear the audio of this NPR broadcast of August 2014: https://www.npr.org/transcripts/338586411

22 Hans Dieter Betz; *The Sermon on the Mount*, Fortress Press, 1995. This 730-page commentary is one of the most thorough and scholarly on the topic—well received by *Review of Biblical Literature* and *Theology Today*. Betz credits the support for work he received on the topic for over two decades including fourteen months of intense study and writing provided by a grant or "*Forschungspreis*." It includes a 90-page introduction covering his approach in five pages and the major problems in a historical and literary perspective. Each section is divided into an introduction, analysis, and interpretation. The commentary is prefaced with a list of works most often cited and closes with his partial bibliography that contains about 700 items.

23 See Douglas Oakman, *Jesus and the Peasants*, "The Lord's Prayer in Social Perspective," p. 199.

2) Provides hope, comfort and opportunities for prayer and meditation throughout the day:

   a. Provides opportunity for greater sense of peace for those in suffering and conflict.

   b. Provides hope and insight for those seeking reconciliation.

   c. Provides comfort and sense of closure for those who have gone through a complete sequence of reconciliation steps but have been rejected by those rejecting reconciliation.

   d. Encourages additional benefits as proposed by participants in these studies.

   e. Provides a way to meaningfully pray for conflict situations as they arise during the day and also prepare for meditative or centering prayer by resolving anxieties, fears or anger that might make it difficult to engage in peaceful meditation.

3) Provides practical steps and processes:

   a. Provides a step-by-step process to acknowledge the loss of peace and its recovery leading the peace-broken to restore their peace and ultimately become the new peacemakers instead of the new peace breakers. The material will indicate this both in the beatitude pairs and the Lord's Prayer.

   b. Provides criteria for mutual communications, feedback, and a checklist to see what needs to be done to establish reconciliation and restoration of a relationship.

   c. Fosters opportunities for Bible studies and meditation groups focused on peace and conflict management.

   d. Encourages caring interactions and programs that meet the needs of others.

   e. Promotes the study of the methods of persuasion, evangelism and Bible learning from ancient media and apply it to modern media and society.

   f. Provokes reconsideration of the Sermon on the Mount in Matthew 5-7 as foundational material for evangelism and disciple-making programs to the extent it was originally intended as the promised "fishing lessons" of Matthew 4:19.

   g. Provides a qualitatively different approach to evangelism and discipleship that begins with listening to the suffering and anger of those who are hurt and brings them to a point of peace where they can become peacemakers.

Imagine one of the more tragic moments in your life due to some conflict with a person, small group or organization that cost you dearly. Then, imagine what it would be worth if that conflict could have been resolved or avoided and not have turned out so badly.

Then try to recall a conflict that was resolved before it turned tragic and imagine how much it would have cost you if it were not resolved. Such conflicts are so great in so many ways that no price tag could be put on them. But, if that were possible, would it be worth a thousand dollars? I know that I have experienced losses where I would gladly have taken out the equivalent of a mortgage to avoid them. I know other conflicts worked out rather well and had they not, the damage would have been impossible to fix regardless of the price I would be willing to pay.

This is just part of the value we might experience from the Lord's Prayer if it were the prayer Jesus asked us to pray for our persecutors, our worst enemy in our worst-case conflict, and would somehow be answered. In the following examination of this prayer as it is found in the Gospel of Matthew, I believe that we can discover how that begins by resolving the conflict within us, and possibly between ourselves and those who are the cause of our conflicts.

Benefits or Value of the Lord's Prayer for conflict resolution: Imagine what the additional value of the Lord's Prayer would be if all it did was resolve just one conflict for each of the two billion people on the planet who know the Lord's Prayer and that was placed at $1,000 each. Then the incremental additional value would be two trillion dollars. If it helped in more than one conflict each, or, if the conflicts were larger, then the total value would really begin to be unimaginable. It would certainly be surprising if the very Lord's Prayer we know was hiding such treasure in plain sight. It might be even more surprising than an old painting of Jesus that was purchased at an estate sale for under $100, was restored to its original state and then sold a few years ago for $450 million at auction. (See the story of the Salvador Mundi.[24]) That potential value monetarily, emotionally, or relationally might make it worth taking another look at something that might otherwise be easy to ignore.

Sunk Investment Cost of the Lord's Prayer: It is easy to take the Lord's Prayer for granted, and to vastly underestimate the investment that has gone into its use. As an anger management tool and disciple making tool, the overlooked value is enormous. For example, the "Global Status of Christianity" report by Gordon Conwell Seminary for 2021 shows the approximate number of Christians globally as 2.4 billion or 32.8% of the world's population.[25] To be conservative and to keep the math simple, imagine that estimated direct costs of an equivalent amount of information to be shared with that many people would be about a US dollar per page to translate, print, produce, and mail one copy to each of 2 billion people. That would total $2 billion. Then add a modest amount of another $100 each to teach the material to someone to the point where they could recite it back by memory. That would be another $200 billion for an approximate $201 billion. Then there would be the estimated cost for memory maintenance which in this case is the weekly (in some cases daily) worship experience of these churches. This might be considered an indirect cost of what is required for these organizations to continue to operate. One year of such operations are estimated by the Global Status report to be at $340 billion for 2021. So, conservatively speaking, the available investment value of the Lord's Prayer as a conflict management or disciple making tool would be $541 billion, a lot of investment to ignore and not put to good use. If coupled with the potential conflict resolution value mentioned above, the total would be many times that number.

Benefits of this Approach to the Lord's Prayer According to Participants and Readers

One pastor in Pennsylvania encouraged his congregation to use this approach to the Lord's Prayer: (See his Lord's Prayer articles in the appendix.)

From: Steve Verkouw <pastor@gracelutheranchurch.com>

Subject: Lord's Prayer in my Newsletter

Date: April 14, 2020 at 12:23:37 PM EDT

To: Charles Manto <chucklmanto@gmail.com>

Hi Chuck!

Hope this finds you well, after a month or so of quarantine. I understand that you have been studying and helping folks prepare for resilience precisely for times like this. I'm sure you have a take on what's going on!

---

24 See live auction video showing the $400M auction price that with fees totaled $450.3M here: https://www.youtube.com/watch?v=_3m-LhkijkOw. See also, Walter Isaacson, *Leonardo da Vinci*, Simon and Shuster, New York, 2017. See also the Wikipedia article: https://en.wikipedia.org/wiki/Salvator_Mundi_(Leonardo)

  The Salvador Mundi for sale at Christie's New York on 15 November 2017 suffered over its 500-year history. Left: in 1904 with overpainting. Right: the painting today, after cleaning and retouching of areas of paint loss Christies Images, 2017. https://images.graph.cool/v1/cj6c28vh912680101ozc2paxj/cj9zj9wo h042e0166qrxzku9t/0x0:810x578/960x960/296_Salvator_Mundi.jpg. See also the recent April 13, 2021, news articles debating whether the painting was a joint work of Leonardo and his studio.

25 See: "Global Status of Christianity" for 2021 at: https://www.gordonconwell.edu/center-for-global-christianity/wp-content/uploads/sites/13/2020/12/Status-of-Global-Christianity-2021.pdf.

Section 1: Introduction

I have been thrown into a situation I never expected - trying to "become a YouTube sensation" overnight, ha-ha!

With my iPhone and a few apps, I have tried my hand at video worship over this last month, slowly learning skills, experimenting, and trying to "bring church to the people" in this way. It's not what I signed up for, but oh well. Old dogs can learn new tricks!

I have also been steadily writing a series of 7 Newsletter articles, beginning in Lent, featuring the understanding of the Lord's Prayer that you have shared with me over the past few years. I tried very hard to put the ideas into my own words. I tried to keep it simple. I repeat a bit from week to week, since it came out in installments. I thought you would enjoy reading it. Since it is inspired by you, feel free to use any or all of it in any way that might be helpful in the quest to encourage peacemaking.

Be well, do good work, stay in touch (as GK used to say).

Blessings,

Steve V

Pastor Stephen P. Verkouw

Grace Lutheran Church, Lancaster Pa.

*Holy Worship * Wholly Serving*

717-397-2748

pastor@gracelutheranchurch.com

Letter from Host Pastor Describing Results of this Approach in Dillon, Colorado:

From: Elena Liliana Stahlberg <liliana_stahlberg@hotmail.com>

Subject: The Conflict in the Lord's Prayer

Date: July 27, 2019 at 11:28:17 PM EDT

To: Charles Manto <chucklmanto@gmail.com>

Lord of the Mountains Lutheran Church in Dillon, Colorado invited Charles Manto to speak on the **Lord's Prayer and the Beatitudes** in the Gospel of Matthew, as conflict resolution inspiration for our daily lives.

There were three sessions and a tandem sermon with Pastor Liliana Stahlberg. The presentations were interactive, actively involving the participants.

The idea that the Lord's Prayer is not only for us but especially for our enemies created a lot of tension, and reactions from the audience.

Charles invited us to pray in this way, "the Father of me and my enemy." It struck all of us as true to the Gospel message, but very difficult to really apply to our daily life. Charles' presentation touched many lives and people retrieved personal stories that were connected to the concept of forgiveness of enemies.

Just last week, a month after the workshop on the Lord's Prayer, a woman from the congregation came to our regular Healing Service on a Wednesday evening, to tell us that she just can't pray the Lord's Prayer anymore because she can't forgive her former husband who had hurt her, and destroyed her life. Her confession generated the opportunity for spiritual companionship. She realized that she was on a journey of self-discovery and that God is leading her to deal with a situation that has been stale for a long time.

Such workshop style presentations are a tool for self-awareness and for discovering ways of healing through forgiveness. I would love to do more presentations with Charles Manto in other congregations.

Yours in Christ,

Pastor Liliana Stahlberg

LOTM

Dillon, Colorado

56 Hwy 6, 80435

cell: 720-341-8096

Excerpts from an Email and Letter from a Business Colleague who Read the Transcripts from Dillon, CO: (See the complete text of his four-page letter in the appendix.)

From: Steve Kramer <stevekrrt@gmail.com>

Subject: The Lord's Prayer in conflict resolution

Date: August 28, 2020 at 11:40:53 AM EDT

To: Chuck <chucklmanto@gmail.com>

Chuck,

I am continuing my "deep dive" into your writings in hopes of gaining a better understanding of Matthew 5-7 and how it relates to your personal struggles as well as to all our struggles. I hope that what I have written provides you with a better understanding of me personally and my spiritual quest. It is often painful to look back and reflect on the trials and tribulations I have gone through. I can see through sharing your life's experiences that you have had much to overcome and conquer too. Thank you for being transparent and exposing the painful realities you have been through. It makes it easier to understand that we are not alone in our sufferings. Jesus gave the ultimate sacrifice by giving his life and his blood so that we all may be given forgiveness. He suffered more than any of us could ever imagine. So, in the end we are going to make it through all of this and live to love another day. Thank you for sharing your knowledge and perspectives and for inviting me to participate in your project.

With much thanks and heartfelt gratitude,

Steve

Chuck,

It was a great surprise for me when I learned of your ongoing perseverance, commitment, and devotion to a life of the gospel after knowing you for years through our common interest in promoting COG. Last summer when I was living in Avon, Colorado you were simultaneously leading classes at The Lord of the Mountains Lutheran Church in Dillon, CO. I was nearing the end of my five-year journey of self-rediscovery that culminated in my retirement from 35 years as a Respiratory Therapist in Los Angeles. During this time, I lived and worked at Sage Memorial Hospital for six months in Ganado, Arizona on the expansive Navajo Indian Reservation. It was a very lonely and oppressive environment, but the land and the people intrigued me. I have always been interested in history and lived a short walk away from The Hubble Trading Post. I almost felt as though I had been transported back to a bygone time….

My life could be characterized as bittersweet. I have been more than fortunate to have had the experiences that I've had in too many ways to count. But I have carried around a lot of pain, resentment, and misery throughout my entire life. This has manifested itself in my occasionally losing control and having anger, animosity, and hostility towards total strangers as well as people I love. It has taken a toll on my own personal health and well-being in addition to damaging the feelings of others I never intended to offend or hurt.

Section 1: Introduction

For most of my life I would simply blame others for my unhappiness. When I recognized that I had a personal responsibility for my own happiness and that I had choices in the methods of resolving conflict, I had more control over the way I felt. I could choose a spontaneous and hostile response when persecuted or provoked that usually had a less than desirable outcome or I could make a conscious decision to shift and divert the negativity of the experience to a more positive one and to feel better about the outcome.

The result could still be something other than the outcome I may have been hoping to achieve but the manner in which I felt mentally and physically at the conclusion of an unpleasant experience was still something I could regulate. The consequences of irrational or emotional responses to persecution or provocation can have profound and long-lasting effects on the nature and the course of our life. Impulsive, reactive, decisions made resulting from the antagonistic or threatening behavior into our personal space physically or verbally will generally not serve our best interests.

I have always admired the basic simplicity of the Christian philosophy. The idea that the Son of God was sent here, to our world and ended up dying on the cross for all of our sins. But we could be redeemed, get salvation and forgiveness, avoid the lake of fire, the depths of hell, and if judged to be fit, earn a place in Heaven with God himself and to live forever without the earthly pain and suffering so common to many of our earthly inhabitants. It sounded like a good deal to me. And all I had to do was to be a good person, ask for forgiveness, be sincere in my beliefs and my actions, and to follow Jesus. I don't take this agreement lightly. I am sincere in my beliefs and convictions. I am trying to be a better father, husband, citizen, human, and person. I am trying to think in terms of Christian values, morals, and interventions, and use what I learn for practical applications in my life. It's a "flying by the seat of my pants" approach but it's been working for me so far throughout my life. Or maybe not so much, but I'm trying to improve on a shaky foundation and incorporate more discipline and tradition with more conventional methods into my regular practices. And besides I still have more to do and contribute before I'm done. If God is willing....

The gift that you have given us Chuck is a useful tool to be able to diffuse and derail many confrontational situations we may find ourselves thrust into. If we too can also learn to turn the other cheek by not only forgiving our confronters but to actually pray for them as well then, we are following Jesus by being more like him. By visualizing and reciting The Lord's Prayer it serves as a catalyst for me to shift a negative thought or behavior into something divine. It allows us to put love into perspective in a split second and to forgive others as Jesus has forgiven us and to pray for his love to be blessed onto our enemies as we would wish onto our own beloved.

For me this line of thinking serves to help promote my own health and wellbeing by keeping my cauldron on a low simmer and enabling me to de-escalate emotionally mentally and physically charged interactions through something as simple and as truthful as The Lord's Prayer. If more of us utilized this technique in these divisive and turbulent times it could be responsible for helping to lower global warming by a few degrees. We all need to chill out a little more and to exercise real tolerance for our fellow man. With everything so polarized and divisiveness being the norm it's more important now than ever to find more positive and productive methods of resolving conflict and channeling aggression. What could be easier than saying The Lord's Prayer and feeling the love, thankfulness, forgiveness, and gratitude it resonates, and for being a Christian.

I am grateful to have met you Chuck and it's a great privilege to have you ask me to help you with this project of yours. I am honored that you have asked me how I utilize The Lord's Prayer in my personal struggles and in conflict resolution. I'm not sure if I have fulfilled your expectations for that but I have attempted to open myself up to you and give you some insight into how I came to try and get right with God and Jesus and how I am continuing to follow the right path towards living a better life and dying a better death when my time comes. I am truly grateful for everything God provides us with and for the wisdom and comfort I feel when reading the Bible. You are a great inspiration and an encouragement to me and I am thankful that our paths have crossed and that the Lord's light that you shine for him illuminates my path and my life and gives me hope for a brighter and more enlightened future. You are someone who I will always treasure knowing Chuck. Because you are not judgmental, and you see the real good in people and that you encourage others in their quest with seeking Jesus and the love of Almighty God. I am enjoying and appreciating your writings. You are helping me to be a better person and motivating me to be a better servant of Christ and The Lord. I pray that I continue to have you in my life and that we can both look forward to better times ahead and to continue to spread the good word of God and Jesus. Thank you for all you do and for having faith and love in me. It means a lot.

With Much Gratitude,

Steve

Section 1: Introduction

The concept may be shared quickly as evidenced by this interaction with a Lyft driver in Atlanta (who was originally from Nigeria):

June 22, 2019 Excerpts from Cab Ride from Emory University to Atlanta Airport

link to video:

https://www.dropbox.com/s/gv6t7p586j2atb1/Lord%27s%20Lyft%20Prayer%20Atlanta%20%281%29.mov?dl=0

CHRISTOPHER: Okay. My name is Christopher Okudowah [spelling uncertain] and you have told me a new way at the Lord's Prayer. I have read Luke and Matthew over and over and I've never looked at it like that. As far as our Lord's Prayer, I recite it almost daily. Sometimes I even rush in my head and I never in-depth thought about it or looked at it the way that you have enlightened me about it.

CHARLES MANTO: And how did I enlighten you? What was different about it today when we talked about it? What was different about the Lord's Prayer?

CHRISTOPHER: The most important thing that you told me is how to look at the word "our." Generally, and I never thought about it. Our father who is in Heaven, and I never really thought about who does that "our" includes? Well, when you broke it down, you let me realize that "our" is me and my enemy, then you make the whole prayer have two different meanings.

CHARLES MANTO: Yes.

CHRISTOPHER: And then, it makes you realize that each time you read it, you see the effect of what you're saying for the prayer out to, you know, to you and your enemy. And in there you find out along the way that, guess what? I need forgiveness, too—because I'm about to... (laughs)

CHARLES MANTO: I want to kill that guy that hurt me.

CHRISTOPHER: I'm about to do some crazy stuff to this person, and then you realize that God gave you a way out in that prayer. Not only for you to pray for your enemy, but for you along the line to realize you have committed sin doing this. So, this is a chance for you to include yourself in that prayer and beg for that forgiveness.

CHARLES MANTO: Wow.

CHRISTOPHER: And that is very powerful.

CHARLES MANTO: And you're from where? Where are you from?

CHRISTOPHER: I'm from Nigeria, and this is Atlanta, Georgia where I live. And I drive Lyft and I met you, and you have made this period—this one hour—the most important one hour of my life!

CHARLES MANTO: Well, thank you so much.

CHRISTOPHER: Because I'm going to teach this to my son and to other people, and I bet you everybody will be amazed. And I appreciate you giving me this knowledge and then teaching me about just a simple—a simple verse in the Bible. And you have given me a way to think about it that I've never been thinking of it before.

CHARLES MANTO: And I can use this in my Sunday School Classes?

CHRISTOPHER: You can use it anywhere you want!

CHARLES MANTO: Thank you.

Section 1: Introduction

Orientation: Approach, Background, Context, Drivers

Approach: Why would anything intended for the original audience of Matthew's Gospel matter to us as its new audience"? Given a compelling message, what's the best approach to this text in Matthew? A casual read? A brief glance at some commentary to see what that writer and a few that he or she quotes have written? Perhaps, thoughtful consideration of a carefully crafted catechism? Or meditation about the text for a while to consider what is being said and why? Or do all that is possible to look and listen carefully to what that ancient writer or presenter is trying to say, to whom and why? The more we discover something that grabs our attention and the more we are compelled by what that text says, the more we may be motivated to use any reasonable method or source to succeed. By thoughtfully examining what was intended for the initial audience, we, in turn, become the new audience that in turn may share that with others who become an even more extended audience. By missing the original audience, we likely miss a key message of the text. By recapturing an understanding of the original audience, we might possibly recover the bulk of the value of that original message.

The world within, behind and in front of the text (or "script")[26]

The world *within* the text: What is the text and where is it?

The text of Matthew is well documented by those who study the earliest manuscripts and various versions. The most significant and most complete ancient manuscripts are documented in Greek Bibles and to a lesser extent in various contemporary language versions and commentaries[27]. With the development of digital libraries, comprehensive copies of all manuscripts will become readily available[28]. But to start understanding what any one word in a text means, the approach I will take is to see what is in that text and where it is situated. That includes how it is used in the sentence where it appears, then seeing how it might be used in the paragraph, then the section or page and then finally the work as a whole. This will reveal other clues that may include patterns that serve either as conceptual or sound maps for the material that make the content easier to memorize and present to the listeners.[29] These patterns often include repetitions of words, word chains, or a group of words or phrases that are presented in one order then presented in reverse order named either chiasmus (chiasm) or inversion when the second set is further elaborated. For a detailed listing see John Harvey's treatment in *Listening to the Text*.[30]

---

26 See the three worlds of textual understanding and exegesis by Paul Ricoeur as expressed Daniel Ulrich and Richard B. Gardner in *A Guide for New Testament Exegesis*, Posted on Bethany Seminary Moodle site for students of Matthew class, B-302. 2020; This is an adaptation of a guide for exegesis developed by Richard B. Gardner, Professor Emeritus of New Testament Studies at Bethany Theological Seminary. The section titled "An Outline of Exegetical Procedures" quotes Ulrich as using "Gardner's exact words with minor changes. I am grateful for his permission to use his work in this way." See, also, Barton, Stephan A.; "Historical Criticism and Social-Scientific Perspectives in New Testament Study," an essay in, *Hearing the New Testament, Strategies for Interpretation*; 2d Edition, by Green, Joel B., Eerdmans, Grand Rapids, 2010, pp. 40-41. He discusses the "world behind the text (the world of the author), the world within the text (the narrated world of the characters, intentions and events), and the world in front of the text (the world of the reader).

27 See various commentaries quoted throughout this resource book. See a sample treatment of various versions of ancient texts in Bruce Metzger's *A Textual Commentary on the Greek New Testament* and details in Greek New Testaments from the United Bible Societies by Aland, et al, used in the Greek text in the commentary section.

28 See the article by Garrick Allen in his article, "The Possibilities of a Gospel Codex GA 2064 (Dublin, CBL W139), Digital Editing, and Reading in a Manuscript Culture", in *The Journal of Biblical Literature*, Vol 140, No. 2021.

29 For an example of sound mapping in the Sermon on the Mount, see Margaret Ellen Lee and Bernard Brandon Scott, *Sound Mapping the New Testament*, Polebridge Press, Salem, Oregon, 2009. Pages 309-383 focuses on the Sermon on the Mount in Matthew and "Q." They also provide insightful comments on the role of the text as it is intended to be heard and how that influences the meaning of the heard text (pp. 386-391). This book has appropriately been praised as a groundbreaking treatment of sound and how it was used in oral media to convey tapestries of information segments more easily through structures and "maps" that are most expedient for the medium. Devices such as oral cues and repetition are examined in depth. The Sermon on the Mount is analyzed from a sound versus written perspective to showcase alternative interpretations to various sections of the material.

30 John D. Harvey, *Listening to the Text, Oral Patterning in Paul's Letters*; Baker Books, 1998. This is a helpful introduction to oral and

Where the text is going: This also makes it useful to understand not only how a word, phrase or sentence or idea of a text can be understood in the segment in which it stands, but to also understand where that text is going. The direction, pace or rhythm, acceleration, manner, and goal often thought of as rhetorical direction or force is vital to fully appreciate the way the text was presented both in writing and orally to the listeners. This holds true of the overall text such as the Gospel of Matthew (a macrotext), a smaller portion of that larger text such as the Sermon on the Mount in Matthew 5-7 (a mini-text), or a subset of that (a microtext), such as the discussion of prayer in Matthew 6:5-15, the focus here. (See the following "Drivers" section for more details.)

Do the text and its context reveal explicit claims as to its audience and purpose that can help provide meaning for the words being used? Are there explicit claims or obvious evidence as to the genre or type of literature that might further shed light on how those words are used? Are the explicit claims consistent with each other or in conflict? Are initial or apparent conflicts being used to grab our attention, show a contrast, make a point, or make the material easier to remember and harder to forget? Are the explicit claims in conflict with implicit claims? The explicit claims would appear to normally have greater weight than implicit claims, especially the ones I or others might infer with less justification from outside the text. These claims may be shown as something Jesus asked the crowds and disciples. It might also be inferred that this is what the writer Matthew is presenting to his audience. These are all questions that some organize as describing the world within the text.

The World Behind the Text: Then it can be helpful to ask how these details match with what is known external to the text about the world of the writer and the audience of the time. These are questions behind the text. That information may come from other texts of various kinds including poetry, laws, religious texts, or information from other artifacts such as coins, statues and archaeological work on ancient settlements or cities including religious buildings, community buildings, housing, and household items. Equally important might be understanding how texts were used in the culture of the time both in written and oral form to persuade and teach others. Information about the world behind the text might also be derived from the material in the text but it can be considered separately.

An interesting example of this orientation can be found while reading Malina and Rohrbaugh's *Social-Science Commentary on the Synoptic Gospels*. In describing the Gospels, such as Matthew, they describe the writing for the "in-group" of disciples or followers and not the "out-group" of those who might become "Jesus followers." "In other words, the Gospels were not written for missionizing or proselytizing."[31] That may be true from the standpoint of merely presenting the writings themselves directly to prospective converts. Yet in the Gospel of Matthew, Jesus explicitly says that he will teach the disciples how to make new disciples. It appears that the Sermon on the Mount spoken by Jesus and heard by the crowds is a proselytizing activity aimed not only at winning new disciples but teaching the disciples how to do just that, namely, "fish for people." These are the words of *the world within the text*. Yet these words in the written Gospel of Matthew appear to be for the "in-group" of disciples for the purpose of training them how to proselytize or win new disciples. So, in that sense, though not intended to be a proselytizing document to be handed out like Bible tracts on a street corner, the Gospel of Matthew does appear to be directed at the disciples or the "in group" of *the world behind the text*. So, while the document was intended for the "in-group," the purpose was to

---

literary patterns in the first century (his Chapter 2) and "Categories and Controls" (Chapter 5). There he discusses jargon used by literary scholars with the example of "chiasmus" that sometimes may cause confusion since different words are sometimes used to describe similar techniques. He compares chiasmus that inverts a series of words ("identical, synonymous, or antonymous words or phrases" at the "sentence level"), whereas inversion is the term used where "a word or phrase on one side of the construction is developed in a sentence or paragraph on the other" (pp. 99, 100). I see these used in various sections of the Sermon on the Mount, though he does not cite usage in Matthew. He does go into a lot of helpful detail about various approaches to memory devices of poetry (p. 59) and other literature (pp. 98-99).

31 See Bruce Malina and Richard Rohrbaugh's *Social-Science Commentary on the Synoptic Gospels*, p. 16. See also their consideration of the blessings in Matthew 5:3-12 as "honorific" and kingdom language as appropriate for the patronage system of Roman Palestine (pp. 41, 17). See also *Honor and Shame in the Gospel of Matthew* by Jerome Neyrey where "blessed" is rendered "honorable" (p. 165) where the dishonored are honored. See also, Parsons and Martin's *Ancient Rhetoric and the New Testament*, pp. 27-38 on *chreia* and *encomium*, pp. 175-230.

help them engage the people of the "out-group." It also appears from the last couple of verses of Matthew (28:18-20), that it was intended not only for the readers alive to read or hear the original Gospel of Matthew for all who follow until the "close of the age." That anticipates a life of *the world in front of the text*.

The World in Front of the Text: Then it helps to compare both the world of the text and behind the text to the views of those who have read and commented on the material since then and through today. These are questions in front of the text. We not only can learn from the knowledge and insights of others but also from their perspectives and prejudices that impact our own perspectives and prejudices. This might be helped by purposely placing ourselves as an audience in a similar environment of the original audience.[32]

Experiencing the text, —or should we say "script?" Interpreting the text is always best done within its context including the way the first receivers of the text experienced it, especially in the way the majority of those who experienced it by "hearing" the text.[33] The text was written for three purposes—one that it would be read, secondly in large measure to be read to someone out-loud, and, third, to be memorized by the reader in order to be spoken without the benefit of a written text to an audience of one or more. In turn, many of those hearers were expected to memorize what they heard so that they could share it with others who would "hear" it from them. The benefit of the written text was that it allowed people to go back and recalibrate what they had memorized to make sure they were still on track. In this sense, these texts could be described as "scripts" not unlike a play meant to be memorized are repeated, taught and "performed" as would telling a story, teaching a lesson or leading an interactive discussion.[34]

Even though this might sound odd to us now, in the time and place that the book of Matthew was received, most of those, even if literate, were not able to purchase and take their own scrolls home with them.[35] Though some may have had the opportunity to read a text, mass production of scrolls for hundreds or thousands did not exist. Both scroll material and the labor involved in writing was expensive, leaving the written material available to institutions and the wealthy but not the average literate person, let alone the illiterate. The need to be able to follow a spoken word required far more attention to aural claims, clues and patterns that made it possible to understand and care about the material in the first place, follow it from segment to segment in the second place, follow it to one or more conclusions in the third place, so that they could remember and apply it in the fourth place and possibly share it with others in the fifth place. By being mindful of how the material was laid out for easier memorization and teaching in these oral settings, we can uncover clues about the organization and integration of the text that can answer questions we would miss otherwise. It might even help to take the time to listen[36] to the text, speak it out loud in any language (especially the earliest Greek), perhaps even trying to memorize it and recite it to ourselves and then others. Though difficult, trying to do that might make it possible to gain insights into meaning of the text and the inherent methods built into to it that make it easier to memorize and share with others.[37] See the section on "Drivers" in this section for more detail on these oral methods of persuasion and memorization.

---

[32] Some may find the works of Umberto Eco helpful on the role of the reader and the meaning of texts.

[33] The works of Tom Boomershine and his colleagues from the Network of Biblical Storytellers and its Scholars Forum consistently encourage the experience of memorizing and performing the texts to understand their oral and mnemonic dynamics.

[34] Note that the well-known scripture verse Romans 10:17 says that "faith comes by *hearing* and *hearing* by the word of God." It did not say "faith comes by *reading*..." Most in that day were exposed to the information by "hearing" the message rather than by "reading" the message. Even though the point of the passage is hearing to the point of understanding, it is interesting to see the significance of "hearing".

[35] See the treatment on the cost of scrolls in the "Drivers" section that follows.

[36] The old pedestrian safety slogan for children applies, "Stop, Look, & Listen!" We can **stop** and further consider the texts that we think we know, then **look** at the context all around the text for clues to its meaning, then **listen** to the text to gain insight of how it is heard when it is spoken to us.

[37] See the example provided by Aaron Milavec where he showed how memorizing the Didache in Greek helped him understand the written text better. He cites the encouragement of the Network of Biblical Storytellers in this regard on pages 64-65. ("When, Why, and for Whom Was the Didache Created: Insights into the Social and Historical Setting of the Didache Communities," from *Matthew and the Didache, Two Documents from the Same Jewish-Christian Milieu?* edited by Huub van de Sandt.

Contemporary brain science demonstrates how arousal, attention, motivation, memorization and retention all are increased by emotion and how the total sense of importance and relevance enhances the effectiveness of persuasion.[38] It is universally understood that a good joke has a story ending with a punch line that makes the entire joke memorable. If the punch line fails to make the joke interesting, both the longer body of the text and the short punch line are all forgotten. The shorter segments are far harder to remember than the longer combination of the successful joke.[39] Reading the joke might be memorable, but hearing it performed and in a memorable situation will make it even more memorable. The more senses involved, the greater the memory.[40] (For this reason, the shortest version of a text might not always be the oldest and the most resilient, but the one that is most memorable.)

Even vision is enhanced within the visual cortex by sound brought from the auditory canal. The human visual cortex uses sound from the ears in addition to information from the eyes to help prepare for the vision that it is about to experience. (See the *Science Daily* report on how sound influences vision and the total experience of an event.)[41] Looking at a text only as a reader could rob the modern reader of the total experience of hearing, memorizing, and retelling a story or text that was known by original audiences of these ancient texts.[42]

Explicit versus Implicit Meaning: All that might be learned from the worlds within, behind and in front of the texts provide insights into the explicit and implicit nature, style, purpose, and genre of the material. Was the meaning, purpose, and genre that of poetry, history, biography, teaching, worship, persuasion, correction, recruitment or evangelism? If there were multiple reasons and applications, was there a key one or two that drove or organized the others? Are there explicit statements throughout the texts that provide insights into its purpose? Most of the problems that have been confessed by scholarly writers commenting on the text appear to arise because of their conflict with the explicit claims of the text. These explicit and implicit elements within any specific text can provide insights to other issues within its context.

After reading and listening to these texts in these ways, we will find it easier to understand how these segments relate to each other and why. I suggest that a carefully crafted set of material like Matthew would be expected to have a purpose. When we initially fail to see it, we could at least admit that such a pattern and purpose may be there even though we don't yet grasp it. This purpose might be better discovered when we seek to see how the text applies to its entire

---

38   J. L. McGaugh, *Maps of the mind. Memory and Emotion: The Making of Lasting Memories.* Columbia University Press. © 2003. See also the works of Merlin Donald such as *Origins of the Modern Mind* (1991) and *A Mind So Rare* (2001) describing multiple integrated brain, nervous system and interpersonal factors in memory, emotion, awareness and relationship.

39   See similar insights throughout the introduction of the work on the Sermon on the Mount by Metropolitan Hilarion Alfeyev, *Jesus Christ: His Life and Teaching, Vol. 2 - The Sermon on the Mount,* St. Vladimir's Seminary Press, 2020. This is the second volume of the six-volume series. It focuses entirely on the Sermon on the Mount, examining the Beatitudes and the Lord's Prayer. He is certain that the audience was both the people of the multitudes and the disciples, or, at a minimum the disciples with the people overhearing, but, not the disciples only. (p.27) He sees the Lord's Prayer in Matthew and Luke as distinct and wholly likely that Jesus spoke differently to different situations and audiences. (p.232) He also sees the use of Father as likely in a universal sense rather than in a soteriological sense. (p. 238)

40   See how different auditory and visual paths influence human experience and memory in the essay by Tom Boomershine in "The New Testament Soundscape and the Puzzle of Mark," "The New Testament Soundscape and the Puzzle of the Mark," Sound Matters, edited by Margaret Lee, Biblical Performance Criticism Vol. 16, Cascade Books, Eugene, OR © 2018 WIPF and Stock Publishers. See sections in pp. 200-225 on "Sensory Systems of the Human Brain" and "Implications for Biblical Scholarship."

41   See: *Science Daily*, May 25, 2014; article at https://www.sciencedaily.com/releases/2014/05/140525155316.htm "Sound and vision: Visual cortex processes auditory information, too"; from: University of Glasgow; *Summary*—"'Seeing is believing,' so the idiom goes, but new research suggests vision also involves a bit of hearing too. 'So, for example, if you are in a street and you hear the sound of an approaching motorbike, you expect to see a motorbike coming around the corner. If it turned out to be a horse, you'd be very surprised,' researchers said."

42   Current work in neuroplasticity and the roles of various sensory inputs such as sound, sight and touch show the complex ways that the human brain and nervous system interact that are just beginning to be understood. See the examples given in the works of Merlin Donald in *A Mind So Rare* and *Origins of the Modern Mind* where he devotes discussion to the emergence of rhetoric and writing on p. 347-356 and throughout both volumes on the role of neural plasticity and "superplasticity" (p. 208 in *Mind So Rare*) that includes the complex interactions of speech, facial recognition, memory and the role of culture and writing in the development of human creativity and communication.

explicit audience, such as the crowds as well as the disciples, even if it may not initially be obvious to us.[43]

In the case of Matthew, explicit claims to the purpose of Jesus' request to the professional fishermen to follow him so that he could "make them fishers of people" in Matthew 4:19, right before the Sermon on the Mount in Chapters 5-7 have not typically been linked to the Sermon itself. Were there actual recruitment or fishing lessons in these Chapters and, if so, what were they? More significantly, these "fishing lessons" have not been applied to the specific blocks of discourse in 5-7, such as the beatitudes, salt and light, antitheses in his treatment of law and conflict, the request to love enemies and pray for persecutors in Chapter 5, the Lord's Prayer in Chapter 6, ask/seek/knock prayer or the warnings about false prophets or "fishermen" of Chapter 7. When this explicit link is missed, then commentators naturally would look for implicit claims, evidence for its purpose elsewhere, or just guess or give up trying.

Other evidence within the text, such as the rhetorical and mnemonic linkages can also be explored to see whether explicit or implicit claims are bolstered by how the material is presented both in written and oral form.

By experiencing the text or script in ways as the original audience did, and by applying insights to one's own conflicts, greater insight into the text and our own lives can be achieved. Groups using this material should feel encouraged to discuss practical applications to the extent appropriate for their groups whether in current events or in their personal lives.

Overview of the Interpretive Method Used Here

Starting with the text and its context, I use the most comprehensive approach that I can using every interpretive method, tool, and insight to the treatment of the text. Study groups could make use of the interests and expertise of group members to explore these different ways to study these texts, their backgrounds, and contemporary applications. I review the range of interpretive methods, their history and genre analysis in greater detail after the bibliography before the appendix.[44] The combination of literary, historic, sociological, psychological, and rhetorical methods seems to be most completely represented in the "socio-rhetorical interpretive" method developed and espoused by Vernon Robbins and his colleagues. I would further add a refinement to rhetorical investigations with "performance criticism" as advocated by Tom Boomershine and his colleagues, where those studying texts are encouraged to listen to, memorize, and perform the text as part of their exploration process.

---

[43] See W.D. Davies in *The Sermon on the Mount*, who points out the connectedness of Matthew and the role of crowds on p. 4. See also Dale Allision in his *The Sermon on the Mount*, p. 9, "This along with 7:28-29, which informs us that Jesus was speaking not just to the disciples (5:1-2) but also to the crowds, means that any interpretation that thinks of the Sermon as addressed to a *corp d'′lite*, as it were, must be mistaken."

[44] See: "Overview of Interpretive Methods and Genre Analysis of Matthew" by Manto after the bibliography before the appendix. Trying to understand what an author of an older text actually meant and then trying to see its significance for both the author and the reader has been written about for millennia. To get an overview of the vastness of such a simple concept, some articles that might be helpful for someone new at this quest can be conveniently found in the Anchor Bible Dictionary. The first two are found under the topic, "Interpretation, the History of" by J.H. Rogerson (pp. 424-433) and Werner G. Jeanrond (pp. 433-443); a third on "Hermeneutics" by Bernard Lategan (pp. 149-155) and a fourth on "Rhetoric and Rhetorical Criticism" by Benjamin Fiore (pp. 710-719). An article demonstrating some of the interactions between those with different views of hermeneutics and rhetoric can be found in the article by Vernon Robbins in the book, *Rhetorics and Hermeneutics*, by Hester and Hester on pp. 105-128. See also, Robbins, Vernon K.; *Exploring the Texture of Texts, A Guide to Socio-Rhetorical Interpretation*; Trinity Press, Harrisburg, PA and Bloomsbury Academic Press, NY & London, 1996. See treatment of five "textures": Inner, Intertexture, Social and Cultural, Ideological and Sacred. See the article on "Form Criticism" on pp. 841-844 in Volume 2 of the *Anchor Bible Dictionary* by Robbins. (See also, Richard Bauckham, *Jesus and the Eyewitnesses, The Gospels as Eyewitness Testimony*, 2d Edition, Eerdmans, Grand Rapids, MI 2006, 2017; Fitzmyer, Joseph A.; *The Interpretation of Scripture*, Paulist Press, 2008. P. 66; See also the publications and conferences promoted by the Network of Biblical Storytellers (NBS). NBS is a group founded by Tom Boomershine. It holds an annual conference and a two-day by-invitation-only Scholars Forum immediately prior to the conference. See their website: https://www.nbsint.org.)

Background

Authorship: The majority of modern scholars such as Craig Keener and Ulrich Luz assumes the author to be unknown, possibly named Matthew, though not likely the disciple, while noting that the use of the title began no later than 100 A.D.[45] Luz describes the author as having a "good feeling" for Jewish style, Greek language, and synagogue training.[46] What appears certain was that Matthew was a Christ-following Hellenized Israelite.

Date: Luz places the date after the destruction of Jerusalem started in 70 A.D. and completed in 72 A.D., but not long after 80 A.D., in large measure because of its use in other documents such as the Didache produced somewhere between 120-150 A.D.[47] Others such as Donald Hagner[48] lean towards a date just before 70 A.D. but open to a date just afterwards. A local writer just before 70 A.D. would be able to know that bad days were ahead and would anticipate the destruction of the temple as Matthew claims Jesus foretold it decades earlier. (The First Jewish-Roman War of 66-73 that led to the destruction of Jerusalem was prefaced by civic strife since 37 A.D.)[49]

Location of writing of Matthew's Gospel: Consensus about the location of the origin of the writing of the Gospel seems to form around Syria but not to the point of naming a city though Antioch seems to be a favorite choice of scholars because of early widespread use of the texts there while some others opt for places around Galilee.[50]

After the destruction of Jerusalem, those in Matthew's Hellenistic Jewish community were pushed outwards into the

---

45   Craig S. Keener, *The Gospel of Matthew, A Socio-rhetorical Commentary*, Wm. B. Eerdmans, Grand Rapids, MI, 2009. Great updated analysis and bibliography exceeding 70 pp. In this edition of what originally came out in 1999, he adds a brief addendum at the front on "Matthew and Greco-Roman Rhetoric," pp. xxv-l. He interprets the material in Matt 5-7 as a collection of materials rather than something taught in a package. See pp. xxxii-iii: "We noted in the commentary that some have proposed rhetorical outlines for this composite speech. But, whereas it is reasonable to view 5:17 or 5:17-20 as articulating a thesis developed in 5:21-48, and 6:1 as a thesis developed in 6:2-18, a full, consistent rhetorical outline seems too much to ask . . . Matthew offers collections of materials rather than genuinely discrete speeches." The interpretation I propose is that the material is organized, whether given initially or collected later, as a means to provide a way to memorize the maximum amount of material in the least amount of time using emotional frameworks and stories. As such, it holds together as one teaching unit or as a collection, or both, since elements could be used separately in different occasions. He shows deference to an uncertain authorship, though possibly but not likely the apostle Matthew, (p. 39), and a location of Syria, possibly Antioch because of the emergence of the Didache (p.41). [Note that both BC/AD and BCE/CE are used interchangeably since those being quoted use either.]

Ulrich Luz, *Matthew*, Hermeneia Edition, translated from German by James Crouch. Fortress Press, 2007. This is a new edition and translation of the 5th German edition of 2002. Luz explains in the most recent preface that he reworked Chapters 3-7 in 1998 and the introduction in the summer of 2000. This represents his life-long work on the topic and is worthy of its wide acclaim as a 3-volume commentary providing well-documented detail of the scholarly work on the Gospel of Matthew. Volume I covers Chapters 1-7, volume 2 covers 8-20, and volume 3 covers 21-28. He includes a bibliography and analysis section for each block of text that includes structure, sources, tradition history and a history of interpretation of each section that will sometimes show how an author's theological bias might influence the interpretation of a section of text. Multiple interpretive perspectives are woven into each section of text as appropriate. An example would be a "social-psychological perspective" of the "woes discourse" of Matthew 23 on p. 177 of Volume 3. Since each section includes its own bibliography, a fourth volume would likely be needed if they were all compiled together in one volume. Footnotes are provided at the bottom of each page as opposed to being end notes.

Luz views the Matthean version of the Lord's Prayer as a "multifunctional text," "useful as a model prayer, as a dogmatic compendium, as a catechetical synthesis, as a private and ecclesiastical prayer, and so on." As covered in his introduction section, he considers it as "grounded in the worship of his community" and "Matthew's redactional language... grounded in worship." He, similar to Betz and others, sees it also as a basic "ethical text." He also restricts the context of the Lord's Prayer to Chapter 6 when he discusses the use of "*our* Father" on p. 316 to "'Our' connects the praying individual with the community; that is also the custom in Jewish prayers."

46   Luz, p. 50.

47   Luz, p. 59.

48   See Hagner in Gurtner's collection of essays and Donald A. Hagner, *Matthew*, Thomas Nelson, Inc., vols 1-2, 2000. Helpful and scholarly two volume series with each section organized with sections on bibliography, translation, form/structure/setting, comment, and explanation. He is of the opinion that the opening of the Sermon on the Mount may indicate for some that Jesus left the crowds but that the end of the Sermon shows that he did not (an observation similar to Keener). However, though it is obvious that Jesus did not leave the crowds and addressed both the disciples and the much larger number who were not, still much of the interpretation treats the sayings of Jesus as if they applied only to the disciples.

49   See the list of incidents outlined in the Wikipedia article at https://en.wikipedia.org/wiki/First_Jewish–Roman_War.

50   See previous note on Keener.

Jewish diaspora, interpreting the significance of its destruction, and considering how were they now going to relate to their Gentile neighbors. The readers of Matthew's Gospel were being recruited to consider embracing a Messiah of peace, become peacemakers who were authorized to love and pray for their enemies using the material in the Sermon on the Mount and all of Matthew to make new disciples of all the nations around wherever they happened to find themselves.

Location of the setting of Matthew's Gospel: The area covered within the Gospel of Matthew setting for the Sermon on the Mount is explicitly described in the text of 4:12-25 and includes the "Galilee of the Gentiles,"[51] so poor that they were described as "living in the valley of the shadow of death" (v.18). The majority subsisted with little after taxes and debt.[52] Understanding that area provides a rich background for the audience of the Sermon on the Mount and much of the Gospel of Matthew (4:12-25) especially in the light of the Greek urban area of approximately ten towns, the Decapolis,[53] also mentioned in Matthew 4. This shows the strong Hellenized influence in the area. The Galilee area is known to have exported smoked fish among other items from Palestine[54] across the empire providing tax revenues from 323 B.C.E. as shown in tax records and coinage. For a history of how scholars have viewed the use of Greek, especially after the discovery of the Dead Sea scrolls and similar finds, see the extensive 2015 treatment by Michael Owen Wise in *Language, Literacy in Roman Judaea*. Funerary inscriptions in Jerusalem and signature-bearing documents in a broader area show widespread use of Greek, Aramaic, and Hebrew.[55] Wise shows a shift from scholars who previously said that Aramaic was the primary language of the area to those who see greater use of Hebrew. Greek has been acknowledged as used in Greek ethnic centers such as the Decapolis and the elite in cities with disagreement about how widespread use would be among peasants in places like Galilee.[56] Scholars may look at the explicit claims of the setting of Jesus within the text of Matthew to help understand the world of Matthew decades after Jesus. Did Matthew over emphasize certain elements of the setting of Jesus' day to make his point more effectively for his audience decades later? Or were these settings for all practical purposes nearly the same? These nuances can be seen as the works of current scholars are read and compared.

For the significance of fishing in the ancient world and for this audience in particular, the standout work on this topic can be found in *The Meaning of 'Fishers of Men'* by Wilhelm H. Wuellner.[57] For centuries, those in Mediterranean and Middle Eastern worlds were aware of the importance of persuading or "fishing for people." It had both positive and negative connotations. If the true prophets, lawyers, politicians, or philosophers did not take the effort to persuade or catch people, then the false prophets would.[58] The contrast of good people fishing compared to evil people fishing is described historically by Wuellner. The apparent purpose of Matthew 5-6 is to show how to persuade or "fish" whereas Matthew 7 shows how not to persuade and warns against those who fish destructively as "false prophets."

---

51 See Wikipedia article quoted on p. 125 and here: https://en.wikipedia.org/wiki/Mount_of_Beatitudes Note that remaining in an undesirable place implies being trapped there, a relatively hopeless situation.

52 See Douglas Oakman, *Jesus and the Peasants* for economics and the work of the Context Group, p. 5.

53 See the extensive article on "Decapolis" in pp. 116-121 of the *Anchor Bible Dictionary, Volume 2*, by Jean-Paul Rey-Coquais, translated by Stephen Rosoff. Whether Jesus visited the Decapolis, or attracted those from there, or whether it was emphasized by Matthew because many of his audience was from Hellenized cities all of which make that place and those Hellenized people a significant audience both within and behind the text. With a million Jews in Egypt at the time, it would not be surprising if nearly every Jewish family in Israel either had a friend or a relative in Greek speaking Egypt. Given that, Matthew shows Jesus as being Greek-friendly and very likely familiar with Greek having spent his language formative years in Greek speaking Egypt.

54 See Meyers and Chancey, p. 17.

55 See Wise, especially, pp. 1-62 for an extensive treatment on the use of Greek and literacy by scholars.

56 Wise, pp. 13-14.

57 See: Wilhelm H., Wuellner, *The Meaning of 'Fishers of Men'*; Westminster Press, Philadelphia, 1967. Shows the history of the concept of persuasion and its discussion as "fishing" for people both in its positive and negative lights throughout ancient culture with an emphasis on Jewish scripture. This is especially significant for Matthew where warnings about "false prophets" are woven throughout the Gospel and serve as a warning about false fishermen and getting caught in their nets.

58 See Parsons and Martin's *Ancient Rhetoric and the New Testament*, p. 84, quoting Wuellner, Hebrew prophets, Plato and Lucian, Mark and Luke for views of people fishing.

By virtue of trade, local government and law including courts, taxation by occupying powers Greek and then Roman, coinage, and Jewish scriptures and literature written in Greek, it is fairly safe to say that most of the people where Jesus taught, (and more so by the time and place of Matthew's writing) were familiar with Greek and that many, especially literate ones and their rabbis, were accustomed to using Greek as their second language to some extent. (I sometimes say that these passages were written in GSL, Greek as a second language, to make the point.) The Greek cultural methods of persuasion and rhetoric used in oral arguments, persuasion and teaching were so much like Jewish practice that the first century C.E. Hellenized Jewish philosopher Philo of Alexandria commented that the Greeks stole their methods from Moses.[59]

Social Environment—Rhetoric, Writing, Literacy, Education: Alexander the Great and successors conquered much of the known world by 332 B.C.E. and established Greek cities and government. The pervasiveness of Greek culture makes itself clear in the dominance of Greek language in business and trade. Greek was used in the writing of the Greek Torah and other Jewish literature by the second century B.C.E.[60]

Contrast the two maps on the following page to see how the region was impacted by the Alexandrian conquests.

Gerhardsson points out the methods used for teaching and memorizing material based on principles of association or catch word phrases throughout Torah and Talmud teachings. "The more elementary technique of mnemonics was practiced by every Rabbi." He quotes others who noted this phenomenon including J. Bruhl's 1884 work in Hebrew, *Die Mnemotechnic des Talmuds*, and the accompanying remarks by Dr. Neusner.[61]

Scholars representing rhetorical and performance criticism perspectives[62] show that many who have previously written on the Gospels have often underappreciated the role of ancient styles of oral and written persuasion in the world known by Jews in the days of Jesus, the writer of Matthew and his audience in the early church. This is covered more thoroughly in the sections commenting on rhetoric and oral teaching as it appears in the texts of Matthew 5-7 in the exegesis section below. The question of rhetoric and its impact ranges across issues such as the experience of common people witnessing public address by those in synagogues, local government and courts. Rhetoric was formalized in

---

59 Marian Hilar, "*Philo of Alexandria (c. 20 B.C.E.- 40 C.E.),*" *Internet Encyclopedia of Philosophy*; Center for Philosophy and Socinian Studies, https://www.iep.utm.edu/philo/ , viewed May 2020. "But it seems that Philo also picked up his ancestral tradition, though as an adult, and once having discovered it, he put forward the teachings of the Jewish prophet, Moses, as "the summit of philosophy" (*Op.* 8), and considered Moses the teacher of Pythagoras (b. ca 570 B.C.E.) and of all Greek philosophers and lawgivers (Hesiod, Heraclitus, Lycurgus, to mention a few). See collected Philo, Loeb Classical Library in 12 volumes, Vol 6, p. 457 (Moses II:12). For Philo, Greek philosophy was a natural development of the revelatory teachings of Moses. He was no innovator in this matter because already before him Jewish scholars attempted the same. Artapanus in the second century B.C.E identified Moses with Musaeus and with Orpheus. Aristobulus of Paneas (first half of the second century B.C.E.) said, "Homer and Hesiod drew from the books of Moses ... translated into Greek long before the Septuagint."

60 See: Eric M Meyers and Mark A. Chancey, *Alexander to Constantine, Archaeology of the Land of the Bible, Volume 3*; Yale University Press, New Haven, CT 2012. This is a general work on archaeology and culture that provides a useful introduction to the impact of Greek culture on the Middle East. See p. 20 as an example where the discussion includes the role of the Septuagint. See also, the extensive work by Michael Owen Wise in *Language & Literacy in Roman Judaea, A Study of the Bar Kokhba Documents* (2015), on the use of Greek (pp. 7, 33, 41) where Greek is considered a rough equal in usage to Aramaic and Hebrew and the extent of literacy (p. 286).

See: Karen H.; Jobes, Moises Silva, *Invitation to the Septuagint, 2d ed*. Baker Academic, Grand Rapids, MI; 2000, 2015. Describes the history and significance of the collection of Hebrew scriptures in Greek by the time of the mid second century BCE used by Jews in Alexandria, Jerusalem, and the diaspora. (See outline on pp. 21-22.)

For a general introduction to Jewish literature of the Second Temple Period, see: Larry R. Helyer, *Exploring Jewish Literature of the Second Temple Period, A Guide for New Testament Students*, Intervarsity Press, Downers Grove, IL, 2002. Written for students and pastors covering the period of 516 B.C.E. and 70 A.D.

61 See pp. 150-154 of Birger Gerhardsson, *Memory and Manuscript, Oral Tradition and written Transmission in Rabbinic Judaism and Early Christianity with Tradition & Transmission in Early Christianity*. Eerdmans, Grand Rapids, 1998. This is a reprint of the 1961 and 1964 work with a helpful forward by Jacob Neusner known for his work on the *Memorized Torah* in 1985. Neusner recounts the personal histories of those that had difficulties understanding the concepts in Gerhardsson's book but are now gaining appreciation.

62 See the treatment in the bibliography and appendix of socio-rhetorical interpretation method of Robbins and the SBL group "Rhetoric of Religious Antiquity" and performance criticism by Boomershine and the "Biblical Performance Criticism" series by Cascade Books at https://wipfandstock.com/catalogsearch/result/index/?q=biblical+performance+criticism&t_series=89424

Section 1: Introduction

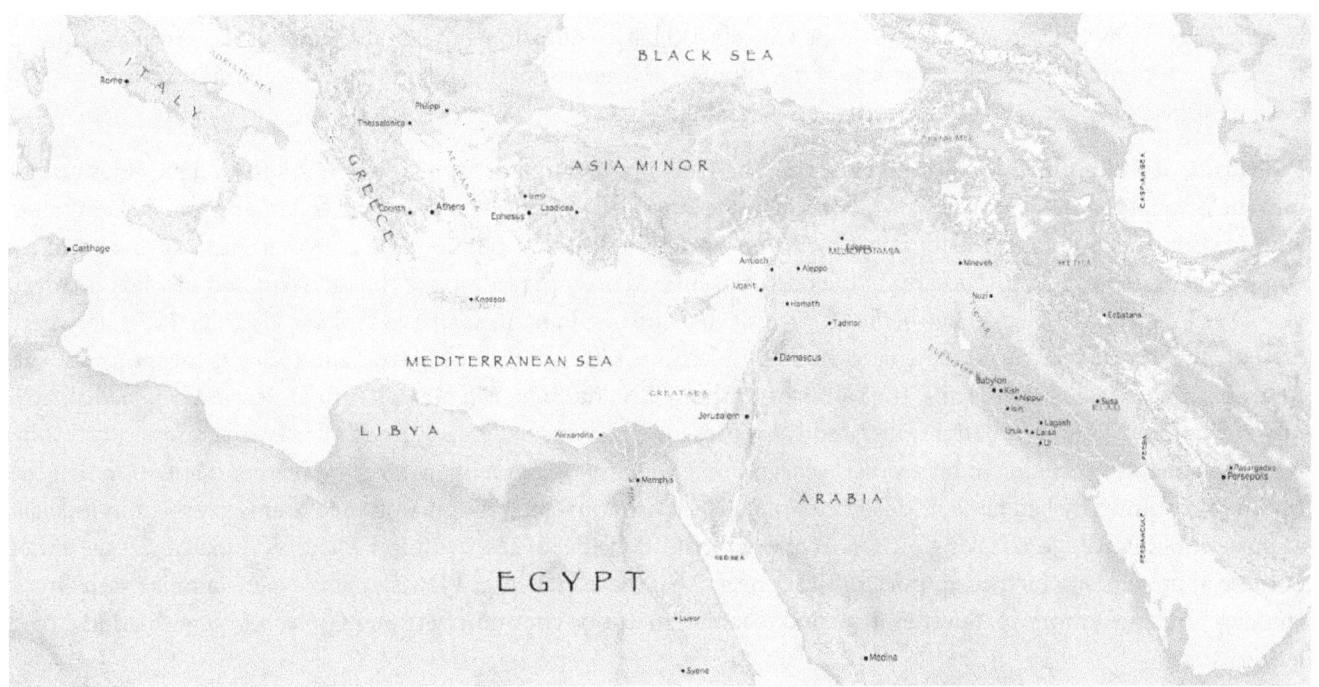

Map of lands comprising areas of the Bible, from *Accordance 13*© 1994-2021 by and used with permission from OakTree Software Inc. for *Accordance Bible Software* licensed to Charles Manto.

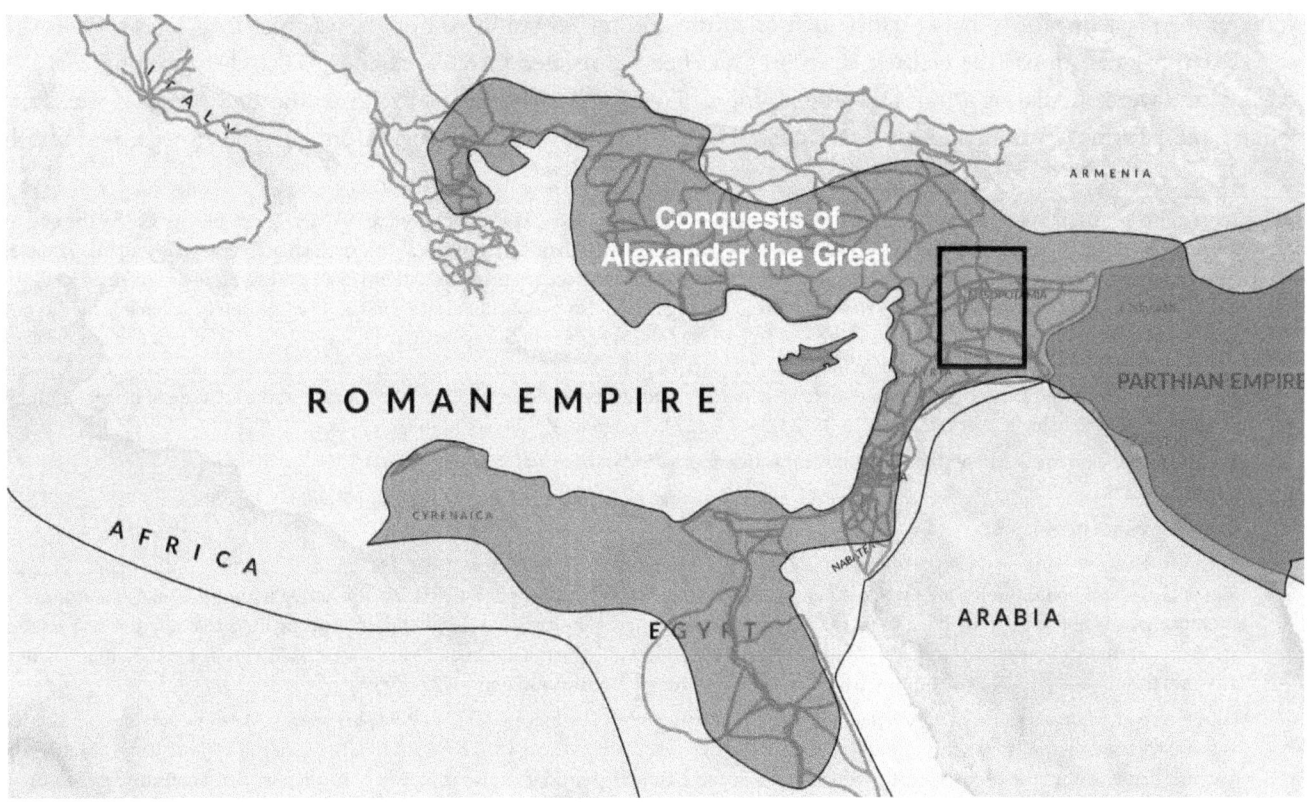

Map of the conquests of Alexander the Great, © 1994-2021 by and used with permission from OakTree Software Inc. for *Accordance Bible Software* licensed to Charles Manto.

higher education venues of their time and influenced the level of education and literacy in general. Estimates range but there are many (as Lemaire) who assume widespread basic education and literacy while others view it as limited to about 15% of the population.[63] Yet 90% of the people had little disposable income after taxes minimized the potential for the average person to own a scroll even if literate.[64]

Political and Religious Background of Syria: The Hellenized nature of the area where Jesus lived provides insight into the diversity of the Jewish leadership in Galilee as opposed to Jerusalem that included Pharisees and Sadducees who were in much greater collaboration with the occupying Roman Empire. For a greater sense of the complex conflicts experienced within this area in the centuries immediately preceding the time of Jesus and the next hundred years, see John Barclay's work, *Jews in the Mediterranean Diaspora, from Alexander to Trajan (323 BCE-117CD)*, where he sees "the term 'Syria' was somewhat vague."[65] Similarly, he states "it is not easy to define what is meant by the cultural complex we call 'Hellenism.'" The works of Anthony J. Saldarini in *Matthew's Christian-Jewish Community* show how the author Matthew is better understood as representing a very Hellenized Jewish Christian community.[66] John Kampen goes a step further in his work *Matthew within Sectarian Judaism* by making the further distinction that the Matthean community had not left Judaism to join a Christian movement but maintained themselves within Judaism as ones who followed Jesus taking on a form of what many consider a "sect" within Hellenized Judaism.[67] I see either of these approaches as further support for the concept that these Hellenized Jewish people were familiar with Greek language, but even more so, the rhetorical and teaching methods common between Greek and Jewish educational leaders.

Furthermore, Matthew was originally written in Greek and used Greek and Jewish rhetoric embedded in the text in a way familiar to many of his readers and hearers who were Hellenized Jewish Christians and encouraged to reach the nations many of whom in their day just happened to use Greek often as a second language. The rhetorical methodology in this Greek Gospel is primarily conceptual and for the most part crosses language boundaries though some of the plays on words that enhance memorization and transmission do not always cross languages such as the earliest Latin translations. The Hebrew scriptures had been translated into Greek after Alexander's conquest in 333 B.C.E.[68] and were circulating around the empire for well over 100-200 years by the time Matthew's Gospel was written in Greek. Rome continued to use Greek as well as Latin as shown by Emperor Domitian's literary games in both

---

63   See: Andre Lemaire, "Writing and Writing Materials," *Anchor Bible Dictionary*, Vol. 6, Doubleday, NY, 1992. Pp. 999-1008. "By the end of the first century B.C., there were schools in most Jewish towns. According to one Talmudic tradition, the high priest Jesus, son of Gamaliel (63-65 A.D.), ordered schoolteachers to be appointed in every town and children brought to them from the age of six or seven. From these indications one may assume that literacy was widespread among the Jewish people in Palestine in the 1st century B.C.; even if Jesus did not attend a high rabbinic school (cf John 7:15), he was able to read the Scripture in the synagogue (Luke 4:7)" (p. 1005). See the discussion of a lower level of literacy in the works of William Harris on p. 14 of his book, *Ancient Literacy*, quoted by Boomershine on p. 2 of *Messiah of Peace*. See Catherine Hezser for estimates of Jewish literacy in Palestine at closer to 3% in rural areas and the critique of her position by Michael Wise proposing higher rates (pp. 26-32, 24-36, 81-82) in *Language & Literacy in Roman Judaea*.

64   See Douglas Oakman's works on the economy of the area and period in *Jesus and the Peasants*, p. 137.

65   John Barclay, *Jews in the Mediterranean Diaspora, from Alexander to Trajan (323 BCE-117CD)*; University of California Press, © T&T Clark, 1996. See p. 242, p. 88.

66   Anthony Saldarini, *Matthew's Christian-Jewish Community*; University of Chicago Press, 1994. He details the context of the people of Matthew's Gospel and community. He provides a comprehensive view of the author as a Christian still active within the Jewish community attempting to establish the Jewish legitimacy of his Christian message. He provides a number of interesting links to contemporary Jewish literature for many of the textual elements of Matthew. An example would be the use of oaths in various Jewish groups at the time. Of note, he views the crowds (p. 37) as distinctive from the disciples though "neutral and good-willed."

67   John Kampen, *Matthew within Sectarian Judaism*, Yale University Press, New Haven, CT, 2019. See his view of Matthew and his community as those who see themselves as part of Judaism who follow Jesus and not as those who have left Judaism. See p. 84 where he ties Matthew's teaching firmly within the apocalyptic traditions of the Second Temple period. See also p. 85 where he disputes the centrality of the Lord's Prayer in Matthew 6 and replaces it with the six antitheses of the Law in Mt 5. I would argue that since the request to love enemies and pray for persecutors is the objective of the six antithesis and outlined in the Lord's Prayer in Mt 6, that both are true, the Lord's Prayer is the ultimate expression of the true law, conflict resolution and prayer all of which are used as an approach used in recruitment of new disciples. See also Charles Ridlehoover *The Lord's Prayer and the Sermon on the Mount in Matthew's Gospel. London: T&T Clark, 2020.* He provides additional support for the centrality of the prayer in Matthew 5-7 and the gospel as a whole.

68   See Jobes and Silva, *Invitation to the Septuagint*, pp. 19-20.

Section 1: Introduction

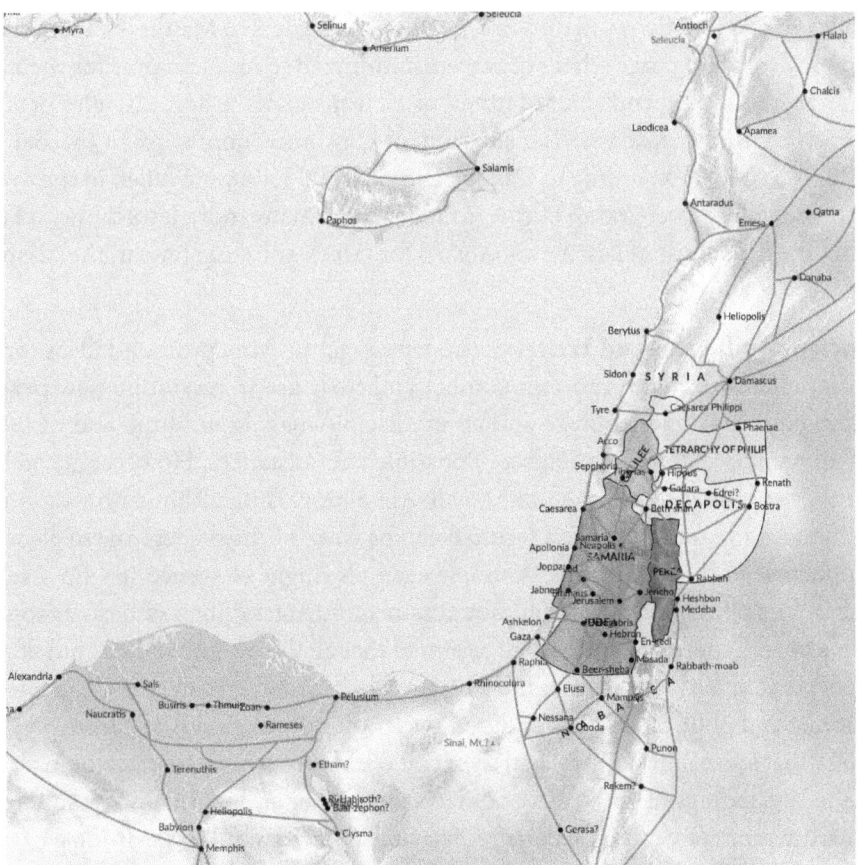

Map of Syria, Israel, Egypt -- regions pertinent to Jesus and the Gospel of Matthew; © 1994-2021 by and used with permission from OakTree Software Inc. for *Accordance Bible Software* licensed to Charles Manto.

languages between 81-96 C.E..[69] Noted Jewish philosopher Philo wrote and spoke primarily in Greek and little in Hebrew or Aramaic. Greek was at least the second language of choice and one that most of the Hellenized Jews and their neighbors throughout the Mediterranean knew in the years following Matthew's publication. Greek was prolific in Rome through the first century C.E.[70]

Fall of Jerusalem: According to contemporary reports, the destruction of Jerusalem in 70-72 C.E., resulted in Josephus claiming a death total of over a million, which if true would likely be about a fifth of Jewish people at the time and resulting in a Jewish tax by Vespasian.[71] During that time, Emperor Domitian pushed to enhance the Roman

---

69 Suetonius, *Lives of the Twelve Caesars*; Public domain online; published in the Loeb Classical Library, 1914. See life of Domitian, sec 4.4: "For there were competitions in prose declamation both in Greek and in Latin;" sec 10.1 See also Barclay, p. 19. "… the Jewish community in Alexandria became extremely large and contained an intellectual elite whose literature (all of it in Greek) became known … to a far greater degree than … other Jewish centers. Most of these papyri originate in the countryside of Egypt."

70 John T. Townsend, "Education, Greco-Roman," *Anchor Bible Dictionary*, Vol. 2, pp. 312-317. "In the world of the NT, educational theory and practice were essentially Hellenistic . . . Even Jewish Hebrew schools were not immune to the pervasive Hellenistic influence, and one can easily interpret rabbinic education as the Jewish adaptation of Hellenistic educational methods and curricula" (p. 312) … "In the western part of the empire Latin language and literature were receiving more emphasis, although the continuing importance of Greek in Roman schools meant that Paul had no difficulty with Christians at Rome understanding an epistle written in Greek. In fact, Greek predominated in Christian worship at Rome until well after the NT period (p. 313), He describes widespread participation in primary schools starting at age 7, and secondary schools that might include textual criticism and translation from classic to contemporary Greek, memorization, and math through geometry. Higher education was experienced by fewer and included the study of philosophy, literature and rhetoric including "the five steps of speech preparation: invention of ideas, arrangement, style, memorization, and delivery" (p.315).

71 Some historians think that the number might have been half that. See the Wikipedia note at https://en.wikipedia.org/wiki/First_Jewish–Roman_War: "The defeat of the Jewish revolt altered Jewish demographics, as many of the Jewish rebels were scattered or sold into slavery. Josephus claimed that 1,100,000 people were killed during the siege, 97,000 were captured and enslaved and many others fled to areas

official religion; both Jews and Christians suffered as a result.[72] The readers of Matthew's Gospel were being recruited to consider embracing a Messiah of peace where they were authorized to love and pray for their enemies and use the material in the Sermon on the Mount and all of Matthew as a means to make new disciples of all the nations around wherever they happened to find themselves. The subsequent continued unrest led to the Bar Kokhba Revolt and Third Jewish War (132-136 C.E.). "According to Cassius Dio, 580,000 Jews were killed in the overall operations, and 50 fortified towns and 985 villages were razed to the ground,[3] with many more Jews dying of famine and disease."[73] These events enhanced the usefulness of Matthew's Gospel for Greek-speaking Jews in the diaspora and their neighbors.

Empathy for the Ancient Audiences and Writers: These passages provide profound ideas for anger, anxiety, conflict management, communications with those in conflict and their use in recruiting new peace-making disciples. The clear intent of the material is to encourage and equip disciple-making until the end of the age which expects that these concepts will hold up globally in each set of possible circumstances. However, it can be easy for someone living millennia after these writings to assume that they live in a more difficult time now or at least a very different time than those two thousand years before. As a result, it can be easy for the reader now to gloss over lightly insights that might be very applicable to their situations. A simple example might be someone who assumes that their times are so hard that those in "the good old days" could not possibly understand their issues. Or someone might assume that it is a waste of time to read these documents if it assumed that all the insight of these old documents would have been learned and incorporated into new ideas rendering a read of the older materials to be unnecessary. But, when one studies the economic and political stresses endured two thousand years ago, it becomes a lot easier to become empathetic and hopeful that something understood then could be helpful now. If so, it would also be valuable to take the time to discover the key findings of the works of old to see whether and when any of those lessons have been appropriated by newer writings or concepts. The benefit of having an open mind towards the past, is that it could result in our being more open-minded to others in our own age but in different circumstances. It might also make us more sympathetic and empathetic to the generations ahead of us who will likely encounter tougher time than our own. That in turn could encourage us to see what ancient lessons might become even more pertinent to the times when manmade and natural disasters are greater than those of the past and the love of most grow cold.

---

around the Mediterranean. A significant portion of the deaths was due to illnesses and hunger brought about by the Romans. "A pestilential destruction upon them, and soon afterward such a famine, as destroyed them more suddenly."[1]

72 Brian W. Jones, "Domitian," *Anchor Bible Dictionary*, volume 2, 1992. (p. 221-222). See discussion of his harassment of Jews and Christians quoting the sources of Suetonius, Pliny and Eusebius. See Suetonius, *Lives of the Twelve Caesars*, Sec. 12.2. "Besides other taxes, that on the Jews was levied with the utmost rigor, and those were prosecuted who without publicly acknowledging that faith yet lived as Jews, as well as those who concealed their origin and did not pay the tribute levied upon their people. I recall being present in my youth when the person of a man ninety years old was examined before the procurator and a very crowded court, to see whether he was circumcised." See: https://en.wikipedia.org/wiki/Fiscus_Judaicus.

73 See: https://en.wikipedia.org/wiki/Bar_Kokhba_revolt

Section 1: Introduction

Context

Prayer and its Elements: within Matthew 6; Matthew 5; Matthew 7; Matthew 18

Each of these three prayers in Matthew 6, 7, and 18 can be shown as conflict prayers. Matthew 5 is included since it provides the immediate context for the prayer in Matthew 6 where the request to pray for persecutors begins in Matthew 5:44 and the conflicts which comprise the relationships between crowd members and their persecutors described from the beginning of the Sermon on the Mount in 5:1 and following. Matthew 7:7-12 appears to reiterate the request to pray for persecutors in the "ask, seek, and knock" prayer culminating in the reminder that the Father in heaven gives good things to those who ask and the conclusion, "whatever you wish that men would do to you, do so to them" similar to the end of the Lord's Prayer in 6:14-15.[74] The first two prayers are pre-emptive in that they are prayers by someone in the spirit of love and forgiveness who is threatened or hurt by an adversary even while they must pray alone because no repentance or reconciliation has yet occurred. The third prayer in Matthew 18 is when the parties reconcile and there is a special presence of Jesus in that prayer of reconciliation.

Characters: Crowds, disciples, gentiles/heathen/nations, hypocrites, tax collectors and Jesus

The *crowds* in Matthew as in Matthew 4:25 are described as "great (or "many") crowds"[75] that followed Jesus from Galilee, the Decapolis, Jerusalem, and from the Jordan. Seeing not just one group, but great or many crowds Jesus goes up the side of the mountain. (Matthew 5:1). Aside from the symbolism[76] of the use of "mountain," this corroborates the intention of Jesus speaking to the entire group including the crowds. Had he not gone on an incline; his voice would not carry[77] through the bodies of those closest to him. So, by leading the crowds uphill, his voice could carry with some help from the sound bounce from the hill or mountainside.[78] These same crowds were there at the end and were astonished at his teaching as being commanding or "authoritative" as if they had no choice but to listen (Matthew 7:28-29). Then the same "great crowds" followed him down from the mountain (Matthew 8:1). This is important to understand as they were the primary audience Jesus was addressing in Matthew 5-7 with the *disciples* looking on. To deny the crowds were there would be in direct opposition to the text. To say that they merely "overheard" Jesus would have Jesus primarily speaking to his disciples who were closest in proximity to Jesus in such a way that most of the "great crowds" would not have even heard him. The only way that the crowds could hear was if Jesus purposely projected his voice to them over the disciples in the front row which would have been odd if only intended for those next to him. The only reason the great crowds would care to listen in the first place and stay until the end of Jesus' last comment would be that the information Jesus was sharing was compellingly relevant to them.

One key reason the teaching was also pertinent to the disciples is that these were the recruiting or "fishing" lessons Jesus just had promised to them near the end of Matthew 4:18-22 when the "great crowds" were introduced in 4:23-25 from whom Jesus was about to recruit and show the fishermen-disciples (4:18) how to do it. He is also teaching the crowds and the disciples how to pray. This audience is different from the one in Luke 11:1-14, after the "Sermon,"

---

74   See the conclusion section comparing the three conflict prayers and ramifications for relationship restoration.

75   See Douglas E. Oakman's comments on the size of crowds in *Jesus and the Peasants*, pp. 46-52.

76   The use of "mount" has been used by many to reflect back on the work of Moses, but it might also have been used to refer to the rhetorical presentation of the material in the Sermon.

77   Note the similar circumstances where elevation is used in amphitheaters or Jesus in a boat (Matthew 13:2) speaking to those on the inclined shore so the audience can hear better. See the November 20, 2018, article in *Physics Today* by Pamela Jordan, "Uncovering Ancient Practices through Acoustics," describing her work in Arcadia, Greece "using a combination of binaural recordings and psychoacoustic analysis tools. I am an architect and heritage specialist by training; as a graduate student and architecture and historic preservation professional." She shows the benefits of using elevation to carry sound to an audience. See the article here: https://physicstoday.scitation.org/do/10.1063/PT.6.1.20180430b/full/

78   See the note above and acoustics work of Jordan and Wikipedia article quoted in the bibliography and here: https://en.wikipedia.org/wiki/Mount_of_Beatitudes

when a disciple privately asked Jesus for prayer coaching. Jesus addresses the disciple differently than he did the crowds in Matthew 6:5-15. Since the disciple presumably agreed with Jesus about the importance of forgiveness, Jesus uses the words "forgive us our sins *for* we forgive (release) everyone who is indebted to us" (Revised Standard Version (RSV)), as opposed to "as we forgive (release) in Matthew. With the audience of the disciples, their forgiving (releasing) others is assumed and is indicative of the relationship already established with the Father; this was not the case for the crowds in Matthew 6:14-15 who were not yet disciples, not yet "caught" and not yet certain of forgiveness. It was still to be determined whether the crowds would forgive, hence the quote at the end of the prayer in Matthew 6:14-15: "for if you forgive (release) people their trespasses, your heavenly Father also will forgive (release) you; but if you do not forgive (release) people their trespasses, neither your Father forgive (release) your trespasses" (RSV).

The *disciples* in Matthew 4:18-22 are only described here as the professional fishermen. If other disciples were present, they were not mentioned. The purpose appears to be that Matthew is emphasizing the nature of the Sermon on the Mount as a recruiting or "fishing" expedition where the professional fishermen were getting "on the job training" or "continuing education" by Jesus to learn how to catch people or make disciples. This focus on "fishing for people" or "disciple-making" is entirely appropriate for the Gospel of Matthew that ends with the command of Jesus to his disciples that they go to the nations to make disciples and that all authority was given to him to pass on to the disciples "on earth as it is in heaven" (ὡς ἐν οὐρανῷ καὶ ἐπὶ γῆς· (in Matthew 28:18) in just the way it was said in the Lord's Prayer in 6:9, the ultimate disciple making tool, when he said "on earth as it is in heaven" (ὡς ἐν οὐρανῷ καὶ ἐπὶ γῆς·).

The *Gentiles, heathen, pagans, nations, nationals* (οἱ ἐθνικοί) (i.e., not Israelites or Judaeans) are mentioned throughout as those with a different world view, God view, and attitude. In the request to pray for persecutors they are mentioned as ones who salute their brothers (5:47) implying not their enemies and in preface to the Lord's Prayer in 6:7 as needing repetitious empty phrases because their inadequate little gods can't hear them otherwise and are ignorant of their needs, unlike the true and infinite God who knows our needs before we do and doesn't require our data in order to be informed (6:8). And later, in the prayer of reconciliation in Matthew 18, if one chooses not to reconcile, they are to be considered as one with a different world or God view, namely a Gentile heathen, or, a tax collector who has the same world view as a fellow Israelite but chooses not to live it (not unlike a hypocrite).[79]

Hypocrites are introduced in the Gospel of Matthew in Chapter 6:2 as those who consistently are concerned about reputation and appearance but not inner realities.[80] This is consistent with inner and outer themes beginning with the alternating pairs of beatitudes, the discussion of salt versus saltiness, and external law versus internal attitudes. Hypocrites give alms, pray, and fast in public (Matthew 6:2-18), the very things that should be done in secret as opposed to the deeds of gentleness, mercy, and peacemaking that should be done in front of others that bring glory to the Father (Matthew 5:3-16). Hypocrites are ultimately described as those who require one thing but do not

---

79   See L. Gregory Jones in Embodying Forgiveness, p.194, "As Stanley Hauerwas [quoting *Christian Existence Today* p.94] has contended, such people 'are acting like those who have not learned that they have been forgiven. To act like one not needing forgiveness is to act against the very basis of this community as a community of peacemaking."

80   Originally defined as "actors." W.F. Albright, and C. S.; Mann, *Matthew*, The Yale Anchor Bible, Yale University Press, 1971. It also has an excellent essay about the historical use of the word "hypocrite" as an actor. See its treatment in the appendix of the introduction of the commentary on pp. cxv to cxxiii. This also provides a fascinating preface describing how the original author dropped out at the last minute requiring the editor to add monographs such as the one on the use of "hypocrite" to fill in material that would otherwise be insufficient for publication (p. v).

See also the entry in *The Theological Dictionary of the New Testament*, Vol. VIII, pp. 559-570, edited by Gerhard Kittel and Gerhard Friedrich, © 1972, reprinted in 2006, Eerdmans, Grand Rapids, MI. This provides a historical use of the word reflecting "explaining," or "acting" with a shift to a negative connotation in the Septuagint and subsequently by Philo and Josephus. Depending on the form of the word, Matthew uses it 13-17 times when Mark uses it once and Luke several times. This could provide some evidence either of the exposure of the writer of Matthew to either Jewish literature accustomed to using the word this way or to greater familiarity with acting within the theater of his day.

Sermon on the Mount © Laura James, used with permission.

live it as in Matthew 23:3, are given woes in 23:13 as blocking others from entry to the "kingdom of heaven" and are blocked from entering it themselves. Hypocrites who promote themselves reflect the opposite of the blessing of Matthew 5:3 and 5:10 where the poor in spirit co-own or possess the "kingdom of heaven." (Note the similarity of hypocrites receiving woes in Matthew 23 for blocking entrance to the Kingdom and persecuting the just.)

Tax collectors: The word for tax-collectors is τελῶναι (telohnai). They were known as Jewish locals who collaborated with the Romans who gave them broad authority to collect taxes which often led to their reputations as abusers of that authority either to extort money or sexual privileges. They may have shared the world view of Israelites as opposed to Gentiles who did not. But the tax collectors, often grouped with the word "sinners" (Matthew 9:10-11), were not living consistently with that world view while being self-serving. In Matthew 18:17, those who refused to reconcile were to be considered either as Gentiles, those who did not share the world view of Israelites whose God is a forgiving or reconciling God, or like the tax collectors who may have believed that was God's job and not their own and hence would not reconcile. (See also Luke 18:11 where the implication of being an evil tax collector may have implied that the epithets of "extortioners, unjust, adulterers" also applied to the tax collector seen as abusing his power, justifying comparison to any or all of the other three.)

In Matthew 5:46 and 5:48, there is a possible play on words where two different words sounded alike to those listening to the words in Matthew. Both the word tax collector, τελῶναι (telohnai) and "be perfect" (τέλειοι) sound alike. They are similarly sounding words. It could also be said that they actually share the same root (tel) that we see in anything with the sense of end, such as telephone, telegraph, television, telescope. In the same way the tax collector is the end point of the imperial government that perfects the reach of the taxing authority into the pockets of the taxed. In that sense a tax collector would literally be called in one word as an "ender" or "perfecter." So, both from the sound of "tel" and its implied usage of perfecter, the listeners in Matthew 5 could be said to hear the rough equivalent of "even the '*perfecters*' love their friends, but I want you to be *perfect* as your heavenly Father is *perfect* and love your enemies." See the phrase, "You must therefore be perfect, just as your heavenly Father is perfect.' (Ἔσεσθε οὖν ὑμεῖς τέλειοι ὡς ὁ πατὴρ ὑμῶν ὁ οὐράνιος τέλειός ἐστιν.) This is a likely impact but might not be what was intended though it appears to have worked out that way. If so, it works in a way like a pun. This is one of the sound-alikes and word plays in Greek which, if present, does not carry over into the oldest Latin texts where the word for "tax collector" is "publican." There are other plays on words and words that work well in sound maps that do not carry over as well into other languages, such as Latin. This one might not be the best example, but I include it so others who are more aware of the use of similar sounding words in ancient rhetoric and the history of that word in Greek may provide some further insight. The use of "tel" here is not an essential point of this view of the Lord's Prayer in Matthew. But readers who familiarize themselves with early Greek versions might be encouraged to discover some of these on their own even if all it does is help them with their own memorization.

Jesus: The first four chapters of Matthew describe a lot about Jesus from the very first verse as "This is a record of the life of Jesus the Messiah, the son of David, the son of Abraham." His identity is commented on by the angel appearing to Joseph in a dream asking him to "name him Jesus because he is the one who will save his people from their sins" (Matthew 1:21 ISV). He is declared king by the wise men (Matthew 2:2). He lived in exile for a while in Egypt before his second birthday (Matthew 2:13-19), likely in a Greek speaking area during the age when he was most capable of becoming bilingual.[81] He was described by Matthew as fulfilling prophesies, described by John the Baptist as the one whose way he is preparing (Matthew 3:1-16) and by the voice from heaven declaring, "This is my Son, whom I love. I am pleased with him."

But for all these declarations, Jesus did not self-identify himself to anyone including his own disciples until Matthew 16:13-20 and then told them not to tell anyone that he was the Messiah. He only gave hints to John the Baptist's

---

[81] See an overview of the use of Greek in Egypt at this time in this article by Peter van Millen: https://library.duke.edu/rubenstein/scriptorium/papyrus/texts/rule.html; and the Wikipedia article: https://en.wikipedia.org/wiki/Ptolemaic_Kingdom; See its description of Greek language usage of Jews in Egypt, "The Jews who lived in Egypt had originally immigrated from the *Southern Levant*. The Jews absorbed Greek, the dominant language of Egypt at the time, and heavily mixed it with Hebrew.[85] The *Septuagint*, the Greek translation of the Jewish scriptures, appeared and was written by seventy Jewish Translators under royal compulsion during Ptolemy II's reign."[86] Estimates of the number of Jews in Egypt at the time are about 1,000,000. See S. Kent Brown; "Egypt, History of (Greco-Roman)," See p. 368, Vol. 2 of *Anchor Bible Dictionary*.

See also the article "The Jews of Ancient Egypt" by Jimmy Dunn on Jewish settlements across all of Egypt here: http://www.touregypt.net/featurestories/jewsinegypt.htm. "Ptolemy I is said to have "removed from the land of the Jews into Egypt up to one hundred thousand people, from whom he armed about thirty thousand chosen men and settled them through the land in the forts" (Ep. Arist. 1213). While Aristea's numbers are likely exaggerated, various papyri, inscriptions and ostraca from the third century B.C. nonetheless testify to the presence of substantial Jewish populations in all parts of Egypt." See also Emil Schurer's comments on the usage of Greek by Jews in Alexandria, "Not many generations after the founding of the community, the Torah was translated into Greek (perhaps under Ptolemy II.; at all events not much later). It was read in Greek in the synagogues; indeed, this was the language chiefly used in the service (Schürer, "Gesch." 3d ed., iii. 93-95). Greek must, therefore, have been the vernacular of the lower classes also." – From the *Jewish Encyclopedia*, http://jewishencyclopedia.com/articles/1171-alexandria-egypt-ancient

disciples in Matthew 11:2-6 who asked him if he was the one. Jesus said to tell John what they saw, namely, that "the blind see, the lame walk, lepers are cleansed, the deaf hear, the dead are raised and the destitute hear the good news."

In Matthew 5, the destitute are the ones surprisingly declared by Jesus to have the "kingdom of heaven." Jesus announces and teaches the crowds of the destitute, not only of physical security, but destitute of hope (the poor in spirit), that God is at work in their lives through their very suffering that would be surprising, good news indeed. John the Baptist would recognize him as the one doing the work of the Messiah just as the demons that he cast out in Matthew 8:29 recognized his power as they exclaimed, "What do you want with us, Son of God? Did you come here to torture us before the proper time?"

These narratives and declarations of the other characters show Jesus as sneaking into the world ahead of the proper time for some unexpected reason, namely as the angel said, "to save his people from their sins." But, according to Matthew, Jesus himself refused to declare that for some time and asked his disciples to keep his true identity under wraps. In the Sermon on the Mount of Matthew 5-7, Jesus was evoking the stories of suffering and injustice of the listeners within the crowds long before telling them his own story. That was ostensibly all part of the way he was teaching his disciples how to "fish for people."

Conflict, Law, and Legal Systems: Compensatory damages section, antitheses section, beatitudes section, Matthew 18 conflict section.

See the discussion on the conflict and conflict resolution orientation of all of Matthew beginning at Matthew 1:21 with the purpose of Jesus to "save his people from their sins" to the beginning of the antitheses section of Matthew 5:17 where Jesus says he has "not come to abolish the law but to fulfill it." Each of the following sections that follow describes the conflict of broken agreements, laws, and relationships and how the crowds are asked to be like the Father to love those in conflict rather than hate, to "pray for" instead of "praying against" them (Matthew 5:44).[82] These will be further addressed in the exegesis section. Whenever someone or some group does something to hurt another, these conflicts result in damages and subsequent claims for compensation (often supported by formal cases before a judge). These claims for compensation become something owed to the person harmed, or a *debt*. For much of the population who is barely getting by after paying taxes, debt could become overwhelming and result in their being placed in prison until the debts are paid, overwhelming to the point of taking away all one's wealth and placing one in and his family in slavery, the ultimate debtors prison. (See Matthew 5:25-26 and 18:34). It could also result in the debtor and his family being sold into slavery (Matthew 18:25). See Betz' description of compensatory damages in the era of Jesus and the Middle East in general[83] and Oakman for the role of debt in Israel at the time of Jesus.[84] Note the common elements between the Jewish law, other ancient Near Eastern systems such as the Code of Hammurabi, Greek and Roman law, how they were expected that these systems would keep the peace and how people were trained to participate in these systems.

This is especially interesting to see how significant these conflicts were in the context of an agrarian society (85% of the population) where nearly all were living off subsistence farming or related activities. There was little "disposable" income after taxes which minimized the potential for purchasing scrolls or hiring others to make them.[85] Douglas Oakman organizes tables and charts of various kinds of ancient agrarian conflicts in his book, *The Radical Jesus, the Bible, and the Great Transformation*.[86] This provides background to the compensatory damages section in Matthew 5 where the use of a conflict matrix in Matthew 5:38-42 shows an extraordinary range of conflicts as the subject of the Lord's Prayer for persecutors.

---

82 See similar concepts in Romans, 12:14-18.

83 Betz, *Sermon on the Mount*, pp., 275-280.

84 Oakman, *Jesus and the Peasants*, pp., 19-39, including the concept of debt as it appears in the Lord's Prayer. See also Oakman's *Jesus, Debt and the Lord's Prayer*, focusing on agrarian debt (pp.17-41) and a social perspective on the prayer (pp.42-91).

85 See the treatment on the economy of the period by Douglas Oakman in *Jesus and the Peasants*. See the "Drivers" section that follows for more details.

86 Oakman, *The Radical Jesus, the Bible and the Great Transformation*, pp. 47-53.

For an overview and history of social-scientific approaches providing insight into conflicts, see the final chapter of *A Marginal Scribe, Studies in the Gospel of Matthew in a Social-Scientific Perspective* by Dennis Duling. He integrates various views of Matthew and his community as a voluntary association with different degrees of connectedness to Jewish roots. For purposes of this study of loving enemies and praying for persecutors with a hope of winning them over, his view of reconciling or reproving offending brothers in Matthew 18 is especially significant.[87]

Comments about the legal system are added in the some of the notes in the commentary sections, such as 5:38 showing connections between the Jewish legal system and Babylonian, Greek, and Roman systems and their related works in legal training and persuasion methods.

---

87   See Duling, *A Marginal Scribe*, p. 334-335.

Section 1: Introduction

Drivers

Capturing the interest of a listener by starting with the listeners own priorities and then leading them to a conclusion provides the framework for a convincing interaction. The material in Matthew 5-7 reveals a collection of these persuasive or rhetorical methods that are combined to show the disciples how to convince others to become disciples and provide the disciples with tools to do that. These methods work together to guide the flow of the writing and drive towards goals that are part of what Matthew believes Jesus is laying out in disciple making.

It's important to keep in mind the role of oral persuasion in a time when the cost of written materials in the ancient world (and the relative poverty of most in the "crowd") meant that rabbis or teachers like Jesus would convey information in such a way that their words and ideas could be grasped and recalled without being written down. Throughout the exegesis section, some care will be given to show the rhetorical force or direction of the material that culminates with the request of Jesus to the crowds that they love enemies and pray for the worst-case, namely the "persecutors" who were pursuing them as in 5:10-12; 25-26 and 5:49.[88] Later, Matthew 18:29-39 places the last woe for persecutors pursuing from town to town in verse 34 in symmetry to the last blessing for the persecuted in 5:10-12 (as the first woe in 23:13 for blocking entrance into the kingdom of heaven is in symmetry to the first blessing for the poor in spirit entering the kingdom of heaven).

The nature of material written to be memorized and presented orally so others might embrace it, memorize it and share it with others orally require a much stronger sense of linkage between the portions of the text compared to us who merely read the texts from relatively cheap materials that we possess. We don't feel the need to memorize the material because we can go back and read it at our convenience.

A scroll might take 4-8 days of labor to complete and a collection of all the scrolls of scripture in the days of Jesus or the early church would comprise 40 or so rolls at roughly 200 days of labor.[89] An average literate person would not likely be able to afford that much of their income, roughly a year of wages for a Bible. If one day of income could possibly be saved per month, it would take 200 months to come up with that much income or about 17 years.

Multiple ancient scrolls can now be seen online. For a sense of the size of a collection of scrolls such as the Bible, see the online version of one of the oldest book style versions of the handwritten Bible the Codex Sinaiticus where there were no spaces between words, likely a space and cost saving practice. See: https://www.codexsinaiticus.org/en/ and Matthew 6 at: http://www.bl.uk/manuscripts/Viewer.aspx?ref=add_ms_43725_f202v .

On the following page is a picture of the page from the Codex Sinaiticus that contains the Lord's Prayer in Matthew 6 from approximately 2d to 3d quarter of the fourth century (325-375 A.D.) The British Museum Library facsimile can be purchased from Henrickson Publishers (https://www.hendrickson.com/html/product/565775.trade.html?category=all). The size is approximately 14.5 x 17.5 x 4 inches and weighs approximately 38 pounds. I assume that a vellum version would weigh more.

Regardless of how you might estimate the cost of a complete Bible, those who were literate and not wealthy would need to memorize the material to study it at home or share it with others.[90] The need to memorize and listen to the

---

88   See John Kampen's *Matthew within Sectarian Judaism*, pp. 80-81 for the seriousness of persecution and added reason to consider the pursuing aspect of persecution.

89   See: Ben Witherington, III; "Books and Scrolls in the World of Jesus"; Patheos online, November 5, 2011. https://www.patheos.com/blogs/bibleandculture/2011/11/05/books-and-scrolls-in-the-world-of-jesus/ "A standard roll of papyrus in mid-first century A.D. Egypt cost four drachmae, which is to say it cost about 4-8 days' pay of an ordinary workman. But let us take for example, the famous Isaiah scroll found at Qumran. A roll thirty feet long took no less than 30 or so hours to fill up. That is—at least three full day's work for a scribe like the one pictured above (my shot from the museum of Egyptology in Cairo). A copy of Isaiah then could cost at least 10 denarii, and that is a low guess. And then you would have exactly ONE book of the OT in your hands. Imagine about 40 more rolls that long and you can imagine an OT on scrolls."

90   For a sense of the size of a collection such as the Bible, see the online version of one of the oldest book style versions of the handwritten Bible the Codex Sinaiticus where there were no spaces between words, likely a space and cost saving practice. See: https://www.codex

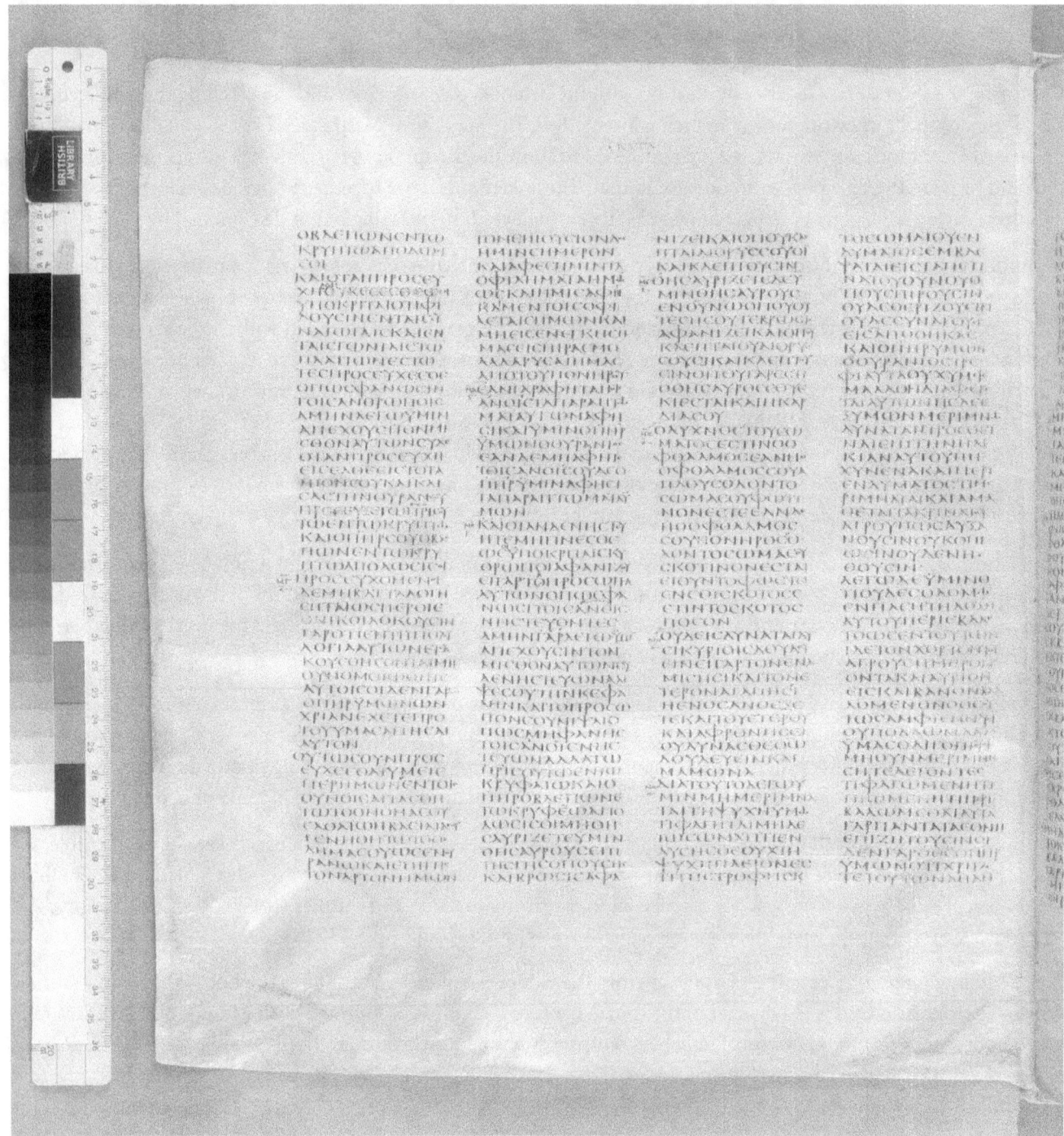

Photo of page of Matthew 6:4 and following from Codex Sinaiticus © and licensed for reproduction to Charles Manto by The British Library Board (Codex Sinaiticus, http://www.bl.uk/manuscripts/Viewer.aspx?ref=add_ms_43725_f202v)

text instead of reading it is of course even more needful for those who could not read. Guesses as to how many people were literate in the days of Jesus vary widely, with the bulk of those estimates saying the majority ranged from illiterate to an elementary capability to read and write. (Refer back to Background section on Social Environment and Literacy where estimates of literacy were shown to be often less than 15%.)[91] To some extent, there may have

---

sinaiticus.org/en/

91   See Boomershine's quote of Harris: Thomas E. Boomershine, *The Messiah of Peace, A Performance-Criticism Commentary on Mark's Passion-Resurrection Narrative*, Biblical Performance Criticism Volume 12, Cascade Books, 2015. This represents 45 years of Dr. Boomershine's

been far greater basic literacy among those serious about their faith.[92] Jewish people were known to read and study the Bible in their gatherings as was shown by accounts in the Gospels and Acts where groups would pass around the scriptures to be read in turn by members of the group. For centuries, verses were to be inscribed on the posts of Israelite homes. But, given the cost of the materials, their studies of written material, whether by reading them or hearing others read them, would have been primarily in central repositories. So, whether the majority were illiterate or capable of reading at a basic level, our modern culture has not experienced such a high level of exposure to oral texts and tends to vastly underestimate the importance of the emotional and conceptual flow of ideas within them which provide mnemonic and performance cues—cues which make it possible to remember and perform the texts in flexible, improvisational ways similar to what would be expected of rhetoricians of that time and place. Modern brain and memory studies[93] reinforce these concepts and show how memory functions work. The bibliography contains works that provide connections to those interested in seeing how these memory and oral methods work in modern psychological and physiological studies.

Listening to the text and following what is heard is easier if the material contains oral guideposts that make it natural and compelling to follow and remember. Some of the methods used to create conceptual and mnemonic links such as symmetry, repetition, chiasmus, inversion, and word links are often overlooked by readers not needing those clues to aid memorization. These are highlighted in my treatment to assist in exegesis and interpretation.

---

activities extending the work of his doctoral thesis. This is an extensive work examining the text in Greek and English that includes links to multi-media performances of the material. It represents the first analytical treatment from the new perspective of performance-criticism and includes helpful appendices on the historical context of the Mark and his audiences, a sound map of the text, pronunciation of Koine Greek and the rhetoric of Biblical storytelling. He quotes William Harris's estimate of literacy in this period as not likely exceeding 15%, a strong reason to understand why oral methods played such a strong role. See also Catherine Hezser and Michael Wise for their works on literacy in this period. Hezser estimates rural literacy as low as 3%. Michael Wise sees it higher than Hezser, provides a history of the treatment of literacy and provides examples in signature-bearing documents showing both the range of literacy and the languages used. He also points to graffiti that provide evidence of a basic literacy that was broader than Hezser assumed. See pp. 1-62 of *Language and Literacy in Roman Judaea*. See also Werner Kelber's, *Imprints, Voiceprints, and Footprints of Memory* and critique by Richard Bauckham in *The Christian World around the New Testament*, p. 102-107.

92 A.R.; Millard, "Literacy, Ancient Israel," *Anchor Bible Dictionary*, Vol. 4, pp. 337-340. "The Bible itself is a witness to Hebrew and Hellenistic literacy, the products of people who wrote in the expectancy that others would read their works" (p. 337). "While the number of ancient Israelites who regularly read and wrote may have been very small and mostly professional scribes, the number who possessed marginal literacy was larger, and still more would likely have been able to recognize and write their own names... In light of the evidence from all sources, it appears that literacy reached beyond the palaces and temples of Israel and Judah to quite small settlements. This means prophetic oracles, hymns, laws could have circulated in written form from an early time to offer an authority and a control on oral tradition. In discussion of the history of the books of the OT the role of Israelite literacy deserves to be given greater prominence" (p. 340).

93 See examples in Rahul Jandial, MD, PhD; *Neurofitness, A Brain Surgeon's Secrets to Boost Performance and Unleash Creativity*, Houghton, Mifflin, Harcourt; Boston, NY, 2019.

Context of the Lord's Prayer Text or Script

Key Finding: Jesus Asks the Crowds in Addition to the Disciples to Pray for their Persecutors in Matthew 5:44 Using the Prayer in 6:9-15:

Once the section in Matthew 6:1-4 is seen as a connector between the prayer request of 5:44 and the prayer in 6:5-15, then it provides the key to the explicit purpose of the Lord's Prayer which is strategically central to the Sermon on the Mount (Matthew 5-7), and strategic to all the Gospel of Matthew. That key is tying the contextual definition of "our" and "Father" in the first words of the prayer (Matthew 6:9)[94] to the request Jesus made when he asked the crowds (5:1-2; 7:28-8:1) to pray for their enemies—including what would have been their worst-case enemies, their pursuing "persecutors" (Matthew 5:44), while the disciples watched Jesus "fish for people" (Matthew 4:19). Crowd members were told to pray in this fashion so that "you may be children of your Father who is in heaven." Another reason why they should pray—and the reason they could pray that prayer even though they were in some way not yet His children—was that "he makes his sun rise on the evil and the good; and sends rain on the just and the unjust" (Matthew 5:45). While the crowds are a collection of groups, each member of the crowds was asked to pray alone for their persecutors with the confidence that they had a common connection with their enemies and persecutors through the Father who gives sunshine and rain to the good and the bad, the just and the unjust. They were asked to use that common connection as a blessing and not as a curse against their enemies. (See such a prayer of curses in Psalm 109:1-20, likely written by David before his murder of Bathsheba's husband.)

Each of these elements grabs the attention of the listening crowds by focusing on their most pressing conflicts, their need for safety, peace and well-being, and their relationship with God and ultimate role in the kingdom of heaven. Then the prayer links each section to the felt needs of the one praying all the way to the goal of forgiveness and restored relationships. It also grabs the attention of the peace-making disciples who were eager to learn how to recruit more peace-making disciples. Ultimately, the disciples discovered that Jesus' method involves the very conflicts that mattered most to their listeners.

This contextual understanding returns the Lord's Prayer to its explicit intention, a versatile anger and conflict management prayer that was requested by Jesus of everyone in the "crowds," not just of the disciples, for any conflict large or small. The context of the Lord's Prayer then changes the definition of the first words "Our Father" from "the Father of me and other disciples," or "the Father of me and other people in general" to "the Father of me (praying alone) and the ones with whom I am conflicted."

"Our" becomes a variable that includes the solitary person praying and any one or any group prayed for that was identified as the worst-case situation, the persecutor. If the worst case can be prayed for, then every lesser case can also be included providing the ultimate in versatility and applicability. The "*necessary* bread" is another variable that stands for any contested necessity that is blocked from or taken from the one praying. This provides a versatile scenario-based approach to conflict management and disciple-making that is typical of ancient Greek persuasion methods known throughout the Hellenic world from 400 B.C. and almost certainly known by educated Greek Jews who were already using a Greek version of their scriptures by the time of Jesus.[95]

To better appreciate the rich flexibility in this scenario-based approach to prayer and its centrality to the Sermon on the Mount in Matthew 5-7, it helps to see it in the context of the two gropus of three "antitheses" contrasting the phrase "you heard it was said" with "but I say." This is used to describe law Matthew 5:21-48 and its application to conflicts that leads to the concluding request of Jesus to love enemies and pray for persecutors. The organization of this set of six antitheses are notably similar to the beatitudes. In the same way that the beatitudes only have two that say, "theirs is the kingdom of heaven," the antitheses only have two that say, "you have heard it was said *by the ancients*

---

94 See the article planned for publication in the Christian Century by Manto, "Who is the 'Our' in the 'Our Father.'"

95 See p. 21 the book of Larry Helyer, *Exploring Jewish Literature of the Second Temple Period*, which not only mentions the usage of the Greek version of the Bible from the fourth century B.C. through 90 A.D., but also the broader Jewish literature of the time.

... but I say." The others leave out "by the ancients." The first antithesis is the one that leads with "you have heard it was said *by the ancients*" and is a treatment on murder (possibly representing offences that are "attacking") (Matt 5: 21-26) and anger. (The role of anger will have an especially important role in the Lord's Prayer as a prayer for one's pursuing persecutors.) The contrast between murder and anger is followed by the antithesis "you have heard it was said … but I say," addressing adultery and lust (possibly representing offences that are "taking") (Matt 5: 27- 30) leading to the unfortunate ramifications of divorce and third parties affected by that divorce (Matt 5: 31-37) that uses a third antithesis "you have heard it said…but I say." This first set of antitheses discuss conflicts that appear to be caused by someone doing "bad" things such as attacking or taking.

The fourth antithesis is like the first in that it says, "you have heard it was said *by the ancients* ... but I say" and discusses oath-taking[96] (Matt 5: 33-37). This might highlight a different type of conflict caused by people wanting to do "good" things but over-promise resulting in someone else becoming over-confident in the "promises." The over-confident recipient of a promise might have taken different actions if it were clear that the promiser might not be able to come through. The difference might be seen as one making a "guarantee" versus a "best effort." This antithesis also has two more that follow. The fifth leads to comments on compensatory damages (Matt 5: 38-42) caused by broken promises just inferred by the comments on "oath-taking." Jesus asks that the listeners not invoke rights to compensatory damages, but turn the other cheek, instead. It, in turn, leads to the sixth and final antithesis describing the preferred ramifications proposed by Jesus (Matt 5: 43-48) that the listeners love their enemies and pray for their persecutors (the ones causing damages) instead of hating them. These six antitheses could be considered two groupings of three making them easier to remember. The second group that ends with a major conclusion of loving and praying for enemies leads to the prayer of forgiveness in 6:9-15 for those same enemies, even the most extreme (persecutors). Forgiveness continues to be developed in the remaining parts of the Sermon on the Mount and echoed elsewhere such as Matthew 18.

Antitheses Matthew 5:21-48									
5:21-26:	You have heard it said **by the ancients**	No murder	But I say	No anger	5:33-37	You have heard it said **by the ancients**	Fulfill oaths	But I say	No oaths
5:27-30	You have heard it said	No adultery	But I say	No lust	5:38-42	You have heard it said	Eye for eye	But I say	Resist not evil
5:31-32	You have heard it said	Safe divorce	But I say	No divorce	5:43-48	You have heard it said	Hate enemies	But I say	Love & pray for enemy

A Bridge to the Lord's Prayer: That section starting with "turn-the-other-cheek" has four key themes that are replicated in reverse order in the "we" section of the Lord's Prayer starting with "give us this day our necessary bread." This way of organizing material in reverse order has been called chiasmus and will be discussed in further detail later. This can be used to link the material in the two sections and makes it easier to remember and present orally.

This chiasmus may have been missed because the two sections are separated by the section of Matthew 5:43-48 which requests prayer for those causing conflict and the section of Matthew 6:1-4, which ties the preceding things that should be done in the presence of third parties versus those that should not be as outlined in 6:1-18. This apparent separation of these two sections that function as a chiasmus is another method that ties the sections together as a quilt or a weave.

---

96 The significance of oath taking in this context is really one of overpromising, which results in disappointment or damages leading up to the section on compensatory damages.

Criss-cross (chiasmus) Connections Show Conflicts and Persecutors for Prayer	
Matthew 5:39-42	**Matthew 6:11-13**
(A) "Do not resist **evil**" (μὴ ἀντιστῆναι τῷ πονηρῷ) in 5:39	(D') "**Give** us today our necessary bread..." (**δὸς** ἡμῖν) in 6:11
(B) "If anyone wants to **judge** (or sue) you" (κριθῆναι), in 5:40a	(C') "**Release** our debts as we release..." (**ἄφες**) in 6:12
(C) "**Release** the coat" (ἄφες), in 5:40b	(B') "Lead us not to **testing**" (**πειρασμόν**) in 6:13a
(D) "**Give**" what is asked" (τῷ αἰτοῦντί σε δός) in 5:42	(A') "Deliver us from **evil**" (ῥῦσαι ἡμᾶς ἀπὸ τοῦ **πονηροῦ**) in 6:13b

Lord's Conflict & Empathy Prayer in Matt 5-7, by C. Manto (c) 2015

This section also provides an example of an extraordinary range of conflicts demonstrating a complex scenario-based matrix of conflicts that provide subject matter for the prayer. That matrix, when placing the items in conflict in columns and the people with whom the conflict is experienced in rows, maximizes data compression and decompression in such a way that the maximum amount of information can be memorized in the shortest amount of time and effort that could be reconstructed later.[97]

The Range of Conflicts Anticipated: Notice that there are two variable types, "who" is challenging down the column on the left and "what" is being challenged across the top row. These reflect the same two variable types in the Lord's Prayer for persecutors of 1) "who" is the persecutor doing the challenging and 2) the "what" that is being challenged symbolized by the "daily necessary bread". Then Jesus provided four examples that run down the diagonal of the matrix, shown above. By mentioning only four examples of conflicts, twelve more are implied for further consideration. See the chart that shows that not only the size of the group can be changed, but, the power positions, and the apparent fault which if that were the case, it would mean that there were 4x4x4x4 number of possible conflict combinations implied by just the four examples given. This would not only provide the greatest number of scenarios to consider or practice, it also provided the would-be disciple maker the maximum flexibility in response to needs on an impromptu basis. Perhaps most importantly, it showed that the love requested by Jesus for the worst-case applies to an unlimited number of conflicts large or small, between one and other individuals, groups or organizations regardless of who was in the power position or at apparent fault. This makes the Lord's Prayer for those we are in conflict a very versatile anger and conflict management prayer. This is one reason why this resource book is designed to provide opportunities for small groups to discuss how this prayer and related forgiveness and restoration might work between individuals and other individuals or groups. For these reasons, the work of professionals whether in counseling, psychology, human resources, health care, project management, quality programs,[98] technical innovation, entrepreneurship, ed-

---

97   See the presentation given to the Scholars Forum of the Network of Biblical Storytellers in 2014 in the paper "Audience and Mnemonics," included in the appendix.

98   The role of feedback is so foundational to "total quality" programs and "continuous improvement" programs, that this prayer in Matthew could be called, "The Lord's Total Quality Prayer" because of the complete feedback between those in conflict within oneself, and then between the parties in conflict and God with the hope of total restoration. The concepts of "total" and "quality" and "continuous improvement" are certainly met or exceeded here.

What Challenged Across > Who Challenges Below: Size, Power, Fault, Type	Cheek (Health, Respect, Honor)	Shirt (Clothing, Warmth, Housing, Possessions)	Walk (Time, Distraction)	Borrow (Ability to manage or gather, use necessities)
1 vs. You (Direct assault by one taking advantage)	X			
Small group vs. You (Agreed contract implied by lawsuit or arrest)		X		
Large group vs You (No due process, conscription requiring 1 mile by Roman Army)			X	
You vs 1 Asks, not insists (Flips power position, loans imply offer to repay)				X

ucation, mediation, law, and international relations[99] are welcomed elements in small group discussions on these Matthew passages.

In addition to the methods of memorization, it is also important to understand the roles that emotion, drama and trauma had in gaining the attention of a listener in the first place and creating memory and recall in the second place. The entire context of the Sermon on the Mount was based on emotion laden conflict and suffering. By evoking the stories of suffering and oppression in the opening beatitudes of Matthew 5, Jesus was overlaying his teaching or data on the pressing concerns of his listeners making his teaching unforgettable. See the work of Robert McIver on *Memory, Jesus and the Synoptic Gospels*[100] for examples.

These 4 by 4 matrices of conflict options show the comprehensive range of conflicts that are the subject of that passage which leads the listeners to understand the breadth of conflicts included in the request to love and pray in Matthew 5:44.[101] Note also the range of reactions that mirror the compensatory damages laws of the day as reflected in the "eye for an eye" laws.[102] This flexibility also makes it an effective disciple-making tool for the disciples who were promised "fishing lessons" near the end of Matthew 4 just before the Sermon on the Mount was given in Chapter 5. These disciple-making or persuasion lessons, known to the Greek and Roman world as "rhetoric lessons" were typical of how most were trained as youth who received basic grammar lessons and then received persuasion lessons

---

99 See the works of Miraslav Volf on forgiveness listed in the bibliography. Dr. Volf leads the Yale Center for Faith and Culture.
100 Robert K. McIver, *Memory Jesus, and the Synoptic Gospels*; 2011, Society of Biblical Literature, Atlanta. See pp. 41-58 on flashbulb memories linking information to a key powerfully experienced emotional event.
101 See the 2014 Manto presentation to NBS in the appendix.
102 Betz shows the range of these laws including the Code of Hammurabi, Greek and Roman traditions and their Jewish counterparts such as Philo. Some examples are provided in the notes in the exegesis sections. More are readily seen in the English translations of these legal traditions provided in the bibliography.

(rhetoric). These lessons provided maximum flexibility so that students could persuasively make their cases in any situation even as improvisational engagements or performances. Such lessons, called *progymnasmata*,[103] provided practice in making flexible use of language and scenarios so that the students would become effective in engaging the attention of their audiences and then lead them to right thinking, decisions, and actions. This method was also evident in Jewish rhetorical leaders and prophets such as Nathan who used this approach effectively with David who held in his person all the military, political and financial power as demonstrated by David's murder of the husband of Bathsheba, whom he impregnated.[104]

In the exegesis sections that follow, the mnemonic and persuasion techniques through linkages between various sections will be shown with special attention to the connections between the conflicts outlined in the "antetheses" section and the "we-petitions" of the Lord's Prayer in the form of a "chiasmus." Additional connections between the conflict section and the four types of over-promising (oaths) will also be shown.

---

[103] Basic persuasion methods called *progymnasmata*, taught to youth after being taught grammar lessons in the Greek cultural world a hundred years or so before the time Jesus.

[104] See Nathan confront David for the murder of Bathsheba's husband in 2 Samuel 11:3-12:24.

Section 2: Commentary

Outline of Lord's Prayer Text, Analysis and Exegesis

Structure and Organization

1) Background in sections prior to 6:5-15 section on the Lord's Prayer

   a) Setting in 4:17- 5:48
      i) 5:1 Jesus, crowds and disciples
      ii) 5:3-16 See beatitudes for similar structure of the alternating pairs of beatitudes organized in two groups of three pairs in alignment with the two bookends aligned with salt versus saltiness, light versus hidden light
      iii) 5:17-20 Law and entry to kingdom of heaven
      iv) 5:21-48 Six key antithesis about conflict and law to goal of loving enemies and praying for persecutors

2) Introduction requesting prayer for those causing conflict 5:44
   a) Request from Jesus of crowds (5:44) to pray for persecutors (worst-case enemies)
   b) Relationship of crowds to the Father (to become children, v45a)
   c) Relationship of Father to the crowds and persecutors (who gives sunshine and rain, v 45b)
   d) Relationship to tax collectors and Gentiles (v. 46-47)
   e) Goal of request to become perfect as heavenly Father (v. 48)

3) Pivot to prayer details section (6:1) "Pay" instead of "pray" and three secrets (6:1-21 instead of three public requests (5:3-16))
   a) How *Not* to Give Mercies 6:2a
   b) How to Give Mercies 6:2b-4

4) Prayer Section 6:5-15 (This is the primary section of three prohibitions in 6:1-17 concerning the three things not to do before people by virtue of 1) its center position, 2) connection to introduction in 5:44, and 3) its connection to 5:16. Its position connects it to the prayer request in 5:44

   a) How *Not* to Pray
      i) Not like hypocrites 6:5-6
      ii) Not like Gentiles/heathen/pagans/nations 6:7-8

   b) How to Pray 6:9a Note the complex audience of 1) "the Father" to whom the prayer is made whose rule and will are asked to be brought to earth, 2) "Our" as defined by the crowds and disciples who were asked to pray, and 3) the persecutors for whom the prayer is offered. (The exegesis section will show how this becomes a flexible anger and conflict management prayer to the knowing Father that can be used to recruit or persuade users within the crowd to become new peacemaking disciples and core part of a formal disciple recruitment rhetoric and training program.)
      i) *Prayer Participants* 6:9b, variable x Who conflict is between (me and persecutor x)
      ii) *You Petitions* 6:9c-10, incursion of kingdom on earth now (as in Great Commission) focusing on relationship conflicts (loving rule of Father, loving desire of Father)
      iii) *We Petitions* 6:11-13, variable x, ('our'=parties in conflict); variable y (items in dispute or whatever conflict is about is the "necessary bread")

iv) Escalation and rhetorical force through forgiveness section.

5) Prayer Conclusion 6:14-15 and Connection to Remainder of Matthew

   i) Role of forgiveness formula "release trespasses as we release…"
   ii) Brief connections to remaining part of Matthew 6 & 7.
   iii) Indicators of kingdom entry as reconciliation in Matthew 5 and 18.
   iv) Three conflict prayers of Matthew 5, 6 and 18.
   v) Quick overview of connections to the passage on fasting and financial security through the end of Chapter 6 and how not to make disciples in Chapter 7 with examples of false prophets, false disciples, and false foundations leading to missing out on the kingdom of heaven.

Section 2: Commentary

Exegesis of 4:17-6:4--, the Preceding Context for the Lord's Prayer in 6:5-15 (for background, see the "Orientation" section above)

USB5	Author and Reader Notes	NASB®	New American BIble
Matt. 4:12 ¶ Ἀκούσας δὲ ὅτι Ἰωάννης παρεδόθη ἀνεχώρησεν εἰς τὴν Γαλιλαίαν. **Matt. 4:13** καὶ καταλιπὼν τὴν Ναζαρὰ ἐλθὼν κατῴκησεν εἰς Καφαρναοὺμ τὴν παραθαλασσίαν ἐν ὁρίοις Ζαβουλὼν καὶ Νεφθαλίμ· **Matt. 4:14** ἵνα πληρωθῇ τὸ ῥηθὲν διὰ Ἠσαΐου τοῦ προφήτου λέγοντος, **Matt. 4:15** Γῆ Ζαβουλὼν καὶ γῆ Νεφθαλίμ, ὁδὸν θαλάσσης, πέραν τοῦ Ἰορδάνου, Γαλιλαία τῶν ἐθνῶν, **Matt. 4:16** ὁ λαὸς ὁ καθήμενος ἐν σκότει φῶς εἶδεν μέγα, καὶ τοῖς καθημένοις ἐν χώρᾳ καὶ σκιᾷ θανάτου φῶς ἀνέτειλεν αὐτοῖς. **Matt. 4:17** ¶ ΑΠΟ ΤΟΤΕ ἤρξατο ὁ Ἰησοῦς κηρύσσειν καὶ λέγειν Μετανοεῖτε, ἤγγικεν γὰρ ἡ βασιλεία τῶν οὐρανῶν. **Matt. 4:18** ¶ Περιπατῶν δὲ παρὰ τὴν θάλασσαν τῆς Γαλιλαίας εἶδεν δύο ἀδελφούς, Σίμωνα τὸν λεγόμενον Πέτρον καὶ Ἀνδρέαν τὸν ἀδελφὸν αὐτοῦ, βάλλοντας ἀμφίβληστρον εἰς	**Note: This section will be used to discuss specific issues about wording, definitions and versions. Some space will be left blank to allow readers to write some of their own notes.** **Version sources are quoted at the top of columns and are used with permission. See copyright page.** 4:25 ὄχλοι πολλοί, might be better rendered, "many crowds" that could also parallel the many places from where they came.	**Matt. 4:12** ¶ Now when Jesus heard that "John had been taken into custody, [b]He withdrew into Galilee; **Matt. 4:13** and leaving Nazareth, He came and [a]settled in Capernaum, which is by the sea, in the region of Zebulun and Naphtali. **Matt. 4:14** *This was* to fulfill what was spoken through Isaiah the prophet: **Matt. 4:15** "[a]THE LAND OF ZEBULUN AND THE LAND OF NAPHTALI, [1]BY THE WAY OF THE SEA, BEYOND THE JORDAN, GALILEE OF THE [2]GENTILES — **Matt. 4:16** "[a]THE PEOPLE WHO WERE SITTING IN DARKNESS SAW A GREAT LIGHT, AND THOSE WHO WERE SITTING IN THE LAND AND SHADOW OF DEATH, UPON THEM A LIGHT DAWNED." **Matt. 4:17** ¶ "From that time Jesus began to [1]preach and say, "[b]Repent, for the kingdom of heaven is at hand." **Matt. 4:18** ¶ "Now as Jesus was walking by [b]the Sea of Galilee, He saw two brothers, [c]Simon who was called Peter, and Andrew his brother, casting a net into the sea; for they were fishermen.	Matthew 4:12-5:1 [12] When he heard that John had been arrested, he withdrew to Galilee. [13] He left Nazareth and went to live in Capernaum by the sea, in the region of Zebulun and Naphtali, [14] that what had been said through Isaiah the prophet might be fulfilled: [15] "Land of Zebulun and land of Naphtali, the way to the sea, beyond the Jordan, Galilee of the Gentiles, [16] the people who sit in darkness have seen a great light, on those dwelling in a land overshadowed by death light has arisen." [17][a] From that time on, Jesus began to preach and say, "Repent, for the

τὴν θάλασσαν, ἦσαν γὰρ ἁλεεῖς. **Matt. 4:19** καὶ λέγει αὐτοῖς Δεῦτε ὀπίσω μου, καὶ ποιήσω ὑμᾶς ἁλεεῖς ἀνθρώπων. **Matt. 4:20** οἱ δὲ εὐθέως ἀφέντες τὰ δίκτυα ἠκολούθησαν αὐτῷ. **Matt. 4:21** Καὶ προβὰς ἐκεῖθεν εἶδεν ἄλλους δύο ἀδελφούς, Ἰάκωβον τὸν τοῦ Ζεβεδαίου καὶ Ἰωάνην τὸν ἀδελφὸν αὐτοῦ, ἐν τῷ πλοίῳ μετὰ Ζεβεδαίου τοῦ πατρὸς αὐτῶν καταρτίζοντας τὰ δίκτυα αὐτῶν, καὶ ἐκάλεσεν αὐτούς. **Matt. 4:22** οἱ δὲ εὐθέως ἀφέντες τὸ πλοῖον καὶ τὸν πατέρα αὐτῶν ἠκολούθησαν αὐτῷ. **Matt. 4:23** Καὶ περιῆγεν ἐν ὅλῃ τῇ Γαλιλαίᾳ, διδάσκων ἐν ταῖς συναγωγαῖς αὐτῶν καὶ κηρύσσων τὸ εὐαγγέλιον τῆς βασιλείας καὶ θεραπεύων πᾶσαν νόσον καὶ πᾶσαν μαλακίαν ἐν τῷ λαῷ. **Matt. 4:24** καὶ ἀπῆλθεν ἡ ἀκοὴ αὐτοῦ εἰς ὅλην τὴν Συρίαν· καὶ προσήνεγκαν αὐτῷ πάντας τοὺς κακῶς ἔχοντας ποικίλαις νόσοις καὶ βασάνοις συνεχομένους, δαιμονιζομένους καὶ σεληνιαζομένους καὶ παραλυτικούς, καὶ ἐθεράπευσεν αὐτούς. **Matt. 4:25** καὶ ἠκολούθησαν αὐτῷ ὄχλοι πολλοὶ ἀπὸ τῆς Γαλιλαίας καὶ Δεκαπόλεως καὶ Ἱεροσολύμων καὶ Ἰουδαίας καὶ πέραν τοῦ Ἰορδάνου.		**Matt. 4:19** And He *said to them, "[1]Follow Me, and I will make you fishers of men." **Matt. 4:20** Immediately they left their nets and followed Him. **Matt. 4:21** Going on from there He saw two other brothers, [1a]James the *son* of Zebedee, and [2]John his brother, in the boat with Zebedee their father, mending their nets; and He called them. **Matt. 4:22** Immediately they left the boat and their father, and followed Him. **Matt. 4:23** ¶ Jesus was going [a]throughout all Galilee, [b]teaching in their synagogues and [c]proclaiming the [1]gospel of the kingdom, and [d]healing every kind of disease and every kind of sickness among the people. **Matt. 4:24** ¶ The news about Him spread [a]throughout all Syria; and they brought to Him all who were ill, those suffering with various diseases and pains, [b]demoniacs, [1c]epileptics, [d]paralytics; and He healed them. **Matt. 4:25** Large crowds [a]followed Him from Galilee and [b]*the* Decapolis and Jerusalem and Judea and *from* [c]beyond the Jordan.	kingdom of heaven is at hand." **The Call of the First Disciples.**[b] [18]As he was walking by the Sea of Galilee, he saw two brothers, Simon who is called Peter, and his brother Andrew, casting a net into the sea; they were fishermen. [19]He said to them, "Come after me, and I will make you fishers of men." [20][c]At once they left their nets and followed him. [21]He walked along from there and saw two other brothers, James, the son of Zebedee, and his brother John. They were in a boat, with their father Zebedee, mending their nets. He called them, [22]and immediately they left their boat and their father and followed him. **Ministering to a Great Multitude.**[d] [23]He went around all of Galilee, teaching in their

			synagogues,[e] proclaiming the gospel of the kingdom, and curing every disease and illness among the people. [24][f]His fame spread to all of Syria, and they brought to him all who were sick with various diseases and racked with pain, those who were possessed, lunatics, and paralytics, and he cured them. [25]And great crowds from Galilee, the Decapolis,[g] Jerusalem, and Judea, and from beyond the Jordan followed him.

Setting for the Sermon on the Mount and the Lord's Prayer, namely, Jesus promising to teach disciples how to "fish" the crowds for new disciples: This section is helpful to review to see the characters and locations in the Sermon on the Mount, the Lord's Prayer, and its connection with the "good news," namely, Jesus, "proclaiming, 'Repent, for the kingdom of Heaven is close at hand.'" This includes the "large crowds" that followed Jesus from "Galilee, the Decapolis, Jerusalem, Judaea and the Transjordan" (v. 25), and the professional fisherman disciples (v. 18-22) as those being asked to follow Jesus so that they would learn how to "fish" for "people" (v. 19).[1] There may have been other disciples there, but the text only points to the professional fishermen showing the purpose of this section as "fishing lessons." This emphasis on the fishermen disciples adds weight to the explicit purpose that the "fishermen" were about to be given the "fishing lessons" just promised. The crowds were those who still needed to be caught and are distinguished from the disciples who were being taught how to catch them and make new disciples.

By missing this distinction, many commentators have assumed that the teachings in the section of Matthew 5-7 were addressed only to those who were already disciples and not the crowds in general who had not yet decided to become disciples and still needed to be caught. Recent scholars have shifted that perspective by showing how the crowds were

---

1   See a thorough historical overview of fishing for people in Wilhelm H. Wuellner's, *The Meaning of 'Fishers of Men'*; Westminster Press, Philadelphia, 1967. Shows the history of the concept of persuasion and its discussion as "fishing" for people both in its positive and negative lights. See also the background section on fishing, persuasion, locations, audience and kingdom.

at least being equally addressed along with the disciples.[2] The crowds attracted by his teachings and healings were the ones from whom disciples would be made. This distinction between crowds and disciples occurs throughout Matthew. In Matthew 9:36-38, "When he saw the crowds, he had compassion for them, because they were harassed and helpless, like sheep without a shepherd.[3] Then he said to his disciples, 'The harvest is plentiful, but the laborers are few; pray therefore the Lord of the harvest to send out laborers into his harvest.'" (RSV) Similarly, in Matthew 13 after speaking to the "great crowds" beside the sea (13:1-9), his disciples asked him why he spoke to the crowds in parables (v.10), demonstrating a difference between crowds (from which some will spring lasting fruit but not all) and the disciples to whom deeper teaching was conveyed.

It can also be seen that Jesus is going around to many places (4:24-25) making the surprising announcements of the good news of the "kingdom of heaven," likely in somewhat different ways to the various crowds given the circumstances in any given exchange. What might possibly make this news good, now, at the end of the age, or anytime in between? This section appears to show what these crowds would hear as they gathered around Jesus to listen to what he was proclaiming. My interpretation is that this section introduces the Sermon on the Mount (Matthew 5-7) that provides specific methods to persuade people to reconcile and how to reconcile, namely the members of the crowds and the disciples to their persecutors. It also shows the disciples how to make new disciples from members of the crowds using these conflict resolution tools.

For discussion:

1) What might be the significance of the description of those in the "valley of the shadow of death"? What is the meaning of "living, sitting or dwelling" there?

2) How might that be a way to describe the "crowds" and the message about to be delivered to them?

3) What is the significance and importance of the challenge to professional fishermen to "fish for people"? What might "fishing for people" mean?

4) How might "fishing for people" tie into the core message of Matthew and its conclusion at the end of the Gospel where the disciples are asked to make disciples?

5) What evidence do you see in these texts that provide a working definition for key words such as "crowds," "fishermen," and "disciples"?

6) How might disciple making relate to the Gospel of Matthew as a whole?

7) How might disciple making relate to the general concept of persuasion or rhetoric?

---

2   In the Matthew 5:1 comments, see the works of Davies, Allison and Pennington who clearly advocate for the crowds being a primary audience. See Robert Gundry who takes an opposing view in his commentary, *Matthew*, on p. 66, where he claims that "Matthew uses 'the crowds' and 'his disciples' interchangeably. "We are not to think that the disciples came from the crowds. They were the crowds (cf Luke 6:17) for Matthew has written in 4:25 that large crowds followed him—an indication of discipleship—and he will yet write that the crowds responded with amazement to this sermon, which he had been teaching them (7:28). Therefore, the disciples about to be taught at the beginning of the sermon must be none other than the crowds that have been taught at the close." I assert that the passages that he quotes actually disproves Gundry's assertions once the connection between the promise of teaching the disciples to "catch people" and repeated distinctions between the crowds and disciples are seen across Matthew (such as Matthew 9:36-38 and 13:1-17). Charles Talbert takes a similar position on p. 74 of *Matthew* where crowds are conflated with disciples merely because the crowds were astonished at his teachings by the end of Matthew 7 when in fact the astonishment would more likely prove that they were not disciples because of the element of surprise. See Leon Morris, *Gospel According to Matthew*, p. 94, where he says, "…the teaching that follows is addressed to disciples rather than the general public." But he does not provide evidence. Similarly, Charles Quarles in *The Sermon on the Mount* (p. 38) assumes that when Jesus teaches "them" that it refers only to disciples and not also the crowds rendering the passage to only train those already disciples rather than helping the disciples learn how to "catch people" who were the crowds which would allow for a dual audience. See also Getz (*Sermon on the Mount*, p. 155) who says, "these texts address…specific communities of disciples" but "the internal evidence is admittedly scarce."

3   See the section on the "setting of Matthew's Gospel" above and commentary on Matthew 5:3 and "first surprise."

UBS5	Author and Reader Notes	NASB®	New Jerusalem Bible
Matt. 5:1 ¶ Ἰδὼν δὲ τοὺς ὄχλους ἀνέβη εἰς τὸ ὄρος, καὶ καθίσαντος αὐτοῦ προσῆλθαν αὐτῷ οἱ μαθηταὶ αὐτοῦ· Matt. 5:2 καὶ ἀνοίξας τὸ στόμα αὐτοῦ ἐδίδασκεν αὐτοὺς λέγων,	**5:1 NJB translation is excellent here since it does not imply abandonment of the crowds as shown in the last two verses of 7 (28-29) and the first verse of 8 where the crowds were there and amazed at the teaching of Jesus.** 5:2 I would prefer keeping the Greek expression of "he opened his mouth and began to speak".	Matt. 5:1 ¶ "When Jesus saw the crowds, He went up on ᵇthe ¹mountain; and after He sat down, His disciples came to Him. Matt. 5:2 ᵃHe opened His mouth and *began* to teach them, saying,	Matt. 5:1 ¶ Seeing the crowds, he went onto the mountain. And when he was seated his disciples came to him. Matt. 5:2 Then he began to speak. This is what he taught them:

5:1 Who were the crowds and where were they? The *crowds* here in 5:1 refer to the same from 4:25. "The large (many) crowds (ὄχλοι πολλοί) followed him from Galilee, the Decapolis, Jerusalem, Judaea and the Transjordan." The geographical range is significant and implies groups such as the Decapolis, the Greek collection of cities, as being substantially affected by Greek rhetoric, culture, commerce, and politics. This would also be the situation of the "nations" to which Jesus will send his disciples at the close of Matthew in 28:18-20 and the increasingly Hellenized world of Matthew the Gospel writer and his readers who experienced dispersion from a destroyed Jerusalem by 72 A.D. The same crowds hearing Jesus stayed there until the end, were amazed at the teaching of Jesus (7:28-29) and followed him down from the mountain (8:1).

How did Jesus' connect to the crowds? "Seeing the crowds, he went onto the mountain." Jesus went up so he could be heard by the crowds not to escape from them. With crowds, the only way to be heard is to make sure that those closest don't absorb the sound. That requires the speaker to either be higher or more likely lower than the crowds so that the front row would not block the sound from back rows. Once on an incline, Jesus could have been either in the higher or most likely the lower position as when in a boat near shore as in Matthew 13:1-2. (Following Jesus down from the mountain in 8:1 might have implied that Jesus had positioned himself at the lower end of the incline making it easier for him to be heard and easier for the crowds to follow him down.) The side of the hill or mountain would also help contain or bounce the sound, as well. (See the discussion on the science of sound and article by Pamela Jordan in the orientation section on crowds.) This all speaks to the claim that Jesus intended to be heard primarily by the crowds with the disciples observing and learning "how to fish" for people rather than Jesus addressing the disciples with messages tailored for them and with the crowds "overhearing" which is the position taken by most commentators in the attached bibliography. Some, as Allison[4] and Pennington,[5] will admit that the sayings must be interpreted as being addressed to the crowds but have not yet shown how these sections including the beatitudes, salt & light and prayer apply to the crowds. Instead, they provide interpretation on how these passages apply to the disciples. See the comments on Gundry's view in 4:25 above where he views crowds and the disciples as one and the same. Nolland, on the other hand, takes a view more consistent with the overall text when he says that the crowds in Matthew 5-7 "are not mere eavesdroppers" and "act as the audience for the sermon" while "disciples…take ringside seats."[6]

---

4   Davies and Allison, *Matthew, 1-7*, p. 422, "…In view of 7:28-8:1, we must think of the crowds overhearing…"

5   Pennington, *The Sermon on the Mount and Human Flourishing*, p. 114, "crowds and disciples." People change their views over time, and I expect that these authors may modify their views on how these sections apply to crowds.

6   See Nolland, *Gospel of Matthew*, p. 191.

View of the Lake of Tibériade (Sea of Galilee) from the Mount of Beatitudes": source Wikipedia, see bibliography

5:2 Why "opened his mouth"? I would prefer keeping the Greek expression of "he opened his mouth and began to speak." The phrase may seem odd since if he had spoken, we would expect that he would have needed to open his mouth making that phrase unnecessary. But this phrasing shows the linkage to the prior section in the episode of the testing of Jesus in Matthew 4:4 which quotes scripture of Deuteronomy 8:3 where it says, "Man shall not live by bread alone but by every word that proceeds *out of the mouth* of God." The implication is that the words out of the mouth of Jesus were the words from the mouth of God. It also weaves the rhetorical link between the words of Jesus and God as both a logical connection and the mnemonic-rhetorical connection to make the material easier for the listener to follow, become memorable and eventually be memorized by the listener who might recite it for another.

UBS5	Author and Reader Notes	NASB®	New Jerusalem Bible
Matt. 5:3 Μακάριοι οἱ πτωχοὶ τῷ πνεύματι, ὅτι αὐτῶν ἐστιν ἡ βασιλεία τῶν οὐρανῶν. **Matt. 5:4** μακάριοι οἱ πενθοῦντες, ὅτι αὐτοὶ παρακληθήσονται. **Matt. 5:5** μακάριοι οἱ πραεῖς, ὅτι αὐτοὶ κληρονομήσουσιν τὴν γῆν.¹ **Matt. 5:6** μακάριοι οἱ πεινῶντες καὶ διψῶντες τὴν δικαιοσύνην, ὅτι αὐτοὶ χορτασθήσονται. **Matt. 5:7** μακάριοι οἱ ἐλεήμονες, ὅτι αὐτοὶ ἐλεηθήσονται. **Matt. 5:8** μακάριοι οἱ καθαροὶ τῇ καρδίᾳ, ὅτι αὐτοὶ τὸν θεὸν	Note on verse order: 5:4 and 5 (second and third beatitude) switched in NJB. Note that the NJB chooses the verse order of a later small set of manuscripts such as the Western Jerome version that places verse 5 ahead of verse 4, apparently to link heaven and earth together. ⁷ The NJB choice is not considered the original choice given all textual evidence. The NJB choice misses the pairing of the original wording. The New American Bible (Catholic Study Bible) maintains the order of the oldest manuscripts and provides a footnote explaining it. The Douay-Rheims replicates the Jerome verse order. 5:6 "Uprightness" --	**Matt. 5:3** ¶ "¹ᵃBlessed are the ²poor in spirit, for ᵇtheirs is the kingdom of heaven. **Matt. 5:4** ¶ "Blessed are ᵃthose who mourn, for they shall be comforted. **Matt. 5:5** ¶ "Blessed are ᵃthe ¹gentle, for they shall inherit the earth. **Matt. 5:6** ¶ "Blessed are ᵃthose who hunger and thirst for righteousness, for they shall be satisfied. **Matt. 5:7** ¶ "Blessed are ᵃthe merciful, for they shall receive mercy. **Matt. 5:8** ¶ "Blessed are ᵃthe pure in heart, for ᵇthey shall see God. **Matt. 5:9** ¶ "Blessed are the peacemakers, for ᵃthey shall be called sons of God. **Matt. 5:10** ¶ "Blessed are those who have been ᵃpersecuted for the sake of	**New Jerusalem Bible** **Matt. 5:3** ¶ How blessed are the poor in spirit: the kingdom of Heaven is theirs. **Matt. 5:4** Blessed are the gentle: they shall have the earth as inheritance. **Matt. 5:5** Blessed are those who mourn: they shall be comforted. **Matt. 5:6** Blessed are those who hunger and thirst for uprightness: they shall have their fill. **Matt. 5:7** Blessed are the merciful: they shall have mercy shown them. **Matt. 5:8** Blessed are the pure in heart: they shall see God. **Matt. 5:9** Blessed are the peacemakers: they shall be recognized as children of

---

7   See Bruce Metzger's treatment in *Text of the New Testament* on p.12 and various textual notes in the Greek New Testaments of UBS5 and Nestle Aland.

Matt. 5:9 μακάριοι
οἱ εἰρηνοποιοί,
    ὅτι αὐτοὶ υἱοὶ θεοῦ
κληθήσονται.
Matt. 5:10 μακάριοι
οἱ δεδιωγμένοι ἕνεκεν
δικαιοσύνης,
    ὅτι αὐτῶν ἐστιν ἡ
βασιλεία τῶν οὐρανῶν.
Matt. 5:11 μακάριοί ἐστε
ὅταν ὀνειδίσωσιν ὑμᾶς καὶ
διώξωσιν καὶ εἴπωσιν πᾶν
πονηρὸν καθ' ὑμῶν
[ψευδόμενοι]² ἕνεκεν ἐμοῦ.
Matt. 5:12 χαίρετε καὶ
ἀγαλλιᾶσθε, ὅτι ὁ μισθὸς
ὑμῶν πολὺς ἐν τοῖς οὐρανοῖς·
οὕτως γὰρ ἐδίωξαν τοὺς
προφήτας τοὺς πρὸ ὑμῶν.
Matt. 5:13 ¶ Ὑμεῖς
ἐστε τὸ ἅλας τῆς γῆς· ἐὰν δὲ
τὸ ἅλας μωρανθῇ, ἐν τίνι
ἁλισθήσεται; εἰς οὐδὲν ἰσχύει
ἔτι εἰ μὴ βληθὲν ἔξω
καταπατεῖσθαι ὑπὸ τῶν
ἀνθρώπων.
Matt. 5:14 Ὑμεῖς ἐστε τὸ
φῶς τοῦ κόσμου. οὐ δύναται
πόλις κρυβῆναι ἐπάνω ὄρους
κειμένη·
Matt. 5:15 οὐδὲ καίουσιν
λύχνον καὶ τιθέασιν αὐτὸν
ὑπὸ τὸν μόδιον ἀλλ' ἐπὶ τὴν
λυχνίαν, καὶ λάμπει πᾶσιν
τοῖς ἐν τῇ οἰκίᾳ.
Matt. 5:16 οὕτως λαμψάτω
τὸ φῶς ὑμῶν ἔμπροσθεν τῶν
ἀνθρώπων, ὅπως ἴδωσιν
ὑμῶν τὰ καλὰ ἔργα καὶ
δοξάσωσιν τὸν πατέρα ὑμῶν
τὸν ἐν τοῖς οὐρανοῖς.

Versions that use the word justice instead are "justified" in that choice as long as the English version can be described as "just relationships" as opposed to "retribution". Similarly, the phrase "upright relationships" might be better in that the sense carries the idea of right behavior and attitudes towards others as opposed to some kind of internal piety that has little to do with others. This is important since the sorrow, oppression and other conflicts or relationships highlighted by Matthew 5-7 which are oriented between people and God, others and themselves. See Ronald Damholt's article on the topic.[8]

5:4 Use of "gentle" is preferred to "meek" or "humble" which does not always connote a relationship to others but may be thought to be either a humble or modest attitude or even one of poor self-esteem.

5: 9 "sons" or "children" of God. Nolland makes a good point when he opts for the literal "sons" of God since there is a strong linkage to special rights of "sons" in traditional Jewish culture that may be significant here.[9]

righteousness, for *b*theirs is the kingdom of heaven.
Matt. 5:11 ¶ "Blessed are you when *people* *a*insult you and persecute you, and falsely say all kinds of evil against you because of Me.
Matt. 5:12 "Rejoice and be glad, for your reward in heaven is great; for *a*in the same way they persecuted the prophets who were before you.
Matt. 5:13 ¶ "You are the salt of the earth; but *a*if the salt has become tasteless, how ¹can it be made salty *again*? It is no longer good for anything, except to be thrown out and trampled under foot by men.
Matt. 5:14 ¶ "You are *a*the light of the world. A city set on a ¹hill cannot be hidden;
Matt. 5:15 *a*nor does *anyone* light a lamp and put it under a ¹basket, but on the lampstand, and it gives light to all who are in the house.
Matt. 5:16 "Let your light shine before men in such a way that they may *a*see your good works, and *b*glorify your Father who is in heaven.

God.
Matt. 5:10 Blessed are those who are persecuted in the cause of uprightness: the kingdom of Heaven is theirs.
Matt. 5:11 ¶ 'Blessed are you when people abuse you and persecute you and speak all kinds of calumny against you falsely on my account.
Matt. 5:12 Rejoice and be glad, for your reward will be great in heaven; this is how they persecuted the prophets before you.
Matt. 5:13 ¶ 'You are salt for the earth. But if salt loses its taste, what can make it salty again? It is good for nothing and can only be thrown out to be trampled under people's feet.
Matt. 5:14 ¶ 'You are light for the world. A city built on a hill-top cannot be hidden.
Matt. 5:15 No one lights a lamp to put it under a tub; they put it on the lamp-stand where it shines for everyone in the house.
Matt. 5:16 In the same way your light must shine in people's sight, so that, seeing your good works, they may give praise to your Father in heaven.

---

8   See, Ronald Damholt, *Rightwiseness and Justice, a Tale of Translation*; Anglican Theological Review, Summer 2105; Chicago, IL p. 413-432. Discusses the historical rendering of the Greek word *dikaiosyne* (justice versus righteousness) in translations, looking into the original Greek uses of the term and ways of handling it in English. This is a helpful thought process regarding the meaning of this word usage in Matthew and other NT texts.

9   See Nolland, p. 206 commenting on 5:9.

	5:13-15 Note that the declaration of salt and light is declared to be applied to all in the audience including the crowds. The only question is not whether any of the listeners might be salt or light but whether they were salty tasting or light giving. This makes it possible to see the connection between the beatitudes and the salt section as two groups of paired beatitudes as shown by the bookends. The first of the pair is an internal perspective and is connected with being salt, the second an external perspective connected with being salty tasting.		

The good news about the "good news": Matthew 5-7 appears to provide the content of the teaching and proclaiming the good news that Matthew 4:23 says that Jesus was doing through the whole region of Galilee, attracting "crowds from Galilee, the Decapolis, Jerusalem, Judaea and Transjordan" (4:25). These declarations of blessings that are surprising, good news sets the stage for the entire sermon on the Mount. The more we can see the organization, flow, and rhetorical force of these blessings as oral teaching, the more we can discern the patterns that will persist throughout the entire passage of Matthew 5-7 and their deep connection with the Lord's Prayer. Whenever this is missed, even scholars honestly share their disappointment in not being able to see how the pieces fit together, or, why elements such as the Lord's Prayer appear where they do. Taking the time to examine the blessings in the way that they were experienced by the listeners will, in fact, provide additional "blessings" to us as readers and listeners now.

A Pair of Blessing Bookends with 3 Blessing Pairs between them: Note how there are two bookends with the phrase "theirs is the *kingdom of heaven*" and how the six blessings in between them form three pairs of blessings that tie into each other. (This highlighting of two beatitudes is similar to what will be done later in sets of contrasts or antitheses where only two refer to "the ancients/ancestors".)

What is the significance of the "kingdom of heaven"[10] in Matthew? Note the significance of the phrase "kingdom of heaven" and its connection to the key message of John the Baptist in Matthew 3:2, to the message of Jesus in 4:17, the announcement of the good news of the kingdom in 5:3&10; status in the kingdom in 5:19, entry to the kingdom in 5:20 and 7:21 and the "kingdom" of the heavenly Father in 6:10 and 6:33. After the Sermon on the Mount, the theme continues throughout Matthew with life in the kingdom discussed in 8:11 and the narrative describing Jesus going to "all the cities and villages . . . announcing the good news of the *kingdom of heaven*" and subsequently speak-

---

10   Professor Ulrich points out "that 'heaven' is a circumlocution for God, and that the genitive case of "heaven" is subjective in character. In other words, the phrase "kingdom of heaven" refers to God's reign or rule. To enter God's reign is to enter the sphere of that rule and thus to receive life. Jack Kingsbury, *Matthew: Structure, Christology, Kingdom* is still relevant on this point. Bruce Chilton, *A Galilean Rabbi and His Bible*, makes a good case for the subjective genitive." See Jonathan Pennington's, *Heaven and Earth in the Gospel of Matthew*, p.5, begins the dissertation-long systematic exception to the circumlocution argument as lacking evidence and being too narrow. Note also his demonstrating the pairing of "heaven" and "earth" throughout Matthew.

ing of it often giving parables about it throughout the rest of Matthew. This good news of the kingdom is what brings peace to the poor in spirit and sorrowful and leads them to become peace-making disciples and ultimately makers of new peacemaking disciples to all the nations. Given the pre-eminence of the role of Jesus as king telling the surprising, good news of the kingdom of heaven, it would not be surprising to see the Sermon on the Mount in 5-7 as the "fishing lessons" he promised the professional fishermen disciples in Matthew 4:19 to catch people for the kingdom of heaven. The importance of gaining entry to the kingdom continues throughout the section of 5-7, especially 7:21-29. It continues throughout Matthew, especially Chapters 18:3, 35 and 25:31-46 where entry into the kingdom of heaven is not certain for everyone but certainly urgent to gain.

Why are these phrases even here and in this order? Why do the beatitudes or blessings appear in the order they appear? Is the order haphazard[11] and meaningless? On the other hand, if the writer of Matthew and Jesus himself uses commonly known persuasion or "rhetorical" methods, then we might be open to see how their order helps engage the attention of the crowd in the first place, makes the information relevant, and how its relevance and order make the material memorable. See the prior section on drivers covering persuasion methods. At the end of the chapter, the crowds proclaim Jesus spoke as one with "authority" likely showing that they were engaged from beginning to the end as if they could not help but listen. What is the connection between the beatitudes and salt and light? Is that just another haphazard collection of sayings or was there a compelling oratorical or rhetorical direction, acceleration, or force? How does that section relate to the section on law and why did Jesus even start on that topic? How does all of that relate to prayer in Chapter 6? Usually, these questions, even when asked, often lead to frustration when the analyst fails to integrate that question with the explicit audience.

What is the significance of "kingdom of heaven" in Matthew 5:3-10? Note that the phrase "kingdom of heaven" is only in the first and eighth beatitude in Matthew 5:3-10 leaving the other six beatitudes between them. If one could discover what makes these bookends a pair, then it might be possible to see how the six in between are really three pairs. If so, they would be much easier to remember. If these can be shown to be pairs, especially if there can be shown a progression between the pairs that made their sequence compelling rather than arbitrary, then it would also be significant to see if one portion of the pairs corresponds to being salt and the other set corresponds to being salty tasting supporting the duality set up in the salt and light passage that immediately follows. For a more complete discussion, see "Audience and Mnemonics," a paper presented to the Network of Biblical Storytellers in 2014 and reproduced in the appendix.

Organization and rhetorical force of the blessings: The first blessing of the "poor in spirit" can be seen as an internal condition likely resulting from external circumstances. It is contrasted with the eighth blessing of the "persecuted" which requires people outside of oneself in order to be persecuted. Similarly, each of the other six blessings alternates between an internal state and a counterpart blessing showing an external relationship. Compare the second as "sorrowful" (internal) vs the third as "gentle" (external), the fourth as "hungering and thirsting" (internal) vs. the fifth as "merciful" (external), the sixth as "purified in heart" (internal) vs the seventh as "peacemaking" (external). The internal portion of the three pairs, as a condition related to external circumstances) comprise three steps of escalating emotion and conflict moving from stage of suffering to oppression that may have caused that suffering which in turn flips to purification and ultimately to peace-making. This approach evokes the stories or circumstances of the listeners who must wonder whether their sorrow or hunger will be blessed. This engages their interest then holds it to a conclusion. Rather than merely providing data about the kingdom, Jesus is relating it to the self-interests of the listeners and evokes their stories before telling them his own. He is using persuasion in the recruitment process among the

---

11 See Davies discussing the purposeful arrangement of the material in Matthew: W.D. Davies, *The Sermon on the Mount*, Cambridge University Press, London, 1966, 1969. This 165-page book covers the setting with section on the "Setting in Matthew," the "Jewish Messianic Expectation," "Contemporary Judaism," "the Early Church," and the "Ministry of Jesus." He reviews the disciplines of "source, form and liturgical criticism: (p. 4-6) provides a mixed approach to Matthew 5-7 as material from "diverse sources" (p. 4), yet considered "Matthew" as the "final author of the Gospel" who "regarded v-vii as a unit" (p. 6). "It reveals a meticulous concern in the arrangement of its details and an architectonic grandeur in its totality." "... It must first be approached in its setting in the structure of Matthew as a whole" (p. 6) See, also, Davies additional work in his three-volume commentary *Matthew* with Dale Allison and Allison's work of the same title, *The Sermon on the Mount*. Davies also produced *The Setting of the Sermon on the Mount*.

crowds and demonstrates effective fishing to the observing disciples as promised in 4:19. This emotional progression of the beatitude pairs reinforced by the salt versus saltiness section that leads to peace-making is a similar process that is apparent in the Lord's Prayer once it is considered from the point of view of a first-time hearer within the crowds. See the following discussion on how the first blessing is an attention-grabbing surprise and how that surprise grows with each escalating pair of blessings. After all, when Jesus was said to have been "preaching the good news," it meant that he was making "surprise announcements of good news," namely, an announcement that was not expected about news that was not anticipated.

The emotional escalation of the surprising blessing pairs or ladder

The first surprise: The first blessing appears to be a reversal of everything assumed by people living in the greatest poverty and despair. They were described in Matthew 4:16 as being those who lived in or were trapped in the valley of the shadow of death. They were those who experienced enough poverty that they lost hope.[12] They may have been told or thought that they didn't matter since, if they did matter, someone might have helped them out of despair. Even God, who certainly was capable enough to help them, did not bother to do so because they apparently did not matter to God. Instead, they are told the surprising, good news that the opposite is true. The good news is that God is working through their bad news[13] in such an amazing way that instead of being at the bottom, the most hopeless of the hopeless are actually at the top. They are in the family that co-owns the kingdom of heaven from which the entire multiverse emerges. That is infinitely better than running three countries for three millennia with a few trillion dollars of pocket change. It is as if the heavenly Father is making an investment within the lives of the poor in proportion to the poverty and suffering that they experience.

The dynamics within the blessing pairs—salt versus salty tasting: The listeners within the crowd who were sorrowful are blessed because God will comfort them. They are already salt because of their sorrow. The question is whether they will be gentle or harsh to others once they receive that comfort from God. If gentle, they will get another blessing. They will inherit the land. When they choose to be gentle, they demonstrate that they have learned something from sorrow. If they have learned something from the great investment made in them through their suffering, then it will show in their gentleness and others will taste their saltiness. If they will be gentle, then they will be salty tasting. Likewise, if they are not gentle, then they act as if they have learned nothing from their suffering and others do not derive its benefit. The salt has lost its taste and most of its value. It is like the well-known problem that abused people often become the new abusers and the oppressed people become the new oppressors.

The dynamics between the blessing pairs: When someone suffers loss of most any kind, that emotional experience is deepened when that person realizes that the only reason why the suffering or loss happened in the first place was because someone caused it. If it were not for someone robbing them of a right or just relationship, the loss never would have occurred in the first place. The emotion escalates from sorrow to anger and rage. This demonstrates the emotional escalation between the blessing pairs. It also serves as growing rhetorical force and makes it easier to follow the line of argument to a climax and ultimately makes it possible for them to memorize the sequencing.

Hungering and thirsting for right or just relationships: The person who was robbed of justice is the one who hungers and thirsts after being denied right or just relationships. The Father will bless them by filling the hunger for right or just relationships. What will they learn as a result? Will they be gentle to everyone else except those who caused their sorrow? Or will they learn from their loss of right or just relationships and share that desire for a right or just relationship with the very person or group that disappointed and robbed them of justice? If they have learned they

---

12 See the introduction section on "location of the setting of Matthew's Gospel" and the stresses most felt who "subsisted on little after taxes and debts," Oakman, *Jesus and the Peasants*, p. 5.

13 This reminds me of my great grandmother, Mrs. Esther Purim who lived in Brooklyn, NY and Miami Beach, FL when she was the subject of several newspaper articles on her birthdays between age 104-113. In at least one of them, when asked for the secret of her longevity, she is quoted to have said, "be good-natured, take care of yourself and most of all, take troubles that come as if they were sent by God." That provides hope to someone experiencing tragedy since if it were sent by God, then something even better will come of it. "113, She Says Visitors Keep Her Youthful" published July 12, 1962 in the Brooklyn section of the Sunday News.

will be merciful to the very one that robbed them of a right relationship. And, when they do become merciful to the one who does not deserve it, they will be blessed and get mercy. In being merciful they shift from being salt to being salty tasting to the one receiving mercy and those who witness that mercy. But, if they don't extend mercy, they will have gone through all that suffering, for nothing and no one will benefit from their being salt.

A worthless blessing? Is the blessing of receiving mercy a worthless blessing? The question remains whether the person who gets the blessing of receiving mercy is getting anything of value especially if they have only ever been an innocent victim not ever needing mercy.[14] That brings us to the next pair of blessings.

Pure in heart? "Blessed are the pure in heart" uses the Greek word καθαροὶ (*katharoi*) similar to the English word "catharsis" that could either mean pure or purified. In Matthew 23:25-26 it does not mean always being clean or pure but having been cleansed or purified like a dirty dish that has been cleansed.[15] So, this word can be used in either of two ways. The first way would be "blessed are those who have always been perfectly pure." That would be an example of someone whose acts and thoughts were blameless. If there were such a person, that person would be blessed and receive the ultimate blessing of being able to see God. But that would be the person who would have never needed mercy, the result of the prior blessing. The second way it can be used is as in "purified" or "cleansed," as in "blessed are the purified…"

Purified in heart? The difference between the two definitions highlights an additional emotional or psychological escalation. Given that sorrow was surpassed by anger or rage from realizing that the sorrow was unnecessarily caused by someone, there is an even greater emotion when a lifelong anger or rage at a certain kind of unjust behavior is turned on oneself. When that anger is nearly murderous to another, it can become suicidal for the ones who realize that they are as bad or worse than the one they hated the most. This is the moment of the greatest pivot in which the one who realizes that he or she is not pure in heart but in need of great mercy. At that moment, he or she may be faced with two alternatives, either they throw themselves on the loving and forgiving mercy of God, or they self-destruct. In the days of Jesus and earlier, when someone realized their great sin against another, he or she would apologize, make amends, and then go to the temple for a sin sacrifice where the innocent sacrifice takes the punishment for the one incurring the moral debt.

In this way, the relationship between this blessing and the next one in the blessing pair can be seen. When the one who is crushed in spirit and goes to the Father for forgiveness based on the price paid through the sacrifice, they become "purified in heart" and as a result "will see God." That is the ultimate blessing. At that moment, they become "salt."

Where are the peacemakers? But, when that person experiences that great blessing of being "purified in heart by this sacrifice," what will they do as a result? If they see others in conflict and they take the risk and effort and possibly sacrifice of themselves to be a peacemaker for others, then they are salty-tasting, and will be called the "children of God." Why are they so described? It is because they are acting like God who makes peace for us based on a sacrifice. (The variety of conflicts in which the peacemaker may work will be further developed in the "turn the other cheek" passage outlining alternatives to compensatory damages.)

The first blessing of each blessing pair is like a tree planted by God in the lives of suffering people. If that tree is planted in good soil, then the fruit of sorrow, loss of justice, and purification of heart will result in gentleness, mercifulness,

---

14   It might be obvious to us that in all conflicts where one party does not believe that he or she is to blame, not all parties in conflict can be in the right. That is the very reason why we have judges and mediators. It is interesting to note how Jesus either in the beatitudes or in the encouragement to pray for persecutors never suggests that the listener might be the party actually in the wrong. In the case of Matthew 5:23-26, where the listener may be the one taken to the judge, the one taken to the judge appears to be presumed innocent by Jesus though still needing to resolve the legal matter prior to getting to the judge. That party might be totally innocent in that situation. But there will be others where the accused may either be wrong or partly wrong. And, if not in that instance, then in others.

15   See some of the parallels between the "blessings" of Matthew 5 and the "woes" of Matthew 23:13-39. The first and last woes are the inverse of the bookend blessing of Matthew 5 in that the first woe discusses failure to get into the kingdom of heaven and the last woe shows those who persecute the just and pursue them from town to town. Between these two woes are the treatment of justice, mercy, faith (v. 23), and purity (v. 24-27).

and peacemaking. The tree is like being salt and the fruit is like being salty tasting or light giving. Furthermore, each pair shows an emotional and conceptual escalation that starts with gentleness (the withholding of harshness by someone with strength), then proceeds to someone showing mercy (the withholding of punishment) to ultimately someone proactively going out and becoming a peacemaker.

What happens to the peacemakers? The last remaining escalation is the understanding that the peacemaker will become persecuted by those accusing the peacemaker in the name of justice or righteousness. This sets up the next section showing how Jesus accuses those who persecute peacemakers for being weak on crime and the law as being the ones who really are the lawbreakers. The same theme arises again when Jesus asks the crowds to pray for the persecutors in Matthew 5:44 asking forgiveness of them in the prayer in 6:9-15. Note the companion set of woes in Matthew 23:13-39, where the first discusses those who block others from the kingdom of heaven and fail to get in themselves and the last woe which goes into detail of how the persecutors attack the righteous and just in the past and the future.

Role of blessings and curses in ancient persuasion (rhetoric) training: Blessings or praises (as well as shaming) are known in the ancient world as a significant part of persuasion techniques. They are detailed in persuasion instructions such as the *progymnysmata* as an essential educational component for those immediately after learning basic grammar. See *Honor and Shame* by Jerome Neyrey that describes the use of blessings or praise as "progymnasmata" and his comments on Matthew 5.[16] They are known to include praise for birth, nurture, training, and deeds. Each of the first pairs of the blessings describe the nurture and training of the receiver of the blessing because of their suffering that God used to bless them. The second blessing is what accrues to them when they choose to be gentle, merciful, peacemaking or persecuted. The approach taken to the Lord's Prayer in Matthew provides evidence that Jesus was not only teaching disciples what it was to be a disciple, but also how to persuade others to become disciples by persuading members of the crowds to become disciples in the presence of those already disciples. This appears to be the primary purpose of the Sermon on the Mount including the Lord's Prayer. The crowds described throughout Matthew, especially Matthew 13, detail the activities that lead some in the crowds to become disciples and the group from which new disciples would be made.

See "Audience and Mnemonics" for a treatment of the beatitude pairs in the appendix for more detail and examples of the emotional escalation in the discussion of the Lord's Prayer skit kit.

Here is another summary of the organization of the beatitudes that is illustrated in the chart that follows:

> (1st and 8th) Blessed are poor in spirit—internal reality; blessed are persecuted— external since outsiders are needed to be persecuted;

> (2d and 3d) Blessed are sorrowful—internal; blessed are gentle, external since need someone with whom to be gentle.

> (4th and 5th) Blessed are hungering and thirsting…—internal reality; blessed are merciful—external since need some on the outside to whom mercy can be shown.

> (6th and 7th) Blessed are pure or purified in heart—internal; blessed are peacemakers—external since those in conflict outside are needed for a peacemaker to do his or her peacemaking.

Each of the first of the pairs is what makes one salt or light; the second of each pair is what makes one salty tasting or light giving. This makes it possible to see how both blessings and salt/light descriptions apply to both crowd members and disciples.

---

16   See Neyrey pp. 72-74 about the role of praise from Aristotle, and categories of praise in the progymnasmata on pp. 78-82, and the role of praise in the beatitudes on p. 167 and role of shame in persecution on p. 168. See also, Parsons and Martin on "Encomium, Crafting Words of Praise and Critique," pp. 175-230 of *Ancient Rhetoric and the New Testament*.

The internal pairs also escalate emotionally in the context of conflict: suffering, outrage at those perceived as the cause, rage turned inward as self is challenged needing purification.

Note the organization of the following chart that outlines how the pairs of beatitudes work in rows with each other in columns of blessings when the listener is weak versus when strong.

Consider how much easier it is to remember pairs that are meaningfully connected as pairs and as a group of pairs when the significance of the pairs become apparent. (I was tempted to write, "a*pair*ent"). Consider how easy it is to fill in the blank for pairings such as "peanut butter and _____; or, "socks and _____" or "raining cats and _____." In this case, the pairs would be "sorrow and gentle," "justice and mercy," and "purified and peacemakers."

Matthew Chapter 5 Beatitude Table with Connection to Salt and Light

Escalation from weak to strong ☐ from smaller to larger motives ☐

	When Weak			When Strong	
Ref	a) Internal Condition ☐	b) Blessing	Ref	a) External Relationship ☐	b) Blessing
v. 3	Poor	*Kingdom of Heaven* (now)	v. 10	Persecuted	*Kingdom of Heaven* (now)
v. 4	Grieving (now)	Comfort (future)	v. 5	Gentle (now) (learned from grief)	Inherit Earth (future or resulting event)
v. 6	Hunger for Justice (now)	Filled (future)	v. 7	Merciful (now) (learned from felt injustice)	Receive Mercy (future or resulting event)
v. 8	Pure (relative and temporary while victim of crime) but becomes in need of purification after own sin (purified) in heart (now) (PIVOT point, sufferer imposes suffering and needs mercy and peace by purification)	See God (future)	v. 9	Peacemakers (now) (learned from purification by sacrifice so makes peace for others on basis of sacrificial act of peace-making)	Called Children of God *since acting like God making peace for others based on sacrificial love* (future or resulting event)
	☐ Salt, Light			☐ Perceived Saltiness, Shining	
v. 13a, 14 a	You are salt (actual now) You are light (actual now)	Actual within self and Potential to others	v. 13b-c, 14 b-16	Salty vs Tasteless (possible future) Shining vs Dark (possible future)	Actualization to others

How crowd members are salt and light: Commentaries have traditionally applied these beatitudes and salt[17] and light declarations only to the disciples or prospective disciples but not to the crowds who are not yet disciples. This is despite the text which clearly states Jesus is addressing the crowds for the purpose of recruiting while the professional fisherman are trying to watch Jesus in action so they could learn how he is fishing for people.[18]

The arrangement of the blessing pairs shows that all members of the crowd were salt by virtue of their suffering and loss of justice. The question was whether they would become salty tasting. Paying attention to the organization of the beatitude pairs may illuminate, rather than frustrate, a modern reader who might give up without understanding how salt and light might apply to crowds.

Understanding how the blessings are organized in a series of pairs as shown by the bookends, and how the second of each pair represents the person's response to what was learned through the first of each pair, can reveal an emotional or psychological progression that can lead to empathy and the goal of recruiting new peace-making disciples from the crowds.

The dual nature of salt versus saltiness or light shining versus a light source hidden as shown in the comments on the beatitudes is further evidence that a pairing may be involved. In this way as mentioned earlier, it may be that any in the crowd is blessed and declared "salt" because of his or her grief and sorrow but is challenged to see if he or she learned from it and refrained from making other sorrowful but chose to be gentle instead. If so, those are considered "salty tasting" because others benefit from what they have learned and done as a result of their being salt. But, if they choose to be the new cause of sorrow, then they failed to learn those lessons and others will not benefit or taste that salt. For more details on how that progression works with growing rhetorical force, see "Audience and Mnemonics in Matthew" in the appendix.

(For an interesting comparison of the first blessing of those who appear to be on the bottom, see Matthew 19:30 & 20:16, and Ps 118:22-24, where the rejected stone becomes the most important.)

Application notes:

"Blessed are the pure/purified…": There is an emotional escalation from the "blessed are the merciful for they shall receive mercy" to the following "blessed are the pure/purified in heart." That is where the "innocent one" discovers their own need for mercy. At that moment, if that one does not choose to ask for mercy and forgiveness, then the lifelong train of anger towards an abusive situation could result in self-anger as illustrated by Judas, a lifelong person so trustworthy that he was the one who was trusted with the disciples' cash yet became the one who betrayed Jesus. Care should be given when walking others through this section to ensure that a balance is struck between their learning of their need for mercy and forgiveness with the accompanying offer of forgiveness by the Father so that they could live on to become the new peacemakers rather than self-destruct in their self-rage.

"Blessed are the peacemakers": When encouraging others to be merciful and forgiving we might consider being careful to not push someone back into a dangerous or life-threatening situation when they should instead seek a safe refuge from serious physical threats. Also, the implication of being a peacemaker implies that one being a peacemaker may include taking steps at one's own risk to help innocent weaker parties from being abused or murdered by others or otherwise harmed by a dangerous environment. Being a peacemaker does not mean that one should appease an abuser and allowing the weak and innocent to be harmed. Instead, a peacemaker attempts reconciliation whether one is suing him (Matthew 5:23-26) or when hurt by and chooses to pursue reconciliation (Matthew 18).[19]

---

17   Many commentaries will aptly point out the reasons why salt was valuable in the ancient world and the ways that it was used for preservation and an antiseptic. See Kurlansky's recent book *Salt, A World History*.

18   See Davies and Allison, Matthew, 1-7, p. 471. "In 5:3 would be disciples are told that they are the salt … not told how to become salt or light." By seeing Beatitudes' pair structure, instead of two groups of four, it becomes clear how they are salt and how they become salty tasting.

19   For an example of the risk of peacemaking, including those who are sincere and serious pacifists, see the description of peacemaking activ-

Current events of pandemics and riots: At the time of this writing, I am experiencing the stay-at-home orders due to a pandemic similar to what I wrote about with two leading experts in public health and medicine ("The Resilient Hospitals Handbook"[20]). The conflicts between individuals, groups, institutions, and an unhealthy environment are certainly numerous and overwhelming to many. Secondly, we are experiencing the reactions including small riots across the country after the public release of videos showing the killing of George Floyd by police officers in Minneapolis. This is gut-wrenching to many including myself who has a black nephew, grew up in the inner-city of Chicago during the riots of the 1960s, and served in the military as a police and corrections officer trained to protect and not seriously injure or kill those, we had to either restrain or arrest so that they could return to duties. All the multitudinous conflicts, inequities, and prejudices between individuals, their communities, the resources they need by way of food, housing, education, medical attention, and jobs are just the beginning of conflicts that inevitably invade the personal well-being, families and marriages of all involved. There will be times when many of these stresses will be experienced at the same time. I hope that every person on the side of every issue regardless of how right or wrong they are can come to the point of praying for those they conflict with by using this prayer of Jesus. I also hope that those wishing to make a difference helping others, often inserting themselves as peacemakers will take advantage of the peace of God that may bring them courage and confidence to help. Perhaps, we can help all of these as we practice using the Lord's Prayer for persecutors for the many conflicts or potential conflicts that we encounter many times each hour. As I write this, I hear the funeral service of the comments of president of North Central University announcing a scholarship fund in honor of George Floyd, a timely peacemaking act. This came just after a Zoom conference call among local church and community leaders discussing the same issue along with housing and food security. Revisiting these passages and discussing them may help us more effectively engage in our own opportunities to become peacemakers and reconcilers for those around us.

For discussion on the beatitudes:

1) What evidence provides a working hypothesis of who the crowds were, the stresses they endured and the extent they would have lost hope?

2) What evidence indicates the nature of the teaching of Jesus and the setting in which he taught?

3) How do the blessing pairs describe emotionally escalating conflicts?

4) What is the significance of the shift from being "pure" in heart to being "purified" in heart?

5) How does the person find "purification"?

6) How does the purification lead to peace instead of anger or resentment?

7) How does the resulting peace connect to the complimentary blessing of "blessed are the peacemakers"?

8) What are the implications for how someone becomes a peacemaker?

9) What are the implications for making new "peace-making" disciples?

10) What might be the connections between peacemakers and persecutors?

11) What evidence do you see in the text, either in English translations or Greek, for working definitions of "meek" or "gentle," "righteousness" or "justice," "pure" or purified," and "persecuted"?

---

ities of antiwar activists in *The Gospel of Rutba*, by Greg Barrett.

20 "Resilient Hospitals Handbook" coauthored by Manto, Motzer, and Terbush can be acquired through Amazon, or available as a free PDF through the HHS public database here: https://asprtracie.hhs.gov/technical-resources/resource/5609/resilient-hospitals-handbook-strhening-healthcare-and-public-health-resilience-in-advance-of-a-prolonged-and-widespread-power-outage

For discussion on the salt and light passage:

Using the material above, including the chart,

1) How might the designation of salt or light apply to the crowds?

2) How might the designation "not losing its saltiness" or "light hidden" apply to the crowds?

3) How might pairs be discussed and taught as memorable units such as "peanut butter and jelly"?

4) How might the application of being salt or being salty tasting, or light seen versus light hidden emphasize the paired nature of the beatitudes and provide insight as to how one becomes salty tasting and light giving?

5) At what point does the member of the crowd transition to becoming a disciple?

6) What implications might there be for the designation of "theirs is the kingdom of heaven"?

7) Later, how might the identification of who "*theirs* is the kingdom" be applied to the Lord's Prayer section in Matthew 6, the ask, seek and knock prayer in 7 and the "depart from me I never knew you" comment in 7, the house built on the foundation of sand or rock in 7, and the unforgiving servant in 18?

8) How might these passages be applied to current events in the news?

9) How might these passages be applied to conflicts known primarily by the study group?

USB5	Author and Reader Notes	NASB®	New American Bible
Matt. 5:17 ¶ Μὴ νομίσητε ὅτι ἦλθον καταλῦσαι τὸν νόμον ἢ τοὺς προφήτας· οὐκ ἦλθον καταλῦσαι ἀλλὰ πληρῶσαι. **Matt. 5:18** ἀμὴν γὰρ λέγω ὑμῖν· ἕως ἂν παρέλθῃ ὁ οὐρανὸς καὶ ἡ γῆ, ἰῶτα ἓν ἢ μία κεραία οὐ μὴ παρέλθῃ ἀπὸ τοῦ νόμου, ἕως ἂν πάντα γένηται. **Matt. 5:19** ὃς ἐὰν οὖν λύσῃ μίαν τῶν ἐντολῶν τούτων τῶν ἐλαχίστων καὶ διδάξῃ οὕτως τοὺς ἀνθρώπους, ἐλάχιστος κληθήσεται ἐν τῇ βασιλείᾳ τῶν οὐρανῶν· ὃς δ᾽ ἂν ποιήσῃ καὶ διδάξῃ, οὗτος μέγας κληθήσεται ἐν τῇ βασιλείᾳ τῶν οὐρανῶν. **Matt. 5:20** λέγω γὰρ ὑμῖν ὅτι ἐὰν μὴ περισσεύσῃ ὑμῶν ἡ δικαιοσύνη πλεῖον τῶν γραμματέων καὶ Φαρισαίων, οὐ μὴ εἰσέλθητε εἰς τὴν βασιλείαν τῶν οὐρανῶν.		**Matt. 5:17** ¶ "Do not think that I came to abolish the ᵃLaw or the Prophets; I did not come to abolish but to fulfill. **Matt. 5:18** "For truly I say to you, ᵃuntil heaven and earth pass away, not ¹the smallest letter or stroke shall pass from the Law until all is accomplished. **Matt. 5:19** "Whoever then annuls one of the least of these commandments, and teaches ¹others *to do* the same, shall be called least ᵃin the kingdom of heaven; but whoever ²keeps and teaches *them*, he shall be called great in the kingdom of heaven. **Matt. 5:20** ¶ "For I say to you that unless your ᵃrighteousness surpasses *that* of the scribes and Pharisees, you will not enter the kingdom of heaven.	17 "Do not think that I have come to abolish the law or the prophets. I have come not to abolish but to fulfill. 18Amen, I say to you, until heaven and earth pass away, not the smallest letter or the smallest part of a letter will pass from the law, until all things have taken place. 19 Therefore, whoever breaks one of the least of these commandments and teaches others to do so will be called least in the kingdom of heaven. But whoever obeys and teaches these commandments will be called greatest in the kingdom of heaven. 20 I tell you, unless your righteousness surpasses that of the scribes and Pharisees, you will not enter into the kingdom of heaven. 21꞊You

Matt. 5:21 ¶
Ἠκούσατε ὅτι ἐρρέθη τοῖς ἀρχαίοις, **Οὐ φονεύσεις·** ὃς δ' ἂν φονεύσῃ, ἔνοχος ἔσται τῇ κρίσει.
Matt. 5:22 ἐγὼ δὲ λέγω ὑμῖν ὅτι πᾶς ὁ ὀργιζόμενος τῷ ἀδελφῷ αὐτοῦ³ ἔνοχος ἔσται τῇ κρίσει· ὃς δ' ἂν εἴπῃ τῷ ἀδελφῷ αὐτοῦ, Ρακά, ἔνοχος ἔσται τῷ συνεδρίῳ· ὃς δ' ἂν εἴπῃ, Μωρέ, ἔνοχος ἔσται εἰς τὴν γέενναν τοῦ πυρός.
Matt. 5:23 ἐὰν οὖν προσφέρῃς τὸ δῶρόν σου ἐπὶ τὸ θυσιαστήριον κἀκεῖ μνησθῇς ὅτι ὁ ἀδελφός σου ἔχει τι κατὰ σοῦ,
Matt. 5:24 ἄφες ἐκεῖ τὸ δῶρόν σου ἔμπροσθεν τοῦ θυσιαστηρίου καὶ ὕπαγε πρῶτον διαλλάγηθι τῷ ἀδελφῷ σου, καὶ τότε ἐλθὼν πρόσφερε τὸ δῶρόν σου.
Matt. 5:25 ἴσθι εὐνοῶν τῷ ἀντιδίκῳ σου ταχύ, ἕως ὅτου εἶ μετ' αὐτοῦ ἐν τῇ ὁδῷ, μήποτέ σε παραδῷ ὁ ἀντίδικος τῷ κριτῇ καὶ ὁ κριτὴς τῷ ὑπηρέτῃ καὶ εἰς φυλακὴν βληθήσῃ·
Matt. 5:26 ἀμὴν λέγω σοι, οὐ μὴ ἐξέλθῃς ἐκεῖθεν, ἕως ἂν ἀποδῷς τὸν ἔσχατον κοδράντην.
Matt. 5:27 ¶
Ἠκούσατε ὅτι ἐρρέθη, **Οὐ μοιχεύσεις.**
Matt. 5:28 ἐγὼ δὲ λέγω ὑμῖν ὅτι πᾶς ὁ βλέπων γυναῖκα πρὸς τὸ ἐπιθυμῆσαι αὐτὴν ἤδη ἐμοίχευσεν αὐτὴν ἐν τῇ καρδίᾳ αὐτοῦ.
Matt. 5:29 εἰ δὲ ὁ ὀφθαλμός σου ὁ δεξιὸς σκανδαλίζει σε, ἔξελε αὐτὸν καὶ βάλε ἀπὸ σοῦ· συμφέρει γάρ σοι ἵνα ἀπόληται ἓν τῶν μελῶν σου καὶ μὴ ὅλον τὸ σῶμά σου

5:24 Note the Greek word for "leave" (ἄφες) your offering is the same as "release" your offering, the same word used to "release" your coat in 5:40 and "release" our debts in 6:12.

Matt. 5:21 ¶ "ᵃYou have heard that ¹the ancients were told, 'ᵇYOU SHALL NOT COMMIT MURDER' and 'Whoever commits murder shall be ²liable to ᶜthe court.'
Matt. 5:22 "But I say to you that everyone who is angry with his brother shall be ¹guilty before ᵃthe court; and whoever says to his brother, '²You good-for-nothing,' shall be ¹guilty before ³ᵇthe supreme court; and whoever says, 'You fool,' shall be ¹guilty *enough to go* into the ⁴ᶜfiery hell.
Matt. 5:23 "Therefore if you are ᵃpresenting your ¹offering at the altar, and there remember that your brother has something against you,
Matt. 5:24 leave your ¹offering there before the altar and go; first be ᵃreconciled to your brother, and then come and present your ¹offering.
Matt. 5:25 "ᵃMake friends quickly with your opponent at law while you are with him on the way, so that your opponent may not hand you over to the judge, and the judge to the officer, and you be thrown into prison.
Matt. 5:26 "Truly I say to you, ᵃyou will not come out of there until you have paid up the last ¹cent.
Matt. 5:27 ¶ "ᵃYou have heard that it was said, 'ᵇYOU SHALL NOT COMMIT ADULTERY';
Matt. 5:28 but I say to you that everyone who looks at a woman ᵃwith lust for her has already committed adultery with her in his heart.
Matt. 5:29 "ᵃIf your right

have heard that it was said to your ancestors, 'You shall not kill; and whoever kills will be liable to judgment.' 22 But I say to you, whoever is angry with his brother will be liable to judgment, and whoever says to his brother, 'Raqa,' will be answerable to the Sanhedrin, and whoever says, 'You fool,' will be liable to fiery Gehenna. 23 Therefore, if you bring your gift to the altar, and there recall that your brother has anything against you, 24 leave your gift there at the altar, go first and be reconciled with your brother, and then come and offer your gift. 25 Settle with your opponent quickly while on the way to court with him. Otherwise your opponent will hand you over to the judge, and the judge will hand you over to the guard, and you will be thrown into prison. 26 Amen, I say to you, you will not be released until you have paid the last penny. 27 "You have heard that it was said, 'You shall not commit adultery.' 28 But I say to you, everyone who looks at a woman with lust has already committed adultery with her in his heart. 29 If your right eye causes you to sin, tear it out and throw it away. It is better for you to lose one of your members than to have your whole body thrown into Gehenna. 30 And if your right hand causes you to sin, cut it off and throw it away. It is better for you to lose one of your members than to have your whole body go

ρληθῇ εἰς γέενναν. **Matt. 5:30** καὶ εἰ ἡ δεξιά σου χεὶρ σκανδαλίζει σε, ἔκκοψον αὐτὴν καὶ βάλε ἀπὸ σοῦ· συμφέρει γάρ σοι ἵνα ἀπόληται ἓν τῶν μελῶν σου καὶ μὴ ὅλον τὸ σῶμά σου εἰς γέενναν ἀπέλθῃ. **Matt. 5:31** ¶ Ἐρρέθη δέ, **Ὃς ἂν ἀπολύσῃ τὴν γυναῖκα αὐτοῦ, δότω αὐτῇ ἀποστάσιον.** **Matt. 5:32** ἐγὼ δὲ λέγω ὑμῖν ὅτι πᾶς ὁ ἀπολύων τὴν γυναῖκα αὐτοῦ παρεκτὸς λόγου πορνείας ποιεῖ αὐτὴν μοιχευθῆναι, καὶ ὃς ἐὰν ἀπολελυμένην γαμήσῃ, μοιχᾶται⁴.		eye makes you ¹stumble, tear it out and throw it from you; for it is better for you ²to lose one of the parts of your body, ³than for your whole body to be thrown into ⁴ᵇhell. **Matt. 5:30** "ᵃIf your right hand makes you ¹stumble, cut it off and throw it from you; for it is better for you ²to lose one of the parts of your body, ³than for your whole body to go into ⁴ᵇhell. **Matt. 5:31** ¶ "It was said, 'ᵃWHOEVER SENDS HIS WIFE AWAY, LET HIM GIVE HER A CERTIFICATE OF DIVORCE'; **Matt. 5:32** ᵈbut I say to you that everyone who ¹divorces his wife, except for *the* reason of unchastity, makes her commit adultery; and whoever marries a ²divorced woman commits adultery.	into Gehenna. 31"It was also said, 'Whoever divorces his wife must give her a bill of divorce.' 32 But I say to you, whoever divorces his wife (unless the marriage is unlawful) causes her to commit adultery, and whoever marries a divorced woman commits adultery.

Matt. 5:17 "Do not imagine that I have come to abolish the Law[21] or the Prophets. I have come not to abolish but to complete them."

Fulfilling the law with a pair of ancient sayings with 3 conflicts each: Why so touchy about the law and why here? Why did Jesus begin talking about abolishing the law here? Was it a change of topic? Or was it his following up on the expectation that peacemakers like himself would be criticized by persecutors as upending their justice system, in this case, their interpretation of the law? These questions cannot be avoided just because a reader might have doubts about Jesus saying these statements. The same questions need to be asked of Matthew who is writing it. Instead of changing the topic, this question provides rhetorical direction, acceleration and force of the beatitudes that leads the listeners to become the new peacemakers by Matthew 5:9; and who consequently will be persecuted by the peace-breakers in the name of their 'justice' that the peacemakers challenge in 5:10-12. So, in the same way that "the best defense is a good offense" Jesus pre-empts the persecutors by showing that they are the ones who lack justice. He demonstrates that the persecution is unwarranted and evil.

From this point, Jesus challenges the "justice system" of the persecutors by showing how they are not consistent with the very law they claim to serve. The series of "antitheses" shown by the phrase, "you have heard but I say…" anticipates that Jesus will be blamed and persecuted for his peacemaking as will his followers. These sections also show how the crowds can persuade their own persecutors to be reconciled with them. In effect, Jesus is showing the disciples how to fish the crowd by showing how the crowd can fish their enemies and reconcile with them.

---

21 See Betz, *Sermon on the Mount*, pp. 167-172 for Greek, Roman and Jewish law related to this text.

Heard not written: Notice also that Jesus counters the devil in Matthew 4 by showing what was "written" in the scriptures, but, to the crowds in Chapter 5 by "what they heard" since many of them might not have read what was there but only heard it either read to them or recited to them from someone's memorized text. This is another illustration of the importance of the oral sharing of the written text whether reading the written text out loud for others to hear or reciting it from memory when the written text is not available requiring motivation and methods capable of making memorization possible.

Matt. 5:20 "For I tell you, if your uprightness does not surpass that of the scribes and Pharisees, you will never get into the kingdom of Heaven."

Never get into the Kingdom of Heaven? [22]

This shows that the greatest conflict of all is not the conflict between members of the crowds and their enemies but between any of them and the kingdom of heaven where the rule of God's love reigns. But, instead of the conflict with the kingdom of heaven being irrelevant to their earthly conflicts, it is absolutely connected as shown in Matthew 6:15, "if you do not forgive men their trespasses, neither will your Father forgive your trespasses" and in 7:21 "not everyone who says, 'Lord, Lord' will enter the kingdom of heaven, but he who does the will of my Father who is in heaven: and, 18:25, "So also my heavenly Father will do to every one of you, if you do not forgive your brother from your heart."

Interpretive comment: As you explore these passages about entry into the kingdom of heaven and receiving forgiveness, see whether you might agree that these comments on living a forgiving way of life is indicative of how one received forgiveness as opposed to causing our forgiveness. In other words, people forgive enemies fully once they experience the gift of forgiveness, of having been fully forgiven for an equal or greater debt, as in the bullying God story in the preface. This would be the opposite of our forgiving way of life causing us to be forgiven. I believe that the ability to best forgive the worst enemy happens when we have experienced that forgiveness first and we feel compelled to forgive in the same way.

Note the warning of the introduction of this section that concludes with the statement challenging assumptions about how one might "enter the kingdom of heaven." It is consistent with Jesus's expressed interest in teaching the disciples how to recruit new disciples from the crowds as promised in 4:19. This discussion of entry into the kingdom is replicated in 5:44 and 6:14-15 and its parallel prayers in 7 and 18. The challenge as to whether one enters the kingdom of heaven highlights the conflict with God as of greater importance than even our conflicts within ourselves and between each other although all these conflicts are connected.[23]

For discussion:

1) What might be the connections between the various statements of "the kingdom of heaven"?

2) What is the importance of having or entering "the kingdom of heaven"?

3) What might be the connections to the promise of showing the professional fishermen of Matthew 4 to become "fishers of people"? How does this theme continue to grow?

4) What is the significance of having "righteousness (or justice)" exceed that of the scribes and Pharisees? How might that be and how might that be accomplished?

5) How might Jesus be pressing those who feel sufficiently righteous towards a consistency that will show up their inconsistency which might result in their also becoming "poor in spirit" and in need of "purification"?

---

22   (Refer to the discussion of the significance of "kingdom" in Matthew 5:3-16. *See* how the connection with the "kingdom" key element in the first and eighth beatitude, "for theirs is the kingdom of heaven' has been tied to the riveting and escalating emotions that comes from being "poor in spirit" and leads to being "persecuted." See Manto's treatment of four beatitude pairs in the paper to the Network of Biblical Storytellers in the appendix. Others have seen two groups of four.)

23   In Matthew 7, disciples are cautioned about how not to go fishing and to avoid false fishermen or prophets.

Matt. 5:21 "You have heard how it was said to our ancestors…"

Why are these the major categories of law and conflict? We have already seen how Jesus now pre-empts any false attack for being weak on "crime" or "injustice." But notice how. He takes what is apparent as outside behavior and applies it to the inside attitude. Jesus turns it around by saying in effect, "I will show you who is weak on justice. Persecutors of the peacemakers merely say don't murder, but I say if you are consistent with loving the way you want to be loved then you will even avoid wanting to commit murder." In fact, he goes further by implying that one crosses the line and may be charged with murder when one moves from being the one who is angry because of one's brother, which can be argued as being healthy and required, to becoming angry at one's brother which is unhealthy, dangerous, and not something we wish others to feel towards us. In each of these antitheses, he provides a different inner versus outer motif (similar to the alternating beatitudes) where each key element of the antitheses is presented in a way that challenges a superficial justice system that ultimately collapses on itself. (This will mirror itself when Jesus asks in the Lord's Prayer that both the "kingdom or rule" of the Father comes (which might align with outer compliance with the law) as well as his "will" or desire for love come, which is an internal reality.)

After the introductory section of 5:17-20, there are two sets of three antitheses: "You heard… but I say." Each of these represented dramatic if not traumatic conflicts that could lead to great loss, imprisonment or death and were of great interest to different members of the crowds. These are definitely high priority concerns that grab the attention of the listeners because they already have such concerns in their lives already. These wound not merely be theoretical concerns but actual ones.

"**Matt. 5:21-22** "You have heard how it was said to our **ancestors**, you shall not kill; and if anyone does kill, he must answer for it before the court." **Matt. 5:22 But I say this to you, anyone who is angry with a brother will answer for it before the court."** In the same way that the beatitudes have two that say, "theirs is the kingdom of heaven," so the contrasts here only have two that say, "you have heard that it was said to *our ancestors (the ancients)*." The first contrast in 5:21-22 makes the contrast between the outward act of murder to the inward attitude of hatred. The one who hates becomes as liable to the court as the one accused of murder. The one who hates and says hurtful words is liable to the high court and the one who hates and says something that dehumanizes the hated one is liable to the fires of Gehenna. This and each of the other elements of these contrasts or antitheses provide the foundation for the Lord's Prayer, not only in the conflicts the one praying is asked to consider but provides the opportunity to discover the common connection with one's persecutor including a common need of forgiveness.[24]

Realizing the self-destructive nature of anger as well as the way it injures others, makes it possible for every person to become humbled and receptive to forgiveness. Otherwise, any one of us who feels that we have never done anything especially bad, might not feel that we need much forgiveness. And, as a result, we might only forgive others of relatively minor infractions, such as the ones we admit to having committed. But we, not having done much evil, might not ever forgive someone of a major atrocity or something purposely hurtful to us.

Matt. 5:23 So then, if … your brother has something against you,

Matt. 5:24 leave your offering … and be reconciled with your brother **Matt. 5:25** Come to terms with your opponent on the way to the court with him, or he may hand you over to the judge and … the officer, and you will be thrown into prison. **Matt. 5:26** … you will not get out ….

Note the switch from anyone including the listener being asked not to be angry in 5:22 to the listener being subject to someone else's anger in 5:23, showing various scenarios of how anger results in damage. In the case of someone believing you have trespassed in such a way to cause damages to them, that person may bring you to court and demand payment for damages. Legal systems were set up to provide a framework for compensatory damages as will be covered later in the chapter when Jesus speaks about the role of "an eye for an eye" when the listeners are being hurt

---

24   For a helpful contemporary discussion of the significance I of anger in conflict resolution by a neuroscientist, see: Dr. Andrew Newberg and Mark Waldman's works, "Words Can Change Your Brain" and "How God Changes Your Brain."

by others and might be owed compensatory damages. In this example, the listeners are asked to consider their own circumstances when someone believes the listeners are at fault. But also note to what extent reconciliation must be done. It is not complete until someone gets tired of trying but until a complete set of steps is taken, or a resolution is achieved. There is no quitting until the moment of the court date. In other words, each party must persist until the other is convinced that the matter is resolved. If not, the case still goes to court. Imagine how often a relationship might be maintained or restored if this advice were to be embraced. This is like the level of effort shown in Matthew 18:15-17 where two or three different attempts may be required to restore a relationship.

Are these links between action and thought unfair and unrealistic?

This is a question worth taking the time to consider and discuss to determine whether we understand and agree with what Jesus was saying about anger. Is Jesus overstating the seriousness of anger or are we underestimating it? Might there be a role for healthy anger because of one's brother as opposed to being angry at or with one's brother?

The same thing could be said about adultery and lust. Might unresolved anger within a marriage result in disappointment that opens one up to considering an outside relationship that appears kinder and more considerate, hence making a connection to the section on lust and adultery? These connections, and others like it, powerfully link all the way through this "Sermon on the Mount" and the rest of Matthew.

As to patterns within this section, notice that in the same way that Jesus begins to talk about the hearers being angry to discussing when someone else is angry with them, note how the switch moves from the listeners being asked to consider their lust to the impact on a third party when their lust results in someone marrying their divorced wife and the ramifications that person inherits. Conflicts are described from the perspective of each of the parties involved and their impacts on others.

For discussion:

1) Are the links between actions and thought reasonable to the listeners? And, if so, what might be the ramifications for their sense of needing purification or forgiveness?

2) What may be the significance of shifting from being angry to having someone being angry with you? What might be the persuasion of teaching significance of the switch?

3) How serious is the issue of someone being angry with you?

4) What is the significance of being pursued and taken to court?

5) What passages after this section also discuss being taken to court or being pursued?

6) What might have been the consequences of being taken to court according to this passage, the one in Matthew 5:38 discussing "eye for an eye" or 5:40 being sued?

7) What are the objective criteria for succeeding at an out-of-court settlement?

8) How might those criteria inform our attempts at communication in conflicts that might avoid a break in a family, work or community relationship or a need to go to court?

9) What were the consequences of having to answer to the king in 18:23-35?

10) What are contemporary examples of being taken to court or pursued?

Why two groupings use the word "ancestors, ancients"? As in the beatitude section where only two beatitudes have "theirs is the kingdom of heaven," with three pairs of beatitudes in between them, of the six antitheses there are only two that have the phrase "to our ancestors," the one beginning in 5:17 and the other in 5:33 indicating a major organized approach to the six categories of conflict. Each of these two groups of antitheses starts with a lead antithesis with a progressive subject division making it easier to memorize and present the material so that others could follow and memorize it to present to others. Following each "to our ancestors" lead antithesis, there is a contrasting antithesis and a follow-up antithesis describing its consequences, for a total of three each. In the first instance it is murder and hate that are contrasted to adultery and lust. It might be possible that anger in a marital relationship might lead to a broken relationship or adultery as described in the text. Both are major offences that could result in the death penalty and may represent a broad category of laws relating to attacking and taking. The third set of conflicts in this group of antitheses ends by showing the impact of the second set of conflicts on third parties, namely on the person who marries the divorced woman. In the second major cluster of conflicts and law, it is oath taking (over-promising), contrasted to compensatory damages that ultimately leads to the third section of consequences Jesus would like to have happen through his request to love and pray for enemies.

Antitheses Matthew 5:21-48									
5:21-26:	You have heard it said **_by the ancients_**	No murder	But I say	No anger	5:33-37	You have heard it said **_by the ancients_**	Fulfill oaths	But I say	No oaths
5:27-30	You have heard it said	No adultery	But I say	No lust	5:38-42	You have heard it said	Eye for eye	But I say	Resist not evil
5:31-32	You have heard it said	Safe divorce	But I say	No divorce	5:43-48	You have heard it said	Hate enemies	But I say	Love & pray for enemy

In this way, the culmination of the entire antitheses section is the request to love enemies and pray for persecutors leading into that prayer outlined in 6:9-13 showing that the antitheses lead to the centrality of the Lord's Prayer for persecutors as the central conflict theme of the antitheses as well as the Sermon on the Mount as a whole.

UBS5	Author and Reader Notes	NASB®	New American Bible
Matt. 5:33 ¶ Πάλιν ἠκούσατε ὅτι ἐρρέθη τοῖς ἀρχαίοις, **Οὐκ ἐπιορκήσεις, ἀποδώσεις** δὲ τῷ κυρίῳ **τοὺς ὅρκους σου.** **Matt. 5:34** ἐγὼ δὲ λέγω ὑμῖν μὴ ὀμόσαι ὅλως· μήτε ἐν τῷ οὐρανῷ, ὅτι θρόνος ἐστὶν τοῦ θεοῦ, **Matt. 5:35** μήτε ἐν τῇ γῇ, ὅτι ὑποπόδιόν ἐστιν τῶν ποδῶν αὐτοῦ, μήτε εἰς Ἱεροσόλυμα, ὅτι πόλις ἐστὶν τοῦ μεγάλου βασιλέως, **Matt. 5:36** μήτε ἐν τῇ		**Matt. 5:33 ¶** "Again, "you have heard that ¹the ancients were told, '²ᵇYOU SHALL NOT ³MAKE FALSE VOWS, BUT SHALL FULFILL YOUR ⁴VOWS TO THE LORD.' **Matt. 5:34** "But I say to you, ªmake no oath at all, either by heaven, for it is ᵇthe throne of God, **Matt. 5:35** or by the earth, for it is the ªfootstool of His feet, or ¹by Jerusalem, for it is ᵇTHE CITY OF THE	. 33"Again you have heard that it was said to your ancestors, 'Do not take a false oath, but make good to the Lord all that you vow.' 34 But I say to you, do not swear at all; ²·³ not by heaven, for it is God's throne; 35 nor by the earth, for it is his footstool; nor by Jerusalem, for it is the city of the great King. 36 Do not swear by your head, for you cannot make a single hair white or black. 37 Let your

		GREAT KING. **Matt. 5:36** "Nor shall you make an oath by your head, for you cannot make one hair white or black. **Matt. 5:37** "But let your statement be, 'Yes, yes' *or* 'No, no'; anything beyond these is ¹ᵃ"evil.	'Yes' mean 'Yes,' and your 'No' mean 'No.' Anything more is from the evil one.
κεφαλῆ σου ὀμόσῃς, ὅτι οὐ δύνασαι μίαν τρίχα λευκὴν ποιῆσαι ἢ μέλαιναν. **Matt. 5:37** ἔστω δὲ ὁ λόγος ὑμῶν ναὶ ναί, οὒ οὒ· τὸ δὲ περισσὸν τούτων ἐκ τοῦ πονηροῦ ἐστιν.			

Significance of Oaths—Why is "oath taking" such a big deal? Note that in 5:33 there is the second use of the term "from our ancestors (ancients)" (τοῖς ἀρχαίοις), the other being 5:21. As in the previous section beginning in 5:21, this is the second major section with two following subsections beginning with the same formula but without the phrase "our ancestors." But in this case, the lead category of conflict and law is "oath taking." Why? A modern reader might wonder how "oath taking" would be so significant that it would be a major heading for law or conflict that has elements underneath it. Asking these kinds of questions facilitate meditation and analysis. In this case, the range of examples used to show how little power the promiser has leads to contemplation of the consequences of the broken promises.

Over-promising and Ties to Compensatory Damages: The examples used to show powerlessness range from heaven, to earth, to Jerusalem, to the hairs on one's head as elements in A, B, C, D order to a list in reverse order of D', C', B', A' of the specific ways of handling compensatory damages in a different way proposed by Jesus when he moves from one person whose cheek was struck, to someone who wants a local government's judge to demand a shirt, to the earthly Roman empire who is the entity that demands someone walk a mile, to the heavens which might be the only clue as to why someone is impacted to the point of needing to make a request for a loan.

A, B, C, D; D', C',B',A' Connections	
Matthew 5:33-37	**Matthew 5:38-42**
A (Don't swear by) Heaven (5:34)	**D'** Cheek, individual head (5:39)
B (Don't swear by) Earth (5:35a)	**C'** Sue (judge) for shirt, local government 5:40
C (Don't swear by) Jerusalem (5:35b)	**B'** Walk (Roman conscription), earth power 5:41
D (Don't swear by) Head (5:36)	**A'** Borrow (beg, not demand, general issue 5:42

See the note below on chiasmus and inversion on the verses of the compensatory damages section and the link to the "we-petitions" of the Lord's Prayer below. Inevitably, those promises lead to disappointment and loss which might only be recovered by someone asking for reimbursement or compensatory damages. The interesting difference between this set and the previous set of conflicts is that the other set appears to be caused by people doing "bad" things (murder/attacking or adultery/taking) whereas this one could be done by a good person trying to do a good thing. This shows another category of conflict -- those done by good people attempting to do good things poorly. It broadens the range of potential conflict scenarios and potential responses offered by the one attempting to reconcile and love enemies. In 5:33, Jesus comments on oath taking which could be considered "over-promising" that leads to disappointment and loss and "evil" since the oath taker has no control of heaven, earth, Jerusalem, or even the hairs of their own heads.

Criss-cross (chiasmus) Connections
Show Conflicts and Persecutors for Prayer

Matthew 5:39-42	Matthew 6:11-13
(A) "Do not resist **evil**" (μὴ ἀντιστῆναι τῷ **πονηρῷ**) in 5:39	(D') "**Give** us today our necessary bread…" (**δὸς** ἡμῖν) in 6:11
(B) "If anyone wants to **judge** (or sue) you" (**κριθῆναι**), in 5:40a	(C') "**Release** our debts as we release…" (**ἄφες**) in 6:12
(C) "**Release** the coat" (**ἄφες**), in 5:40b	(B') "Lead us not to **testing**" (**πειρασμόν**) in 6:13a
(D) "**Give** what is asked" (τῷ αἰτοῦντί σε **δός**) in 5:42	(A') "Deliver us from **evil**" (ῥῦσαι ἡμᾶς ἀπὸ τοῦ **πονηροῦ**) in 6:13b

Lord's Conflict & Empathy Prayer in Matt 5-7, by C. Manto (c) 2015

UBS5	Author and Reader Notes	NASB®	New American Bible
Matt. 5:38 ¶ Ἠκούσατε ὅτι ἐρρέθη, Ὀφθαλμὸν ἀντὶ ὀφθαλμοῦ καὶ ὀδόντα ἀντὶ ὀδόντος. **Matt. 5:39** ἐγὼ δὲ λέγω ὑμῖν μὴ ἀντιστῆναι τῷ πονηρῷ· ἀλλ' ὅστις σε ῥαπίζει εἰς τὴν δεξιὰν σιαγόνα [σου], στρέψον αὐτῷ καὶ τὴν ἄλλην· **Matt. 5:40** καὶ τῷ θέλοντί σοι κριθῆναι καὶ τὸν χιτῶνά σου λαβεῖν, ἄφες αὐτῷ καὶ τὸ ἱμάτιον· **Matt. 5:41** καὶ ὅστις σε ἀγγαρεύσει μίλιον ἕν, ὕπαγε μετ' αὐτοῦ δύο. **Matt. 5:42** τῷ αἰτοῦντί σε δός, καὶ τὸν θέλοντα ἀπὸ σοῦ δανίσασθαι μὴ ἀποστραφῇς.	Note on 5:40 ff. ἄφες αὐτῷ καὶ τὸ ἱμάτιον· If anyone wishes to go to judgement with you to get your shirt, release your cloak as well. The word judgment is key as it relates to testing used in the testing in the wilderness earlier and in the Lord's Prayer later. Consistency helps identify the common themes and the mnemonic devices and rhetorical rhythm and force being developed. Also, ἄφες is used both here and in the Lord's Prayer for release of debts. This is also important and becomes part of an inverse chiasm between this section and the we section of the Lord's prayer with the other two being "evil" and "give".	**Matt. 5:38** ¶ "You have heard that it was said, ᵇAN EYE FOR AN EYE, AND A TOOTH FOR A TOOTH.' **Matt. 5:39** "But I say to you, do not resist an evil person; but ᵃwhoever slaps you on your right cheek, turn the other to him also. **Matt. 5:40** "If anyone wants to sue you and take your ¹shirt, let him have your ²coat also. **Matt. 5:41** "Whoever ¹forces you to go one mile, go with him two. **Matt. 5:42** "ᵃGive to him who asks of you, and do not turn away from him who wants to borrow from you.	38 ²⁵ "You have heard that it was said, 'An eye for an eye and a tooth for a tooth.' 39 But I say to you, offer no resistance to one who is evil. When someone strikes you on (your) right cheek, turn the other one to him as well. 40 If anyone wants to go to law with you over your tunic, hand him your cloak as well. 41 Should anyone press you into service for one mile, ²⁶ go with him for two miles. 42 Give to the one who asks of you, and do not turn your back on one who wants to borrow.

Connecting Over-promising's Compensatory Damages to Conflicted Daily Necessities: Each of these sections accelerates a connection to the following section with growing rhetorical force. The request to not swear oaths that only leads to evil in 5:37 leads to the antithesis. Matthew 5:38 begins a discussion of compensatory damages[25] such as "an eye for an eye" where Jesus requests the crowds to do something different, namely "not resist evil" but "turn the other cheek," etc. Note that the "eye for an eye" section reflects a "law of equal retribution" which limits or eliminates a concept of revenge and replacing it with a concept of proportional punishment or substitutional compensation.[26] In this passage, Jesus goes a further step by asking the listeners in the crowd as well as the disciples, to engage lovingly by offering more than what the other is requiring. It is also interesting to see that these categories are examples of when the listeners are being hurt in some way and would be expected to use the law of compensatory damages to recover losses or debts as opposed to the earlier comments in 5:23-26 when Jesus asks those who are subject of lawsuits of compensatory damages to settle out of court.

Why so complicated?

> **Matt. 5:39 But I say this to you**: offer no resistance to the wicked. On the contrary, if anyone hits you on the right cheek, offer him the other as well;
>
> **Matt. 5:40** If someone wishes to go to law with you to get your tunic, let him have your cloak as well.
>
> **Matt. 5:41** And if anyone requires you to go one mile, go two miles with him.
>
> **Matt. 5:42** Give to anyone who asks you ...

Why does the writer of this section make the list so much more complex than it could have if all that was needed to be accomplished was to talk about four categories of conflict? Why did Matthew go into such detail mindful of his audience that used Greek as a second language and needed to keep it simple especially for memorization? For example, I thought of this while contemplating memorizing this material in Greek after looking at the simple patterns in the beatitudes using repetitive phrases such as "blessed are the ..." That repetition was not only poetic, but it was also easier to remember.

So, why would not Matthew say something like, "If someone assaults you, turn the other cheek: if someone assaults you for your shirt, give him your cloak; if someone assaults you to walk a mile, walk for two; if someone assaults you for your money, give them more money." He could have used the assault or hit-on-the-cheek phrase four times—but he did not. He changed the people and the actions in the scenarios each time making them more complicated initially (and in my case, including Greek vocabulary and grammar). Ultimately, he makes it possible to have at least four times four combinations of conflict covered by these four different expressions. The first is caused by someone assaulting or insulting one on one. The next is a conflict with a small group including a judge that might be corrupt but could decide in favor of the defendant since a court implies some level of due process. The being forced to walk a mile was a commonly known situation before and during the time of the Romans when a group of soldiers drafted a civilian to carry a load for a mile. There was no due process there and the group is larger. The fourth is the only time the power position is reversed since someone is asking not demanding something.

---

25 See Betz on compensatory damages comparing Jewish, Middle Eastern, Greek, and Roman concepts on pp. 275-279 revealing a link between compensatory damages due to conflicts and the "debts." These "debs" are the same as those asked to be "released in the Lord's Prayer in 6. Note how hitting a cheek may incur different compensatory damages depending on the class of people and other circumstances even in the Code of Hammurabi in the edition by James Pritchard in section 202-205 (p. 175). Someone of a lower class hitting someone of a higher class incurred greater punishment than someone hitting someone of the same or lower class. Though Philo objected to inequality of punishments (Special Laws III, 181-182), he still made room for special consideration for those who "strike" a "father" or "abuse of a ruler." Yet "all other similar facts must be carefully considered with a view to making the punishment greater or less." (Special Laws III, 184; Loeb Classical Library, Philo VII, p 589-591). For contemporary examples of compensatory damages, see various works on torts, such as: Dan B. Dobbs, *Torts and Compensation, Personal Accountability and Social Responsibility for Injury*.

26 See Betz, p. 276.

In this verse, **Matt. 5:42** "Give to anyone who asks you, and if anyone wants to borrow, do not turn away," what is being asked is not specified. That has the advantage of allowing any item to be considered, allowing for more flexibility. Later in Matthew 25:35-36, the range of what might be borrowed could include a range of resources from food, drink, welcoming, clothing, and support in prison, the worst-case situation for a distressed peasant who will be forced to give up all and be sold into slavery if that all is not enough to satisfy the debt. Each of the previous alternatives covers compensatory damages when a loss is imposed on the listener resulting in a debt to the listener. In this case, the request is not imposed but still results in a debt to the listener, one that might not be repaid. All these debts will soon be included in the concept of debt release in the prayer requested for persecutors in Matthew 5:44 and outlined in 6:9-15. Providing such a loan at the expense of the one making the loan could be seen as the work of a peacemaker described earlier. In this case, the opportunity presents itself to the listener in the form of a loan request. Peacemakers might also be proactive in offering help even when not asked.

By only choosing one item from each column and row, a diagonal across the spread sheet can be seen such that four choices make it possible to add twelve others later outlining a total of 16 possibilities. Each of these groups represented on each row is of a different size, power dynamic, and possibly different perceptions of apparent fault. If so, the one matrix could represent four matrices or an even broader group of conflicts.

So, see the following chart of examples of conflicts from the compensatory damages section in Matthew 5:39-42 just prior to the request:

What Challenged Across > Who Challenges Below: Size, Power, Fault, Type	Cheek (Health, Respect, Honor)	Shirt (Clothing, Warmth, Housing, Possessions)	Walk (Time, Distraction)	Borrow (Ability to manage or gather, use necessities)
1 vs. You (Direct assault by one taking advantage)	X			
Small group vs. You (Agreed contract implied by lawsuit or arrest)		X		
Large group vs You (No due process, conscription requiring 1 mile by Roman Army)			X	
You vs 1 Asks, not insists (Flips power position, loans imply offer to repay)				X

These 4 by 4 matrices of conflict options show the comprehensive range of conflicts that are the subject of that passage which leads the listeners to understand the range of conflicts and resulting debts included in the request to love and pray in Matthew 5:44.[27,28]

---

27   See the 2014 Manto presentation to NBS in the appendix.

28   Douglas Oakman organizes tables and charts of various kinds of ancient agrarian conflicts on pp. 47-52 in his book, *The Radical Jesus, the Bible, and the Great Transformation*. This provides background to the compensatory damages section in Matthew 5, where the use of a

Note also how each of the items showcasing the conflict might have multiple components. For example, the hitting of the other cheek appears to be an abuse of power of one person over another with no ability to strike back, such as a servant. That abuse of power may be a threat to reputation by shaming and a threat to something greater such as health or well-being.[29]

This complexity reveals more than an order-of-magnitude data compression and decompression technique that minimizes the amount of information needed to be memorized in order to capture the maximum amount of information. See the treatment on the significant flexibility, motivation, mnemonic, and data compression accomplished by this section in the "Audience and Mnemonics" paper in the appendix and briefly on the related discussion on the conflict matrix above (p. 42). This provides not only a rich mnemonic technique, but a flexible persuasion or rhetorical method that can be applied to any conflict. Thinking and discussing through various conflicts as examples of how to use the Lord's Prayer that follows will demonstrate its rhetorical value. (A possibly related use of columns and rows have been seen in ancient Babylonian trigonometry tables as in the Plimpton 322 tablet.[30])

Photo copyrighted and used with permission from the University of New South Wales, Australia.

---

        conflict matrix in Matthew 5:38-42 shows an extraordinary range of conflicts as the subject of the Lord's Prayer for persecutors.

29   See the treatment of honor and shame in the ancient world in book of Jerome Neyrey, pp. 204-205 describing the backhanded slap with the unclean hand as the ultimate shaming.

30   See the article reinterpreting the use of the method as the first and most accurate trigonometry table: https://www.sciencealert.com/scientists-just-solved-a-maths-problem-on-this-3-700-year-old-clay-tablet (see section at end prior to bibliography) and the journal article describing the method used by the tablet: https://www.sciencedirect.com/science/article/pii/S0315086017300691; *Historia Mathematica*, Volume 44, Issue 4, November 2017, pp. 395-419.

Chiasmus/Chiasm with the We-Petitions of the Lord's Prayer: Note that this section on compensatory damages begins with the eye-for-an-eye section in 5:38 where he asks the crowds not to "resist evil" in 5:39 (μὴ ἀντιστῆναι τῷ *πονηρῷ*[31]). The connection between the use of the word "evil" here and the last word of the Lord's Prayer, "evil," has been pointed out by John Piper and leads him to demonstrate how the prayer for persecutors is tied to the Lord's Prayer.[32] Additional links that further support the connection made by Piper can be shown by comparing the phrase asking to submit in 5:39 to going to the court test and judgment in 5:40a (*κριθῆναι*), "release the coat" in 5:40b (*ἄφες*), and "give" what is requested in 5:42 (τῷ αἰτοῦντί σε *δός*) of those who ask. These all happen to be what are in the "we-petitions" of the Lord's prayer in reverse order as if it were a chiasmus.[33] This crisscross method of organizing material looks like the letter X, which in Greek is the letter chi, from which the word "chiasmus" comes. Compare these elements here and in the chart that follows: A (*evil* in 5:39), B (*judge* in 5:40a), C (*release* in 5:40b), D (*give* in 5:42); D' (*give* in 6:11), C' (*release* in 6:12), B' (*test* in 6:13a), A' (*evil* in 6:13b).

Criss-cross (chiasmus) Connections
Show Conflicts and Persecutors for Prayer

Matthew 5:39-42	Matthew 6:11-13
(A) "Do not resist **evil**" (μὴ ἀντιστῆναι τῷ **πονηρῷ**) in 5:39	**(D')** "**Give** us today our necessary bread…" (**δὸς** ἡμῖν) in 6:11
(B) "If anyone wants to **judge** (or sue) you" (**κριθῆναι**), in 5:40a	**(C')** "**Release** our debts as we release…" (**ἄφες**) in 6:12
(C) "**Release** the coat" (**ἄφες**), in 5:40b	**(B')** "Lead us not to **testing**" (**πειρασμόν**) in 6:13a
(D) "**Give**" what is asked" (τῷ αἰτοῦντί σε **δός**) in 5:42	**(A')** "Deliver us from **evil**" (ῥῦσαι ἡμᾶς ἀπὸ τοῦ **πονηροῦ**) in 6:13b

Lord's Conflict & Empathy Prayer in Matt 5-7, by C. Manto (c) 2015

Note that the word "judgment" (κριθῆναι) is similar but not identical to "test" (πειρασμόν) in 6:13. Matthew quotes Jesus as choosing the word judgement that echoes the 5:25-26 anger passage whereby one is taken to court and the word "testing" that reflects back to the testing of Jesus in the wilderness in 4:1. See John Harvey's treatment on the

---

31   Ambiguity of the options of having the Greek word in either the neuter or masculine case would allow evil to refer either to circumstances or a person, both of which appear relevant in these two sections using the word "evil."

32   See John Piper's extensive comments on pp. 141-152 of his key work, *Love Your Enemies* where such a link is proposed. Although others have shown a similarity in themes between the sections, this is the only contemporary citation I could find apart from the footnote in R.T. France's *Matthew*, where the direct connection to the Lord's Prayer is mentioned.

33   See the discussion by Harvey on "chiasmus," pp., 98-100, inversion, alternation, inclusion, ring-composition, word chains, refrain and concentric symmetry in his book, *Listening to the Text*. John D. Harvey, *Listening to the Text, Oral Patterning in Paul's Letters*, Baker Books, 1998. This is a helpful introduction to oral and literary patterns in the first century (see his Chapter 2) and "Categories and Controls" (Chapter 5).

use of chiasmus that does not require exact wording. "For the purpose of this study, then, chiasmus will be defined as *the transposition of corresponding words or phrases at the sentence level. Identification of this pattern is made relatively simple by the fact that identical, synonymous, or antonymous words or phrases are used.*"[34] This section that starts with the request to not "resist evil" happens to lead to the concluding antithesis section starting in 5:43 where Jesus asks that the crowds love their enemies and pray for their persecutors which ultimately asks that the one praying and the persecutors be "delivered from evil." Harvey continues his discussion of chiasmus to show similar mnemonic devices named "inversion" and "alternation." These methods, such as chiasmus, help the listener follow the oral presentation and eventually memorize it for transmission to others or in discussions with others.

This linkage is a similar practice across Matthew to interweave connections and make the material easier to memorize and orally present without a written manuscript in hand. Recall the similar linkage of Jesus starting in 5:1 to speak with the addition of "opening his mouth," reminiscent of "man shall not live by bread alone but by every word that proceeds from the mouth of God" in 4:4.

USB5	Author and Reader Notes	NASB®	New American Bible
Matt. 5:43 ¶ Ἠκούσατε ὅτι ἐρρέθη, **Ἀγαπήσεις τὸν πλησίον σου** καὶ μισήσεις τὸν ἐχθρόν σου. **Matt. 5:44** ἐγὼ δὲ λέγω ὑμῖν, ἀγαπᾶτε τοὺς ἐχθροὺς ὑμῶν⁵ καὶ προσεύχεσθε ὑπὲρ τῶν διωκόντων ὑμᾶς⁶, **Matt. 5:45** ὅπως γένησθε υἱοὶ τοῦ πατρὸς ὑμῶν τοῦ ἐν οὐρανοῖς, ὅτι τὸν ἥλιον αὐτοῦ ἀνατέλλει ἐπὶ πονηροὺς καὶ ἀγαθοὺς καὶ βρέχει ἐπὶ δικαίους καὶ ἀδίκους. **Matt. 5:46** ἐὰν γὰρ ἀγαπήσητε τοὺς ἀγαπῶντας ὑμᾶς, τίνα μισθὸν ἔχετε; οὐχὶ καὶ οἱ τελῶναι τὸ αὐτὸ ποιοῦσιν; **Matt. 5:47** καὶ ἐὰν ἀσπάσησθε τοὺς ἀδελφοὺς ὑμῶν μόνον, τί περισσὸν ποιεῖτε; οὐχὶ καὶ οἱ ἐθνικοὶ⁷ τὸ αὐτὸ ποιοῦσιν; **Matt. 5:48** Ἔσεσθε οὖν ὑμεῖς τέλειοι ὡς ὁ πατὴρ ὑμῶν ὁ οὐράνιος τέλειός ἐστιν.		**Matt. 5:43** ¶ "ᵃYou have heard that it was said, 'ᵇYOU SHALL LOVE YOUR NEIGHBOR ᶜand hate your enemy.' **Matt. 5:44** "But I say to you, "love your enemies and pray for those who persecute you, **Matt. 5:45** so that you may ¹be "sons of your Father who is in heaven; for He causes His sun to rise on *the* evil and *the* good, and sends rain on *the* righteous and *the* unrighteous. **Matt. 5:46** "For ᵃif you love those who love you, what reward do you have? Do not even the tax collectors do the same? **Matt. 5:47** "If you greet only your brothers, what more are you doing *than others*? Do not even the Gentiles do the same? **Matt. 5:48** "Therefore ¹ᵃyou are to be perfect, as your heavenly Father is perfect.	43 "You have heard that it was said, 'You shall love your neighbor and hate your enemy.' 44 But I say to you, love your enemies, and pray for those who persecute you, 45 that you may be children of your heavenly Father, for he makes his sun rise on the bad and the good, and causes rain to fall on the just and the unjust. 46 For if you love those who love you, what recompense will you have? Do not the tax collectors [28] do the same? 47 And if you greet your brothers only, what is unusual about that? Do not the pagans do the same? 48 So be perfect, [30] just as your heavenly Father is perfect.

The Prayer Request for Persecutors—The beginning of the request for prayer providing flexible conflict scenarios: The request to love enemies[35] instead of hating them and then pray for the worst-case (the persecutors) is a

---

34 See Harvey, p. 100.

35 In many circles in contemporary culture, many might think that the word "enemy" is excessively strong and that they do not have enemies. The point of the passage is to consider each and every conflict (including the worst case) with any person, group or organization as one

contrast that is revisited through the rest of this section where even tax collectors and Gentiles are said to love and respectfully greet their friends. This request to love and pray for every case including the worst case is the conclusion and the rhetorical "ask" of the prior conflict section outlined by antitheses above where the result is that the crowds were asked to love and pray for all cases including the worst. It was scenario-based so that it could include any lesser conflict the individual in the crowd or disciple might face with anyone over anything. Note also the theme echoed from Matthew 5:3, 10 where those in conflict with persecutors for justice's sake are blessed and pronounced heirs of the kingdom of heaven.

Jesus used these flexible examples to help and persuade the crowd learn how to persuade their enemies. He did that at the same time he was persuading the disciples how to persuade the crowd to become new disciples as he just promised in Matthew 4:19 just before the Sermon on the Mount began in 5:1.

Flexible scenario-based persuasion methods used in the "technai" or more introductory "progymnasmata" in the Greek cultural world of Jesus' day are still used today to teach prospective lawyers who are asked to practice being both the prosecutor and defense attorney for a hypothetical client.[36]

Where's the prayer? As important as this conclusion to pray for persecutors may be in this section, nearly all the commentators focus on the "love your enemies" portion of the text and brush over lightly the portion on praying for persecutors. Few seem to ask, "how would one actually go about praying for persecutors?" I have discovered two that do. R.T. France in his commentary, "The Gospel of Matthew" does by noting that Jesus asks that one pray for persecutors but cannot see any place where the content is specified.[37] Fortunately, he does quote John Piper's extensive comments on pp. 141-152 of his key work, *Love Your Enemies*[38] where such a link is proposed. But France does not appear to fully embrace what Piper appears to have proposed or, perhaps, he would have said more about it.[39] While Piper's book is not a commentary, per se, this section is noteworthy and reflects Piper's lifelong work expanding his doctoral dissertation on loving enemies.

The Piper lost in France: Note Dr. John Piper's connection between the request to pray for persecutors in 5:44 and the Lord's Prayer in 6:9-13: "Not only has Mt brought into this context words on how one is to pray but also on what one is to pray. That the Lord's Prayer (6:9-13) should be read in close connection with the preceding commands of Mt 5 is shown by the essential relation between the commands and the petitions." Piper even notes the connection between 5:39 "do not resist evil" with the phrase in the prayer of 6:13 "deliver us from evil." (See commentary on Matthew 5:39 for more details on each of the four elements that are common between 5:39-44 and 6:9-13.)

---

that should be loved and not hated. Persecutors would be the more serious cases that are pursuing their adversaries such as the one forcing someone to show up at court in Matthew 5:25-26 to face charges and possible requirement for payment of damages that could lead to giving up all wealth and freedom.

36 See references in the discussions on rhetoric in works such as Burton Mack & Vernon Robbins, *Patterns of Persuasion in the Gospels*, (Sonoma, CA: Polebridge Press, 1989; Wipf & Stock, 2008) 1989, 2008.

37 See R.T. France, *The Gospel of Matthew*, The New International Commentary of the New Testament, William B. Eerdmans, Grand Rapids, MI, 2007. This is another respected and useful scholarly commentary designed for pastors and teachers interested in a serious presentation relatively easy to follow. As to the discussion on prayer, however, it also is disjointed. Note the reference on p. 226 to MT 5:44c where Jesus asks to pray for persecutors, "without specifying its content."

38 See John J. Piper, *Love Your Enemies, Jesus' Love Command in the Synoptic Gospels and the Early Christian Paraenesis*; 2012 edition of 1979 version. Crossway, Wheaton, IL. The preface is worthwhile biographical material showing how he worked his 2004 doctoral thesis throughout his career. (Similar to Boomershine who reworked his 2004 thesis on "The Messiah of Peace"). See especially his section linking the prayer request to pray for persecutors of Matthew 5:44 with the Lord's Prayer in 6:9-13 on p. 143 (in the section from p. 134-170). "Not only has Mt brought into this context words on how one is to pray but also on what one is to pray. That the Lord's Prayer (6:9-13) should be read in close connection with the preceding commands of Matt. 5 is shown by the essential relation between the commands and the petitions." He even notes the connection between 5:39 "do not resist evil" with the phrase in the prayer of 6:13 "deliver us from evil."

39 Nolland also shows a link to 5:44 when commenting on 6:9 but does not develop it apart from saying that "prayer for others ... has already been touched on." See p. 285 of Nolland's *Gospel of Matthew*.

Love One Another © by Laura James, licensed and used with permission.

For discussion:

1) What is the significance of the range of conflicts in this section compared to the conflicts of the crowd from Chapter 4 until here, after this section and until the end of Matthew?

2) What are implications of the legal system for compensatory damages in this era ("eye for an eye") compared to our own?

3) How might the context show how the word "enemies" was used and how does it compare to how we tend to use the word now? What were "persecutors" and how might it have been distinguished from "enemies"? How is that similar or different from use today?

4) What are the relationship dynamics of being pursued for compensatory damages with the use of the word "persecutors"?

5) How is "loving enemies and praying for persecutors" positioned as the climax of the entire Sermon (5:1 and following) to this point?

6) What are the range of conflicts, losses and debts under consideration?

7) What are the ramifications for conflict engagement, forgiveness, and reconciliation?

USB5	Author and Reader Notes	NASB®	New American Bible
Matt. 6:1 ¶ Προσέχετε [δὲ] τὴν δικαιοσύνην ὑμῶν μὴ ποιεῖν ἔμπροσθεν τῶν ἀνθρώπων πρὸς τὸ θεαθῆναι αὐτοῖς· εἰ δὲ μή γε, μισθὸν οὐκ ἔχετε παρὰ τῷ πατρὶ ὑμῶν τῷ ἐν τοῖς οὐρανοῖς. **Matt. 6:2 ¶** Ὅταν οὖν ποιῇς ἐλεημοσύνην, μὴ σαλπίσῃς ἔμπροσθέν σου, ὥσπερ οἱ ὑποκριταὶ ποιοῦσιν ἐν ταῖς συναγωγαῖς καὶ ἐν ταῖς ῥύμαις, ὅπως δοξασθῶσιν ὑπὸ τῶν ἀνθρώπων· ἀμὴν λέγω ὑμῖν, ἀπέχουσιν τὸν μισθὸν αὐτῶν. **Matt. 6:3** σοῦ δὲ ποιοῦντος ἐλεημοσύνην μὴ γνώτω ἡ ἀριστερά σου τί ποιεῖ ἡ δεξιά σου, **Matt. 6:4** ὅπως ᾖ σου ἡ ἐλεημοσύνη ἐν τῷ κρυπτῷ· καὶ ὁ πατήρ σου ὁ βλέπων ἐν τῷ κρυπτῷ ἀποδώσει σοι¹.	"*Pay attention* not to parade your acts of justice" (in Greek, see the discussion on "*pay attention*" (Προσέχετε) versus "*pray*" (προσεύχησθε). Also note, just the one word "*justices*" as in "*acts of justices*" (as opposed to 'judges') is used that connects with "mercies" before men to attract attention (6:3)... Note the link backwards to the beatitudes and the link forward to the end of Matthew 6, "seek first the kingdom and his *justice*" (δικαιοσύνην). It would be better to keep a consistent word for δικαιοσύνην in each instance so that the linkages shown by the Greek could carry through in a subsequent language such as English. 6:2 So that when you give *mercies (alms)*, do not... The link between justice and mercy is tight here and, in the beatitudes, but is lost when alms is substituted for mercies here.	**Matt. 6:1 ¶** "Beware of practicing your righteousness before men ᵃ"to be noticed by them; otherwise you have no reward with your Father who is in heaven. **Matt. 6:2 ¶** "So when you ¹give to the poor, do not sound a trumpet before you, as the hypocrites do in the synagogues and in the streets, so that they ᵃ"may be honored by men. ᵇTruly I say to you, they have their reward in full. **Matt. 6:3** "But when you ¹give to the poor, do not let your left hand know what your right hand is doing, **Matt. 6:4** so that your ¹giving will be in secret; and ᵃyour Father who sees *what is done* in secret will reward you.	**Teaching About Almsgiving.**[a] 1 "[But] take care not to perform righteous deeds in order that people may see them; otherwise, you will have no recompense from your heavenly Father. ² When you give alms, do not blow a trumpet before you, as the hypocrites[b] do in the synagogues and in the streets to win the praise of others. Amen, I say to you, they have received their reward. ³ But when you give alms, do not let your left hand know what your right is doing, ⁴ so that your almsgiving may be secret. And your Father who sees in secret will repay you.

Fastening the Lord's Prayer to Prayer Request & Beatitudes—Context of the Lord's Prayer: A casual reading of Matthew 6:1-4 might lead one to believe that Matthew had Jesus change the subject from loving enemies and praying for persecutors to a different topic, namely almsgiving. That may be a key reason why many commentators have not strongly linked the request to pray for persecutors in 5:44 with the Lord's Prayer beginning in 6:9. However, a closer examination of the context[40] reveals that Matthew 6:1-4 was used to connect themes previously discussed with what is about to be discussed instead of changing the topic.

---

40 For an example of the importance of the understanding the Lord's Prayer in its context in Matthew and its significance of catechisms and their accompanying essays, see the introduction of the Lord's Prayer in the most recent theological commentary on the Catholic Catechism by Ugo Vani. See, also, the article submitted for publication to *Christian Century*, "Who is 'our' in Our Father" in the appendix.

The text of 6:1-4 in its context of 5:1 through 8:1 achieves this by at least five specific methods.

1) Repeating words such as "pray," "justice/righteousness," or "mercy/mercies" and themes such as "inner versus outer."

2) Using a key word as a *pivot*, "pay-attention" instead of "pray" in Matthew 6:1.

3) *Weaving* a connection between things that should be done before people (Matthew 5:3-16) versus three things that should not (Matthew 6:1-18).

4) Placing two similar sets of words in reverse order to each other (called a chiasmus), between a segment occurring before and after this section. In this case, the chiasmus is the set of four key words (Evil, Judge/test, release, give) from the "turn-the-other-cheek" section of demands of persecutors (5:39-42) repeated in reverse order in the request section "give us our daily bread" (6:11-13).

5) 4) *Centering* prayer in 6:1-18 and section 6:1-18 between 5:1- 48 and 6:19 - 8:1.

Note how the combinations of these are interwoven in a way that connects these passages together.

Criss-cross (Chiasmus) Connections					
Matthew 5:33-37			**Matthew 5:38-42**		
		D Head (5:36)		D' Cheek, Individual (5:39)	
	C Jerusalem (5:35b)				C' Sue (for shirt, local government (5:40)
B Earth (5:35a)					B' Walk Roman empire conscription (5:41)
A Heaven (5:34)					A' Borrow Ask, beg, general heaven issue (5:42)

Criss-cross (Chiasmus) Connections – Requests					
Matthew 5:38-42			**Matthew 6:11-13**		
		D Give (5:42)		D' Give (6:11)	
	C Release (5:40b)			C' Release (6:12)	
	B Judge (5:40a)				B' Test (6:13a)
A Evil (5:39)					A' Evil (6:13b)

Repetition: This repetitive use of the concept of inner versus outer and words such as "pray" either as inclusions or word chains makes it easy for a reader to connect the dots but, even more so, a listener who hears these words repeatedly over the course of one minute of discourse, will find it easier follow, memorize, and recite later. This combination of evidence is so strong, that it appears conclusive that the immediate context of 6:5-15 begins with the request to pray for persecutors in 5:44.

Pivot-- Why did Matthew wait to start talking about prayer in 6:5 instead of 6:1 while still on the topic of prayer at the end of Chapter 5? These links show that Jesus did not abruptly change the subject at the beginning of what we call Chapter 6 when he talks about giving alms or "mercies", but ties them together to make it easier to recall and connect the portion that preceded with what is about to be spoken next.

The pivot to "pay attention" where "pray" was expected: In New Testament Greek, the connection becomes clearer through the pivotal first word. As the writer of Matthew completes the last line in Chapter 5 calling on those in the crowd to pray for the worst-case enemies, you might expect him to give you a clue regarding how to do what seems an impossible prayer. At just the moment you would expect him to say "pray", instead you hear him say "pay … attention." In the same way that "pay" sounds like "pray" in English, the first word of Chapter 6 is *prosexeteh* which means, "Pay attention!" (Προσέχετε). We are expecting him to say, *prosuxestheh* ("Pray," προσεύχεσθε) which he just said moments before because this would continue the thought from above in 5:44 and will again be used in 6:5. This sound-alike thus adds rhetorical force inserting an "intercalation"[41] that works as a cue and mnemonic for the speaker, makes the listener pay closer attention and helps the listener attempting to remember this. It is especially the case when the listener would need to remember it in order to repeat to someone else. In this pivot, Jesus is saying, in effect, "Before I tell you how to pray for those who persecute you, pay attention! Let me tell you how not to pray for them: don't make big public gestures of justice or righteousness." By doing this, he further ties this material about how to pray, give mercies[42] and fast to the section on publicly giving glory to the Father just mentioned just five minutes previously in his section on the beatitudes and light in Chapter 5:16.

Weaving—**Contrasting public versus private good works**: The interposition of 6:1-4 is also surrounded by the word *repetition* of "pray" showing that this is an insertion that works to link groupings on either side of it. This section starts with a sound alike word in Greek to "pray" with "pay-attention" used as a pivot described below. This section highlights the first of three items that Matthew quotes Jesus as saying should not be done in front of people (almsgiving, prayer and fasting) that brings attention to themselves. It appears to purposely be contrasted as a mnemonic weave to the three things Jesus had just said should be done in front of people that bring glory to the Father, namely being gentle, merciful and peacemaking in Matthew 5:16. "Let your light shine so that people see your good works and glorify the Father." This contrast creates further rhetorical tension and makes the passage easier to remember by weaving the passages together.

It also *repeats* a theme of "inner and outer" shown in the pairings of the beatitudes to the salt versus saltiness and light versus light received and the contrasts (antitheses) between the salt & light section and the prayer request. This is covered in more detail below where the significance of the placement of "prayer" in the center position of "almsgiving, prayer and fasting" is discussed.

Chiasmus—The third example of "chiasmus," repeating a group of words in reverse order is described above in Matthew 5:38 and later in 6:11.

Together, this section of Matthew 6:1-4 strengthens the links between the request to love enemies and pray for persecutors and the Lord's Prayer and all that comes before and after it within the Sermon on the Mount in Matthew 5-7. It also sets the stage for the central and most significant of the three items of what not to do before people, namely, pray for persecutors.

Significance of the *Center* Position: This section and the ways that tie the prayer sections together as a group creates a center piece, or possibly a virtual hill, where the Lord's Prayer is in the most important and center position among the three things that should not be done before people in the same way that the Lord's Prayer becomes placed in the

---

41   See David Bauer's discussion on compositional relationships including repetition, contrast, comparison, substantiation, climax, the pivot, statement of purpose, interchange, chiasm, and intercalation on p.13-19. "Intercalation is the insertion of one literary unit in the midst of another literary unit (a, b, a). David R. Bauer, *The Structure of Matthew's Gospel*, Almond Press of Sheffield Academic Press, 1988, 1989. He mentions the prior work of Joanna Dewey's doctoral dissertation, Dewey, Joanna, *Markan Public Debate: Literary Technique, Concentric Structure, and Theology in Mark 2:1-3:6* (SBL Dissertation Series, Number 48), SBL, Atlanta, 1980. See her work discussing interpositions, frames and word repetition to tie together ring compositions (pp. 67-68.)

42   As others such as Daniel Ulrich will point out, "The giving of alms might be seen as an act of justice as well as mercy. Note also the connection to 5:42." Note also the juxtaposition of justice and mercy in the beatitude pairs.

center or top of the "Sermon on the Mount." Another possible connection is that this section works as a contrast or way to say in effect, "before I tell you how to pray for persecutors, let me tell you how not to pray for persecutors." The following discussion will demonstrate the ways that the request to pray for persecutors is continued in Chapter 6, the peak of the mount.

		What Not to Do before People (vs What to Do)		
		Matthew 6:1-18		
		Pray (6:5-15) (vs Merciful in 5:7)		
	Give alms (mercies) (6:1-4) (vs Gentle in 5:5)		**Fast** (6:16-18) (vs Peace-making in 5:9)	

As just mentioned, Matthew 6:1-4 is the first of three sections that describe what people *should not do* noticeably before people, namely righteousness (or justice) such as almsgiving (mercies), praying and fasting. The significance of prayer in the center position will be described in detail in a moment. The Lord's Prayer has long been considered as the center of the Sermon on the Mount.[43] Its use in the center of the three items here sets up the Lord's Prayer as central point of these three prohibitions just as it is central within the "Sermon on the Mount". It is as if Matthew created this large hill of Chapters 5-7 of the Gospel of Matthew where he places a small hill of section 6:1-18 on top of it. In doing so, Matthew has Jesus connecting the Lord's Prayer in 6:9-13 to the context of prayer immediately before it in 5:44. He also links it to the treatment of conflict and law in the "turn the other cheek" section, to oath-taking, the antitheses section as a whole, and its context which in turn flowed from the section on blessings, salt and saltiness, light and covered light at the beginning of Chapter 5.

The practice of placing something in the center for emphasis is just one of a number of ways to connect thoughts with each other in ancient literature, especially that devoted to persuasion or rhetoric. The use of a central position is described further in the next section. It and other techniques are described by Harvey in his discussion of "inclusion" or "ring-composition," "word chains" and "refrains" following his treatment of chiasmus. An inclusion uses single words whereas ring-composition uses sentences "in which a speaker returns to a previous point in the discussion, either concluding or resuming his train of thought." That concept is continued in his discussion of word chains and refrains.[44] In this case, the same word "pray" (προσεύχεσθε) is used to link the material from 5:44 through 6:15 denoting both the beginning and end of the context as well as material linked to it throughout the section. This includes the related rabbit trail (how "not to pray" before showing "how to pray") in the use of the homonym in 6:1 (Προσέχετε) and the use of "pray" (προσεύχεσθε)" in 6:5 that resumes the topic of prayer for enemies.

---

43 Many scholars have noted the strategic positioning of the Lord's Prayer in the Sermon on the Mount. See Luz p. 309, "It was certainly Matthew who located the prayer in the center of the Sermon on the Mount." See Betz, SoM, p. 373, "…the Lord's Prayer stands in the middle of SM, this prominent location is not an accident. Occupying the center of the cultic instruction of 6:1-18, the Lord's Prayer stands also in the middle of the SM as a whole."

44 Harvey, pp. 102-104, see also p. 56 and the strategic role of the center position. This is covered in more detail in comments on Matthew 6:5.

Exegesis of Microtext 6:5-15—the Model Prayer requested in 5:44.

UBS5	Author and Reader Notes	NASB®	New American Bible
Matt. 6:5 ¶ Καὶ ὅταν προσεύχησθε, οὐκ ἔσεσθε ὡς οἱ ὑποκριταί, ὅτι φιλοῦσιν ἐν ταῖς συναγωγαῖς καὶ ἐν ταῖς γωνίαις τῶν πλατειῶν ἑστῶτες προσεύχεσθαι, ὅπως φανῶσιν τοῖς ἀνθρώποις· ἀμὴν λέγω ὑμῖν, ἀπέχουσιν τὸν μισθὸν αὐτῶν.	"And when you pray, do not *become* as the hypocrites …" I chose the word become in this instance to be consistent with other uses of the word ἔσεσθε.	**Matt. 6:5 ¶** "When you pray, you are not to be like the hypocrites; for they love to "stand and pray in the synagogues and on the street corners [1b]so that they may be seen by men. 'Truly I say to you, they have their reward in full.	**Teaching About Prayer.** [5]"When you pray, do not be like the hypocrites, who love to stand and pray in the synagogues and on street corners so that others may see them. Amen, I say to you, they have received their reward.

The Significance of Matthew 6:5-15: This section contains the text of the "Lord's Prayer", known by 2.4 billion people living at the time of this writing.[45] It is considered by many commentators to be the centerpiece of the Sermon on the Mount, Matthew 5-7, the foundational teaching of Matthew. The placement here and the connections between what precedes show three key concepts often overlooked, namely, 1) the content and method of how to pray for persecutors as requested in 5:44, 2) why the Lord's Prayer is placed where it is and 3) what is its purpose, namely its role as the prayer for persecutors and anyone in conflict. As a conflict prayer, it can be shown to be a way to resolve anger and anxiety in a step-by-step approach, similar to what occurs when the beatitudes of Matthew 5 are seen as pairs of blessings. The apparent goal is to comfort those whose peace has been broken and guide them to become new peacemakers instead of new peace breakers. Together in the overall context of Matthew 5-7, the Lord's Prayer can also be shown as part of the method to disciple-making as promised by Jesus to the fishermen in Matthew 4:19.[46]

Resumption of Prayer: There are a number of reasons why this section beginning with Matthew 6:5 can be shown to resume the discussion of prayer begun in Matthew 5:44. The opening phrase, "when you pray" is the next statement on prayer after the request by Jesus of the crowds to "pray for their persecutors." (**Matt. 5:44** ἐγὼ δὲ λέγω ὑμῖν, ἀγαπᾶτε τοὺς ἐχθροὺς ὑμῶν[5] καὶ **προσεύχεσθε** ὑπὲρ τῶν διωκόντων ὑμᾶς[6]).

Section 6:1-4 provides at least several mnemonic and conceptual links between the request to pray for persecutors in 5:44-48 to the section beginning in 5:3-16 and the section beginning in 6:5 discussing prayer and fasting. As discussed in the comments on 6:1-4, these are well-known rhetorical methods to enable the material to be effectively memorized and delivered to an audience.[47] The use of these rhetorical patterns augments the apparent connections between these elements to show flow and continuity rather than disrupt them.

In this case, the prior section of 5:3-16, listeners were asked that they let their "light shine" so that people see three works of gentleness, mercy, and peacemaking in order that people might give glory to the Father in heaven. By contrast, in Chapter 6, three things are shown that should not be done in front of people, namely, alms giving (6:1-4); prayer (6:5-15); and fasting (6:16-18) since it only brought attention to themselves. This section in Chapter 6 also ends with a discussion on light saying, "if the light within you is darkness, how great is the darkness" (6:23).

One of the attention getting and memorable ways Jesus does here, is that when Jesus asks that his listeners refrain from doing these three acts of righteousness (justice) in the presence of people, he seems to contradict what he just

---

45   See estimate of global population by religion from Gordon Conwell Seminary's "Status of Global Christianity" annual report. For 2021, the total Christian population is estimated at 2.4 billion for about 32.3% of total population. See the appendix and: https://www.gordonconwell.edu/center-for-global-christianity/wp-content/uploads/sites/13/2020/12/Status-of-Global-Christianity-2021.pdf

46   For additional background, see comments and notes on each verse throughout the commentary text along with related comments in the introduction and appendix searchable by those same verses.

47   See the prior notes above by Bauer, Dewey and others describing various rhetorical devices especially in the Introduction's Approach section including "experiencing the text," the "Background" section on rhetoric, and the "Drivers" section.

said moments before in 5:16 when he asked the same listeners to "let your light so shine before men that they may see your good works and give glory to your father in heaven." Such apparent contradiction arouses emotion and incites analysis as to why three are done before people and another three are not and serves as a memory bridge between the two segments. This is essential when performing, especially extemporaneously and even more so interactively with oral material without the aid of a written document. It is even more important when the listener needs to remember and memorize the material for further study and possibly teach others.

As mentioned in the comments of 6:1-4, this contrast of those things that one should or should not do before others is one of at least three or four ways[48] that concepts of conflicts, the love of enemy and prayer for persecutors enhance the connections between the prayer request for persecutors of 5:44 and its detailed fulfillment in the Lord's Prayer of 6:5-15. This contrast also repeats the theme of comparing inner versus outer relationships begun in the pairing of the beatitudes into salt versus salty-tasting and the contrasts of the law externally versus the law internally covered after the beatitudes.

The significance of prayer in the center position: As described in detail in the comments on Matthew 6:1-4, the fact that the prayer segment is in the center position of 6:1-18 does not render it secondary in importance among the three topics of alms (mercies), prayer and fasting. Rather it is in the primary position, a practice used in ancient literature and oral rhetoric. Note Harvey's discussion of Greek literature in which "significant words, phrases or events were often placed at the center of literary work."[49]

The significance of the continuity of prayer: Discussions of the narrative phenomenon of "markedness" and "the principle of continuity" as described by Stephanie Black shows that a discussion is expected to be part of what preceded unless the reader or listener is told otherwise.[50] Commentators have often read the discussion on alms-giving for four verses starting in Chapter 6 as a change of topic while these links signal that the topic of prayer from the bottom of Chapter 5 has not changed.

It might seem reasonable to have started this section of Matthew 6 beginning in verse 5 and place it instead as verse 1 where the sequencing of the three sections began in 6:1 begins with the word that is a sound-alike to **pray**, namely, "**pay** attention." This word which may arouse attention as something different from what was expected serves as the second of at least three ways that the request to pray for persecutors and the Lord's Prayer is connected.[51] It also made it possible to place the discussion of prayer in a central position between almsgiving and fasting.

The pivot from or to prayer? Another attention getting and mnemonic device is a pivotal play on words. As mentioned in the comments on 6:1, Προσέχετε (prosecheteh) is spelled almost exactly and pronounced almost the same as προσεύχεσθε (prosuchestheh) with only changing the **έ to εύ and the χεσθε to χετε** with the same number of syllables in each of the two different words. It maintains the rhythm and the sound almost exactly. Just when the listener expects to hear the word for "pray" he hears "pay…" showing a pivot to what looks like a side comment or rabbit trail that provides the opportunity for Jesus to explain how they should *not* pray, namely before people, before he explains how they should pray alone. This is the beginning of the rabbit trail that served to bridge the two segments between 5:1-16 and 6:1-18 in a technique known be some as quilting or weaving. It has also been shown by recent brain scan studies as a superior method to aid memory by connecting two different memory locations in the brain.[52]

---

48   It may be possible to look at the use of inclusions or "inclusios" as not only standing on their own, but interwoven in such a way to connect various portions of a longer text together.

49   Harvey, p. 56. See his further discussion, "Cedric Whitman has also examined 'geometric structure' in Homer's works. He contends that a geometric approach was central to classical Greek art. He notes that in the case of epic poetry, however, the initial impulse for composition of this sort was mnemonic."

50   Note Stephanie Black's comments on "marking" on p. 30. Daniel M. Gurtner & John Nolland, editors; *Built upon the Rock, Studies in the Gospel of Matthew*, 2008, Eerdmans, Grand Rapids, MI. Black's article on syntax lays a groundwork for elements that would be useful in a rhetorical approach with built-in mnemonic devices.

51   See all three in the comments above on "Matt. 6:1, Προσέχετε [δὲ] τὴν δικαιοσύνην ὑμῶν μὴ ποιεῖν ἔμπροσθεν τῶν ἀνθρώπων" with details on the chiasmus in the comments of Matthew 5:38.)

52   See works in the bibliography on brain and memory studies such as those in this book: Rahul Jandial, MD, PhD; *Neurofitness, A Brain Sur-*

But when you pray, "do not imitate the hypocrites." The hypocrites (originally the Greek word for actors)[53] who perform on the outside something different than what they really are. The word "hypocrites" is used in each of the three things that one should not do before people (give alms in 6:2, pray in 6:5 and fast in 6:15). The difference between the inside and outside can be seen in patterns in the beatitudes of 5:16 and especially the antitheses in 5:21- 45. It is also significant in Matthew 23:13 that shows how they fail to enter the kingdom of heaven and block others from doing so.[54]

And when *who* prays? "And when you pray" (Καὶ ὅταν **προσεύχησθε, οὐκ ἔσεσθε** ὡς οἱ ὑποκριταί,) requires us to ask, "who are 'you'"? In the context it might be surprising to most to see that it refers to the request just given in 5:44 that includes the individuals in the "crowds" to "pray (**προσεύχησθε**) for their persecutors" and not merely the disciples who are observing from front row seats next to Jesus who is providing the promised "fishing lessons" in Matthew 4:19. The members of these crowds were described in Matthew 4:16 as trapped in the region of darkness, the shadow of death. These and other descriptions of the crowds show that they were the most distressed and desperate.[55] This enhances the idea that the request to love and pray was also intended as part of the fishing lessons showing the disciples how the members of the crowd may become engaged and possibly recruited as new disciples. This might be difficult for some to understand if they believe that only the disciples could pray and be heard. Yet here, the crowd is asked to pray *before* they become disciples. In fact, it appears that this very prayer is somehow instrumental in their becoming disciples. This can be seen in part in the very way that they were to pray. The way that crowd members were to pray is as the way they were to gives alms in 6:1-4, mainly in such a way that they "*not* become as the hypocrites…" Notice the words used to "not become" hypocrites (which implies that they are not yet necessarily hypocrites) reflects back to 5:44-5 where the audience is asked to love and pray for the worst-case persecutors so that they "may become children of your father in the heavens" (ὅπως **γένησθε** υἱοὶ τοῦ πατρὸς ὑμῶν τοῦ ἐν οὐρανοῖς). Does that imply that they are not yet heirs or children? It may sound odd since if they are to become children of the Father that they already have. Fatherhood assumes being related to the Father in some way. There are two ways this could happen. One possibility is that they are children in one sense (such as being created and sustained), but not as another (redeemed and enrolled in the kingdom of heaven). The comparison is that by doing what Jesus asks they might become "children of their Father in the heavens" while not doing so would result in not becoming children of their father but "becoming hypocrites." Another possible interpretation would be as John Nolland offers where the phrase means 'act consistent with your sonship,' as in "like Father, like son".[56] In this sense, they are being asked to act like the children that they already are.

---

geon's Secrets to Boost Performance and Unleash Creativity, Houghton, Mifflin, Harcourt; Boston, NY 2019. A helpful orientation to recent brain science applicable to mnemonics and rhetoric.

53 See the treatment of the word "hypocrites" in the introduction. See also p. CXII and the monograph inserted into the 'appendix' within the introduction beginning on CXV-CXXIII by Albright and Mann in the Anchor Yale Bible series commentary on Matthew: *Matthew*, The Yale Anchor Bible, Yale University Press, 1971. Work makes use of Qumran material and Palestinian archaeology. This also provides a fascinating preface describing how the original author dropped out at the last minute requiring the editor to add monographs such as the one on the use of "hypocrite" to fill in material that would otherwise be insufficient for publication (p. v.). In the same way that "tax collectors and Gentiles" are used in contrast in 5:44-48 and 18:17, "hypocrites" and "Gentiles" are linked in this section providing opportunities to consider the relationship between "hypocrites" and "tax collectors."

54 Note also the links between the concept of hypocrites and the "false prophets" in Matt 7:13-23 and its expansion in Matt. 25:31-46 and by implication "false followers" through the concept of trees and its fruit. The parent tree causes the fruit, the fruit does not cause the parent tree. Either way, there is much talk throughout Matthew about entering the kingdom of heaven and obtaining forgiveness all of which is consistent with Jesus addressing the crowds who are not yet disciples as he recruits them and trains the disciples in how to recruit ("fish") and make new disciples. The word for hypocrites here is the same word for hypocrites in Matt 23:13 who block others from entering the kingdom of heaven and fail to enter themselves. That happens to appear in the phrase of the first "woe" of Matthew 23, the opposite of the first "blessing" which speaks of the "poor in spirit" referred to as "theirs is the kingdom of heaven" in Matthew 5:3. Again, these links in the text serve both conceptual as well as mnemonic goals.

55 Craig Keener emphasizes this a number of times in *The Gospel of Matthew*, "This is a prayer for the desperate", p. 216. Lachs further describes this as a "danger" prayer in *A Rabbinic Commentary on the New Testament*, p. 118.

56 See p. 268 where Nolland comments on "your Father in heaven" of verse 5:45, and references back to the sense of the Father is the Father of the Jewish people, p. 206 commenting on 5:9, p. 214 commenting on 5:16; John Noland, *The Gospel of Matthew*, 2005, Eerdmans, Grand Rapids, MI.

A method to resolve this fatherhood definition is to determine to whom Jesus is speaking in this context. Nolland and others opine that Jesus is only referring to disciples who would be redeemed children expected to be in the kingdom of heaven and not merely children by virtue of being created and sustained by the Father. Once it becomes apparent that Jesus is also referring to members of the crowds who are asked to pray[57] and yet are the same ones needing to be fished (4:19), becoming a child in the sense of becoming forgiven and one that enters the kingdom of heaven is still a possible interpretation. Note the difference in the forgiveness section of the Lord's Prayer and the comment afterwards which both show that forgiveness is not resolved (6:12-15). This is the opposite of Luke's version (Luke 11:1-5) where forgiveness is asked because the disciple already forgave.

Nevertheless, Nolland's perspective of acting consistently is a viable theme in its own right and supports either interpretation of being "a child of the Father." It is like the prayer of forgiveness in the Lord's Prayer and the story in Matthew 18, where acting in love and in forgiveness is not so much causal of a person becoming forgiven as much as it is indicative of their status of forgiveness in the first place. They forgive because they embraced forgiveness and reconciliation by mercy and grace and are so moved by that love that they in turn show it by how they forgive and reconcile by grace. When they fail to embrace forgiveness and reconciliation by grace, they then show it by how they fail to forgive and reconcile by grace.

In summary, this section on prayer in 6:5-15 is in the center place of three items from 6:1-18 that describes three things Jesus asked that the crowd and disciples NOT to do, before people, namely, give alms (mercies[58]) pray before people or fast before people. The section in 6 ends with an admonition to not seek what the Gentiles seek 6:32a (as will be mentioned below) since the Father knows what they need 6:32b (also in the section below in 6:8) and to "seek first his kingdom his justice" also connecting to the previous beatitudes and salt and light passage in 5:1-16 where the poor in spirit and persecuted are blessed in kingdom participation.

USB5	Author and Reader Notes	NASB®	New American Bible
Matt. 6:6 σὺ δὲ ὅταν προσεύχῃ, εἴσελθε εἰς τὸ ταμεῖόν σου καὶ κλείσας τὴν θύραν σου πρόσευξαι τῷ πατρί σου τῷ ἐν τῷ κρυπτῷ· καὶ ὁ πατήρ σου ὁ βλέπων ἐν τῷ κρυπτῷ ἀποδώσει σοι².	"But when you pray, enter into the storage closet…" Any of the translations that show a prayer in private works well.	**Matt. 6:6** "But you, when you pray, "go into your inner room, close your door and pray to your Father who is in secret, and ᵇyour Father who sees *what is done* in secret will reward you.	⁶But when you pray, go to your inner room, close the door, and pray to your Father in secret. And your Father who sees in secret will repay you.

Praying a conflict prayer alone in secret:

Praying where? —(Alone) in the secret place—For some such as Betz, the admonition to go and pray alone does not make sense seeing as the Lord's Prayer begins with "Our Father" instead of "my Father." He apparently sees the Lord's Prayer much as he and most of us experienced it, as a liturgical prayer said by a group in a setting of community worship[59]. That is perfectly understandable and is one of a handful of possible interpretations of the Lord's Prayer when pulled out of the context of Matthew.

---

57 See the prior comments on Matthew 5:44 and in the article in the appendix in the paper "Who is the 'Our' in the Our Father" about the relationship of the crowds to the Father who are asked to pray since the Father gives sunshine and rain to the just and unjust. Members of the crowds not yet disciples can pray and have that same relationship to their persecutors that allows and compels them to pray.

58 Note the connection between not doing "justices (uprightness, righteousness)" before men in 6:1 then starts with "mercies" in 6:2. Back in 5:6, doing "justice (righteousness, uprightness) is contrasted with "Showing mercy" in 5:7. **Matt. 6:1** Προσέχετε [δὲ] τὴν **δικαιοσύνην** ὑμῶν μὴ ποιεῖν ἔμπροσθεν τῶν ἀνθρώπων πρὸς τὸ θεαθῆναι αὐτοῖς· εἰ δὲ μή γε, μισθὸν οὐκ ἔχετε παρὰ τῷ πατρὶ ὑμῶν τῷ ἐν τοῖς οὐρανοῖς. **Matt. 6:2** Ὅταν οὖν ποιῇς **ἐλεημοσύνην**,

59 For a discussion and example of one of the oldest musical renditions of the Lord's Prayer, see: https://www.npr.org/transcripts/338586411. For a popular current rendition in English, see: https://www.youtube.com/watch?v=u8jImIjg4UY

See his reasoning from his marvelous Matthew commentary where his comment shows tension and inherent contradiction within the text: "… the prayer instruction 6:7-8… presupposes that the Lord's Prayer was to be used as a 'private' prayer, but, I have already pointed out that this context is secondary and in tension with the invocation of vs 9b ('Our Father'), which points to a group prayer."[60] It is as if Matthew, the author or redacting editor, (if not Jesus himself being quoted as saying all this) is immediately contradicting himself. If, on the other hand, Betz had seen the connection to 5:44, he could have reframed the definition of "our" and eliminated the tension and contradiction by having "our" refer to the lone individual praying to the Father of him or herself and the one or more with whom the one solitary person is praying. (For example, "our Father" would thus be "the Father of me and the one(s) persecuting me" (per Matthew 5:44). See the how the definition of "our" that includes the crowds would make the following changes in logic:

Alternative 1: "the one praying" **and with** (*therefore, not in secret*) "some larger group of people" such as

"those that are praying alongside him or her," or

"all the other disciples, or participants in that faith community,"

Alternative 2: "the one praying" **alone** (*in secret*) **for** the "persecutor(s)" (not participating in the conflict prayer here or in Matthew 7 but possibly included in Matthew 18 if reconciliation occurs).

This explicit use of the Lord's Prayer as a conflict prayer is in harmony with the genre of a Jewish "short prayer" described by Samuel Tobias Lach as a prayer "in tannaitic sources, designated a prayer to be recited in place of danger", and not in a liturgical setting.[61]

Note, "the Father who sees in secret will reward" continues the theme of inner versus outer that will continue throughout the Sermon on the Mount. So, the reasonable conclusion would be that the Lord's Prayer as used in Matthew was not used as a group prayer in the context of worship, but, as a private conflict prayer adaptable to any conflict with the goal of having the one praying come to a place of personal and interpersonal peace when arriving at a place of forgiveness of even their worst enemy and hoped for reconciliation. Note that the later request to release debts and trespasses AS we release debts and trespasses, implies if we do not do it, or only do it halfway, we will not receive the release we want.

USB5	Author and Reader Notes	NASB®	New American Bible
Matt. 6:7 Προσευχόμενοι δὲ μὴ βατταλογήσητε ὥσπερ οἱ ἐθνικοί, δοκοῦσιν γὰρ ὅτι ἐν τῇ πολυλογίᾳ αὐτῶν εἰσακουσθήσονται.		**Matt. 6:7** ¶ "And when you are praying, do not use meaningless repetition as the Gentiles do, for they suppose that they will be heard for their ᵃmany words.	7 [In praying, do not babble like the pagans, who think that they will be heard because of their many words.

Gentiles: The Gentiles (ἐθνικοί) here as in 5:47-48, 6:32 and later in Chapter 18 are those with a different world view and view of God and less likely to pray for persecutors. A god of the Gentiles is less capable and is not readily aware of their prayer and as in the next verse depicting how gods need information from the one praying to help the one praying.

---

60   Betz; See p. 373, column 2 at bottom. See also p. 376, column 2 in discussion of group vs. private prayers. See a brief organization of interpretations presented by Luz in *Matthew 1-7*, p. 313-314. See also *Matthias' The Perfect Prayer* on p. 3 where he claims that the Matthew version was intended for public worship, the opposite of what Matthew says Jesus requested for use of this prayer in private and not in public.

61   See Samuel Tobias Lachs, *A Rabbinic Commentary on the New Testament, The Gospels of Matthew, Mark and Luke*, KTAV Publishing House, Hoboken, NJ, 1987. See p. 118, citing L. Ginzberg, *A Commentary on the Palestinian Talmud*. See p. 118. The Hebrew for the short danger prayer genre is "*tephillah qezarah*".

USB5	Author and Reader Notes	NASB®	New American Bible
Matt. 6:8 μὴ οὖν ὁμοιωθῆτε αὐτοῖς· οἶδεν γὰρ ὁ πατὴρ ὑμῶν[3] ὧν χρείαν ἔχετε πρὸ τοῦ ὑμᾶς αἰτῆσαι αὐτόν.		**Matt. 6:8** "So do not be like them; for "your Father knows what you need before you ask Him.	[8] Do not be like them. Your Father knows what you need before you ask him.

Who is Father? In 5:45, he is the Father who gives sunshine and rain to the evil and the unjust reminding crowd members to pray for enemies and persecutors. In 6:8 Father is the Infinite Knower. The Father knowing what you need links also to the Father in 6:32-33 who knows their needs. They are asked to seek first the kingdom as in 6:10 and his justice as in 6:1. This stands in contrast to the Gentiles who have a smaller less knowing God. The Gentiles seek things over the relationship inherent in the Father's kingdom and justice. Now if there were Gentiles in the crowds, or Israelites that thought or acted like them (as might tax collectors who would ostensibly hold their world view but did not act on it), they might possibly pray this prayer also in a moment of vulnerability like one we know as an "atheist in a foxhole." Being in such overwhelming danger, calling for a short prayer as shown by Lachs[62], may suddenly change their philosophy and theology as they call out to the infinite God who is communicative enough to hear them in the din of battle, big enough to get them out alive and caring enough to do so. But this is the gentle reminder to Jews and Gentiles that the Father of the heavens is that infinite God who knows what we need before we ask.

UBS5	Author and Reader Notes	NASB®	New American Bible
Matt. 6:9 Οὕτως οὖν προσεύχεσθε ὑμεῖς· Πάτερ ἡμῶν ὁ ἐν τοῖς οὐρανοῖς· ἁγιασθήτω τὸ ὄνομά σου·		**Matt. 6:9** ¶ "Pray, then, in this way: 'Our Father who is in heaven, Hallowed be Your name.	**The Lord's Prayer.** [9] "This is how you are to pray: Our Father in heaven,[f] hallowed be your name,

This is the section beginning the text of the "Lord's Prayer" and linking it to the prior passage with the word "therefore" opening up a world of its purpose and applications explicitly demonstrated by the passage as a whole. [63]

Contrasting Attitudes of law and prayer: "Therefore" certainly refers to the immediate section before the admonition regarding how not to pray ... not publicly and not as hypocrites in 6:5 (as in 'tax collectors' in 5:46) and Gentles (as in 5:47) in 6:7, who care only for their friends (5:46-47). "Therefore" could also refer back to "pray" (προσεύχεσθε) in 5:44 when Jesus asks the crowds to "pray" (προσεύχεσθε) for persecutors and thereby providing the purpose of the Lord's Prayer.

Who is "Our?" "Our Father..." (Πάτερ ἡμῶν) As explained above, "Our" in this text cannot refer to some group praying together as in a worship service since Jesus had just asked the crowds to go to pray alone.

Ernst Lohmeyer in his book, *Our Father, an Introduction to the Lord's Prayer*, also shows his uncertainty about the "our" here. He concludes that it refers to the "community," but concedes "we have hardly any concrete features of the community which it indicates in this way."[64]

Again, I would propose that the "our" could instead refer to the combination of the individual praying and the per-

---

62 As noted previously, see Lachs, p. 118.
63 See Betz, *Sermon on the Mount*, p. 373, discussing the placement and purpose of the Lord's Prayer here where he says, "What did Jesus intend by the creation of this prayer? One can only speculate about this question because none of the sources is explicit about it." This integrated treatment provides the "explicit" answers built into the text of Matthew when the linkages pointed out here are considered.
64 See Lohmeyer, p. 59.

secutor for whom he or she is praying just as it was requested in the paragraph before at the end of Matthew 5. From the perspective of a listener to these words in Matthew, the time between the end of Chapter 5 to Chapter 6 verse 5 is about one minute. That is too brief a time to think that the listeners forgot that Jesus was talking about prayer especially when all the other rhetorical and mnemonic devices were linking to it. As to the identity of the one asked to pray, the prayer request Jesus made was primarily to the crowds with the disciples observing as Jesus asked them to do in 4:19. "Father" primarily refers to the one who had a common connection with the both the persecuted in the crowds and persecutors all of whom received sunshine and rain from the Father.[65]

Where is "Father"? The location enhances the identification. Father "in the heavens", (ἐν τοῖς οὐρανοῖς·) is the one from the location where the rain and sun are given to the just and unjust alike and where it is the will of that Father that we pray for persecutors (5:44). As the one infinite God, the Father is unique as his name that not only distinguishes the creator from the creation but suggests an invitation to unique communication. This emphasizes the comment earlier that these praying are not praying as Gentiles to a smaller god, nor as those who may merely be expressing intentions harmonious to the universe but not before the personal and capable Infinite One who can hear, understand, and respond to the prayer—much like the hope of the prayer of an atheist in a foxhole hopes to be rescued by One capable of hearing and intervening.

"Hallowed be your name" or "sanctify your name" shows that it is to be set apart or considered unique. It could include not only a distinction of who the Father is apart from all creation, but, how uniquely capable, ready and willing the Father is to hear our prayers. This is the same Father in heaven who gives sunshine and rain on the just and unjust, the good and the evil in Matthew 5:45 and asked that prayers be made on behalf of the persecutors in 5:44.

UBS5	Author and Reader Notes	NASB®	New American Bible
Matt. 6:10 ἐλθέτω ἡ βασιλεία σου· γενηθήτω τὸ θέλημά σου," ὡς ἐν οὐρανῷ καὶ ἐπὶ γῆς·		Matt. 6:10 "'Your kingdom come. ᵇYour will be done, On earth as it is in heaven.	10 your kingdom come,[g] your will be done, on earth as in heaven.

His kingdom come and will be done contrasted with our coming into his kingdom and will; Our coming into his kingdom is essential from the passages before and after the above passage. Entry to his kingdom of heaven is the most important of all as shown by 1) the beatitudes, 2) the justice or uprightness that exceeds the scribes and pharisees (5:1-20) and 3) on judgement day where not all identifying with Jesus will be let in (6:21). It also seems to be the conclusion of the Lord's Prayer (6:12-15) which shows that our forgiveness of others is indicative of our status of forgiveness from the Father and whether we enter his kingdom.

But, in this moment, the one praying is asking that the rule of the Father come into this world now. The kingdom (rule) of God and the will (desire) of God is being summoned to break through into this moment in this request of the persecuted for both themselves and the ones doing the persecuting. If the rule and desire of the Father for love be done on earth now, there would be no conflict in the first place or, at the least, there would be resolution of the conflict and reconciliation. This request for the kingdom and will of the Father is not only an intellectual connection, but a heartfelt priority for the conflict at hand that propels the listener into the prayer for persecutors in the first place.

---

65 See "our" in relationship to 5:44 and previous paragraphs on conflicts. See also crowds in 4:25- 5:2. See Craig Keener, *The Gospel of Matthew*, p. 216 who insightfully shows that this prayer is for the "desperate" and ties the prayer back to the beatitudes of 5:3-12 but describes Jesus here as one who "summons his disciples to pray." On p. 218, "Jesus summons his *disciples* to appropriate this intimacy more deeply." Warren Carter outlines the work of many assuming that the Lord's Prayer is for the disciples on p. 93 in *What Are They Saying about Matthew's Sermon on the Mount?* Paulist Press. In *Matthew and the Margins, A Sociopolitical and Religious Reading*, Orbis Books, Maryknoll, NY, 2000 he goes into greater detail on pp. 163-169, where he states that the "our" in "our Father" is considered to refer to the "community of disciples."

It also about to be made solid in the request for "our necessary bread."

Later: Future arrival of the kingdom: His kingdom rule will come on earth ultimately as described in Matthew 25:21-36 when sheep are let in but goats are not.

Now: Meanwhile his kingdom authority is already given, precisely worded "as in heaven and (also) on earth" (ὡς ἐν οὐρανῷ καὶ ἐπὶ γῆς)" in this verse of the prayer in 6:10 and in the Great Commission of 28:18-20 where Jesus' authority "in heaven and (also) on earth" (ἐν οὐρανῷ καὶ ἐπὶ γῆς)") is given to disciples to make new disciples among the nations. This is further evidence that this prayer for the crowds is the disciple-making tool that disciples use not just among themselves in prayer but in the conflict-laden and peace-deprived lives of the crowds around them. How that works is shown in the "we-petitions" that follow.

Jesus in this passage in Matthew is claiming that the will of the Father now is that the listeners in the crowds and disciples begin to pray for their persecutors and begin the path of being peacemakers. In just a couple of verses, failing to do so will be shown to result in their not being forgiven (6:14-15), not being allowed entry to the kingdom which would be catastrophic hence the request to be delivered from evil.

UBS5	Author and Reader Notes	NASB®	New American Bible
Matt. 6:11 τὸν ἄρτον ἡμῶν τὸν ἐπιούσιον δὸς ἡμῖν σήμερον·	See commentators who seek to define ἐπιούσιον by seeing the two parts of this unusual word (ἐπι-ούσιον) in such a way that it becomes "give us today our *necessary* bread." It could also be "following day" as in "give us today the following day's" bread. Either highlights the point of the conflicts between individuals of the crowds and their persecutors who are threatening any of a number of things needed for life as shown in the variety of conflicts in the compensatory damages section.	Matt. 6:11 "Give us this day ¹our daily bread.	[h]Give us today our daily bread;

This section shifts from petitions of the one praying for the Father to petitions from the Father to the "us" in these verses, often called the "we-petitions" or requests for the one praying. These requests are like the requests made of the listeners in Matthew 5:38-42 (turn the other cheek, walk the extra mile, release coat when sued for your shirt, give when begged) and is reflected in the phrase here "give us this day our necessary bread." See the details below of 1) who is the "us," 2) what is being requested, and 3) how these two elements make for a maximally flexible anger management, conflict management and reconciliation prayer.

***Chiasmus*—Give what to whom?** To see whom Jesus is referring here, it helps to see the context and the words being used to emphasize that. As shown in the discussion of 5:39-42, "*Give us this day our necessary bread.*" (δὸς ... ΄τὸν ἄρτον ἡμῶν τὸν ἐπιούσιον δὸς ἡμῖν σήμερον·), each key phrase in this "how to" section of the prayer coincides[66] with four key elements in the compensatory damages section earlier in Chapter 5 that leads to the crescendo of "love enemies and pray for persecutors" requested in 5:44. In this phrase of the Lord's Prayer in 6:11, the crowd is guided

---

66 Refer back to the discussion in 5:39 and 6:1 about the pattern of chiasmus here.

to ask the Father to "*give*" them "their necessary bread" just as Jesus asked those in 5:42 "*give* to him who begs from you" (RSV).[67]

Give: Note that the word to "give" is the same Greek word used in both 5:42 and 6:11, *dos* "δὸς" and that the one praying is not in the power position by virtue of asking and not demanding. There appears to be an implied link between generosity to those in need in 5:42 and 6:11 that is affirmed in Matthew 25 when generosity to those in need is an indicator of kingdom entry as is full forgiveness expressed in 6:14-15 and 18: 15-35. It might be possible to consider this as an opportunity to see how those in relative power, whether one who is persecuted or one who might actually be the persecutor, may be the one in power being asked for a loan. How might the one being begged pray for the beggar? This would be relevant whether the one being begged may or may not actually be the one at fault. Only after working through the prayer, including the "forgive our debts" portion might the persecutor realize their complicity in the conflict.

Daily: Many but not all of the English translations maintain the traditional phrase, "give us this **day** our **daily** bread," or as above, "give us **today** our **daily** bread." The second use of day in "daily" is really a different word (*epiousios*) from the first for day (*saymeron*). Most commentators will point out that the second word is unusual in that it is only used twice in the New Testament, here and in Luke's version in Luke 11:5, and nowhere else in extant Greek manuscripts.[68] Others, again pointed out by France,[69] seeing it as formed from "he" and "*epiousa*" used five times in Acts (7:26, 16:11,20:15, 21:18, 23:11) as "the following day." Some will point out the two frequently used portions of the word "epi" and "*ousia*" may be intended rendering the meaning "needed for existence." Given the uncertainty, either appear to be workable to me, though the compound rendered as "necessary" fits the concept of what is important for conflicts is preferable though the "following day" rendition also fits that context of what is needed.

For a detailed treatment of the options for the definition and use of the word "*epiousios*," see the treatment by Douglas Oakman in *Jesus, Debt and the Lord's Prayer*.[70] There he covers both the word *epiousios*, but also the similar Greek word, *periousios*, and its usage in places such as the Greek Septuagint (Old Testament). In this case, the meaning shifts just a bit from the "necessary" bread to bread "in abundance" implying also that bread may not be in sufficient supply. In the Aramaic, he also shows the usage may imply the "estate's" bread or the "kingdom's" bread.

Any one or combination of these may be understood and included the concept of what is needed and the subject of the conflict.

Why give? "Why should I ask the Father to give what the persecutor took from me? That persecutor does not deserve it. He is the bad guy. I am the one who worked hard for that reputation, shirt, food, home or money, not the persecutor. In fact, that persecutor (usually unjust and evil) does not even need that home or food because that no good "so and so" has mine!

This request for prayer by Jesus of the member of a crowd for the worst-case enemy certainly grabs the attention of the person in the crowd who might find it hard to go to the Father and pray for the persecutor. It relates to what this conflicted person cares about most. And this is precisely what someone trying to persuade or recruit someone needs to do and what is compellingly relevant, in this case of Jesus persuading someone to pray for persecutors.

---

67 See the connection of the four words described earlier in reverse order between the section in 5:38-42 and 6:11-13, (evil, sue/test), release, give linking these groups of texts together. This placement of a chiasmus here—a section or two removed from the "turn the other cheek" section does not reduce the force and rhetorical value of this chiasmus, but rather strengthens it in the mind of the one speaking it and in the mind of the listener who can hear the connections. It provides an aural and memorable weave of the sections that also provides teaching or persuasive discussion opportunities.

68 See R.T. France, *Matthew*, p. p.247-249. Lachs quotes E. Nestle as showing 13 definitions with others adding more, on his *Sermon on the Mount*, p. 119.

69 Ibid., p. 147.

70 Oakman, Douglas E., *Jesus, Debt and the Lord's Prayer, First Century Debt and Jesus' Intentions*, Cascade Books, Eugene, Oregon 2014. See pages 63-67.

The two-variable agile prayer formula: This part of the Lord's Prayer completes a very robust core of this two-variable anger management and conflict management prayer. Any conflict with any person or group can be substituted for these two variables of 1) **who,** the conflicting parties as represented by 'our' which means 'me' as anyone in that crowd and 'my persecutor,' namely any person, group, entity or environment who is threatening or fighting me as illustrated in the compensatory damages section; and 2) **what,** "the necessary bread" which is whatever necessity we are fighting over.[71] (Compare the same two variable in Matthew 5:39-42 and the matrix showing the "who" that is challenging "whom" and the "what" that is being challenged (cheek, shirt, walk, borrowing).

In the same way that the "our" in "our Father" can be substituted with "the Father of me and my persecutor", the use of plurals here would be the same when we move from "our" Father to "our" bread in verse 11 and "our" debts in verse 12. Knowing who "us" (ἡμῶν, *haymone*) is, just like in the opening line, "the Father of us" substantially changes the emotion felt by the listener who is a member of the crowds being asked to pray for their persecutors especially in the light of what, "the necessary bread", they are fighting over, the second variable in the model prayer.

If you are part of a discussion group, consider discussing various ways that this two-part conflict or anger management formula can be used in any conflict where the person or group we are in conflict (the persecutors) combined with ourselves make up the "our" or "us" and the "necessary bread" stands for the object of the conflict. See the following examples of the types of "persecutors," what necessity might be at stake and how surprising it must have felt to have heard this prayer request.

Imagine how it must have felt for a first-time listener in the crowds who was denied something essential such as reputation, food or housing by a persecutor. Imagine asking the Father to give the very thing denied by the persecutor to both the persecuted individual suffering the loss and for the persecutor causing that very loss. Such a prayer would sound like, "the Father of me and the one hurting my reputation, give us both good reputations," "the Father of me and the one who stole all my family's food, give us both the food we all need." Or "the Father of me and the one who made me homeless, give us both homes." The first time that we hear that request we might likely object in anger and amazement that such a request would even be given.

This two-variable combination can cover an infinite number of conflict combinations as shown in the compensatory damages section in 5:38-44 that could be used in various disciple-making or recruitment situations. After all, rhetoricians were trained to use scenario-based conflicts for their own persuasion or rhetorical training whether in the courts, political arena or business in the most advanced *technai* or most elementary and broadly taught *progymnasmata*.[72]

With this phrase, "give us this day our necessary bread," this two-variable conflict scenario prayer has started by understanding the conflict of the persecuted individual in the crowd who is assumed at this point to be the innocent party. The recruitment of the individual within the crowd has begun. The suffering of the abused listener in the crowd has been recognized not unlike the blessing for the suffering one was just covered in the beatitude pairs spoken less than ten minutes before in the beginning of Chapter 5 when he said, "blessed are the sorrowful" (5:4). Now the full sense of outrage against the one who caused the sorrow or suffering will be engaged in the next phrase focused on the need for forgiveness.

---

71   In the same way that the Lord's Prayer was recommended to be used at least three times a day by the *Didache*, Chapter 8, (prior to 120 AD); and Tertullian's "On Prayer," Chapter 25, the Lord's Prayer can be adapted to any conflict throughout the day. It may also be used as preparation for centering prayer or meditation because of the way it can help deal with conflicts leading to distraction, anxiety, fear or anger so that the one wishing to meditate can do so with minimal distraction.

72   See the section on rhetorical and performance criticism for details.

UBS5	Author and Reader Notes	NASB®	New American Bible
Matt. 6:12 καὶ ἄφες ἡμῖν τὰ ὀφειλήματα ἡμῶν, ὡς καὶ ἡμεῖς ἀφήκαμεν τοῖς ὀφειλέταις ἡμῶν·	καὶ *ἄφες* ἡμῖν τὰ ὀφειλήματα ἡμῶν, should really be "***release*** us of our debts" since that is the same word just used in the compensatory damages section for "releasing the survival coat" when sued for the shirt off your back. The word "release" would make sense both in the case of debts and the coat in 5:40 instead of "let him have it…" Using the same word consistently in translation makes it easier to follow the line of reasoning from one section to the next as well as show the mnemonic value of the material.	**Matt. 6:12** 'And "forgive us our debts, as we also have forgiven our debtors.	[12] and forgive us our debts,[i] as we forgive our debtors;

Second Use of the Two-variable Agile Prayer Formula—Release what? *"Release"* **our debts as in** *"release"* **your coat:** This is the second use of a two-variable formula in that "us" and "our" can refer to the one praying alone in combination with any person(s) with whom the praying person is in conflict and "debts" can be the resulting loss or harm of any possible conflict. "And forgive us our debts" (καὶ ἄφες ἡμῖν τὰ ὀφειλήματα ἡμῶν). Note the word "forgive" (*ahfes*, ἄφες) here is actually "release." See how "release us our debts" is identical to the request to "release the coat" (ἄφες αὐτῷ καὶ τὸ ἱμάτιον) when sued for the shirt earlier in Matthew 5:40, or "release the gift" (ἄφες ἐκεῖ τὸ δῶρόν) at the altar in 5:24 when being sued and there is still an opportunity for an "out-of-court" settlement. The listener would have heard the prior use of "release (ἀφῆτε)" less than a minute earlier. As described earlier, it is the second of four such connections between the compensatory damages section that led to the request to pray for persecutors in 5:44 and the Lord's Prayer here and shows that these connections were intentional.

The significance of this connection emerges primarily in this second step of the emotional, psychological, and rhetorical acceleration of this next stage in the conflict management and recruitment process. Each person in the crowd was hearing this outrageous sounding prayer request for the first time. (For an example of a prayer against a persecutor, see Psalm 109:1-20 where David is likely praying prior to his murder of Bathsheba's husband and may have not yet been humbled enough to pray for enemies.)

What do you mean, by "debts"? Compounding the surprise and outrage: Less than a minute before in Matthew 5:40, the listeners in the crowd just heard Jesus ask them to *release* their coat to the persecutor, the very person taking their shirt. Then, in the same way the members of the crowd were asked to "give" to the one who asked them for a loan, they are now asked to go to the Father and ask that the Father "give" both them and the persecutor whatever the persecutor has taken from them, the necessary bread. Then, if that is not surprising and outrageous enough, an even greater outrage is presented.

Now the crowd member is supposed to ask that the Father "release" the debt of the persecutor in the same way that the victim had to "release" their coat to the very same persecutor. This is an added insult to injury if there ever was one since the crowd member is asked to love the person or group causing the conflict both by asking that the persecutor be given what they took from the victim but then also by "releasing" or forgiving the persecutor of their theft.

What do you mean by "our"? Then challenge intensifies further. In this case the request for forgiveness or "releasing" the debt is not just for the one causing the conflict or debt but for the victim who was not the one causing the conflict or debt. The victim at this point is even more outraged. The one praying might say, "Why blame the victim? I worked hard for that shirt, food, or house. I deserve it. I have nothing to be forgiven for. That no good persecutor who stole mine is the one who needs forgiveness not me. Now that I think about it, I am not so sure that I want that evil person to be forgiven at all. In fact, if that person comes here right now, I will attack him and take my stuff back."

The person praying at that moment is experiencing the increased emotion felt when he or she realizes that the suffering was unnecessary. The person praying suffered only because he or she had been robbed of justice by the person for whom he or she was supposed to be praying. The feelings of the person praying have now escalated from the sorrow of loss to the rage of anger. This is very similar to the progression of blessings in the conflict scenarios of 5:3-6 when progressing from being blessed for being sorrowful to being blessed for hungering and thirsting for the justice that was deprived when someone unnecessarily caused one to suffer. Now, the personal story of suffering has escalated to a story of understandable rage or "righteous indignation" as someone abused or oppressed.

Why forgive? Emotional upset continues to grow. The one praying might think, "I am not the one who needs forgiveness. He does. But I don't want him forgiven. I want to him to rot in hell forever after what he did to me and my family." That rage is understandable and possibly even typical.

Note also that Jesus does not accuse the member of the crowd of causing the conflict. In fact, he reinforces that in Matthew 7: 1-6 when he asks not to judge and throw valuable pearls of wisdom before wild swine or dogs who would prefer tasty treats. However, since nearly all people in a conflict feel they are not to blame, the reality must be that half of those in a conflict are at least partially at fault. Furthermore, in both the beatitudes and the Lord's Prayer, Jesus is engaging the listeners to consider their own stories. In effect, Jesus evokes the stories of the listeners before he tells them his own story or even his version of their stories. At this point, Jesus has been listening to the story of their suffering and feelings of injustice. Only now does he help them begin to see another perspective and possibly gain empathy for the very person causing their disappointment, loss, or sense of threat.

The threat experienced by the listener from their conflicts that cause fear, anxiety, and anger can block the potential for empathy in the first place. Whether by nature or nurture, these feelings in extreme circumstances can lead one to think or act like a narcissist or psychopath. Elizabeth Segal asks how various experiences from conflict can block empathy and how an understanding of the "golden rule" may reverse that.[73] She also takes time to discuss bullying and cyber bullying with an emphasis on how the bystanders can help or hinder their own empathy by the roles they choose while witnessing a bullying event.[74] She cites Emily Bazelon's work, *Sticks and Stones: Defeating the Culture of Bullying and Rediscovering the Power of Character and Empathy* and her description of 'othering' that bullies use to "cut off victims from any outside support". "How many of us can remember being made fun of? And what relief there was when the target of the joke was someone else?" (See the "Joke" skit kit in the appendix as a method to help youth discover that problem and how the Lord's Prayer could be used to create empathy to solve it.)

Flipped by Jesus: In that moment of dismay, the listener may have recalled Jesus explaining just a minute or two before that the one who is angry at his brother is liable for murder charges before a court. Now, the listener who is railing before the judge of judges against the thief has just provided evidence that the listener is a murderer. This is especially true when the one that the praying person is addressing is not a small god of the Gentiles, but the infinitely powerful heavenly Father who knows the need before the one praying knows or asks. The Father is the one who can and does act as shown by his provision of sunshine and rain on both the good and the bad, the just and unjust. It is the Father who *knows* and is not some mindless universal principle exemplifying some cosmic karma of "what goes around comes around," but the one who does judge. And now, the petitioner when praying against the persecutor out of their anger, instead of praying for the persecutor, succeeds in providing prima facie evidence of their being a

---

[73] See Segal's chapter on stress and depression's impact on empathy in the chapter beginning on p. 151 and her treatment of the "golden rule" in forming empathy on p. 152. *Social Empathy, The Art of Understanding Others.*

[74] Segal, p. 165-166.

murderer (according to Matthew 5:21-22) and providing that evidence convincingly before the supreme judge.

Now the listener has been flipped from being a pure innocent victim to becoming someone guilty of something as bad or worse. At last, the listener realizes his own need of forgiveness, and, ultimately, the need to forgive the persecutor. Recall the beatitude pairs when the blessing for the pure in heart, the pure innocent victim who did no wrong suddenly discovers that he or she needs purification and can instead become purified in heart. In each case, this works as a flip or pivot in which the victim sees him or herself needing purification as much or more than the one who caused their suffering. This works when the person is truly the victim of the persecutor, only misunderstanding and not persecuted at all, or when the persecutor is the one praying likely not realizing his or her participation as a persecutor.

The prayer now sets up a grand bargain. It asks that the listener be forgiven based on how forgiving he is towards the persecutor. A listener might wonder, "How well will that work"?

"Forgive us as…": How much forgiveness is that? If it is determined by the intent to be fully resolved as in Matt 5:24 resulting in reconciliation and a cancelled lawsuit, then it is more than just no longer feeling upset. If it is like the reconciliation described throughout the entire chapter of Matthew 18, then it would result either in reconciliation or the one refusing reconciliation denying the reconciling action of the heavenly father. If we tell the one whom we supposedly have forgiven to "depart from me," then perhaps the forgiveness that we are aligning with at that moment is the kind of forgiveness that we will hear when in the words of Jesus in Matthew 7:23 he will have no choice but to say, "I never knew you, depart from me, you evil doers." This may hold true for the one bearing fruit that denies someone thirsting for water or thirsting for reconciliation when they themselves fail to appropriate the radical forgiveness and reconciliation of the heavenly father and naturally fail to show it to others. Consider the significance of the role of this kind of forgiveness and the practical impacts in your own personal relationships and those around the world, especially those areas of conflict that resulted in genocide and war. One example can be seen in the doctoral thesis and subsequent book by Dr. Isaac K. Mbabazi on interpersonal forgiveness in Matthew and his application to the Democratic Republic of the Congo. [75] Another example is the work of Rev. Dr. Celestin Musekura on the role of forgiveness in creating communities of reconciliation in the books *Forgiving as We have been Forgiven: Community Practices for Peace* and his doctoral thesis and subsequent book *Assessment of Contemporary Models of Forgiveness* as well that his practical missionary work with African Leadership & Reconciliation Ministries founded by Rev. Celestin Musekura, Ph.D. Their website, alarm-inc.org, explains their work this way:

> ALARM is faith-based and was founded in 1994 in response to the Rwandan genocide. Hundreds of thousands of people were murdered, many were forced to seek refuge in neighboring countries. The church was also affected. Over 70 percent of Rwandan pastors were either killed or forced to flee.
>
> Similarly, violent ethnic, civil and political events were escalating in Uganda, Southern Sudan, and Democratic Republic of Congo (DRC) among other countries in East and Central Africa. These events adversely affected the Christian church in those areas and continue to do so to date.
>
> As a result, ALARM, seeks to promote servant leadership, biblical forgiveness and reconciliation, conflict management in Africa. As an Africa-based and African-led organization, ALARM has expanded and currently operates in eight countries in East and Central Africa, namely, Burundi, Democratic Republic of Congo, Kenya, Rwanda, South Sudan, Sudan, Tanzania, and Uganda, with its headquarters in Nairobi, Kenya

Forgiving that completely can understandably be difficult. It may also be elusive in that any one conflict may be like a multiple layered onion where one conflict covers another or creates others. For example, if one were unfairly slandered on a job and without due process and was fired, then there could be implications about having enough money

---

75   Mbabazi, Isaac Kahwa, Ph.D., *The Significance of Interpersonal Forgiveness in Matthew's Gospel*, University of Manchester, © 2011 and WIPF, Eugene OR 2013.This work links forgiveness and reciprocity in the Gospel of Matthew, compares it to other literature of the time and its importance to recovery in the Democratic Republic of the Congo.

for food, rent, medical care or stability of the marriage or family. In some cases, it might be helpful to use this prayer for each of the resulting other conflicts or needs to fully address each of the issues involved so that none remain unaddressed. The flexibility of these two variables of conflict, the parties in the conflict and the items contested provide for the capability of addressing any conflict and those they in turn may cause.

By reflecting on the conflict that causes upset, anxiety, worry, grief, or anger, it might also help heal the one suffering from conflict. Continued emotional stress is known by brain scientists to enhance the emotional center of the brain often at the expense of the center of creative thought. By praying through these issues, the brain may be able to shift from the emotional centers of the brain and help heal emotional trauma similar to the ways journaling may help. See Amy Shulman and her work providing an overview of this and her own healing from loss and grief by journaling.[76]

Application Note: It might be helpful to consider various ways to inject a given conflict using the Lord's Prayer for Persecutors where the "our" represents the conflicting parties and the "necessary bread" is what is being fought over. See the appendix for the article expected to be published in the *Christian Century* magazine in 2021, the skit kit written in 2017 for examples and templates for how the Lord's Prayer might be used this way along with the interactive Bible studies, and sermons on the Lord's Prayer discussing it. Using these examples, memorizing, and then applying these principles in conflicts that impact you or those around you, will help place you in a similar position as the original audience. As such, you are applying performance criticism exercises that will help you experience and validate what may been the original purpose of the material. It might also help provide you far greater value than the purchase price of the Bible you bought to do this study.

UBS5	Author and Reader Notes	NASB®	New American Bible
Matt. 6:13 καὶ μὴ εἰσενέγκῃς ἡμᾶς εἰς πειρασμόν, ἀλλὰ ῥῦσαι ἡμᾶς ἀπὸ τοῦ πονηροῦ[4].	See benefit of using "test" instead of "tempt" to avoid the connotation of "alure". As to use of "evil": As **Matt. 5:39** ἐγὼ δὲ λέγω ὑμῖν μὴ ἀντιστῆναι τῷ πονηρῷ·, so, ἀπὸ τοῦ πονηροῦ[4]. Suggests that the best translation should provide consistency. In this case it might be related to an evil person as one presenting the conflict in Matthew 5:39 or possibly the "evil one" such as the tempter of Jesus representing the kingdom not of God, or (possibly more likely) the evil consequences of not being forgiven which could actually embody all of the above combinations. Note that the oldest	Matt. 6:13 'And do not lead us into temptation, but "deliver us from [1b]evil. [2][For Yours is the kingdom and the power and the glory forever. Amen.']	and do not subject us to the final test,[i] but deliver us from the evil one.

---

76 See Lisa M. Shulman, M.D. *Before and After Loss, A Neurologist's Perspective on Loss, Grief, and Our Brain*; Johns Hopkins University Press, ©2018. The author describes integrates her personal loss of her husband to her professional understanding of how the brain works. She describes three principles of healing the mind and brain after loss: 1) subconscious-conscious integration, 2) immersion-distraction, 3) (p. 63). She reviews the roles of nine brain regions (p.95) and their connections to hormones, the immune system and sleep (.98-99). She promotes the benefits of journaling to address issues as opposed to ignoring them, which does not promote healing. These insights support the practical value of praying for "persecutors" or others creating our conflicts so that one might be able to come to a place of peace. It also supports the concept of praying the Lord's Prayer for Persecutors to calm oneself and prepare one for a more effective time of meditation.

	translations end at "evil" and do not include the doxology, "for thine is the kingdom, and the power, and the glory forever. Amen."		

As **Matt. 5:39** ἐγὼ δὲ λέγω ὑμῖν μὴ ἀντιστῆναι τῷ πονηρῷ·; , so, ἀπὸ τοῦ πονηροῦ[4]. Suggests that the best translation should provide consistency. In this case it might be related to an evil person as one presenting the conflict in Matthew 5:39 or possibly the "evil one" such as the tempter of Jesus representing the kingdom not of God, or (possibly more likely) the evil consequences of not being forgiven which could actually embody all of the above combinations.

Note that the oldest translations end at "evil" and do not include the doxology, "for thine is the kingdom, and the power, and the glory forever. Amen."

Skipping the test: Compare this to the compensatory damages talk about leading to judgement to sue for one's shirt in 5:40 ("wants to *sue*" θέλοντί σοι κριθῆναι) (similar to an earlier section of 5:23-26 when brought to a judge by an angry person). In the same way, here one is asked to not be led to "testing," exactly what happens at a court before the judge and like the test given to Jesus in the wilderness in Matthew 4:1. This "test" is the third common element between the compensatory damages section earlier and this section of the Lord's Prayer with the "we-petitions."

Save us from the consequences of failing such a test: Having the judge who cannot be fooled test the listener to see if the listener is releasing the debt of his debtor (the persecutor) at the height of the listener's rage would be dangerous. For that reason, it is reasonable to ask not to be given that *test*. Because if the listener failed the test, the results would be disastrous, hence, deliver us from *evil (ponayrou, πονηροῦ)*, the very thing that was asked to not be resisted in the beginning of the compensatory damages section of 5:33 and the fourth item in this half of the chiasmus (*give, release, test, evil*).

For discussion:

1) What might be sample conflicts addressed in the Lord's Prayer?

2) How might these examples substitute "our" and "us" with oneself and the person or group causing the conflict and substituting the "necessary bread" with what the conflict is over?

3) How might the initial conflicts reveal related secondary or tertiary problems that result from the primary conflict?

4) Questions that might follow could include: how might these bring a sense of peace, solidarity with the one causing the conflict, and the options for eventual peacemaking attempts suggested in Matthew 18?

5) How might the concept of "forgive (release) us AS we forgive (release)" relate to the extent we forgive and restore relationships?

6) How might the use of this prayer be used as a disciple making tool?

7) How would you compare the conflict progression in the beatitude pairs with the pattern in the Lord's Prayer?

USB	Author and Reader Notes	NASB*	New American Bible
Matt. 6:15 ἐὰν δὲ μὴ ἀφῆτε τοῖς ἀνθρώποις⁵, οὐδὲ ὁ πατὴρ ὑμῶν ἀφήσει τὰ παραπτώματα ὑμῶν.	Note the use of "release" (ἀφῆτε) is used here but switches to "transgressions" (παραπτώματα), suggesting a strong connection between debts and transgressions.	**Matt. 6:15** "But ᵃif you do not forgive ¹others, then your Father will not forgive your transgressions.	¹⁵But if you do not forgive others, neither will your Father forgive your transgressions.

To release or not release, that is the question: These two verses show that whether the listener within the crowd will "release (forgive) the debt," is uncertain. This is understandable because the ones asked to pray are members of the crowd and not yet disciples[77] and may not buy into the concept of forgiving enemies and praying for persecutors.

Compare this section to the forgiveness, reconciliation, and restoration in Matthew 18:15-35. There the one asked to go to attempt a restoration is told that it is uncertain whether the other party will accept the three-fold attempt at a restoration. If they accept, they can then pray together (as opposed to the prayer in Matthew 6:5-15) and whatever those two or three ask (from the context, presumably the one trying to reconcile, the witness and the person trying to be restored) will be granted and Jesus promised in Matthew 18:19-20 to be amid them (those agreeing on the restoration)[78]. These attempts show efforts at creating communication and feedback loops needed for effective communication that can lead to full restoration of a relationship.[79]

Also note the parable of the unforgiving servant of Matthew 18:23-35, the beatitude of "blessed are the pure/purified in heart" in 5:8 and the discussions of fruit in Matthew 7:15-20 all of which point to a concept reflecting the indicative nature of forgiveness in that how we forgive and the extent to which we forgive is indicative of how we embrace God's forgiveness. If we forgive, it is out of the appreciation of how we have been forgiven and not the cause of our forgiveness. Similarly, if we fail to forgive, or fail to attempt restoration, it might be indicative of how we did not fully appreciate and comprehend the forgiveness offered to us in the first place as in the parable of the unforgiving servant.[80]

Note once again how the two phrases of 6:14-15 begin with the positive and end with the negative. Also, see the climax of the argument is focused on whether we comprehend forgiveness and evidence it in the way in which we forgive others, also reinforced in Matthew 18. See the links between "release" of forgiveness of "debts" in 6:12 and "transgressions in 6:14-15. Luke does something similar in Luke 11:4 when he says, "release us our sins for we release our debtors". Michael Hudson makes this connection within the Luke version of the prayer, connects it to Matthew 18 and the Jewish concept and celebration of Jubilee.[81] This reflects the ancient thought that creditors can forgive debts while only God can forgive sins.

Practicing the Prayer: Given the significance of this prayer as a conflict resolution prayer, readers are encouraged to use this prayer throughout the day substituting the "our" and "us" with the person praying and the person or group with whom the person praying is in conflict at that moment and the "necessary bread" is what is the object of the

---

77 This is different from the similar prayer in Luke 11:1-4 where it was told later than the sermon and where it was a response to the prayer coaching request of a disciple. In this case, the forgiveness phrase is different and is phrased, "forgive us for (or because) we have forgiven." This is because the audience is different because the one praying in Luke is not in the crowds but a disciple who already has agreed to the concept of forgiveness.

78 See the *Gospel of Matthew Study Guide (aka Matthew: Jesus as the Fulfillment of God's Promises)* by Pinson, Blair and Trammel, p. 106 showing the context of the "where two or three are gathered" refers to reconciled parties.

79 Feedback loops are well understood in biology, counseling and even the total quality movement and continuous improvement programs embraced by business and industry. Discussion group members could welcome comments from those experienced in using feedback in their respective professions. One example of a feedback loop can be seen here: https://courses.lumenlearning.com/ap1/chapter/feedback-loops/

80 See the treatment of the unforgiving servant and comparison of "Gentiles and tax collectors" by L. Gregory Jones in *Embodying Forgiveness* on p. 193-196.

81 See Michael Hudson on p. 226 of *... and forgive them their debts*.

conflict. And, in remembering the context introducing love for enemies and prayer for persecutors back in Matthew 5:39-44, the conflicts range from large to small, intentional to unintentional, and practicing the prayer can be applied to situation between us and any person, group, or organization. Study groups might discuss how that might work with hypothetical examples or those from literature, current events, history, or, when appropriate, personal examples.

Matthew 6:16- 7:29: The rest of the material through the end of Chapter 7 further reinforces the Lord's Prayer teaching, its role in disciple-making and can be covered in a more detailed treatment of this entire set of material in Matthew 5-7 known as the "Sermon on the Mount." Briefly, the material following the prayer covers another item to do in secret, namely fasting. This may result in the crowd member wondering what tangible benefits might come from this sacrificially loving lifestyle that appears to give more than it ever gets, especially if one can't even receive public relations benefits, which some might argue are helpful tools in providing a good example. As soon as the discussion on fasting is completed that answer is given in a treatment of present rewards and financial security in the remaining part of Chapter 6 when it recommends, "seek first his kingdom and all these things will be added to you" (6:33). This reminds the hearers of the foundational discussion of the kingdom of heaven in the beatitudes of Chapter 5.

USB5	Author and Reader Notes	NASB®	RSV
Matt. 6:16 ¶ Ὅταν δὲ νηστεύητε, μὴ γίνεσθε ὡς οἱ ὑποκριταὶ σκυθρωποί, ἀφανίζουσιν γὰρ τὰ πρόσωπα αὐτῶν ὅπως φανῶσιν τοῖς ἀνθρώποις νηστεύοντες· ἀμὴν λέγω ὑμῖν, ἀπέχουσιν τὸν μισθὸν αὐτῶν. **Matt. 6:17** σὺ δὲ νηστεύων ἄλειψαί σου τὴν κεφαλὴν καὶ τὸ πρόσωπόν σου νίψαι, **Matt. 6:18** ὅπως μὴ φανῇς τοῖς ἀνθρώποις νηστεύων ἀλλὰ τῷ πατρί σου τῷ ἐν τῷ κρυφαίῳ· καὶ ὁ πατήρ σου ὁ βλέπων ἐν τῷ κρυφαίῳ ἀποδώσει σοι⁶. **Matt. 6:19** ¶ Μὴ θησαυρίζετε ὑμῖν θησαυροὺς ἐπὶ τῆς γῆς, ὅπου σὴς καὶ βρῶσις ἀφανίζει καὶ ὅπου κλέπται διορύσσουσιν καὶ κλέπτουσιν· **Matt. 6:20** θησαυρίζετε δὲ ὑμῖν θησαυροὺς ἐν οὐρανῷ, ὅπου οὔτε σὴς οὔτε βρῶσις ἀφανίζει καὶ ὅπου κλέπται οὐ διορύσσουσιν οὐδὲ κλέπτουσιν· **Matt. 6:21** ὅπου γάρ ἐστιν ὁ θησαυρός σου, ἐκεῖ ἔσται καὶ ἡ καρδία σου. **Matt. 6:22** ¶ Ὁ λύχνος τοῦ σώματός ἐστιν ὁ ὀφθαλμός. ἐὰν οὖν ᾖ ὁ ὀφθαλμός σου ἁπλοῦς, ὅλον	(Note version change from New American Bible to RSV)	**Matt. 6:16** ¶ "ᵃWhenever you fast, do not put on a gloomy face as the hypocrites *do*, for they ¹neglect their appearance so that they will be noticed by men when they are fasting. ᵇTruly I say to you, they have their reward in full. **Matt. 6:17** "But you, when you fast, ᵃanoint your head and wash your face **Matt. 6:18** so that your fasting will not be noticed by men, but by your Father who is in secret; and your ᵃFather who sees *what is done* in secret will reward you. **Matt. 6:19** ¶ "ᵃDo not store up for yourselves treasures on earth, where moth and rust destroy, and where thieves break in and steal. **Matt. 6:20** "But store up for yourselves ᵃtreasures in heaven, where neither moth nor rust destroys, and where thieves do not break in or steal; **Matt. 6:21** for ᵃwhere your treasure is, there your heart will be also. **Matt. 6:22** ¶ "ᵃThe eye is the lamp of the body; so then if your eye is ¹clear, your whole body will be full of light.	Concerning Fasting

¹⁶ "And when you fast, do not look dismal, like the hypocrites, for they disfigure their faces that their fasting may be seen by men. Truly, I say to you, they have received their reward. ¹⁷ But when you fast, anoint your head and wash your face, ¹⁸ that your fasting may not be seen by men but by your Father who is in secret; and your Father who sees in secret will reward you.

Concerning Treasures

¹⁹ "Do not lay up for yourselves treasures on earth, where moth and rust[c]consume and where thieves break in and steal, ²⁰ but lay up for yourselves treasures in heaven, where neither moth nor rust[d] consumes and where thieves do not break in and steal. ²¹ For where your treasure is, there will your heart be also.

The Sound Eye |

τὸ σῶμά σου φωτεινὸν ἔσται·
Matt. 6:23 ἐὰν δὲ ὁ ὀφθαλμός σου πονηρὸς ᾖ, ὅλον τὸ σῶμά σου σκοτεινὸν ἔσται. εἰ οὖν τὸ φῶς τὸ ἐν σοὶ σκότος ἐστίν, τὸ σκότος πόσον.
Matt. 6:24 ¶ Οὐδεὶς δύναται δυσὶ κυρίοις δουλεύειν· ἢ γὰρ τὸν ἕνα μισήσει καὶ τὸν ἕτερον ἀγαπήσει, ἢ ἑνὸς ἀνθέξεται καὶ τοῦ ἑτέρου καταφρονήσει. οὐ δύνασθε θεῷ δουλεύειν καὶ μαμωνᾷ.
Matt. 6:25 ¶ Διὰ τοῦτο λέγω ὑμῖν, μὴ μεριμνᾶτε τῇ ψυχῇ ὑμῶν τί φάγητε [ἢ τί πίητε]⁷, μηδὲ τῷ σώματι ὑμῶν τί ἐνδύσησθε. οὐχὶ ἡ ψυχὴ πλεῖόν ἐστιν τῆς τροφῆς καὶ τὸ σῶμα τοῦ ἐνδύματος;
Matt. 6:26 ἐμβλέψατε εἰς τὰ πετεινὰ τοῦ οὐρανοῦ ὅτι οὐ σπείρουσιν οὐδὲ θερίζουσιν οὐδὲ συνάγουσιν εἰς ἀποθήκας, καὶ ὁ πατὴρ ὑμῶν ὁ οὐράνιος τρέφει αὐτά· οὐχ ὑμεῖς μᾶλλον διαφέρετε αὐτῶν;
Matt. 6:27 τίς δὲ ἐξ ὑμῶν μεριμνῶν δύναται προσθεῖναι ἐπὶ τὴν ἡλικίαν αὐτοῦ πῆχυν ἕνα;
Matt. 6:28 καὶ περὶ ἐνδύματος τί μεριμνᾶτε; καταμάθετε τὰ κρίνα τοῦ ἀγροῦ πῶς αὐξάνουσιν· οὐ κοπιῶσιν οὐδὲ νήθουσιν⁸·
Matt. 6:29 λέγω δὲ ὑμῖν ὅτι οὐδὲ Σολομὼν ἐν πάσῃ τῇ δόξῃ αὐτοῦ περιεβάλετο ὡς ἓν τούτων.
Matt. 6:30 εἰ δὲ τὸν χόρτον τοῦ ἀγροῦ σήμερον ὄντα καὶ αὔριον εἰς κλίβανον βαλλόμενον ὁ θεὸς οὕτως ἀμφιέννυσιν, οὐ πολλῷ μᾶλλον ὑμᾶς, ὀλιγόπιστοι;
Matt. 6:31 μὴ οὖν μεριμνήσητε λέγοντες, Τί φάγωμεν; ἤ, Τί πίωμεν; ἤ, Τί περιβαλώμεθα;

²³ But if your eye is [a]bad, your whole body will be full of darkness. So if the light that is in you is darkness, how great is the darkness!

²⁴ "No one can serve two masters; for either he will hate the one and love the other, or he will be devoted to one and despise the other. You cannot serve God and [b]wealth.

The Cure for Anxiety

²⁵ "For this reason I say to you, [c]do not be worried about your [d]life, *as to* what you will eat or what you will drink; nor for your body, *as to* what you will put on. Is life not more than food, and the body more than clothing? ²⁶ Look at the birds of the sky, that they do not sow, nor reap, nor gather *crops* into barns, and *yet* your heavenly Father feeds them. Are you not much more important than they? ²⁷ And which of

²² "The eye is the lamp of the body. So, if your eye is sound, your whole body will be full of light; ²³ but if your eye is not sound, your whole body will be full of darkness. If then the light in you is darkness, how great is the darkness!

Serving Two Masters

²⁴ "No one can serve two masters; for either he will hate the one and love the other, or he will be devoted to the one and despise the other. You cannot serve God and mammon.[e]

Do Not Worry

²⁵ "Therefore I tell you, do not be anxious about your life, what you shall eat or what you shall drink, nor about your body, what you shall put on. Is not life more than food, and the body more than clothing? ²⁶ Look at the birds of the air: they neither sow nor reap nor gather into barns, and yet your heavenly Father feeds them. Are you not of more value than they? ²⁷ And which of you by being anxious can add one cubit to his span of life?[f] ²⁸ And why are you anxious about clothing? Consider the lilies of the field, how they grow; they neither toil nor spin; ²⁹ yet I tell you, even Solomon in all his glory was not arrayed like one of these. ³⁰ But if God so clothes the grass of the field, which today is alive and tomorrow is thrown into the oven, will he not much more clothe you, O men of

Matt. 6:32 πάντα γὰρ ταῦτα τὰ ἔθνη ἐπιζητοῦσιν· οἶδεν γὰρ ὁ πατὴρ ὑμῶν ὁ οὐράνιος ὅτι χρῄζετε τούτων ἁπάντων. **Matt. 6:33** ζητεῖτε δὲ πρῶτον τὴν βασιλείαν [τοῦ θεοῦ] καὶ τὴν δικαιοσύνην αὐτοῦ⁹, καὶ ταῦτα παντα προστεθήσεται ὑμῖν. **Matt. 6:34** μὴ οὖν μεριμνήσητε εἰς τὴν αὔριον, ἡ γὰρ αὔριον μεριμνήσει ἑαυτῆς· ἀρκετὸν τῇ ἡμέρᾳ ἡ κακία αὐτῆς.		you by worrying can add a single [e]day to his [f]life's span? ²⁸ And why are you worried about clothing? Notice how the lilies of the field grow; they do not labor nor do they spin *thread for cloth*, ²⁹ yet I say to you that not even Solomon in all his glory clothed himself like one of these. ³⁰ But if God so clothes the grass of the field, which is *alive* today and tomorrow is thrown into the furnace, *will He* not much more *clothe* you? You of little faith! ³¹ Do not worry then, saying, 'What are we to eat?' or 'What are we to drink?' or 'What are we to wear for clothing?' ³² For the Gentiles eagerly seek all these things; for your heavenly Father knows that you need all these things. ³³ But [g]seek first [h]His kingdom and His righteousness, and all these things will be [i]provided to you. ³⁴ "So do not worry about tomorrow; for tomorrow will [i]worry about	little faith? ³¹ Therefore do not be anxious, saying, 'What shall we eat?' or 'What shall we drink?' or 'What shall we wear?' ³² For the Gentiles seek all these things; and your heavenly Father knows that you need them all. ³³ But seek first his kingdom and his righteousness, and all these things shall be yours as well. ³⁴ "Therefore do not be anxious about tomorrow, for tomorrow will be anxious for itself. Let the day's own trouble be sufficient for the day.

| | | itself. [k]Each day has enough trouble of its own. | |

Then a discussion on what to do if no initial results occur from using the Lord's Prayer of chapter 6 is covered in Chapter 7 when it asks the person to keep on praying in the "ask, seek, and knock" prayer passage. It ends with a rephrasing of the golden rule starting with the perceived needs of the listeners, "whatever way you wish people would do to you, do so to them; for this is the law and the prophets" (7:7-12). That is very similar to the reciprocity comment of the Lord's Prayer above in 6:14-15 where Jesus in effect says you will be forgiven or not forgiven in the same way that you forgive or fail to do so. This prayer becomes an echo of the Lord's Prayer. It encourages continued use of the Lord's Prayer for the persecutors rather than giving up and resorting to giving unwanted advice or judgement, namely casting of pearls before wild dogs and swine. In effect, the "ask, seek and knock" prayer says, "if at first you don't succeed, pray and pray again."

USB5	Author and Reader Notes	NASB®	RSV
Matt. 7:1 ⁋ Μὴ κρίνετε, ἵνα μὴ κριθῆτε· Matt. 7:2 ἐν ᾧ γὰρ κρίματι κρίνετε κριθήσεσθε, καὶ ἐν ᾧ μέτρῳ μετρεῖτε μετρηθήσεται ὑμῖν. Matt. 7:3 τί δὲ βλέπεις τὸ κάρφος τὸ ἐν τῷ ὀφθαλμῷ τοῦ ἀδελφοῦ σου, τὴν δὲ ἐν τῷ σῷ ὀφθαλμῷ δοκὸν οὐ κατανοεῖς; Matt. 7:4 ἢ πῶς ἐρεῖς τῷ ἀδελφῷ σου, Ἄφες ἐκβάλω τὸ κάρφος ἐκ τοῦ ὀφθαλμοῦ σου, καὶ ἰδοὺ ἡ δοκὸς ἐν τῷ ὀφθαλμῷ σοῦ; Matt. 7:5 ὑποκριτά, ἔκβαλε πρῶτον ἐκ τοῦ ὀφθαλμοῦ σοῦ τὴν δοκόν, καὶ τότε διαβλέψεις ἐκβαλεῖν τὸ κάρφος ἐκ τοῦ ὀφθαλμοῦ τοῦ ἀδελφοῦ σου.		7 "Do not [l]judge, so that you will not be judged. ²For in the way you judge, you will be judged; and [m]by your standard of measure, it will be measured to you. ³Why do you look at the [n]speck that is in your brother's eye, but do not notice the log that is in your own eye? ⁴Or how [o]can you say to your brother, 'Let me take the [p]speck out of your eye,' and look, the log is in your own eye? ⁵You hypocrite, first take the log out of your own eye, and then you will see clearly to take the [q]speck out of your brother's eye!	Judging Others

7 "Judge not, that you be not judged. ²For with the judgment you pronounce you will be judged, and the measure you give will be the measure you get. ³Why do you see the speck that is in your brother's eye, but do not notice the log that is in your own eye? ⁴Or how can you say to your brother, 'Let me take the speck out of your eye,' when there is the log in your own eye? ⁵You hypocrite, first take the log out of your own eye, and then you will see clearly to take the speck out of your brother's eye. |

Matt. 7:6 Μὴ δῶτε τὸ ἅγιον τοῖς κυσὶν μηδὲ βάλητε τοὺς μαργαρίτας ὑμῶν ἔμπροσθεν τῶν χοίρων, μήποτε καταπατήσουσιν αὐτοὺς ἐν τοῖς ποσὶν αὐτῶν καὶ στραφέντες ῥήξωσιν ὑμᾶς. Matt. 7:7 ¶ Αἰτεῖτε καὶ δοθήσεται ὑμῖν, ζητεῖτε καὶ εὑρήσετε, κρούετε καὶ ἀνοιγήσεται ὑμῖν· Matt. 7:8 πᾶς γὰρ ὁ αἰτῶν λαμβάνει καὶ ὁ ζητῶν εὑρίσκει καὶ τῷ κρούοντι ἀνοιγήσεται. Matt. 7:9 ἢ τίς ἐστιν ἐξ ὑμῶν ἄνθρωπος, ὃν αἰτήσει ὁ υἱὸς αὐτοῦ ἄρτον, μὴ λίθον ἐπιδώσει αὐτῷ; Matt. 7:10 ἢ καὶ ἰχθὺν αἰτήσει, μὴ ὄφιν ἐπιδώσει αὐτῷ; Matt. 7:11 εἰ οὖν ὑμεῖς πονηροὶ ὄντες οἴδατε δόματα ἀγαθὰ διδόναι τοῖς τέκνοις ὑμῶν, πόσῳ μᾶλλον ὁ πατὴρ ὑμῶν ὁ ἐν τοῖς οὐρανοῖς δώσει ἀγαθὰ τοῖς αἰτοῦσιν αὐτόν.ᵃ Matt. 7:12 Πάντα οὖν ὅσα ἐὰν θέλητε ἵνα ποιῶσιν ὑμῖν οἱ ἄνθρωποι, οὕτως καὶ ὑμεῖς ποιεῖτε αὐτοῖς· οὗτος γάρ ἐστιν ὁ νόμος καὶ οἱ προφῆται. Matt. 7:13 ¶ Εἰσέλθατε διὰ τῆς στενῆς πύλης· ὅτι	6 "Do not give what is holy to dogs, and do not throw your pearls before pigs, or they will trample them under their feet, and turn and tear you to pieces. **Prayer and the Golden Rule** 7 "[t]Ask, and it will be given to you; [s]seek, and you will find; [t]knock, and it will be opened to you. 8 For everyone who asks receives, and the one who seeks finds, and to the one who knocks it will be opened. 9 Or what person is there among you [u]who, when his son asks for a loaf of bread, [v]will give him a stone? 10 Or [w]if he asks for a fish, he will not give him a snake, will he? 11 So if you, *despite* being [s]evil, know how to give good gifts to your children, how much more will your Father who is in heaven give good things to those who ask Him! 12 "In everything, therefore, [y]treat	Profaning the Holy 6 "Do not give dogs what is holy; and do not throw your pearls before swine, lest they trample them under foot and turn to attack you. Ask, Search, Knock 7 "Ask, and it will be given you; seek, and you will find; knock, and it will be opened to you. 8 For every one who asks receives, and he who seeks finds, and to him who knocks it will be opened. 9 Or what man of you, if his son asks him for bread, will give him a stone? 10 Or if he asks for a fish, will give him a serpent? 11 If you then, who are evil, know how to give good gifts to your children, how much more will your Father who is in heaven give good things to those who ask him! 12 So whatever you wish that men would do to you, do so to them; for this is the law and the prophets. The Narrow Gate

πλατεῖα ἡ πύλη¹ καὶ εὐρύχωρος ἡ ὁδὸς ἡ ἀπάγουσα εἰς τὴν ἀπώλειαν καὶ πολλοί εἰσιν οἱ εἰσερχόμενοι δι᾽ αὐτῆς· **Matt. 7:14** τί² στενὴ ἡ πύλη³ καὶ τεθλιμμένη ἡ ὁδὸς ἡ ἀπάγουσα εἰς τὴν ζωὴν καὶ ὀλίγοι εἰσιν οἱ εὑρίσκοντες αὐτήν. **Matt. 7:15** ¶ Προσέχετε ἀπὸ τῶν ψευδοπροφητῶν, οἵτινες ἔρχονται πρὸς ὑμᾶς ἐν ἐνδύμασιν προβάτων, ἔσωθεν δέ εἰσιν λύκοι ἅρπαγες. **Matt. 7:16** ἀπὸ τῶν καρπῶν αὐτῶν ἐπιγνώσεσθε αὐτούς. μήτι συλλέγουσιν ἀπὸ ἀκανθῶν σταφυλὰς ἢ ἀπὸ τριβόλων σῦκα; **Matt. 7:17** οὕτως πᾶν δένδρον ἀγαθὸν καρποὺς καλοὺς ποιεῖ, τὸ δὲ σαπρὸν δένδρον καρποὺς πονηροὺς ποιεῖ. **Matt. 7:18** οὐ δύναται δένδρον ἀγαθὸν καρποὺς πονηροὺς ποιεῖν οὐδὲ δένδρον σαπρὸν καρποὺς καλοὺς ποιεῖν. **Matt. 7:19** πᾶν δένδρον μὴ ποιοῦν καρπὸν καλὸν ἐκκόπτεται καὶ εἰς πῦρ βάλλεται. **Matt. 7:20** ἄρα γε ἀπὸ τῶν καρπῶν αὐτῶν	people the same way you want [z]them to treat you, for this is the Law and the Prophets.

The Narrow and Wide Gates

¹³"Enter through the narrow gate; for the gate is wide and the way is broad that leads to destruction, and there are many who enter through it. ¹⁴For the gate is narrow and the way is constricted that leads to life, and there are few who find it.

A Tree and Its Fruit

¹⁵"Beware of the false prophets, who come to you in sheep's clothing, but inwardly are ravenous wolves. ¹⁶You will [aa]know them by their fruits. [ab]Grapes are not gathered from thorn *bushes*, nor figs from thistles, are they? ¹⁷So every good tree bears good fruit, but the bad tree bears bad fruit. ¹⁸A good tree cannot bear bad | ¹³"Enter by the narrow gate; for the gate is wide and the way is easy,[g] that leads to destruction, and those who enter by it are many. ¹⁴For the gate is narrow and the way is hard, that leads to life, and those who find it are few.

A Tree and Its Fruit

¹⁵"Beware of false prophets, who come to you in sheep's clothing but inwardly are ravenous wolves. ¹⁶You will know them by their fruits. Are grapes gathered from thorns, or figs from thistles? ¹⁷So, every sound tree bears good fruit, but the bad tree bears evil fruit. ¹⁸A sound tree cannot bear evil fruit, nor can a bad tree bear good fruit. ¹⁹Every tree that does not bear good fruit is cut down and thrown into the fire. ²⁰Thus you will know them by their fruits.

Concerning Self-Deception

²¹"Not every one who says to me, 'Lord, Lord,' shall enter the kingdom of heaven, |

ἐπιγνώσεσθε αὐτούς.
Matt. 7:21 ¶ Οὐ πᾶς ὁ λέγων μοι, Κύριε κύριε, εἰσελεύσεται εἰς τὴν βασιλείαν τῶν οὐρανῶν, ἀλλ᾽ ὁ ποιῶν τὸ θέλημα τοῦ πατρός μου τοῦ ἐν τοῖς οὐρανοῖς.
Matt. 7:22 πολλοὶ ἐροῦσίν μοι ἐν ἐκείνῃ τῇ ἡμέρᾳ, Κύριε κύριε, οὐ τῷ σῷ ὀνόματι ἐπροφητεύσαμεν, καὶ τῷ σῷ ὀνόματι δαιμόνια ἐξεβάλομεν, καὶ τῷ σῷ ὀνόματι δυνάμεις πολλὰς ἐποιήσαμεν;
Matt. 7:23 καὶ τότε ὁμολογήσω αὐτοῖς ὅτι Οὐδέποτε ἔγνων ὑμᾶς· ἀποχωρεῖτε ἀπ᾽ ἐμοῦ οἱ ἐργαζόμενοι τὴν ἀνομίαν.
Matt. 7:24 ¶ Πᾶς οὖν ὅστις ἀκούει μου τοὺς λόγους τούτους καὶ ποιεῖ αὐτούς, ὁμοιωθήσεται[4] ἀνδρὶ φρονίμῳ, ὅστις ᾠκοδόμησεν αὐτοῦ τὴν οἰκίαν ἐπὶ τὴν πέτραν·
Matt. 7:25 καὶ κατέβη ἡ βροχὴ καὶ ἦλθον οἱ ποταμοὶ καὶ ἔπνευσαν οἱ ἄνεμοι καὶ προσέπεσαν τῇ οἰκίᾳ ἐκείνῃ, καὶ οὐκ ἔπεσεν, τεθεμελίωτο γὰρ ἐπὶ τὴν πέτραν.
Matt. 7:26 καὶ πᾶς ὁ ἀκούων μου τοὺς λόγους τούτους καὶ μὴ ποιῶν αὐτούς

fruit, nor can a bad tree bear good fruit. [19] Every tree that does not bear good fruit is cut down and thrown into the fire. [20] So then, you will [ac]know them by their fruits.

[21] "Not everyone who says to Me, 'Lord, Lord,' will enter the kingdom of heaven, but the one who does the will of My Father who is in heaven *will enter.* [22] Many will say to Me on that day, 'Lord, Lord, did we not prophesy in Your name, and in Your name cast out demons, and in Your name perform many [ad]miracles?' [23] And then I will declare to them, 'I never knew you; leave Me, you who practice lawlessness.'

The Two Foundations

[24] "Therefore, everyone who hears these words of Mine, and [ae]acts on them, will be like a wise man who built his house on the rock. [25] And the rain fell and the [af]floods

but he who does the will of my Father who is in heaven. [22] On that day many will say to me, 'Lord, Lord, did we not prophesy in your name, and cast out demons in your name, and do many mighty works in your name?' [23] And then will I declare to them, 'I never knew you; depart from me, you evildoers.'

Hearers and Doers

[24] "Every one then who hears these words of mine and does them will be like a wise man who built his house upon the rock; [25] and the rain fell, and the floods came, and the winds blew and beat upon that house, but it did not fall, because it had been founded on the rock. [26] And every one who hears these words of mine and does not do them will be like a foolish man who built his house upon the sand; [27] and the rain fell, and the floods came, and the winds blew and beat against that house, and it fell; and great was the fall of it."

[28] And when Jesus

ὁμοιωθήσεται ἀνδρὶ μωρῷ, ὅστις ᾠκοδόμησεν αὐτοῦ τὴν οἰκίαν ἐπὶ τὴν ἄμμον· **Matt. 7:27** καὶ κατέβη ἡ βροχὴ καὶ ἦλθον οἱ ποταμοὶ καὶ ἔπνευσαν οἱ ἄνεμοι καὶ προσέκοψαν τῇ οἰκίᾳ ἐκείνῃ, καὶ ἔπεσεν καὶ ἦν ἡ πτῶσις αὐτῆς μεγάλη. **Matt. 7:28** ¶ Καὶ ἐγένετο ὅτε ἐτέλεσεν ὁ Ἰησοῦς τοὺς λόγους τούτους, ἐξεπλήσσοντο οἱ ὄχλοι ἐπὶ τῇ διδαχῇ αὐτοῦ· **Matt. 7:29** ἦν γὰρ διδάσκων αὐτοὺς ὡς ἐξουσίαν ἔχων καὶ οὐχ ὡς οἱ γραμματεῖς αὐτῶν. **Matt. 8:1** ¶ Καταβάντος δὲ αὐτοῦ ἀπὸ τοῦ ὄρους ἠκολούθησαν αὐτῷ ὄχλοι πολλοί.	came, and the winds blew and slammed against that house; and *yet* it did not fall, for it had been founded on the rock. ²⁶ And everyone who hears these words of Mine, and does not [ag]act on them, will be like a foolish man who built his house on the sand. ²⁷ And the rain fell and the [ah]floods came, and the winds blew and slammed against that house; and it fell—and its collapse was great." ²⁸ [ai]When Jesus had finished these words, the crowds were amazed at His teaching; ²⁹ for He was teaching them as one who had authority, and not as their scribes. **Jesus Cleanses a Man with Leprosy** **8** When [aj]Jesus came down from the mountain, [ak]large crowds followed Him.	finished these sayings, the crowds were astonished at his teaching, ²⁹ for he taught them as one who had authority, and not as their scribes. **Jesus Cleanses a Leper** **8** When he came down from the mountain, great crowds followed him;

In the same way that Chapters 5-6 cover how to "fish" for new disciples, Chapter 7 shows how not to "fish" by offering our pearls of wisdom uninvited. Offering uninvited wisdom often appears to be the method of choice of many modern evangelism programs. It would be interesting to discuss how outreach programs might be developed around an approach more closely aligned to what Matthew claims Jesus teaches here. This section also describes the work of "false fisherman" or "false prophets" and how many including those naming and serving the name of Jesus will miss out on the Kingdom of Heaven because they have not experienced the kind of forgiveness and restoration that is as complete as that which Jesus is advocating in Chapters 5-6. "On that day, many will say to me, 'Lord, Lord, did we not prophesy in your name, and cast out demons in your name, and do many mighty works in your name?' And then I will declare to them, depart from me you evil doers" (Matthew 5:23). The implication is that there will be many who use the name of Jesus and work in his name but reject his concept of forgiveness and for that reason are not really connected like they think they are.

An interpretive option for Matthew 7:24-27: It appears that the end of Chapter 7 shows that those who build on the rock through a purified heart of forgiveness will survive the onslaught of one's own self judgment while those who build their house on a flimsy foundation of the sand of their self-righteousness will find their own self-judgement beating against their house and destroying it.

The crowds at the end of the teaching in Matthew 7:28-8:1: "And when Jesus finished these sayings, the crowds were astonished at his teaching, for he taught them as one who had authority, and not as their scribes. When he came down from the mountain, great crowds followed him." According to this section, the audience is identified as it was in the beginning of Matthew 5:1-2 as the "crowds" and described as those who were fully engaged until the end at not merely those who overheard what was meant only for the disciples. The messages built from the beginning of the blessings through the Lord's Prayer and up until the warning of final judgement were crafted and presented to the crowds with the disciples paying close attention.

Conclusion of the Lord's Prayers and the 3 Conflict Prayers

Conclusion of the Lord's Prayer, Good news invitation ending in bad news? —The way we forgive and reconcile is indicative of how the Father will forgive and welcome us into his Kingdom: Matthew 6:14-15 is the end of the Lord's Prayer section showing that we will be forgiven in the same way that we forgive and that the way we practice forgiveness is indicative of the type of forgiveness we have embraced. It almost sounds like "a downer" since it ends on an ominous note. It could have reversed the order and said if you fail to forgive you will not be forgiven but if you do forgive you will be forgiven. But this ends with the negative scenario causing the listener to consider the bottom line. It ends with a challenge just like the challenge to bear good fruit was followed by the warning about bearing evil fruit (7:17), those let into the kingdom of heaven (7:21) were followed by those rejected (7:23) and the house built on the rock was followed by the one built on the sand (7:24-27). This is not only a tactical placement of a warning at the end of these couplets, but it also reflects what current brain science shows that people show greater concern for negative things that impact them as much as five times more than positive things. his is known as the "negativity bias."[82] This bad news challenge compels us to consider the good news we may be missing.

The Three Conflict Prayers of Matthew: The Lord's Prayer of 6:9-15 is echoed in the "ask, seek, and knock" section of Matthew 7:7-12 that also ends in a similar fashion in verse 12 when it says that the way you want to be treated by others, you should treat them. (Notice the order of the phrase is reversed in the Greek from other expressions of the command to love others as ourselves since this use starts with the felt need of the listener. Note also how this is placed in Chapter 7 which shows how not to make disciples, namely not providing answers uninvited, making the "ask, seek, knock" prayer a request to not give up on the approach given in the Lord's Prayer in Chapter 6.)

In the first two teachings about prayer of Matthew 6 and 7, the one praying may not even be on speaking terms with

---

82   See the article online from *Psychology Today*: https://www.psychologytoday.com/us/articles/200306/our-brains-negative-bias. See also the bibliography section that includes work on recent brain studies and memory showing the importance of emotion on memorization and the role of trauma in remembering and forgetting.

the persecutor and the forgiveness happens before the persecutor even repents if ever. The teaching on prayer in Matthew 18:18-20 is also presented in the context of conflict but somewhat differently. It is the only conflict prayer where all parties reconcile in the prayer itself. It refers to those who are confronting each other over an offense that they resolve. Hence, when those "two or three" in a conflict with each other subsequently reconcile (18:19) and as a result gather in Jesus' name," anything they ask, it will be done for them by my Father in heaven". Jesus is amid those reconciled in a special way. Like the case in 5:23-26 where the person being brought to court is encouraged to negotiate their way out of the lawsuit before arriving to court when it might be too late, so, in Matthew 18:15-17 the one who is offended is required to take all of the steps required to reconcile with the offender including going first alone, then with one or two witnesses, and failing that the group.

Perhaps, in the first meeting, each side could listen to the other so well that they could take turns telling what the other person is concerned about in their own words so that each party can have confidence that they are heard and understood.[83] At that point, the parties in conflict might discover that they have misunderstood each other, or that their differences could easily be resolved. If not, it might take a second or third attempt to fully reconcile and restore the relationship. But, if one refused to reconcile after all those attempts, as in Matthew 18:17, "let him be to you as a Gentile and a tax collector." In other words, after several attempts at reconciliation, the person refusing to reconcile could be left to go their own way either because they are like Gentiles without a worldview of a reconciling God, or a tax-collector who has that world view but refuses to live by it. This challenges us to consider whether we have fully forgiven if we have not gone through this process to re-establish the relationship. Can we maintain the relationship or agree to part in love and peace? When do we know we did all we could on our end? When we feel tired and hurt so much that we don't want to do more? Or when we go through and complete an objective process? What objective test can we give ourselves to help us understand whether we have fully forgiven or not?

That discussion of reconciliation is followed by the story of one who failed to forgive someone who owed him money. It is a parable about forgiveness that reflects on the prayer for persecutors in Matthew 6:5-15. The servant's failure to forgive was indicative of how he failed to apprehend a prior offer of forgiveness. In the same vein, Jesus says in Matthew 18:35, "So also my heavenly Father will do to every one of you, if you do not forgive your brother from your heart." The warning to the readers or listeners of this message is stark since the extent to which we forgive and reconcile is indicative of our being forgiven or reconciled by the Father. (18:35). Or, in the words of Matthew 7 when Jesus says, "the bad tree bears evil fruit" (7:17) and many of those who identified with Jesus and worked in his name are the very ones who are told, "I never knew you, depart from me you evil doers" (7:23). If we are the ones who tell those who offend us to depart from us, might that be indicative of our relationship with the Father who will have no choice but to tell us "depart from me"? Our willingness to reconcile gives us a chance to revisit how we accepted the love and reconciliation of the Father. Did we accept his forgiveness based as a complete gift? Did we wish to be accepted into his kingdom or left alone on the outside? Does that reflect how we would like others to forgive and reconcile with us? Does that reflect on how we forgive and restore the relationships of the significant people in our lives? If it does not, does that give us an opportunity to either revisit our acceptance of the forgiveness of the Father or application of it to others? What is at stake is not only our practice of forgiveness and reconciliation but our entry to the kingdom of heaven since our willingness to reconcile is indicative of the forgiveness we do or do not have. It also may impact how we may help others enter the kingdom or block others from entering.

Are we In or Out? This material guides us using the Lord's Prayer as a tool to reconsider and resolve our own anger and enable us to reconcile rather than continue estrangement. This helps us validate our own connection with the concept of reconciliation and our own fruit that shows us what tree we are from. Will we be satisfied if the Father fails to forgive us in the same way we fail to forgive others? Will we be satisfied if the Father refrains from welcoming us

---

83 Many family and relationship counseling styles, and mediation methods encourage an approach to listening and then repeating back to each other until all parties are convinced that they are heard. For examples, see "Imago Relationship Therapy" developed by Harville Hendrix and Helen Hunt in 1980 at (https://www.psychologytoday.com/us/therapy-types/imago-relationship-therapy), practitioners of the "four attachment" theories of relationships (https://en.wikipedia.org/wiki/Attachment_theory), or Virginia Satir on "The New Peoplemaking."

and says "depart from me" as we fail to welcome and reconcile with others? The Father could just say, "I am not upset with you anymore, but I don't want to be around you, you are not welcomed into my kingdom." Does the phrase, "forgive us as we forgive" cause us to have any concern if how we forgive is indicative of how we are forgiven? Are we from the tree that yields the fruit of forgiveness and reconciliation or the tree that maintains distance and estrangement? Perhaps, we would prefer to be replanted or grafted on to a "sound tree bearing good fruit" that naturally results in forgiveness and reconciliation. So, the question comes back to whether we are in or are we out. Are we all in for releasing others of their debts and strive for reconciliation because it reflects the forgiveness we received? Or are we out either because we don't believe that there is an infinite God who forgave us just that way, or if we hope God does, we are still not motivated to accept that it is our consequential job to do the same as a result? Are we in the kingdom or out? Are we all in for making others reconciling peace-making disciples or are we out?

The Lord's Prayer as the Ultimate Conflict Resolution and Disciple Making Tool: These questions in turn are the same questions we get to share with others who face their most harsh disappointments and heartbreak. In effect, this section served as a persuasive recruiting or disciple-making program intended for the early Jewish Christian community to use as they were sent or scattered throughout the world.[84] Will they be able to walk through the process of having their peace restored to the extent that they will become new peacemakers? Will they be the ones who give water to the very people who made them thirsty? Or will they harbor bitterness and anger to the hurt of others and the destruction of themselves? The Lord's Prayer for persecutors makes it possible for each of us to walk through that process and then subsequently enable those in the crowds, those not yet disciples, those not yet ready to reconcile, to consider the love, forgiveness and the reconciliation of the Father who wants to welcome them into his kingdom and share it with them. All of this can happen because the Lord's Prayer for the worst-case enemies in the worst-case times, and all the lesser cases, was provided for all of us.

For discussion:

1) How central or important is the concept of conflict, forgiveness, and restoration in these passages of Matthew 5-7 and 18?

2) What differences might there be in seeing how we forgive others as either causative or indicative of our own forgiveness and entry into the kingdom of heaven?

3) What do these passages suggest are the objective criteria used to discover whether we fully forgive someone?

4) What implications are there for attempting reconciliation have for the concept of feedback loops in communications that might avert conflict in the first place or resolve it in the second place?

5) What might be examples and ramifications of forgiving partially and not fully?

6) How might the concept of "forgive us AS we forgive" illustrate these ramifications and a working definition of "forgive?"

7) When might there be reason to forgive and attempt restoration but hold back actually restoring a connection when it is not safe to do so?

8) How might the "ask, seek, knock" prayer in Matthew 7 be used to reflect the Lord's Prayer in Chapter 6 and especially in the section on how not to make disciples?

---

84 See the genre section of the essay by Manto, "Overview of the Interpretive Methods and Genre Analysis of Matthew" following the bibliography where instruction was given to disciples as to how to recruit new disciples while Jesus was actually recruiting them as he spoke to the crowds.

Section 2: Commentary

9) What might examples of full or partial forgiveness look like in the circumstances of those in this discussion group, those we know or examples from history?

10) How might a parable of the half-forgiving servant be relevant or not in various conflict scenarios? See the outline of a potential alternative parable for an example.

Unforgiving Servant and Half-forgiving Servant Examples:

Matt 18:23-35

Unforgiving Servant

Problem 1: (v. 23-25a) Servant (an upper-level servant) owed 10,000 talents to king but could not pay.

Resolution Part 1: (v. 25b) Captured servant required to make partial recovery was ordered to be sold into slavery along with his wife and children in addition giving all his possessions (likely ten cents on the dollar recovery).

Resolution Part 2: (v. 26) Servant implores for patience; (v. 27) king forgives releasing servant's debt (and keeps servant in his job).

Problem 2: (v. 28) Upper-level servant came upon a fellow lower-level servant who owed him 100 denarii (one talent) who could not pay. Upper-level servant seized fellow lower-level servant by the throat and demands payment.

Resolution part 1: (v. 29) Lower-level fellow servant implores for patience.

Resolution part 2: (v. 30) Upper-level servant refuses and places lower-level fellow servant in prison.

Problem 3: (v. 31) Other fellow servants hearing of imprisonment were distressed and told the king.

Resolution 1: (v. 32) King summons upper-level servant and declares: "You wicked servant! I forgave you all that debt because you besought me; (v. 33) and should not you have mercy on your fellow servant, as I had mercy on you?" (v. 34). And in anger his lord delivered him to the jailers, "til he pays all his debt."

Jesus' declaration: (v.35) "So also, my heavenly Father will do to every one of you, if you do not forgive your brother from your heart."

Half-forgiving Servant: Servant who owed the 10,000 talents is in upper management who has other lower-level servants reporting to him (such as a subservient fellow servant), whom he can hire and fire. Subservient fellow servant owed his servant upper-level boss 100 denarii (1 talent). Upper-level boss servant grabs subservient lower-level servant and demands payment.

Resolution part 1: Subservient fellow servant implores for patience. Servant boss releases subservient servant from the debt of 1 talent and does not collect the debt but fires the subservient servant from his job and bans him from the premises to manage on his own.

Resolution part 2: Other fellow servants hearing of firing were distressed and told the king.

Resolution part 3: King summons fellow servant and declares: "'You wicked servant! I forgave you all that debt and did not fire you because you besought me; and should not you have mercy on your fellow servant, as I had mercy on you?' The king did not collect any of the debt but in anger his lord fired the upper-level management servant and banned him from the official kingdom premises to continue on his own."

Jesus' declaration: "So also, my heavenly Father will do to every one of you, if you do not forgive your brother from your heart."

For discussion:

1) Does the release of the debt constitute half forgiveness when he still fires the servant and does not want his presence on the job?

2) Given reconciliation discussions in Matthew 5 and 18, what objective criteria might be used to establish due-process, and restoration of the relationship?

3) How would thorough conversations using that objective criteria make it possible maintain a relationship in the first place and avoid breaking it?

4) What would Jesus say to us who half-forgives by releasing obligations but keeps us the other at a distance? Would he say, "depart from me?"

5) From the passages here, why or why not?

6) In what ways might the beatitude pairs leading to peacemaking be used as an evangelism or disciple-making method?

7) In what ways might the Lord's Prayer for persecutors be used as an evangelism or disciple-making method?

8) What are the steps or stages of each of these and how might they be used to provide a pathway to that shift to peace, forgiveness, entry to the kingdom of heaven and the encouragement to do the same for others?

9) How might these approaches to disciple-making be successful in an otherwise hostile environment and even with a hostile audience?

10) How might the prayer for the worst-case enemies, the persecutors, work in the worst of times in Matthew 24?

11) How might these methods be empowering as the disciples find themselves dispersed among the nations as in Matthew 28:16-20 even as some wavered in confidence?

12) What other questions come to mind that might be added to the discussion?

Section 2: Commentary

Ancient Use of Columns and Rows

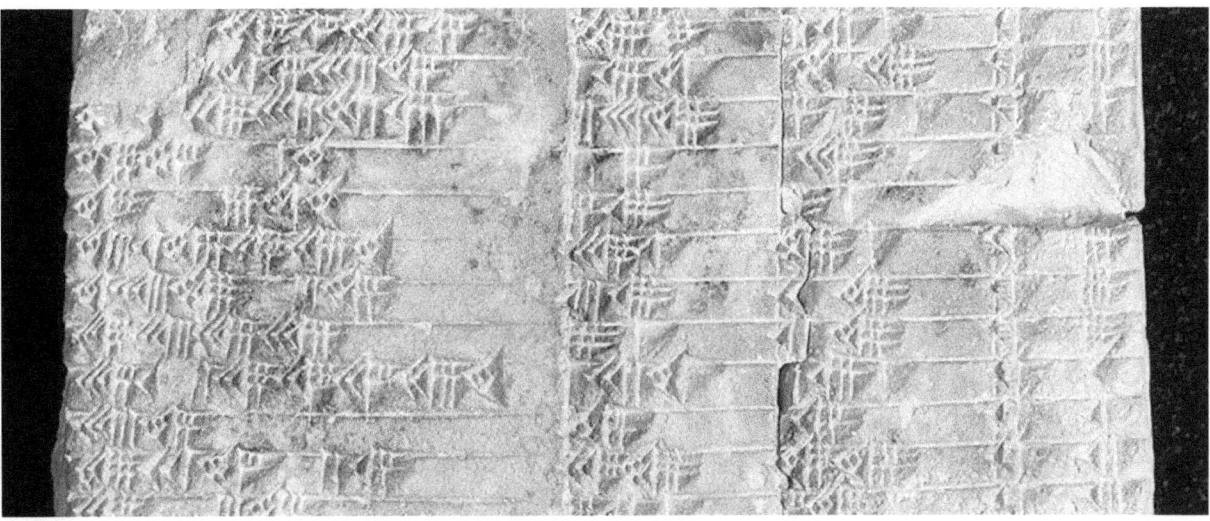

Photo © University of New South Wales, used with permission. Article © by ScienceAlert used with permission. https://www.sciencealert.com/scientists-just-solved-a-maths-problem-on-this-3-700-year-old-clay-tablet

This 3,700-Year-Old Babylonian Clay Tablet Just Changed the History of Maths

DAVID NIELD

24 AUGUST 2017

A Babylonian clay tablet dating back 3,700 years has been identified as the world's oldest and most accurate trigonometric table, suggesting the Babylonians beat the ancient Greeks to the invention of trigonometry by over 1,000 years.

The tablet, known as Plimpton 322, was discovered in the early 1900s in what is now southern Iraq, but researchers have always been baffled about what its purpose was.

Thanks to a team from the University of New South Wales (UNSW) in Australia, the mystery may have been solved. More than that, the Babylonian method of calculating trigonometric values could have something to teach mathematicians today.

Overview of Interpretive Methods and Genre Analysis of Matthew

Overview of Interpretive Methods: Trying to understand what an author of an older text meant and then trying to see its significance for both the author and the reader has been written about for millennia. To get an overview of the vastness of such a simple concept, some articles that might be helpful for someone new at this quest can be conveniently found in the Anchor Bible Dictionary. The first two are found under the topic, "Interpretation, the History of" by J.H. Rogerson (pp. 424-433) and Werner G. Jeanrond (pp. 433-443); a third on "Hermeneutics" by Bernard Lategan (pp. 149-155) and a fourth on "Rhetoric and Rhetorical Criticism" by Benjamin Fiore (pp. 710-719). An article demonstrating some of the interactions between those with different views of hermeneutics and rhetoric can be found in the article by Vernon Robbins in the book, *Rhetorics and Hermeneutics*.[85] The following proponents show how these various approaches continue to be used across various religious and scholarly traditions.

Historical-Critical Method: The goal of such an approach would be similar to what was simply said by Joseph A. Fitzmyer, S.J., a renowned Catholic biblical scholar, in his 2008 book, *The Interpretation of Scripture*,[86] "to determine the meaning of the text as it was intended and expressed by the human author moved long ago to compose it." (Such a goal can be seen in extant Greek writings from the 4th century BC and various writers within ancient Jewish scriptures.) He continued by describing the goal of exegeting or drawing out the intended meaning of a text "to include not only the textual meaning (the sense of its words or phrases), but, also its contextual meaning (their sense in a given paragraph or episode), and its relational meaning (their sense in relation to the book or corpus of writings as a whole). The relational meaning is called at times its biblical-theological meaning, because it seeks to interpret the words and phrases according to the synthesis of ideas of the biblical reader."[87] He describes this as a combination of historical and literary methods named the "historical-critical" method that includes works discussing "literary," "form," "source," and "redaction criticism."[88] The historical-critical approach to get to that meaning has been viewed at times by other modern scholars as essential but incomplete since it has paid insufficient attention to other available tools of interpretation.

These historical and literary methods appropriately care for the text by emphasizing the need to carefully read and draw out what is there (exegesis) as opposed to hastily reading into the text definitions or ideas from outside the text (eisegesis). This is especially critical for the analysis and exegesis of the Lord's Prayer in Matthew since our own experience of the Lord's Prayer in our own worship experience and devotional treatments of it create a sense of what is obvious or generally accepted. These deeply held and useful understandings of the prayer in our own contexts in the world in front of the text may blind us and prevent us from taking a closer look at what we thought was obvious in the world within the text. Why bother taking the time to examine what is obvious? The obvious that we brush over lightly may provide contextual clues to the most important elements that are hiding in plain sight. When we can examine words and the intent of the prayer by what is explicit in the context as opposed to assuming what they mean, we might find clues that can help us remove the layers of the veneer of our experience so we can restore and experience the author's prayer as opposed to the obscured copy we have been glancing at.

Literary-Historical-Sociological Method: Others such as Stephen A. Barton have suggested that it is possible to go even further than the exegetical examination of the text by giving detailed attention to the social context of the world within and behind the text which was written and ultimately read or recited aloud to listeners.[89] By that expansion, a

---

85 Hester, John D., Hester, David J, editors: *Rhetorics and Hermeneutics*, Emory University, T&T Clark, Atlanta, © 2004. This collection of essays discusses the nature of rhetoric and hermeneutics and their relationship over time as the terms have been interpreted and changed over time. See article by Robbins on pp. 105-125; "Where is Wuellner's Anti-Hermeneutical Hermeneutic Taking Us?"

86 Fitzmyer, Joseph A.; *The Interpretation of Scripture*, Paulist Press, 2008. P. 66. Note that he was roughly 88 years old at the time of its publication.

87 Ibid., pp. 68-69.

88 Ibid., pp. 64-65.

89 This dual nature of written scripture has been noticed by others. For an example, see Alter, Robert; *The Art of Biblical Narrative*, Basic

broader approach would be "a literary-historical-sociological analysis."[90] This is helpful even for the world within the text since those other insights from sociological perspectives might help define the words used and their contexts within and behind the texts. In Matthew, it can be especially helpful to see the role of Matthew's writing as a Hellenistic Jew and his audience affected for decades after its writing by the destruction of Jerusalem in A.D. 70-72.

Rhetorical Criticism: An array of additional perspectives under the rubric of "rhetorical criticism" are described by C. Clifton Black in his essay, "Rhetorical Criticism" bundled by Green in the same collection of essays as Barton's.[91] As others, he shows some regrets of the word choice of "rhetoric" because of the way modern use has rendered the word using the *Random House Dictionary of the English Language* by way of example: "the undue use of exaggeration or display, bombast.[92] He also shows concern that "rhetorical criticism," like the term "literary criticism," has been used to mean too many things resulting in some confusion. But he fully appreciates the classical use of it for oral and written composition and discourse with a goal towards persuasion and provides a historical overview of the spread of Greek rhetoric from the time of Alexander the Great and its Latin counterparts of the Roman empire through a revitalization of interest in recent biblical scholarship. He notes its influence on Hellenized Jewish teachers such as Caecilius (late first century B.C.E.) and the early church fathers. Black sees how Jesus and his disciples would have been steeped in a culture shaped by use of classical and Jewish rhetoric.[93] In current usage, he expresses optimism for work that Burton Mack and Dr. Vernon K. Robbins[94] have done on the influence of "*chreiai*, didactic anecdotes" and "elaboration (the complete argument)" in the formal handbooks of rhetoric for advanced practitioners known as the *technai* from the 4th century B.C.E. (such as Aristotle's *Rhetoric*) and for beginners in programs such as *progymnasmata* well established by the first century B.C.E. and C.E. by those such as Theon.[95] See their pertinent work, *Patterns of Persuasion* in the Gospels, particularly, "*Chreia* and Pronouncement Story in Synoptic Studies" by Robbins.[96]

These perceptions are especially helpful in Matthew as it is written by a Hellenistic Jew who not only was aware of all these persuasion techniques, but can be shown, as I hope to begin to demonstrate in this writing, to use them profusely throughout the entire Gospel as if it were a handbook for disciples being taught how to recruit and train new disciples.

Socio-Rhetorical Interpretation and "the New Rhetoric": The work of Vernon Robbins[97] here is especially helpful when considering the full range of persuasion elements woven throughout the Sermon on the Mount that I will outline in the background, context and driver sections that follow[98] and in greater detail in the specific texts. Robbins

---

Books © 1981. See p. 90 concerning the oral purpose and use of written scriptures in his Chapter on repetition.

90 Barton, Stephan A.; "Historical Criticism and Social-Scientific Perspectives in New Testament Study," an essay in *Hearing the New Testament, Strategies for Interpretation*; 2d Edition, by Green, Joel B., Eerdmans, Grand Rapids, 2010, pp. 40-41. He discusses the "world behind the text (the world of the author), the world within the text (the narrated world of the characters, intentions and events), and the world in front of the text (the world of the reader).

91 Ibid., pp. 166-168.

92 Ibid., p. 166.

93 Ibid., pp. 166-167.

94 Ibid., p. 173. See quotes of George Kennedy and others citing the *Progymnasmata* of Theon and others.

95 See also original works of George Kennedy including his translation of *Progymnasmata* and the Greek text presented by Lederlini, et al. cited in the bibliography.

96 Mack, Burton; Robbins, Vernon K.; *Patterns of Persuasion in the Gospels* (Sonoma, CA: Polebridge Press, 1989; Wipf & Stock, 2008), 1989; 2008. See Robbins on elaboration on pp. 5, 8, 20, 20-24, 27, and "Chreia and Pronouncement Story in Synoptic Studies" on pp. 1-30; See Mack on "elaboration (the complete argument)" on his Chapter on "Elaboration of the Chreia in the Hellenistic School" (pp. 31-68) and the section pp. 51-67. Note the distinction of the "technai" handbooks for more advanced "teachers, rhetors, and other theoreticians advanced in their professions" from the 4th century B.C.E. such as the "Rhetoric" of Aristotle and the handbooks for beginners from the 1st century BCE named the *progymnasmata* on p. 33. See also, Parsons and Martin on "Ecomium, Crafting Words of Praise and Critique," pp. 175-230 of Ancient Rhetoric and the New Testament.

97 Robbins, Vernon K.; New Boundaries in Old Territories, Peter Lang Publishing, NY, 1994. See Chapter 7, "Jesus' Blessing of the Children," especially pp. 155-161 describing the range of rhetorical methods and the way they were taught.

98 I believe that the full range of memory devices (mnemonics) and other rhetorical elements in the sense of persuasion provide evidence that the Sermon on the Mount in Matthew 5-7 was a formal set of persuasion or disciple-making lessons just as Jesus promised the fisher-

has gone on to create what appears to be an even broader approach than Barton's "literary-historical-sociological" of interpretation by adding "rhetorical insights" resulting in his "socio-rhetorical interpretation" (SRI) method[99] used by the group within the Society of Biblical Literature (SBL), The Rhetoric of Religious Antiquity (RRA).[100] Participants of the RRA are producing a series of commentaries using this method.

Performance Criticism: The SRI method could be further enhanced by the rhetorical insights provided by those who try to memorize and perform the material for oral presentation and have come up with the concept of "performance criticism". See the work of many led by Tom Boomershine at the Network of Biblical Storytellers[101] and the group at SBL, The Bible in Ancient and Modern Media[102], who have produced a series of books published by Cascade in "Biblical Performance Criticism"[103] and are beginning to create commentaries using "performance criticism" insights.

Their experience of memorizing the texts so that they might recite or perform them before an audience provides more thorough opportunities to consider the nature of these written texts expected to be read to audiences, and in many cases, memorized and recited from memory. My own difficulties in trying to memorize this material in either English or Greek were so overwhelming, that I had to give up and do pattern recognition on the texts to see if any memorization aids might emerge. I was surprised by what I found and continue to be surprised by asking questions of the texts that I see so that I might discover how they were heard and whether word selection or their sequencing were purposeful. These experiences from attempting to memorize and perform the material are very helpful and can enhance efforts in rhetorical analysis. This turns out to be especially helpful in Matthew and the interpretation of the material that was intended for the "crowds" *listening* to Jesus.

Black continued to express appreciation for those he includes as representatives of the "New Rhetoric" who see rhetoric through its goals to persuade, motivate and influence people to 'act right' showing a "practical and social thrust." He highlighted the work of Wilhelm Wuellner who sees this type of rhetoric as a 'practical exercise of power.' Black ended his essay with a challenge to all those practicing "rhetorical criticism" of any type to not miss the point of the text of the passage and not get hung up on the methods.[104]

Genre Analysis: Literary and classical rhetorical interests can also broaden the range of approaches when viewed through a concept of "genre analysis," described in another essay in Green's volume by James L. Bailey. He described genre as "conventional and repeatable patterns of oral and written speech that facilitate interaction among people in specific social situations."[105] He then continued to describe over forty examples of genre that include "prayer, praise, blessing, diatribe, vice and virtue lists, chiasm, biography, history, parable, and call story."[106] All of these appear in Matthew and the Sermon on the Mount. The question is how these fit together, and whether any one or two form organizing structures that help us better understand the texts. Those who look at the text from this perspective are especially helpful when seeing Matthew even if it is to get a sense of what the commentators conclusions were and

---

    men near the end of Matthew 4.

99   Robbins, Vernon K.; *Exploring the Texture of Texts, A Guide to Socio-Rhetorical Interpretation*; Trinity Press, Harrisburg, PA and Bloomsbury Academic Press, NY & London, 1996. See a somewhat formal approach by looking at five "textures": Inner, Intertexture, Social and Cultural, Ideological and Sacred.

100   See the SBL RRA site: https://www.sbl-site.org/publications/books_RhetoricReligiousAntiquity.aspx

101   NBS is a group founded by Tom Boomershine. It holds an annual conference and a two-day by-invitation-only Scholars Forum immediately prior to the conference. See their website: https://www.nbsint.org.

102   See the SBL BAMM site: https://www.sbl-site.org/meetings/Congresses_CallForPaperDetails.aspx?MeetingId=12&VolunteerUnitId=56 and here: https://www.biblicalperformancecriticism.org/index.php/54-news/announcements/sbl-2015-atlanta/325-s21-209-bible-in-ancient-and-modern-media

103   Hearon, Holly and Ruge-Jones, Philip; *The Bible in Ancient and Modern Media, Story and Performance, Biblical Performance Criticism, Volume 1*; Cascade Books, Eugene, OR, 2009.

104   Black, pp. 176, 186.

105   Op. Cit., p. 143.

106   Ibid., pp. 150-151.

how those influence their decisions about the world within the text.

Gospel Genre: Ulrich Luz described the question of genre of the Gospel of Matthew in his 2007 commentary, *Matthew*,[107] as lacking consensus but covers five: 1) Gospels (which he endorses as an original genre form), 2) sayings or remembrances, 3) lectionary or catechism (with its problem of not accounting for 'narrative'), 4) biography[108] or 5) kerygmatic history (such as Chronicles) which he views preferable over biography but imprecise because it does not account for its theological presentations.[109] He sees many of these elements but organizes them under the concept of biography. Specific elements such as the Lord's Prayer also have multiple functions. Luz views the Matthean version of the Lord's Prayer as a "multifunctional text," "useful as a model prayer, as a dogmatic compendium, as a catechetical synthesis, as a private and ecclesiastical prayer, and so on."[110] This is covered in his introduction section, he considers it as "grounded in the worship of his community" and "Matthew's redactional language ... grounded in worship."[111] He, similar to Betz and others, sees it also as a basic "ethical text."

Disciple Teaching Genre: Hans Dieter Betz recognizes the genre categories used to describe the Sermon on the Mount including sayings, pronouncements, compendium, speech, teaching, (especially ethical teaching), summary, rules, training, catechism-like, and epitome (proposed by Betz). He views the Sermon on the Mount (SM) as "*epitomai*, consisting of sayings of Jesus grouped together according to systematic points of doctrine considered to be of primary importance."[112] The literary function of the SM, according to Betz, was the "'advanced' teaching for those who have already become disciples ... the personal instruction not only of the four disciples addressed, but of all disciples." Note his explanation to the "seeming inconsistency" of the inclusion of the "crowds."

> "While according to the beginning in 5:1, only the disciples received the SM, 7:28-29 reports that somehow 'the crowds' (οἱ ὄχλοι) came to know it, too. Rather than an oversight on the part of Matthew, the seeming inconsistency shows 'progress'; Matthew seems to have been aware that the SM was originally intended for the disciples only, but that it had become public knowledge.... Indeed, for Matthew 'the crowds' (οἱ ὄχλοι) are the pool from which new church members are to be recruited. That the 'crowds' also receive the SM (7:28-29) shows how this change took place and that the SM played an important role in attracting people to the church. The SM has played this role during the entire history of the church up to the present."[113]

---

107 Luz, Ulrich; *Matthew*, Fortress Press, 2007. This is a 3-volume commentary, volume I covers Chapters 1-7. He includes a history of interpretation of each section and will sometimes show how an author's theological bias might influence the interpretation of a section of text. He also restricts the context of the Lord's Prayer to Chapter 6 when he discusses the use of "*our* Father" on p. 316 to "'Our' connects the praying individual with the community; that is also the custom in Jewish prayers." See p. 13-15 in the first volume covering Matthew 1-7.

108 Luz opposes the label "biography" due to lack of ancient examples and too few criteria while those such as Keener use the "biography" framework similarly to the way Luz approaches the Gospel genre. See: Keener, Craig S.; Wright, Edward T.; *Biographies and Jesus, What Does It Mean for the Gospels to be Biographies?* Emeth Press, Lexington, KY, 2016. See, also, the work of R Bauckham, who without having to argue about the genre of biography discusses the rhetorical significance of eyewitness testimony and its reliability: Richard Bauckham, *Jesus and the Eyewitnesses, The Gospels as Eyewitness Testimony*, 2d Edition, Eerdmans, Grand Rapids, MI 2006, 2017. "...Oral transmission is quite capable of preserving traditions faithfully, even across much longer periods than that between Jesus and the writing of the Gospels, and we shall see reason to support those scholars who see the early Christian transmission of Jesus traditions as a relatively conservative process. Other scholars, however, working with the dictum that the Jesus traditions are in the first place evidence about the Christian communities that transmitted them, conclude that they tell us much more about those communities than about Jesus" (p. 240). "...The three main models of oral interpretation ... used to understand the transmission of Gospel tradition in the early church. They are associated with the names Rudolph Bultmann, Birger Gerhardsson, and Kenneth Bailey." (p. 241).

109 Luz, p. 14.

110 Luz, p. 313, column 2.

111 Luz; p. 43.

112 Betz, Hans Dieter; *The Sermon on the Mount*; Fortress Press, Minneapolis; 1995. See pp. 70-81.

113 Ibid. p. 81.

Note while saying that it had a role in "attracting people to the church" it was not expected that it provided instructions or step-by-step methods to do so.

Disciple-making (recruitment, persuasion, rhetoric, teaching) genre: I would propose to build on the approach of Betz on genre by seeing the material as useful in teaching disciples, but by actually teaching the disciples "how to make new disciples" by addressing the crowds and showing them how with a live audience. By seeing all the persuasion elements of the SM, including the methods of persuasion contained with the pairings of the beatitudes and the similar progression within the Lord's Prayer, this reverses the purpose of the SM and the Lord's Prayer in the following way. Instead of being primarily focused on those already disciples and somehow later figuring out how the crowds fit in, I would propose that the primary intent was for the material to be provided to the crowds as Jesus' persuasive engagement to make new disciples from the crowd[114] in such a way that the disciples having a front row seat could see how new disciple making is done as stated in Matthew 4:19 and 5:1-2. In other words, the SM was not merely instructions for those already chosen to be disciples, but interactions directly aimed at the crowds as lessons for the disciples in how to recruit or persuade others to become disciples. In that way, Jesus projects purposely to the crowds with the disciples watching and listening intently, as opposed to Jesus speaking to a few people in front of him with the crowds happening to eavesdrop on some of his comments.

By seeing the purpose of the SM and the Lord's Prayer as material designed to be used with the "crowds" so that they may become disciples, this material functions as a collection of multiple genres) all organized for the purpose of persuasion as if it were a formal disciple-making training program for the disciples. (Perhaps, this serves as a primary, coordinating, or uber-genre.) It not only states the teaching of Jesus, not only proposes what the mission of the disciples would be but shows HOW to make disciples. This approach of seeing the SM and the Lord's Prayer as real-time disciple making lessons, requires a new set of disciplined questions for those reading the Lord's Prayer and the entire SM, namely, how does the material engage and relate to the primary audience, the crowds. This approach would solve the "tension" and apparent contradictions that Luz[115] and Betz[116] see while finding the purpose of the Lord's Prayer that both Betz[117] and Luz[118] admit difficulty in finding. All of these issues combined also provide opportunity to see not only the intended audience and writing in its sociological and rhetorical context of persuasion, but, also in the psychological context of how the human brain, mind and body work in the areas of engagement and motivation and the ways anger and conflict management, persuasion, memorization, meditation and teaching work within the body. Current studies in brain science, trauma and memory can augment our understanding on ways the rhetorical patterns in Matthew's SM and Lord's Prayer function. In effect, Jesus in Matthew, the Sermon on the Mount, and its Lord's Prayer for persecutors, is shown to be a master of persuasion or disciple making by starting first with the perceived trauma of the listeners in the context of their own stories, then overlays data that allows them to progress to a place of peace and ultimately peace-making. At the end, the listeners become part of the Jesus story. Jesus most effectively communicates his story by first evoking their own. To open some of those doors, I will make occasional reference to

---

114 As Betz sees the Sermon on the Mount be used primarily to teach the disciples but used secondarily for the crowds as the "pools" from which they would be recruited by the church, then I would describe Matthew 5-7 as primarily being the "tools" that were designed to recruit from those crowds.

115 Luz, Ulrich; *Matthew*, Fortress Press, 2007. This is a 3-volume commentary, volume I covers Chapters 1-7. He includes a history of interpretation of each section and will sometimes show how an author's theological bias might influence the interpretation of a section of text. He also restricts the context of the Lord's Prayer to Chapter 6 when he discusses the use of "*our* Father" on p. 316 to "'Our' connects the praying individual with the community; that is also the custom in Jewish prayers."

116 Betz, p. 373. Note his comment that shows tension and inherent contradiction within the text: "It does agree with the prayer instruction 6:7-8, which presupposes that the Lord's Prayer was to be used as a 'private' prayer, but I have already pointed out that this context is secondary and in tension with the invocation of vs 9b ('Our Father'), which points to a group prayer."

117 Betz, Hans Dieter; *The Sermon on the Mount*, Fortress Press, 1995. This 730-page commentary is one of the most thorough and scholarly on the topic—well received by Review of Biblical Literature and Theology Today. See the section on p. 373 (column 2), "Original Purpose and Function" of the Lord's Prayer: "What did Jesus intend by the creation of this prayer? One can only speculate about this question because none of the sources is explicit about this." That might be true if the context of Chapter 5 was not already explicit about it when it asks to pray for those who persecute us. However, it may seem to be distant by a couple of paragraphs, but perhaps would be considered much closer when the memory methods of weaving interrelated concepts are considered.

118 Luz, p. 314, "The petitions of the Lord's Prayer are so short and open that seldom is one able to establish their meaning unambiguously."

relevant studies in these areas. To begin such a fully comprehensive approach, it will also be helpful to see the primary thrust of the background, context, and direction that the text is heading using every tool at our disposal to understand these texts and their explicit intentions.

Partially Annotated Bibliography for the Sermon on the Mount

The purpose of my own working annotated bibliography: I decided to make my own bibliography so that I can gather key publications, especially those that have their own bibliographies so that with them I would have a fairly comprehensive gathering of key works on the topic. One purpose behind annotating them is to make sure I can remember key portions for my own use and help others to find specific elements that might be of common interest in our mutual discussions. Lack of comments on this version of the bibliography is not a reflection of significance of a given work as much as it shows a lack of my own time devoted to writing in a work in progress. I continue to invite others to share works on the topic that I might include in the bibliography along with some of the reasons why those works are considered significant. In addition to work on the text itself, there is a lot to be gained from commentaries and scholarly studies on the topic and applications such as related theological, literary, pedagogical, rhetorical, psychological, rhetorical and sociological areas. Not all of these are cited in the resource book but are intended to provide a basis for future publications and studies of the author and readers.

Albright, W.F. and Mann, C. S.; *Matthew, The Anchor Yale Bible.* New Haven: Yale University Press, 2011 / New York: Doubleday, a division of Random House, 1971, © 1971by Yale University as assignee from Doubleday. Work makes use of Qumran material and Palestinian archaeology. It also has an excellent essay about the historical use of the word "hypocrite" as an actor. This also provides a fascinating preface describing how the original author dropped out at the last minute requiring the editor to add monographs such as the one on the use of "hypocrite" to fill in material that would otherwise be insufficient for publication (p. v.).

Aland, Barbara; Aland, Kurt; Karavidopoulos, Johannes; Martini, Carlo M.; and, Metzger, Bruce; editors; *The Greek New Testament, Fifth Revised Edition.* Stuttgart, Germany: Institute for New Testament Textual Research, Deutsche Bibelgesllschaft, American Bible Society, United Bible Societies, © 2014. See the helpful version for students with a "Running Greek-English Dictionary" compiled by Barclay M. Newman.

Aland, Barbara and Karavidopoulos; Johannes; Martini, Carolo; Metzger, Bruce M.; editors; *Novum Testamentum Graece et Latine, 28th edition.* Stuttgart, Germany: German Bible Society, Institute for New Testament Textual Research (Munster/Westphalia) under the direction of Holger Strutwolf; 2014. Greek Text *Novum Testamentum Graece* Based on the work of Eberhard and Erwin Nestle, This text with Greek on one side and Latin on the other makes it easier to trace textual and rhetorical differences as they pass from Greek to Latin. Note controversy over the use of some of the Vulgate translations that differ from those of Jerome described in places such as Wikipedia as follows: " *Houghton, H. A. G. (2016).* "Editions and Resources". *The Latin New Testament: A Guide to Its Early History, Texts, and Manuscripts.* Oxford University Press. p. 133. *ISBN 9780198744733.* There are approximately 2,000 differences between the *Nova Vulgata and* the critical text of Jerome's revision of the Gospels in the Stuttgart Vulgate, most of which are very minor. Following the appearance of the *Nova Vulgata,* Nestle's *Novum Testamentum Latine* was revised by Kurt and Barbara Aland: the Clementine text was replaced with the *Nova Vulgata* and an apparatus added showing differences from eleven other editions, including the Stuttgart, Oxford, Sixtine, *and* Clementine Vulgates; the first edition of 1984 was followed by a second edition in 1992. The *Nova Vulgata* is also the Latin text in the Alands' bilingual edition, *Novum Testamentum Graece et Latine."* See: https://en.wikipedia.org/wiki/Nova_Vulgata

Aland, Kurt, ed.; *Synopsis of the Four Gospels, Greek-English Edition of the Synopsis Quattuor Evangeliorum with the Text of the Revised Standard Version.* Stuttgart, West Germany: United Bible Societies, 1972. This is a very helpful side-by-side comparison of the four Gospels with Greek texts (with variants) on the left page and English on the right.

Alfeyev, Metropolitan Hilarion, *Jesus Christ: His Life and Teaching, in Six Volumes, Vol. 2 - The Sermon on the Mount.*: Yonkers, New York: St. Vladimir's Seminary Press, © 2019. This is the second volume of the six-volume series. It focuses entirely on the Sermon on the Mount, examining the Beatitudes and the Lord's Prayer. He advocates a coherent organization of Matthew 5-7 and does not conflate Matthew's Sermon on the Mount with Luke's Sermon on the Plain.

Allen, Garrick V.: "The Possibilities of a Gospel Codex GA 2064 (Dublin, CBL W139), Digital Editing, and Reading in a Manuscript Culture", in *The Journal of Biblical Literature*, Vol 140, No. 2021.

Allen, O. Wesley; UI, *Mark and Luke*, 2013. St. Louis: Chalice Press, 2013.

Allen, O. Wesley; *Reading the Synoptic Gospels, Basic Methods for Interpreting Matthew, Mark, and Luke*. St. Louis: Chalice Press, 2013.

Allison, Dale C.; *The Sermon on the Mount, Inspiring the Moral Imagination*; New York: Crossroad Publishing, 1999. This provides very engaging connections of the practical value of the passage and the issues that it has provoked over the 2000 years since it was first circulated. See his helpful comments on the need to include "the crowds" as part of the audience of the Matthew 5-7 on p. 9, "This along with 7:28-29, which informs us that Jesus was speaking not just to the disciples (5:1-2) but also to the crowds, means that any interpretation that thinks of the Sermon as addressed to a *corp d"lite*, as it were, must be mistaken." Yet, on p. 117 he does not appear to apply this audience to the Lord's Prayer. Though crowds needing to be "caught" are a key part of the audience, he concludes, "We have here a prayer for the church, for those who have become through Jesus brothers and sisters as children of God (cf. 5:45). He refers to 5:45 showing that the crowds might become children of God as if that somehow limits it to disciples when in fact it appears to do the opposite.

Alter, Robert; *The Art of Biblical Narrative*. New York: Basic Books © 1981. See p. 90 concerning the oral purpose and use of written scriptures in his chapter on repetition.

Aristotle; *The Rhetoric and Poetics*, (translated by Roberts and Bywater). New York: Modern Library, 1955.

Aune, David; *The Gospel of Matthew in Current Study*. Grand Rapids: Wm B. Eerdmans, 2001. See Graham Stanton's work on recently discovered papyri that show a mixed collection of written materials ranging from less costly copies to those more artfully and carefully designed. (p. 50 ff.)

Bailey, James L.; *Contrast Community, Practicing the Sermon on the Mount*. Eugene, OR: WIPF and Stock, 2013.

Bailey, Kenneth E.; *The Cross and the Prodigal, Luke 15 Through the Eyes of Middle Eastern Peasants*, Downers Grove, IL: IVP Academic, , ©2005.

Bailey, Kenneth E.; *The Good Shepherd. A Thousand-Year Journey from Psalm 23 to the New testament*. Downers Grove, IL: IVP Academic, © 2014. Note his comparison of the rhetoric of Psalm 23 and the Lost Coin in Luke on p. 144.

Bailey, Kenneth E.; *Jacob and the Prodigal, How Jesus Retold Israel's Story*. Downers Grove, IL: IVP Academic, , ©2003.

Bailey, Kenneth E.; *Jesus through Middle Eastern Eyes*. Downers Grove, IL: IVP Academic, 2009, © 2008.. Interesting coverage of the beatitudes of Matt 5 and the Lord's Prayer of Matt 6,

Barclay, John M.G.; *Jews in the Mediterranean Diaspora, From Alexander to Trajan (323 B.C.E. – 117 C.E.)*; Berkeley: University of California Press, © 1996, 1999. Provides background into the strained relationships between Jewish and various political groups in places such as Syria in the establishment of a homeland for Jewish people.

Barrett, Greg; *The Gospel of Rutba,—War, Peace, and the Good Samaritan Story in Iraq*; Maryknoll, NY: Orbis Books, © 2012. This story covers biographical elements of Shane Claiborne some of whose works are included in this bibliography and Pastor Weldon Nisley, an active member of the Scholars Forum of the Network of Biblical Storytellers.

Bauer, David R.; *The Structure of Matthew's Gospel*. United Kingdom: Almond Press of Sheffield Academic Press, 1988, 1989, merged into T&T Clark. His first chapter provides a broad overview of various approaches to the literary structure of the Gospel of Matthew leading to his approach of looking at the book primarily in its final form while paying attention to pertinent historical and literary influences. He details fifteen types of "compositional relationships" that can be used by the author to highlight "relationships both between and within these units" of literary structure (pp. 13-19). His second chapter emphasizes that most scholars agree with W.D. Davies that the book of Matthew as a whole has been "meticulously structured" (p. 21). See also the other topics of compositional relationships including purpose, pivot, causation and substantiation, climax, and intercalation on pp. 13-22.

Bauckham, Richard; *The Christian World around the New Testament*. Grand Rapids, MI: Baker Academic, © 2017. This is a companion publication to an earlier collection of essays, *The Jewish World around the New Testament* (WUNT 233).

Bauckham, Richard; *Jesus and the Eyewitnesses, The Gospels as Eyewitness Testimony, 2d Edition*. Grand Rapids, MI Eerdmans, © 2006, 2017. "…Oral transmission is quite capable of preserving traditions faithfully, even across much longer periods than that between Jesus and the writing of the Gospels, and we shall see reason to support those scholars who see the early Christian transmission of Jesus traditions as a relatively conservative process. Other scholars, however, working with the dictum that the Jesus traditions are in the first-place evidence about the Christian communities that transmitted them, conclude that they tell us much more about those communities than about Jesus (p. 240). "…The three main models of oral interpretation… used to understand the transmission of Gospel tradition in the early church. They are associated with the names Rudolph Bultmann, Birger Gerhardsson, and Kenneth Bailey" (p.241).

Bazelon, Emily; *Sticks and Stones: Defeating the Culture of Bullying and Rediscovering the Power of Character and Empathy*. New York: Random House, © 2013.

Bergen, Benjamin K.; *Louder than Words, The New Science of How the Mind Makes Meaning*. New York: Basic Books, 2012. His discussion of "embodied simulation" to describe how the brain works has interesting implications about how our thoughts influence our interpretations, communications and actions.

Betz, Hans Dieter; *Essays on the Sermon on the Mount*. Philadelphia: Fortress Press, ©1985.

Betz, Hans Dieter; *The Sermon on the Mount*, Fortress Press. Philadelphia: 1995. This 730-page commentary is one of the most thorough and scholarly on the topic—well received by *Review of Biblical Literature* and *Theology Today*. Betz credits the support for work he received on the topic for over two decades including fourteen months of intense study and writing provided by a grant or "Forschungspreis." (p.xv) It includes a 90-page introduction covering his approach in five pages and the major problems in a historical and literary perspective. Each section is divided into an introduction, analysis, and interpretation. The commentary is prefaced with a list of works most often cited and closes with his partial bibliography that contains about 700 items.

Betz believes that the Lord's Prayer was already known to the readers of Matthew's Gospel as an oral text and in multiple forms which makes sense from the core evidence being the two forms in Matthew and Luke.[119] Betz also notes the "performative language"[120] of the Lord's Prayer as opposed to a theologically "descriptive language" although he sees

---

119   Betz, see p. 370, column 1. Betz; see p. 370, column 2.
120   Betz; See p. 377, column 1. Despite his acknowledgment of its "performative nature," he appears to limit that performance to group wor-

that it contains theological concepts. Despite his acknowledgment of its "performative nature," he appears to limit that performance to group worship, and not the "performance" or the improvisational work of someone trying to convince or persuade someone of something, not unlike one who was trained in ancient "rhetoric" or "disciple-making." Betz sees the preponderance of the evidence pointing to a Greek language origin and not Aramaic or Hebrew.

See the section on p. 373 (column 2), "Original Purpose and Function" of the Lord's Prayer: "What did Jesus intend by the creation of this prayer? One can only speculate about this question because none of the sources is explicit about this." That might be true if the context of Chapter 5 was not already explicit about it when it asks to pray for those who persecute us. However, it may seem to be distant by a couple of paragraphs, but perhaps would be considered much closer when the memory methods of weaving interrelated concepts are considered.

As to the type of literature and its purpose see: Betz views the Sermon on the Mount (SM) as *epitomai*, consisting of sayings of Jesus grouped together according to systematic points of doctrine considered to be of primary importance." The literary function of the SM, according to Betz, was the "'advanced' teaching for those who have already become disciples … the personal instruction not only of the four disciples addressed, but of all disciples." Note his explanation to the "seeming inconsistency" of the inclusion of the "crowds" "While according to the beginning in 5:1, only the disciples received the SM, 7:28-29 reports that somehow 'the crowds' (οἱ ὄχλοι) came to know it, too. Rather than an oversight on the part of Matthew, the seeming inconsistency shows 'progress'; Matthew seems to have been aware that the SM was originally intended for the disciples only, but that it had become public knowledge … Indeed, for Matthew 'the crowds' (οἱ ὄχλοι) are the pool from which new church members are to be recruited. That the 'crowds' also receive the SM (7:28-29) shows how this change took place and that the SM played an important role in attracting people to the church. The SM has played this role during the entire history of the church up to the present." I would further demonstrate that the Sermon on the Mount was material developed for the disciples showing them how to make new disciples in fulfillment of the promise to make them "fishers of people" in Matthew 4:19.

Bevere, John; *Bait of Satan, Living Free from the Deadly Trap of Offense, 10th Anniversary Edition*. Lake Mary, FL: Charisma House, © 1994, 2004. See p. 158 discussing Matthew 5:25-26 where someone is offended by you and where you are to try to reconcile with them and compare that to p. 159 where he discusses Matthew 18:15 where someone offends you and you are to try to reconcile.

Black, Stephanie L.; "How Matthew Tells the Story, A Linguistic Approach to Matthew's Narrative Syntax," pp. 24-52 from: **Gurtner, Daniel M. & Nolland, John; editors**. *Built upon the Rock, Studies in the Gospel of Matthew*. Grand Rapids, MI: Eerdmans, 2008

Boomershine, Thomas E. *The Messiah of* Peace, A Performance-Criticism Commentary on Mark's Passion-Resurrection Narrative, Biblical Performance Criticism Volume 12. Eugene, OR: Cascade Books, 2015. This represents 45 years of Dr. Boomershine's activities extending the work of his doctoral thesis. This is an extensive work examining the text in Greek and English that includes links to multi-media performances of the material. It represents the first analytical treatment from the new perspective of performance-criticism and includes helpful appendices on the historical context of the Mark and his audiences, a sound map of the text, pronunciation of Koine Greek and the rhetoric of Biblical storytelling. He quotes William Harris's estimate of literacy in this period as not likely exceeding 15%, a strong reason to understand why oral methods played such a strong role.

Boomershine, Thomas; "The New Testament Soundscape and the Puzzle of the Mark," *Sound Matters, Biblical Performance Criticism Vol. 16* edited by Margaret Lee. Eugene, OR: Cascade Books, © 2018 WIPF and Stock Publishers. See sections in pp. 200-225 on "Sensory Systems of the Human Brain" and "Implications for Biblical Scholarship."

---

ship, and not the "performance" or the improvisational work of someone trying to convince or persuade someone of something, not unlike one who was trained in ancient "rhetoric" or "disciple-making."

Bonhoeffer, Dietrich; *The Cost of Discipleship*; from German, *Nachfolge*, 1937; English translation, NY: Simon and Schuster, © 1959. Substantially a commentary on the Sermon on the Mount, see the sections on "the Enemy," "the Hiddenness of Prayer," and the "Disciple and Unbelievers."

Boring, Eugene M.; *The Interpreters Bible, New Testament Articles, Matthew, Mark*. Nashville, TN: Abingdon Press, 1995. This provides a helpful overview of the background of the Gospel and its chiastic structure (p. 113). He views the Sermon on the Mount as primarily being addressed to the disciples (p.175). Although, he sees the crowds there until the end as "potential disciples at this point in the narrative". In the Manto thesis, the crowds are the primary audience being "fished" by Jesus as part of the promised "fishing lessons" he gave to his fishermen disciples in Matthew 4:19 making the disciples a secondary audience. Boring sees the beatitudes as "pronounce blessing on authentic disciples in the Christian community" (p. 178). Similarly, Boren views the Lord's Prayer as "the authentic prayer of his disciples" (p. 201) "as a pattern for the disciples" (p.202). He recognizes the Lord's Prayer as the "structural and technological center of the Sermon on the Mount, with the Lord's Prayer the core of this center." (p. 201)

Botha, Peter J.J.; *Orality and Literacy in Early Christianity, Biblical Performance Criticism, Vol. 5.* Eugene, Oregon: Cascade Books, 2012.

British Museum Library; *Codex Sinaiticus, Facsimile Edition;* Peabody, MA: Hendrickson, 2010; "Hendrickson Publishers, in conjunction with the British Library, is now releasing a limited number of full color facsimiles of the preserved *Codex Sinaiticus*. *Codex Sinaiticus* is the oldest known complete manuscript featuring the full canon of the Christian Bible in Greek. It was originally produced in the middle of the fourth Century (ca. 350A.D.) in the southeastern Mediterranean. Originally *Codex Sinaiticus* was produced on parchment whose total number exceeded 730 leaves, approximately 1,460 pages. It contains the oldest complete New Testament, and at one time the entire Old Testament."

Brown, Jeanine K. *The Disciples in Narrative Perspective, The Portrayal and Function of the Matthean Disciples.* Atlanta: Society of Biblical Literature, 2002.

Brown, Jeanine K.; Roberts, Kyle; *Matthew;* 2018. Grand Rapids, MI: Eerdmans. As most others, the Lord's Prayer is seen as a pattern for disciples, see pp. 69-70. Sections such as Matthew 5:21-48 and 7:21-23 "as an audience already following Jesus" (p.57).

Brown, S. Kent; "Egypt, History of (Greco-Roman)," *Anchor Bible Dictionary*.New York/London/Toronto/Sydney/Aukland: DoubleDay, © 1992. See p. 368, vol 2 of

Brown, Michael J.; *The Lord's Prayer through Africa Eyes.* T&T Clark, 2004.

Burke, Kenneth; *The Rhetoric of Religion.* Los Angeles: University of Cal Press, , 1970

Burridge, Richard A.; *Imitating Jesus, An Inclusive Approach to Ethics.* Grand Rapids, MI: Eerdmans, 2007

Calvin, John; *Commentaries;* on-line collection as of Mar. 1, 2014 here: http://www.ccel.org/ccel/calvin/calcom31.ix.xli.html?scrBook=Matt&scrCh=5&scrV=1#ix.xli-p11.1

"*He went up into a mountain.* Those who think that Christ's sermon, which is here related, is different from the sermon contained in the sixth chapter of Luke's Gospel, rest their opinion on a very light and frivolous argument. Matthew states, that Christ spoke to his disciples on a mountain, while Luke seems to say, that the discourse was delivered on a plain. But it is a mistake to read the words of Luke, *he went down with them, and stood in the plain* (Luke 6:17,) as immediately connected with the statement that, *lifting up his eyes on the disciples,* he spoke thus. For the design of both

Evangelists was, to collect into one place the leading points of the doctrine of Christ, which related to a devout and holy life. Although Luke had previously mentioned a *plain, he does not observe the immediate succession of events in the history, but passes from miracles to doctrine, without pointing out either time or place: just as Matthew takes no notice of the time, but only mentions the place. It is probable, that this discourse was not delivered until Christ had chosen the twelve: but in attending to the order of time, which I saw that the Spirit of God had disregarded, I did not wish to be too precise. Pious and modest readers ought to be satisfied with having a brief summary of the doctrine of Christ placed before their eyes, collected out of his many and various discourses, the first of which was that in which he spoke to his disciples about true happiness.*"

Carter, Warren; *Matthew and the Margins, A Sociopolitical and Religious Reading*, Maryknoll, NY: Orbis Books , ©2000. In pp. 163-169, the "our" in "our Father" is considered to refer to the "community of disciples," missing the role of the crowds to which the prayer is principally addressed. On p.11, he discusses a revival of the role of Matthew as the first produced Gospel from which Mark copied. This might also explain why the "Sermon on the Mount" was not in Mark, ostensibly because it was already provided by Matthew.

Carter, Warren; *What Are They Saying about Matthew's Sermon on the Mount?*. MahWah, New Jersey: Paulist Press. ©1994. Received his Ph.D. from Princeton Theological Seminary and teaching at Saint Paul School of Theology in Kansas City, he summarizes scholarship with an emphasis of structure, function, and content. In his discussion of the Lord's Prayer, he assumes the view of others that this was for the disciples and has no explanation for its role with the crowds starting with the question, "What do disciples pray for in the Lord's Prayer?". p. 93-95.

Carruthers, Mary; *The Book of Memory, A Study of Memory in Medieval Culture*. Cambridge, United Kingdom: Cambridge University Press, © 1990, 2013.

Carruthers, Mary; *The Craft of Thought, Meditation, Rhetoric and the Making of Images 400-1200*. Cambridge, United Kingdom: Cambridge University Press, 1998. She discusses the essence of memory as one of images in places. See her discussion of the history of thought on the topic and her description of Albertus making such a claim around 1246 through his treatise, "On the Good" (p. 13).

Case-Winters, Anna, *Matthew*. Louisville, KY: Westminster John Knox, 2015. Though following a discussion of loving enemies on p. 100, by 107, the "our" of the "our Father" of the Lord's Prayer refers to the community of the church and does not envision the crowds outside the church praying this.

Chrysostom, *Homilies on the Gospel of Saint Matthew*, 388 A.D., from *Nicene and Post-Nicene Fathers of the Christian Church, edited by Philip Schaff, Editor (Oxford edition, 1851, American edition, 1888;* Grand Rapids, MI: Wm. B. Eerdmans Publishing Company, 1975. These English volumes provide easy access to key writings of the church fathers. Notable in Homily XV on p. 97 is the linkage of the salt and light passage with the beatitudes but ascribes salt to the believers without distinguishing any difference between those who are salt and salty tasting that would make it possible to apply "you are salt" to the crowds who were not yet believers. In Homily XIX on the Lord's Prayer in Matthew 6, Chrysostom makes the connection with the Father giving sun on the evil and the good from Matthew 5 (see p. 137) and sees a major point of the prayer as forgiveness of enemies and wrong doers (p. 137-138). I don't believe it would not be a stretch to see Chrysostom as one who might assume that the Lord's prayer would be a prayer said in for the persecutor, but in that case would be limited to a prayer by a believer for the persecutor (and the one praying) as opposed to a prayer by anyone being persecuted on behalf of the persecutor and themselves. If true, the Chrysostom would see the one praying as being in solidarity with the person persecuting the one praying but would not be able to see the pre-believer making such a prayer. In section 6 on page 134 and section 9 on page 135, Chrysostom sees the one calling on the Father only as the believers, but, as equals without regard to earthly rank (section 7 page 134), though requiring to forgive those even outside the faith (p. 137).

Claiborne, Shane; Wilson-Hartgrove, Jonathan; Okoro, Enuma; *Common Prayer, A Liturgy for Ordinary Radi-*

cals. Grand Rapids: Zondervan, 2010. (as of 2012 part of Harper Collins Christian Publishing).

Claiborne, Shane; *The Irresistible Revolution, Living as an Ordinary; The Simple Way*. Grand Rapids, MI: Zondervan, © 2006, 2016. See comments throughout on the Sermon on the Mount on Chapter 10, Extremists for Love, p 257.

Cobb, Sara Ph.D; Federman, Sarah; Castel, Alison; *Introduction to Conflict Resolution, Discourses and Dynamics*. London, England and Lanham, MD: Rowman and Littlefield, ©2019.

Cobb, Sara Ph.D.; *Speaking of Violence: The Politics and Poetics of Narrative in Conflict Resolution (Explorations in Narrative Psychology*. New York: Oxford University Press, 2013. This approach to conflict resolution draws attention to core cultural constructs that form the basis for conflict and its management. This provides profound hope for use of ideas and themes of items like the Lord's Prayer that could be leveraged in anger and conflict management.

Conzelmann, Hans; Lindemann, Andreas; *Interpreting the New Testament, An Introduction to the Principles and Methods of N.T., Exegesis*. Peabody, MA: Hendrickson Publishing, © 1988.

Crossan, John Dominic; *The Greatest Prayer*. San Francisco: Harper One, 2010. Crossan suggests that the prayer may be "neither a Jewish prayer for Jews or a Christian prayer for Christians… but a prayer from the heart of Judaism on the lips of Christians for the conscience of the world" (p. 2). He calls it a "revolutionary manifesto and a hymn of hope… proclaiming a radical vision of justice that is the core of Israel's biblical tradition." On page 4, he also discusses the nature of climactic or crescendo parallelism where the content increases to a climax. He shows an example from Habakkuk 3:17. I certainly see this type of parallelism through the entire sermon on the Mount leading to, through and beyond the Lord's Prayer. From pages 29-52 he focuses on the phrase "our Father" (or literally, "Father of us") to discuss the nature of father, but, only devotes three sentences to the "our" or "of us" element by saying it is meant to be a communal prayer and not merely a personal one. He does not make the connection to the persecutor.

Dallaire, Romeo; *Shake Hands with the Devil, the Failure of Humanity in Rwanda*. New York: Carroll & Graf Publishers, © 2003. This is a powerful book recommended to those who care about forgiveness in the face of genocide as discussed by authors Musekura, Jones, and Larson. But it is important to read the foreword by Ambassador Samantha Power leading Harvard's Carr Center for Human Rights (https://carrcenter.hks.harvard.edu) and the preface by Lieutenant-General Dallaire. In the preface he recounts a question by a Canadian Forces priest who asked if he still believes in God after all he saw. Dallaire answers, "I know there is a God because in Rwanda I shook hands with the devil." (p. xxv) In the preface, there is an implied challenge by Power about the entire "world's failure to protect and his own failure to persuade". (p. ix) Similarly, what are the consequences if we fail to persuade the world of the primary intent of the Lord's Prayer as the prayer for our persecutors?

Damholt, Ronald; "Rightwiseness and Justice, a Tale of Translation;" *Anglican Theological Review*, Summer 2105; Chicago, IL p. 413-432. Discusses the historical rendering of the Greek word *dikaiosyne* (justice versus righteousness) in translations, looking into the original Greek uses of the term and ways of handling it in English. This is a helpful thought process regarding the meaning of this word usage in Matthew and other NT texts.

Davies, Margaret; *Matthew*, 2d ed.; S. Yorkshire, UK: Sheffield Phoenix, 2009. She is one that recognizes the use of Father in this Lord's Prayer as the Father of "all people" (p. 61) but does not call out the request to be the Father of me and my persecutor, that robs the passage of its rhetorical punch of praying for every case including the worst case enemy.

Davies, W.D.; *The Sermon on the Mount*. London: Cambridge University Press, 1966,1969. This 165-page book covers the setting with section on the "Setting in Matthew," the "Jewish Messianic Expectation," "Contemporary Judaism," "the Early Church," and the "Ministry of Jesus." He reviews the disciplines of "source, form and liturgical criticism" (p. 4) as providing unnecessary bias for considering the material as a haphazard collection.

His view is expressed on p. 5 where he says, "This emphasis is that we should think of Matthew, as of the other composers of the Gospels, not as mere editors, manipulating sources with scissors and paste, so to speak, to produce a mosaic of snippets, but as themselves in a real sense 'authors.' Dependent on a tradition there were, but they were not passive transmitters of it. By what they preserved, by the way they changed it and, above all, arranged it, they left their impress on it. This is particularly true of Matthew … And in light of this we must insist that Matthew, the final author of the Gospel (note we write *'author'* not *'editor'*), did himself regard v-vii as a unit. The concluding formula in vii.28-9 makes this clear. The section finishes with these words: 'and it came to pass when Jesus had ended these sayings the people were astonished at his doctrine, for he taught them as one having authority and not as the scribes.'… So that v-vii do constitute for him (Matthew) an essential unity." Davies also emphasizes the significant role of the beginning and ending sections of the gospel encouraging readers to consider it as tightly connected sections.

Davies, W.D.; *The Setting of the Sermon on the Mount*. Atlanta, GA: Scholars Press, 1989, © Brown University, 1989. The author's preface of February 3, 1963, dates this to an earlier publication, this copyright notwithstanding, and emanates from a series of lectures he gave in 1957 in Wales.

Davies, W.D. and Allison, D.C.; *Matthew*, Volumes 1-3 *International Critical Commentary*. London and New York: T&T Clark, ©1988, this edition 2004, reprinted 2005, 2007. This is a very thorough and scholarly treatment of the Gospel of Matthew with each section consistently treated under the topics: "Structure, Sources, Exegesis, Concluding Observations, and Bibliography." Each section of text uses the koine Greek text represented by the Nestle-Aland *Novum Testamentum Graece* and the Huck-Greeven *Synopse der drei ersten Evangelien*. (See p. 147 of their 148-page introduction. They also have 32 pages of abbreviations and bibliography at the front of the book.) Volume 1 covers Chapters 1-7, volume two Chapters 8-18, and volume 3 Chapters 19-28. In the preface of the third volume, it was explained that Davies expected to produce a draft of each of the three volumes first. That worked out for the first volume but not the remaining two where he was only able to review the work of Allison. Note also that Davies wrote a separate volume, *Sermon on the Mount*, beginning in 1969 through 1990, and the *Setting of the Sermon on the Mount* in 1989. Allison also wrote a separate book, *The Sermon on the Mount, Inspiring the Moral Imagination,* in 1999. Those not conversant in Greek may wish to use their English language Bible while reading it. Like many scholarly works, this one took years to produce with the support of the universities where they worked or collaborated.

The introduction makes the case that the Gospel of Matthew is well crafted from end to end. "Clearly the hand of one man has been active throughout. Secondly, devices such as foreshadowing, repetition, *inclusio*, show up the impressive unity of the gospel. The beginning and the end hang together, as do the various parts that make up the whole" (volume 1, p. 96). While considering the Sermon on the Mount as an essential unity in volume one, the strong connections with other sections in MT is re-emphasized in the preface to the second volume, "The Sermon on the Mount is retrospective: it is inseparable from what precedes it in Chapters 1-4. But it is also prospective, equally inseparable from what follows it in Chapters 8-28." See vol. 2, p. ix.

Unresolved interpretive problems in Matthew 5-7: Who is "salt and who is "our"? In my opinion, two key unresolved issues arise from failing to apply the explicit audience of the crowds with the disciples looking on to the specific passages within Mt 5-7. For example, "who is salt"? when Jesus addresses the crowds, saying, "you are the salt of the earth." Who is the "our" in "our Father" when Jesus asks the crowds to pray?

Who is Salt? See p. 471 of volume 1 for Davies and Allison's description of salt. Davies and Allison assume that only disciples are identified as salt but with no discernible justification for why the crowds are left out. Therefore, the identification of "who" is salt is incomplete at best. This is despite the fact they both recognize that Jesus addresses the crowds. Note their comments on pp. 421-422 of volume 1, "The impression created by this and the previous clause is that Jesus, having seen the crowds, goes up the mountain to get away from them (cf. Jn 6.3). Yet in view of 7.28-8.1, we must think of the crowds as overhearing the discourse. So there are two circles around Jesus, an inner circle (the disciples) and an outer circle (the crowds)."

While they see the crowds and disciples in two circles who both hear Jesus, commentators who suggest that Jesus primarily addressed the disciples but that the crowds "overheard" fail to fully appreciate the nature of speaking outdoors to not one but many "crowds" and how the "crowds" would be amazed at the end. The "crowds" only hear if Jesus purposely addresses the crowds so that they all could hear including those at the furthest distance from Jesus the speaker. In fact, going up to the side of the mountain makes it possible for Jesus to project over the bodies of those near the front so that those in the back could hear. This is similar to when Jesus goes into a boat to speak to crowds as in an amphitheater so those in the back are not blocked by those in the front.

Merely overhearing Jesus speaking to the disciples close at hand would neither make it possible for them to hear Jesus in the first place or be so captivated by them at the end so that they declared that he spoke as one with "authority," implying that they had no choice but to keep on listening. Also, addressing the interests of the disciples would not engage or keep the attention of those in the "crowds" who were not being addressed. Whatever Jesus had to say to the crowds needed not only to be capable of being heard, but capable of capturing and holding their attention. This, of course, would be exactly what would be expected if Jesus was intending to show the disciples how to recruit from the crowds. Understanding the explicit audience as primarily being the crowds being recruited for the benefit of the disciples who were promised "recruiting lessons" is the only way to make sense of the text in its context and its explicit audience. With this understanding, one can then answer the questions, "who is salt?" and "who is 'our'?"

Davies and Allison do, however, go into detail about how salt functions (pp. 472-473). As a result, he concludes his thoughts on p. 473 by saying, "Given the various uses for salt (cf. Pliny, *Nat. His.* 31.73-92, 98-105) and its several symbolic associations, it is quite impossible to decide what one characteristic is to the fore in Mt 5:13. Thus while it would make sense to affirm that the disciples are, for example, the world's wisdom, it would also be reasonable to think that the pure in heart (5:8) purify the world, or, (as Origen, *C.Cels.* 8.70 has it) that Jesus' followers preserve the world, or that they are willing to sacrifice themselves (cf. Schnackenburg (v), pp. 195-196). But as implied by two facts, the 'ambiguity of salt need not trouble; for salt was equivocal and multivocal for the evangelist" (p. 473). As in his introductory comments in his exegesis of Mt 5:13 on p. 471, he says "In 5:13 would be disciples are told that they are the salt of the earth, in 5:14-16 that they are light of the world. The statements are quite general. The reader is not told how to become salt or light."

In my view, Davies and Allison admits to missing how one might become salt and light and how it applies to the crowds because they miss the rhetorical pairings of the beatitudes immediately prior in Mt 5:3-12. They overlook the difference between being "salt and light" as opposed to being "salty tasting and light giving" and hence miss how one becomes salt in the first place, namely by going through sorrow and being deprived of justice and what one must to as a consequence, namely becoming gentle and merciful.

It would be a lot easier for Davies and Allison to then see how the categories of salt and light applied to all including the crowds when any in the crowds are "sorrowful, deprived and therefore hungering for justice." Similarly, they miss the point of how being salt or light by virtue of their sorrow, provides those who suffer with insights into becoming salty tasting and light giving when they are "gentle, merciful and peace-making." If the crowds learn the lessons from their suffering, then others become blessed by their gentleness, mercifulness and peace-making. But, if the members of the crowds fail to be gentle, that means that those in the crowds who have suffered have failed to learn their lessons, failed to be gentle and failed to bless others who are then robbed of experiencing their saltiness or light. In that case, it is as though those members of the crowds went through all that suffering for nothing.

Once it can be shown that Jesus was primarily addressing the crowds with the disciples overhearing, then it can be shown to be a progression of concepts that comfort the sorrowful and justice-deprived while ultimately turning them into new peace-making disciples instead of the new peace breakers. By missing the pairings and the inherent psychological progression that restores peace promoting empathy and peacemaking, it is easy to see why commentators such as Davies and Allison totally miss the disciple making process inherent in the progression of the beatitude pairs and its fulfillment of the promise to receive "fishing lessons" promised in Mt 4: 19. Note that the text of Mt 5:13 shows that Jesus says that the "crowds" are already salt and light while being salty tasting or light providing is still in question. "You are the salt of the earth; but if salt has lost its taste, how shall its saltness be restored?" This same failure to address the explicit audience of Matthew 5-7 as both the crowds and the disciples, not only causes Davies and Allison to not understand "who is salt," they fail to apply the request of Jesus for the crowds to pray for their enemies and miss the major point of the Lord's Prayer.

Who is "our"? Note their comment on Mt 6:9, on "our Father," their definition of "our" totally leaves out the "crowds." "Concerning the injunction to pray to God as Father and the related concept of the believer's sonship in Matthew, two points are to be made (1). "Your Father" and "Our Father" include the disciples but not the populace at large. This is because sonship depends upon Jesus, the Son of God. Specifically, those who obey the will of God and follow his Son themselves become sons of God (c.f. 5:9, 45)." As one might see, Davies and Allison completely contradict the text and themselves. The text of Matthew explicitly states that Jesus explicitly addresses the crowds who, while sons of the Father in the respect that they as their persecutors receive sunshine and rain, are not yet sons of the Father until they love and pray for their worst-case enemies. Note the odd phrase, "so that you may become sons of your Father." How is that they have the Father but are not sons yet? Davies and Allison, as most all recent commentators, have missed the strangeness of this line and the explicit audience of the text, namely the crowds, and the disciples as those getting "fishing or disciple-making lessons." As a result, they miss the possible definition of "our" as the combination of the individuals in the crowds who were to pray alone for their persecutors, and the "persecutors" for whom they would pray. By doing that, it that will lead the individuals within the crowds in time to become sons of their Father and new peace-maker disciples. Whenever someone assumes that Father only relates to those like disciples who have already entered into the kingdom family, that person misses the opportunity to see how this prayer was used to reach those who are not yet disciples and the same tool expected to be used to reach the nations as described the Great Commission.

Davis, Rabbi Menachem; *Siddur for Weekdays with an Interlinear Translation*. Brooklyn, NY: Mesorah Publications; © 2002.

Dewey, Joanna; *Markan Public Debate: Literary Technique, Concentric Structure, and Theology in Mark 2:1-3:6* (SBL Dissertation Series, Number 48). Atlanta: SBL, ©1980. This work provides an overview of rhetoric methods employed in Mark and is quoted by Bauer in his work on Matthew's structure.

Dewey, Joanna; *The Oral Ethos of the Early Church*, Eugene, OR: Cascade Books, ©2013. Her Chapter 1 on "Textuality in an Oral Culture" provides views of the extent and role of literacy in the time of Christ and the writing of the Gospels; and Chapter 4 on "Mark as Interwoven Tapestry" shows the method of weaving themes throughout a longer work as a method to enhance memorization of a work being taught.

Dibelius, Martin; *The Sermon on the Mount*. New York: Charles Scribner's Sons, 1940.

Dobbs, Dan B.; *Torts and Compensation, Personal Accountability and Social Responsibility for Injury*. St. Paul, Minnesota: West Publication Co., © 1985. This is a modern treatment of lawsuits to establish compensation for damages not unlike the "eye for an eye" section in Matt.5.

Dodd, C. H., *The Parables of the Kingdom*. New York: Scribners, 1961.

Donald, Merlin; *A Mind So Rare*. NY/London: W.W. Norton, © 2001.

Donald, Merlin; *Origins of the Modern Mind*; Cambridge, Massachusetts / London: Harvard University Press, © 1991. See discussion to the emergence of rhetoric and writing on pp. 347-356.

Duling, Dennis C.; *A Marginal Scribe, Studies in the Gospel of Matthew in a Social-Scientific Perspective*. Eugene, OR: Cascade Books, © 2012.

Durston, Chris "Historical Interpretation of the Sermon on the Mount," pp. 42-49, *Scripture Bulletin 18* (1988). Oxford, England: Catholic Biblical Society, © 1988. The author compares historical treatment with contemporary culture and religious life where many are encouraged to not take the teachings too seriously because of the apparent difficulty in engaging them.

Eco, Umberto, *The Limits of Interpretation*. Bloomington, IN: Indiana University Press, © 1990.

Eco, Umberto, *The Role of the Reader, Explorations in the Semiotics of Texts*. Bloomington, IN: Indiana University Press, © 1979.

Eco, Umberto; *Semiotics and the Philosophy of Language*. Bloomington, IN: Indiana University Press, © 1984.

Eco, Umberto; *A Theory of Semiotics*. Bloomington, IN: Indiana University Press, © 1976.

Enright, Robert D.; Fitzgibbons, Richard P.; *Helping Clients Forgive, An Empirical Guide for Resolving Anger and Restoring Hop.;* Washington, D.C.: American Psychological Association, © 2000, 3d printing 2002.

Estes, Douglas; *Questions and Rhetoric in the Greek New Testament*. Grand Rapids, MI: Zondervan, 2017.

Farrer, Austin; *St. Matthew and St. Mark*. Westminster/ London: Dacre Press, 1954. In his preface on p. v, he makes the case that the material is purposely organized as a literary work and not merely a haphazard collection of material. The book includes an essay on the Lord's Prayer.

Fisichella, Archbishop Rino; *Catechism of the Catholic Church, with Theological Commentary, Direction and Coordination of the Theological Commentary*. Vatican City State: Vatican Publishing House, © 2017. See Ugo Vanni's essay on "the Lord's Prayer" on p.1205-1237; Our Sunday Visitor, Huntington, IN, © 2019.

Fitzmyer, Joseph A.; *The Interpretation of Scripture, In Defense of the Historical-Critical Method*. Paulist Press, NY; 2008. Helpful orientation to the history of the method and its role in Catholic and Protestant circles.

Fleer, David; Bland, Dave (editors); *PREACHING the Sermon on the Mount, The World it Imagines*. St. Louis: .Chalice Press, © 2007,

France, R.T.; *Matthew, Evangelist and Teacher*. Eugene, OR: WIPF and Stock Press, © 2004 Previously published by Paternoster Press ©1989.

France, R.T.; *The Gospel of Matthew, The New International Commentary of the New Testament*, Grand Rapids, MI: William B. Eerdmans, 2007. This is another respected and useful scholarly commentary designed for pastors and teachers interested in a serious presentation relatively easy to follow. As to the discussion on prayer, however, it also is disjointed. Note the reference on p. 226 to MT 5:44c where Jesus asks to pray for persecutors, "without specifying its content." He assumes Matthew was not specifying content because France failed to see the many links between that request for prayer the Lord's Prayer in MT 6. (Father gives sunshine and rain to just and unjust.) As others in the commentary traditions, no link is made between asking to pray for persecutors with the following prayer in Chapter 6 of the "Lord's Prayer." When commenting on the Lord's Prayer in Matthew 6 on p. 245, France says, "… God as the heavenly Father of disciples. When Jesus prays to God as "Father" (11:25, 26) it is sometimes explicitly to "*my* Father" (26:39, 42; Jesus speaks of God as 'my Father' a further fourteen times in Matthew) and never in the form 'our Father' which he here teaches his disciples to use." Note his assumption that this is directed primarily or solely to his disciples and not to the crowd to whom he is primarily addressing. Note subsequent assumptions as on p. 247 when France says about 6:11 and "give us our daily bread" becomes give us disciples our daily bread: "The first of the petitions for the disciples' own needs concerns material provision (cf. Prov 30:8, 'feed me with the bread I need'). In contrast, I (Chuck Manto) would ask, "What about the crowd's need? What about the combined need of the crowd and those attacking the crowd for whom they are to pray?"

At the end of the treatment on the Lord's Prayer, France correctly sees the singular comment of Jesus on the importance of forgiveness on p. 249 but does not notice that as a bracket that helps link the prayer here for the request for loving enemies and praying for them as requested at the bottom of Matthew 5.

Franzman, Martin H. *Follow Me, Discipleship According to Matthew.* by St. Louis, MO: Concordia Publishing House, 1982 reprint of 1961 ©. On p. 36 he makes clear his opinion that the Sermon on the Mount was meant for the disciples since Jesus departed from the crowds. The beatitudes are organized in two groups of four and not pairs (p. 38). Both beatitudes (p. 36), the salt and light designation (p. 42) and the Lord's Prayer (p. 54) are for the disciples and not the crowds.

Freedman, David Noel; *The Anchor Bible Dictionary.* New York: Doubleday, 1992. See useful and well documented articles on topics, places and movements ranging from rhetoric, Hellenism, Galilee, Decapolis, Septuagint and so on.

Huther, Brian; Ben Auxier, Ben; and Macchi, Seth. *GOP Jesus, sketch.* Friend Dog Studios, Chicago, IL. https://www.youtube.com/watch?v=SZ2L-R8NgrA ; Premiered November 3, 2018

Gardner, Richard B., *Matthew.* Scottdale, PA/ Harrisonburg, VA Herald Press, 1991. See p. 118 where he speaks of the "our" in "Our Father" as familial or soteriological. In other words, it is the Father of me and those in the Jesus Community (see link to same in treatment of the beatitudes on p. 91).

Gerhardsson, Birger; *Memory and Manuscript, Oral Tradition and written Transmission in Rabbinic Judaism and Early Christianity with Tradition & Transmission in Early Christianity.* Grand Rapids: Eerdmans, 1998. This is a reprint of the 1961 and 1964 work with a helpful forward by Jacob Neusner known for his work on the Memorized Torah. Neusner recounts the personal histories of those that had difficulties understanding the concepts in Gerhardsson's book but are now gaining appreciation. See Gerhardsson's discussion of the role of "arranging oral traditional collections in such a way as to make them easier the [sic] memorize and recite." p. 149.

Gibbs, Jeffrey A.; *Matthew 1:1-11:1.* St. Louis: Concordia Publishing House, 2006. He sees the "our" as the Father of the one praying and the other "disciples ... set in community with one another." P. 322.

Goodman, Martin (editor); *Jews in a Graeco-Roman World*; Oxford. Clarendon Press: 1999. Essays.

Gonzales, Justo L.; *Teach Us to Pray: The Lord's Prayer in the Early Church and Today.* Grand Rapids: Eerdmans, 2021.

Gorman, Michael J.; *Elements of Biblical Exegesis, A Guide for Students and Ministers, Revised and Expanded Edition.* Ada, MI: Baker Academic, 2009.

Green, Joel B., *Hearing the New Testament, Strategies for Interpretation, 2d. Ed.* Grand Rapids, MI: Eerdmans, 2010. This is a collection of essays, two of which have special relevance, namely "Genre Analysis" by James L. Bailey and "Rhetorical Criticism" by C. Clifton Black.

Greenman, Jeffrey P.; Larsen, Timothy; Spencer, Stephen R. (Editors). *The Sermon on the Mount through the Centuries, From the Early Church to John Paul II.* Grand Rapids, MI: Brazos Press, © 2007. These contain scholarly essays on the use of the Sermon by Chrysostom, Augustine, Hugh of St Victor, Dante and Chaucer, Luther, Calvin, Wesley,

Spurgeon, D Bonhoeffer and John Yoder, Pope John Paul II and Leonardo off and John Stott. The article on Calvin correctly points out through Calvin's commentary on the Sermon on the Mount that Calvin could not see many connections and that the material was a collection of pulled together in no significant order.

Guelich, Robert A. *The Sermon on the Mount, A Foundation for Understanding.* Waco, TX: Word, 1982

Gundry, Robert H. *Matthew, A Commentary on His Handbook for a Mixed Church Under Persecution, 2d edition,* Grand Rapids: Eerdmans, ©1982, 1994. On the Lord's Prayer, p. 104-105, claims that Matthew "removes the prayer from its original context, and inserts it here to teach that Jesus' disciples ought to pray with an economy of words." He in effect conflates the two prayers and the two audiences as being one when in fact the text explicitly states otherwise. Surprising in one sense that a very conservative seminary professor would do that here but not in that he is repeating traditions of interpretation.

Gurtner, Daniel M. & Nolland, John; editors. *Built upon the Rock, Studies in the Gospel of Matthew.* Grand Rapids, MI: Eerdmans,, 2008. Black's article on syntax lays a groundwork for elements that would be useful in a rhetorical approach with built-in mnemonic devices. Note Stephanie Black's comments on "marking" on p. 30.

Gurtner, Daniel M.; Willits, Joel; Burridge, Richard A.; *Jesus, Matthew's Gospel and Early Christianity, Studies in Memory of Graham N. Stanton.* London: Bloomsbury T&T Clark, 2011, 2013. See the essay by Donald Hagner on the dating of Matthew in his essay, "Determining the Date of Matthew," pp. 76-92. He provides a range of evidence that while for him is not conclusive, strongly leads to a date just prior to 70 A.D. as opposed to just afterwards by as much as a decade (see his conclusion on p. 91).

Hagner, Donald A., *Matthew, vols 1-2, Word Biblical Commentary vol. 33A-B.* Nashville/Dallas: Thomas Nelson, Inc., © 2000. Helpful and scholarly two volume series with each section organized with sections on bibliography, translation, form/structure/setting, comment, and explanation. He is of the opinion that the opening of the Sermon on the Mount may indicate for some that Jesus left the crowds but that the end of the Sermon shows that he did not (an observation similar to Keener). However, though it is obvious that Jesus did not leave the crowds and addressed both the disciples and the much larger number who were not, still much of the interpretation treats the sayings of Jesus as if they applied only to the disciples. (This may or may not be due in part to a loving pastoral heart of commentators who have their Christian congregations in mind as they comment on the material, something I have also observed in some of the writings of the early church fathers.)

Hare, Douglas R.A., *Matthew, Interpretation—A Bible Commentary for Teaching and Preaching.* Louisville, KY: Westminster John Knox Press, 2009. This is not as detailed as those with a more scholarly audience in mind and at times not as careful. For example, in the beatitudes section, Hare attempts to make the point that the 8th beatitude is different from the others in that it uses the 2d person plural as does Mark. In reality, the blessing itself ("Blessed are the persecuted…") is not in the second person, only the explanatory material that follows it. The actual beatitude portion is the last bookend similar to the first in that it is in the present tense and uses the phrase "theirs is the kingdom of heaven." The use of the second person helps show that the material shifts from the 4 pairs of material to continued commentary on the persecution issue where a defamation campaign could be used to prevent other would-be peacemakers to come to the aid of the one being persecuted. This additional detail sets up the following section where Jesus defends his remarks from the charge of being weak on justice and the law.

Harris, William V.; *Ancient Literacy.* Cambridge: Harvard University Press, 1989.

Harvey, John D., *Listening to the Text, Oral Patterning in Paul's Letters.* Grand Rapids, MI: Baker Books, 1998. This is a helpful introduction to oral and literary patterns in the first century (his Chapter 2) describing oral culture in detail and use of structure with special treatment of the center position. See "Categories and Controls" (Chapter 5). There he discusses jargon used by literary scholars with the example of "chiasmus" that sometimes may cause confusion since different words are sometimes used to describe similar techniques. He compares chiasmus that inverts a series of words ("identical, synonymous, or antonymous words or phrases are used" at the "sentence level"), whereas inversion is the term used where "a word or phrase on one side of the construction is developed in a sentence or paragraph on the other" (p. 100). I see these used in various sections of the Sermon on the Mount, though he does not cite usage in Matthew. He does go into a lot of helpful detail about various approaches to memory devices of poetry (p. 59) versus similar or different words (pp.98-99) in other literature.

Hearon, Holly E. and Ruge-Jones, Philip, *The Bible in Ancient and Modern Media, Story and Performance*. Eugene, Oregon: Cascade Books, 2009. This is an extremely helpful collection of essays on the role of oral media in light of the expense of early writing and its limited availability to those minority who were literate and the majority who were not. Essays include discussion of oral methods such as repetition that are required for easy understanding by an audience but also necessary for easier memorization. Areas of study such as "performance criticism" are proposed.

Helyer, Larry R.; *Exploring Jewish Literature of the Second Temple Period, A Guide for New Testament Students*. Downers Grove, IL: Intervarsity Press, 2002. Written for students and pastors covering the period of 516 B.C.E. and 70 A.D.

Hendriksen, William *Exposition of the Gospel According to Matthew*. Grand Rapids, MI: Baker Book House, 1973. This is an example of a commentary written to provide a scholarly insight into work used primarily for pastoral purposes. As such, there are insights that can be gained from the author who has great care and sensitivities of his own contemporary audience. See his identification of salt and light of Matthew 5:11-12 on his p. 282 as referring to "Christ's followers", and today, as "believers in the Lord Jesus Christ" (p.261). Most significant is his statement on the Lord's Prayer. Because he makes the assumption that "Father" could only be used in this passage "in a definitely soteriological or redemptive sense." (p. 326), Then commenting on Matthew 6:9b he continues by saying, "Once this is understood it becomes clear that this model prayer is for believers in the Lord Jesus Christ, for them alone." His comparison of other texts at the neglect of this immediate context results in his extraordinarily strong claims that this prayer would not be for the crowds but only disciples. In my view of this passage, Jesus uses prayer to draw the one who is "not yet redeemed" or "not yet a disciple" to a place where they can be as part of the "fishing lessons" he promised in Matthew 4:17. Dr. Hendriksen winds up missing out on much of the value presented in this passage as a result, only being able to apply it to the disciples and not the crowds.

Henry, Matthew, *Matthew, A Commentary of the Holy Bible, Vol 5, A New and Illustrated Edition with essay by John Stoughton*. New York: Funk & Wagnalls, 1890. . On his commentary of Matthew 5:1-2, He says the following. "III. The auditors were his disciples, who came unto him came at his call, as appears by comparing Mark iii.13. Luke vi.13. To them he directed his speech, because they followed him for love and learning, while others attended him only for cures. He taught them, because they were willing to be taught; (the meek will he teach his way;) because they would understand what he taught, which to others was foolishness; and because they were to teach others; and it was therefore requisite that they should have a clear and distinct knowledge of these things themselves … But though this discourse was directed at the disciples, it was in the hearing of the multitude; for it is said (Ch. vii.28). The people were astonished … Note it is an encouragement to a faithful minister to cast the net of the gospel where there are a great many fishes in hope that some will be caught." In his commentary on salt in Matthew 5:13, he considers the disciples as salt. In 5:14, "All Christians are light in the Lord (Eph.v.8.), and must shine as lights, (Phil.ii.15.) but ministers in a special manner." In 5:43, he mentions in section II. "Note, it is the great duty of Christians to love their enemies." And later, "we must pray for them." Likewise on Matthew 6:5, "When thou prayest; (v.5) it is taken for granted that all the disciples of Christ pray." As to "Our Father," "We must pray, not only alone and for ourselves, but with and for others; for we are members one of another and are called into fellowship with each other." In that section I, he continues, "We must address ourselves to him as our Father and must call him so. He is a common Father to all mankind by creation", Mal.ii.10. Acts xvii.28. He is in a special manner a Father to the saints, by adoption and regeneration (Ephi.5 Gal.iv.6.).

Hester, John d.' Hester, David J, editors: *Rhetorics and Hermeneutics*. Atlanta: Emory University / T&T Clark, © 2004. This collection of essays discusses the nature of rhetoric and hermeneutics and their relationship over time as the terms have been interpreted and changed over time.

Hezser, Catherine; *Jewish Literacy in Roman Palestine (Texts and Studies in Ancient Judaism)*. [*Der jüdische Gebrauch der Schrift in der römischen Antike*. Von Catherine Hezser.]

2001. IX, 557 pages. Tubingen: Mohr and Siebeck, © 2001. Born 1960; 1986 Dr. theol. at the University of Heidelberg; 1992 Ph.D. at the Jewish Theological Seminary New York;

She expresses appreciation for the opportunity to begin her research on this topic at the Hebrew University in Jerusalem in 1997-1998.

Hilar, Marian; "*Philo of Alexandria (c. 20 B.C.E.- 40 C.E.),*" Internet Encyclopedia of Philosophy; Center for Philosophy and Socinian Studies, https://www.iep.utm.edu/philo/, [Retrieved May 2020].

"But it seems that Philo also picked up his ancestral tradition, though as an adult, and once having discovered it, he put forward the teachings of the Jewish prophet, Moses, as "the summit of philosophy" (*Op.* 8), and considered Moses the teacher of Pythagoras (b. ca 570 B.C.E.) and of all Greek philosophers and lawgivers (Hesiod, Heraclitus, Lycurgus, to mention a few). For Philo, Greek philosophy was a natural development of the revelatory teachings of Moses. He was no innovator in this matter because already before him Jewish scholars attempted the same. Artapanus in the second century B.C.E identified Moses with Musaeus and with Orpheus. According to Aristobulus of Paneas (first half of the second century B.C.E.), Homer and Hesiod drew from the books of Moses which were translated into Greek long before the Septuagint."

Hoffman, Oswald C. J., *The Lord's Prayer*. San Francisco: Harper & Row, 1982. This is a clearly devotional and evangelistic work known as his work as speaker on the "Lutheran Hour." It is interesting how he defines "our Father" on p. 10, "When Christ said, 'our,' he meant *our*. Christ did not just teach people to pray; he himself joined in." Dr. Hoffman is one who chooses to define "our Father" as the father of me and Jesus. However, he does not maintain the use of the plural that way consistently through the prayer and certainly does not make that association later when he gets to the phrase, "forgive us" since he would not believe that Jesus needs to be forgiven (pp. 54-67).

Hogan, Katrina Martin; Goff, Matthew; Wasserman, Emma; *Pedagogy in Ancient Judaism and Early Christianity*, Atlanta: SBL Press, 2017.

Horsley, Richard; *Oral Performance, Popular Tradition, and Hidden Transcript in Q*; Atlanta: Society of Biblical Literature, 2006.

Hudson, Michael; *... and forgive them their debts*. Dresden: by ISLET-Verlag, 2018. P.59 This book covers the earliest history of credit, debt and money and continues it to the concept of forgiveness of debts in the Lord's Prayer in Matthew and Luke. (p. 224-227).

Jaech, Richard E.; *Transforming Church Conflicts*. Camas, WA: Aachen Press;, © 2011.

Jandial, Rahul, MD, PhD; *Neurofitness, A Brain Surgeon's Secrets to Boost Performance and Unleash Creativity*. New York: Houghton, Mifflin, Harcourt; Boston 2019. A helpful orientation to recent brain science applicable to mnemonics and rhetoric.

Jensen, Richard A.; *Preaching Matthew's Gospel*. Lima, Ohio: CMS Publishing, 1998.

Jobes, Karen H.; Silva, Moises; *Invitation to the Septuagint, 2d ed*. Grand Rapids, MI: Baker Academic, 2000, 2015 Describes the history and significance of the collection of Hebrew scriptures in Greek by the time of the mid second century BCE used by Jews in Alexandria, Jerusalem, and the diaspora. (See outline in pp. 21-22.)

John II, Pope John; *Catechism of the Catholic Church, 2d edition*, Rome: Libraria Editrice Vaticana, 2006, 2010, 2019, http://ccc.usccb.org/flipbooks/catechism/IV/, http://ccc.usccb.org/flipbooks/catechism/VI/ , http://ccc.usccb.org/flipbooks/catechism/XVI/. See LP coverage on pp. 661-686. These hyperlinks are for an online edition. See various catechisms including the one from Cardinal Ratzinger.

Jones, Brian W.; "Domitian," *Anchor Bible Dictionary, volume 2*. New York: Doubleday, 1992. (pp. 221-222). See discussion of his harassment of Jews and Christians quoting the sources of Suetonius, Pliny, and Eusebius.

Jones, Gregory L.; *Embodying Forgiveness, A Theological Analysis*; Grand Rapids, MI: Wm. B. Eerdmans,. © 1995. See. p. 194 (in section 192-197) on the role of Matthew 18 in confronting those who offend and the consideration of those who refuse as "Gentiles and tax collectors.

Jones, Gregory L.; Musekura, Celestin. FORGIVING As We've Been FORGIVEN, *Community Practices for Making Peace*. Downers Grove, IL: InterVarsity Press © 2010. This compelling book describes the events related to the genocide in Rwanda in 1997-1998. It walks through the issues revolving how one goes about forgiving and reconciling with those who murdered or help murder your family members and how those who did so might be reconciled to their victims and to themselves. These questions are pertinent to all of us who seek to understand what it means to ask, "forgive AS we forgive". See his chapter 5 on "Communities of Forgiveness" where his forgiving his father who abandoned him led to his father's conversion. This is exactly the model of disciplemaking advocated in Matthew 5-7 and the Lord's Prayer for our persecutors. This approach to forgiveness resulted in ongoing work in the two organizations of these authors, the Duke Divinity School Center for Reconciliation and African Leadership and Reconciliation Ministries (ALARM).

Jordan, Pamela; "Uncovering Ancient Practices through Acoustics," *Physics Today*, © November 30, 2018 online at: https://physicstoday.scitation.org/do/10.1063/PT.6.1.20180430b/full/. Note the similar circumstances where elevation is used in amphitheaters or Jesus in a boat (Matthew 13:2) speaking to those on the inclined shore so the audience can hear better. See the November 20, 2018 article in *Physics Today* by Pamela Jordan, "Uncovering Ancient Practices through Acoustics," describing her work in Arcadia, Greece "using a combination of binaural recordings and psychoacoustic analysis tools. I am an architect and heritage specialist by training; as a graduate student and architecture and historic preservation professional." She shows the benefits of using elevation to carry sound to an audience. See her articles "Listening Beyond the Visible", "Sound Archives and Online Repositories", and "Overhearing History, Sound as Historical Material", in *Sounding Heritage*, University of Pennsylvania Press, Volume 9, Number 2 Fall 2019, pp.118-131, 132-144 and 256-258 respectively.

Josephus; *The Wars of the Jews or the History of the Destruction of Jerusalem*;

See this excerpt on death count estimates of those in Jerusalem including those visiting for holidays, available in the public domain here: http://www.ultimatebiblereferencelibrary.com/Complete_Works_of_Josephus.pdf

"3. Now the number (32) of those that were carried captive during this whole war was collected to be ninety-seven thousand; as was the number of those that perished during the whole siege **eleven hundred thousand**, the greater part of whom were indeed of the same nation [with the citizens of Jerusalem], but not belonging to the city itself; for they were come up from all the country to the feast of unleavened bread, and were on a sudden shut up by an army, which, at the very first, occasioned so great a straightness among them, that there came a pestilential destruction upon them, and soon afterward such a famine, as destroyed them more suddenly. And that this city could contain so many people in it, is manifest by that number of them, which was taken under Cestius, who being desirous of informing Nero of the power of the city, who otherwise was disposed to contemn that nation, entreated the high priests, if the thing were possible, to take the number of their whole multitude. So these high priests, upon the coming of that feast which is called the Passover, when they slay their sacrifices, from the ninth hour till the eleventh, but so that a company not less than ten (33) belong to every sacrifice, (for it is not lawful for them to feast singly by themselves,) and many of us are twenty in a company, found the number of sacrifices was two hundred and fifty-six thousand five hundred; which, upon the allowance of no more than ten that feast together, amounts to **two millions seven hundred thousand and two hundred persons** that were pure and holy; for as to those that have the leprosy, or the gonorrhea, or women that have their monthly courses, or such as are otherwise polluted, it is not lawful for them to be partakers of this sacrifice; nor indeed for any foreigners neither, who come hither to worship."

Jousse, Marcel; *Memory, Memorization, and Memorizers, The Galilean Oral-Style Tradition and its Traditionists; Biblical Performance Criticism, Vol. 15.* texts selected, edited and translated by Edgard Sienaert, forward by Wermer H Kelber; Eugene, OR: Cascade Books, , © 2018.

Kampen, John, *Matthew within Sectarian Judaism.* New Haven, CT: Yale University Press, 2019. See his view of Matthew and his community as those who see themselves as part of Judaism who follow Jesus and not as those who have left Judaism.

Keener, Craig S.; Wright, Edward T.; *Biographies and Jesus, What Does It Mean for the Gospels to be Biographies?* Lexington, KY: Emeth Press, 2016.

Keener, Craig S., *The Gospel of Matthew, A Socio-rhetorical Commentary*. Grand Rapids, MI: Wm. B Eerdmans, 2009. Great updated analysis and bibliography exceeding 70 pp. In this edition of what originally came out in 1999, he adds a brief addendum at the front on "Matthew and Greco-Roman Rhetoric," pp. xxv-l. He interprets the material in Matt 5-7 as a collection of materials rather than something taught in a package. See p. xxxii-iii: "We noted in the commentary that some have proposed rhetorical outlines for this composite speech. But, whereas it is reasonable to view 5:17 or 5:17-20 as articulating a thesis developed in 5:21 48, and 6:1 as a thesis developed in 6:2-18, a full, consistent rhetorical outline seems too much to ask. ... Matthew offers collections of materials rather than genuinely discrete speeches." The interpretation I propose is that the material is organized, whether given initially or collected later, to provide a way to memorize the maximum amount of material in the least amount of time using emotional frameworks and stories. As such, it holds together as one teaching unit or as a collection, or both since elements could be used separately in different occasions. He shows deference to an uncertain authorship, though possibly but not likely the apostle Matthew, (p. 39), and a location of Syria, possibly Antioch because of the emergence of the Didache (p.41).

Kelber, Werner H., *Imprints, Voiceprints, & Footprints of Memory*. Atlanta: Society of Biblical Literature, 2013. These are his collected essays from 1985-2011 that provides an in-depth treatment of issues related to the history of oral versus written methods including memorization.

Kennedy, George A., *The Art of Persuasion in Greece*. Princeton, NJ: Princeton U Press, 1963.

Kennedy, George A., *The Art of Rhetoric in the Roman World*. Princeton, NJ: Princeton U Press, 1972.

Kennedy, George A., *Classical Rhetoric and Its Christian and Secular Tradition, 2d edition,* Chapel Hill &London: University of N Carolina Press, 1999. This is one of a life-long series of works on classical and Christian rhetoric which provides substantial insight into the ways those in the first century used to convey their thoughts and convince others.

Kennedy, George A. *New Testament Interpretation through Rhetorical Criticism*. Chapel Hill N.C. and London: University of North Carolina, 1984.

Kennedy, George A., *Progymnasmata, Greek Textbooks of Prose Composition and Rhetoric, Translated with Introductions and Notes by George A. Kennedy.* Atlanta, Society of Biblical Literature, 2003.

Kingsbury, Jack Dean, *Matthew: Structure, Christology, Kingdom.* Philadelphia: Fortress Press, © 1975.

Kissinger, Warren S.; *The Sermon on the Mount, A History of Interpretation and Bibliography.* Lanham, MD: The Scarecrow Press, 1975. This is an amazing bibliography of roughly 2500 titles as part of an interpretive history of the material that forms part of a story of a lifelong work of collecting resources by Harold Rowe and continued by Warren Kissinger.

Kittel, Gerhard and Friedrich, Gerhard (editors); *The Theological Dictionary of the New Testament, volumes I-X.* Grand Rapids, MI: Eerdmans, © 1972, reprinted in 2006. This provides a historical use of the word reflecting "explaining," or "acting," with a shift to a negative connotation in the Septuagint and subsequently by Philo and Josephus. See vol. VIII, pp. 559-570.

Kruger, Michael J.; *Christianity at the Crossroads, How the Second Century Shaped the Future of the Church.* Downers Grove, IL: Intervarsity Press,; US edition © 2018; © 2017 UK edition.

Kurlansky, Mark; *Salt, A World History.* London: Penguin Books, © 2002.

Lachs, Samuel Tobias, *A Rabbinic Commentary on the New Testament, The Gospels of Matthew, Mark and Luke.* Hoboken, NJ: KTAV Publishing House, 1987. See p. 117-123 for the Lord's Prayer, with a discussion on "daily" and role of "debts".

Lapide, Pinchas. *The Sermon on the Mount.* Maryknoll: Orbis, 1986.

Larson, Catherine Claire. *As We Forgive.* Grand Rapids, MI: Zondervan, © 2009. A straightforward challenge to our concepts of forgiveness and reconciliation. It also provides a historical chronology from 1885 through 2003 when Rwandan President Paul Kagame decreed that those who confessed their crimes would be released, approximately 60,000 at the time of its writing.

Larson, Matthew D. C. *Gospels before the Book.* Oxford: Oxford University Press, 2018.

Leas, Speed; Kittlaus, Paul; *Church Fights, Managing Conflict in the Local Church;* Louisville, KY: Westminster Press, © 1973.

Lee, Margaret Ellen; *Sound Matters, New Testament Studies in Sound Mapping.* Eugene, OR: Cascade Books, © 2018.

Lee, Margaret Ellen and Scott, Bernard Brandon; *Sound Mapping the New Testament.* Salem, Oregon: Polebridge Press, 2009. This book has appropriately been praised as a groundbreaking treatment of sound and how it was used in oral media to convey tapestries of information segments more easily through structures and "maps" that are most expedient for the medium. Devices such as oral cues and repetition are examined in depth. The Sermon on the Mount is analyzed from a sound versus written perspective to showcase alternative interpretations to various sections of the material.

Lemaire, Andre; "Writing and Writing Materials," *Anchor Bible Dictionary, vol. 6.* New York: Doubleday, NY, 1992. Pp. 999-1008. "By the end of the first century B.C., there were schools in most Jewish towns. According to one Talmadic tradition, the high priest Jesus, son of Gamaliel (63-65 A.D.), ordered schoolteachers to be appointed in every town and children brought to them from the age of six or seven. From these indications one may assume that literacy was widespread among the Jewish people in Palestine in the 1st century B.C.; even if Jesus did not attend a high rabbinic school (cf John 7:15), he was able to read the Scripture in the synagogue (Luke 4:7)" (p. 1005).

Levy, Carlos; "Philo of Alexandria," *Stanford Encyclopedia of Philosophy,* Metaphysics Research Lab, Stanford University, © *https://plato.stanford.edu/entries/philo/* 2018.

See: "Through the many studies Manuel Alexandre (1999) devoted to Philo's rhetoric, we can more precisely gauge Philo's position in this central debate within Greek culture: the conflict between philosophy and rhetoric, or better, between philosophers and rhetors. Philo displays a sound knowledge of rhetoric. His affinity with Platonism impelled him to address very harsh critics of the "lesser" rhetoric, that of sophists, who represent the opposite pole of his own thought. *Sophisteia*, sophistry, is in Philo a frequent concept attached to a range of negative meanings. But, as in Plato (where Socrates opposes the idea of a greater rhetoric to Gorgias' lesser rhetoric in the *Phaedrus*), in Philo we see the possibility of a positive use of rhetoric. For Philo, rhetoric is neither an activity nor an abstract ideal but a human reality, the nature of which is laid out in the Bible. Moses is the man who saw God in the Sinai, but he by himself would have been unable to speak to Pharaoh and persuade him to let his people go. Moses needed the presence of Aaron to obtain what he sought. Moses represents the metaphysical truth, Aaron its implementation in reality, akin to the two faces of *logos*: while the *logos prophorikos* is that of communication, the *logos endiathetos* is the internal world of thoughts, and each is impossible without the other. It can be added that Abraham is said by Philo (*Mut.* 66) to have been the "father of the sounds," a strange expression that, alongside many similar allusions to music, shows that Philo was not the philosopher of sight alone. Another path of research is that of *parrêsia*, a complex term of political origin that appeared in the context of the Athenian democracy. In literary and philosophical texts, it means freedom of speech, frankness, and honesty. For Philo, however, *parrêsia* is neither a political ideal nor an individual achievement, but something given by God; and it must be used without harming relatives or friends."

Lloyd-Jones, D. Martyn; *Studies in the Sermon on the Mount, 2d edition*. Grand Rapids, MI: Eerdmans, 1971, 1976. See p. 328-329. He takes an approach which looks at the material as a whole and believes that there is meaning in the sequencing and that the collection is not merely accidental or haphazard. (See p. 33.) But theological issues seem to significantly impact his methodology or process of interpretation. One example might be his treatment of prayer: "It is only those who are true believers in the Lord Jesus Christ who can say 'Our Father.' It is only the people of whom the Beatitudes are true who can say with any confidence, 'Our Father.'" Lloyd-Jones does little to justify his position from the context but more from his theology. He also assumes the people of the Beatitudes as also being believers as opposed to both the disciples and the crowds. He also wrestles with some dispensational theologians who view the beatitudes as only applicable to the disciples or a future kingdom but not 'contemporary' Christians between the time of the disciples and the new millennial kingdom of the future (p. 11). Lloyd-Jones views this as applicable to all Christians while trying to sort out differences between law and grace in questions such as how we obtain forgiveness. If it is by forgiving others, then it is by law. If we forgive others because we have been forgiven, then it is by grace (pp. 12-13). He also sees the requirements of the Beatitudes as crushing (p. 13). He also sees a "spiritual order and sequence"; "Our Lord does not say these things accidentally; the whole thing is deliberate." He also sees the beatitudes as applying to all Christians including the laity (p. 25) but distinguishes them from non-believers or "non-Christians" (p. 32). He admits on p. 577 that by the end of the teaching there were crowds though it only started with Jesus and his disciples. He applied no discussion of the opening verses of Chapter 5 as to the disappearance of the crowds at the beginning but merely assumes it.

His view of "salt" is consistent with his view of the listener of the beatitudes as being the disciples only. In the Chapter, "Salt of the Earth" (p. 129), he states, "We now come to a new and fresh section in the Sermon on the Mount. In verses 3-12 our Lord and Saviour has been delineating the Christian character. Here at verse 13 He moves forward and applies his description. Having seen what the Christian is, we now come to consider how the Christian should manifest this ... We are poor in spirit, and merciful, and meek, and hungering and thirsting after righteousness in order, in a sense, that we may be 'the salt of the earth' ... We are told very clearly the relationship of the Christian to the world in general." Here he shows that there is a connection between the beatitudes and the declaration that those depicted in the beatitudes are somehow salt and light and encourages his readers to attempt to be and do the same.

Lohmeyer, Ernst; *"Our Father," An Introduction to the Lord's Prayer.* New York: Harper and Row Publishers, © 1962 from German, *Das Vater-Unser* by Vandenhoeck & Ruprecht, 1952. He views Matthew 6:5-15 in the context of Matthew 6:1-18 (on his p. 20) and sees connections to the Luke version but does not note the difference between the audience between Matthew and Luke, nor does he make the connection of the Lord's Prayer in Matthew 6 to the request to pray for persecutors in Matthew 5. As a result, he has difficulty finding sufficient information in the text to determine what community is being considered when the word "our" is used. See his interpretation of 'our' on p. 57, "…Our is not meant to unite the disciples who pray with the master who teaches them this prayer; the language of the Gospel always distinguishes between Jesus and the disciples, as it does between 'my Father' and 'your Father' … thereby referring the 'our' to the community asking for Gods' blessing." On p. 58, Lohmeyer asks, "What objective justification is there of this 'our' and what are the historical characteristics of a group which prays so humbly and yet so proudly to 'our Father?'"

But, on p. 59, he concedes that we cannot know much and, "As a result, we are led to the conclusion that his 'our', too, primarily denotes a community and a sum of individuals. The significant thing about it is that we have hardly any concrete features of the community which it indicates in this way. It is a community of people who pray, or rather, the community constitutes itself praying to 'Our Father,', just at itself constituted through him. So, we can also see why those who pray are justified in using the word 'our' to associate themselves with the Father."

Long, Thomas G.; *Matthew, Westminster Bible Companion Series.* Louisville, KY: Westminster John Knox Press, © 1997. He views the "crowds" being addressed "through the disciples", p. 46 so thereby anticipating reaching the world". He acknowledges that the Matthew version of the Lord's Prayer is more rhythmic and easier to say it out loud (p.69). But, instead of seeing this as an indication of something used in oral settings and easily memorized showing that it would be an early version, he opts for an interpretation that this was a later version adapted for worship services. He considers the Lucan version as the earlier version of the same prayer as opposed to the same prayer with a different audience. Those praying are considered "God's holy people" (p. 70) and "addressed to the church, to believers, to the followers of Jesus" (p 71). This does not succeed in showing how this might apply to the crowds prior to them becoming disciples.

Loubser, J. A. (Bobby); *Oral and Manuscript Culture in the Bible, Studies on the Media Texture of the New Testament – Explorative Hermeneutics, Biblical Performance Criticism, Volume 7.* Eugene, OR: Cascade Books, 2013. This series of essays provides a comparison of oral versus written material from prehistory to the periods during and immediately after the period of the New Testament, e.g., his chart on p. 182 that he uses to set the stage for comparing the various ways that written and oral methods may have impacted each other. The respective advantages of oral or written material persist today and in more complex situations where technology now makes it possible to widely disseminate in-person presentations to those who can listen or watch it online in far greater numbers than previously experienced. Yet it is still nearly impossible to capture "gesture, body language, facial expression, eye contact, intonation, etc." in writing (pp. 185-186). These issues are routinely confronted when in-person presentations are video, or audio recorded and then transcribed for print. The best transcriptions are now those that are hyperlinked to the original in-person presentation so that the reader of the transcript can also follow the video recording. This problem is also the reason many try to use interactive video whenever possible than a phone conference even though an audio connection allows for experiencing audio clues such as timing change or pacing, volume, speed, intensity changes and other nuances which can indicate rabbit trails or other interpretive clues while missing the visual clues such as body language. Often, these may be inferred from written material, but not always. The discussion of oral methods impacting written methods is also highlighted (see pp. 187-188) when habits of explanation and revisiting information in a speech may be used in writing that might make it appear that a document is really written on two occasions, when it may instead be a communication habit used in oral circumstances and applied to a written document or dictated letter.

Luria, A.R. *The Mind of Mnemonist, Translation from the Russian by Lynn Solotaroff.* NY, New York: Basic Books, Inc, Discus Books, Avon Press of the Hearst Corporation, 1968. Reviewed positively by Michael Cole in *Psychology Today*, this treatment includes work of Luria as a psychologist from the 1920's in Russia with a patient named "S" (p.7). This work includes methods that S used to memorize material by assigning meaning to otherwise meaningless details as location or stories. However, his approach to memorizing details did not provide a meaningful framework that would allow him to forget non-essential details. I am not sure if that lack of a framework contributed to the inability to forget or do critical thinking. he examples shown by Luria demonstrated that the frameworks that S used were not stories that were relevant to him. But it seems reasonable that remembering stories that are relevant to us and interpreting them in a way that makes it possible to improve as a result, then the stories can be highly valuable as opposed to an accumulating pile of unrelated and distracting detail. S apparently had difficulty forgetting. Relevant to our work is that he wrote things down in order to allow his mind to relax and forget what he had previously memorized (p.70).

Luz, Ulrich; *Matthew, Hermeneia Edition, translated from German by James Crouch.* Philadelphia: Fortress Press, 2007.[121] This is a new edition and translation of the fifth German edition of 2002. Luz explains in the most recent preface that he reworked Chapters 3-7 in 1998 and the introduction in the summer of 2000. This represents his life-long work on the topic and is worthy of its wide acclaim as a 3-volume commentary providing well-documented detail of the scholarly work on the Gospel of Matthew. Volume I covers Chapters 1-7, volume 2 covers 8-20, and volume 3 covers 21-28. He includes a bibliography and analysis section for each block of text that includes structure, sources, tradition history and a history of interpretation of each section that will sometimes show how an author's theological bias might influence the interpretation of a section of text. Multiple interpretive perspectives are woven into each section of text as appropriate. An example would be a "social-psychological perspective" of the "woes discourse" of Matthew 23 on p. 177 of volume 3. Since each section includes its own bibliography, a fourth volume would likely be needed if they were all compiled together in one volume. Footnotes are provided at the bottom of each page as opposed to being end notes.

Luz views the Matthean version of the Lord's Prayer as a "multifunctional text," "useful as a model prayer, as a dogmatic compendium, as a catechetical synthesis, as a private and ecclesiastical prayer, and so on."[122] As covered in his introduction section, he considers it as "grounded in the worship of his community" and "Matthew's redactional language…grounded in worship."[123] He, similar to Betz and others, sees it also as a basic "ethical text." He also restricts the context of the Lord's Prayer to Chapter 6 when he discusses the use of "*our* Father" on p. 316 to "'Our' connects the praying individual with the community; that is also the custom in Jewish prayers."

Mack, Burton; Robbins, Vernon K.; *Patterns of Persuasion in the Gospels.* Sonoma, CA: Polebridge Press, 1989; Eugene Oregon:Wipf & Stock, 2008, 1989; 2008.

Malina, Bruce J. & Rohrbaugh, Richard I.; *Social Science Commentary on the Synoptic Gospels; 2d edition.* Minneapolis: Augsburg Fortress Press, © 2003.

Manto, Charles L.; "Electromagnetic Pulse Triage & Recovery", *DomPrep Journal, Nov. 2014.*

Severna Park, MD: DomesticPreparedness.com, 2014. Cost effective EMP protection techniques and processes based on triage. Provides tips and a civilian EMP protection rating system that can be applied to local, national, and global networks of communications, computing, power, and other lifeline infrastructure.

Manto, Charles L.; "EMP Executive Order & Self-Funding Resilient Microgrids", *DomPrep Journal, Jun.26, 2019.*

---

121 Luz, Ulrich; *Matthew*, Fortress Press, 2007.
122 Luz; p. 313, column 2.
123 Luz; p. 43.

Severna Park, MD: DomesticPreparedness.com, 2019. This article links the National Space Weather Strategy and the Presidential Executive Order on EMP that came out in March 2019 with resilient Microgrids systems solutions that the emergency management community can deploy. The article also discusses funding methodologies and sources especially helpful for organizations with limited resources.

Manto, Charles L.; "Solar Storm Near Miss Threats to Lifeline Infrastructure", *DomPrep Journal, Sep. 24, 2014.* Severna Park, MD: DomesticPreparedness.com, 2014. Updates space weather events influencing perspectives on high-impact threats to critical infrastructure including electromagnetic pulse and cyber-attacks.

Manto, Charles L.; "Space Weather - A Historic Shift in Emergency Preparedness", *DomPrep Journal, June 15, 2016.* Severna Park, MD: DomesticPreparedness.com, 2016. Reviews the historic shift of emergency preparedness in the new National Space Weather Strategy and Action Plan asking for the "whole-of-community" to begin planning for long-term nationwide power outages due to extreme space weather and other high-impact low frequency events relatively likely in our lifetimes. The article also covers the DoD concern for power grid vulnerability due to EMP and the DHS RRAP program findings for cyber industry vulnerability to various types of electromagnetic threats.

Manto, Charles L.; "Summary of Audience and Mnemonics of the Sermon on the Mount" (Oral Presentation Given to the Network of Biblical Storytellers Scholars Forum; August 5, 2014).

Manto, Charles L., editor; *High-Impact Threats to Critical Infrastructure, Dupont Summit 2012.* Washington, D.C.: Westphalia Press, © 2013.

Manto, Charles L., editor; *Mitigating High-Impact Threats to Critical Infrastructure, Dupont Summit 2013.* Washington, D.C.: Westphalia Press, © 2014.

Manto, Charles L., "Modeling's Grand Challenge -- Long Term Nationwide High Impact Threats", *Insight, Vol. 19, Issue 4, p. 12-17.* Hoboken, New Jersey: Wiley, A publication of the International Council on Systems Engineering (INCOSE), December 10, 2016. This journal's entire issue is devoted to related topics hosted by INCOSE's Critical Infrastructure Protection and Recovery (CIPR) Working Group. It begins with an overview from the three CIPR Working Group co-chairs (deLamare, Juhasz, Walker) and covers various issues regarding assessment, modeling and systems engineering perspectives of high impact threats. Manto's article sets the stage for the complexity and approaches needed by specialists such as systems engineers to work through complex threats with cascading interdependencies for their respective organizations.

Manto, Charles L. and Lokmer, Stephanie, editors; *Planning Resilience for High-Impact Threats to Critical Infrastructure, Dupont Summit 2014.* Washington, D.C.: Westphalia Press, © 2015.

Manto, Charles L. and Lokmer, Stephanie, editors; *Engaging Communities for High-Impact Threats to Critical Infrastructure, Dupont Summit 2015.* Washington, D.C.: Westphalia Press, © 2016,

Manto, Charles L. and Lokmer, Stephanie, editors; *Best Practices for High-Impact Threats to Critical Infrastructure, Dupont Summit 2016.* Washington, D.C. Westphalia Press, © 2017.

Manto, Charles L.; Child, Joseph R.; *System and method for providing certifiable electromagnetic pulse and RFI protection through mass-produced shielded containers and rooms;* US Patent #8,849,595; U.S. Patent Office, Washington, D.C., September 30, 2014, filing date October 27, 2005. **Abstract**: "Disclosed are a system and method for providing certifiable shielded cabinets and rooms, or pods, to protect devices, equipment and people from electromagnetic interference such as electromagnetic pulse and directed energy attack. The method simulates the separate electric and magnetic shield requirements and capabilities of each type of materials, simulating them separately and together to form a combined set of materials layered for an enhanced electromagnetic shield that is lighter weight and less expensive. Further disclosed is a system and method for SCADA, RFID, and OID monitoring and controls to enable initial and ongoing testing and control."

The filing date shows that Manto was doing the research for this patent while he was doing research on the Sermon on the Mount in Greek looking for mnemonic patterns. The patent covering mitigation measures for threats that could become a worst-case disaster scenario, was issued on September 30, 2014, just less than two months after he presented his biblical research findings to the Network of Biblical Storytellers on August 5, 2014, "Summary of Audience and Mnemonics of the Sermon on the Mount".

Manto, Charles L.; "Summary of Audience and Mnemonics of the Sermon on the Mount" (Oral Presentation Given to the Network of Biblical Storytellers Scholars Forum; August 5, 2014).

Manto, Charles L.; "Who is the 'Our' in the 'Our Father,'" *Christian Century* magazine, accepted for release in 2021.

Manto, Charles L.; Terbush, Dr. James; Motzer, Dr. Earl; *Resilient Hospitals Handbook*. Washington, D.C.: Westphalia Press, 2017. Also available online at https://asprtracie.hhs.gov/technical-resources/resource/5609/resilient-hospitals-handbook-strhening-healthcare-and-public-health-resilience-in-advance-of-a-prolonged-and-widespread-power-outage.

Matera, Frank J.; *New Testament Ethics, The Legacies of Jesus and Paul*. Louisville, KY: Westminster John Knox, 1996.

Matthias, Philip; *The Perfect Prayer, Search for the Kingdom through the Lord's Prayer*. Minneapolis: Augsburg Books, 2005. This journalist concentrates mainly on the Luke version of the prayer, but, following the lead of many commentators who see Matthew's version as a public worship prayer, he views the Luke version as a different prayer but one for private use saying Matthew is "adapting Jesus's prayer to public worship". "Luke's version is more rewarding to contemplation in private.", p.3. This despite the phrase in Matthew 6 where Jesus requests that this prayer be said in private.

Maxey, James A.; *From Orality to Orality, A New Paradigm for Contextual Translation of the Bible; Biblical Performance Criticism, Vol. 2*; Eugene, OR: Cascade Books, (c)2009.

Maxey, James and Wendland, Ernst R., *Translating Scripture for Sound and Performance, New Directions in Biblical Studies, Biblical Performance Criticism, Volume 6,* Eugene, OR: Cascade Books, 2013. One sound mapping discussion I thought interesting was the use of 'ideophones' in Greek and Hebrew and the attempt to bring them to other language translations brought out by David Rhoads on p. 32 and similar discussions of Dan Nasselqvist on p. 54-55 discussing the usage of *marturia* and *fos* (witness and light) in John 1. I similarly thought that the use of consistent wording as opposed to using synonyms to avoid redundancy in modern English, is useful in showing the literary connections and enhancing the oral connections in the in-person presentation or performance. However, I also thought that this makes it easier to do two things for the translator, which is the case for those who were often using Koine as the common commercial language most were using as a second language requiring them to learn the material in Greek (the common language) and then teaching it to others in their respective native languages. First, it helped maintain the literary and oral connections of the common word regardless of the sounds in the target language where text was being translated. Secondly, it helped those trying to learn the common commercial second language since the repetition kept the material simpler to understand and learn where the root word was maintained while altering case endings or conjugation forms.

Mbabazi, Isaac Kahwa, Ph.D.; *The Significance of Interpersonal Forgiveness in Matthew's Gospel*, Ph.D. dissertation, University of Manchester, © 2011; published as *The Significance of Interpersonal Forgiveness in the Gospel of*

Matthew. Eugene, Oregon WIPF & Stock, (c)2013, This work links forgiveness and reciprocity in the Gospel of Matthew, compares it to other literature of the time and its importance to recovery in the Democratic Republic of the Congo.

McGaugh, J. L. *Memory and emotion (Maps of the mind): The making of lasting memories.* New York: Columbia University Press. © 2003. Abstract from PsycINFO Database Record (c) 2016 APA, all rights reserved. "Whether implicit or explicit, our memories connect the past to the present and allow us to form expectations of the future. They are our most important assets, and without them life as we know it would be impossible. But memories come in many different forms and vary substantially in strength; some can be very brief, while others can remain etched in our minds till the day we die. Of all memories, those of emotionally arousing events tend to be the best remembered. Here, James L. McGaugh explains why this is. Along the way he reveals exactly what we know, and what still remains mysterious, about this most intriguing of subjects. Against a historical background, he asks: how are memories made and preserved? Are long-term memories simply rehearsed and strengthened short-term memories? Why do most experiences fade and disappear with time, and would it be a good thing if they didn't? How do stress hormones influence the consolidation of memories and might drugs improve our ability to learn? What do studies of extraordinary memories and disorders tell us about the workings of the brain systems involved in memory formation? And lastly, why is remembering a creative act that can, and often does, produce faulty memories of our experiences?"

McIver, Robert K.; *Memory Jesus, and the Synoptic Gospels*. Atlanta: Society of Biblical Literature, 2011.

McKendrick, Scot; Parker, David; O'Hogan; *Codex Sinaiticus, New Perspectives on the Ancient Biblical Manuscript*; London/ Peabody, Mass: British Museum Library/ Hendrickson, 2015.

McKnight, Scot; *Sermon on the Mount*; Grand Rapids, MI: Zondervan, 2013. He applies "our" to the audience that "includes the disciples but does not include the hypocrites and Gentiles". (p. 175) He does not address the role of the crowds in the prayer and certainly not the persecutors. In advice to preachers regarding the Lord's Prayer on p. 169, "Don't try to say anything new because you'll be wrong".

Meier, John P; "Gospel of Matthew," *Anchor Bible Dictionary*, pp 622-641. New York / London: Doubleday, 1992.

Mendonca, Jose Tolentino; *Our Father, Who Art on Earth, The Lord's Prayer for Believers and Unbelievers*; New York, Paulist Press, 2011. Note his comment on "our" as those who are not the crowds in the following quote from pp. 30-31: "But when he taught the Our Father to his disciples, Jesus said "Our Father" as if he wished to explain the mystery of communion that unites us in him. When we pray *Our Father*, we really are partakers in Christ. His being, his way, his style become ours, because "his Father" is "our Father." In other words, he shares with us this vital and interior architecture, his interior framework, the One towards whom he turns continually. The Prologue to Saint John's Gospel tells us: 'But to all who received him, who believed in his name, he gave power to become children of God' (John 1:12)."

Merkle, Benjamin L. Ph.D; Plummer, Robert L. Ph.D.; *Greek for Life, Strategies for Learning, Retaining, and Reviving New Testament Greek*. Grand Rapids, MI: Baker Academic, a division of Baker Publishing Group, 2017. See chapter 4, "Use Your Memory Effectively", and chapter 8, "How to Get it Back" and the segment on writing it out by hand, p. 132-133.

Messenger, Will (editor, producer) *Matthew, the Bible and Your Work*. Peabody, MA: Hendrickson, 2015. A Bible study workbook suggesting applications for work that includes brief discussion on the beatitudes and the use of the Lord's Prayer.

Metzger, Bruce M.; *A Textual Commentary on the New Testament, 3d edition*. London, NY: United Bible Societies,

1970. This arranges the major textual differences as they appear in the text.

Metzger, Bruce M.; *The Text of the New Testament, 2d edition;* NY and Oxford: Oxford University Press ©1968, first edition 1964. This is a very helpful orientation to the making of ancient manuscripts and books with a history and overview of the key manuscripts for the New Testament.

Meyers, Eric M; Chancey, Mark A.; *Alexander to Constantine, Archaeology of the Land of the Bible, Volume 3;* New Haven, CT: Yale University Press, 2012.

Millard, A.R.; "Literacy, Ancient Israel," *Anchor Bible Dictionary, Vol. 4.* New York / London: Doubleday, 1992 pp. 337-340. "The Bible itself is a witness to Hebrew and Hellenistic literacy, the products of people who wrote in the expectancy that others would read their works" (p. 337). "While the number of ancient Israelites who regularly read and wrote may have been very small and mostly professional scribes, the number who possessed marginal literacy was larger, and still more would likely have been able to recognize and write their own names … In light of the evidence from all sources, it appears that literacy reached beyond the palaces and temples of Israel and Judah to quite small settlements. This means prophetic oracles, hymns, laws could have circulated in written form from an early time to offer an authority and a control on oral tradition. In discussion of the history of the books of the OT the role of Israelite literacy deserves to be given greater prominence" (p. 340).

Morris, Leon; *The Gospel According to Matthew,* Grand Rapids: Eerdmans, and Intervarsity Press. 1992. On. p. 143, he mentions that is would be reasonable that Jesus would teach the prayer in different words for different audiences and hence has no problem with the different wording between Matthew and Luke as both being contemporary with Jesus. He sees the request by a disciple in Luke but sees the "our" in the "our Father" as relating to the one praying and "other believers" p. 144, typical of most who miss the prayer as being directed to the crowds and results in the "our" referring to the one praying and "the other believers." He is consistent given his interpretation of the entire section of 5-7 as aimed at disciples and not the "general public" (p. 94).

Musekura, Celestin ; *An Assessment of Contemporary Models of Forgiveness.* New York, Washington, D.C./Baltimore, Bern, Frankfurt, Berlin, Brussels, Vienna, Oxford: Peter Lang, © 2010. Covers psychological and biblical models of forgiveness in the context of community. The introduction challenges the culture of churches that while not embracing or preaching ethnic hatred, often fails to emphasize concepts of love and forgiveness (p. 4). He engages Hebrew and Greek linguistic issues including the concept of "release" in the word forgiveness, p. 30.

Neusner, Jacob; *The Memorized Torah, The Mnemonic System of the Mishnah,* Brown Judaic Studies 96. Chico: Scholars Press, CA: ©1985. His work demonstrates the importance of understanding concepts that provide motivation and insight creating the potential to memorize large amounts of text.

Neusner, Jacob; *Recovering Judaism.* Minneapolis, MN: Augsburg Fortress Press, © 2001.

Neusner, Jacob; *The Way of Torah, 7th Edition.* Australia, Canada: Thomson, Wadsworth, © 2004.

Newberg, M.D. Andrew; Waldman, Mark Robert; *How God Changes Your Brain.* New York: Ballantine Books, 2010 © 2009. These authors cover the concept of anger and its ramifications, including anger often engaged for religious purposes.

Newberg, M.D. Andrew; D'Aquili, M.D., Ph.D., Rause, Vince; *Why God Won't Go Away;* © 2001, *Epilogue* 2002; New York: Balantine Books, Random House. Demonstrates how the brain functions in various modes including various means of achieving insight and the capability of comprehending or authoring myths and concepts of God.

Newberg, Andrew; **Waldman, Mark Robert**; *Words Can Change Your Brain*; Penguin Group, NY, © 2012.

Neyrey, Jerome H.; *An Encomium for Jesus.* United Kingdom: Sheffield Phoenix Press, University of Sheffield, 2020. See p. 102-103 concerning reciprocity and forgiveness in Matthew 6.

Neyrey, Jerome H.; *Honor and Shame in the Gospel of Matthew.* Westminster John Knox Press, Louisville, KY, 1998. See his chapter 8 beginning on p. 164 regarding the use of "honor" instead of "blessed" (*makarios*) for the beatitudes in Matthew 5.

Noland, John; *The Gospel of Matthew.* Grand Rapids, MI: Eerdmans, © 2005.

Oakman, Douglas E.; *Jesus and the Peasants.* Eugene, OR: Cascade Books, Wipf and Stock Publishers, ©2008. See his statistical analysis of the size of "large crowds" (Chapter 4, pp. 46-52). He estimates virtually no disposable income for the majority of the population (p.101). He also discusses the role of debt in such an economy (pp. 22-41, 104 and following) and the difference between rural and city dwellers (p. 112 and following). He provides a significant essay on the "social significance of the Lord's Prayer" from pp. 199-242 and the role of indebtedness. He concludes on p. 141, "The Lord's Prayer is surprisingly more concerned with specific problems and human welfare in the here and now than might otherwise been suspected."

Oakman, Douglas E.; *Jesus, Debt, and the Lord's Prayer: First-Century Debt and Jesus' Intentions.* Eugene, Oregon: Cascade Books, Wipf and Stock Publishers, © 2014. See pp. 42-91 on the Lord's Prayer in social perspective and pp. 63-67 on "epiouisios."

Oakman, Douglas E.; *The Radical Jesus, the Bible, and the Great Transformation.* Eugene, Oregon: Cascade Books, Wipf and Stock Publishers, ©2021. See the combinations of agrarian conflict in tables and charts on pp. 47-52.

Packer, J.I., *Praying the Lord's Prayer.* Wheaton, IL: Crossway, 2007. It would not be fair to take a scholar's devotional writing and expect the same rigor that would be expected of an academic work. However, devotional works provide an honest perspective of the author's views of important issues. This is especially true in the case of works on the Lord's Prayer. The orientation of the prayer on page 22 shows that the "our Father" implies that the prayer is for "his committed disciples ... adopted into God's family by grace." Furthermore, he states that "we must love our *brothers* by constant care and prayer for them. The Lord's Prayer schools us in intercession for the family's needs: Our Father … give us … forgive us … lead us … deliver us… 'Us' means more than just me! For God's child, prayer is no 'flight of the alone to the Alone' but concern for the family is built into it" (pp. 30-31).

Parsons, Mikeal C.; **Martin, Michael Wade**; *Ancient Rhetoric and the New Testament, The Influence of Elementary Greek Composition.* Waco, TX, Baylor University Press, 2018.

Patte. Daniel; *The Challenge of Discipleship.* Valley Forge. Trinity Press International. 1999.

Patte. Daniel; *Discipleship According to the Sermon on the Mount: Four Legitimate Readings, Four Plausible Views of Discipleship and their Relative Values.* Valley Forge: Trinity Press Interanational, 1996.

Patte. Daniel; *The Gospel According to Matthew, A Structural Commentary on Matthew's Faith.* Philadelphia: Fortress Press © 1987. Patte takes an interesting view of the crowds on p. 62 where he states on one hand that, "Matthew assumes that his readers thought that the Sermon was addressed to the narrow circle of disciples." Yet he also says that "this teaching is addressed to all his disciples, a group that includes international crowds (4:25), that is a group not limited to the band of disciples that followed him during his ministry." He appears to conflate the "crowds" of Matthew 4:19-8:1 that were distinct from the disciples and blend them with future disciples. This misses the opportunity to see how these teachings would be relevant to the crowds of the text that were not disciples. It is not surprising then that "the Lord's prayer asks God to give the disciples the good things they need in order to fulfill their vocation…" (p. 102).

Pelikan, Jaroslav; *Jesus through the Centuries, His Place in the History of Culture.* New Haven, CT: Yale University Press, 1985. See the section commenting on Jesus speaking to crowds on pp. 15-16.

Pennington, Jonathan T.; *Heaven and Earth in the Gospel of Matthew.* Grand Rapids, MI & Leiden: 2009; Baker Academic & Brill, 2007. This is his revision of his doctoral dissertation.

Pennington, Jonathan T.; *The Sermon on the Mount and Human Flourishing, A Theological Commentary.* Grand Rapids, MI: Baker Academic, 2017.

Pennington, Jonathan T.; *Small Preaching.* Bellingham, Washington: Lexham Press, 2021. See his recommendation of listening on p. 24 and on the role of loving witness instead of argumentation on p. 28. I view these as key elements of the Beatitudes and Lord's Prayer as methods of disciple making and as such are relevant to Matthew 5-7.

Philo; *Philo's Works, 10 Volumes & 2 Supplements, Loeb Classical Library.* Cambridge, Mass: Harvard University Press, © 1929.

Pink Arthur W., *The Lord's Praye.;* Memphis, TN: Bottom of the Hill Publishing, 2011.

He views the one praying as the one reborn and the Fatherhood as that of savior as opposed to sustainer as mentioned in MT 5. See pp.15-16. On p. 48 he points out that "daily bread" stands for any type of any temporal necessity, and quotes Matthew Henry by agreeing that one needs to exist physically in order to have spiritual needs. He appears to miss the contention over a temporal necessity that drives the conflict and need for forgiveness, understandably since the connection to the prayer for persecutors is missed.

Pinson, Bill' Blair, Joe; Trammell, Tim; *Matthew: Jesus as the Fulfillment of God's Promises.* Dallas, TX: Baptist Way Press ©2001. See the extent of forgiveness in their discussion of Matthew 18 on p. 106 and their coverage of caring practical outreach of love in their chapter "Are You Ready? Beginning on p. 121. There is no coverage of the prayer for persecutors or Chapters 6-8.

Piper, John; *Love Your Enemies, Jesus' Love Command in the Synoptic Gospels and the Early Christian Paraenesis,* 2012 edition of 1979 version. Wheaton, IL: Crossway. The preface is worthwhile biographical material showing how he worked his 1974 doctoral thesis throughout his career. (Similar to Boomershine who reworked his 1974 thesis on "The Messiah of Peace." See especially his section linking the prayer request to pray for persecutors of Matthew 5:44 with the Lord's Prayer in 6:9-13 on p. 143 in the section from pp. 134-170. See: "Not only has Mt brought into this context words on how one is to pray but also on what one is to pray. That the Lord's Prayer (6:9-13) should be read in close connection with the preceding commands of Mt 5 is shown by the essential relation between the commands and the petitions." He even notes the connection between 5:39 "do not resist evil" with the phrase in the prayer of 6:13 "deliver us from evil."

Pritchard, James B.; *Ancient Near Eastern Texts Relating to the Old Testament,* 3d edition with supplement. Princeton, NJ: Princeton University Press, © 1969, 1950, 1955 (third printing 1974). See Code of Hammurabi (who ruled from 1728-1686 B.C.E.) as translated by Theophile J. Meek on pp. 163-180. See examples of compensatory damages, including hitting on the cheek in sections 202-205. Eye for eye in 197 and tooth in 200. In each of these sections, what is owed is dependent on the class of the offender versus the offended, and in some cases create a monetary debt.

Purim, Esther; "113, She Says Visitors Keep Her Youthful". New York: Brooklyn section of the *Sunday News*, July 12, 1962. "Be good-natured, take care of yourself and most of all, take troubles that come as if they were sent by God."

Quarles, Charles L.; *Matthew, Exegetical Guide to the Greek New Testament*. Nashville, TN: B&H Publishing Group, © 2017.

Quarles, Charles L.; *A Theology of Matthew*. Phillipsburg, NJ: P&R Publishing Co., © 2013.

Quarles, Charles L. *Sermon on the Mount, Restoring Christ's Message to the Modern Church, NAC Studies in Bible and Theology*. Nashville, TN: B&H Publishing Group, 2011. This carefully and lovingly written volume is intended for evangelical audiences with an expressed concern to engage ethical issues inherent in the material and is reflected in its brief overview of the history of its interpretation. It is of exceptional value because of the way it represents the vast majority of thinking on the use of the prayer and the definition of the word "our" in "our Father" among evangelicals. Noteworthy is the compelling discussion of what it must have meant to pray for those presently persecuting the person asked to pray in Matthew 5.

Consistent with other treatments is the lack of linkages from the request to pray in Matthew 5 with the Lord's Prayer in Matthew 6. Furthermore, he makes the customary assumption of many evangelical writers on pp. 187-8 that the "our" in "Our Father" was not viewed in this instance as the "…Father of all people in general. Instead, God is the Father of Jesus' followers exclusively […] Because of this exclusive relationship to God, Jesus' followers can be confident that he is attentive to his prayers."

This contrasts with Manto's thesis that "Our Father" means the "Father of me and my persecutor" and that the prayer was intended not just for the disciples but for the crowds whose qualification was that they had a conflict (the worst case which would be with a determined persecutor). Note: "The use of the first-person 'our' *(hemon)* rather than the first-person singular pronoun 'my' shows that Jesus expected his disciples to pray together as a group." This, of course is explicitly incompatible with Jesus's request that the listeners go into a closet alone, not with disciples, and pray. It was not expected that the person praying consider the Father as the Father in common with disciples, but as the Father in common with the persecutor. His interpretation of the use of the plural "our" is instructive not only how his interpretation but many others. However, his interpretation not only does injustice to the context but to his own evangelical position and concern for discipleship.

Racine, Jean-Francois; *The Text of Matthew in the Writings of Basil of Caesarea*. Atlanta: Society of Biblical Literature, 2004.

Ratzinger, Joseph; *Catechism of the Catholic Church*. New Hope, KY & Rome, Italy: Urbi et Urbi, 1992, pp. 661-668 on Lord's Prayer (see definition of "our" as all in the church, p. 669, sections 2790-2792)

Rauschenbusch, Walter; *For God and the People: Prayers of the Social Awakening*. Boston, New York, Chicago: Pilgrim Press, The Philips Publishing Company, 1909, 1910 . On p. 11 of the preface, he expects criticism for challenging accepted norms of the use of the prayer by looking at actual conflicts and social needs of those who are hurting. This treatment comes close to making the application I suggest for a conflict prayer but WR's treatment reflects the personal need of the person praying in a social context but not the combined need of the one in need and the person or group causing the need. Hence, some of the other concepts are not fully developed but get close. See the following from pp.17-18: "When he bade us say, 'Our Father,' Jesus spoke from that consciousness of human solidarity which was a matter of course in all his thinking. He compels us to clasp hands in spirit with all our brothers and thus to approach the Father together. This rules out all selfish isolation in religion. Before God no man stands alone. Before the All-seeing he is surrounded by the spiritual throng of all to whom he stands related near and far, all whom he loves or hates, whom he serves or oppresses, whom he wrongs or saves. We are one with our fellow man in all our needs. We are one in our sin and our salvation … No one has a clear right to ask for bread for his body or strength for his soul, unless he has identified his will with this all-embracing purpose of God, and intends to use the vitality of body and soul in the attainment of that end."

In this case, I would suggest that the prayer requires us to pray for the "bread for body…or soul" of his own and the one who blocks him from it or takes it from him. He then continues with a request to be modest in the request so that the granting of that prayer does not injure someone else. "With that understanding we can say that the remaining petitions deal with personal needs. … But he lets us pray only for the bread that is needful, and for that only when it becomes needful … This prayer can never be used to cover luxuries that debilitate, nor accumulations of property that can never be used but are sure to curse the soul of the holder with diverse diseases of mammonism … In this petition, too, Jesus compels us to stand together. We have to ask in common for our daily bread. We sit at the common table in God's great house, and the supply of each depends on the security of all. The more society is socialized, the clearer does that fact become, and the more just and humane its organization becomes, the more will that recognition be at the bottom of all our institutions."

Then WR discusses the inner life which is a mix of personal and societal. "The remaining petitions deal with the spiritual needs. Looking backward we see that our lives have been full of sin and failure, and we realize the need of forgiveness. Looking forward, we tremble at the temptations that await us and pray for deliverance from evil." He notes then that temptations are what often comes as a result of ineffective and unjust social institutions. So, he concludes (on p. 23) that the Lord's Prayer is the great prayer of social Christianity … It assumes the social solidarity of men as a matter of course. It recognizes the basis of all moral and religious life even in the most intimate personal relations to God. By looking at this prayer as the conflict resolution prayer, it includes the spiritual needs of both the one praying and the one with whom we are in conflict.

Rhoads, David; "Performance Criticism, An Emerging Methodology in Biblical Studies," https://www.sbl-site.org/assets/pdfs/Rhoads_Performance.pdf.

Rhoads, David; *Reading Mark, Engaging the Gospel.* Minneapolis: Augsburg Fortress Press, 2004. David Rhoads describes the development of literary criticism to include "narrative criticism" which in time has encompassed a stronger appreciation of the time in which it was written that would include a wholistic approach to the material as a whole. This minimizes fragmentation and provides insight into the unity of material that makes a story comprehensible and memorable. He also has a chapter on memorizing and performing the Gospel of Mark. His success came largely from understanding how the story unfolds rather than rote memory of the material. Further understanding comes from interactions with the audience and the interpretation of the story which implies believability as a function of understanding the story and conflicts underlying the story.

Ricoeur, Paul; *Figuring the Sacred; Religion Narrative and Imagination, translated by Pellauer.* Minneapolis: Fortress Press, 1995.

Ricoeur, Paul; *Time and Narrative, Volumes 1-3, translated by McLaughlin and Pellauer.* Chicago: University of Chicago Press, © 1984; originally published as *Temps et Recit, Editions de Seuil,* © 1983; Vol. 2, © 1985, 1984; Vol 3. © 1988, 1985.

Ridlehoover, Charles Nathan; *The Lord's Prayer and the Sermon on the Mount in Matthew's Gospel.* London: T&T Clark, 2020. He provides additional support for the centrality of the prayer in Matthew 5-7 and the gospel as a whole.

Robbins, Vernon K.; "Pronouncement Stories, and Jesus' Blessing of the Children, A Rhetorical Approach." *Semeia,* SBL, 1983.

Robbins, Vernon K.; *Exploring the Texture of Texts, A Guide to Socio-Rhetorical Interpretation.* Harrisburg, PA: Trinity Press, 1996.

Robbins, Vernon K.; von Thaden, Robert Jr. H; Bruehler, Bart B.; *Foundations for Sociorhetorical Exploration, A Rhetoric of Religious Antiquity Reader*. Atlanta: Society of Biblical Literature, Rhetoric of Religious Antiquity © 2016. This contains Robbins articles on "Sociorhetorical Criticism" and "Rhetography."

Robbins, Vernon K.; *New Boundaries in Old Territory, Form and Social Rhetoric in Mark*. New York, Peter Lang, 1994.

Robbins, Vernon K.; *Patterns of Persuasion in the Gospels* (with Burton L. Mack). Sonoma, CA: Polebridge Press, 1989; Eugene, OR: Wipf & Stock, 2008), 1989; 2008.

Roberts, Alexander and Donaldson, James; *Ante Nicene, Nicene and Post Nicene Fathers*, Grand Rapids, MI: Wm B Eerdmans, (reprinted 1975).

This set of the early church writings provides a wealth of writing and commentary related to biblical materials and the first few hundred years of the church. See vol 7 of Ante-Nicene Fathers for the 'Teaching of the Twelve (Didache)" and the "Apostolic Constitutions." In Chapter I of the Didache, the very first paragraph teaches the way of life following the two great commands to love God and neighbor with an immediate appeal to the Sermon on the Mount of Matthew: "And of these sayings, the teaching is this: Bless them that curse you, and pray for your enemies, and fast for them that persecute you." Then later in section VIII, it speaks of praying and fasting quoting the Lord's Prayer of MT 6 with the words, "Thrice in the day pray thus." Similarly, in the Apostolic Constitutions, in the second part of section I, it says, "For so says He again in the Gospel, 'Love your enemies, do good to them that hate you, and pray for them which despitefully use you and persecute you...'" Then again in Section II part XXIV the reader is instructed to use the Lord's Prayer of MT 6 with the instruction, "Pray thus thrice in a day, preparing yourselves ahead of time."

See volume 6 of the Nicene Post Nicene Fathers, series 1, for Augustine's commentary on the Sermon on the Mount (pp 1-63) and his Harmony of the Gospels (pp. 65- 236). On page 33 he closes out what we know as Chapter 5 with continued instructions to pray for enemies and those who persecute us. On page 34, he begins Book 2, where the first words on Chapter I-1 are: "The subject of mercy, with the treatment of which the first book came to a close, is followed by that of the cleansing of the heart which the present one begins." From this point onwards, he construes the context for the Lord's Prayer is being in Chapter 6 of Matthew. (Though chapter divisions are first credited to Stephen Langdon in 1205, these logical sections were obvious and noted by Augustine.) On p. 39, when Augustine treats "Our Father," he believes that the phrase refers to those who are "called to an eternal inheritance, that we might be fellow heirs with Christ, and attain to the adoption of sons, is not from our deserts, but of God's grace; we put this very same grace in the beginning of our prayer, when we say "Our Father." And by that appellation both love is stirred up—for what ought to be dearer to sons than a father?—and a suppliant disposition, when men say to God, 'Our Father:' and a certain presumption of obtaining what we are about to ask; since before we ask anything, we have received so great a gift as to be allowed to call God 'Our Father.'"

Rodin, Judith; *The Resilience Dividend*. Rockefeller Foundation, New York: PublicAffairs, a division of Perseus Books, ©2014.

Rubin, Israel; *The How and Why of Jewish Prayer*. Beit Shemesh, Israel: Arba Kamfot Press, © 2011.

Rubin, Israel; Who Were the Krymchaks? – A Vanishing remant of rabbinic Jews, unpublished paper, Israel, ©2008: Mr. Rubin shows family documentation, Encyclopedia Judaica and other sources regarding Jews from the province of Judaea arriving in Crimea after the Bar Kochba revolt *(132-135 CE).

Runeson, Anders; Gurtner, Daniel M.; *Matthew within Judaism: Israel and the Nations in the First Gospel*. Minneapolis, MN: Fortress, 2016.

Saldarini, Anthony; *Matthew's Christian-Jewish Community*. Chicago: University of Chicago Press, 1994; He details the context of the people of Matthew's Gospel and community. He provides a comprehensive view of the author as a Christian still active within the Jewish community attempting to establish the Jewish legitimacy of the Christian message. He provides a number of interesting links to contemporary Jewish literature for many of the textual elements of Matthew. An example would be the use of oaths in various Jewish groups at the time. Of note, he views the crowds (p. 37) as distinctive from the disciples though "neutral and good-willed."

Satir, Virginia M.; *Conjoint Family Therapy, 3d Edition.* Palo Alto, CA:Science and Behavior Books, Inc., ©1983

Satir, Virginia M.; *The New Peoplemaking.* Palo Alto, CA: Science and Behavior Books, Inc.; ISBN 13: 9780831400705; © 1988.

Sande, Ken & Moore, Kay; *Peacefakers, Peacebreakers, and Peacemakers.* Garland, TX: Hannibal Books © 2005. See ministry and publication history at: https://peacemaker.training/about/.

Schnackenburg, Rudolph; *The Gospel of Matthew.* Grand Rapids. MI: Wm B Eerdmans, 2002. Though he states that Matt 5-7 is addressed to crowds and disciples alike (p. 46), he refers to the prayer as being directed to Jesus's disciples (p. 65).

Schurer, Emil; *The History of the Jewish People in the time of Jesus Christ.* Edinburgh: T&T Clark, 1890; See the previous German and subsequent English retranslation and related information in the Wikipedia article: "His elaborate work on the history of the Jews in the time of Christ, *Geschichte des jüdischen Volkes im Zeitalter Jesu Christi* (1886–1890; 4th edition 1901–1909), made him one of the best known of modern German scholars in Great Britain and the United States.[2] The second edition was translated into English under the title *A History of the Jewish People in the Time of Jesus Christ* (1885–1891). Later, a revised English version of the work was created under the editorship of Géza Vermes, Fergus Millar and Matthew Black, with the slightly different title of *The History of the Jewish People in the Age of Jesus Christ* Edinburgh: T&T Clark (1973–1987). In its earliest form, this work appeared as *Lehrbuch der neutestamentlichen Zeitgeschichte* (1874).[3]" https://en.wikipedia.org/wiki/Emil_Schürer

Segal, Elizabeth A.; *Social Empathy, The Art of Understanding Others.* New York: Columbia University, 2018. Her chapter "What if stress, depression and other health factors block empathy?" supports the approach used by Jesus in the Sermon on the Mount to create empathy.

Senor, Donald; *Matthew.* Nashville: Abingdon Press, 1998. He quotes Luz on p. 70 stating that the SoM is for the crowds as well as the disciples but does not discuss the audience of the Lord's Prayer or define "our" though notes its inclusion here and not in Luke's version (p. 84).

Shively, Elizabeth E.; Oyen, Geert Van; *Communication, Pedagogy, and the Gospel of Mark.* SBL Press, Atlanta, GA; © 2016.

Shulman, Lisa.M., M.D.; *Before and After Loss, A Neurologist's Perspective on Loss, Grief, and Our Brain.* Baltimore: Johns Hopkins University Press, ©2018. The author describes integrates her personal loss of her husband to her professional understanding of how the brain works. She describes three principles of healing the mind and brain after loss: 1) subconscious-conscious integration, 2) immersion-distraction, 3) (p. 63). She reviews the roles of nine brain regions (p.95) and their connections to hormones, the immune system and sleep (.98-99). She promotes the benefits of journaling as a means to address issues as opposed to ignoring them, which does not promote healing. These insights support the practical value of praying for "persecutors" or others creating our conflicts so that one might be able to come to a place of peace. It also supports the concept of praying the Lord's Prayer for Persecutors to calm oneself and prepare one for a more effective time of meditation.

Sim, David; *The Gospel of Matthew and Christian Judaism: The History and Social Setting of he Mattheaqn Community.* Edinburgh: T.&T. Clark, 1998.

Soysal, Oguz; Soysal, Hilkat; Manto, Charles Leo, Assignee: Instant Access Networks, LLC: *Method and instrumentation for sustainable energy load flow management system performing as resilient adaptive microgrid system* : US Patent 10,169,832; U.S. Patent Office, Washington, D.C., January 1, 2019, filing date May 8, 2013. **Abstract:** Disclosed is a method and instrumentation for predictive and adaptive controllers devised to ensure uninterrupted operation of standalone electrical supply systems powered by sustainable energy sources. The device hereby referred to as SelfMaster.TM. is an expert system that manages the energy conversion, storage, and consumption in an isolated electric grid based on data collected during past and current operation of the system and predicted future states of the primary energy sources, storage level, and demand. The sustainable primary energy sources managed by SelfMaster.TM. may include, but not limited to, wind force, solar radiation, and biofuels. The energy storage system is a combination of batteries, hydrogen, biofuel, and hot water tanks. Electric demand consists of critical, non-critical, and deferrable loads identified according to the activities supported by the supply system.

Stanton, Graham N.; *A Gospel for a New People: Studies in Matthew.* Louisville, KY: Westminster John Knox Press, 1992. He has an interesting chapter 13 on "the origin and purpose of the sermon on the mount" where he focuses on Betz' claim on p. 310 and following that the Sermon on the Mount was previously developed material that Matthew uses. This seems altogether plausible as oral teaching that could stand on its own.

Stanton, Graham N., editor; *The Interpretation of Matthew.* Philadelphia/London: Fortrress Press, 1983.

Stassen, Glen H.; *Living the Sermon on the Mount, A Practical Hope for Grace and Deliverance.* San Francisco: Jossey-Bass, a Wiley Imprint, , 2006.

Stott, John R.W.; *The Message on the Sermon on the Mount.* Downers Grove, IL: Intervarsity Press, © 1978, Originally published as *The Christian Counter-Culture.*

Strecker, Georg; *The Sermon on the Mount: An Exegetical Commentary.* Nashville: Abingdon, 1988.

Suetonius, *Lives of the Caesars ,vol.1 &2, with an English translation by J.C. Rolfe, Loeb Classical Library.* Cambridge, MA & London: Harvard University Press,1997, 1998, first published 1913, 1914. Public domain online; published in the *Loeb Classical Library*, 1914. See life of Domitian, sec 4.4: "For there were competitions in prose declamation[15] both in Greek and in Latin;" sec 10.1 "But he did not continue this course of mercy or integrity, although he turned to cruelty somewhat more speedily than to avarice." Sec 12.2 Besides other taxes, that on the Jews was levied with the utmost rigour, and those were prosecuted who without publicly acknowledging that faith yet lived as Jews, as well (p. 367) as those who concealed their origin and did not pay the tribute levied upon their people. I recall being present in my youth when the person of a man ninety years old was examined before the procurator and a very crowded court, to see whether he was circumcised. Sec 23.1 "The senators on the contrary were so overjoyed, that they raced to fill the House, where they did not refrain from assailing the dead emperor with the most insulting and stinging kind of outcries. They even had ladders brought and his shields and images torn down before their eyes and dashed upon the ground; finally they passed a decree that his inscriptions should everywhere be erased, and all record of him obliterated.[76]"

Swanson, Richard W. *Provoking the Gospel of Matthew, A Storyteller's Commentary;* Cleveland, OH: The Pilgrim Press, 2007. This is one of a series on the Gospels that brings insight that comes from speaking and acting the material before audiences. This approach facilitates understanding the relationships between the teller and the audience including the emotions that make the material relevant, believable, memorable, and sharable. It is a multi-media publication that includes a DVD illustrating the process of script development.

Syreeni, Kari; *The Making of the Sermon on the Mount: A Procedural Analysis of Matthew's Redactional Activity, Part I: Methodology and Compositional Analysis.* Helsinki: Suomalianen Tiedeakatemia, 1987.

Talbert, Charles H., *Matthew.* Grand Rapids, MI: Baker Academics, 2010.

Thatcher, Tom; Keith, Chris; Person, Jr, Raymond F.; Stern, Elisa R.; Odor, Judith; *The Dictionary of the Bible and Ancient Media.* London, New York: Bloomsbury T&T Clark, (c) 2017.

Theola, Sister Mary, s.s.n.d; *My First Communion Prayer Book, revised 5th edition,* Belgium: Regina Press, 1997, 1952,. The dedication page mentions this as "one of the most popular Communion books ever published … translated into 14 languages." On p. 61, it has a page on the Sermon on the Mount with a focus on the Lord's Prayer which is quoted. This summary, titled, "Jesus Speaks to the People" is interesting for how it boils down the sermon into one paragraph. The author paraphrases the Matthew 5-7 passage in this way, "One day Jesus went to the mountain top and he spoke to the people. He said, 'Love everyone, even those who are not kind to you. Treat others as you want them to treat you. Ask God your Father for whatever you need. Here is how you are to pray to him…" his is so close to the intent of the prayer because of the proximity of the teaching to love enemies. But the prayer is focused on the need of the child and not the combined need of the child and the one who might be hurting or otherwise impacting the child.

Theonis (Ed. Lederlini, Johannis Henrici); *Progymnasmata,* Stuttgart, Germany: 1834, reprint in India 2015. Greek texts with comments in Latin.

Tipping, Colin; *Radical Forgiveness;, A Radical Five-Stage Process to Heal Relationships.* Boulder, CO: Sounds True Inc. 2009. This includes worksheets and story templates to help the reader work through the issues that can result in healing a relationship. Author founded the Institute for Radical Forgiveness Therapy and Coaching.

Toledano, Rabbi Eliezer; *The Orot Sephardic Shabat Siddur.* Lakewood, NJ & Gateshead, England: OROT, Inc. © 2002. This is a "Sephardic Siddur with English translation with an anthologized commentary including laws and customs of Sephardic communities in all parts of the world."

Toledano, Rabbi Eliezer; *The Orot Sephardic Weekday Siddur;* Lakewood, NJ & Gateshead, England: Orot, Inc., © 2002.

Townsend, John T.; "Education, Greco-Roman," *Anchor Bible Dictionary, Vol 2.* New York / London: Doubleday, 1992, pp. 312-317. "In the world of the NT, educational theory and practice were essentially Hellenistic . . . Even Jewish Hebrew schools were not immune to the pervasive Hellenistic influence, and one can easily interpret rabbinic education as the Jewish adaptation of Hellenistic educational methods and curricula" (p. 312); … "In the western part of the empire Latin language and literature were receiving more emphasis, although the continuing importance of Greek in Roman schools meant that Paul had no difficulty with Christians at Rome understanding an epistle written in Greek. In fact, Greek predominated in Christian worship at Rome until well after the NT period" (p. 313). He describes widespread participation in primary schools starting at age 7, secondary schools that might include textual criticism and translation from classic to contemporary Greek, memorization, and math through geometry. Higher education was experienced by fewer and included the study of philosophy, literature and rhetoric including "the five steps of speech preparation: invention of ideas, arrangement, style, memorization, and delivery" (p. 315).

Ulrich, Daniel & Gardner, Richard B.; "*A Guide for New Testament Exegesis,*" Posted on Bethany Seminary Moodle site for students of Matthew class, B-302. 2020;" This is an adaptation of a guide for exegesis developed by Richard B. Gardner, Professor Emeritus of New Testament Studies at Bethany Theological Seminary. The section titled "An Outline of Exegetical Procedures" uses Gardner's exact words with minor changes. I am grateful for his permission to use his work in this way."

Van Bruggen, Jakob; *Christ on Earth, The Gospel Narratives as History; translated by Nancy Forrest-Flier.* Grand Rapids, MI : Baker Books, , © 1998; Netherlands, ©1987.

Van de Sant, Huub, *Matthew and the Didache*. Philadelphia: Fortress Press, 2005. This is a collection of essays about the early church document which makes heavy use of the sayings used in Matthew. The strong emphasis of "turning the other cheek" and praying for enemies shows the early church orientation to this approach to evangelism and discipleship. One particularly helpful essay by Aaron Milavec shows the value of trying to memorize a text in order to understand the oral methods of organizing material for memorization, teaching and preservation, crediting encouragement from the Network of Biblical Storytellers.

Van der Kolk, Bessel, M.D.; *The Body Keeps the Score, Brain Mind and Body in the Healing of Trauma.* New York: Penguin Books, 2014.

Vanni, Ugo; "The Lord's Prayer", *Catechism of the Catholic Church, with Theological Commentary, Direction and Coordination of the Theological Commentary by Rino Fisichella. pp. 1205-1237.* Vatican City State: Vatican Publishing House, © 2017, Huntington, IN: Our Sunday Visitor © 2019 .;;, ,. See p. 1208, "The liturgical text used in the Lord's Prayer uses the formula found in the Gospel of Matthew (Mt 6:9-13) which forms part of the great Sermon on the Mount (Mt 5-7). In order to fully understand the formula, one must first and foremost pay attention to the context, then to the text that expresses it, and finally to the implications that it contains and that are then expanded upon elsewhere in the Gospel of Matthew."

Volf, Miraslav; *The End of Memory, Remembering Rightly in a Violent World.* Grand Rapids, MI: Wm. B. Eerdmans Press. © 2006.

Volf, Miraslav; *Exclusion and Embrace, A Theological Exploration of Identity, Otherness, and Reconciliation.* Nashville, TN: Abingdon Press, ©1996. See the center he founded at Yale for faith and culture. https://faith.yale.edu/people/miroslav-volf.

Volf, Miraslav; *Free of Charge, Giving and Forgiving in a Culture Stripped of Grace.* Grand Rapids, MI: Zondervan Press, 2005.

Wesley, John; *Sermons, Vol 1,* Carlton and Phillips, 1856. See the *Sermon on the Mount,* Sermon xxvi, Discourse 6, p. 237. Note the very universal sense in which Wesley refers to the "our" in "our Father" in that he applies it to all people, not just followers of Jesus. "'Our Father' not mine only who now cry unto Him, but ours in the most extensive sense. The God and 'Father of the spirits of all flesh,' the Father of angels and men . . . The Father of the universe of all the families both in heaven and earth.' Note also, p. 240 where the universality of the Father is narrowed somewhat to our wants and those of the church as a whole: "'Give us this day our daily bread.' In the three former petitions, we have been praying for all mankind. We come now more particularly to desire a supply for our own wants . . . But this may be used for the whole church of Christ upon earth.' Bread is also referred to as "all things needful whether for our souls or bodies."

Wikipedia; *Mount of Beatitudes,* online on May 2020 at https://en.wikipedia.org/wiki/Mount_of_Beatitudes

See this article that includes the following: "The **Mount of Beatitudes** (Hebrew: רשואה רה, *Har HaOsher*) is a hill in northern Israel, in the Korazim Plateau. It is where Jesus is believed to have delivered the Sermon on the Mount.

Contents: "The traditional location for the Mount of Beatitudes is on the northwestern shore of the Sea of Galilee, between Capernaum and the archeological site of Gennesaret (Ginosar), on the southern slopes of the Korazim Plateau. Its negative altitude (around 25 metres below sea level, nearly 200 metres above the Sea of Galilee) makes it one of the lowest summits of the world. The actual location of the Sermon on the Mount is not certain. [1]

The specific location of a likely location of a place where the Sermon on the Mount may have been given is not certain, but the present site (also known as Mount Eremos) has been commemorated for more than 1600 years. The site is very near Tabgha. Other suggested locations for the Jesus' Sermon on the Mount have included the nearby Mount Arbel, or even the Horns of Hattin. The overall idea of making use of an incline to be heard by larger groups would make sense to those familiar with the area."

View of the Lake of Tibériade (Sea of Galilee) from the Mount of Beatitudes" (from Wikipedia, above)

Wilson, Victor M.; *Divine Symmetries, The Art of Biblical Rhetoric.* Lanham, MD: University Press of America; © 1997. Presents patterns and outlines of the material in the Gospels.

Wilson, William G.; *Alcoholics Anonymous, 4th Edition.* New York: Alcoholics Anonymous Worldwide, © 2001. Students of the Lord's Prayer intended for the crowds will find great value in seeing the approach to a "higher power" in the chapter four, "We Agnostics", the 12 steps in chapter five p. 59 in "How it Works", and a section on itemizing resentments and the chart on p. 65.

Windisch, Hans; *The Meaning of the Sermon on the Mount: A Contribution to the Historical Understanding of the Gospels and to the Problem of their True Exegesis.* Philadelphia: Westminster, 1050.

Wink, Walter; "Beyond Just War and Pacifixm: Jesus' Nonviolent Way", *Review and Expositor 89 (1992): 197-214.*

Wink, Walter; *The Powers that Be, Theology for a New Millennium.* New York: Doubleday, © 1998. Touches on Gospels and his discussion of violence and its use.

Wise, Michael Owen; *Language and Literacy in Roman Judaea: A Study of the Bar Kokhba Document.;* New Haven: Yale Bible Reference Library, © 2015. Shows evidence of a higher amount of literacy and language usage of Hebrew, Aramaic, and Greek in this period.

Wise, Michael Owen; Abegg Jr, Martin G.; Cook, Edward M.; *The Dead Sea Scrolls, A New Translation, Revised Edition.* New York: Harper Collins, 1996, 2005. This revised edition provides additional scrolls not available at the first edition. While not producing every fragment, it is representatively comprehensive for most general audiences. In addition to introductory essays of nearly fifty pages, each of the texts have short introductions of their own, making it possible for general readers to grasp the significance of many of the texts.

Witherington, Ben III; *Matthew.* Macon, Georgia: Smyth and Helwys, 2006. This comes with a CD-ROM that includes research tools. Discusses consideration of some such as J. Jeremias seeing the Sermon on the Mount (SoM) as a catechism but sees this as an anachronistic usage of a later genre for inculcating theology (p. 116). I see this as something that could be resolved by seeing the material as it was explicitly stated, namely as persuasion teaching inherent in disciple making training.

Witherington, Ben III; "Books and Scrolls in the World of Jesus". Patheos online, November 5, 2011. https://www.

patheos.com/blogs/bibleandculture/2011/11/05/books-and-scrolls-in-the-world-of-jesus/ "A standard roll of papyrus in mid-first century A.D. Egypt cost four drachmae, which is to say it cost about 4-8 days pay of an ordinary workman. But let us take for example, the famous Isaiah scroll found at Qumran. A roll thirty feet long took no less than 30 or so hours to fill up. That is—at least three full days work for a scribe like the one pictured above (my shot from the museum of Egyptology in Cairo). A copy of Isaiah then could cost at least 10 denarii, and that is a low guess. And then you would have exactly ONE book of the OT in your hands. Imagine about 40 more rolls that long and you can imagine an OT on scrolls."

One of the major differences between scribes working in Jesus' world and those in the Greco-Roman world is that they were not slaves. They were instead free artisans practicing their trade, and they were without question in huge demand, mainly for the composition of practical documents—wills, property deeds etc. Another difference would be that Jewish scribes copying scrolls did not do so in scriptorium fashion writing while listening to someone read the document. No, they composed by comparing. They acted alone so far as we can tell. The largest single group of such scribes would have been connected either with the Temple, or the various palaces of rulers. But in every town, there would have been someone who could draft documents on demand, and most people would not want to go to despised tax collectors to do the job.

The ordinary person in Jesus' world was assumed to be able to read: 1) decrees, 2) edicts, 3) signs, 4) inscriptions, and 5) placards like that hung round Jesus' neck on the way to execution. A rudimentary kind of literacy was assumed for a wide audience by the governing officials."

Work, Telford; *Ain't Too Proud to Beg, Living Through the Lord's Prayer*. Grand Rapids, MI: Wm. B. Eerdmans, © 2007.

Wuellner, Wilhelm H., *The Meaning of 'Fishers of Men*; Philadelphia: Westminster Press, 1967. Shows the history of the concept of persuasion and its discussion as "fishing" for people both in its positive and negative lights.

Young, Brad H.; *Meet the Rabbis, Rabbinic Thought and the Teachings of Jesus*. Peabody Mass: Hendrickson Publishers, 2007.

Matthew Class April 24, 2020, Bethany Theological Seminary

By Charles Manto

Review of Three Commentaries: Betz, Davies & Allison, Luz – a Discursive Bibliography

Betz, Hans Dieter; *The Sermon on the Mount*, Fortress Press, 1995. This 730-page commentary is one of the most thorough and scholarly on the topic—well received by *Review of Biblical Literature* and *Theology Today*. Betz credits the support for work he received on the topic for over two decades including fourteen months of intense study and writing provided by a grant or "Forschungspreis." It includes a 90-page introduction covering his approach in five pages and the major problems in a historical and literary perspective. Each section is divided into an introduction, analysis, and interpretation. he commentary is prefaced with a list of works most often cited and closes with his partial bibliography that contains about 700 items.

As to the type of literature and its purpose see: Betz views the Sermon on the Mount (SM) as "*epitomai,* consisting of sayings of Jesus grouped together according to systematic points of doctrine considered to be of primary importance." The literary function of the SM, according to Betz, was the "'advanced' teaching for those who have already become disciples … the personal instruction not only of the four disciples addressed, but of all disciples." Note his explanation to the "seeming inconsistency" of the inclusion of the "crowds." "While according to the beginning in 5:1, only the disciples received the SM, 7:28-29 reports that somehow 'the crowds' (οἱ ὄχλοι) came to know it, too. Rather than an oversight on the part of Matthew, the seeming inconsistency shows 'progress'; Matthew seems to have been aware that the SM was originally intended for the disciples only, but that it had become public knowledge . . . Indeed, for Matthew 'the crowds' (οἱ ὄχλοι) are the pool from which new church members are to be recruited. That the 'crowds' also receive the SM (7:28-29) shows how this change took place and that the SM played an important role in attracting people to the church. The SM has played this role during the entire history of the church up to the present."

Betz believes that the Lord's Prayer was already known to the readers of Matthew's Gospel as an oral text [1] and in multiple forms which makes sense from the core evidence being the two forms in Matthew and Luke [2]. Betz also notes the "performative language" [3] of the Lord's Prayer as opposed to a theologically "descriptive language" although he sees that it contains theological concepts. Despite his acknowledgment of its "performative nature," he appears to primarily interpret that performance as being applicable to group worship that he assumes is evidenced by the use of "our Father." He does not notice the "performance" or the improvisational nature of the prayer as useful in the work of trying to convince or persuade someone of something. A recruitment or persuasion intention would be familiar to one who was trained in ancient "rhetoric" or "disciple-making." Betz sees the preponderance of the evidence pointing to a Greek language origin and not Aramaic or Hebrew.

Unresolved Interpretations Issues for Betz, missing purpose, contradictory function:

Missing Purpose:

See the section on p. 373 (column 2), "Original Purpose and Function" of the Lord's Prayer: "What did Jesus intend by the creation of this prayer? One can only speculate about this question because none of the sources is explicit about this." That might be true if the context of Chapter 5 was not already explicit about it when it asks to pray for those who persecute us. However, it may seem to be distant by a couple of paragraphs, but perhaps would be considered much closer when the memory methods of weaving interrelated concepts are considered.

Contradictory Function:

Because Betz fails to link this to the context beginning in 5:44, he not only fails to see the explicit purpose that the context provides for the Lord's Prayer; he fails to make sense of the prayer provided for private use in 6:6 "But when you pray, go into your room and shut the door and pray to your Father who is in secret…" with the use of the words "Our Father" … at the beginning of the prayer in 6:9 that make it appear to Betz as a public prayer. Note his comment that shows tension and inherent contradiction within the text: "It does agree with the prayer instruction 6:7-8, which presupposes that the Lord's Prayer was to be used as a 'private' prayer, but, I have already pointed out that this context is secondary and in tension with the invocation of vs 9b ('Our Father'), which points to a group prayer."[4] It is as if Matthew, the author or redacting editor, (if not Jesus himself being quoted as saying all this) is immediately contradicting himself. If, on the other hand, Betz had seen the connection to 5:44, he could have reframed the definition of "our" and eliminated the tension and contradiction. See the how the definition of "our" makes the change:

from "the one praying" **and with** (*therefore, not in secret*) "some larger group of people" such as "those that are praying alongside him or her," or "all the other disciples, or participants in that faith community,"

to "the one praying" **alone** (*in secret*) **for** the "persecutor" (not participating in the conflict prayer here or in Matthew 7 but hopefully included in Matthew 18).

Because Betz cuts off his consideration of the Lord's Prayer from 5:44, he also fails to note the other connections between that section of Matthew 5:43 on loving enemies, and each of the elements of the don't resist "evil" section in Matthew 5 with the petition on "evil" in the Lord's Prayer, and the other mutual elements of that section with the "we" petitions of "giving," "releasing" and "testing" [5]. Though recognizing the apparent contradiction [6], Betz also misses the rhetorical benefit and links of the three items to not do in public (almsgiving (mercies), prayer, and fasting) compared to the three we ought to do before men (being gentle, merciful and peacemaking) as mnemonic weaves that provide the rhetorical direction and force throughout the SM culminating in the Lord's Prayer and its application. It is understandable that those who are accustomed to read linearly to see Chapter 6 as a change of focus that would be separate from the material in Chapter 5. It is easier to see those connections when the material is seen as interwoven links for progressive rings that make the entire collection of material in Chapters 5-7 easier to remember and subsequently share. The links also help remember or perform the larger texts with a sense of where they were heading.

The failure of Betz to see the Lord's Prayer in its context of Matthew 5:44 is also indicative of how he misses the clear claims of the text as directed to the "crowds" and for the purpose of providing "fishing lessons" or discipleship making lessons to the fishermen disciples in 4:19. While many of the lessons of the SM and the Lord's Prayer are certainly applicable to disciples, the life of the community of disciples and their worship as they spread across the nations and into the end times, Betz does not connect the offer of "fishing lessons" in Matthew 4:19 as the stated purpose of the material in Matthew 5-7 as disciple making lessons that disciples were to use in order to make new disciples. As a consequence, he misses the nature of the interaction directly with the crowds addressed in Matthew 5-7 and the Lord's Prayer that they were asked to pray for their persecutors. In the same way, Betz is left bewildered by the purpose of the Lord's Prayer and its position, this also impacts Betz's view of the genre or type of literature of represented by the Lord's Prayer and the Sermon on the Mount as a whole.

Davies, W.D. and Allison, D.C.; *Matthew*, Volumes 1-3. T&T Clark, London and New York, 1988. International Critical Commentary. This is a very thorough and scholarly treatment of the Gospel of Matthew with each section consistently treated under the topics: "Structure, Sources, Exegesis, Concluding observations, and Bibliography." Each section of text uses the koine Greek text represented by the Nestle-Aland *Novum Testamentum Graece* and the Huck-Greeven *Synopse der drei ersten Evangelien*. (See p. 147 of their 148-page introduction. They also have 32 pages of abbreviations and bibliography at the front of the book.) Volume 1 covers Chapters 1-7, volume two Chapters 8-18, and volume 3 Chapters 19-28. In the preface of the third volume, it was explained that Davies expected to produce a draft of each of the three volumes first. That worked out for the first volume but not the remaining two where he was only able to review the work of Allison. Note also that Davies wrote a separate volume, *Sermon on the Mount*, beginning in 1969 through 1990, and the *Setting of the Sermon on the Mount* in 1989. Allison also wrote a separate book, *The Sermon on the Mount, Inspiring the Moral Imagination*, in 1999. Those not conversant in Greek may wish to use their English language Bible while reading it. Like many scholarly works, this one took years to produce with the support of the universities where they worked or collaborated.

The introduction makes the case that the Gospel of Matthew is well crafted from end to end. "Clearly the hand of one man has been active throughout. Secondly, devices such as foreshadowing, repetition, *inclusio*, show up the impressive unity of the gospel. The beginning and the end hang together, as do the various parts that make up the whole" (volume 1, p. 96). While considering the Sermon on the Mount as an essential unity in volume one, the strong connections with other sections in MT are re-emphasized in the preface to the second volume, "The Sermon on the Mount is retrospective: it is inseparable from what precedes it in Chapters 1-4. But it is also prospective, equally inseparable from what follows it in Chapters 8-28." See vol. 2, p. ix.

Unresolved interpretive problems in Matthew 5-7: Who is "salt and who is "our"? In my opinion, two key unresolved issues arise from failing to apply the explicit audience of the crowds with the disciples observing and learning from Jesus who is showing them how to recruit or "fish" for people among the crowds addressed in the specific passages within Mt 5-7. For example, "who is salt"? when Jesus addresses the crowds saying, "you are the salt of the earth." Who is the "our" in "our Father" when Jesus asks the crowds to pray? Davies and Allison admit that they cannot see how one becomes salt nor can they figure out for sure how salt generally functions in the text. They claim to know who the "our" is in the Lord's Prayer but fail to account for the prayer that Jesus requested of the crowds whom they believe he left out of the request.

Who is Salt? See p. 471 of volume 1 for Davies and Allison's description of salt. Davies and Allison assume that only disciples are identified as salt but with no discernible justification for why the crowds are left out. Therefore, the identification of "who" is salt is incomplete at best. This is despite the fact they both recognize that Jesus addresses the crowds. Note their comments on pp. 421-422 of volume 1, "The impression created by this and the previous clause is that Jesus, having seen the crowds, goes up the mountain to get away from them (cf. Jn 6.3). Yet in view of 7.28-8.1, we must think of the crowds as overhearing the discourse. There are two circles around Jesus, an inner circle (the disciples) and an outer circle (the crowds)."

While they see the crowds and disciples in two circles who both hear Jesus, commentators who suggest that Jesus primarily addressed the disciples but that the crowds "overheard" fail to fully appreciate the nature of speaking outdoors to not one but many "crowds" and how the "crowds" would be amazed at the end. The "crowds" only hear if Jesus purposely addresses the crowds so that they all could hear including those at the furthest distance from Jesus the speaker. In fact, going up to the side of the mountain makes it possible for Jesus to project over the bodies of those near the front so that those in the back could hear. This is similar to when Jesus goes into a boat to speak to crowds as in an amphitheater so those in the back are not blocked by those in the front.

Merely overhearing Jesus speaking to the disciples close at hand would neither make it possible for them to hear Jesus in the first place or be so captivated by them at the end so that they declared that he spoke as one with "authority," implying that they had no choice but to keep on listening. Also, addressing the interests of the disciples would not engage or keep the attention of those in the "crowds" who were not being addressed. Whatever Jesus had to say to the crowds needed not only to be capable of being heard, but capable of capturing and holding their attention. This, of course, would be exactly what would be expected if Jesus was intending to show the disciples how to recruit from the crowds and teach both the crowds and disciples how to persuade those in conflict. Understanding the explicit audience as primarily being the crowds being recruited for the benefit of the disciples who were promised "recruiting lessons" is the only way to make sense of the text in its context and its explicit audience. With this understanding, one can then answer the questions, "who is salt?" and "who is 'our?"

How does one become salt? Davies and Allison do, however, go into great detail about how salt functions (pp. 472-473). As a result, he concludes his thoughts on p. 473 by saying, "Given the various uses for salt (cf. Pliny, *Nat. His.* 31.73-92, 98-105) and its several symbolic associations, it is quite impossible to decide what one characteristic is to the fore in Mt 5:13. Thus while it would make sense to affirm that the disciples are, for example, the world's wisdom, it would also be reasonable to think that the pure in heart (5:8) purify the world, or (as Origen, *C.Cels.* 8.70 has it) that Jesus' followers preserve the world, or that they are willing to sacrifice themselves (cf. Schnackenburg (v), pp. 195-196). But as implied by two facts, the 'ambiguity of salt need not trouble; for salt was equivocal and multivocal for the evangelist" (p. 473). As in his introductory comments in his exegesis of Mt 5:13 on p. 471, he says "In 5:13 would be disciples are told that they are the salt of the earth, in 5:14-16 that they are light of the world. The statements are quite general. The reader is not told how to become salt or light."

In my view, Davies and Allison admit to missing how one might become salt and light and how it applies to the crowds because they miss the rhetorical pairings of the beatitudes immediately prior in Mt 5:3-12. They overlook the difference between being "salt and light" as opposed to being "salty tasting and light giving" and hence miss how one becomes salt in the first place, namely by going through sorrow and being deprived of justice and what one must do consequently, namely becoming gentle and merciful. These links become more apparent once the beatitudes are seen as pairs, the first being the bookends and the six in between as pairs of alternating states within oneself and an accompanying connection to those outside oneself. (See the treatment on salt and light by Manto in the paper presented to the Network of Biblical Storytellers.)

It would be a lot easier for Davies and Allison to then see how the categories of salt and light applied to all including the crowds when any in the crowds are "sorrowful, deprived and therefore hungering for justice." Similarly, they miss the point of how being salt or light by virtue of their sorrow, provides those who suffer with insights into becoming salty tasting and light giving when they are "gentle, merciful and peace-making." If the crowds learn the lessons from their suffering, then others become blessed by their gentleness, mercifulness and peace-making. But, if the members of the crowds fail to be gentle, that means that those in the crowds who have suffered have failed to learn their lessons, failed to be gentle and failed to bless others who are then robbed of experiencing their saltiness or light. In that case, it is as though those members of the crowds went through all that suffering for nothing.

Once it can be shown that Jesus was primarily addressing the crowds with the disciples overhearing, then it can be shown to be a progression of concepts that comfort the sorrowful and justice-deprived while ultimately turning them into new peace-making disciples instead of the new peace breakers. By missing the pairings and the inherent psychological progression that restores peace promoting empathy and peacemaking, it is easy to see why commentators such as Davies and Allison totally miss the disciple making process inherent in the progression of the beatitude pairs and its fulfillment of the promise to receive "fishing lessons" promised in Mt 4: 19. Note that the text of Mt 5:13 shows that Jesus says that the "crowds" are already salt and light while being salty tasting (or not tasted) or light providing (or light hiding) is still in question. "You are the salt of the earth; but if salt has lost its taste, how shall its saltness be restored?" This same failure to address the explicit audience of Matthew 5-7 as both the crowds and the disciples, not only causes Davies and Allison to not understand "who is salt," they fail to apply the request of Jesus for the crowds to pray for their enemies and miss the major point of the Lord's Prayer.

Contradiction of Who is "our"?

Claiming leaving out the crowds: Note their comment on Mt 6:9, on "our Father," their definition of "our" totally leaves out the "crowds." "Concerning the injunction to pray to God as Father and the related concept of the believer's sonship in Matthew, two points are to be made. (1) 'Your Father' and 'Our Father' include the disciples but not the populace at large. This is because sonship depends upon Jesus, the Son of God. Specifically, those who obey the will of God and follow his Son themselves become sons of God (c.f. 5:9, 45; 12:46-50)." As one might see, Davies and Allison completely contradict the text and themselves. The text of Matthew explicitly states that Jesus explicitly addresses the crowds who, while sons of the Father in the respect that they, like their persecutors receive sunshine and rain, are not yet sons of the Father until they love and pray for their worst-case enemies.

Text Used that Contradicts Their Own Position: Note the odd phrase, "so that you may become sons of your Father." How is it that they have the Father but are not sons yet (Mt 5:44)? Does it merely mean "become like your Father"? If so, like a father in what way? Or does it imply that this refers to the disciples only as true children? Or might it be how they might be children in one way but not another? Children in one sense now but another sense later? Davies and Allison claim that the prayer is for those who are already disciples and not the crowd because the disciples are already children, yet they see and quote the request to pray for enemies because in doing so they will become children (Mt 5:44), so in this case the text they quote shows that the ones praying are NOT the children that Davies and Allison makes them out to be. Davies and Allison, as most all recent commentators, have missed the strangeness of this line and the explicit audience of the text, namely the crowds, and the disciples as those getting "fishing or disciple-making lessons." As a result, they miss the possible definition of "our" as the combination of the individuals in the crowds who were to pray alone for their persecutors, and the "persecutors" for whom they would pray. By doing that, it that will lead the individuals within the crowds in time to become sons of their Father and new peace-maker disciples. Many tend to read their theology of the concept of sonship and Fatherhood into the text and miss the opportunity to further support their perfectly correct theology and desire to reach the nations as described the Great Commission.

Luz, Ulrich; *Matthew*, Hermeneia Edition, translated from German by James Crouch. Fortress Press, 2007[7]. This is a new edition and translation of the fifth German edition of 2002. Luz explains in the most recent preface that he reworked Chapters 3-7 in 1998 and the introduction in the summer of 2000. his represents his life-long work on the topic and is worthy of its wide acclaim as a 3-volume commentary providing well-documented detail of the scholarly work on the Gospel of Matthew. Volume I covers Chapters 1-7, volume 2 covers 8-20, and volume 3 covers 21-28. He includes a bibliography and analysis section for each block of text that includes structure, sources, tradition history and a history of interpretation of each section that will sometimes show how an author's theological bias might influence the interpretation of a section of text. Multiple interpretive perspectives are woven into each section of text as appropriate. An example would be a "social-psychological perspective" of the "woes discourse" of Matthew 23 on p. 177 of volume 3. Since each section includes its own bibliography, a fourth volume would likely be needed if they were all compiled together in one volume. Footnotes are provided at the bottom of each page as opposed to being end notes.

Luz views the Matthean version of the Lord's Prayer as a "multifunctional text," "useful as a model prayer, as a dogmatic compendium, as a catechetical synthesis, as a private and ecclesiastical prayer, and so on" [8]. As covered in his introduction section, he considers it as "grounded in the worship of his community" and "Matthew's redactional language ... grounded in worship" [9]. He, similar to Betz and others, sees it also as a basic "ethical text." He also restricts the context of the Lord's Prayer to Chapter 6 when he discusses the use of "*our* Father" on p. 316 to "'Our' connects the praying individual with the community; that is also the custom in Jewish prayers."

Unresolved Difficulties in Interpretation: As Betz, Luz admits that there are difficulties in interpretation. "The petitions of the Lord's Prayer are so short and open that seldom is one able to establish their meaning unambiguously" [10]. Again, Luz does not make meaningful connections to the prayer context beginning in Matt 5:44.

As a result, Luz needs to read into the text definitions of "our Father" (Πάτερ ἡμῶν) from his theological insights that come from outside the context. Note, "Thus by addressing God as Πάτερ, the Lord's prayer begins with a promise of salvation. It is a prayer of God's children" [11]. In so doing he misses both the dual nature of fatherhood mentioned in the context of Matthew 5:44-45, "so you might become children of your Father in heaven" (where those addressed in Matt 5:44 are children of the Father and also not yet children) and the specific connection to prayer and the Father who "makes his sun rise on the evil and on the good, and sends rain on the just and the unjust" (Matthew 5:45) as their creator, sustainer and protector but not their "redeemer or savior from sin."

Luz restricts the context of the Lord's Prayer to Chapter 6 when he discusses the use of "*our* Father" on p. 316 to the praying community according to his statement, "'Our' connects the praying individual with the community; that is also the custom in Jewish prayers" that are discussed in some detail.

By missing the connection of the Lord's Prayer for persecutors, he fails to show the linkages with each of the section within the prayer and the goal of forgiveness and also shows some difficulties making the connections between the "you petitions" well known in Jewish prayers which focus on the coming reign of God in the world which will resolve our conflicts and needs with the "we petitions" which focus on the very things that are threatened by the persecutors, "the necessary bread" which in turn propels us into our need of forgiveness as a result of that conflict over "necessities."

Again, the simplicity, unity and the rhetorical force and direction of the Lord's Prayer in the context of Matthew 5-7 is missed by not understanding the "our" in "our Father." Hence, each of the following phrases within the Lord's Prayer are also under-appreciated for their rhetorical force and stronger linkages and symmetry. This is especially evident when the commentary here is compared to the rest of the SM, especially the "ask, seek, and knock" prayer, and the subsequent conflict prayer in Matthew 18.

[1] Betz; See p. 370, column 1.

[2] Betz; See p. 370, column 2.

[3] Betz; See p. 377, column 1. Despite his acknowledgment of its "performative nature," he appears to limit that performance to group worship, and not the "performance" or the improvisational work of someone trying to convince or persuade someone of something, not unlike one who was trained in ancient "rhetoric" or "disciple-making."

[4] Betz; See p. 373, column 2 at bottom. See also p. 376, column 2 in discussion of group vs private prayers.

[5] See my discussion on the chiasmus between the 'turn the other cheek' section and the 'we petitions' of the prayer. Note also the identical wording of "on earth as it is in heaven" in the prayer and the end of Matthew's "great commission."

[6] Betz; See p. 346 column two and footnote 126. The apparent contradiction provides emotion and motivation to enhance memory and conceptual linkage between the two groups of three. This is a practice of rhetorical weaving and is supported by new awareness in the way memory works in the human brain shown by brain imaging.

[7] Luz, Ulrich; *Matthew*, Fortress Press, 2007.

[8] Luz; p. 313, column 2.

[9] Luz; p. 43.

[10] Luz; p. 314, column 1.

[11] Luz; p. 315, column 2.

Epilogue and Final Application Note

Just before submitting final responses to copy edits of this text to the publisher, I unexpectedly brushed up against some poison plants and experienced extreme itching and burning rashes that made it hard to concentrate for a week forcing me to take some medication that reduced the skin irritation but made me drowsy. So, I got behind in my scheduled work. During that delay, I got an inquiry from my cousin Maureen about a contact through 23&me who was given up for adoption at six months of age and is now, while in his sixties, trying to find his biological family. Maureen knew I would be interested since she knew that I met her after my own quest to find my father's family ever since I was forbidden to do so when I was nine years old, at the birth of my youngest brother, Mark. Now, after 60 years on that path of reconciliation, I discovered my half-brother David Cassens who was born two blocks from where I lived at the time just eleven months before my younger brother Sam was born. Now, suddenly, and certainly unexpectedly, I have not only been able to round out my family with a brand-new sixty-six-year-old baby brother, I found a collaborator who has deep connections with both the Eastern church with whom he fellowships and with the Roman Catholic scholarly community whom he serves as Dean of Libraries at St. Louis University where my niece Samantha and her husband Brian took courses. David was able to provide me with some bibliography that brought me up to date on a Russian scholar I had not known. If I did not brush up against the poison plants, I would not have met David in time for him to see the final draft and make it possible for me to include a meaningful Russian Orthodox perspective by Dr. Alfeyev.

I have often told my friends that if you knew my ethnic nationality, Finish on my mother's side and Russian on my father's side, you would understand my personality: "I am always rushin' because I'm only half finish'". And so, with this book. I am rushing to get it done knowing that it is a foundation for several other items I need to publish both for general audiences on one hand and scholarly and professional audiences on the other. I could wait a little longer to smooth out the writing in this resource book a little more, but, then it would delay the others which in themselves may make for more focused writing on specific topics that this resource book seeks to address. So, as I ask forgiveness for being half finish', you at least will know that I have an authentically good excuse. I really can't help it, at least this time. Maybe I can finish this in the studies and writings to follow.

Section 3: Appendix

Including Limited Distribution Papers by Manto and Colleagues

Most of the following documents are examples of interactions regarding the Lord's Prayer in Matthew 5-7 showing how the material in Matthew 5-7 lends itself to interactive discussions. (Note that a Kindle version of this book can be used as a search tool and index. For an example of how to search on Kindle, see items on the web such as: https://smallbusiness.chron.com/can-search-word-within-book-kindle-73592.html)

- **Summary of Audience and Mnemonics of the Sermon on the Mount, August 2014 presented to the Scholars Forum of the Network of Biblical Studies and discussed within the group**
- **Draft publication for CC, "Who is the 'our' in the Our Father?" 2020 accepted for publication by** *Christian Century* **magazine**
- **Use of the Lord's Prayer for Persecutors by Dr. Verkouw in his Lenten series for his congregation in March 2020 and his email introduction of the material**
- **Lord's Prayer Sermon by Dr. Laura Truax, Pastor, LaSalle Street Church, Chicago**
- **Interactive Bible Study, Video Link & Transcript, Matthew 5; June 28, 2019 with commentary by Pastor Stahlberg on July 27, 2019**
- **Interactive Bible Study, Video Link & Transcript, Matthew 6; June 29, 2019**
- **Interactive Lord's Prayer Tandem-Preached Sermon, Video Link & Transcript, Dillon, CO; June 30, 2019**
- **Interactive Discussion on Lord's Prayer for Enemies with Atlanta Lyft Driver from Nigeria, Video Link and Transcript; June 22, 2019**
- **Lord's Prayer as Preparation for Meditation**
- **"The Joke," Lord's Prayer Skit. Manto, 2017**
- **Quick Overview of My Stake in Conflict Resolution** *(response to request for author's background in conflicts)*
- **Discussion Questions Used in Body of Text**
- **Letter Regarding Anger and Conflict Resolution from Reader**
- **"Relationships Come First—Maslow's Hierarchy of Needs Contradicts the Facts of Human Existence"**
- **Script without Spacing Exercise**
- **Status of Global Christianity Charts**
- **Bible Manuscript and Greek language resources**

    Volume II Study Guide (forthcoming)
    Volume III Alternative Texts (forthcoming)
    Volume IV Prayer Journal (forthcoming)

Summary of Audience and Mnemonics of the Sermon on the Mount

(Oral Presentation Given to the Network of Biblical Storytellers Scholars Forum August 5, 2014)

Matthew's Gospel (Chapters 5-7) contains what is often known as the Sermon on the Mount which showcases the most famous sayings of Jesus before four new disciples who were challenged to watch Jesus fish for people and a large crowd that would likely have met the description of Matthew Chapter 4 as "those who lived (or were trapped) in the valley of the shadow of death." By the end of the sermon, the crowd was so **amazed** that they said that they never **heard** anyone speak with such **authority**. What was so amazing and authoritative that demonstrated that these crowds were in the nets of Matthew's Jesus?

At the center of the Sermon on the Mount, Matthew's Jesus had just been guiding some thoughts leading up to the famous section of conflict management where he encourages those who had been hurt and were accustomed to ask for an eye for an eye to instead "turn the other cheek" and "walk the extra mile." (These conflict **scenario kernels** are slightly modified from each other to provide the maximum number of relevant **story combinations** with the fewest possible words. See the appendix for computing as many as 4x4x4x4-3 times the number of relationships as possible combinations.)[1]

In addition to those actions, he encourages an internal attitude of "loving enemies." Having just outlined a broad range of conflict, he encourages them to their use their common connection with God through prayer—to bring blessing instead of a curse on the worst-case scenario of conflicts —the persecutor. (This would imply that if you were to pray for the person in the worst-case scenario, you would do the same for any lesser case.) Some, even modern scholarly commentators on that section at the bottom of Chapter 5 lament that Jesus did not show us how to do such a prayer (see sample NICNT commentary by France). I propose that when you discover some of the memory devices that **weave** these sections together in a paragraph or so later, *Jesus indeed goes into the very prayer to use for those with whom you have conflict, namely what we know as the "Lord's Prayer."*

If the "Lord's Prayer" is the prayer for persecutors, then I as the person praying would think of "our Father" as the "father of the just (me) and the unjust (my persecutor) who is hurting me or blocking me from what I need most. In that prayer I ask the Father to give us both the very critical thing that the persecutor has taken from me (our daily bread).

I believe that these concepts are woven together in such a way as to provide the maximum amount of information in the fewest possible words, thus making communication and memorization easier. Then, I also see these elements built on an **escalating emotional framework** that taps into my motivation and renders the material unforgettable. In this case, the "Lord's Prayer," echoing the beatitudes, culminates in a crescendo of an even greater emotional flip or pivot that then asks for forgiveness of me, and my persecutor based on how well we are forgiving each other. This is something that is so hard, that the praying person then asks to be excused from that test ("deliver us from testing") since it would only lead to destruction ("deliver us from evil"). But it creates an extraordinary amount of empathy, humility, and a sharing of mercy that is remarkable. This pattern has already been set up from the very beginning of the Sermon on the Mount in the beatitudes or blessings that have already been built on an **escalating emotional framework** that also has an **emotional pivot** that makes the sequence of 4 pairs of blessings easy to remember and hard to forget.

Because of limited time, I will not go into the way I discovered the pattern but will merely describe the emotional framework that I see.

Only two of the beatitudes have the phrase "theirs is the kingdom of heaven," the first and the eighth. The first pattern element is one of an internal condition when suffering, "Blessed are the poor in spirit"; and the second, is an external relationship when strong, "blessed are those who are persecuted." (You need someone else to persecute you.)

Then the six in between are actually three pairs that replicate this pattern of inner and outer, of weaker versus stronger.

"Blessed are the sorrowful" (inner and weaker)

    vs "Blessed are the gentle" (outer—*needing someone to be gentle with*—and stronger),

"Blessed are those who hunger and thirst for justice" (inner and weaker—*weaker because they were hurt from the action that deprived them of something that caused them to crave justice they were denied*)

    vs "Blessed are the merciful" (outer and stronger)

"Blessed are the pure in heart" (inner and weaker)

    vs "Blessed are the peacemakers" (outer and stronger)

Now we have a simpler set of three pairs surrounded by an introduction and an ending blessing that reflect the pattern of inner to outer and weaker to stronger. Then there is a memorable sequencing of emotional escalations between each pair and a flip or pivot at the "blessed are the pure in heart."

Emotional escalation within the blessing pair: those who have been hurt ("blessed are the sorrowful") have a choice when they recover and become strong ("for they shall be comforted") to either continue the cycle of abuse or instead be gentle ("blessed are the gentle") and hence "inherit the earth." (The oppressed people can recover and grow to become the new oppressors.)

Emotional escalation between the blessing pairs: But what happens when that person who had been deprived of justice and has been hungering and thirsting for justice (or for the injustice to have never happened) recovers and becomes strong and comes across the very person who caused all that suffering? The desire for revenge is so powerful, is such an emotional escalation, that it might not be so easy for that person to be merciful to the perpetrator. But if he does show mercy, he or she is said to be "blessed" with the promise of receiving mercy in the future.

Emotional flip or pivot: It is hard for that innocent victim who in the moment of that harsh treatment might be considered as "pure in heart" to think that he or she would be as bad as the perpetrator and ever need mercy like that. But this is where even greater emotional escalation and a flip or pivot comes in. Because at some point in each of our lives, we discover, that we did the very thing we detested most and became like the person we most abhorred. It would be like King David when challenged by the prophet Nathan, was driven to demand of Nathan, who this man is who did such a terrible thing and deserves to die (2 Sam 12:6-7)? Then, we like David are told, "Thou art the man!" (*Jesus is playing a Nathan to everyone in the crowd—each of whom is a David.*)

At that moment, all my moralizing momentum is turned on me like a judo flip and I discover that I am the one who did what I detested most, and I have joined the most impure of all. This message becomes authoritative for me as it was for David or the crowds because it addresses my greatest concern with what I am most aware. At that moment I have my greatest crisis of identity, my greatest emotional discouragement. At that moment, I also have a choice. I can stay in that place and die like Judas, or, I can go apologize, make what compensation I can, and go to God for forgiveness which then gives me peace with God that comes not from how wonderfully moral and loving I am but solely on the mercy that comes from God through an innocent sacrifice and declares that I have been purified from what I have known to be the greatest of impurities.

So, this blessing for "the pure in heart" serves as a **switch or pivot**. At one moment, just for a time when we were victimized, we were relatively innocent and pure. But later when being the ones in need of mercy and purification, we can experience being "purified in heart" with the promise of "seeing God."

Then, the following blessing in that pair shows what happens when that one gained peace with God through the mercy that comes from sacrifice. This is also an **escalation** because it is the first time in the second half of the blessings when the strong one shifts from merely restraining from continuing the cycle of abuse by being gentle; or merely refrains from revenge by showing mercy but injects him or herself into the path of danger by being a peacemaker and thus creating peace. Those who see that declare the "God thing" before their eyes and call the peacemaker a child of God because that is precisely what God does, make peace for people based on an innocent sacrifice. And that is just what the peacemaker had done, namely, make peace for another on the basis of the sacrifice of his or herself.

The following bookend then makes even more sense. Those who were stopped by the peacemaker now have a new agenda. They must focus all their attention on the peacemaker who blocked them from their form of justice and now begin to persecute the peacemaker—ironically, in the name of justice. "Blessed are the persecuted for justice's sake for theirs is the kingdom of heaven."

This is why at the end of the blessings, Jesus says that they who have suffered (and are sorrowful, deprived of and hunger for justice, and have been alternately pure or purified in heart) are declared to be salt and light. The Good News is that God has already been at work in their bad news and has invested in them proportionately to their suffering and has given them insights by virtue of their suffering. But, when strong will they act out what they have learned and be "gentle, merciful and peacemaking" and hence be salty tasting and light giving? Or will they waste all that investment of their suffering and not be salty tasting and hide the light under a basket?

This emotional framework with a pivot maps the most traumatic experience of the listener into the blessings of the Good News that becomes readily recognized and unforgettable.

When I have asked numbers of people who have read the beatitudes dozens or hundreds of times how many there were or could recite them back, very few (maybe one or two) could do so. But after discussing the emotional escalation this way and asking what they thought of being salt (been sorrowful, deprived of justice, in need of purification themselves) or salty tasting (being gentle, merciful, or peacemaking), they remarkably can repeat all the blessings. How long they remember might be a matter of how closely these were mapped against their own drama and trauma. But for me, who does not have a very good rote memory, this emotional framework is much more meaningful and memorable. Perhaps it was for others, also, who could not afford paper but had to rely on memorized material.

I recently returned from Rwanda[1] that is still recovering from genocide that some experts have thought might have been exasperated by dwindling resources needed by too many people. In our country, we are facing the possible collapse of our overly centralized infrastructure from any of a half dozen causes that could create an even greater loss of resources and loss of life. In my day job, I develop technology to protect critical infrastructure from hazards such as electromagnetic pulse and develop local power generation and storage systems. I also lead a nationwide volunteer organization with industry and government, sponsored by the FBI, that focuses on any of these half dozen ways critical infrastructure might fail nationwide for more than a month. When a Katrina like event happens to the whole country, it may take months if not a year for outside help to arrive. When that fragile infrastructure inevitably collapses, will we discover our relationships to be similarly fragile, or robust so that we will be the peacemakers that minimize the conflict (possibly a genocide) before the fact or help us navigate through them after the fact? If so, it might be timely to reconsider these ideas.

---

[1] While in Rwanda with my son Jason who completed a six-year tour of duty as a technical adviser to the One Acre Fund, I had the opportunity to visit The Evangelical Restoration Church Rusororo in Kigali, the capital of Rwanda. There I attended an evening worship service and met with a staff member who spoke great English having spent time in Ohio. We spent an hour discussing these concepts of the Lord's Prayer for persecutors.

Matthew Chapter 5 Beatitude Table with Connection to Salt and Light

Escalation from weak to strong ☐ from smaller to larger motives ☐

	When Weak			When Strong	
Ref	a) Internal Condition ☐	b) Blessing	Ref	a) External Relationship ☐	b) Blessing
v. 3	Poor	*Kingdom of Heaven (now)*	v. 10	Persecuted	*Kingdom of Heaven (now)*
v. 4	Grieving (now)	Comfort (future)	v. 5	Gentle (now) (learned from grief)	Inherit Earth (future or resulting event)
v. 6	Hunger for Justice (now)	Filled (future)	v. 7	Merciful (now) (learned from felt injustice)	Receive Mercy (future or resulting event)
v. 8	Pure (relative and temporary while victim of crime) but becomes in need of purification after own sin (purified) in heart (now) (PIVOT point, sufferer imposes suffering and needs mercy and peace by purification)	See God (future)	v. 9	Peacemakers (now) (learned from purification by sacrifice so makes peace for others on basis of sacrificial act of peace-making)	Called Children of God *since acting like God making peace for others based on sacrificial love* (future or resulting event)
	☐ Salt, Light			☐ Perceived Saltiness, Shining	
v. 13a, 14 a	You are salt (actual now) You are light (actual now)	Actual within self and Potential to others	v. 13b-c, 14 b-16	Salty vs Tasteless (possible future) Shining vs Dark (possible future)	Actualization to others

Who is the Our in the Our Father?[2]

When Jesus begins the prayer that has come to be called The Lord's Prayer with the words, "Our Father," who is included in his "our"?

Throughout the tradition of the prayer's interpretation, "our" has been understood expansively—the crowd, all people, all of creation—and narrowly: the children of Abraham, the Jewish people, anyone who has accepted that Jesus is the Christ, the disciples.

---

[2] This article was accepted for publication by the *Christian Century* for 2020 but as of this date not yet slotted for a given issue. See bibliography.

But one possibility that has been missing from the debate is that the "our" in the Our Father is at once far more universal and far more specific than the tradition has allowed. The "our" in the Our Father includes both the person praying and the enemies of the person praying. The prayer is teaching us how to pray for our enemies.

We can come to this understanding by considering the context of the Sermon on the Mount. In the Sermon on the Mount, Jesus gives the crowd extensive instructions on how to deal with those whom they consider their enemies and those who are persecuting them. Ultimately, he tells the crowd, "love your enemies and pray for your persecutors" (Matthew 5:44). This context is essential in understanding what it means that Jesus tells the people to be the "salt of the earth" or what to do if someone takes you to court. That same focus is present when Jesus teaches the crowds how to pray: the "our" is both us and those with whom we are fighting.

If this sounds unusual to us, it would have sounded even more so to Jesus' first listeners. These aren't just any people. Jesus' crowd is the poor, the underclass, the socially despised—and they would have been persecuted by many people, and many people with a great deal of power over them. The question of how to be in relation to these people was not an abstract one, and this is one reason that Jesus focuses so extensively on it.

Reading and preaching the Sermon on the Mount for decades, I missed this context myself until I decided to memorize the text in biblical Greek and set it to music. I recognized how awful my rote memory skills were and decided to look for patterns in the text that would make my task easier. I discovered a number of them including one placed right at the end of what I took to be the section on praying for persecutors. These patterns showed me how the Lord's Prayer in Matthew 6:9 is not in a separate section at all, but is directly connected to Jesus' insistence on praying for persecutors in Matthew 5:44.

After telling the crowd to love their enemies and pray for their persecutors, Jesus then tells them why they should do this. They have a common connection with those people. That common connection is the Father (our Father) who gives sunshine and rain on both the "good" and the "bad." That also explains why he asked them to pray for their persecutors. Initially this would likely sound as outrageous as asking them "to love" instead of to hate their enemies. Yet Jesus then reminded them that, "Even the most despised tax collectors can love their friends," and asked them to do better than that: to be perfect like the Father who gives sun and rain to the good and the evil, the just and the unjust.

Does he then change the subject at the beginning of what we call Chapter 6? I would argue he does not. In New Testament Greek, the connection becomes clearer. In the same way that "pay" sounds like "pray" in English, the first word of Chapter 6 is *prosexeteh* which means, "Pay attention!" (Προσέχετε). We are expecting him to say *prosuxestheh* ("Pray," προσεύχεσθε), because this would continue the thought from above. This sound-alike thus adds rhetorical force. Jesus is saying, in effect, "Before I tell you how to pray for those who persecute you, pay attention! Let me tell you how not to pray for them: don't make big public gestures of righteousness." This is the centerpiece of three items that Matthew quotes Jesus as saying should not be done in front of people (almsgiving, prayer and fasting) in comparison to three things Jesus had just said should be done in front of people that bring glory to the Father, namely being gentle, merciful and peacemaking. "Let your light shine so that people see your good works and glorify the Father" (Matthew 5:16). This contrast creates further rhetorical tension and makes the passage easier to remember by weaving the passages together.

Jesus then turns to the matter at hand: how to pray for those who persecute you. First you acknowledge the connection that you share: Our Father. Then you acknowledge that over which you are in conflict: our daily bread. Now the Lord's Prayer becomes a prayer about conflict and ultimately a prayer that teaches peace and empathy. Furthermore, each of the phrases begins to connect to every other phrase in far more powerful ways than would a haphazard collection of things to pray about.

Although it is impossible to know how the first listeners heard this, I can imagine it must have grabbed their attention. It must have seemed outrageous compared to what they would normally do, that is, pray *against* their enemies. And in each phrase of the prayer for persecutors, the outrage and rhetorical force only grows.

Imagine how it must have felt to hear: "Our Father," that is, "the Father of me and the one who is taking my food, livelihood, health, shelter, safety, family…." Jesus focus's attention to their conflict by asking the crowd to pray," Your kingdom come, your will be done on earth as it is in heaven." Because if it that will was being done, my persecutors would not be hurting me like this. God's will is to fix this, right?

Then Jesus' apparently outrageous demand grows. "Give me and my persecutors the very necessity they are denying me." Why should I ask that the bad guys who stole my bread, housing, or family be given the very things they are taking from me? They don't deserve those things. They are the bad guys. I deserve them. I am the one who worked for them. If they came by here now, I would attack them and take my bread back. The "rhetorical force" of the prayer is growing, as is my attention and likely outrage as I consider this odd sounding request to ask that the Father give what is needed to survive, the "necessary bread," to the very ones who have taken it from me.

But the frustration does not end there; it grows even more in the next phrase. "Forgive us…" That is, forgive me and the person who has taken from me. I am the one who worked hard for that bread, that home, that family. I didn't steal it. The thieves stole it, not me. They need forgiveness, not me.

And now as my rage races and accelerates, I am so angry at those people who are hurting me and my family that I am far more inclined to ask God in the middle of this prayer to make those people rot in hell forever after what they have done.

Just then something remarkable happens. In the height of my rage, perhaps I remember the words I heard Jesus speak only moments before: "Everyone who is angry with his brother shall be guilty," guilty as if they had committed murder. Becoming angry like this lands me in the company of the persecutors. Not only have I discovered that I may have done something similar to the persecutors at some time in my life, but that at this very moment, I have done a greater evil.

Jesus has just done a "judo flip." I was the pure innocent victim only in solidarity with other victims; now I am in solidarity with my victimizers, the persecutors. At this moment, I have the opportunity to gain peace by both receiving forgiveness and giving it to the ones who robbed me of mine.

Finally, the grand bargain appears. At the height of my rage, I'm told to ask that the "Father forgive me/us" based on how forgiving I am towards this person I want to murder a million times over. The implicit question becomes, "If the Father (the judge of all judges) gives me a pop quiz to examine how forgiving I am, would I pass or fail?" The obvious answer is that I would fail. No wonder then that the very next phrase in the prayer is "and lead us not into testing" because if we were to be tested, we would fail, and the consequences to us would be most disastrous since we would become the ones not forgiven. And then the inevitable conclusion: "deliver us from evil," from the consequences of our failure to forgive.

If there were any doubt about the rhetorical force of this instruction on how to pray for the persecutors, Jesus concludes the prayer in Matthew with a challenge, "So if you forgive them, then the Father will forgive you; but if you don't forgive them, then He will not forgive you." This is the closing bracket to the difficult question of how to pray for those who persecute you. Jesus has offered the crowd of persecuted people a step-by-step way to peace for those whose peace has been broken, and how to become peacemakers even to those who were responsible for their loss. The way to peace and freedom is to find solidarity with the persecutors, recognize them as members of your own family, and then to ask and to offer forgiveness. By adopting a way to pray for those responsible for our worst-case conflict, it makes it possible for us to pray for all the lesser cases. The alternative to not forgiving in this way would be to miss experiencing peace, miss becoming a new peacemaker and to ultimately become the new peace breaker.

Lord's Prayer for Persecutors—interactions with a scholarly pastor and his congregation:

The following email and newsletters are reproduced with permission by Dr. Steve Verkouw, the pastor of Grace Lutheran Church in Lancaster, Pennsylvania. It is an example of how an understanding of the Lord's Prayer of Matthew 6:5-15 as the prayer for persecutors requested by Jesus in Matthew 5:44 can be applied to conflicts in a powerful way. Pastor Verkouw has done a great job thinking through these ideas on his own and applying them with his congregation. Note the introductory email and his attribution at the end showing the interactive nature of this material and how easily it can be shared.

From: Steve Verkouw <pastor@gracelutheranchurch.com>

Subject: Lord's Prayer in my Newsletter

Date: April 14, 2020 at 12:23:37 PM EDT

To: Charles Manto <chucklmanto@gmail.com>

Hi Chuck!

Hope this finds you well, after a month or so of quarantine. I understand that you have been studying and helping folks prepare for resilience precisely for times like this. I'm sure you have a take on what's going on!

I have been thrown into a situation I never expected - trying to "become a YouTube sensation" overnight, haha!

With my iphone and a few apps, I have tried my hand at video worship over this last month, slowly learning skills, experimenting and trying to "bring church to the people" in this way. It's not what I signed up for, but oh well. Old dogs can learn new tricks!

I have also been steadily writing a series of 7 Newsletter articles, beginning in Lent, featuring the understanding of the Lord's Prayer that you have shared with me over the past few years. I tried very hard to put the ideas into my own words. I tried to keep it simple. I repeat a bit from week to week, since it came out in installments. I thought you would enjoy reading it. Since it is inspired by you, feel free to use any or all of it in any way that might be helpful in the quest to encourage peacemaking.

Be well, do good work, stay in touch (as GK used to say)

Blessings,

Steve V

--

Pastor Stephen P. Verkouw

Grace Lutheran Church, Lancaster Pa.

*Holy Worship * Wholly Serving*

717-397-2748

pastor@gracelutheranchurch.com

1. Introduction—The Lord's Prayer

How many prayers have you memorized? Maybe more than you think! "Lord, have mercy" is a prayer. Many use one or more prayers at meals, like: "God is great, God is good…" Hymn texts are prayers of a sort, some more so than others. But certainly anyone who has been worshipping regularly has also memorized some version of the "Lord's Prayer," also called the "Our Father" —the prayer's opening address.

Found in Matthew 6:9-13 and Luke 11:2-4, and traditionally found in the Sunday liturgy for Lutherans as the conclusion to the Great Thanksgiving for Holy Communion, this brief prayer is probably the most widely offered prayer by Christians around the world, usually by memory. It shows up in the orders for daily morning and evening prayers, at weddings and funerals, and again at the graveside. It is recommended from ancient times as a prayer to be repeated over and over again as a basic spiritual exercise.

As one of the most basic texts of worship and of our personal prayer lives, the Lord's Prayer has often been the subject of reflection by pastors and theologians across the ages. Martin Luther's teaching in his Small Catechism has been studied for nearly 500 years by Lutheran confirmation students around the world, and this teaching sets the standard for a brief commentary on this prayer, offered by Jesus to his disciples and by the Spirit, through the scriptures to the Church. I mentioned earlier that this prayer of Jesus appears twice in the gospels. The difference between these two appearances may not appear too significant, at least at first … but let's look a little more closely.

At the end of Luke 10 there is a familiar story about Jesus in the home of Mary and Martha, which ends with Jesus seeming to take sides with Mary, who was listening to his teaching, over against Martha, who complained that Mary wasn't helping in the kitchen, leaving her to serve dinner alone. But as Chapter 11 begins, Luke takes us to a whole new setting: Jesus is now somewhere else, "praying in a certain place." When he is finished, his disciples ask him for help and direction: "Lord, teach us to pray, as John taught his disciples." The answer Jesus gives is a very specific one, which we could summarize as, "When you pray, say this," followed by what we now call Lord's Prayer.

Here, let us notice, the Lord's Prayer appears as a general instruction, seemingly offered out of the blue as an answer to the disciples' request for a basic, all-purpose prayer. This context is overwhelmingly the way the Lord's Prayer has been understood.

"What does this mean?" asks Luther in the Small Catechism, petition after petition, and his answers expand the specific petitions—for God's will to be done, for daily bread, for forgiveness, for relief from temptation and trial,—into much wider lists of things. For instance, "daily bread" becomes, "everything included in the necessities and nourishment for our bodies, such as food, drink, clothing, shoes, house, farm, fields, livestock, money, property, an upright spouse, upright children, upright members of the household, upright and faithful rulers, good government, good weather, peace, health, decency, honor, good friends, faithful neighbors, and the like." Wow! Everything from soup to nuts, as they say. Even world peace! nd, it seems, anything else you might think necessary— "and the like." There is much precedent for reading and praying the Lord's Prayer in this expanded way. And yet…

The context in Matthew 6 is quite different. Here the prayer appears, not as an answer to a question at all, but in the middle of that major dissertation, usually called, "The Sermon on the Mount," spanning three Chapters (111 verses total). Perhaps you could read it this week (Matthew 5-7). And then you'll be better prepared to read my second installment, in the next *Grace News*!

2. The Lord's Prayer and the Sermon on the Mount

In my introduction to this series on the Lord's Prayer in last week's *Grace News*, we learned that this fundamental Christian prayer appears twice in the gospels: in Matthew 6 and Luke 11. We saw that in Luke, Jesus offers the prayer as an answer to a specific request from his disciples: "Lord, teach us to pray…" From this context, it has been taken up and used as a basic, all-purpose prayer for the church. It begins with some very general petitions: "hallowed be your name," and "your kingdom come on earth as in heaven." Then the prayer offers some much more specific petitions: for daily bread, forgiveness, and protection from temptation and evil.

The prayer is both widely comprehensive— "your will be done on earth as it is in heaven," and narrowly practical. As such it can serve well as a memorized prayer for daily personal devotion, public worship, and everything in between. When you want to pray and aren't sure how to start, begin with the Lord's Prayer and see where the Holy Spirit leads your prayers after that!

In contrast, the Lord's Prayer appears in Matthew in a very different setting, the middle of Jesus' "Sermon on the Mount." I suggested that you read those Chapters (5-7) of Matthew last week. Did you? If so, you began with the poetry of the Beatitudes, and continued through a series of short teachings, which at first glance may have seemed a bit random and unrelated. But we know that Matthew's gospel very deliberately sets out to expand the shorter gospel of Mark. We know this, because almost every word and phrase of Mark is included by Matthew; Mark's narrative forms the basic outline of Matthew (and Luke, for that matter). Matthew fills out this basic structure with more vivid details, with unifying themes and connections including many quotations from the Hebrew Scriptures, and longer sections of Jesus teaching and interpreting those scriptures and Jewish theology. How likely is it that these teachings are chosen at random or without deliberate consideration of how they would reinforce each other? In fact, the Sermon on the Mount holds together very well, if we take time to register the connections.

Though we don't have time to trace the entire Sermon here, we must notice the intensity that is building throughout the verses of Chapter 5. After declaring the blessings of God upon those who might be feeling "un-blessed" because of poverty, mourning, meekness, injustice, persecution and the like, Jesus begins to teach about the difficult path of "righteousness." What does it mean to do God's will? Beginning with verse 21, he teaches by interpreting basic scenarios of human conflict with a simple pattern. "You have heard that it was said…" followed by "But I say to you…" With this pattern, Jesus teaches about what righteousness means, first, in basic interpersonal conflict, then adultery, then divorce, then swearing oaths. The final section is about revenge.

"You have heard that it was said, 'You shall love your neighbor and hate your enemy.' But I say to you, Love your enemies and pray for those who persecute you…" (Matt 5:43-33). What does it mean to "love your enemy?" It means first of all, to "pray for those who persecute you." Hmm. Now we are talking about prayer again! The Lord's Prayer lies ahead. But we're not there yet! See you at worship, I hope, this weekend. And I'll be back here in this space next week. To be continued…

3. The Lord's Prayer and our Enemies

In last week's *Grace News*, we noticed the intensity that is building through the teachings of Jesus in Matthew 5, interpreting the idea of righteousness—doing God's will—using scenarios of typical human conflict, and ending with time-honored idea of revenge. "You have heard that it was said, 'an eye for an eye and a tooth for a tooth.' But I say to you, Do not resist one who is evil. But if anyone strikes you on the right cheek, turn to him the other also, and if any one would sue you and take your coat, let him have your cloak as well…"

This idea of "turning the other cheek" is hard to understand, and we could get distracted here by diving more deeply into what it means to apply this teaching to our daily lives. Should disciples of Jesus really not defend ourselves if someone means us to do harm? Can we apply this teaching to our communities, or even our nation? Is Jesus recommending that we let criminals run amok, or not have a military to defend our nation? These are reasonable questions! But for today, let us simply notice the difficulty of living out this "but I say to you" from Jesus. It seems un-natural, to say the least. Then comes the final teaching in this series.

"You have heard that it was said, 'You shall love your neighbor and hate your enemy. But I say to you, Love your enemies and pray for those who persecute you, so that you shall be children of your Father who is in heaven … For if you love those who love you ... do not even the tax collectors do the same? ... You, therefore, must be perfect, as your heavenly Father is perfect" (Matthew 5:43-48). The command to love our enemies and pray for them might sound somewhat easier than turning the other cheek in a fight or avoiding military conflict where the defense and protection of innocent life is at stake. Love and prayer seem more like "spiritual exercise" than serving as a punching bag for my enemy! But they are no more natural or easy to do. Why waste any of my prayer time on an enemy? Jesus gives the answer: because you are both children of God, who "makes his sun rise on the evil and on the good, and his rain fall on the just and on the unjust" (Matthew 5:45).

We are almost back to the Lord's Prayer itself, but one other series of teachings interrupts this call to pray for our enemies ... a teaching about how NOT to pray! "Beware of practicing your piety before others in order to be seen by them; for then you will have no reward from your Father who is in heaven." So begins the sixth chapter. At church, we read these verses on Ash Wednesday. Jesus offers us teachings about giving alms (offerings to help the poor), praying and fasting. All of these are spiritual exercises that can be mis-used in a public way, in order to manipulate our reputation in the eyes of others. Yet right here, we may remember that back in Chapter 5, Jesus has encouraged his disciples by calling them the "salt of the earth," and the "light of the world," and called them to "Let your light shine before others, that they may see your good works and give glory to your Father in heaven." What's with the confusion? Are good works to be done in public to "give glory" to God? Or in secret, so that God will "reward you?" Perhaps we can resolve this confusion ... in next week's segment! I hope to see you at worship this Sunday, ready to practice good hand-washing and "social distancing" to keep the corona virus at bay.

God's peace, for peacemaking –

Pastor Verkouw

4. The Address of the Lord's Prayer—Our Father in Heaven

In last week's *Grace News* segment, we ended by noticing two things. First, early in the Sermon on the Mount, Jesus teaches disciples to "Let your light shine before others so they may see your good works and glorify your Father in Heaven" (Matt. 5:16). But after teaching disciples to "love your enemies and pray for those who persecute you" (Matt. 5:44), a further instruction begins with a word that in Greek sounds very similar to "pray." It is the word "Beware." As in "Beware of practicing your piety before others in order to be seen by them" (Matt. 6:1). He goes on to single out giving offerings for the poor, prayer and fasting as good works that should be done "in secret." How to understand the apparent contradiction?

Included in the Beatitudes at the beginning of Chapter 5, there are three good works that Jesus blesses that seem to apply to situations of human conflict: meekness or gentleness (vs. 5), mercy (vs. 7), and peacemaking (vs. 9). Such good works are not easily manipulated or offered in pretense. They are part of a way of life that seeks to make peace with our enemies, a way of life that sees everyone as included in the family as children of God. When such works are accomplished, everyone benefits, not just the individual doing them. But works of prayer, fasting, and giving offerings in a public way might be done simply, "in order to be seen by others," but not to give glory to God by bringing any real righteousness to light. So we are to share, pray, fast, but also to beware—what are our motives.

Let's pull back now and see the big picture of this extended introduction to the Lord's Prayer. Jesus has been weaving various strands of righteousness together, including meekness (gentleness), mercy (forgiveness), and peacemaking from the . He then weaves these good works together with several intensifying scenarios of human conflict—disagreement, adultery, divorce, and revenge, including the command to "Love your enemies and pray for those who persecute you." Finally, he weaves a third braid: sharing, prayer and fasting with a warning: "Beware" the temptation of doing these things simply to make yourself look good in the eyes of others.

It is here, then, in the midst of his teaching about prayer, that Jesus introduces the Lord's Prayer with these words: "When you pray, do not heap up empty phrases as the Gentiles do; for they think that they will be heard because of their many words. Do not be like them, for your Father knows what you need before you ask him. Pray then, like this"

(Matt. 6:7-9). Here is a very interesting thing! Just before offering his exemplary prayer, Jesus very clearly says what it is NOT to be about. Prayer should not be a long list of many words about what we think we need. Why? Because our Father already knows our needs. The Lord's Prayer in Matthew does not seem to be offered as a general prayer that sums up all the possible needs we may have. What is it, then? It is a prayer to "Our Father." Who, besides the pray-er, is included in the word "Our?" Why not "My Father?"

When the Lord's prayer is understood as a basic general prayer, such as it is presented in Luke's gospel, the "Our" might include such groups as: all of us praying together right now, or all of us who believe in God, or all Christians in every time and place. But in the Sermon on the Mount, it seems like Jesus is trying to be much more specific. What if the "Our" Father is a prayer to God not just about me, nor about all of us, but exactly two of us … me … and my enemy? We will take up this startling thought next week!

God's peace, for peacemaking,

Pastor Verkouw

5. The Lord's Prayer—A Prayer for Peacemaking?

In our previous four segments of teaching on the Lord's Prayer this Lent, we have learned that:

- Luke's gospel shows Jesus offering the Lord's Prayer as an all-purpose prayer, a direct answer to a request from the disciples.

- Very differently, Matthew sets the Lord's Prayer in the midst of Jesus' teaching in the Sermon on the Mount, after an extended introduction.

- Jesus' teaching there focuses on the gentleness, mercy and peacemaking in the Beatitudes, deepens through his consideration of different kinds of human conflict, and culminates in his commandment to "love your enemies and pray for those who persecute you."

- In this context, the Lord's Prayer then appears as an instruction on how to pray in obedience to this command, beginning in the very address to God as "Our Father"—very specifically understood as the father of me … and my enemy.

But now we notice: the vast majority of commentary on the address "Our Father" in the Lord's Prayer is focused on the word "Father," not the word "Our." Commentators, theologians, devotional writers all communicate a point that I will summarize informally: Look, they say, Jesus talks to God like a parent! Amazing that Jesus addresses God with an Aramaic word that might best be translated "Daddy!" No one else ever did this before. How new, how different, how non-traditional, or something like that.

It is true: the word "Abba" (Aramaic for Papa/Dad/Father) does seem to be a deeply personal form of address for God into which Jesus invites us—precisely in his role as "the only begotten Son of the Father." But such intimate address for God on our part only "works" in contrast and in parallel with the many other forms of address that are found in the Bible. For example, titles like Lord, King, Sovereign, Ruler, Almighty, etc … all point to the majesty of God, a completely different idea or emphasis that goes missing in the intimacy and familiarity of calling God "Our Father." Creator, Redeemer, Holy One of Israel, Spirit of Life, Eternal One, Holy Trinity, are all biblical titles for God and expressions of God's lively and active relationship with us and through the ages, calling us and challenging us even through the words we use to call upon God. And the more descriptive titles and metaphors used to address God are too numerous to mention; some familiar ones are Shepherd, Fire, Light, Mother Hen, Eagles Wings, Wind, Breath, Vine and Branches. This whole subject provides much to ponder. But in all the fuss about the word Father, not to mention the feminist critique that says, "Isn't there also a mothering side to God?" to which the biblical answer is also yes, there just isn't much notice taken of the word "our." Without paying close attention to the Sermon on the Mount as we have been doing, we may easily assume that "our" just means, "mine and everybody else's." God, Our

Father, everybody's heavenly Father.

It seems very likely that, in the Sermon on the Mount, Jesus is offering this prayer at least somewhat differently. Here, he introduces it, teaches it and offers it as a gift for those who are wondering: how on earth will I ever be able to "love my enemies and pray for them?" Do it like this, Jesus seems to be saying. Start by remembering that you, and your enemy, are both children of your heavenly Father.

Next week we will look at some of the implications of praying the word "Our" in this specific way. How does the Lord's prayer take shape if we pray it especially with "my enemy" in mind? And who is my enemy, anyway? And how might God answer such a prayer, offered in obedience to Jesus? We will take up these questions in Holy Week, when we hear Jesus praying: "My Father, let this cup pass from me…" (Matt 26:39), and in Luke, "Father forgive them, for they know not what they do" (Luke 23:34). I look forward to meeting you in the *Grace News* again, next week!

God's Peace, for peacemaking,

Pastor Verkouw

6. Loving our Enemies

How does the Lord's Prayer take shape when we pray it especially with our enemy in mind? This is the question with which we ended last week. What happens when praying, "Our Father" means that we are praying to, "The Father of Jesus, of me, and of my enemy?" This change in emphasis or context in the very address of the Lord's Prayer flows out into the rest of the petitions, connecting them in ways that are not so obvious when we read them as just a general list of basic things that we need or want. Phrase by phrase, let me try to give some examples.

"Hallowed be your name" — "Hallowed" means holy, unique, sacred, powerful, and able to save is your name, but now we offer this praise to God who is the Father of me AND my enemy, the one who is taking something from me. This petition of praise for the holiness of God acknowledges God's righteous rule over me and my enemy, alike. It circles back to the very beginning of the prayer, the way we name God as "Our Father" in the first place. That God is the God of me and my enemy is an expression of God's holiness itself. There is no other God to turn toward, other than this holy one, the creator and redeemer of my enemy as well as me. The Lord's Prayer begins by helping the one praying it to remember that this is so.

"Your kingdom come; your will be done on earth as it is in heaven" —God's kingdom is the reality of God's will being done by his children, the outward expression of God's inner desire or will. Now we pray that this be done not only in heaven, where all are right with God and one another, but also on earth, here where my enemy and I are fighting over something. To pray such a prayer is to recognize that somehow, I am reinforcing this boundary between earth and heaven. This boundary runs between me and my enemy, but also right through my own heart, my own anger, my own desire to demonize my enemy. Even if all I can name in this moment is that I am in some sense a victim, that I am hurt, insulted, depleted, laid low, usurped, or otherwise diminished by my enemy. This is not about whose "fault" it is, not yet. It is simply the recognition that having an enemy exposes our mutual distance from God's Kingdom, which is supposed to be "drawing near."

"Give us this day our daily bread." Here, "daily bread" may mean food, if that is what my enemy and I are fighting over. In many places in the world, God's children do not have daily bread, the necessary food and sustenance to grow, to live, and to work with health and strength. This is a scandal, in a world overflowing with abundance! Something is awry in a world where people are deprived, by the economic arrangements favored by the wealthy, of enough daily bread to survive. Over the past decades, let us be thankful, the hard work of many people has ensured that a smaller part of the world's population is facing famine or critical food shortages. But many are still hungry. And so, our first and most necessary hunger—for food—becomes a way to express our hunger for whatever it is that my enemy is taking from me.

But now I'm almost out of space for this week … and it is the week when we remember the story of Jesus and his enemies. Who were they? The Roman soldiers who arrested him, the leaders and teachers of his own people who were threatened by his teaching and popularity, his disciples, like Judas, who betrayed him, or the other disciples who could not stay awake with him and pray, who ran away or denied their relationship with him, presumably to protect themselves.

Jesus knew what it was like to have enemies. As he faces them he seems to be guided, in his own thoughts, words and actions, by this prayer that he taught his disciples, by the goal of making peace between God and us. Blessed Holy Week to you all, and …

God's Peace, for peacemaking,

Pastor Verkouw

7. The Lord's Prayer, My Enemy, and Stealing

When I teach the 10 commandments in confirmation class, I always ask the students to ponder this question—is there one commandment there that might somehow shed light on all the others? What is the one verb, the one thing that "Thou shalt not DO," that is happening when each of the commandments is being disobeyed? There are a number of possible right answers I suppose. Sometimes, one of the kids guesses the one I'm thinking about. It's stealing, for me, some kind of stealing that is going on when each of the commandments is being actively disobeyed. There is the stealing of God's uniqueness when we make idols of all that is not God; there is the stealing of God's name to use it for our own purposes; there is the stealing of Sabbath time away from God and others who need us to be present and open in those relationships; there is the stealing of our parents' proper role when we do not honor them; there is the stealing of a spouse or a parent when adultery happens, there is the stealing of the truth and trust when lies are told, and what is coveting, if not the beginning of thinking and scheming about how to get what my neighbor has, for myself?

As we think and pray through the Lord's Prayer from this perspective of praying about my enemy and the peace that is missing between us, it may seem frustrating to have an enemy intrude on our time with God. Why dwell on the negative? It often seems easier to push all that stuff aside, to pretend that we don't have enemies. But Jesus knows that as we put our own enemies out of mind, it becomes much easier to forget that there may be someone who might also be praying this prayer—who might have you or me in mind as an enemy!

Let's reflect on the word "enemy." Most of us use this word in English in a very strong sense: enemies are usually thought of as a very serious adversary who seeks to destroy our lives. When Jesus is calling us to love our enemies, there is no doubt he has such people in mind. But they are simply the hardest cases. Such enemies do not exclude or rule out the other enemies that we have, the ones that are somehow our adversaries in day-to-day in life, who affect our own happiness and well-being. Could your spouse, dear friend, child or parent, someone whom you love deeply, also show up on your list of enemies? Could they be, at some point on any given day, someone who wants what they want and in order to get it they need you to give something of yourself up, something that you don't feel ready, able, or willing to give? Maybe it's their need for affection, or their unwillingness to share it—always tricky to keep all that in balance! Maybe it's more about time together, or a choice of activity you'd rather do instead. Our loved ones need us to sacrifice ourselves in some way and very often we find ourselves negotiating difficult conversations about blame and guilt and what's normal and what's manipulative.

Let's face it. We humans are very good at making ourselves feel better about ourselves by making someone else feel worse. We can literally steal someone else's sense of self and make it our own. It happens all the time, it keeps therapists in business and in the end such habits can damage destroy the very relationships that give us life and worth and well-being.

The Lord's Prayer is given for the healing of such enmity. It's unlikely that the leaders of warring nations would reach across "enemy lines" and pray for each other, although surely a Christian leader might feel moved to pray such a prayer from one side. But it seems quite likely that this prayer could be the perfect way out of a conversation that has become difficult with someone who has become in our life a sort of enemy, someone who wants our daily bread, whatever that may be.

Jesus' mission was to bring peace—peace in the cosmic sense, between our creator and the rebellious creatures we so easily become, and peace between each of us and our enemies. "Peace I give to you," the risen Jesus tells his disciples. "As the Father has sent me, so I send you" (John 20:21). As we are sent to be peacemakers in His name, let us not forget this most practical tool of all, the peacemaking prayer that brings each of us before God WITH our enemy in mind. It is the peacemaking prayer of the Lord. The Lord's Prayer of peace. May we not be afraid to use it!

A Final Note:

In my experience, this setting of the Lord's Prayer in Matthew is rarely taught, written about, or studied in a way that takes the unity of Jesus' teaching about enemies in the Sermon on the Mount into account. I owe this insight to my friend, Chuck Manto, a layperson who knows his Greek, his Bible and his own heart better than many pastors I know! While the writing over these past weeks has been mine, I was provoked to read the Sermon on the Mount and understand the Lord's Prayer in this way thanks to his essays and encouragement. His hope and prayer is that the Holy Spirit might find more hearts open to peacemaking if even a small number of Christians who pray the Lord's Prayer often would be able to pray it not only as they have learned from Jesus in Luke's gospel, or from Luther's Small Catechism, but also in the peacemaking, reconciling way of the Sermon on the Mount.

So, thank you Chuck for your inspiration!

(sig) Pastor Verkouw

We are here for All of us.

Sermon Series on The Lord's Prayer Wk3
LaSalle Street Church, Chicago, Illinois

October 22, 2020

(*Sermon video recording: https://www.youtube.com/watch?v=EJZapuZGyHY&t=2810s*

Post service interview of Charles Manto can be found at: https://youtu.be/BP7ftsjfPfA)

Matthew 6:

I propose to show the framework for TLP inverts the power dynamics of our life to the end that our prayer would become our life.

Good morning sisters and brothers. Welcome to the virtual assembly of the faithful known as LaSalle Street church. We're glad you are joining us from wherever you are. We're in the third week of our series called, *We are here for all of us*. A worship series on the Lord's prayer from Matthew 6.

We call it the Lord's prayer because Jesus is the one who teaches it to us. Meaning that when we pray this prayer we are using words taught to us by none other than God! The apostle Paul took it seriously when he wrote: "we don't know how to pray as we ought." Jesus apparently took our ignorance seriously enough to teach us how to do it!

We don't know how to pray. We are accustomed to thinking of prayer as a "good strategy for getting what we want." But the prayer Jesus teaches us is less about getting what we want and more about bending our wants toward what God wants.

As Methodist bishop William Willamon writes, "By learning to pray the Lord's prayer, we do not become better than other people—at least not in the sense that "better" is used in our society. We do not become better; ***we become Christian.***"

In other words, we become what we pray. In the Latin of the early church fathers, *Lex Orandi, Lex Credendi*, what we pray becomes what we believe.

Or, to echo what many a parent might say: **We are what we eat.**

The early church had a sense of what this prayer would do in their lives. 2nd century church leader, Tertullian, urged believers to pray this prayer at least 3X a day.

We know in the first few hundred years of the Christian era, saying this prayer was regularly outlawed. In part because officials didn't want their people praying to forgive their enemies ... because they wouldn't be as willing to go to war against them.

Now, there's a thought.

Speaking of war, there was an antidote from a WW2 veteran about his experience of this prayer while in a Japanese POW camp in Burma. Even though worship was forbidden, the man recounted that some of the captured soldiers would pray the Our Father in their own cells.

That the prayer would start to grow as others joined into the familiar words. their voices one by one gathering in strength and momentum, till by the end these American soldiers hearing one another in cell after cell after cell were thundering the final phrase:

For THINE is the KINGDOM

    and the POWER

        AND THE GLORY FOREVER. AMEN!!

Wow. When was the last time you prayed in a way that demanded something from you? That the act of praying was so unsettling, that you might have well been **asking for mountains to move**?

We become what we pray, but do we understand what we're praying for?

The Lord's Prayer is subversive. And you don't have to be a POW to know that. It inverts the framework of how the world works.

It is a demanding, bracing call to **unlearn** the ways of the world, and to begin again. And I suspect **if we understood that** we would pray it a lot slower and with more reverence that what we've been taught. As Martin Luther said, "This is certainly the very best prayer that ever came to earth or that anyone would ever have thought up."

Each week we've read a portion of Matthew 6 to alert us to the bigger context. Jesus teaches it during the sermon on the mount. His longest, uninterrupted teaching lecture in the book of Matthew. Jesus in front of the crowds of people who have followed him for instruction. He is address people who are **oppressed.** Who are **poor.** The ones who are mourning, crying for justice.

Just verses before this prayer, Jesus had advised them to turn the other cheek, to offer up their coat, to shame the injustice of the powerful by acting justly.

Jesus then goes on to explain, that in God's eyes: the "show-offs" the hypocrites who pray loudly in the streets (and btw, hypocrites is the Greek word for actors) so, the actors, and those who make a great show of giving money to the poor—that the only reward coming to them is that pride they feel about being above others. That's it.

That pride of being above, that power that one feels about having more,

    knowing more,

        being more—it's the way the world works. But it's not of God.

Beware. Beware Jesus says. *I'm warning you!*

Give in such a way that the poor don't even know who paid their rent. The hungry don't know who their benefactor was. Pray in such a way that the focus is on God not your eloquence.

Because here's the thing: when we do these "good and right" actions anonymously, we are actually **performing a sacrifice**—we are sacrificing the recognition of others. We give up the ego of our false selves. We start to edge closer toward humility—doing these things for the sake of LOVE.

We start to move from the hierarchies of power that "dominate" our world and into a place of mutuality. Solidarity.

Returning to the prayer: look at this—Jesus has been deconstructing the apparatus of rankings and pecking orders and now—right in the middle of it all—he gives us this prayer, **Pray like this.**

And right from the beginning he gives the massive leveling—**Our** Father. the call that we don't do this alone, even when we are alone, that this God isn't held by just me, this is a God for all of us. A God concerned with *all of us.*

And then Jesus pushes even deeper: orientating us to kneel before one God alone.

It is **God's kingdom** we seek, not our own domain where we are in charge, rule everyone and everything. In one stroke putting both our kingdom of self, and pride on the shelf. But also any kingdom of nationalism or ethnic pride.

It is God's will we want. Meaning, as I pray this I am deliberately, intentionally, asking for my will to be bent toward God. I am saying when a decision comes my way and there is fork in the road in front of me, and I can go the way of vulnerability, sacrifice, humility, or I can take the power move, the self-aggrandizing step, I will seek the way of Jesus. I will seek to listen before I speak, be moved by love of God and love of others first.

But deeper still, Jesus moves into the places where we live: daily needs. Human angst. Our relationships where we have been wronged.

To this group of hungry people, oppressed people, Jews who are stepped on by their government, peasants who are taxed to death by their own complicit religious leaders—Jesus tells them to pray for ***our bread***—meet the daily needs of both Nancy Pelosi AND Mike Pence.

He urges prayer for the 545 children along our border whose parents can't be found. And for the policy makers who separated them in the first place.

As LaSaller Chuck Manto writes, *(and the person I'll be doing the post-sermon conversation with)* this is the equivalent of saying I'm here, standing next to the guy who stole my car, asking that you would provide transportation to both of us—the wronged and the thief alike.

Then, the icing on the cake is when Jesus links our forgiveness to God with how we forgive others. *Forgive us our debts as we also have forgiven our debtors.*

Isn't this an **echo of the sacrifice theme Jesus** was talking about just before the prayer? Things have to change if **me and this stranger are both getting bread**—or our daily needs.

In 2015, and 2018, and 2019, the president of the Federated State of Micronesia has stood in the UN begging the nations of the world to do something about climate change, the rising seas threaten to swallow the pacific island nations. Their nation will disappear.

Where will our citizens go? Peter Christiansen asked. Become refugees in a world where countries have quite literally closed our doors to them?

"Give us this day OUR daily bread" Jesus is connecting their survival to our own. Their needs to our own. This petition endorses that the hungry should demand their bread, GIVE US OUR BREAD!!! And that those with too many loaves need to give some up, give ALL OF US our bread.

This is not an easy prayer.

This is the kind of prayer that *makes us Christian.* And being a Christian is a pretty bracing thing to be.

Jesus is praying into being a new creation.

New People who are consistently walking to a different beat.

Jesus lived the way he prayed.

When Jesus prayed, ***Thy kingdom come,*** it meant that he, the God-Man, was praying that his heart and his will would be prepared for whatever was going to befall him.

He was getting ready for what was going to happen not too long later in the **garden of Gethsemane.**

There is that mysterious passage in Hebrews, that Jesus **learned obedience.** At first blush you wonder how did Jesus **learn** anything? He was born perfect.

Yes. But the God-Man bent his free will to the will of his Father. Day after day after day. ***Our Father.* Thy** will. **Our** bread.

Thy kingdom come! *He had prayed.* ***Thy will be done!*** *He had asked. And now, here it was … God's will. What was the Son going to do with it?*

Here's what he's going to do: After three years of living among others, loving others, of healing the tender hearted and laughing at dinners and raising children above his head and blessing them, **Jesus realized it was soon coming to an end.**

That his death would be horrible.

That his pain would be physical—nailed to a cross, hung to suffocate by crucifixion; but the pain would also be emotional and spiritual:

He would die alone.

No crowds would demand justice.

There would be no protests in the street, no laws passed so "this never happens again."

Instead, there would be guards throwing dice for his clothing. Crowds jeering on the sidelines.

He would die a failure.

This is the kind of prayer that leads to sacrifice for the sake of the other.

Since I opened with a war story, let me close with one too. This one is from Ernest Gordan, the writer best known for the film, *"The Bridge over the River Kwai."*

Gordon was in a concentration camp in Burma—where, the guards had so intimidated the prisoners and violated every code of civilized treatment that "Each man was out for himself," Gordan wrote.

"Prisoners stole food and medical supplies for themselves,

robbed each other,

ratted on other prisoners in order to get favors from the guards,

and isolated new prisoners who came into the camp.

Anything to survive.

One day as they were coming in from work detail and putting away the tools, the guards discovered that a shovel was missing. The angry guards lined the prisoners up and threatened them:

"If the person who stole this shovel does not come forward in ten seconds, we are going to shoot all of you."

After a long silence, the guards cocked their guns, preparing to shoot when one of the prisoners stepped forward.

The guards pounced on him, beat him with their gun butts, and shot him dead on the spot.

But when the guards told the prisoners to finish putting away the tools, they realized that all the shovels were there.

No shovel had been missing after all. In shock and silence the prisoners went back to the barracks. One of the prisoners had voluntarily given his life so that the rest would not be shot. He had sacrificed himself for them all.

Gordan writes, "Life in the camp changed after that."

Other acts of sacrifice began to take place.

Prisoners began to share medical supplies with each other.

They formed teams to attend to each other's wounds and illnesses.

Some sick prisoners gave their food to weak prisoners who had a better chance for survival.

Others risked death by sneaking outside the camp to procure food for the sick.

Together they established a secret system of communication to give each other information and support. They welcomed new prisoners and quickly incorporated them into their network.

In the midst of the most horrible conditions, there emerged a remarkably humane society of prisoners, all made possible because of the effect of this one fellow prisoner who gave his life for them to live.

Our father … **Thy** kingdom. **Thy** will … **Our** daily bread. Forgive us as we forgive others…

Be careful what you pray for—we become what we pray.

Become as God created you to be.

Become whole.

Become Christian.

Let us pray.

The following interactive classes were video recorded and transcribed with the support of Lord of the Mountains Lutheran Church in Dillon, CO.

The following email outlines the perspective of Pastor Stahlberg who hosted the sessions.

From: Elena Liliana Stahlberg <liliana_stahlberg@hotmail.com>

Subject: The Conflict in the Lord's Prayer

Date: July 27, 2019 at 11:28:17 PM EDT

To: Charles Manto <chucklmanto@gmail.com>

Lord of the Mountains Lutheran Church in Dillon, Colorado invited Charles Manto to speak on the **Lord's Prayer and the Beatitudes** in the Gospel of Matthew, as conflict resolution inspiration for our daily lives.

There were three sessions and a tandem sermon with Pastor Liliana Stahlberg. The presentations were interactive, actively involving the participants.

The idea that the Lord's Prayer is not only for us but especially for our enemies created a lot of tension, and reactions from the audience.

Charles invited us to pray in this way, "the Father of me and my enemy." It struck all of us as true to the Gospel message, but very difficult to really apply to our daily life. Charles' presentation touched many lives and people retrieved personal stories that were connected to the concept of forgiveness of enemies.

Just last week, a month after the workshop on the Lord's Prayer, a woman from the congregation came to our regular Healing Service on a Wednesday evening, to tell us that she just can't pray the Lord's Prayer anymore because she can't forgive her former husband who had hurt her, and destroyed her life. Her confession generated the opportunity for spiritual companionship. She realized that she was on a journey of self-discovery and that God is leading her to deal with a situation that has been stale for a long time.

Such workshop style presentations are a tool for self-awareness and for discovering ways of healing through forgiveness. I would love to do more presentations with Charles Manto in other congregations.

Yours in Christ,

Pastor Liliana Stahlberg
LOTM
Dillon, Colorado
56 Hwy 6, 80435
cell: 720-341-8096
720 341 8096

Transcript of Friday June 28, 2019
Lord of the Mountains Lutheran Church, Dillon, Colorado
Matthew 5 Session 1 Part 1 and 2
Presented by Charles Manto, Hosted by Pastor Stahlberg
Video Archive https://video.ibm.com/recorded/122534694 [3]

Pastor Stahlberg:	Good evening.
Multiple:	Good evening.
Pastor Stahlberg:	Good evening. We will start with a short prayer. Graceful and merciful Creator, thank you for bringing us tonight to talk about theology, which is our love for God and trying to understand your message for this world through the words and teachings of Jesus. We give you thanks for our speaker, Charles Manto, who traveled all from—
Charles Manto:	Maryland.
Pastor Stahlberg:	Maryland. Oh, I always confuse it. Anyway. To start the conversation with us. May God bless you and keep you in His grace. Amen.
Multiple:	Amen.
Pastor Stahlberg:	All right. So, this—I want to welcome everybody. And for those who are not from the congregation, but they know it already, the bathrooms are on this hallway, and if you need those. We are going to—I know there is a concert at the amphitheater, but we'll see if we can finish sooner than this. It's interesting, so I hope we can still go to the concert after this presentation.

I want to say that we have advertised this event, and we didn't check the times very well. Tomorrow morning, we meet from 9:30 to noon, and some people have seen I think in our announcement that it's 10:00 AM, but it's 9:30. We will have lunch here. After that, actually, we will have he lunch here so we can continue conversation. So make sure to come, and I hope there will be even more people tomorrow. I know some could not be here tonight.

It is time to present our biblical scholar, Charles Manto. He and I met a year ago at the Network of Biblical Storytellers in Dayton, Ohio. And he told me a personal story—he's going to share that with you—that really touched my heart and kind of took me on a journey of understanding how we can become peacemakers, and that's—we are trying to use the Lord's Prayer and the Sermon on the Mount to turn from peace breakers to peacemakers.

Charles will enchant you with his personal story. I only wanted to say a few words about him, but he will now tell you the story. It is called "Life in Five." That's his— |
Charles Manto:	But we're going to introduce them first, right?
Pastor Stahlberg:	You will do that.
Charles Manto:	Okay, great.

---

[3] These are alternative video clips from a different camera angle and with audio that might be easier to hear: Friday Session 1 Matthew 5 (Beatitudes) Part 1: https://www.dropbox.com/s/emm4mxu6yt0w8v2/Friday%20June%2028%20Matthew%205%20Session%201%20part%201%20%2859%3B50%29%20.MP4?dl=0; Friday Session 1 Matthew 5 (Beatitudes) part 2: https://www.dropbox.com/s/33s51lfix70wtm5/Friday%20June%2028%20Matthew%205%20Session%201%20part%202%20Q%26A%20%2848%3A56%29%20.MP4?dl=0

Pastor Stahlberg:	So let us welcome Charles Manto.
	[Applause]
Charles Manto:	So, many of you've already been spending some time with me because of choir practice last night or the hike this morning. But maybe we could just go around the room and have everyone say your name and just 10 seconds of something about yourself so everybody can hear you name, so that later on when we interact, we'll be familiar with you. Maybe we'll start in the back with Nancy Spears and just work our way around. Nancy?
Nancy Spears:	Hi. I'm Nancy Spears. I think I've been here since 2003.
Female:	Louder, please.
Nancy Spears:	Oh, I'm Nancy Spears, and I've been coming to this church since 2003, and it just—everything about this church touched my heart. It's different than any other church I've ever gone to.
Charles Manto:	Thank you, Nancy.
Brian Smith:	I'm Brian Smith. Jane and I are part-timers. We live in St. Louis when the weather is nice, and we live out here in Dillon when it's nice, too. *[Laughter]*
Jane Smith:	Hi, I am Jane Smith, and we started coming here probably—I don't know—2005 about, maybe more. And we enjoy coming.
Carl Rasmussen:	And I'm Carl Rasmussen, and I've been to this church about 10 years.
Les Wall:	Jan and Les Wall. She's from North Dakota. I'm from Minnesota. But now we're residents of Arizona most of the time, and we're here like three months.
Susan Knopf:	Susan and Jonathan Knopf. We're full-time residents here about five years. We got our home here about 10. We're members of the Interfaith Council and members of Synagogue of the Summit, and we just love this church. We come here quite often. And if we don't, Liliana beats us regularly. *[Laughter]*
Bill:	Bill. I'm a member of the church. I live in Silverthorne.
Lydia Wittman:	Lydia Wittman. Been here a couple years as an adult, but I did live in Summit County in the 1990s as a teenager and went to this church back then. I'm so happy to be living here now among you all.
Bonnie Brown:	I didn't know that. I'm Bonnie Brown. I'm probably the oldest member here. I've been coming as associate and then as a full-time member for probably over 30 years.
Moderator:	And she's the president of our council.
Karen Johns:	I'm Karen Johns. I am a full-time resident. Newly retired and loving every second of it. Probably been part-time off and on here for four years and full-time for two years.
Cindy Bardell:	Hi, I'm Cindy Bardell, and I've lived here 20 years.
Moderator:	And I'm the pastor here. I've been here almost three years in September, end of August.
Amy Simper:	I'm Amy Simper. Full-time since 2010, part-time since '07, but I came here for Christmas Eve service in 1998 and I was sold.

Male:	Twenty years.
Doug Muschett:	Excuse me. I'm Doug Muschett. Mostly retired, but still trying to be relevant. And for most of my life until we moved out here and joined Lord of Mountains around 2007, I was known as Pastor Darleen's husband. *[Laughter]*
Darleen Muschett:	Oh, geez. I'm your driver's spouse. You've met this morning. Darleen Muschett. We moved here in '08, and it's great. Welcome.
Charles Manto:	Thank you. And you were a pastor somewhere?
Darleen Muschett:	Yeah, in Rochester, New York, and I served on the staff here for 10 years. Not as pastor, but in different capacities. Now I'm—I think I'm retired. Almost.
Susan Knopf:	I doubt it. *[Laughter]*
Ron:	I'm Ron and love it here. I think we first started coming here because Greg really wanted to be here, and I had a job in Pennsylvania teaching at Penn State. But because of this church, I know this is the place I want to be. So Greg is probably now happy that I really want to be here.
	So we're gradually coming here more and more, and it's interesting to find out we're not alone and that a lot of people are from somewhere else. A lot of people are here part-time and somewhere else part-time. But eventually we're going to be here 100 percent. I'm looking forward to today because I love the Sermon on the Mount and want to understand it better.
Greg Wright:	I'm Greg Wright, and most people know me as Ron's husband. *[Laughter]* And I think he said it all. I was a resident of Colorado and northwestern Colorado for a lot of years and then left to pursue a career in the east and have been pining to get back here ever since. So that's starting to happen.
Nina Nichols:	I'm Nina Nichols, and I'm a friend of Chuck's. I'm from Denver and very interested by his teachings and scholarly work. We've had a number of really great discussions, so I'm delighted to be present for the workshop and helping film.
Charles Manto:	And helping film so you guys can look over it later.
Nina Nichols:	And helping film.
Charles Manto:	Figure out what we can do to further improve or totally reverse what we talk about today. So now what I'm supposed to do—she's going to help me keep it to five minutes. So, I got to go over my life in five minutes just so you can get a sense of who I am, where I come from, and why I'm saying what I'm saying.
Pastor Stahlberg:	Can everybody hear him?
Charles Manto:	Am I okay?
Multiple:	Yes.
Charles Manto:	And also, if you need me to either slow down or you want to wave at me or give me a timeout sign, I'm very easily interrupted. I don't take offense at that. And she's going to help me, give me like a two-minute warning and a one-minute warning just to hope that I stay somewhat on time so we can keep moving. And we have slides that will sort of help us in a little bit as well. We're hoping to keep this informal. The point of the slides is just to make certain we're keeping everything moving.

So just a little bit about my life, and I guess we can start with my father, who was born in—well, actually was conceived in Crimea in 1923 when the United States passed their most extreme immigration law ever, where only 100 people from undesirable countries were allowed to come. And at that time, because of the Russia Revolution moving south, his family decided to move out and went to Istanbul. So, he was actually then born in what was called Constantinople at the time when Ataturk took over. And they lived there until 1929 when he moved here.

And lucky for him, even though there were only 100 visas, his was number 63, and he came and arrived in Brooklyn. Some time passed. He met my mother in Chicago. That's where I was born and raised. And I was just a secular child. Had no religious background at all. My father was a Russian Jewish guy who, for lots of reasons, decided to be an atheist.

And when my youngest brother was born, he gave me my life lessons in like two minutes or less; and there were three life lessons. And one of them was: "Even though I'm an atheist, there are no atheists in foxholes." He's been in the Battle of the Bulge and he wanted to emphasize that.

The next thing he told me, which made sense that he didn't talk much about it before because he was an atheist: He said, "Son, I want to tell you something really important. You're Jewish, and you're never supposed to be ashamed that you're Jewish. Now don't go telling anybody because if you do, it's just going to get you in a lot of trouble." *[Laughter]* So, "You can't tell," and maybe other people have experienced that as well.

And the third one was, "Blood is thicker than water. Whatever you do, you've got to take care of your two brothers." And I said, "Hey, dad. Do you have any brothers?" He said, "Yeah." "What's his name?" "Max." "How come I've never seen him?" "Shut up, kid. Mind your own business." *[Laughter]*

So, from that day, even though I was refused to know anything about the family except his mother's name, Reva; my grandmother was called Babushka *[Russian word for grandmother]*. They came from Kerch in Crimea and showed up in Brooklyn. I knew nothing *[else about them]*, and it started me on a path from age about nine to find my father's family. It took about 30 years. That's another story. I'm not going to tell you about it *[today]*.

But I wound up being in Chicago as a child, and before I was long involved with a church, I was a member of the Chicago Junior Academy of Sciences. Loved what everything nature and science had to offer but had no religious background. If I wanted to play with my friends, though, on Sunday, the parents would say, "Well, you can do that if you go to Sunday School first," and things such as that.

So I would go to some Sunday School lessons once in a while. By fifth grade, somebody invited me to something called vacation Bible school at some church where if you went there you got to play with the woodworking equipment and get Bible stories. And some woman in the neighborhood, in our apartment building, actually, knew I was going, and she said, "Hey, kid, do you have a Bible," and I said, "no." She said, "Well, why don't you take mine?" I said, "Sure, if you're not using it."

And when I got it, the words of Jesus were in red, and I thought that was interesting because a Bible seemed to be a really important book, but it was way too big to read and a little too complicated. But if I just get the red words down, I'd get the shortcut and that's all I really needed to get the basic idea down. *[Laughter]*

Now, these words of Jesus were interesting because they were things like, "Prioritize your life. Why gain the whole world if you lose your own soul?" Or "Better to gauge out your eye and cut off your hand and go wounded into Heaven than go whole into Hell." And I said, "So I sort of get that, but I think I'm going to run out of body parts." *[Laughter]*

And then the other one was like, "Turn the other cheek." Well, if you grow up in Chicago from the youngest age, you scrap all the time in the playgrounds, and you deal with bullies. And when you face down bullies, there's usually three ways to deal with them. You either take out the big guy, you talk your way out of it, or you cut and run. I usually would talk my way out of it. But I never imagined that looking in the face of a bully and then loving the bully while he's abusing you and then turning the other cheek and letting him hit you another time. Said *[to myself]* I've never seen anybody do that, but that was pretty impressive.

Speed up to eighth grade, aged 12. Some of the guys said, "Hey, you want to play softball in the wintertime in Chicago?" I said, "Well, of course. How do you do that?" He said, "Well, this church has an auditorium, and you get to play softball there." *[I asked]* "Well, how much does that cost?" And he said, "Well, it doesn't cost you anything except for a half-hour they've got to tell you Bible stories." I said, "Okay, that sounds a little weird, but I've been to some of these classes, and they're safe." So I went ahead and did it.

And in that place, they taught other Bible verses, like, "God so loved the world he gave his only son. Whoever believes in him has eternal life." "God loved you when you couldn't care less." "You didn't love God, but he loved you. And even when you were his enemies." He loved you, even going to the point of the cross." And that was sort of a different set of verses. And I went home, and I was trying to make sense of all of this, and I was pulling it all together.

So here's the image that came to my mind at age 12, and it'll give you an understanding of what connected with me. I imagined I was in the playground in Chicago, at age 12. Little kid comes up to me, and I slap him around, push him down, bloody his nose, make him cry. And when I'm going to smack him another time, the little kid looks up to me lovingly and turns the other cheek for me.

And it dawns on me in that moment, what happened is that God snuck into the world in disguise as a little boy, and I was beating up God in the playground, not realizing he could beat me up and everybody else in the playground, in the city, in the planet, in the universe. In fact, he could snap his finger and restart the multiverse.

And so the infinitely powerful was letting the infinitesimally small, and what little power I had was derived from the infinite, smack him again, which was really troublesome because I was 100 percent in the wrong and the guy with all the power was 100 percent in the right. And that sort of shocked me because I thought that would be the biggest love model possible, where the one with all the power was 100 percent in the right and was loving me with infinitesimal power and the one in the wrong. And I said, "Wow, that's pretty powerful."

And not only growing up by that time with bullies in the schoolyard, but in the Cold War, having been taught what happens when a nuclear weapon goes off, looking for fallout shelters on the way home from my public school in Chicago, I realized that this world's a pretty dangerous place. And like the "Wizard of Oz," if we could keep people on the Yellow Brick Road and not destroy each other, that could be pretty neat. And that's okay even if the guy at the end of the Yellow Brick Road behind the curtain's a phony, because if everybody stays on the Yellow Brick Road, we don't destroy each other.

Then I was thinking, "Now, what could be more interesting or more powerful than that?" I said, "Well, I'm only 12 years old. I don't know. You can't get any bigger than infinite. You can't be more in the right than a hundred percent," and I said, "What could be more powerful than a model like that?"

And I said, "Well, the only thing that could be more powerful is if the model were true," and said, "Well, how in the world would you ever figure that out? If I had 100,000, 500,000 years to live and as many PhDs and I can go in every nook and cranny in the multiverse, I probably still wouldn't get enough data to figure that out. How am I going to figure this out?"

Then it dawned on me, when I was thinking about this god who does all this wonderful creation and all this stuff with science, discovered in physics, how photosynthesis works and how rocks work and everything in it that you can imagine; every time you turn around you're in total awe, it just dawned on me. I said, "It would be just like God to do that. Somebody that smart, that big might actually pull that off and do it." And so that just became an awareness for me that, "Wow, this is really cool," and it's not because I was able to prove it. It was just this sense of awareness.

So, from that moment on, I was very impressed with this idea of how do we possibly pull off loving people, including the people bent on our destruction, in such a way that we can make reconciliation happen. And even growing up in the city, I was thinking of like during the riots that were—I was watching firsthand. I had this image of KKK, Ku Klux Klan, Black Panthers, Young Lords, Jewish Defense League, Palestinians all in the same room loving each other. And I said, "Wow, that's really powerful. If you can make that happen, that's cool."

Now, fast forward to, oh, 2004. I was driving into the city of D.C. and, to not waste a lot of time in traffic and to be environmentally conscious, I decided to go to the train station, which is the end of the line on the *[DC Metro]* train system. I had this long ride into the city, and I didn't want to waste a lot of my time. I said, "How do I make good use of this time on the train?"

And I just heard this thing on the radio saying some medical report said if you do languages and music, your aging brain can do better. So, I said, "Okay, I know what I'll do. I'll memorize the Sermon on the Mount that I was looking at as a child in ancient Greek and set it to music." But the reason I tried to dare myself was because I had this fond memory of beating up God in a playground. There's something else very significant going on in that. Why that caught my attention and led to tonight is that—

Pastor Stahlberg: You are cutting in and out, so I'm going to adjust your mic and that connection may come in later. So I give you the two-minute warning.

Charles Manto: Let me take off my glasses. And take this off and put this one on?

Pastor Stahlberg: That was "Life in Five."

Charles Manto: So, the short version there is that I wanted to figure out how to remember all this. How could I possible memorize all this stuff? To do that, I just started to try to ask, "how could they remember all this if they could not afford to take the scrolls home?" I wondered when these guys wrote this stuff, whether they placed built-in memory tricks. So, I started looking for memory devices that were built into the Sermon on the Mount because there was no way I was going to remember this stuff by rote since I have the world's worst rote memory and no patience at all to do it.

And that led me, when I had to start looking for that to really examine these passages a little bit more, and that caused me to stumble across a couple of really interesting things, two of which we're going to do tonight. But we're going to start by saying like why we are here and go to the next slide.

And I had done back in Maryland a six-class session on the Sermon on the Mount, and tonight and tomorrow—we're only going to do class number two and class number five. At some other point, we'll be able to do more. And, so, we're going to do a little *[slide]* skipping, and that's going to be okay. We'll make it work. And so let's go to the next slide and talk about what we're going to focus on.

So, what we're going to do starting tonight and then tomorrow, we're going to look at two things. We're going to look at Matthew 5 where these beatitudes are, "Blessed are the poor in spirit, blessed are the sorrowful," all these that you've heard before. But we're going to start by looking at setting the stage at the end of 4. And then tomorrow we're going to look at Matthew 6 where the Lord's Prayer is. A couple of billion people on the planet know this prayer.

But to look at it, we're going to examine it in the context of Matthew 5, which we're going to be studying tonight a little bit. So we're going to use what's a little bit before these passages to set the stage, to see what was going on when these guys wrote this in the first place.

And you can remember, like I just said, the reason why I was focusing on this is because of what happened to me as a child and thinking this through and how I put all this together—and this is what we're going to have to discover together, whether or not this makes sense to you—is whether or not these discussions can transform us when bad things happen to us and our peace has been broken. And as broken people, can we move to the point where we're no longer broken, but become strong and then become peacemakers instead of the next peace breaker?

Because, as you know, when people are abused, they often become the next abuser. When oppressed people grow strong, they become the next oppressors. How do you break that cycle? That's what we want to do. Our discussion is to discover whether or not this is going on in the text. And then, if it does, how do we make it work in our lives? Next slide.

Now, this is a picture of an ancient Greek manuscript, and the purpose of mentioning this is just a couple of things and why it's important to do the kind of thing we're doing. Even if we were literate 2,000 years ago, it would have cost us maybe a couple hundred thousand dollars to have a bunch of scrolls the size of a Bible, and we couldn't afford it.

So, we would have to then go to the church or synagogue and memorize this stuff if we wanted to study it and study it at home from memory. And for that to happen, there has to be something to make it easier to make that happen, and it has to be relevant to somebody in the first place. It's got to be compelling. It has to be easy to remember, and something's got to be going on for this to even work. Next slide.

This is to some of the points that we started talking about. Background this time. If you are not literate or you're not wealthy, you couldn't do this. I told you about my train ride. I was looking for patterns. We're going to see some of these patterns today maybe. We are going to discover patterns together this evening to see if this is true or not. Next. So many slides to go through.

Now, I'm making a couple of sections—just so you know, these weren't just slapped together haphazardly if people were going to be able to remember them or care about them. They're there on purpose, and it causes us to ask, "Well, why is this phrase next to that phrase? Is there something significant or not?" And we're going to ask some of those same questions. Is there some reason why these things are next to each other? Is there anything unusual? Is something jumping out at us? That's what we're going to do in a moment. Next.

Now, to start with, we're going to start our conversation now, and we're going to pass out one version of the Bible that on one side is going to have Chapter 4 and the other Chapter's going to have Chapter 5. The reason we're going to take just as moment to look at Chapter 4 is we're going to set the stage. So if you're going to be seeing something like the Sermon on the Mount, you're going to basically say, "Well, why is this here? What's going on here," and we're going to find this out.

So, what we're going to do is have some—once you get these, Pastor Stahlberg, Pastor Lili, however you liked to be called best.

Pastor Stahlberg: That's fine.

Charles Manto: She will help call out people who might want to read certain sections. And just—so the first thing we're going to do is there's three things going on in the background.

Female: You don't have to share.

Charles Manto: You have enough for everybody?

Pastor Stahlberg: Sharing is caring.

Charles Manto: And how about does everybody have one? Oh, one for Nina.

Pastor Stahlberg: Oh, I'm sorry, Nina. You have—everybody's got some?

Charles Manto: So the first question I would like is just to have somebody read in Matthew 4, verses 14 and through 16, about three verses. We're going to want to open something about this setting. Would somebody read that?

Pastor Stahlberg: Darleen? Pastor?

Darleen Muschett: I'll read it. "This was to fulfill what was spoken through Isaiah the prophet. The land of Zebulun and the land of Naphtali, by the way of the sea, beyond the Jordan, Galilee of the Gentiles. The people who were sitting in darkness saw a great light and those who were sitting in the land and shadow of death upon them a Light dawned."

Charles Manto: Now we're going to just ask each of these, we're going to ask a quick question. Probably if you've been in Christmas pageants, you might hear this passage being read, right? And all of these places seem sort of foreign, except we also heard about Galilee, right?

So the question I've got is what do you think—what significance is going on about this passage, about what's going to happen later? How are they setting the stage in this little section? Any ideas at all? What you might notice, anything at all and just—from where you are, just tell us loudly enough to hear. What do you think might be going on?

Pastor Stahlberg: I was wondering if Susan and Jonathan can tell us about the land of Zebulun and Naphtali. Do you know anything about that?

Susan Knopf: No, I haven't studied it that much. I'm sorry. In our scripture, but not studied it.

Jonathan Knopf: I will say if you take this passage out, the capitalization of the word "light" seemed significant.

Charles Manto: And what about the land of darkness? What's going on there? Those land of shadow—valley of the shadow of death, where have you heard that before, that phrase?

Multiple: Psalm.

Charles Manto: And what's it say there in the psalm?

Male:	"I shall fear no evil."
Charles Manto:	"Though I walk through the valley of the shadow of death." Now, I've always viewed the shadow of death as like if I'm standing over this pulpit and I'm casting a shadow, that means I'm so close, I could snatch that person any time and there's nothing they can do about it. It's like a very treacherous place to be in, and the psalm says because God's with me, I don't have to fear all this evil while I'm going through this valley, because it's a dangerous place, right?

And many of us have all been through something like the valley of the shadow of death where we're sort of helpless, we want to get out of there as soon as we can, and we're trusting in God we can make it, right? How many people want to volunteer to go through another valley like that? *[Laughter]* How many people want to take permanent residence in such a place?

Now, I've noticed what this is saying is these are the people who live there. Now, some versions will say dwell there, sit there. There's all these different versions. But they're not leaving. And so one of the things that struck me odd about this when I gave it some thought, another way of saying this is these are the people trapped in the valley of the shadow of death. They're not getting out. Their poverty's so extreme. Something happened to their society. Their economy's never going to get any better. They've got a lifelong disease they're never going to get over. They might be in prison forever, one kind of prison or another.

But so in effect, this prophesy, whatever it all means and what all of these places are is to say that, to the most hopeless of hopeless trapped in the valley of the shadow of death, the great light will first appear to them. The good news or the brightness or the answer is going to get first to them. They're the ones who need it the most or deserve it the most or something like that is going out.

So that's start one of the stages that's being set, that these are the people trapped in the valley of the shadow of death. Now, someone else can read that next section, about 18 to 22, the fisherman part? |
| *Pastor Stahlberg:* | Doug? |
| *Doug Muschett:* | "Now as Jesus was walking by the Sea of Galilee, He saw two brothers, Simon, who was called Peter, and Andrew, his brother, casting a net into the sea, for they were fishermen. And He said to them, 'Follow me, and I will make you fishers of men.' Immediately they left their nets and followed him. Going on from there He saw two other brothers, James the son of Zebedee, and John his brother, in the boat with Zebedee their father, mending their nets; and He called them. Immediately they left the boat and their father and followed Him." |
| *Charles Manto:* | So just a background on like Galilee. This is an area where there's a lot of fishing going on. That was where they made their money. In fact, this is why they were internationally significant. The Roman Empire realized they made enough money; they would tax that fishing industry. So fishing was really important and talking in fishing language here was really important.

But what's going on in your mind when he's saying, "I'm going to show you how to fish for people"? What's going on there? What's he saying? What's happening? "Once you get challenging, I'll show you how to fish for people." What does that mean? |
Female:	Missionary work.
Charles Manto:	Okay, how so?
Female:	You're going to recruit people to walk in faith.

Charles Manto:	Yeah. So that means you've got to engage them, and you got to persuade them to come over to your side. So, what he's promising them is salesmanship lessons maybe, persuasion lessons. In the ancient world, we would call that rhetoric, right? In the early church, you would call what exactly you would say. They would call that evangelism or whatever, or proselyte or whatever word you use for that.

The idea is how do you effectively engage people? Now, think of our society right now. Are we effectively engaging each other when we have different points of view? |
Multiple:	No.
Charles Manto:	Are we winning people over to our side?
Multiple:	No.
Female:	No, because we're not listening. Sometimes I don't listen it. Put it on me.
Charles Manto:	Yes. So the idea is I can get in front of you and I could win my argument and I could just traipse you and I've won my argument, but have I won you? I may have won all my backers who think, "Go, Chuck. Give it to them," right? But I haven't won them. And he's promising fishing lessons. That's part of the settlement.

The next section. Somebody read 25—*[Pastor Stahlberg raises her hand]* sorry, go ahead. She has a question. |
| *Pastor Stahlberg:* | So, the fishing lessons are for who? Who does he want to fish? |
| *Charles Manto:* | Okay, so that's a good point. So, what we know—what little we know is Jesus is going to guys who are fishing. He says, "You're catching fish. Would you like to learn how to catch people?" He doesn't tell you how or why. He doesn't tell you much, but he's saying, "Wow, I know how important it is to catch fish. If I could learn how to catch people, that would even be better, whatever that means."

And one of the things I'm trying to do as we look through this is not read too much into it, because we all have biases and understandings. It's really better to sort of read and say, "What can we get out of it, and the other stuff we'll put on the side and we'll figure out later." |
| *Pastor Stahlberg:* | My question has a purpose, because it's connected to what you said before. I don't think that like if Jesus were alive today or a rabbi, and he would say, "I'm going to fish for the Republicans only, or I'm going to fish only for the Democrats. I'm going to fish only for the blacks." I think that it's a message—a general message for—it's not directed to just a special category. |
| *Charles Manto:* | And, yes, that's very important. And here's something that dawned on me recently thinking about this. When you're fast tracking it all the way to the end of the Sermon on the Mount in 7, now how do you—when everybody's busy and overwhelmed, how do you get through to them? How do you break through? Especially if you have no power.

Now, if I have lots of money, I say, "Hey, I'll get you a job," you might listen to me. Or I tell you, "I'm going to fire you from my job if you don't do something." And you say, "I don't want to lose my job." You listen to me, right? Or if I have military power, "You do this, or I'm going to blow your brains out," right? "What do I have to do? I don't want you to blow my brains all over their ground. What do I have to do?"

But if you have no military power, political power, financial power, or anything else, how do you get anybody to stop what they're doing and listen? What kind of authority do you have when you're at the bottom and have no power? |

Male:	You become a pastor.
Charles Manto:	There you go. But then you've got to have people who want to listen to you, and then does she have any power over you or maybe not? We've got to find out. So this is what these guys are being promised. "We're going to give you the ability, though you have no military, financial, political power or whatever, to still grab people's attention and hook them and win them over," which is something we'd all like to do.
Pastor Stahlberg:	And there is another preacher who says that he did not do it by force, but by fascination.
Charles Manto:	There you go, and you've got a hook. Because if they don't care—
Pastor Stahlberg:	Exactly. How do you entice people in an honest, authentic way rather than manipulative or using power of force?
Charles Manto:	Anyone else? I heard a voice.
Female:	You love them.
Charles Manto:	Yes. Well, we're going to find out. We're going to find out in just a moment. Now, can someone read verse 23 through 25? Are you going to help me pick someone?
Pastor Stahlberg:	Yeah. Susan?
Susan Knopf:	"Jesus was going throughout all Galilee, teaching in their synagogues, and proclaiming the gospel of the kingdom, and healing every kind of disease and every kind of sickness among the people. The news about Him spread throughout all Syria; and they brought to Him all who were ill, those suffering with various diseases and pains, demoniacs, epileptics, paralytics; and He healed them. Large crowds followed Him from Galilee and Decapolis and Jerusalem and Judea and from beyond the Jordan."
Charles Manto:	So this is in further setup. This is setting the stage for the play you're about to hear. So what's he saying in this passage that's setting it up for us? What do you notice? What is he setting up?
Male:	He's making an impact.
Charles Manto:	He's making an impact.
Amy Simper:	He was a modern-day televangelist.
Charles Manto:	Without the television. Yeah. So big crowds are following him, and he's making an impact.
Female:	He's healing.
Charles Manto:	He's healing. What else?
Darleen Muschett:	Teaching.
Charles Manto:	Teaching. Anything else?
Female:	He's engaging.
Charles Manto:	Engaging.
Pastor Stahlberg:	I think he meets people where they are because they had all these things and he was not going to—

Charles Manto:	They weren't coming to him. He's going to them.
Pastor Stahlberg:	He's going to them.
Charles Manto:	And where are they? Where is he going? Where's he doing all this? Where's the geographical place name there?
Susan Knopf:	Beyond the Jordan.
Charles Manto:	And all-around Galilee. So he's doing all that stuff they just talked about before where it said, "The great Light must first go to the people who are trapped in the valley of the shadow of death," this part is saying, "Now he's doing it, and there's these great crowds following him. He's having an impact." That's setting the stage. Now we're going to go to the meat.
Pastor Stahlberg:	I just want to add that now, at least to me, it makes sense that those who were suffering the various diseases and pains, demoniacs, epileptics, paralytics were in the valley of the shadow of death.
Charles Manto:	Yes. They were hopeless.
Pastor Stahlberg:	So these are the people living in the valley of the shadow of death.
Charles Manto:	Now, these are the people who are the most hopeless. Now, in that world, maybe we should review what that meant to view the most hopeless. If you are the most hopeless, does that mean you had much power?
Multiple:	No.
Charles Manto:	Did you have—what's that?
Male:	Ostracized, separated.
Charles Manto:	How about friends in high places?
Multiple:	No.
Charles Manto:	If you had friends in high places, you wouldn't be in this predicament, right? Now, what were people's thinking? Like if I were one of these wretched, poor souls, what would people think my relationship with God would be?
Ron:	You're damned.
Darleen Muschett:	Probably think they were being punished by God.
Charles Manto:	"I did something wrong." Or being punished. What else?
Male:	Irrelevant.
Charles Manto:	Irrelevant. You don't matter. And why would that be?
Male:	Because you can't believe.
Charles Manto:	But why does that prove that I'm irrelevant to God?
Female:	God wouldn't allow me to have this disease, if I was with God.
Charles Manto:	Right. If I was important, God is big enough to do something about it. The fact that I'm in this is proof, prima facie evidence that I don't matter.

Greg Wright:	Proverbs says that.
Charles Manto:	What does it say?
Greg Wright:	That those who are doing well is because they were good to God or against God didn't—
Charles Manto:	The bad guys get clobbered, right? So, I either am a bad guy or I just don't matter. Anyone else have anything about that? So, this is quite the setup. Now, this is why it's going to be really interesting to read Matthew 5:1-16. So, let's start with just the first two verses before Jesus actually starts talking. Can someone read the first couple of verses? One to two before he starts talking.
Female:	The pages starts with verse 3.
Charles Manto:	—oh, you don't have it. I'm sorry. I'm sorry. That's my fault. So, does anybody want to guess what it says or have a Bible? We can tell you.
Pastor Stahlberg:	Well, he gathers—so he sees the crowds, and he goes up the mountain. And, so, the crowds are there, but then he calls his disciples around him. I mean, they will—let's say that Amy is my disciple, but you are the crowds. But there is a nearness, but the crowds are also there. And then he begins teaching.
Charles Manto:	Yes. There you go. So, what's going on in 5:1-2, it says, "So all these crowds"—and just like they set up all of these crowds that he's been impacting, the hopeless ones, they are the ones that are big numbers coming. And there are so many of them, if I didn't have a microphone and they're just standing in front of me, if I tried to talk to them, the guy in the fifth or 10th or 20th row's not going to hear it. So, I got to go up the incline a little bit so my sound doesn't get absorbed by their bodies, and my voice can project, right? But what did I just tell the fishermen a few minutes before?
Multiple:	Fishers of men.
Charles Manto:	So they're getting on-the-job training to see the master fishermen at work fishing these crowds who are not yet his followers, right? So, all of the things that are supposed to happen according to the setup is now about to unfold right before your eyes if you're following the story. You don't have to believe the story. But if you're going to even read the story and even reject the story, at least you got to give the story writer a fair shot at telling you what he's saying. That's what we're doing here. So the huge crowds come. Jesus backs up so he can just be heard. And then what does verse three say? Just read verse three. You got verse three. Oh, one second while the mic is coming. Right before that, now the phrase says, "And Jesus opens his mouth, teaching them." And what's really interesting is, well, of course if he's going to teach them, he's going to open his mouth. Why did they say he's going to open his mouth?
Pastor Stahlberg:	We don't know.
Charles Manto:	Well, the quotes are from the older part of the Bible that man shall not live by bread alone. Like he just went through the temptation, but by what?
Pastor Stahlberg:	By the word of God.
Charles Manto:	By every word that comes from the mouth of God. So now Jesus, they just said Jesus himself challenged tempter in the wilderness, and you have to follow every word that comes from the mouth of God. Now the mouth of Jesus is opening. There's a connection going on some-

	how. I don't know what it is. Now let's read verse three for the first thing he says. The first thing out of his mouth was what?
Female:	"Blessed are the poor in spirit, for theirs is the kingdom of heaven."
Charles Manto:	Now, this sounds pretty outrageous if you think about it. We have already set the stage that the people who are trapped in the valley of the shadow of death, they don't matter, right? They not only don't matter to the important people; they don't matter to God.

So Jesus is going around and preaching—the word preaching the gospel. Preaching means announcement. Like, "We interrupt this program for the next tornado's coming in five minutes. Take cover." Sorry about that. Maybe too broad with my hands. Surprise announcement that happens, and gospel just means good news.

So Jesus comes up with this surprise announcement that says everything in existence is working upside down from what you think. Because the people you thought are the ones who mattered least matter most, and the people who are totally crushed, they're not just living a nicer life to age 150 with a spare trillion dollars of pocket change and running a couple of countries. They actually are co-owners of the kingdom of heaven. This is the rule of God that is before the multiverse.

So these are the guys who are co-owners of the multiverse. You are co-owners of all the solar systems in the galaxies. And not just in this dimension, but others you don't have a clue about. It is the absolute infinite inverse of what you think it is. It is totally surprising. And everybody's saying, "Oh, really?"

Now why don't you read a few more? Read a couple of more of these. |
Female:	Number four. "Blessed are those who mourn, for they shall be comforted. Blessed are the gentle, for they shall inherit the earth."
Charles Manto:	Why don't you go ahead and read all of them because they're not that many? The next person read the next handful.
Ron:	Where are we? "Blessed are those who hunger and thirst for righteousness or justice, for they shall be satisfied. Blessed are the merciful, for they shall receive mercy. Blessed are the pure in heart, for they shall see God. Blessed are the peacemakers, for they shall be called sons of God. Blessed are those who have been persecuted for the sake of righteousness or justice, for theirs is the kingdom of heaven."
Pastor Stahlberg:	Okay, let's stop there.
Charles Manto:	Let's go to the next—oh, before we change the slide, let's just ask a couple questions about these. We're not going to take too long. Just really fast. Out of all that stuff you just heard, what are the parts that might even be memorable to you or well-known? And then we're going to ask in a moment which ones either raised questions or difficulties or words—

So first—or we could probably answer those together. First, maybe one or two or three of you might say which ones have you heard before or seem to be the most well-known either in your life or people around you? Any ideas at all? Any of those? |
Darleen Muschett:	Maybe blessed are those who mourn, for they shall be comforted. It comes to mind.
Charles Manto:	And is that helpful or troubling?
Darleen Muschett:	I don't know yet.

Charles Manto:	Because sometimes they're just well-known and you're not sure. The jury's out. Is this good or bad, or is it helpful or not? Greg has a—
Greg Wright:	I would just say that, to me, the beatitudes don't mirror what I see when I walk around in life on the planet. So it is the exact opposite. Like Darleen, I don't really know what to make of that. Sometimes I go, "Well, this has got to be a load of BS because that's not what I see."
Charles Manto:	And that's a very good attitude to have. You're going to sound sacrilegious almost but let me tell you why it's good. When you read something that hits you right in the face, it says, "There's something not right with this picture," and those guys were about as smart as we were 2,000 years ago when they're writing this. Do they not get that? No, of course they got that.

So, they are smacking us in the face and waking us up on purpose, and they're causing us to say, "Well, how does this make any sense," right? And they're forcing us to think about something, and they're engaging us, right? And so—and it's good to ask those questions because if it's obvious to you, it's probably obvious to them, too. And then you got to figure out like, "Well, what's going on here," right?

And then when you figure out what's going on there, then you can say, "Do I like this or not?" Or "Have I figured it out, or do I got to put it aside and come back to it later?" Anybody else? Anything else from that passage that jumped out at you that has been either helpful or troubling to you or memorable? Yes? |
Female:	Blessed are the peacemakers. That's something that we need to be tuned into today in the world we're living in.
Charles Manto:	So that's something that's encouraging or challenging in a nice way, right? This is something, if we could figure out how to do this—
Female:	Well, when I see peacemakers, I go, "Listen up."
Charles Manto:	And that's one of the things I think I think is growing there. This is going to—this is driving us somewhere. It's driving us to become peacemakers, and it's so unusual in this environment. How are these guys going to be peacemakers? They have no money. They have no power. They have no military. They have nothing, right? So it's interesting. Anyone else? If not, we're going to move on. Yes?
Pastor Stahlberg:	I think the most jarring for me—I mean, they're all of them are just—but blessed are the gentle, for they shall inherit the earth. And if we look—I mean, this is not true because—
Charles Manto:	The military powers inherit the earth. The Roman Empire's got the earth.
Pastor Stahlberg:	More than that. Right now we have an environmental crisis. The rich people are and the powerful are going to buy their way out of the crisis because they can, they have money. Build the, I don't know, higher streets. Who suffers most right now is the poor in coastlands, on coastlands. And so—and then they are coming to our doors and it's—so it's—
Charles Manto:	Living in Bangladesh is not a prized place to live right now, right?
Pastor Stahlberg:	It is not true that the gentle will inherit the earth.
Charles Manto:	Now this goes back to a quote from Psalm 37, and this was already said in Psalm 37 where they're talking about the people with power and the bad guys doing bad things to people, and somehow God's changing this up even back in the Psalm 37. So, this idea of not again like the meek, but the sense of who's got the power and how is power being used. Some-

thing's going on here. We don't have to figure it out now, but that's a good one to take note of in this whole concept.

Anything else to take note of before we move to the next bit? Yeah, I see the hand.

Lydia Wittman: It's helpful for me in the part that we read to notice the tense that is the blessedness is now, present, and the good thing is in the future. And that—for me that helps the cognitive dissonance of why I can't see it, because it's not here yet. We didn't read the part where it's all present tense, and that's a little bit harder for me because it's like when people are insulting you right now, you're blessed, and that I have more dissonance with because it doesn't feel that way.

Charles Manto: So, you're right. Blessed are the people in this state because God's going to do something, and he will comfort you or will fulfill your hunger and thirst for justice or whatever it is. And then the same thing, blessed are those who are—and the contrast with bookends—we're going to get to that in a moment. Some of them are saying yours is the kingdom versus you will get something.

And the something could be, "Yeah, you keep doing the good thing and like good karma is going to come around to you in the next year or five years, or maybe 500,000 years from now when God puts us all straight and he's really powerful, going to make that happen." It could go either way. The jury is out yet as to what that is.

But there's something going on between what's going on now and what's going to happen in the future, and that's something we get to play with a little bit as we look at this. Next slide. Yes?

Darleen Muschett: You can tell me if this is correct, but I've been given to understand that the word "blessed" does not mean happy. And if that is true, that helps me deal a little more with the cognitive—what is it?

Charles Manto: Dissonance. Happy doesn't mean—so, happy gives a sense of, "Wow, I just found 50 bucks on the street, and I'm happy." "I won the lottery." My circumstances are making me happy, as opposed to I'm in a special state and that—and then we've got to figure out what that is. That's a good point. I see other hands.

Greg Wright: I was just going to mention to Lydia's point about the thing about the present is blessed are you now because you'll get something in the future.

Charles Manto: That's true.

Greg Wright: It seems to lend itself to the Protestant idea of all of our stuff is going to be in the afterlife and inhabit us. So, if we suffer through life now and have a miserable time, but we're going to get—

Charles Manto: Or it's like another might be the concept of an inheritance. I am underage, I'm 14 years old, but my father's a billionaire. Just wait until I'm 21 or my trust fund starts kicking in. So, I know it's mine and it's coming to me eventually, but I'm going to have to wait for a while. And it might be a year, 10 years, a thousand years, whatever it might be.

Pastor Stahlberg: But I need to comment on that because there was a time so when people poor—Mary's Magnificat is the dad has thrown the mighty down from their thrones and uplifted the humble of heart and the rich go hungry, but the poor will eat and be satisfied and so on. I think that's very wishful thinking, I have to say.

And when people figured out—I grew up in the church that said that. "Oh, let us, the rich one, be happy on this earth. You, the poor guys, are going to be happy in the next life." And that people figured out that that ain't going to happen.

Female: It's not going to work.

Charles Manto: Well, and this is the whole problem with—

Pastor Stahlberg: And that's how you have the movements that have appeared for justice in this life, because people are not sure about the next life because the pearly gates and all these kinds of things is kind of wishful thinking. Like the streets of gold in heaven but let us be poor. So, I have big problems with that.

Male: And that's in the Lord's Prayer about let it be done on earth as it is in heaven.

Pastor Stahlberg: Exactly, the Lord's Prayer.

Charles Manto: That's right. And you're going to see this come out even here later when we get to this next spot. Like in the peacemaker section and then even at the end of Matthew where interesting things happen with peacemakers because of what they did in the here and now. Yes?

Greg Wright: I just wanted to point out that, in my experience, when poor people become rich, they don't behave any differently than rich people did.

Pastor Stahlberg: No, exactly.

Charles Manto: That's the whole point of this is—and then we can get to that in a moment. That's going to be a good—but one more hand, and then we're going to switch over.

Susan Knopf: So a couple of things. One, there's two meanings of blessed. So sometimes we say, "I feel so blessed," meaning thankful for some blessing that you have, some goodness. "I feel so blessed to live in Summit County and not in downtown Detroit. I really feel blessed about that." But then it can also mean blessed is something that will happen in the future, which we've discussed.

I'm kind of disturbed, the along the same lines you've been talking about, Liliana, blessed are those who have been persecuted for the sake of righteousness, justice for theirs is the kingdom of heaven. When you look at the Christians persecuted, Jews persecuted, gays persecuted, blacks persecuted, I don't know about the kingdom of heaven, but I sure think everybody'd like a square meal and a decent roof.

Charles Manto: And that's why we're going to go to the next one and start seeing how this plays out. Next. Now this is what you have. Then the few that don't have it, we get leave that on the screen. Go next.

Now we're going to start looking at the beatitudes themselves. We looked at the things that like jump out and sort of like disturb us or comfort us and so on. What I'm asking as a quick question is as you scan that whole page, what patterns do you see there? Because if there's going to be like a driver to get us someplace, what patterns are you seeing? We're just going to take just a quick moment to see if anything jumps out at you. We're going to play with some in just a minute. And if you see patterns, why might they be significant or helpful?

So when you look at all of them that are all—because they were written in there on purpose. They were placed next to each other on purpose. What kind of patterns do you seem to notice even initially, without having to figure it all out or understand what it all means? What kind of patterns do you notice?

Male:	It's all about hope.
Charles Manto:	There's a lot of hope in there.
Darleen Muschett:	Up is down.
Charles Manto:	Up is down.
Darleen Muschett:	Grace comes to mind.
Female:	Blessed are for they.
Charles Manto:	So there's a repetition of this phrasing, right? "Blessed are," and then something after. So, there's a pattern of blessed and then they. What else do you see in patterns? And word patterns is good. You don't even have to do theological patterns so much as this. Even what you see in the words.
Doug Muschett:	One of the things you said, it comes through on all of these that if you suffer now, it will give you your reward in the future.
Charles Manto:	So there's something—there's a now and a future thing going on. That's a pattern. What else do you see as patterns?
Lydia Wittman:	It's using very logical words. "If this, then this," for something that doesn't seem very logical.
Charles Manto:	So that was a pattern there. What else do you see as a pattern? Any other patterns?
Female:	Be aware and recognize the disenfranchised.
Charles Manto:	Anything else you see?
Pastor Stahlberg:	The kingdom of heaven appears. We have not read up to the end, but I actually see and that's—it's in bold, "for theirs is the kingdom of heaven", "for theirs is the kingdom of heaven." And then the last one we have not read is let your light shine.
Charles Manto:	So, it's interesting. How many of these beatitudes have theirs is the kingdom of heaven in there?
Pastor Stahlberg:	Three.
Charles Manto:	How many?
Multiple:	2; 3 and 10.
Charles Manto:	Two. 3 and 10. And so one's near the front and one's near the end, right? So, is that—is there something going on there?
Greg Wright:	Must be because it's in bold.
Charles Manto:	There you go. The original manuscripts all had this in bold. *[Laughter]* Doing a little cheating here. What's that?
Male:	It's a reinforcement.
Charles Manto:	Reinforcement because one's at the beginning and one's at the end.
Female:	Kind of like bookends.

Charles Manto:	Kind of like bookends. See like bookends?
Female:	It's kind of the middle.
Pastor Stahlberg:	Middle because there are two more after.
Charles Manto:	What are the two more?
Lydia Wittman:	They become more personal; I think. It's talking about them and now it's talking about you.
Charles Manto:	And notice what the subject matter of those other two are. It's like he's going into more detail. Like, blessed are the persecuted, but when people do this to you and that to you and this this to you and that to you, it's sort of like, "And let me give you a few more examples," right? So that's why—yes?
Male:	Jesus was preaching off-the-cuff. This is a literary pattern. Are these patterns of Jesus or are these—
Charles Manto:	That's a very good question. And as you see more of these, this is going to be interesting, and the reverse question could be answered. We have a way of writing logically in a narrative style since the printing press was common. We have lots of words, and they're cheap. We could do a very easy narrative flow and transition into things, so we don't lose our audience, right? And when you're trying to get people to memorize massive amounts of stuff and you want to do data compression, you tend to shrink things down and you don't always make the smooth, easy to follow transitions. So, you've got two things at play here. What is Matthew the writer doing? What is the person doing the oral teaching doing? What is the listener who doesn't have a piece of paper in front of them doing? All of these questions—

[End of Friday June 28 Matthew 5 Session 1 part 1 (59;50)]

[Beginning of Friday June 28 Matthew 5 Session 1 part 2 Q&A]

Charles Manto:	You're asking about the relationship between the writer and the listener and the reader and the hero are all important.
Male:	This is a half a century later.
Charles Manto:	Yeah, exactly. It's a half a century later, and that draws in the whole questions that we will get into maybe a little bit here and there, is how does human memory work? How does using persuasion work? Well, anybody heard of post-traumatic stress disorder?
Pastor Stahlberg:	She said the repetition.
Charles Manto:	Repetition.
Amy Simper:	But here's a different question I have here, is these are all promises for people that are currently in a struggling situation. And what about me that things are relatively hunky dory? Am I left out of the boat?
Charles Manto:	So, it's an interesting question because in Luke when you do this—so Matthew later on has

	some woes for the people who don't seem to care and don't seem to get it, but they think everything's fine. Not the average people like you're talking about.
Amy Simper:	So, I'm screwed either way.
Charles Manto:	Yeah. So maybe. The jury's out. So, when we do this kind of discussion, what we're asking all of us to do is to work with like a whiteboard or something like this. We can tear a piece of paper and throw it out, right? We're making scenarios, and we picked maybe 10 facts, and maybe there's three different ways to look at these 10 facts. We don't have to jump into the first way and agree that that's the only way to do it. There might be three different ways to look at this.

And so—and then, so let's go back to this bookends thing for a moment. Bookends could be interesting for emphasis. They could be, like you're saying, to sort of frame something. Like you're writing something and purposely outlining something on purpose. What else could bookends be useful for? |
Female:	Which ones are you calling the bookends?
Charles Manto:	"Theirs is the kingdom" because one's at verse 3, "kingdom of heaven." Then the other one's sitting there about verse 10, "theirs is the kingdom." The others after that are really sidebar conversations with added detail. So, if you put the sidebar—because they're the ones that go to the second person.
Pastor Stahlberg:	To you. They are not general.
Charles Manto:	The first ones say for all those people theirs is, "blessed are they for theirs is," "blessed are they for theirs is." And then when he finishes the second "Theirs is the kingdom of heaven," then he goes off and says, "And when they do this to you and when they do that to you and they do that to you," you can see those because they are all in the second person as being like a little addition, a little separate.
Pastor Stahlberg:	Yeah. Maybe it's because you and I have talked so much about this, but Charles says that these are fishing lessons for people. And I think that for the first 10 ones, he is evoking the story of the listeners. Those who have been hurt, "Oh, it's about me." Those who have been poor, "Poor, it's about me." Those who the merciful—because you are merciful.
Amy Simper:	Sometimes.
Pastor Stahlberg:	Sometimes. Yeah. Well, you can be more. *[Laughter]* You will receive mercy. So, I think it's a book. The first 10 ones are like it's about you. You are the subject of these things.
Charles Manto:	Yes.
Pastor Stahlberg:	So that's the first. And then comes the commission. We have not read the rest of it, because it says but you are also—I mean, now you have identified with those who are blessed. So you win the—why don't you tell the lottery ticket thing?
Charles Manto:	Well, let's imagine if I was going to buy lottery tickets for you guys tonight with the scratch-off numbers that are winners and then hand them all out to you. I figure that's not a very good thing to do in a church. But if I gave out scratch-off lottery tickets and I posted the numbers, you'd be real eager to scratch off the number to see if you won 50,000 bucks, right? Because it's your lottery ticket.

Well, Jesus is sort of doing the same thing. He's evoking something inside you. I've wondered if this great fortune of being co-owners of the kingdom of heaven is for me. All the |

suffering—all I've had is a life of suffering. Nothing's gone good for me. Is this thing he's talking about going to be for me? —I'm going to scratch off this lottery ticket to see if it's for me. So what he's doing by doing that is—

Female: The next meal.

Charles Manto: Yeah, exactly. So, he—all these people, they're caused—what Jesus is doing is saying, "Your story, your circumstances, your suffering is what matters." He wasn't saying, "Okay, now, I don't know who you are. And it's obvious God doesn't care about you, and you don't matter. But my message really matters, and you need to listen to my message." You see, he doesn't do that. He's starting in the reverse. "I want to hear your story. Your story is what I want to start with. Not my story." Yes, go ahead.

Male: So, are you saying that every good fisherman needs a lot of bait?

Charles Manto: I think every good fisherman—if this is true—needs to start by listening.

Male: Right. But are these promises considered his process of—

Charles Manto: Of pulling people in.

Male: Pulling people in.

Charles Manto: We're going to find that out. So let's see about—so we're going to start—let's start with the first, the bookends for a moment, and I'm going to throw out an idea that came to me about the bookends. Next slide.

Now, I was wondering about this partly because I'm the world's worst—I have the world's worst memory when it comes to rote memory, and I'm totally impatient, right? If you want to give me $10,000 for remembering a bunch of Bible verses, I probably wouldn't do it.

Now, I was wondering if the bookends are a pair, if I could figure out what made them a pair, I'm wondering if the six in between might just be three pairs. Because if they are, I could remember three things. I just can't remember six, seven, eight, or nine. It gets beyond me. So I'm saying, I'm wondering if something is going on here with the pairs. What is going on there that might make them a pair and, if so, so what?

And so the question I've got fused is—let's just ask the question for a moment. When you look at these two bookends and you just look at them all by themselves, is there some kind of logical or emotional or some kind of relationship going on between those two that might make them meaningful as a pair? And if you don't figure it out, that's okay. Because when you don't have a lot of time, so—

Male: Like sons of God inherit the earth are similar.

Charles Manto: Yeah. So there's some things that are similar, and then they're—like, theirs is the kingdom of heaven, right? That's similar. What's different about them?

Female: Going back to your first one, I see 3 and 10 are the ones where people are really hurting. I mean, I see if you're mourning, that's healthy. If you're being gentle, that's healthy. If you're merciful, that's a good trait. The third and the tenth one are ones that are pretty painful. If you're really poor in spirit. If you're being persecuted.

Charles Manto: Now, if we only looked at the third and the tenth and skip all the ones in the middle for the moment, what would be different between the third and the tenth?

Female:	One and three is how other people feel, and 10 is because someone's done something to them.
Charles Manto:	Wow. Okay. Repeat that a little louder.
Pastor Stahlberg:	We need the microphone.
Female:	I said 3 is how they feel internally and 10 is what people have done to them.
Pastor Stahlberg:	One is internally, one is external.
Charles Manto:	Okay, next slide. Next slide. Here's a tentative pattern for our whiteboard, what she just said. Poor in spirit. That's an inner condition or an inner result of maybe something happening to you, but it's your circumstance inside you because you are poor in spirit. You are crushed. You are like trapped in the valley of the shadow, and you have no hope. You're poor in spirit. That's inner. External, you need somebody on the outside to persecute you or fight you or whatever. Now, let's see if this holds up with any of the others. Next slide.
Male:	But then can result in 3.
Charles Manto:	What's that?
Male:	10 could result in 3.
Charles Manto:	Exactly. Exactly right. It could be a cycle. When somebody persecutes me, now I'm even poorer in spirit again. But you notice there's two things going on in the two that's different, just for words without having to figure out too much, is with all that stuff going on in the world, it results in my being poor in spirit.

Now, something else was going on in this other one where there's something on the outside going on. So if there's something on the inside going on, could be very complicated, like you're suggesting. Could even be some kind of circular thing going on. But the words are saying something is on the inside, and then something else is going on, on the outside.

We're not trying to make any significance out of it. We're just noticing that that's something there. And without trying to figure out what it is, the question is does that kind of pattern hold to the next seven now? |
Amy Simper:	I've got a question. I'm the resident skeptic here.
Charles Manto:	Sure, please.
Amy Simper:	We're probably pretty educated people in this room, and this isn't the first walk in the park reading this stuff, yet the people that were in that original audience may not have been the most educated. They're suffering and starving and stuff.
Charles Manto:	And hearing it for the first time.
Amy Simper:	What was their attention span? They're not thinking, "Okay, how is this relevant to me? Am I going to take this home?" How did these original people—
Charles Manto:	So that's why we need to go through—so that's why—and this is why when we're seeing this 2,000 years later in written form, we have to ask ourselves these very questions. How does a listener get engaged with this? And this is all you've got going on. Those are the right questions to ask. Just like his question was the right one to ask. The thing that just jumps out at us, those are the right questions. Doesn't mean we have answers right away. And that's why we've got to go and look—

Pastor Stahlberg:	But I do have a little answer. The brilliance of this writer of the text is that although, like Amy is saying, we feel excluded because we are honky dory, actually because of the pair and the internal versus external, we might not be persecuted, but everybody here in this room is poor in spirit in a way because—at some point in your life. I'm so grateful because she makes me think.
	Blessed are the pure in heart for they shall see God is really something for everybody, whether you are materially poor or very wealthy. If you may—you can be pure in heart. And so I think if we think of this as fishing lessons, he touches just about everybody, and everybody can identify with that either in those days or today.
Amy Simper:	But it doesn't say aspires to be pure in heart. It says are pure in heart.
Pastor Stahlberg:	We want this conversation actually, because that's stimulating.
Ron:	That comes from what you were saying. You said, Amy, that you can be merciful. So that's something we can do. We can also be gentle and we can also be peacemakers.
Charles Manto:	Very interesting. Let's do the next slide while we're doing this. Next slide. Notice what's going on in the next one? "Blessed are the sorrowful." Sorrowful, that's an inner condition, right? And you were just talking about that. Notice what happens—and it's an inner condition, like you were suggesting earlier. It could be from all these bad things happening, goes from the outside, right? That's just I don't wake up and be sad. I have a reason for it, right? But the condition is sorrowful is inside.
	And the next one is, "Blessed are the gentle." Now, some versions have "blessed are the meek", and this is one for some discussion and thinking. But most of the scholarship and some of the translations are basically saying the next one is like, "Blessed are the sorrowful ..." that's an inner condition, "... for you shall be comforted." The next one is, "Blessed are the gentle." That implies that I have to be gentle with somebody as opposed to harsh with somebody. It's not like I can be gentle with myself or harsh with myself.
	The meekness word might say, "Well, I have a bad self-esteem, and I'm really shy, and I'm really, really worried about what you think about me, and I don't feel really confident." And that could maybe throw us off. And if it's just that—and this is an admission here. If it's just that, then this inner/outer thing might not work so well. So, I'm putting all of those notes on the whiteboard before I make up my mind, right?
	But notice this thing about sorrowful/inner, gentle/outer. And then let's go to the next pair before we make up mind our minds. See the next one. Next. "Blessed are those who are hungry and thirsting." Hungering and thirsting, is that inside? Hungering and thirsting is inside for righteousness or justice. And justice here means like right relationships. Like, "If everybody was loving everyone the way they're supposed to, these guys wouldn't be hurting me like this," right?
	Now, what's the one after, "Blessed are those who are hungering and thirsting"?
Female:	"Blessed are the merciful."
Charles Manto:	"Blessed are the merciful." I need somebody to be merciful to. So now we're almost seeing whatever it means there's an inner condition and an outer something, an inner condition and outer something. Let's go to the next one. Pure in heart. "Blessed are the pure in heart." Is that inner?
Multiple:	Inner.

Charles Manto: What about a peacemaker?

Multiple: Outer.

Charles Manto: I got to have somebody out there for me to break up the fight. If two guys are fighting, I go and break up the fight. I might get beat up, but I'm being the peacemaker and I'm breaking up the fight. Notice inner/outer, inner/outer. Interesting tentative theory going on. And what's interesting for me with the lousy memory, that so happens, hey, I got three pairs. I just see that.

Now, the next question is, what's going on between the two inner and outer, and does the sequencing mean anything? Let's just see what the next slide is, because I forgot what we put in there. So, this is reviewing the pairs. Does the inner/outer hold the same—kind of sort of, right? Would we all sort of agree that might be something there? We don't have to be convinced. We can just say, "I can see the logic in it, even though I don't yet buy into it." Might we have a pattern? Next slide.

Are they there in some sequence on purpose or not? And look at the last bullet. Are there patterns or pairs that make them meaningful and memorable? Let's go to the next slide. Just get through these. And we've just put them in a list. That's just a chart. I don't know if that helps us or not, but we can talk about escalation.

But I wanted to bring something out that you said. Just skip to the next slide and see if what you said already appeared. What connection or progression might be going on? Let's do the next slide. I wanted to go to the—you mentioned something a moment ago.

Greg Wright: I was thinking the gentle can help those who are mourning. The merciful can help those who are hungry. And the peacemakers can help the pure.

Charles Manto: So let's do—let's start with the blessed are the sorrowful for they should be comforted. So let's say God does some crazy, wonderful thing and you do become comforted in this life. Now you're stronger. Now imagine somebody you know—and somebody else just mentioned the same thing. You have a person who grew up abused, but they become stronger and they sort of get over it, and now they're no longer in an abusive situation. They're in a strong situation. Or you have an oppressed people group. They've been oppressed. Now they become powerful. They throw off your presence. Now the question becomes they're at a fork in the road. They have a choice. They can continue the suffering, or they can take a different path and be gentle. They could be oppressed and be robbed of justice and so angry at the person who caused this, they find that person, they have two choices. They could go for revenge, or they could break the cycle and choose to be merciful.

So what's interesting is the inner side is something that happens to us where we sort of have no choice in the matter. We're like the pure, innocent victim of this thing. "I didn't ask for anybody to rob me, to kick me to, abuse me, to run over my country and make us all homeless and kill half the kids or take all the women, or whatever they did that was terrible. I didn't ask for any of that. But when I become strong, now I have a choice."

And I think that's something that's really interesting, and it goes back to that what do you do in this world? What practical help happens now? Because if I am the one that can move from being the peace broken or the person whose peace is broken, maybe instead of becoming the new peace breaker, maybe I can become something else. And what's the pattern to that?

And let's look at this thing about peacemaker and see what's going on there. Let's go to the next one. Now let's look at this thing about pure in heart. And how are we doing on time? We've got a half-hour, 10 minutes?

Female:	Half-hour.
Charles Manto:	We have a half-hour. I'm just trying to—because I'm not doing this and I don't see the big clock. You are very kind to your pastor. Do you know why?
Female:	There's no clock.
Charles Manto:	You don't have a giant clock over the exit sign that's counting down. Countdown clock. Very gentle.
Female:	We need to buy.
Charles Manto:	Oh, no, let's not do that.
Female:	What did she say?
Charles Manto:	She said something we need to buy. There's this big blank there.
Pastor Stahlberg:	We can never finish in one hour.
Charles Manto:	So think about all the people and people groups that you know that have been hurt. They usually aren't asking to be hurt, right? So they are, in that instance anyway, the pureness of victim. And it's sort of like if some guy stole all of your family's food, you worked hard for that food. You deserved the food. You didn't do anything wrong. You went to work for it, right?
	The jerk who's the thief, he came over and took all your food, and 2,000 years ago there's not a 7/11 down the street. That means you've got to work harder. You're working tired. You're working more. You might have health problems. You might lose children. I mean, being hit by a thief is dangerous, right?
	So, in a sense, blessed are the pure in heart. If you're the good guy and you're just the innocent victim, you're in a good spot. Even though you've been clobbered, like you were saying. Life's not been working out, and every time you turn around, somebody else is kicking you in the teeth. Well, you're still alive, but they're still kicking you in the teeth. Where's God? Where's anybody to help you, right? All that pessimism is realistic.
	Now, he's basically saying the following. So if in life you have always been the pure innocent victim and you never took your turn at being the bad guy, you never did anything evil, you never even thought anything evil, you just always were good, and all you did was get clobbered. But you were always the pureness and victim, and you're really pure heart. You're not even a little bit tarnished, a little bit dirty. Like some people are awfully dirty. You're not. You're pure in heart. What's the good news? You get to see God. That's like the best blessing of all.
	Now, what happens, though, when the person who despised bullies all of their life discovered that they just took their turn at being a bully and just clobbered some guy, and his children died as a result or something like that, and he just realized the thing he most despised in his life is what he himself has become? That I think is a bigger emotional escalation than even revenge.
	Remember how this emotions work. I suffer. That's sad. I'm grieving. I'm hurting. But if I realize half my children died or I became homeless and jobless because some jerk over there did something totally unnecessary, I go into rage. That's an even more powerful emotion. What's more powerful than rage at someone else? Rage at yourself. So if you've got this life-long freight train coming at you, full speed ahead, you don't want anybody jumping in front of that freight train, right? You're going to be crushed.

What happens when you step in front of your own freight train, or what happens when I'm really upset at this guy who stole my food and my family could have died, and I'm going to show that guy I found out where he lives and I'm going to kill? Now, when he did his terrible thing to me, he almost killed me, but he didn't kill me. But if I let my rage get out of control and I go to kill him or want to kill him, what's my—am I pure anymore? I took my turn at being a bad guy not because I stole anything. I became the bad guy why? Because I'm going to kill the guy.

Now, here's an interesting word. That word pure in heart. You heard the word "catharsis" before? This is the Greek word for it, and it's used two different ways. And later on in Matthew, it's used two different ways. You can have a coffee cup that's pure because nobody ever drank out of it and it's pure and clean. Or you could spit in it, and the vile, sickest people spit in it over and over, and it's kicked over. But if you wash that cup and then sanitize it and sterilize it, you'd be purifying that cup. You've purified it. Same word works.

So this is a double entendre or a pivot or like a judo flip. In the old days as a Jewish person, if you discovered you were that bad after having this lifelong guilt thing working for you and you stepped in front of your own freight train, you had two choices basically. You go hang yourself like Judas because your whole id, your whole ego has just collapsed. Or you go and make amends, you apologize, you make amends, you say you're sorry. Then you'd go to the temple, realizing I just did sin against this person, I sinned against God.

And for you to get right with God, God takes the hit for you because he has a sacrifice with either the innocent lamb or the innocent dove or whatever's going on there. And, so you get in this position of peace with God because God's forgiving you and God's taking the hit for you, and that's how Jewish people at that time would in effect become purified in heart. They would own up to it, they would make their amends, and then they would go to God and own up to it with God, and then God would make peace for them based on the sacrifice.

Now, what's interesting about this is saying if you've discovered you're the bad guy and you've discovered you deserve to die, instead of doing yourself in, don't do that. Let God take the hit for you like he wants to do. Receive the joy of his forgiveness, and now you are purified in heart, and guess what? You will see God just like the guy who never did anything wrong. Of course, there aren't many people like that, right? But blessed are the purified in heart because you get to see God.

Now, the question is, that's the internal thing. What's the external thing that goes with blessed are the pure in heart? What's the next one after blessed are the pure in heart?

Multiple: Peacemakers.

Charles Manto: So the idea is what did the guy do to get peace with God in the first one to become purified? In owning up to it, he had to let God pay the price in a sacrifice. Now, I love the idea of being forgiven when I was a jerk by God himself. And a mere mortal offends me, am I willing to forgive you? If God forgave me, how much less—how much more do I need to forgive you? And if God took this hit for me, how much more should I take the hit for you?

And if you guys are fighting—like look at how nice they are to each other. They're sitting right there, and then you are cat fighting. And I go in, and I break up the fight. Well, if God did all this for me and made peace for me and took the hit for me, I should be willing to break up the fight even though she hit my friend and she starts beating up on me. Never interrupt a domestic quarrel, right?

But anyway, that's what's going on. I think there's this inner/outer, inner/outer thing that's going on which says blessed are the peacemaker for they shall be called what?

Multiple:	Children of God.
Charles Manto:	Why does that make sense?
Amy Simper:	It doesn't because it's just for men. *[Laughter]*
Charles Manto:	It means children of God, but you're right. It's just for men. Why does it matter? Because women never do anything wrong. They don't need to go through all this. I'm just joking. For everybody. So, what's this being called the children of God significant about? What's that mean? What's going on?
Male:	Well, if I did the forgiving first, then as children of God, you emulate.
Charles Manto:	Like chip off the old block. And, in fact, God even pays a price to do it, right? It's not, "Well, it's no big deal." Like if you just broke something that cost me $100,000 and I got to replace it and I don't have insurance, I'm self-insured, I might lose my retirement. I may have to work another five—I know guys who put their money with Madoff, and he made off with all the money. Now they got to make up for it, right?
	So, if I'm taking the hit, it's not like, "Oh, no big deal," when your 100,000 is lost. No, it is a big deal. Or you hurt me tremendously. It is a big deal, but I still forgive you because I take the big hit. Why? Because God took a bigger hit for me. If God, the infinite one, takes a bigger hit for me, how could I not take the hit for you, right? Isn't that interesting?
	And when we act like God did when he takes the hit for us and forgives us, then other people see that and say, "Wow, that's a God thing. That person's acting like God." They called you a child of God because you are doing a God thing, right? You're making peace as a peacemaker. Now, notice there's still a bookend. What's coming next after blessed are the peacemakers?
Male:	Those who have been persecuted.
Charles Manto:	For what reason?
Darleen Muschett:	For righteousness.
Charles Manto:	Or justice. So, let's say I go—so I have this wonderful thing. I was about to kill—maybe in the process of hiring a hitman to kill the thief. And then I got called on it and instead of like committing suicide, I throw my life on the alter and say, "God, forgive me," and God takes the hit for me. And then I have my turn, and I see a guy being lynched, and I throw myself in the lynch mob. Use a little bit of the judo I learned as an MP and all that. I still get the crap beaten out of me, right?
	But the guy's happy with me because he's not hung tonight. The objective neighbors thought, "Hey, that was a cool thing he did. He didn't have to get involved. And he got the crap beaten out of him, but he's saved the guy's life. That's cool. He's a child of God." Who's not happy with me?
Darleen Muschett:	The persecutors.
Pastor Stahlberg:	The family.
Charles Manto:	Which family?
Pastor Stahlberg:	The family of the one who got into the fight.
Charles Manto:	So how about the lynch mob? The lynch mob. I stopped the lynch mob from lynching this guy. So, the family of the guy who saved me likes me, assuming you like him.

Pastor Stahlberg:	No, but my own family will suffer because I lost my life.
Charles Manto:	Oh, yeah, my family might not be happy that I got myself beat up. That's true. That's a very, very good point, by the way. And that should not be forgotten.
Pastor Stahlberg:	And they might take revenge.
Charles Manto:	Yeah, exactly. That's a very good point. We should not ever forget that. But the first one is the lynch mob. The lynch mob would be upset for what reason?
Female:	They didn't get to lynch.
Charles Manto:	They didn't get to lynch, because that's their form of justice. So the lynch mob's going to go up to me and say, "Who do you think you are? You are getting in the way of our justice system. We're going to lynch this guy now, and you're insisting on a fair trial. We don't trust that stuff. We want to kill this guy now. You are interfering with our criminal justice system that we want to impose. So, we're taking our tracking—our targeting system, and we're aiming it at you. You are the ones we're going to take out now because we've got four more people to hang, and if you keep getting in the way, we're never going to get this job done." That's why it makes sense that after you see, "Blessed are the peacemakers," you see, "Blessed are the persecuted in the name of justice." How ironic that somebody is going to persecute you in the name of justice when you're the peacemaker, but it only makes sense if the person doing it is the lynch mob. So now you have this total package of what's going on inner and outer that starts with our being clobbered in this world with no hope at all and allows me in whatever way I receive peace from God—and let's say I never become wealthy and let's say I'm still living hand to mouth. Guess what? I still get to break up a fight with other hands to mouth guys who are fighting. I still get to be loving and kind and forgiving somebody who insulted me or somebody in my family. I get to be a peacemaker right now. Maybe all I can do is give this guy a cup of water who really need something to drink or half my sandwich because that's all I've got. But I can be a peacemaker now and turn everything upside down. I don't have to use my poverty as an excuse and say, "Well, I would've helped you right now, but I'm sorry, buddy, I don't have any money." "No, wait a second. I got a quarter, or let's go get a sandwich together and we'll split it." I can be a peacemaker now. And this is a path where you take the people who have been pre-spoken and bring them to become peacemakers. Now let's look quickly at the salt. Let's go to the next one.
Pastor Stahlberg:	I just wanted to say that the reality of things is that the poor people are more merciful and more giving.
Charles Manto:	Than the rich.
Pastor Stahlberg:	Yeah, absolutely. In the homeless communities, people—yeah.
Charles Manto:	Even in the Bible, we have problems with rich Corinthians.
Amy Simper:	They can be as mean to each other as we are. Poor people, they're bad to each other, too.
Charles Manto:	Well, it works both ways.
Amy Simper:	They're judgmental, too.
Pastor Stahlberg:	When you say "they," you generalize. There are people who—

Amy Simper:	You're generalizing too, though.
Pastor Stahlberg:	We are fighting now.
Charles Manto:	I'll break up the fight later, but we're going to let it go on a little bit further before I break it up. So you see this slide. We already talked about this. There's a judo flip.

So this is like a play. This is like a drama where there's escalating conflict, and it gets to a pinnacle where you're going to have total destruction and then there's a flip at the height of the conflict. There's a judo flip, right? And now the peace broken, instead of becoming the new peace breaker, it becomes the peacemaker, right? Beautiful drama here, right? If you were going to write a script for Hollywood or play, this is how you would do it. This is where the flipping comes. Next slide.

Now, when we—we didn't go too much—we got choices. When I find out I could've committed—the other thing I could have done is minimize it. Or I killed off these people, but that's no big deal. That's another way to confront my own evil. I can minimize it, I could commit suicide in self-destruction, or I can surrender to God. We did that. Next slide.

We talked about if God made peace for me, that's the judo flip. This is the persuasion technique, by the way. Jesus is starting by listening to the suffering, listening to the outrage, listening to what it is to be the pure innocent victim, but still hanging in there until the time when the judo flip happens. Interesting persuasion technique. Very different. He's winning people, not winning arguments, and he's being the peacemaker himself or finding people to be the peacemaker. You're winning people over by loving them. You're loving them into the kingdom. You don't argue them into the kingdom.

Next. Escalation, we talked about that. Next. Next. See, we covered all this. We can review all this. We can talk about the driving to this point of flipping and then becoming the peacemaker. Next.

We can talk a little bit about examples, and I might want to come back—we might, if we have some time, if not today, we might want to come back tomorrow before we start the other one and talk about examples from our own lives about the things that drive us crazy the most and when we've been flipped, and we can go through examples of how this might actually work in life, because we haven't had much time to discuss it.

Next. Now, the connection to salt. Here's something interesting. Do you have the Bible verses there that we just read? After the beatitudes, there's something that says you are the salt of the earth. Can someone read that?

Male:	"You are the salt of the earth; but if the salt has become tasteless, how can it be made salty again? It is no longer good for anything, except to be thrown out and trampled underfoot by all. You are the light of the world. A city set on a hill cannot be hidden. Nor does anyone light a lamp, and put it under a basket, but on the lampstand; and it gives light to all who are in the house. Let your light so shine before all in such a way that they may see your good works and glorify your Creator who is in heaven."
Charles Manto:	So, the question is, who is salt? Who is salt, and what's the difference between being salt and being salty tasting? Who is salt? Now, who's Jesus addressing in this group? Who's in the crowd?
Pastor Stahlberg:	The crowds.
Charles Manto:	The whole crowds. Jesus just told everybody, not just the followers in the front row, "Hey, you guys following me, you're salt and the rest of the people are not worth anything." Salt is

very precious and valuable. He told the whole crowd, "You are salt." How could that possibly be? These people trapped in the valley of the shadow of death, God could care less for them, right? How is it that they are all salt?

Male: Again, it's more encouragement. Trying to give people hope, encourage them to be good. And then once they're good, to share their good.

Greg Wright: This may be very similar, but even the stronger you are good and you really need you—you really add to this recipe.

Charles Manto: Now, here's another question. If you go back to the beatitudes we just read and there's all this blessing-ness, like the blessings are the co-owners of the kingdom of heaven, right? All the other blessed, like blessed are the sorrowful. You'll be comforted, right? What is it that got you that comfort and put you in that position of being co-owners to the kingdom of heaven? What got you here? Big bank account?

Female: God.

Charles Manto: What else? What did the text say?

Female: Poor.

Charles Manto: You were poor in spirit or you were sorrowful. So the fact is this sorrow that you've experienced turns out to have great value, right? And so basically what he's telling everybody in the crowd is if you have sorrow, you are salt. If you are crushed in spirit, you are salt. If you've been robbed of justice, you're hungry and thirsting for justice—like relationships, not revenge.

Because, boy, if everybody's just been loving each other the way they're supposed to, this never would've happened, right? And you were on the bad end of that, right? That is highly valuable because you were in the bad end of that. That in itself is valuable, right?

So, basically what he's saying is all of you who have been suffering, considered worthless and scumbags and the bottom dwellers, the fact of all of that stuff that puts you in that position, you are salt. It's that combination somehow. You are already salt.

He didn't say, "If you become my followers like these guys up in the front row, you'll become salt, too. If you start following me and do what I say or give me money or become whatever I want you to become"—never said that. "You are already salt," right? Now, the question wasn't whether or not they were salt. The question is what?

Pastor Stahlberg: If they are salty.

Charles Manto: Salty tasting. They were already light. The question is, would anybody see the light? So, imagine it—I imagine it this way, but you've got to decide if this makes sense to you. We can talk more about this in the examples tomorrow.

So, the idea is the more you've suffered, the more investment God's been making in your life. And how many of you, when you went through something terrible, you'd say to me, "Boy, if I had $10,000, I'd avoid that. It was so painful. I'd give $1 million to not have my marriage breakup or my kid to die or 10 million." That's a huge investment.

Now the question is, no doubt about it that you've had this huge investment, this huge suffering. The question is, have you learned anything from it? Because if you've just learned from all that suffering, like $1 billion of suffering and that's $1 billion of salt, and all you do is go right out and cause 10 more billion dollars of suffering or a trillion dollars of suffering to someone else, you've just taken that investment and flushed it down the toilet.

Now what do you think about all that terrible stuff? You think it was worthless? I mean, you're the one who's telling me or telling God that that was a terrible thing. Was it really terrible? Was it really meaningful? So you can just flush it all down the toilet like it meant nothing?

Pastor Stahlberg: Well, actually, I know many people who—anyway, I know a person right now in the congregation who has cancer and is witnessing that that brought him closer to God. So suffer is the wounded healer that you are talking about.

Charles Manto: Yes, exactly.

Pastor Stahlberg: When we are wounded, we can make something out of it or we can be a victim.

Charles Manto: Or you could say, "I know what got me cancer, and I've only got another six months live. I'm going to make certain those 10,000 people get cancer, too." There are people who have said that, and there are people who've done that and on the public record for having done that.

Now, most people fortunately who get clobbered that way say, "I wouldn't wish this on my worst enemy," but there are some who do. In fact, there are some who say, "And I really not only wish it on my worst enemy. There's a whole bunch of people I don't even know, but I wish it on them too," because they can't get over that.

So the idea is it's one thing if you're salt. The question: are you salty tasting? Guess what? We got another pair going on. All the people on the left-hand side who are in this condition, you're salt. The question is, what are you going to do with it? Are you going to be gentle? Are you going to be merciful? Are you going to be peacemaking? Because if you are, you're salty tasting.

And same thing with light. You went through all this. Why would anybody want to put a bushel over the light? And, in fact, he seems to me to be appealing. "Your suffering is so big. You can't even hide it. The whole world knows how bad you've had it. There's no way you cannot appreciate it, because we appreciate the terrible suffering you've gone through. So let your light shine so other people can get the benefit out of it." Isn't that beautiful, if this in fact happens this way?

Cindy Bardell: I think what you mean more was when you said, "He looked out to the crowd and said you are the salt. He knows our nature. It wasn't the person I agree with. You all are salt."

Charles Manto: Yeah. And you're all suffering. You're all suffering. We're all in this together.

Cindy Bardell: Have the capacity to suffer, have the capacity to be pure of heart, but that he knows that even when we don't know that we are, that he knows us. The condition—but not my condition, because I'm right. It's the condition of every human person around me.

Charles Manto: Now it's up to you to go home tonight and come back tomorrow and think about the patterns to see whether it's there. Because if you do, you will have discovered something on your own which is very significant. Because many people, when they're in a hurry to read through this stuff, which we all are, they basically see Jesus saying nice things to people and we have a "my side" bias.

"If Jesus says, 'Blessed are you, and you're salt, and you're the light of the world,' who is he talking about? He must be talking to people like me. I'm a nice guy. He's talking to the disciples. This couldn't possibly apply to the riff raff. The crowds are now following him."

But if all of these sayings are just to the people who are following him, like the guys in the front row who were already caught, what kind of fishing lessons are going on? If he's only talking to the people—it's like going to me and say, "Chuck, go catch some fish," and I go to the cupboard and I bring you a can of sardines. "No, those guys are already caught. I didn't mean those," right? And so are there fishing lessons here or not?

Now, what's interesting is we live in a world where we have lots of divisiveness, lots of anger, lots of violence, not the ability to win people, only win arguments at the cost of people. We need more than ever to learn how to effectively engage and find whatever lessons we can from wherever, even if it's in our millennium-old core teachings of the church and this stuff that you see in the Sermon on the Mount. It could be applicable to everybody: the atheist in the foxhole, to people not yet Christians, to people who are Jewish, people who are Muslims. Everybody has these conflicts.

And so the question is, what would we do with it and, if so, maybe these are fishing lessons. Yes, go ahead.

Female: I'm guessing that you're going to beautifully connect all fishermen, all people, all, all, all with our Father.

Charles Manto: Yes. That's what we're going to do tomorrow. And what I'm going to ask you to do tomorrow when we do this, is we all have good ideas, reasonable ideas about what all these words should mean. I mean, most of these words are all common words, and every word has three, four, five different definitions. And so we've got a scenario in mind that says, well, I know who "all" are. I know "our" is. I know who the "father" is.

And what I'm going to ask you to do tonight when you come in the morning is to set aside all of those perfectly reasonable ideas and discipline yourself, if you can, to just use the information in the setup of 4 and in 5 and when you began to reach 6 to say—using only the information there as to how to define the terms. Like when somebody says a new word and we use it in a sentence. Let's see how he used it in a sentence and see how he used it in a paragraph and let that define "father," let that define "our" and see what kind of scenario that leads us to.

It may surprise us in interesting ways. That's my thought. Any other questions? How are we doing for time?

Pastor Stahlberg: We are not—Amy has a good point that she—when Jesus says we are the salt of the are the earth, the light of the world, these are all beautiful metaphors suggesting many things. But the Gospel, all the gospels are stories, and if you take anything out of the story and just analyze it on itself, we'll lose something.

So, for me, this whole thing ends up, as we were talking, with Matthew 25 that tells us what it means to be salt and salty, what it means to be liked, for I was hungry and you gave me food, for I was thirsty and you gave me—so it has a practical side because I can say, boy, I'm such a light to look at—teach people. But what is the incarnation of being salty and being a light?

Charles Manto: That's exactly right.

Pastor Stahlberg: And so we need to read the whole story because he is building up towards something very—

Charles Manto: In fact, if we had those whole six classes, a lot of this is already in Matthew 7. He lays it out in Matthew 7 clearly as juxtaposing just that, and then later at the end, you're in Matthew 25 when the big day appears, people show up before heaven, and some people are saying, "Hey, come on over." And they say, "Why should I come over?"

	He says, "Well, I know you. You used to give me food when I was hungry, and you gave me"—and the guy says, "I never knew you. I never did anything for you. What are you talking about?" And then he turns around and says, "Well, when you did it for the least of these, you did it for me." And so there were—there's an idea that those peacemaking activities, as trivial as they may have been in the hands of people who had trivial amounts of power, were infinitely valuable—
Pastor Stahlberg:	And powerful.
Charles Manto:	And powerful internally. Now, they made a powerful impact for the person who received that measly drink of water or morsel of food. Powerful in that person's life even though we look at it and say, "Oh, that's nothing. Doesn't mean much." It meant a lot to God and this infinite one who has responsibility and ownership of the multiverse, is big enough to not only appreciate what happened back then in these what we think are measly little ways that don't amount to much, ascribes to an infinite value.
	But you can see that more—but we will come to how this plays out in 5:44. There's a whole section there about turning the other cheek, walk the extra mile, you love your enemies. That's going to be the set up to the Lord's Prayer, because he's going to say, "I want you not only to love your enemies, I want you to pray for them." And this is going to be the set up. So you can think about that a little bit tonight, and then we can sort of recap in the morning and then go into how this plays out.
	[Applause]
Pastor Stahlberg:	Thank you very much. I hope you will come tomorrow. Actually, I'm very happy that Susan and Jonathan are here because I'm very grateful for the Jewish faith that has produced these conversations for millennia. And—
Charles Manto:	And I hope you appreciate my father's admonition. "Don't ever be ashamed to be Jewish, but don't go tell anybody because it's just going to get you in a lot of trouble."
Pastor Stahlberg:	No, but they say and we are proud, so it's amazing.
Jonathan Knopf:	I never question what a father says.
Pastor Stahlberg:	Thank you so much. I'll see you tomorrow morning at 9:30. We have lunch after the talk.
	[End of Audio]

Section 3: Appendix

Saturday June 29 Session 2, Matthew 6
Lord of the Mountains Lutheran Church, Dillon, Colorado
Presented by Charles Manto, Hosted by Pastor Stahlberg

LOM Video Archive: *https://video.ibm.com/recorded/122552587*

https://video.ibm.com/recorded/122555099 [4]

Pastor Stahlberg:	And during lunch time you are welcome to sit with Charles and ask him tough questions. He likes tough questions. I keep asking him the hard ones. I like when he says, "I just don't know." So that's very honest. We will have yesterday—I will invite Charles to tell those of you who were not here what we talked about yesterday very shortly. Because there are new people, he will tell us a little about himself for those who were not here yesterday. Maybe not "Life in Five," but "Life in Three." And then he will introduce us to his presentation to the Lord's Prayer.
	[Charles' Phone rings]
Charles Manto:	If anyone wants to soften their cell phones, this is a good time to do it.
Pastor Stahlberg:	Yes, that's a good time to do it. Without further ado, I present to you Charles Manto.
	[Applause]
Charles Manto:	We have two mics because we like to do a lot of interaction. One should be on one side of the room, one on the other so it doesn't have to take so long. Maybe somebody could be the mic person.
Pastor Stahlberg:	I will. If you have a question, I'm going to bring the mic to you so that your question can be recorded. If you just speak, it will not be recorded.
Charles Manto:	And maybe somebody could help you with one on each side because we've got two mics today.
	[Crosstalk]
Charles Manto:	And one of the things we did yesterday is go through a quick round of like who we are. But at least I thought we would start today by getting a show of hands. How many people were here yesterday? Okay. How many people weren't here yesterday? Okay. So maybe what we should do at least is have the people who weren't here yesterday tell their names and just a sentence about how you're connected here or how you showed up here

---

4 These are alternative videos of the same workshop where the audio might also be easier to hear and is clipped to eliminate portions not part of the actual workshop. For example, the first video clip above can be chosen but the session does not start until minute 5 of the clip.

Saturday Session 2 Matthew 6 (Lord's Prayer) part1: https://www.dropbox.com/s/r54220iuhr1dtfw/Saturday%20June%2029%20Matthew%206%20Session%202%20part%201.MP4?dl=0

Saturday Session 2 Matthew 6 (Lord's Prayer) part2:https://www.dropbox.com/s/ntzw72dppiqs8n5/Saturday%20June%2029%20Matthew%206%20Session%202%20part%202%20%2815%3A44%29%20.MP4?dl=0

Saturday Session 2 Matthew 6 (Lord's Prayer) part3: https://www.dropbox.com/s/nhvn4crhuqpnlbo/Saturday%20June%2029%20Matthew%206%20Session%202%20part%203%20.MP4?dl=0

	today or something like that. So let's start from like this side. Who was not here yesterday? Okay. So woman in the back, Sally, and then Linda.
Sally Brown:	Sally Brown from Summit Cove. I'm two years, second summer here. I love Lord of the Mountains.
Charles Manto:	And by the way, this is sort of informal, but we're recording it for your benefit so later on you can review it. The only reason for the mic is not so that we can hear you, but so the recording can hear you. Because we know you can all speak loudly enough.
Linda Wakefield:	I'm Linda Wakefield. I've been here something slightly less than 20, I think. I can't quite remember. And I'm a member of Lord of the Mountains.
Charles Manto:	And anyone else on this side? Okay. How about on this side? We're going to start in the front.
Pastor Stahlberg:	With Fred.
Fred Wilson:	My name is Fred Wilson. I come from the Houston area. My wife and I have been coming up here for years. And I met Charles yesterday on the hike, and that's why I'm here. *[Laughter]*
Lamont Wright:	Hey, my name is Lamont Wright. Originally from Sioux City, Iowa. I came here in February. I was invited to the church and just really enjoyed it. So, thanks.
Alan Szymanski:	Alan and Carla Szymanski. We have been here since 2018, locals. We live by the golf course, and we attend St. John's the Baptist campus.
Carla Szymanski:	And we've just began full time living in Breck because we lived for 45 years in Houston. That was for his benefit.
Carol Mezwell:	Carol Mezwell from Breck. I'm a member here.
Jim Llewellyn:	Jim Llewellyn from Summit Cove. I'm a member here. Anybody else?
Ben:	My name's Ben. My wife and I have lived here for about seven years. We're just really excited to attend things in the area that have to do with theology and just the community coming together to support spiritual education. So this is wonderful, so happy to be here.
Charles Manto:	And today also we're hanging out for lunch. We've mentioned that already.
Pastor Stahlberg:	Yeah, we will hang out for lunch.
Charles Manto:	So instead of life in five—yesterday I tried to tell my life story in five minutes. Of course, if you know me, I could go on for five days. So that was pretty good that we shrunk it to five. Now we're going to do it in three, which means I'm not going to tell you my family history from Russia all the way to Brooklyn. We're going to skip all that.
Pastor Stahlberg:	Well, a little. Go ahead. Just say it, because I think it's so interesting.
Charles Manto:	If I talk twice as fast out of both sides of my mouth, *so you can get four times the data. [Laughter]* Father, conceived in Crimea. Born in Constantinople, 1923, when we had our most restrictive immigration laws passed. Only a hundred undesirables from these undesirable countries were allowed in, such as Turkey. My father was lucky. He was number 63, so he and his mother and brother and grandmother came.
	Didn't know much about that until my youngest brother was born. I was nine years old. My father sat me down and said, "I've got to give you life lessons." He did it all in a minute. Life

lesson one: "There's no such thing as atheists in a foxhole. I'm an atheist, but I've been in a foxhole," and that was his World War II set of stories.

Lesson number two was, "I didn't tell you this before, but you're Jewish. Don't be ashamed. There's nothing—you've got to be proud that you're Jewish. Just don't go telling anybody. It's only going to get you in a lot of trouble."

And number three was, "Blood's thicker than water. Always do what you can to take care of your little brothers, one of which is about to be born." And I said, I go, "Dad, you have any brothers?" And he said, "Yeah." I said, "What's his name?" "Max." "How come I don't see him?" "Shut up, kid. Mind your own business."

So—and from that moment on I started looking for my family. Took me about 30 years before I found them. I finally discovered my grandmother when she was 82. Resulted in the reconciliation with my father. That's an interesting story in itself. I went from having no relatives on my father's side to having hundreds and hundreds from New York to Miami Beach, and that's a separate story.

It leads up to the idea that I grew up as a secular child with no religious background. But if I wanted to play with my friends on a Sunday, the parents would say, "Well, if you want to play with my kid today, you got to go to Sunday School first." So every once in a while I'd get a little bit of teaching.

By about fifth grade, we had something in the neighborhood called Vacation Bible School. If we would go, we'd get to play with woodworking equipment, which was sort of cool, but of course the price of admission is you had to listen to Bible stories. The woman in the neighborhood in the apartment building in Chicago said, "You have a Bible, kid?" I said no. "Well, you can take mine. I say, "Well, if you're not using it, okay."

The nice thing about her Bible was the words of Jesus were in red. And I looked at that big, fat book all my friends were studying and I understand it was a really important book. It's just a little too big to read, a little too much, little too complicated. But the words of Jesus were like a short cut. If I just read those, maybe I'd get the basic idea and I wouldn't have to read the rest of it.

And I was intrigued by those red words, which we talked about yesterday. Like better to gain the whole—or why gain the whole world and lose your own soul? Better to gauge out your eye and cut off your hand than go wounded into heaven as opposed to going to hell whole. And as I said yesterday, I get that, but I'm going to run out of body parts.

And then I liked the idea of turning the other cheek, was intriguing to me because if you're in a schoolyard with bullies, you've learned really fast there's like three different ways to deal with it. You either take out the big guy, or you talk your way out—which was my preferred method—or you cut and run. I wasn't fast enough to cut and run, so I had to talk my way out of it.

I never imagined being able to look in the eye of the bully and love the bully and turn the other cheek for the bully. And I thought, "Wow, that's pretty powerful. I've never seen anybody do that." And I just set that aside, and that was just what I learned up until that fifth-grade moment.

Eighth grade. "You like to play softball in the winter?" "Yes." "Well, there's this church that has a gym. You get to do that if you want." "What's the price of it?" "You got to listen to some Bible verses." "Oh, boy, here we go again, but okay. They're safe. I can do that." This time the verses were "God loves you even though you didn't love him. Even to the point of going to the cross. Even though you were his enemy, God loved you." And I said okay. I went home and tried to figure out what all this stuff meant.

So I pulled those ideas together and I imagined myself being in a playground, only this time I was the bully and I get the little kid that comes up to me. I don't know him, but he's small enough. I could push him around, make his nose bleed, make him cry, taunt him, tease him. And then when I'm going to go to hit him another time, the little boy looks at me lovingly and turns the other cheek for me.

And in that moment, I realized "Oops. God just snuck into the world in disguise as a little boy, and I'm bullying God." And I thought that was pretty impressive because this little boy who was sneaking into the world could beat me up if he wanted to, but he didn't. He instead turned the other cheek. In fact, he could beat up everybody in the playground, the entire city of Chicago. He could take out the country, the planet, the universe, and he can snap his finger and take out the multiverse if he chose to because he had infinite power.

On the other hand, I had infinitesimal power. What little I had came from him. The bad news about that is, in this case, I was 100 percent wrong and he was 100 percent in the right. So that gave me this huge model of love that I couldn't imagine before where the infinitely powerful was infinitely loving and a hundred percent in the right when I was not.

And I said, growing up in that time, eighth grade, 1965, Cold War, we always had films in school about what nuclear weapons do when they blow up. We sort of mapped out all the fallout shelters on the way home in case the sirens went off. In fact, the planes would be buzzing by Chicago doing sonic booms, just to remind us of that. And so I realized we were in a dangerous world not just because of the bullies, and I thought what would really be interesting is if people could love each other this way even though they thought they were enemies.

It'd be sort of like the "Wizard of Oz" where everybody stayed on the Yellow Brick Road. And even if this idea of the story is not true and the guy behind the curtain's a phony, we could really use something to keep us all on the Yellow Brick Road so we don't all self-destruct. So I thought that was pretty impressive, and I asked myself what could be more powerful than a message like that, since I'm on this kick. And I was saying, "Well, I don't know if I can think of anything more powerful except maybe if the guy behind the booth isn't a phony."

What happens if God really did love us that much that he would sneak into the world as a little boy and turn his cheek for us, right? And I said, "Well, how do you know whether or not that's true?" And I said (to myself), "Well, maybe if I live 500,000 years, have that many PhDs, could go over every nook and cranny of the multiverse, maybe I could gather enough data to figure it out. But I don't think I've got that much time. I'm not that smart. I'll never be able to pull it off."

And then it dawned on me: "Well, God is pretty smart, and he's pretty powerful. And if these guys can think of this story, maybe God can think it up. In fact, it would be just like God to do that." And so it was an awareness that came over me that says I'm just now convinced that God does love us that much. And if God loves us that much, how much easier is it for us to love each other that much?

So that was sort of my story of how I got into this. And the reason that was important is later on when I was picking something to do on a train ride into D.C. every day and not wanting to waste time, I heard if you're getting old, it's good to do languages and music. I decided to memorize these passages in the Sermon on the Mount in ancient Greek and set it to music. And the funny thing about doing that, aside from realizing right away I have the world's worst rote memory so bad I forgot how bad it was, I started looking for memory tricks that might make it easier for me to do that.

And that led to all these studies, and we're going to do what we did yesterday, but that's sort of the life in five. I tried three, but maybe four. Yesterday we pointed out that—and this is like a six-session class that I've been teaching to adults. Yesterday we did session two, and we'll review that. Today we're going to go to session five, which is the Our Father or the Lord's Prayer.

Pastor Stahlberg:	Can we review the answer to—I think most people here know the passage with salt. You are the salt of the world. Who was the salt?
Charles Manto:	Yes. So yesterday we were trying to figure out when Jesus—the whole point of this passage of the Sermon on the Mount is all these crowds are following Jesus. They all show up to be taught, and the disciples have the front row seat. And then Jesus starts pronouncing all these blessings. "Blessed are the poor in spirit, blessed are the sorrowful." And then when he's all done with these blessings, he turns around to the whole crowd—not just to the guys in the front row, his followers—and that they are all salt.

And we were trying to figure out yesterday who is salt and what made all these guys salt? He could say, "If you follow me and become one of these wonderful disciples like the guys in the front row, you'll become salt." He declared that they were already salt, and we were trying to figure out what was so valuable, what was going on that the entire crowd was already salt. And anybody remember from yesterday what we thought that was, and then that goes through another question that sort of summarizes. |
Pastor Stahlberg:	Let's see what people remember.
Charles Manto:	Now, by the way, when people answer, it doesn't mean that we all agree with this. These are my ideas that you're considering. And if it makes sense for you, you might agree with them or choose not to. Anyone from yesterday? Who was salt and why could the crowd be salt? Oh, we've got microphones.
Pastor Stahlberg:	Yes. Who wants to say who was salt? Cindy I think was yesterday, so tell us.
Female:	Well, we're all salt, but not just us. Everyone that's out there. The context in Matthew 4 was that Christ was walking among the people and telling them his story, and then they followed him, all of them. And they were the people who didn't have a lot, and he looked down on all of them and said, "You are all salt. You are all light." And so it was the context of him walking among them and telling them his story, and then the beatitudes and then saying to them—not just the disciples, to everyone.
Charles Manto:	Anyone else have ideas from yesterday or thoughts? You need to refresh my screen or password? Can you hear me over there? Do you need my password? If you cut off my finger, it will take the fingerprint. Or do one and then Mac with the M is capitalized and then Book where the B is capitalized and Pro where the P is capitalized. And then I think it might be the one after that. Try that. And now the whole world knows my password. Want to take a one-minute break, and I'll go back there and give my fingerprint. I'll come back with my finger.
Pastor Stahlberg:	I can continue about yesterday. We talked at the beginning of the beatitudes, we discovered that those who are blessed, that the wretched of the world, those who are poor, those who are mourning, everybody who is in pain, those who suffer for justice or righteousness, so these are all people who are walking through the valley of the shadow of death. And there the message you get when you are destitute is that you don't count, you don't matter.

And the beatitudes tell these people that actually God loves them and they matter most. So it's a complete reversal of the values of the world where if you are a homeless, stinky person, you don't count. But in the beatitudes, we hear that everybody counts and everybody is salt. So I just did that review for you.

Charles Manto: So I didn't get to hear her answer, so we get to compare all these answers. *[Indistinct conversation with sound technician from back of room]*. And I was giving him one digit off so now the whole world doesn't know my password. *[Laughter]*

So, anyway, what we were saying—I'll put it in my own words—is that all of these people who were crushed, poor in spirit to people who are sorrowful, people who are hungering and thirsting for the justice they never got, because they went through all of that, they were salt and they were light.

The question is when you went through all of that, that was like God's investment in you, and you went through all of that difficulty. At the end of that, did you learn anything from it? If you went through all the suffering and abuse, did you just put everyone else through more of that same suffering and abuse? Because it promised you if you were sorrowful, God's going to comfort you, so you got comforted. Now you're in a strong position. You can put everybody else in the same discomfort you were in and keep that cycle going.

Or you could choose instead, because you've learned what it was to be in all that discomfort, misery, abuse, oppression, whatever it was, you can choose instead to break the cycle and be gentle. And if you're gentle instead of harsh, you get another blessing. Blessed are the gentle, for they shall inherit the land or the earth or whatever.

Same thing if you were the one who was the victim of injustice and you're hungering and thirsting for it, and God fills you and now you're in a strong position. And you've got somebody else in your life who shows up, and they're a jerk, or you've got the person who hurt you. You could do revenge, or you could instead choose to do mercy. And so what he's basically saying in this passage earlier that we talked about yesterday is we're all salt and light. The question is are we salty tasting or light giving?

If we choose to be gentle and merciful and peacemaking, we are salty tasting and we are light giving. But if we choose to not do any of those things, we've lost the opportunity to not only benefit ourselves, but lose the opportunity for other people to benefit from what we've learned. And that's what was going on in the salt/light passage, and that was like who was salt. The surprise is if that's true, the salt was not the believers. The salt was everybody in the crowd, and the question wasn't whether you were salt. It's whether you're salty tasting.

And now we were going to ask—one of the questions we're going to talk about today, pastor, when we were talking a little bit about examples of restorative justice. Because one of the things we talked about yesterday was what do we do with all that? And do we like—for example, when we finally get the strong position, exact revenge or we instead eventually work our way to becoming peacemakers?

Pastor Stahlberg: Right. So what Charles—yes, you are right. As we were preparing for today, I told Charles what you are talking about is actually restorative justice. Our legal system here and all over the world is based on retributive justice. You have done something wrong. You are locked up, you are punished. You are being punished, and hopefully you will be reformed if some people help you. But it is a punishment-based system.

Retribution is our natural tendency. It's not natural actually. It is what we learn from society. Natural would be restorative. But we learn that if somebody slaps me, I will slap back. If somebody does something to me, I will report him to the authorities. The beatitudes and the Lord's Prayer are about restorative justice, where the person who did something wrong is restored and the victim is not a victim anymore. But they build that relationship and there is forgiveness.

So we have an example. I told him that examples stay with us at this church. Right after I became—I came here as a pastor, it was a cold evening, cold winter night. And when we came to church the next morning, we found out that the police have been here and somebody had broken into our church. They broke a window to get warm. Now, it was a very young man, and he had frostbite in his toes. And, actually, I saw them and they were black. The pain must have been unbearable. I would have broken into the church too, to be honest with you.

The question was whether we should press charges or not. And then at that point I said—remember I sent an email to our council and I said, "But who is this young man? Where is his family? He is not a nobody. Let's find out what is going on. Why did he do that? He didn't steal anything. He just broke in the church to get warm."

A family from the church tracked him down through—with the help of the police. We found out he had a brother. We visited with the brother. This young man went to the hospital, almost lost his toes. But because he's younger, he actually didn't lose his toes. His body could recover. He couldn't walk for a long time. My husband and I, we visited both with him and his brothers, and we began a relationship and found out that they're wonderful people. That was the situation. It was not that he was evil and wanting to hurt us.

At the end of the story is that both brothers gave us money to replace the window, and then this young man came here in front of the congregation and apologized and cried and thanked us for not sending him to prison, but giving him another chance. He is around and works at Red Mountain Grill and has another job. So he has been restored. The congregation here has forgiven you. He has apologized. So the relationship was healed.

That is healing and restoration rather than retribution, and that's the point of the beatitudes, and so to give each other another chance and not be victim and abuser.

Charles Manto: (I was trying to stay not too close so I wouldn't cause reverb maybe or conflict with those two mics.) So I'm going to give you a moment to think of another example or two that—but if you remember from yesterday, you start in the beatitudes where a person is crushed, broken, hurting, sorrowful, and something is driving through the beatitudes towards the end where they now become peacemakers instead of the new peace breakers.

Because very often what happens to the abused, the abused becomes the new abuser. The oppressed people becomes the new oppressor. But in this case they were walking you through a sequence where something happened. And in the case of the beatitudes, do you know where those were—remember what the flip was, where the person turned from being the innocent victim to getting ready to become the peacemaker? What flips them, if you recall from yesterday? And if you can't, that's okay, and I'll just remind everybody. I'll just tell you just to save time.

So you go from, "I'm sorrowful," to, "I'm angry because I've been robbed of justice." I'm the pure, innocent victim. Lucky me, because it says "blessed are the pure in heart *[for they shall see God]*." We shall see God until the day comes when I discover and take my turn at being the bad guy." Or maybe I think that I've never done anything wrong. And I'm so angry at the guy who stole my food, I'm ready to kill him, which turns me into a murderer suddenly, right?

And so I realize I'm not the pure, innocent victim all the time. I take my turn at being the very bully I despise. And that is a really tough emotion to go through if you're sincere and you're not just saying, "Oh, it's no big deal," because if you realize how angry you are at other people for being a jerk and then you yourself discover that you've taken your turn at being that, that's a stronger emotion because your entire ego, your entire identity is crushed.

And so you have two choices at that point. You either give up on life, commit suicide, roll over and die, or you throw yourself on the mercy of God and you let God restore you. And what people would do [in that case] is they would apologize, make their amends, go to the temple, do the temple sacrifice. In effect, then God was saying, "I'll pay that price for you. I'm going to forgive you. I'm going to take the hit." So that person becomes purified in heart. So the flip, when you go through this progression in the sermon and the beatitudes is you flip from being the pure, innocent victim to, "I'm taking my turn, and it's not enough to be pure in heart. I have to be **purified** in heart."

ow, if God purifies me in heart, what do I do with that? Nothing. Or do I go out in life and forgive other people, love other people the way God loved me, make peace for other people like God made peace for me, make myself a lifelong peacemaker? And that normally means pay the price. If you break up a fight, most likely one of those guys is going to deck you and you're going to take a hit, right? And when you do that, you're being just like God. And people see that and recognize that and say, "That's a God thing." It's a chip off the old block. And it says when you are a pacemaker, you're blessed because why?

Pastor Stahlberg: You are a child of God.

Charles Manto: You'll be called a "child of God." You are already a child of God when you received that peace, but now you'll be called a child of God because you're living like an offshoot of God, making peace for other people based on a sacrifice (including yourself). You're going to be called a child. So that's the progression there. And so that's what was happening about the beatitudes being this way of taking people from being broken and crushed to becoming peacemakers. It's not just a bunch of haphazard blessings that have no connection with each other.

Sometimes people have thought that, because we don't always take the time to think how these things might relate to each other. And if we don't do our homework to figure out how they might relate to each other, we might think they don't relate to each other. It's just a hodgepodge collection of Jesus' sayings. And many famous theologians gave up on it too quickly and said just that, but today we discovered maybe there is a connection. And if it is, it could be this thing that takes us from being the peace broken to being peacemakers. And that's what we did yesterday.

How about an example? Have you ever seen that in your life? She mentioned one from church. How about either an example from your life where you've experienced restorative justice, where the bad guy not only is restored, but goes out and now restores other people? How about examples from literature or the movies? I see a hand. Microphone. Microphone. Oh, there's one right there. There's one right there.

Male: This is probably my favorite, where Jean Valjean was staying at the priest's house. He sneaks out later that night with one silver candlestick. The police catch him and bring him back to the priest's home and say to the priest to press charges, as you were talking about here for the church.

The priest says, "Oh, he forgot the second one. Remember I gave you two of them?" He gives him the second silver candlestick, and he says separately to Jean Valjean, "Remember that the price is that you walk for God," or something like that. And the rest of the "Les Mis" is that he does go on to be this wonderful holy person.

Pastor Stahlberg:	He transformed this man's life with this one thing.
Charles Manto:	He was just being with the priest and stealing his stuff. And the priest turned around and said, "You forgot the other stuff," and gave him more. He was literally turning the other cheek. It would be as if we were—I was talking to this this way. It's like as if the guy broke in and we caught him in the act, and we realized as we looked at his feet that he was going to die out there, and our response would be, "Here, let me break another window for you. Let me pay for your medical bills."
Pastor Stahlberg:	Or if somebody takes your coat, you give the shirt, too.
Charles Manto:	Yeah.
Pastor Stahlberg:	These are very upside down.
Charles Manto:	And it's interesting. In Luke, that's how they do it. They say if a guy takes your coat, give them the shirt off your back. In Matthew, it's the flip. He says if a guy goes to court to sue you for the shirt off your back—which sounds on its face totally ridiculous, right? Why would anybody do that? And if that's happened, it's probably because he's got the fix with the judge. The fix is in, and it's an evil court in the first place. And then he says what do you do when— he says if a guy takes you to court for the shirt off your back, what are you doing in Matthew? Because we didn't talk about this yesterday.
Female:	Give it to him.
Charles Manto:	You give him what? Because you're already taking the shirt off your back. What do you give them in Matthew if they take the shirt off your back?
Female:	Shoes.
Charles Manto:	The coat. That's flipped. It's the coat. Now the reason this is important is this is what's going on in the turn the other cheek passage. It's not only a loving thing. It gives the person who has no power and is being sincerely loving an opportunity to claim self-respect and do something really interesting.

In the case of the coat, Jewish law said you were never allowed to take anybody's overcoat overnight as a security deposit, because in those days that's what kept you alive. It kept you from freezing at night and dying of hypothermia. So if you ever were to—so if I came into your business and I said, "Oops, I forgot my wallet in the car here. Hold my coat for a moment, and I'll go get my wallet," that's acceptable. But if you find out I can't find my wallet and I'm really sorry, you're not allowed to keep my coat overnight. If you do, you're violating a huge law, and it sort of like goes to the top of God's inbox of things that are going bad down there, right?

And so what you do is when you offer your coat and if the judge accepts your coat, you've just proven to the judge, everyone in the room and to the whole community when you walk out that it is an unjust judge and an unjust legal system. And that's why everyone's out the door with no shirt and no coat. Now, you'd no longer have a coat if he takes it, but you've actually been able in a very loving way show, "I'm loving you anyway, but you just proved to the world that you are an unjust judge." It's an interesting— |
| *Pastor Stahlberg:* | Preserve your dignity. |
| *Charles Manto:* | You preserved your dignity. Same thing with being slapped in the face. You turn the other cheek. We're going to go to that, and we're going to go through how this all fits together. We're going to give you—so yesterday when we did this, we talked a little bit before the be- |

atitudes in Chapter 5, we took a little bit of time to look at the setting of the stage, what was going on at the bottom of Chapter 4. We're going to do this, and I'm going to pass out some pages, and I will review some stuff from Chapter 5, which is setting the stage for Chapter 6.

And all that stuff we did now with the Jean Valjean example, with if the guy steals your shirt, give him your coat; or if he wants your coat, give him your shirt. We went through that example. Does anyone else have a quick one they want to say while we're passing these out? Yes. Go ahead. Microphone right next to you. Doug, thank you.

Female: I was raised by a father who sometimes was very physically, verbally abusive, and the other time he was very loving. I never knew which was coming. And I remember him taking me for a driving lesson, and I didn't do very well. I slammed on the brakes, and I waited for his angry putdown, and he got up from bashing his head on the dashboard and looked at me and smiled and said, "Daughter, we stopped."

Charles Manto: So that was a nice change of pace.

Female: That was a flip. That was unexpected restoration.

Charles Manto: And was he a charged person after that, or did he still go back and forth and you really didn't know?

Female: Until he was 68 he went back and forth, and then Jesus grabbed him. Beautiful ending.

Charles Manto: Sometimes that process takes a little while.

Female: Took his lifetime.

Charles Manto: So we've seen who is salt, and we're seeing this pattern. Now we've going to look and ask a similar question. Who is the "our" in Our Father? Like the old "Lone Ranger" joke, "What do you mean we, Kimosabe?" I don't know if any of you know that "Lone Ranger" joke. We won't go into that now. If you didn't grow up here, so you wouldn't know the "Lone Ranger" stories.

So we're going to go into this, and we're going to look at the setup, and what we're going to do is have people maybe read a few verses, and pastor will sort of pick on you to—if you're ready to read.

Pastor Stahlberg: Linda, why don't you read because you have the mic there?

Charles Manto: And find and see which one you're going to start with first.

Pastor Stahlberg: It's Matthew 5:16 and then we go to 38. Here, I have a copy. Charles, here.

Charles Manto: So let's have somebody just read 5:16.

Female: "Let your light shine before men in such a way that they may see your good works, and glorify your Father who is in heaven."

Charles Manto: So the reason I pointed this out—and sometimes to save a little time I'm going to tell you why I think this is a setup. What's going on in 5 right before the Lord's Prayer session as setting the stage? So setting the stage here, what we talked about yesterday in the salt and light passage, you'll notice when he finishes talking about salt and light, he says, "So therefore let your light shine so everybody sees these wonderful, good things"—being gentle, merciful, peacemaking. "Let the whole world see them so they see that and glorify your Father in heaven because of your good deeds."

You're going to see later that he's going to say there's a bunch of stuff you don't do in front of people. So you're going to—this is going to be a setup. You're going to see this almost contradicted in 6, and we're going to figure out why is this apparent contradiction there. Now, somebody else maybe read 38 through 42.

Pastor Stahlberg: Amy?

Female: "You have heard that it was said, 'AN EYE FOR AN EYE, AND A TOOTH FOR A TOOTH.' But I say to you, do not resist an evil person; but whoever slaps you on your right cheek, turn the other to him also. If anyone wants to sue you, and take your shirt, let him have your coat also. Whoever forces you to go one mile, go with him two. Give to him who asks of you, and do not turn away from him who wants to borrow from you. You have heard that it was said, 'YOU SHALL LOVE YOUR NEIGHBOR, and hate your enemy.'"

Charles Manto: That's good enough for now. Stop there for a moment. We have the next slide. So we talked about that word—and let's go to the next one. So skip over the next two, because they have that, and go to the third. Skip that one, because I think we meant to take that one out. Go to the next one.

So now you see the setup again is going—is still talking about conflict, still talking about what our alternatives are instead of doing the retribution. You're seeing this section that we're not getting into a lot of detail, but they give examples of how to do something different. And it culminates in this section, the next section that's setting up the Lord's Prayer, which is about loving enemies and praying for them. And maybe somebody may want to read now verse 43, which you started, and go to 48.

Female: "You have heard that it was said, 'YOU SHALL LOVE YOUR NEIGHBOR, and hate your enemy.' But I say to you, love your enemies, and pray for those who persecute you so that you may be sons of your Father who is in heaven; for He causes His sun to rise on the evil and the good, and sends rain on the righteous and the unrighteous. For if you love those who love you, what reward you have. Do not even the tax collectors do the same? If you greet only your brother, what more are you doing than others? Do not even the Gentiles do the same? Therefore, you are to be perfect, as your heavenly Father is perfect."

Charles Manto: So any thoughts or questions about any of those sections? I know you've heard these phrases before. In this section, walk the extra mile, turn the other cheek, love your enemy, probably the most well-known verses of the Bible, even though people don't even know they come from the Bible, right? Pastor?

Pastor Stahlberg: There is a progression because actually the Jewish law, an eye for an eye and a tooth for a tooth, was a progressive law. People—like if somebody stole a sheep from you, you would go and kill 10 sheep or more sheep. So the people would take revenge double or triple. An eye for an eye and a tooth for a tooth was really progress where if somebody did something wrong, I would repay, I would take revenge but do the same thing and not more. And that—and so Jesus goes a hundred steps further from an eye, and so he takes us on a much higher level of consciousness.

Charles Manto: That's a very good point. It's sort of like saying, "You took out my eye? I'll take out both of yours. I'll take out all your teeth." And society says, "No, you're not going to do that. You only get to take out the one tooth." So that was progress. Now this is something different. Although this all may sound a little foreign to us, any other questions or thoughts about this? And you're seeing this whole setup about the audience is still in conflict very often.

In fact, when we read the—going back to eye for an eye, tooth for a tooth, who is empowered on these verses from 38 to 42? Who's in the power position, and who's in the weak

	position? So if somebody is coming to slap you on the cheek, are you in the strong position? Probably not. But they're giving you the chance to turn the other cheek.
	What's the next one? If they're going to sue you and taking you to court, who's in the power position?
Multiple:	They are.
Charles Manto:	There are in the power position. In fact, it's not looking good for you. Because if you—if somebody walked in right now and pulled me away in handcuffs, you say, "Oh, Charlie must have done something bad." That's what we first think, right? So if there's apparent fault as well, it must be the bad guy. Sometimes it's the other way around.
	What's the next one? Who forced you to go one mile? When did that happen in the ancient world?
Pastor Stahlberg:	The soldiers would ask people to carry their load.
Charles Manto:	Yeah. That's an interesting one because even before the Roman army, in the Middle East ancient armies would be empowered and told when you're going to go to work in the morning on a work detail or you're going to battle, if this guy's standing out along the way and you just happen to come across him, you must force him and draft him for an hour basically to carry your pack so when you get to the job site you're more rested. But the basic rule of thumb was you don't get to do it for two or three miles. Why?
Female:	It would be usury.
Charles Manto:	For forcing him to do too much. What's another one? Think of it from the standpoint of the Roman army. Why would it be bad for the Roman army, I'm a centurion and I'm drafting you for an hour to go for miles carrying his pack? Why would it be bad for me for him to go two, three miles?
Female:	He might go against you.
Male:	Might slow him down.
Charles Manto:	Slow him down because he's not as fit as all of us guys who are like the NFL, superhero, warriors, right? He's not a superhero or a warrior. After about a mile hike, like we took the hike yesterday, you make him hike two miles, you're going to slow the whole thing down. Now, guess what happens when he offers to go the next mile? Imagine I'm a poor guy. "Oh, by the way, Roman soldiers. I'm so glad I bumped into you today. If it wasn't for you, we wouldn't have these nice roads. Oh, you want me to carry your pack? Let me carry two. Let me carry three."
	So this old man is carrying the pack two to three miles. What's happening? They either get to the battle late or the work job late. But if it's the battle late, they lose the battle. And if they lose the battle, they might lose the war. And if they lose the war, the entire Roman Empire could collapse. Imagine this: the old man who carries the pack for a second mile can actually take down the entire Roman Empire if he's allowed to do it.
	But he can be loving. It's not like, "Oh, he's going to—he's messing with me. I'm going to take him out right now for being a jerk." But if you really truly are loving and the guy's got to think it over, that's a really interesting position to be in.
Pastor Stahlberg:	And the one carry the load for more miles is regaining power and dignity. It's again over and over, it's the reverse of those who seem to be powerless regaining their dignity and power.

Charles Manto:	And, see, by the way, just like in the beatitudes, the first one is the one on weak, and what do you do with it? You could have power and you could flip it around, right? But you're still doing it in love.
	Now let's go to this next one, 42. Who's in power?
Female:	The one who asks of you.
Charles Manto:	What do you think?
Female:	I think the opposite.
Charles Manto:	You think it's the opposite. How many think it's the one who's asking, and how many who thinks it's the one being asked? How many thinks the person asking's in power? Raise a hand. How many thinks the one being asked is in power? Aha. I think the second group has it.
	Now, here's what's interesting. If the guy had the power, like the guy's going to just hit you and make you turn the other cheek or bring you to court or the Roman Empire with all the military might, they could just say, "I'm taking your money. I'm sorry," right? In this case, they're asking. Why are they asking? Because they can't take it. You're in the power position.
Male:	Because you have more money.
Charles Manto:	Or you have more power. That could be like we're all relatively equal in power, but I'm just a little tougher than you, or I've got a few friends. And so here's a situation where it's reversed where you're in power. So it's interesting, is this section shows all kinds of conflicts, from smaller one-on-one to a larger group, like the court, to the entire Roman Empire. And even on the off chance that you're the one in the power, they give you a whole wide range of conflicts that we're talking about here.
	So this is the setup. So all of this stuff that happened in the beatitudes, and the salt and light, and the stuff about the law that we skipped over in those other two classes, and now this is setting this up and it's talking about—then he goes to love your enemies.
	And now let's look at why prayer is relevant. Let's look at verse 45. Why is prayer relevant? Look at verse 45. What is going on with me and the Father that I'm supposed to pray—and we're going to need a microphone. I'll just tell you.
Pastor Stahlberg:	Who wants to answer it? Come on.
Charles Manto:	What's going on here? Why would you bother to—why would even Jesus be telling you to pray? Aside from the fact that—
Female:	So you can be a child of God, because he loves you and wants you to be his child.
Pastor Stahlberg:	A chip off the old block.
Charles Manto:	And what's going with the father of me? Chip off the old block would be one. Now what about the father of me and the bad guy? What's the connection between the three? Now I've got a three things going on. Many relationships, not only the writer of this and us reading it, but in the story itself. You've got the person in the conflict, the person causing the problem, and you've got the father. There are three parties in this, right? Did I hear another answer?
Female:	Prayer can change not only the bad—prayer can change everybody, not just the so-called bad person. Can change everybody.

Charles Manto:	Okay. And why can it change?
Female:	Because God's power can—I believe God's spirit is in every person. That power can change all of us.
Male:	I was thinking that we'd be more like God, and God is giving reign to everybody. So God loves everybody, so we should be more like God.
Female:	I'm just thinking of God, I need to be in prayer because he's my support system, and I need to continue a conversation with him to say I need to stay on the path and you are my need. I need to be with you in prayer so that the two of us are communicating.
Charles Manto:	Okay. So I'm going to merge a couple of those into—basically, I am facing this conflict. Most of the time I'm not in any power. Lucky for me, I have a friend in a really high place, and this friend that I have is very, very powerful. And this friend is also not only connected with me but also connected with that other person I'm in this fight with.

So, in this case, the father gives sunshine and rain to whichever one I'm in the conflict with and every hour might change. But the moment I get out in the conflict with the Roman Empire, that entire Roman Empire get sunshine and rain from the father. My connection with the father is even a higher place than the entire Roman Empire. There is nothing and no one and no system I can be in conflict with that God isn't bigger.

Now, this only assumes you've got a big god. If you've got a little itty bitty god or mediocre, it doesn't count. You're hopeless. But only for the people with the big gods. Even like the atheist in the foxhole, you could have a really lousy theology one day, but in the foxhole you're saying, "I've got a really big god, I hope. Because I'm in a pickle here, and only a really big one's going to get me out of this one," right?

So, in that moment, your theology—and this is what it's saying. You've got a common connection with the Father who gives sunshine and rain to whatever entity you're in conflict with. Now you have a choice, and you will see examples of this in the psalms that goes either way. I have a common connection with the Father, and I can use it like a voodoo weapon, a knife, and bring down the wrath of God and crush that enemy. Whether it's my no-good boss or the unjust judge, my Father can crush the entire Roman Empire. "We'll see who's tough now. Wait till I tell dad."

Or you could do something very unusual. You could ask that the Father who has power over the entire Roman Empire, the unjust judge, the nasty boss, or whoever it is you're dealing with and give them a blessing instead of a curse. Total flip. Might be outrageous for some people. "Why should I do that? Why should—if I got a common connection, then I got an in with God, the Father, who gives sunshine and rain. Why don't I just ask for him to flood the guy out and drown him to death rather than just have his crops grow?" There's a choice here, and Jesus is asking us to take that choice that is the very way that the guy wants us to hurt us, we're supposed to go to the Father and ask for a blessing. So this is the setup going on.

So the Father, when he's talking about fatherhood now, in that sentence, what is the Father up to? If you knew nothing about what the word "Father" meant, you had no theology, you had no Bible, and you never had one second of conversation with anybody religious at all ever in your life, totally empty brain on this, and the first moment you see is this sentence only, 45, what do you know about Father?

Female:	He says everybody gets an equal shot.
Charles Manto:	He's fair. What else do you notice?

Female:	He's generous.
Female:	He cares for you.
Charles Manto:	I'm sorry, what? Oh, we didn't have the microphone. Microphone. Grab a mic.
Pastor Stahlberg:	He's more than fair.
Charles Manto:	He's generous.
Pastor Stahlberg:	He's more than fair. From our standards, it is unfair from a human—from our broken self that the sun rises over the evil and the good, because we would like that to reward the good and punish the evil. But it doesn't work that way. So this is very—it's, again, a higher level of consciousness.
Female:	I think it's because God cares for you. Your father cares for you and takes care of you, and then—
Charles Manto:	He's a caretaker is what you're saying.
Female:	Right, right.
Charles Manto:	Another? Another? No. It's only five bucks to get the mic. You know every time you get the mic you pay five bucks. No, or it's the other way around. Every time you get the mic, you get paid five bucks.
Female:	I'll stick around. Grace. God's free gift to good and evil, grace. Free gift of love.
Charles Manto:	Microphone. You've got one. Pass the other one while he's talking. Pass it to Cindy.
Male:	There's a New Testament professor at Vanderbilt and she's Jewish, but she's the professor of New Testament. And she came and gave a talk to our group one time and said, "This is the area where Jesus was very radical in the Jewish world, because the Jewish world had actually progressed from an eye for an eye, tooth for a tooth and now we have the—some of the more—the later Jewish writers and prophets and even the Pharisees were actually more liberal." She said even Jesus might've been a Pharisee.

So he was talking to some of his friends sometimes when he was criticizing them, but she said Jewish people still sort of felt that God was good to the good and not good to—not punish the bad. And so this was—so it was really hard when she first told me that actually the Jewish faith was pretty good by then when Jesus talked about helping the cow out of the ditch even though it's the Sabbath, Jewish people had already gotten to that. Love was really important. But on this she said this is where Jesus was very radical, and that God loved everybody and we should love everybody. |
| *Pastor Stahlberg:* | This reminds me of the insight that Martin Luther had. So in the Lutheran church, Luther said that we are hundred percent saints and hundred percent sinners. So this is—all these writings are paradoxical. They put together two things that seem they don't go together, but they do. And when the father makes the sun rise on the evil and the good, that's me. I'm both evil and I am both good, one hundred percent.

And so it's when we—when I read this first, I'm thinking, "No, those evil people out there and the"—but the next step is to see that I am the bad girl sometime. I'm not—I want to be good, but I fail. So the good and evil is in all of us. It's not only I'm good and the other way around. |

Female:	And your question was what would you know about the Father just by reading this. He's in heaven. Begs the question of where's heaven? And he talks about heaven in the Lord's Prayer, too.
Charles Manto:	And what's interesting, there's this—now you just mentioned my take on the Jewish concept. When you see these things throughout the Bible about heaven, you see the father or something, you see all these angels just singing love songs all the time, and it's sort of like a declaration that the eternal infinite one always maintains a constant loving connection to the creation, and that's what heaven is. Heaven is that place where God is maintaining the constant loving connection. And in that place, the outer rule of God, the exterior rule of God is love.
	Imagine I know I was going to just get away with walking in here and start picking fights with any of you, because the rest of you are going to come to their aid. They're going to wait till you get away from there. And just like little kids don't want to do something bad in front of their parents. Same way in the presence of God. Nobody's getting away with bad stuff. And the desire of God is love, and that's going to all come out in the Lord's Prayer. So this is interesting that you pointed that out.
	Now let's go to—because we're going to go to the next one. Just a moment. Oh, not the next slide. I meant the prior slide. We're going to go—no, go down again. Where we were a moment ago. That one. So he gives sunshine and rain, and he's asking us to love. So in 44, he says, "Love your enemies and pray for them." And now going back to everything we said, because if you—you have this common connection.

[End of Saturday June 29 Matthew 6 Session 2 part 1]

[Beginning of Saturday June 29 Matthew 6 Session 2 part 2 (15_44)]

Charles Manto:	With the Father, you're not praying against them. You're praying for them. That's the switch we just talked that's very different. So verse 44 is the first time in this whole section he's talking about prayer, and this is why this is the setup for the later conversation about prayer. Notice he's asking that we pray for our enemies.
	Now, the question might be as you're reading this, he says, "Okay, you should love your enemies. Anybody could love their friends. You should pray for your enemies. Anybody can pray for their friends, right?" Well, how do you go about praying for your enemies? Does he give us any instruction on that page in Matthew 5? How would you go about doing that?
	Or is it just tossed in? Did he just sort of throw it in there? "Love, love, love, love. A little bit about prayer. Pray for him, too." But there's no real big discussion about prayer yet. Any information in that verse, those verses in Chapter 5 about you how go about doing that?
Male:	Well, you could pray for your enemy's destruction.
Charles Manto:	Yes, you could. And you can pray for his benefit, but they don't—does it give you any information yet how you do it? Not in 5, not here.
	Now, he does have this interesting thing about tax collectors, and I think there's a fun play of words going on there, because the word for tax collector is "*telones*" and whatever the ancient root of that is, the word—like telephone, telegraph, telephone, television, and so on. But it meant by that point the guy who's getting the taxes. So they knew it as a tax collector,

but it had that sound "tel." And then he basically says, "I want you to be perfect like your heavenly Father is perfect." The word is also "tel."

So he's basically doing a play on words, so he's basically saying even the tax collectors—and end up to be like saying, "Even the perfectors can love their friends. But I don't want you to merely love your friends like the perfecting tax collectors. I want you to be perfect like your heavenly Father is perfect." Play on words.

So, so far we see all this. We see all this stuff about prayer, and then we might be hoping he would tell us more about prayer. And now we're going to flip the page and go to the next section where we would think he's going to tell us about prayer. Somebody read verse 6:1?

Male:	"Beware of practicing your righteousness before men to be noticed by them; otherwise you have no reward with your Father who is in heaven."
Charles Manto:	Now just leaving it on just that sentence only, notice he doesn't say pray. He says beware. You won't know this—there's a play on words here. We're not going to get into it much. But like instead of pray, he's saying **pay** attention. In Greek the word for "**pay** attention" is almost exactly like **pray**. They just threw a couple of words around. So he's throwing a hominem at them. When you're expecting him to say, "Okay, now let me tell you how to **pray**," he's going into this whole section about how not to do a whole bunch of stuff including prayer.
	It's like he's going off on a rabbit trail and, in fact, it's sort of an abrupt, frustrating rabbit trail. Because what does he say beware about doing or pay attention not to do something? What is he telling us not to do?
Female:	Show off.
Charles Manto:	Show off or doing things in front of people, whether your intentions are good or not. It might be you're very sincere. "I need to be a good example for the rest of you. That's why I'm doing all this stuff in front of you. I'm setting an example. You should be like—it's all about me of course. It's about the example." So even if your intentions are well, but he says it can be problematic.
	But notice what he's saying. "Don't do stuff in front of men." Now, what we talked about in the setup at the very beginning of—let your light shine before men.
Pastor Stahlberg:	Now that's in contradiction.
Charles Manto:	Jesus, which way are you going to have it? One moment you tell us do this stuff in front of people so the light shines on us and the Father gets glorified. The next minute you say don't do stuff in front of people. You're going to have it one way or you're going to have it the other?
Pastor Stahlberg:	It's paradoxical.
Charles Manto:	Yes. What's going on here? Microphone. *[offering microphone to audience member]*
Male:	Let your light shine before men in such a way.
Charles Manto:	And so one of the things you might do—set in such a way. Now, notice what he's doing there. He's trying to make sense of this apparent contradiction. What's going on in the three that you're supposed to do versus what are the kinds of things you don't do, right? It might be the manner in which you do it. What else might be the difference?
	Because those three things you're going to—and you've seen this passage before, and you

can sort of skim down the whole thing. He's going to say don't do alms in public. Don't pray in public. Don't fast in public. Those are a little different than being gentle, merciful, and peacemaking. Maybe you see some other differences between the three that he's comparing. Maybe not. You don't have to figure it out all at once.

Pastor Stahlberg: What are the three?

Charles Manto: So there are three things in Matthew 5 he says to do to let your light shine. What was he saying is good? In Matthew 5, the good stuff was being gentle, being merciful, being peacemaking instead of being harsh, revengeful, and not peacemaking. You could just mind your own business and not be a peacemaker. You'd get the peace from God. You'd get the forgiveness of God, and just keep to yourself on that. Don't mind anybody else's business. Don't stop that mob from lynching the guy. You're only going to get hurt. Mind your own business. No.

Pastor Stahlberg: But if you are merciful and gentle, all this—

Charles Manto: Peacemaking.

Pastor Stahlberg: Peacemaking. I think on Matthew where it says not, he's talking about self-righteousness, which is so seductive. So, "Here, look how good I am. I'm doing this so then—when I am self-righteous because I am such a good person, what the next step is, I judge my enemies, I judge my friends, and then I'm not gentle and merciful and all of these things."

Female: Thanks. And following up on what I just heard my pastor say, for me a key difference in Matthew 5:16 and the one in 6:1 is who is getting the glory. Is what we're doing bringing joy and light to God, or is it how wonderful I am?

Charles Manto: And so it could be a question of attitude or it may just be consequential. So, for example, let's say I have the best of intentions and I can decide when I'm going to give away money in public. I can decide when to pray in public. I can decide when to fast in public. It's all under my control. Even if I have the best of intentions, everybody knows it's under my control.

And they could look at me and say, "You've got your own PR program going on. You're getting—you really are a sincere guy, and that's good stuff you're doing. Before you, nobody would be giving money to the poor, and they wouldn't be praying. We're really happy that you do it. But it's your own PR program. Even if you don't intend it this way, it is."

Now, here's what's interesting about this. There's a word for what's going on here when they group this, and I'm going to mention it in two contexts. When you study ancient literature or memorizing things, they call this weaving. When you group something together over here and connect it to something over there, you got these two groups going on. And when you're weaving like that, it's easy to remember two groups. Remember I said before too many beatitudes, I couldn't remember them? But if I could figure out how six might just be three pairs, it's easier.

Weaving is the same thing. There's a bunch of stuff Jesus said to do, and then you got to think about, "What did he say," and then you go back and you figure it out. And then there's a bunch of stuff he said not to do. You can go back and think about it, figure that out. That weaving technique is a way to make it easy to remember.

And if you recall, a lot of this stuff, even though written down somewhere, most people even could not afford to take the Bible home. Those scrolls would be too pricey. It's like hundreds of thousands of dollars. You could be as literate as you want. Too bad. You don't have them at home. So what did you do? You had to remember them. Well, these guys, if they're serious about it, they came up with some interesting ways. This is one of them.

And modern approaches—there's a new book about neuro fitness that just came out by a brain surgeon and a brain scientist, and he talks about the same thing, clunking and clustering. There's a group of things over here, and that's clunking. There's a group of things over here, and that's clunking. There's a group over here, and I'm clunking them. There's a group over there, and I'm clunking them.

The brain works best when you not only clunk things, but you take the time to link the clunks together in a cluster, and it forces your brain to go into different parts, and they can do brain scans and see the brain light up in different ways. And when you do all of that, it actually helps your brain and it helps in memory.

So modern brain science is sort of replicating and showing all of the wisdom that these guys are doing by how they were writing this material to make it easy to teach orally. And it's sort of like a—and it also helps like a punchline of a joke. We were talking about this last night. All of this is driving what some people call rhetorical force, but it's the idea of you got a story going on, and you start from being crushed and it goes to like a movie or a play.

When you get to the climax and then you're waiting for the big event to happen, and in this case the innocent victim becomes a—realizes they're the victimizer, and they get flipped. That's the crescendo, and it goes on. It's like the punchline of a joke. You need to know the whole story to make it memorable. If you don't remember the punchline, what was that joke all about? Or you remember the punchline, but you don't remember what leads to the punchline. That didn't do you any good.

That's why we're always looking at these contexts to see what was going on, what's the driving force behind this. And now we're getting into this thing where he's about to tell us about prayer, and he takes a moment out to say, "Before I tell you guys how to pray, let me tell you how not to pray."

And it sounds like Jesus is changing the topic because, when you start reading the first four verses of 6, he's starting to talk about don't give your money in public. And because there's a whole paragraph about money, people are basically thinking, "Jesus changed the topic. He's no longer talking about loving enemies and praying for them. He's now going off on money giving and about showing off, and now he's on to something totally different. And so we really never got any advice or help to figure out how would we go about praying for the bad guy anyway."

But what I'm suggesting with this whole context is if you understand how this memory technique of weaving goes and you see this rabbit trail of like how not to do stuff is a way to help remember all this stuff, when you take this little rabbit trail off the table, the very next words after, "I want you to pray for the enemy because anybody can pray for their friends," is verse 5.

Somebody then—in other words, we pick up the prayer theme again. It's not very far from a moment ago when he said to pray for the enemy. It's just a paragraph later, and he picks it up again. It's not like he lost it. Somebody read verse 5-8. Anybody with a microphone can start and then we'll—go ahead.

Male: "When you pray, you are not to be like hypocrites; for they love to stand and pray in the synagogues and on the street corners, so that they may be seen by men. Truly I say to you, they have their reward in full. But you, when you pray, go into your inner room, close your door, and pray to your Father who is in secret, and your Father who sees what is done in secret will reward you. And when you are praying, do not use meaningless repetition as the Gentiles do, for they suppose that they will be heard for their many words. So do not be like them; for your Father knows what you need before you ask Him."

Charles Manto:	So here's the question to think about when you go on break, which is this: if in fact he's been telling you to pray for enemies and he just took a moment out just to say, "Here's how not to do it," and then he goes back and starts to pray, and he says—and then somebody read just the first nine of the first verse of the Lord's Prayer, which is—anybody read verse 9, whoever has the mic? Can be the same guy. Doesn't matter. Whoever's got the mic, just read the first nine.
Male:	"Pray, then, in this way: Our Father who is in heaven, Hallowed be Your name."
Charles Manto:	There you go. Now, so the question becomes, if we have the Lord's Prayer just all by itself, Our Father could mean all kinds of things, and they're all reasonable. The father of me and everyone in the multiverse. The father of me and everyone in the universe. The father of everybody on the planet earth, or the father of me and all my fellow Roman Catholics who are in the right church, so therefore he is the father and then we get to pray this prayer.
	Or the father of me and all the Protestant born again people, because we're born again. I now have a relationship with the father and I get to say the prayer, but those other people can't do the prayer. Or it could be the father of everybody here in the room together, or the father of me and all of my friends.
	Or the father of me—and I said I couldn't figure out what other kind of our father could be, and some guy in college gave me one I never thought of. It could be the father of me and all my split personalities. *[Laughter]* Or it could just be the father of me and Jesus. All of those make perfectly good sense depending on what the context is.
	But if the context happens to be, "I want you to pray for the enemy," what is a one-word definition of "our" [as 'me and my ____] that we might consider in our long list of possible definitions?
Female:	The enemy.
Charles Manto:	Yes. Now it becomes the father of "me and my enemy." A totally different option we would never consider unless we looked at the Lord's Prayer in the context of 5 when he asked us to pray in the first place. So, while we're going on break, when you think about that—10 minutes because we went a little over. Ten-minute breaks, on your mark, get set, go. We covered a lot.

[End of Saturday June 29 Matthew 6 Session 2 part 2 (15_44)]

[Beginning of Saturday June 29 Matthew 6 Session 2 part 3]

Charles Manto:	*[Describes a display pile of sample books on Matthew 5-7 at back of room]* But to show you how much work people have done, this is—see the thick book here? This is one guy just writing on three pagers or the three chapters on the Sermon on the Mount. And a couple of other fat books back there is either one person's commentary on Matthew or the first of three volumes on it.
	Here's a book called "Memory, Jesus, and the Synaptic Gospels." Here's somebody who's writing on these concepts of how moral teaching works and what is new memory and brain science teaching us about all that. Lots of interesting stuff. Show and tell, that's all that is while you're getting back here. You're welcome to flip through it.

Pastor Stahlberg:	I want to say that we are reading as a congregation this book called "The Inspired" by Rachel Held Evans, and we have ordered copies. It's $10. In August we're going to talk about it. It's fascinating, and it's easy to—it's the storytelling of this young woman who unfortunately passed away recently out of the blue. She made a move from growing Fundamentalist Baptist to becoming a beacon of hope for progressive Christianity, and she goes through the biblical stories and reinterprets them. It's fascinating. So I have copies after the presentation, $10.
Charles Manto:	So what we were doing at the end of the break was connecting all of the stuff we saw before in Chapter 5, leading up to how to pray for the bad guy, the enemy, the persecutor. Persecutor is just the worst-case version of an enemy. It's trying to say that's the most extreme case, the guy who's gunning for you and has the ability to get you.

And the idea behind it is if you pray for the worst case, you could pray for all the lesser cases. But if you start with just praying for your friends, you might not go much beyond that. Maybe sort of a friend and an acquaintance, but not the bad guy, right? So this is getting us to pray for the worst-case version.

And so basically what we were suggesting as a possibility by the break time was maybe the prayer for the persecutor is the Lord's Prayer. And that would be very amazing if it would be because it would have—it would make a huge impact on how we not only pray the Lord's Prayer—and we're going to do that in a moment with this in mind—but it links all these passages together in a meaningful way. It's like getting the point of the story or the punchline of a joke or whatever.

And so now let's go to the next slide after this one and see—because what we're going to do is—and then basically we're going to ask the question, is if all of this material when Jesus says pray for the bad guy, pray for the persecutor is this what the Lord's Prayer is about? In the Lord's Prayer we've got "**Our** Father, … give **us**."—Who's the "us"?—**Our** daily bread. Forgive **us**. You got all these plurals.

And the idea would be for the next exercise I'm going to do with you now is to do an algebraic substitution. Every time it's our Father it becomes the "Father, me *and* the person I'm fighting with," and the daily bread is what "we're fighting over," We're going to go through this and see how that works.

Let's see the next slide. And then going over that whole thing we did about turning the other cheek and walk the extra mile we did a moment ago, how the old man could take out the entire Roman Empire and so on. You can see there's all kinds of conflicts. So, theoretically, if this works this way—we navigate through conflict continually all day long. That changes every hour.

Theoretically, this prayer could be used differently every hour with every conflict, no matter whether if it's with a person, a system, a business, a nation, or whatever, political party. I know you all love Republicans dearly, and you have welcomed them as your neighbor, and Democrats and Socialists and people that want to restore the monarchy. Anyway, we won't go there.

Next slide. Later on we'll talk about the kinds of things that might be the things we would contest: housing, clothing, safety, jobs, and anything you can imagine. You probably have 10 more in your mind. Next slide.

Now let's start with we have a few slides, and we could talk about them briefly and ask how this might work out. The very first one is—oh, let's go back to the verses in the Bible. We have the Lord's Prayer right in front of us. And the first verse again, let someone read verse

	9. Anyone who has a mic can read verse 9. Just real fast.
Female:	"Pray, then, in this way: Our Father who is in heaven, Hallowed be Your name."
Charles Manto:	I'm going to think of potential conflict. Let's say it's a thief who stole all your family's food. And now you—then there's no 7/11. You had to go way out of your way to find food. Maybe your kids get sick because of it. You're dead tired. Maybe you lose your job, get in trouble with your boss, whatever it is. Let's pretend that it's the thief who stole all our food.

Now we're going to do a substitution for "Our Father." Every time we do the plural, let's substitute it with that to see how that plays out. So Our Father becomes what? The father of me and— |
Female:	Everybody.
Charles Manto:	No, the thief. You're going to be surprised how this plays out.
Pastor Stahlberg:	I have another example. I think for me—I'll speak for myself. I have a very hard time with shooters in schools. So is it my father and of the shooters.
Charles Manto:	Yes, that's a very good one. In fact, our pastor's—we've been talking about this for some time. They started to do a summer series on the Lord's Prayer, and she has come to the conclusion after working with me on this for years that this is the prayer for the persecuted. And she became, in fact, very concerned about the same thing and uses that example, because a shooting just happened the week before, and she said, "How are we going to pray for the shooters?"

So, let's do the shooter one. So, now it's the shooter. Is it the shooter at the workplace or the shooter at the school? Which shooter did you have in mind? |
Pastor Stahlberg:	School. Shooters in schools.
Charles Manto:	Is it a grown up or a child? Grown up coming back? Like 18 and 20-year-old?
Pastor Stahlberg:	Eighteen.
Charles Manto:	Somebody 18 or older. Just so we have the same thing in mind. So the bad guy we're praying for is the shooter, and the school is maybe the school where our kids go to and our neighbor goes to. So we know the people. Maybe our own family is there. It's not just somebody across the way that we don't know anything about. So, Our Father's now the father of me and?
Multiple:	The shooter.
Charles Manto:	Who is in heaven, Hallowed be your name. Somebody read verse 10?
Female:	"Your kingdom come. Your will be done, On earth as it is in heaven."
Charles Manto:	Now let's think about this for a moment. It's outside and inside. Kingdom is the outside world. Your will is inside. It's interesting how this inner and outer thing goes. So if God's kingdom and power and presence, like the constant loving connection in heaven, if his kingdom were here, would any shooting be going on?
Female:	No.
Charles Manto:	No one would dare. No shooting would be going on right in front of the Father's face. Are you kidding me? And he's praying your kingdom come, your will would be loving. If everybody was loving and your will be done on earth—that we all love each other, would there be

any shooting? Notice so far that if you're keeping this in mind, you're not beginning to pray about the shooter and drifting off into some other—okay, we're finished with the shooter. Now let's just talk about the Kingdom of God and the—no. It's all tied to the shooter. And our upsettedness is growing, not diminishing.

Just like in the beatitudes, Jesus wants to know are you suffering and are you suffering because somebody messed with you? Now you're outraged, so your outrage is growing. By the way, this is told to the crowd. Not just the disciples. The people who've never done this prayer before, never thought of loving enemies before.

Now somebody read the next one, 11.

Female:	"Give us this day our daily bread."
Charles Manto:	Now let's figure out how we do this exercise. It's no longer us. Let me start with the word "us." Who's—so give...
Multiple:	Me.
Charles Manto:	Me and?
Multiple:	The shooter.
Charles Manto:	Now if you recall many sermons on the daily bread, "Give us this day our daily bread," they're sort of figuring out what's this double daily thing in there for? And one of them is really this day. The other's sort of like our necessary bread. And so this is an algebraic opportunity, substitution opportunity where whatever it is that's important to us is what we substitute for daily bread. So what is it that we need at the—because I'm upset because of what the shooter's doing. What am I at risk for? What's my conflict that's going on because of the shooter? Microphone?
Female:	That I might get shot.
Charles Manto:	And because you might get shot, you need safety, right, so you don't get shot, right?
Pastor Stahlberg:	Your daily bread is safety.
Female:	I need a gun of mine own. *[Laughter]*
Charles Manto:	But you need safety. The gun of your own is just a way to get to safety. What you're really wanting is the safety. Now, what else—microphone, please. Posterity is listening to you. Go ahead.
Female:	Peace.
Charles Manto:	Peace. You need peace, because your peace has been taken from you with this guy who's going around shooting. Maybe he's going to shoot you next. Maybe shot your friend or your child or your grandchild. Anyone else? Daily bread relative to the shooter. Microphone to the—Sally needs a mic.
Female:	Forgiveness.
Charles Manto:	You need to—no, we're going to start with you. Do you need forgiveness? You're the victim here. So we're starting from you.

Female:	To accept it.
Charles Manto:	So you need acceptance so you can be free from the anxiety. So you've got anxiety because of this, so you want peace, you want safety, you want emotional safety because you're all upset, and you want to have—and so any conflict, by the way, as you know is like a layered onion. It starts with the shooter, but now I'm anxious and that's another layer of the onion. There may be some peace. There may be other things that we can unpeel this onion further.
Male:	Just to throw a little monkey wrench into this, some people would say their daily bread would be justice.
Charles Manto:	So I want justice. So now—that's a good one. Now all of these we place on our whiteboard. We can write it down. So let's make the list. One was safety from the shooter. One was peace. One was the anxiety. And you just mentioned justice.
Female:	I want to go back to what Sally said. Give me forgiveness of the shooter.
Charles Manto:	I need to forgive the shooter because I'm upset with the shooter. So put that on the list.
Male:	I was wondering, Doug, what did you mean by justice?
Charles Manto:	Give him the microphone so he can answer.
Male:	Well, justice in the sense of retribution against the shooter.
Charles Manto:	I not only want him stopped, I want him to learn a lesson so he doesn't do it anymore. The next guy doesn't do it. That's the whole point of retributive justice, right? We got to stop stuff from happening, and we got to teach him a lesson, hopefully he gets restored, and then teach the next guy not to do it. Because you don't get away with this, because that's part of the kingdom of God.

If the rule of God was on earth, you wouldn't pull this stuff off. And so I want the rule of God here and if you do it, God's going to either stop you or if he's a little late on the job, maybe he'll stop you after the fact and give you a spanking and so on. Then you'll learn not to do it again. |
| *Pastor Stahlberg:* | Microphone. There are examples—not many, but there are examples of a mother, for instance, whose son was shot. And they went to trial and so on, and she adopted the shooter who became her son. For me, that's restorative justice. I mean, that's living at such a high level of consciousness, but that's the level Jesus is inviting us.

The other example is the Mennonites—or the Amish, when the shooter killed their children. They fed his wife, and they took care of the shooter's family. So there are—yes. |
Charles Manto:	Microphone to the back.
Female:	I read an article a few years about two gentlemen who became very good friends as a result of the grandson of the gentleman—grandson of one of the men went and stole a gun and shot this other man's son delivering pizza for someone. And they became—the two fathers became very good friends, and now they will be going from various prisons around the country talking about what it's like—
Pastor Stahlberg:	They witness to—
Female:	So I think they become a witness, and they've done wonderful things.
Charles Manto:	Wow. I would love to collect some of these stories in literature, the ones that are there. There's

a lot of interesting ones. Now let's look at this list that we have here. I'm wanting to go back and sort of step this through one step at a time. Because there's sort of a progression, just like there was in the beatitudes. And I'm going to sort of play the role of cynic who's hearing this for the first time and going to tell you my personal outrage at your request that I do this prayer.

I don't like to be victimized by the shooter. I am doing everything I can to make a nice, peaceful community. I want peace and safety. I don't want to have anxiety. I want good stuff to reign. I want justice to be there, and I want this for myself. Father, I want peace from being shot at. I want to be safe. I'm not so sure I want that other guy to be safe. He doesn't deserve to be safe. He's the bad guy. He's the guy going around shooting people just because he feels like it. He doesn't deserve to be safe.

I, my children and my grandchildren, and those nice teachers over there working way below the level they should be paid, and they're sacrificing every day, I love those teachers. And there's this guy's killing those teachers or shooting at those teachers. I want them to be safe. I don't want the bad guy to be safe. What's this thing about "give both of us safety"? I'm not sure I want that for you.

You see how that happens? If you're first coming at this for the first time and then it leads to—somebody read the next one, verse 12. Anybody with a microphone.

Male: "And forgive us our debts, as we also have forgiven our debtors."

Charles Manto: So I'm playing the role of cynic. What do you mean by "we?" What about us? Why are you blaming the victim? I didn't go to school and shoot anybody. In fact, I was over there helping the patrol boys or something. I was there volunteering. Why are you blaming the victim? I didn't do anything. Did I cause that guy to go? Did I dare him to go shoot the kids? "I dare you to go…"—I didn't do any of this. Why are you blaming the victim?

I don't have anything to be forgiven about in this particular conflict. Because we're talking about this particular conflict. So I'm the innocent victim. Who are you to blame the victim? I don't need any forgiveness here. And so, in fact, come to think of it, not only does the bad guy—he's the one who needs the forgiveness. Not me. I'm not even sure I want this guy to be forgiven.

How many people by a show of hands have heard this phrase before: "I want that soul to rot in hell forever after what he did to me and those kids." Raise your hand if you've heard anybody say that phrase. Everybody's heard that phrase, right? So now—

Pastor Stahlberg: "I hope they rot in hell."

Charles Manto: Rot in hell forever. So imagine what's happening here where we've already set the stage. I need a god really big to be able to figure this out, and he's big enough to hear me in all the cacophony of the multiverse. He's big enough to do something about it. He's caring enough to do something about it. So talk about being a really smart god, he's really smart, and he's a really smart judge. I'm asking him to judge this guy, beat that guy down, right?

So I'm standing before the judge of judges who has an infinite amount of power, capable of doing all of this, and I'm railing against the bad guy. I'm the poor, innocent victim here. I don't need any forgiveness, and I'm not sure you should forgive him either. Kill him in hell tonight on Monday and again on Tuesday. It's like "Godfather" on steroids. On Wednesday and on Thursday for the next million and a half days, kill him again, over and over and over again.

Now, Jesus had just had this conversation a moment before the Lord's Prayer, saying—and we didn't get into this. It's one of these classes we didn't do, but you're all familiar with this. We cross the line when we go from it's healthy to be angry because of our brother. Somebody hits you with a rack, it's healthy to feel the pain, to duck to stop it from happening. But we cross the line from when we become angry because of our brother, to becoming angry at our brother.

And what he was saying just a moment before is when we cross that line, it's not enough to just refrain from murdering people. He says when we want to murder people, we cross that line and we become guilty of murder. Now that's true—notice what just happened to me.

Pastor Stahlberg: You become the bad guy.

Charles Manto: I become the bad guy, and I'm doing it in front of God, and I'm giving God prima facie evidence why I'm the bad guy. I'm not only as bad as the shooter who maybe didn't even kill anybody yet or maybe killed one person, I'm now convicting myself of serial murder because I want this guy to be unforgiven and to be killed every day forever in eternity. So suddenly I've been flipped.

Just like in the beatitudes, blessed are the pure in heart. If I'm the pure, innocent victim and I've never done anything bad ever and never had anything but pure thoughts, good for me. I get to see God. But the moment I take my turn at being the bad guy, suddenly I need to be purified in heart. I'm going through the same exact progression through the Lord's Prayer if I'm praying for the enemy. Because even though I am the pure, innocent victim because I'm not the shooter, I'm not the thief, I'm not the this, I'm not the that, suddenly I've found I've taken my turn at being the bad guy or worse.

Pastor Stahlberg: So are you saying that in our desire for revenge we become—

Charles Manto: Yes. We become maybe a different bad guy. So maybe all the guy did was steal all my food, but I want to kill the guy. He was a thief. I'm a murderer. Maybe this guy shot five people. Well, I want to kill this guy 500, 5,000 times. So if he's a serial murderer, I'm a bigger serial murderer. Jesus has just done a judo flip on me. I went from being the pure, innocent victim to taking my turn at being the bad guy.

Now suddenly "forgive us" makes sense, and the "forgive us" is the judo flip or the pivot in this story that talks about people whose peace has been broken. And notice how Jesus starts this with—both the beatitudes and the Lord's Prayer—the fact that you are a victim is true. Nobody's diminishing your suffering. The terrible thing you went through is really terrible. Even think of the guy with the foot about to be cut off. Just that would bring you to tears. Breaking the window to save your life. If his leg was cut off, how many windows would you break to restore his leg? You'd break all the windows.

Pastor Stahlberg: You cannot restore his leg.

Charles Manto: And you can't restore his leg. And that's just a guy who broke in to stay one night, right? So God starts with our suffering, and he doesn't say your suffering is meaningless and doesn't matter and the justice you've been robbed of doesn't matter. It matters a lot. And when we are the pure, innocent victim, that's absolutely true in that moment. We're not blaming you, the victim.

But where the flip happens is when we take just as seriously our turn at being the bad guy and we discover that the thing that we hate most in the life—is like a freight train you don't want to get in front of it. We stepped in front of our own freight train, and we're going to get crushed. That's the moment when we decide and discover we need the forgiveness, too.

	That's the pivot. That's the emotional flip. That's like the crescendo of the musical concert. That's the play when—whatever that is, when that magic moment happens in the program or in the short story at the very end, when everything flips around.
	And now we got the grand bargain. What's the grand bargain? Somebody read us the grand bargain. What's 12, what's the grand bargain? We just read it. How do we get this forgiveness?
Multiple:	As we forgive others.
Charles Manto:	Now I'm standing before God, who is the judge of judges and the professor of professors. I'm at the height of my rage saying, "I want you to kill this guy a billion times and to the billionth power. Don't ever stop killing him." I'm at the height of my rage, and I'm asking God, "But I want you to forgive me based on how loving and forgiving I am."
	If God gave me a pop quiz at the height of my rage, how would I do on that pop quiz? Up or down? All the people who say up, let me see hands. *[No hands go up.]* All the people say down, show of hands. *[Most hands go up.]* I had flunked the quiz. Now what is the next phrase? Somebody read verse 13?
Male:	"And do not lead us into temptation, but deliver us from evil."
Charles Manto:	Very good. Now this goes back to Deuteronomy 8, among other places, where God says, "I'm going to put you to the test to see what's really going on inside you," and he says that in Deuteronomy why? Because God's sort of dumb and he'd like some data? Is it a dumb god who needs some data, he's going to put you to the test because he really doesn't know which way you're going to be depending on which way you—no, because we need the data. He's not testing us because he's sort of a second-rate god, not so smart, and needs a little education from us. He's leading us to test for our benefit.
	And it's the same word which basically says lead us not to testing—God's not trying to seduce you to see if —and he's not asking this—don't need to ask God not to lead us to temptation. But like the spirit led Jesus into the world, it's the same way. He is saying lead us not to testing. Why? Because if I make this grand bargain at the height of my rage, just like the pop quiz question, lead me down to testing because if you test me to see how loving and forgiving I am right now, I might fail the test. And if I fail the test, what happens? I don't get forgiveness.
	Now I'm the guy who gets killed a million times over. I don't get to go to the kingdom, right? I'm not getting all of that. The consequences are disastrous with a capital D, or evil, and now I can see how every phrase of the Lord's Prayer is tightly coupled with the phrase before and is a driving force all the way to the end, because basically this guy is saying, "God, we got this grand bargain. Forgive me based on how well I'm doing, but I hope you've got a plan B here because I'm not so sure how plan A is going."
	And then at the end of the Lord's Prayer—somebody read the next verse, verse 14 and 15.
Female:	"For you are forgiven, forgive others of their transgressions for the heavenly Father will also forgive you. But if you do not forgive others, then your Father will not forgive your transgressions."
Charles Manto:	Now this is sort of interesting. So he's basically saying to the whole crowd—these are not just his followers. He's telling the whole crowd gets to pray this prayer. You don't get qualified to do the Lord's Prayer because you decided to be a follower of Jesus.

Pastor Stahlberg:	Not everyone was a follower.
Charles Manto:	What I'm saying is even if you're not a follower, what you qualify to have this is you have to have conflict. If you've got a conflict, you've got a prayer. Like if you've got a phone, you got a lawyer or whatever that commercial is. So if you've got a conflict, you've got a prayer. Everybody's invited to this. Not just the disciples. The people who are uncertain. What qualifies you is that you have—and you care about your conflict, like the atheist in the foxhole, and you hope God's big enough to do something about it.
	So he says, "Guys, if you forgive that jerk, that persecutor, the worst-case version of an enemy, the scoundrel, no good guy who's shooting up your kids in the playground, if you forgive him, then the Father's going to forgive you. But if you're not, He's not going to forgive you." Now, this is a really interesting point because what he's saying is when he's giving this Lord's Prayer to the crowd who are not yet truly following, they're not disciples yet, it's not a sure bet whether they're going to drink this Kool-Aid.
	We don't know whether they will forgive—and Jesus is saying, "So how's it going to be, guys? You're going to forgive that jerk or not? I'm not sure. You tell me." It's not clear because these guys haven't declared I'm going to—I guess I'm going through the process. I forgot the forgiveness for myself, now therefore I'm going to go out and do it. It's unclear whether they're following through this process yet or not.
	And so at the beginning of 5:44, Jesus says, "I want you to pray for..." That's where he starts the conversation about prayer.
Female:	Enemies.
Charles Manto:	And enemies. "I want you to pray for the persecutor." That's in 5:44. That's the beginning of the section. And now you have this closing of the section, like putting parentheses around this whole passage. This is the context of the prayer context. The prayer context doesn't start in the middle of *[Chapter]* 6 here. It starts at 5:44. You can see how all this fits together. And it's a driving force to have us to really get to the point where we will do this forgiveness.
	... Here's my take on it. But, I'd like this for discussion and maybe we can think of a few other examples other than just the shooter to see how we play this out. Well, let's go back to the other examples, other than shooters. Anybody else have examples about a conflict that we might do this through? Let's run this through real fast with a different conflict other than a shooter.
Female:	Someone stole all your money.
Charles Manto:	Somebody stole the money. You need the money. What happens if you don't have money? Maybe you don't pay the rent. Maybe you're going to be homeless, right? You're not going to eat. So if the Father—so let's go to "give us this day our daily bread." "Give me and the guy who stole our money, give us both money." Give us money. But because it's money, let's say because I don't have any money, now I'm not going to eat.
	"The Father of me and the guy who stole my money and I can't afford to eat, give us something to eat." The guy stole all my money—and maybe I'm not going to pay the rent on time, I'm going to be evicted. "The Father of me and the guy who's causing me to be evicted, give us both a situation where we won't be evicted."
	Isn't this interesting? We're beginning to draw empathy. Even though I don't fully understand that another guy, I can't fully see the world through his eyes because I don't know him all that well, I don't know his culture, but I have something in common with him. The thing

I do have in common with him is this conflict, and the very thing I'm in conflict with is the very thing I'm praying about. And it starts there, the money, but you get to unravel the onion a little bit. It's the money and the fact that I might be homeless now or then I might lose my job.

Each of these specific things are sort of a guidebook as to how I pray for the bad guy. Now you're going to see how this works. Let's say we do marriage, and you're going to see why Jesus says do this prayer in the closet, not the church. Imagine if I go to the prayer meeting and she's going to start prayer meetings.

Did she tell you this? We're starting a whole new prayer meeting for enemies, and I'm going to come there and say, "Father, I want you to pray for my no-good girlfriend. She just doesn't get me." Wouldn't that be embarrassing? People say leave that as an unspoken request. Don't go airing your dirty laundry in front of all the church. Jesus, by the way, he says, "Do this prayer in the closet. Other people don't have to hear this stuff." Now you understand why you don't want me praying about my spouse in front of the whole church necessarily.

Or imagine if you're my boss and everybody knows you're my boss. I come to the prayer meetings and say, "I've got a prayer request. My boss is a real jerk. He's mistreating me this way. He makes me work overtime. He doesn't pay me. He cuts me down in front of the other people. I feel miserable. I don't even want to work for him anymore." Half of it might not even be true, but is he *[the boss]* going to be very happy? I'm going to have a libel lawsuit on my—libel/slander lawsuit.

These prayers, it makes sense why Jesus says—it's not only just about bragging. It's like it's the ramification of doing this prayer publicly. So we had one. What was the other one? Somebody pick one real fast.

Female:	Because of the divisiveness in our country, those who have different political ideologies that we have, who we both—we disagree with.
Charles Manto:	So let's pick one. Pick a favorite one then.
Female:	Abortion I think is a big one right now.
Charles Manto:	So let's pick—now this is interesting. Let's have two people praying the same prayer for the people on the imposing side of abortion. So I'm the woman who is struggling with abortion, and I'm saying, "The father of me and the person who does not want me to get the medical care I need for my situation where I really think to be able to stay healthy, I need to get this abortion, but they won't do it. So, "the father of me and the one preventing me from getting medical care, give us both medical care." "The father of me and the person who is maybe going to result in my dying, give us both the life that we need." And there might be three, four others. I'm not a woman who thought through abortion, and I've not thought through it. I don't think it through like a woman does, right?

And then the other person might be the person who believes abortion is bad. "My parents didn't care much about kids, and they let me live. But the other one was just an inconvenience, and they just aborted them because they really didn't care. They're self-centered, and I don't like this abortion movement, pro-abortion, pro-choice movement. And so I think that they are promulgating irresponsible behavior to people like me. And if my parents had their way, they would've aborted me. And I know that they don't love me, and then they didn't love my kid brother and my kid sister who they knew was going to be a girl, and they killed them."

And so what's that person's prayer? "The father of me and the people who are not taking children or almost children—whatever you're going to call them—seriously, let us all take children seriously and let us treat the unborn seriously as if they were the grown-up woman we want to love." And so now you've got people praying on opposite sides in a way that's becoming more empathetic to each other, even though they don't like that other person's position.

And maybe it's not so easy to reconcile that position, and maybe the only way to reconcile that position is to get deep, deep in the weeds and find out what's going on. So if you are a pro-life person, maybe the only way to go through that thing is to personally take the responsibility to raise a million dollars to help those mothers who are at risk and those children who are never going to have a decent home, and you take the responsibility to place those children, because that's what a peacemaker is. Or if I'm on the other side and you want people to understand your rights for free choice, are you willing to take a million dollars of your money and go and talk to those people on the other side and say, "What can we do to solve this problem together?"

Now the problem in our society is we don't do this. In fact, we're not going to get to this next section, but the very next section after Chapter 5 and Chapter 6, how to lovingly engage people where we listen to their suffering, we listen to their sense of injustice, and then we—eventually, when we become forgiven, we want to forgive others, and now we're going to be the new peacemakers. Jesus says that.

By the way, I'm going to show you how to do this. And you've heard this phrase: "Judge not lest you be judged, and don't put your pearls before the swine." So let's say I get 10 PhDs and real fast, and I'm only 50. And I got all those PhDs, and I'm the smartest guy in the world. I also have this great experience that I've gone through all this great suffering too, and I have all this wonderful wisdom, and now I've got to listen to all my friends who all have PhDs.

I am a really smart dude, and now because I love all of you, I'm going to walk up to you and say, "I really don't know you that well, but let me tell you, I know what your problem is. You didn't even ask me to talk to you about your problem, but I care about you. You don't realize it but, man, you've got a problem, and let me tell you what your problem is."

And here's how it comes out. If I'm religiously conservative, "You know you're a sinner." I don't know them personally. I don't know what their sin is, but you're an evil guy. "You're a jerk, and you're a jerk of all jerks, and you're going to hell. I can prove it to you from the Bible. You don't have to tell me anything. Anything you say can be used against you in the Bible, and it says that you're a jerk, and I can prove it to you."

Are you going to like that? Or if I'm not getting into the sinner stuff, "I don't know you really. I don't care to know about you. I don't have time. I'm a really busy guy because I'm really smart. But let me tell you, I already know what your problem is. The problem is that you're uneducated and you're illogical and your priorities are all messed up. And if you just got enlightened like me, you wouldn't be such a mess." *[Laughter]* Would you be welcoming that message from me?

Female: Not very well.

Charles Manto: So what did we do on both sides to get the most conservative people we really don't like—and pick your favorite group and the person you most despise—and just get your goat every time? You can't stand them. Get that picture in your mind. Put them here. Get the most liberal, progressive person you love or vice versa. On the other hand, whichever end of the spectrum you are, imagine that person, and that person has great pearls of wisdom.

Jesus is saying don't debate them into the kingdom. It's not going to work. Love them into the kingdom. You don't start to persuade somebody by telling them what their problem is. You start by listening to find out what they think their problem is. Even if it's not the real one, even if you know better, you start by listening to them to find out what their problem is and why they're outraged by it and walk them through it to the point where you do what Jesus did. You be a peacemaker for them, and then you find out alongside them because you love them in that way, you find out with them when they discover they took the turn at being the bad guy. And that's a very dangerous moment, because you remember what happened to Judas when he discovered that? He hung himself.

So if you're going to be really effective and prove how immoral that person is, you'd better be careful. Because when you prove them, they're going to go hang themselves. If you're going to prove them how stupid they are and how worthless they are, they're never going to amount to anything because they don't have a decent education and they just can't think straight, they might just give up on life because they may believe you. You have to be careful what you wish for because you might get it.

And so this is what Jesus is basically saying to us. There's a way to persuade people, but it might not be the way we're accustomed to doing it. Anyway. I went and cheated and went all the way to the end. And it sounded like a sermon.

[Applause]

Pastor Stahlberg: Some questions to Charles this moment urgent? Yes.

Male: Not urgent. I just wanted to mention what the desire for retribution does to the insides of a person who desires it, and there's also that. I mean, there's actually—for me, I can say a physical effect of hating somebody. So if Donald Trump does his latest atrocity and I just—I feel my chest tighten, that has a direct impact not only on people around me, but for yourself. So getting to a place where you can forgive is also a way to kind of unload that so that I can feel healthy.

Female: Shifts the power.

Male: So one of the things that I grapple with, let's suppose that I'm aware that there's a terrorist cell in Somalia and I consider them my enemy, and I have a tendency to want to pray for them and forgive them. Pray meaning a number of different things and asking God to forgive him. But at the same time, I don't necessarily think that it's inconsistent that I want to see them destroyed before they can do harm. And that's something that I can't quite sort out completely.

Female: You're not alone.

Charles Manto: So I think one more, and then I'll give a quick response, and then we could do more of this over lunch. We're not going away. And I don't know about tomorrow, if we're doing lunch tomorrow or not.

Pastor Stahlberg: Tomorrow we'll go out.

Charles Manto: We'll go out for lunch. So we can do more of this twice, today and tomorrow. Go ahead.

Female: Matthew 5:48 where it says be perfect. I had long understood that that word perfect from the Greek does not mean get it all right, but it means be complete and be fulfilled. And if that is the case, then as we seem to follow this path of Jesus, we will be complete.

Charles Manto: Be mature like—so don't be mature like the tax collectors, because they claim that. Don't be perfect like them. Be perfect, mature or complete like your heavenly Father is by doing this.

And then let me comment briefly on the other two parts. I have a friend of mine in business who declared that he grew up as a Catholic, he's become an agnostic for all the obvious reasons. And he had the same thing that sort of crushed him and I think led them that way in part was a close, dear friend in business cheated him of all of the money and left him really hurting because his nest egg was gone. And it was a big deal.

But he's confided that, "The anger inside me and the destruction from my anger was far greater than all the money I lost." And so he asked me about the—how does this stuff I do in the day job in business relate to this stuff, and I told him the little story about my beating up God in the playground and then I told him about the "Our Father." It sort of connected with him to figure out how you could love even that person that ruined your life and release all that anger which was destroying him.

And he's not sure where he's going to wind up in terms of reevaluating his being an agnostic, although he said that idea of loving enemies and the Father being our father is helping him reconsider it. Because I think that's one of the reasons why he took that position anyway. He was personally discouraged. And this person who hurt him was a very religious person, by the way. To make matters worse, that often happens.

And the other person, I grew up in the inner city of Chicago. I saw a lot of bad stuff, even before getting ready for facing like the Vietnam War and all of that. Plus, understanding the Cold War. And the idea of being a loving person who's turning the cheek doesn't mean you just let somebody run and shoot and kill your kids and take advantage of people or just hang the guy.

So let's say we've got a mob outside who wants to hang this guy. Now the guy they're going to hang could be a liberal Democrat or it could be a conservative Republican. Either could happen in Colorado, right? And you could go in and rush into that mob and stop the hanging. They may beat the crap out of you. But what's more noble? To rush in and stop the hanging—and say, "Hey, we're going to do this right. Take your time. We're going to bring this guy to trial and figure it out."

And the guys are going to say, "No, we need justice and we need it now. You got in the way of our justice system." Is it better for you to be the peacemaker, to pay the price and take the hit to save that guy and be a peacemaker even though you're going to be persecuted, ironically, in the name of justice for doing it? Or are you going to just mind your own business and just turn the other cheek yourself and let that other guy turn his cheek on the hangman's noose? So there's a question.

There's a difference between turning your cheek and standing idly by and letting some other guy turn his cheek. Are you willing to get your cheek slapped to stop that guy from being hung or not? And in fact, there's a progression in the beatitudes which says when you're gentle, that means I've got power. I can take you out. But I'm restraining myself. I've got this thing about I've been hungry and thirsting for justice, and I'm full and I found the bad guy. And I can take them out and have revenge, or I could restrain myself and be merciful.

The first major shift in the progression—again, this driving force to this pinnacle—is when I become a peacemaker, I'm no longer just restraining my power or withholding punishment and being merciful. I am going out of my way and inserting myself as a peacemaker, and I'm paying the price and taking the hit for you just the way God did for me. If God would do it for me, how can I not do it for you? And the bigger the picture we make of God's love and the bigger we let it get, then the more compelling it is for me to do it for you.

But when we minimize the love, the bigness of God, the goodness of God, the love of God and His grace and love for me, and I try to—and not maximize my complicity, but I'm trying to say, "Oh, my complicity's no big deal," I miss the opportunity to be overwhelmed by this love of God and just let it compel me to be a peacemaker for others.

And that's the challenge. We need to work because multiple theologies and multiple concerns about what's going on in the world gets us all confused. And what I'm wondering is whether or not going back to these very basic, simple ideas of what's in the beatitudes as a way to go from peace broken to being a peacemaker. And the same thing in the Lord's prayer, being the pure, innocent victim, not needing forgiveness, to being the one that does. And that if I do it, I can't help myself to loving someone else, and the evidence of my loving somebody else shows that it worked.

But if I'm not loving someone else, something along the way, I'm not loving that other guy, there's something along the way that I've missed that didn't make it so compelling for me to do it. Maybe because I'm pretty good myself. *[and don't need much forgiveness and have little motivation to forgive others]*

Pastor Stahlberg: I keep saying—I think I've said it several times here that loving somebody and engaging in conversation does not necessarily mean that we will agree.

Charles Manto: Exactly, the same thing about being a peacemaker.

Pastor Stahlberg: Exactly.

Charles Manto: You may take action to prevent that person from—"You want me to vote for you? I'm not voting for you."

Pastor Stahlberg: Yeah, but that should not stop the relationship between the human beings and the loving. I might not like you, but I love you. I mean, I don't like your opinion, and that's fine because we all have different—which is part of God's creation to be—to have this diversity. But I think that we still be empathetic and compassionate.

Charles Manto: Maybe we can give examples of how you've seen or how you've done it. And all of us who have done it, by the way, we also have not done it. So just because we give an example of how we've done, it doesn't mean that we're this wonderful person. But it'd be good to give examples of that so people can get encouraged that's possible to do that.

Pastor Stahlberg: There is a person here in the congregation—I mean, least one, but maybe more, I don't know. And we had a conversation on guns. I'm absolutely anti-gun, but I said I would take a bullet for you because that—I disagree with that person, but different shooter comes in, I will stand in front of that to prevent him from dying because my love for him is bigger than my opinion about guns.

Charles Manto: Very good. Thank you. Let's go to lunch. See you tomorrow, for those who are here.

[End of Saturday June 29 Matthew 6 Session 2 part 3]

Sunday June 30 AM Team-preached Sermon on the Lord's Prayer

Sunday Tandem-Preached Sermon June 30, 2019 at Lord of the Mountains Lutheran Church, Dillon, CO

by Pastor Elena Liliana Stahlberg and Charles Manto

Matthew 6 (Lord's Prayer)(reading starts at 18:35):

https://www.dropbox.com/s/9xptf9evzzgh5ct/Sunday%20June%2030%20AM%20team%20preached%20LP%20%2859%3A50%2C%20reading%20starts%2018%3A35%29.MP4?dl=0

See also LOTM Sermon Archives at: http://www.ustream.tv/recorded/122588380

Archives include Workshop Sessions of June 28-29 and Q&A session on June 30.

Pastor Stahlberg: *(At the front, inviting Charles to come forward)*

(Charles joins)

Pastor Stahlberg:	When Jesus saw the crowds, he went up the mountain. And when he sat down, his disciples came to him and he began teaching them, saying, "Blessed are the poor in spirit, for theirs is the kingdom of God. Blessed are those who mourn, for they will be comforted."
Charles Manto:	"Blessed are the gentle, for they shall inherit the earth."
Pastor Stahlberg:	"Blessed are those who hunger and thirst for justice, for they will be filled."
Charles Manto:	"Blessed are the merciful, for they will receive mercy."
Pastor Stahlberg:	"Blessed are the pure in heart, for they shall see God."
Charles Manto:	"Blessed are the peacemakers, for they shall be called the children of God."
Pastor Stahlberg:	"Blessed are those who are persecuted for justice's sake, for theirs is the kingdom of heaven."
Charles Manto:	"Blessed are you when people revile you and persecute you and utter all kinds of evil against you falsely, on my account. Rejoice, and be glad, for your reward is great in heaven, for in the same way they persecuted the prophets who were before you. You are the salt of the earth."
Pastor Stahlberg:	"But if the salt loses its taste, what can make saltiness be restored? It is no longer good for anything, but it is thrown out and it will be trampled under foot."
Charles Manto:	"You are the light of the world."
Pastor Stahlberg:	"A city built on a hill cannot be hidden. And the lamp is lit, you don't put it under a bushel basket. You put it on a lampstand so that all living in the house can receive the light." And this is the gospel, the good news of our Lord. Please be seated.

So this weekend we studied here with Charles the beatitudes, the blessedness, as well as the Lord's Prayer. In both of these, the underlying theme is peace. Peace with yourself. Unless we have peace with ourselves, it is very hard to have peace with others.

But then peace with others is as important, but here in this congregation, in Summit County, in the country and in the world, we would love to have peace with one another. It is one of the biggest wishes. I remember when the Miss Universe contests were taking places. They were saying, "What do we want to do for the world?" "I want to bring peace in the world." It is a big desire in people's hearts.

And then we need peace with God, and maybe everything starts with a peace with God. The funny part is that—or the interesting part is that Jesus promises to us that peace. More than that, he said, "My peace, I leave with you." So you've got it. You've got it right now if you believe it.

The peace of Christ, though, is not as the peace of the world. Not that the world couldn't be at peace, but it is a deeper peace. So you and I have already the peace of Christ inside us, and yet we need to practice that peace. We need to study, and that's what we were doing this weekend. Looking how can we achieve a peace with ourselves? Jesus invites us to have peace with our enemies and peace with God.

Charles had a claim that the Lord's Prayer, if understood, if we don't just say it by rote, but we pay attention to the words, is a tool, an instrument for bringing peace in our hearts, among each other and in the world. And that starts with a question, and I will give just two, three seconds for you to ponder on the question that he raised. Who is "our" in the prayer, "Our Father"? Who is "our"? When you say "our father," who are you thinking of? Just of yourself? Just of your family?

So, Charles, who is "our" in our father?

Charles Manto (facing Pastor): Well, it's interesting because when I looked at these passages, one could come up with four or five different definitions, all of which are perfectly reasonable. It could be the father of me and everybody in the room, the father of me and everybody in the multiverse, the universe, the planet Earth, all fellow Roman Catholics who are in the true church and they could really have the Father and can pray, or the Father of all born-again people who now have connection with the Father and now for the first time we pray, or just the people in your family, you and all the other nice guys, you and a handful of people that you are close to. And any of those might fit.

The time that sort of surprised me is when I started looking at the texts to figure out, "where did the conversation about prayer actually begin"? So by looking at that, I could see, like when somebody asks what's the definition of a word and the responder might say, "Please use it in a sentence so I can get some clues." When you use the phrase "our Father" and you looked in the paragraph before for clues, you come up with one more choice that would not otherwise be readily apparent.

Pastor Stahlberg: Please speak to the congregation, because I know this. *[Laughter]*

Charles Manto (Turns toward congregation): What's really interesting about where this starts, amazingly enough, you actually know by heart already where the Lord's Prayer reference actually begins before the Lord's Prayer.

Pastor Stahlberg: It's the context. We cannot take the Lord's Prayer out of the context.

Charles Manto: Trying to figure out how this writer of the Lord's Prayer in Matthew is setting the stage, you look for what comes before and go back until you find the first thing about prayer. And you back up a couple of paragraphs to probably the most well-known phrase from the Bible. Right after, "Turn the other cheek, walk the extra mile," comes the phrase, "And love your enemies," in Matthew 5:44, just a couple of paragraphs before. But the part of that very sentence most people don't know is this: "Love your enemies and pray for your persecutors." Pray for your persecutors.

Now, that part of that very sentence is usually not very well known, and I admit to you personally why I had basic prejudice against it was because it wasn't something I would pay attention to, because I grew up as a secular child, and I did my first degree at Urbana, Illinois in psychology. It was the number two school at the time.

We learned early on that Freud thought anybody religious was delusional. And the DSM (Diagnostic and Statistical Manual of Mental Health Disorders), the manual to help figure out what kind of mental health problem a person has so a practitioner could get paid *(by insurance companies for providing mental health services)* still says that if you have a persecution complex, typical among some religious people, you have a mental health disorder.

I know a bunch of religious people who are so odd and act out in such a strange way that other people are constantly pushing back at the odd acting religious people and then those religious people feel persecuted. And I sort of feel embarrassed for that whole situation. And so when people talk about persecution, I think persecution complex, all that mess, and I just don't want to hear about it. So when I see that (conversation about persecution), I just go over it very lightly and don't pay any attention to it.

But in this case I had to pay attention, and in the context of Matthew, these were people who had some really serious, tough problems. The things they needed to survive day-to-day were at risk. They really did have huge conflicts. They had people who were actually gunning for them sometimes, the persecutors.

And while that was going on in this text, Jesus was saying in effect: God is with you in the most difficult situation in your life imaginable, even when somebody's gunning for you, and he wants you to be able to not only love, but pray for the worst case. Because if we can do that for the worst case, we can do it in every case.

Pastor Stahlberg: So what is the benefit of praying for the persecutors?

Charles Manto: Well, it's sort of interesting. It's similar to what we discovered in the beatitudes where it starts off by saying, "Blessed are the crushed in spirit." That's sort of a surprise, by the way, because those sorts of people aren't very blessed. Or those who are sorrowful. And in the beatitudes, you see this whole range leading to a crescendo like a drama where the people who are crushed and their peace has been lost, they not only get it restored, but they become instead of the peace breakers, they become peacemakers.

Pastor Stahlberg: Peacemakers.

Charles Manto: And the same thing happens in the Lord's Prayer. If you look at this as your conflict prayer, your anger management prayer, that gives you a step-by-step progression as to how you can engage with the very person ruining your life.

Pastor Stahlberg: I never thought of the Lord's Prayer as a conflict management prayer, but—

Charles Manto: But it becomes a peace prayer.

Pastor Stahlberg: It is a peace prayer.

Charles Manto: By the way, an interesting thing about the Matthew prayer, this is not just for the Christians. This was for the crowd, most of whom had not yet found Jesus. Yeah, there were some disciples getting some on-the-job training about how to reach out to people, but the bulk of the people were not followers. This prayer is for anyone who has a conflict. If you have a conflict, you have a prayer.

Pastor Stahlberg: Okay, I have a conflict. Let's say that there are two spouses. Could be male or female, male and male, or female and female. And relationships are hard, and there are moments where your spouse becomes your enemy. I remember a movie with Julia Roberts called "Sleeping with the Enemy." *[Laughter]* That was her husband. So how are spouses supposed to pray for each other, and what would be the—how does this play out?

Charles Manto: So, first of all, because lots of times we think, "Well, we're not people with enemies. We don't have enemies." But sometimes we have relationships where they're so difficult, that for me to raise one question that between me and the person I love is so overwhelming, I feel like I'm going to die if I have to face this. I'd rather not face that. I'd rather get a divorce first, right?

So let's see how this works. So every time you see the word "our" or "us," you have to do a little substitution like in algebra. So instead of "our father," it's the father of me and the person I'm fighting. In the case of a spouse, it's the father of me and the spouse who's not loving me, or maybe the father of me and the spouse who is not loving me and also being mean to me and is distancing from me, or maybe using distancing as a way of punishment.

And so now you're going to the prayer like this:

"The father of me and the spouse who's fighting with me, our father who art in heaven, the constant loving connection between God and his creation. Your kingdom come. If your rule of love come and your desire will be done, your desire for love be done on earth as it was in heaven, then my spouse and I wouldn't be fighting like this."

So it's forcing me to look at the very thing that's bothering me with my spouse. And the very next phrase, "Give us this day our daily bread," the daily bread is what we're caring about, and the "us" is me and my spouse, so we word it this way.

"The father of me and the spouse who's fighting with me, was not loving me and was hurting me" What am I missing? What, from my selfish point of view, what am I missing and how not doing well? So, "Father of me and the spouse who is not loving me, give us both." What?

Pastor Stahlberg: "Give us both the love we need."

Charles Manto: Yes.

"The father of me and the person who is not being patient with me, give us people who are patient with us."

"The father of me and the person who is hurting me and not being patient with me, give us both people who are gentle and patient with us."

Now, when I say that, though, if I'm really upset and I'm thinking, "I do all this stuff for my spouse. I do everything I could, and after all the nice things I do for them and then they treat me like this." And the more I think and brood about all the bad ways they're treating me, after all the things I've been nice to them about, I start saying, "Well, wait a second. I don't know that that person deserves the love."

Pastor Stahlberg: Deserves the love.

Charles Manto: I deserve the love because I'm the good guy. I'm the one who's giving and giving and giving, and that jerk over there is hurting me and running off with somebody else and not caring about me. I'm not sure I even want them to have that love. So now sort of, because I'm being honest, this idea of praying for instead of praying against is hard. Easier to say "teach them a lesson and punish them" or not have to pray since this is so outrageous. So the first in this context is "Give me and the person I'm fighting, the very thing that's been taken from me" then the next part of the prayer.

Pastor Stahlberg:	My question is, what is the effect of that prayer on you?
Charles Manto:	Well, when you go to the next phrase, remember the next phrase after, "Give us this day our daily bread?" What is after that?
Pastor Stahlberg:	"Forgive us our trespasses."
Charles Manto:	"Forgive us our trespasses." So, I might have a problem with that. Why do we blame the victim? "I did nothing to hurt that spouse, and yet he or she's treating me like this. That's the person who needs forgiveness. They're the jerk. They're the bad guy. Not me. I don't need any forgiveness here."
Pastor Stahlberg:	Oh, you are self-righteous. *[Laughter]*
Charles Manto:	Just in this situation. So here's how it begins to apply, is interesting. I started off being a pure innocent victim who didn't do anything wrong to anybody.
Pastor Stahlberg:	You were the pure in heart. The beatitudes.
Charles Manto:	Yes. And because I'm pure in heart, I never do anything wrong to anybody. Lucky me. I get to see God. "Blessed are the pure in heart." They get to see God. But in some point in time when you work through this, go to counseling or you think about it, you might discover that the same way your spouse was inpatient with you, you were impatient with someone else.
	Or going back just to your spouse in the prayer, the second phrase says, "Forgive us." "But, no; I don't need forgiveness. I'm the innocent victim." And why say, "Well, forgive us? That is the person who needs forgiveness is that no-good spouse over there."
Pastor Stahlberg:	"The jerk over there."
Charles Manto:	"In fact, I'm so mad because after all the things I did over and over and over again, they treat me like this over and over and over again. They're hurting my life, and I can't stand it anymore. I'm not sure I even want that person forgiven. They're the one who…"
Pastor Stahlberg:	So what is your emotion then?
Charles Manto:	"I am so angry. I wish…" Now you have to be pretty extreme in a relationship to think like this, but how many of you have ever heard the phrase, "That person is so bad, I want them to rot in hell forever after what they've done?" We've all heard phrases like that. So the idea is…
Pastor Stahlberg:	I have a whole list of people. *[Laughter]*
Charles Manto:	So here I am, I'm standing before God. He knows every thought. He's all-powerful. Knows every motivation. And I'm really upset and say, "God, why do I—I don't need any forgiveness. That jerk over there needs the forgiveness, but I don't want you to forgive him. Because you have the power, God, I want you to put that person in hell and punish them on Monday, Tuesday, like the godfather on steroids, I want you to kill them a million times over and keep on doing it."
Pastor Stahlberg:	Charles, you are horrible and you need forgiveness right now. *[Laughter]*
Charles Manto:	Well, that's exactly what happened. Because as I'm raving against that no-good person and then I'm remembering this comment Jesus made a minute before. In effect he says, "Yeah, it's okay. It's healthy to be angry because of your brother. Somebody does something bad to you, you're supposed to be upset because you don't want that bad thing to happen. But you

	cross a line when you move from getting angry because of your brother and you become angry at your brother." And Jesus knows when you cross that line, you're guilty of … murder.
Pastor Stahlberg:	Murder. Even if you are only angry at your brother, you are guilty of murder.
Charles Manto:	But why are you guilty? When you're so angry at them. When you're angry at them, you're guilty of murder. So I'm standing before the judge of judges and in front of the courtroom, I'm giving Him prima facie evidence that I am guilty of murder. I've got a rotten spouse. If I've got a rotten spouse and God agrees with me, right? But what did I do to myself? What did I convict myself of?
Pastor Stahlberg:	The same thing.
Charles Manto:	No, worse. I've convicted myself of murder. Not only murder, serial murder. *[Laughter]* How do I get forgiveness for that?
Pastor Stahlberg:	No forgiveness.
Charles Manto:	So I've convicted myself of murder. Now, what Jesus is doing, he's letting me start with appreciating my true sorrow, the fact that I really was treated unjustly, and I've been a victim of injustice, and the anger is certainly understandable. But when I crossed that line and became angry at them, I realized that I too…
Pastor Stahlberg:	Need forgiveness.
Charles Manto:	Now, notice in the Lord's Prayer, it says, "Give me and my spouse daily bread." I'm not sure I want that, and then, "Forgive us." I'm not sure I want them to be forgiven. And now I realize, oops, I'm in big trouble, and now we strike the grand bargain. The father, forgive us how?
Pastor Stahlberg:	As we forgive.
Charles Manto:	Based on how I forgive. Now imagine that this prayer was really effective, and all of my rage has been uncovered, and I'm at the height of my rage, wanting to destroy this person over and over and over again, and God chooses at that moment to give me a pop quiz.

How well would I do on the pop quiz if the pop quiz is, "Forgive me based on how loving and forgiving I am"—how well would I do? Show of hands. How many people think I would pass the pop quiz? *[Laughter, no hands go up.]* Show of hands, how many people think I would fail the pop quiz? *[Nearly all hands go up.]* Woo. That's why the very next phrase, the Lord's Prayer, is, "Lead us not into testing." Not that God is trying to tempt us. |
Pastor Stahlberg:	Don't give us a pop quiz.
Charles Manto:	Don't give me this pop quiz because, if you do, I would fail and the consequences would be disastrous because I wouldn't be forgiven. That's why it then says deliver us from?
Multiple:	Evil.
Charles Manto:	And then at the end of the Lord's Prayer, Jesus says, "So, guys, do you want the father in heaven to forgive you? And then you forgive those jerks over there, the father will forgive you. But if you don't, he won't forgive you."

So what Jesus is doing in this prayer is driving us to consistency where basically we say, "God, I'm not so sure how I'm doing with this plan A. I hope you've got a good plan B. Just forgive me and love me because you can," and we get crushed and we have no alternative, but let God do that for us as a totally free gift and we receive it. And if I felt like I was just |

terribly reduced before God himself as the serial killer and God forgives me, how can I not then forgive my spouse?

Pastor Stahlberg (turning to congregation): Okay, you give me a conflict that he will walk through the Lord's Prayer. Something tough. Something that makes you really angry, and we want to punish those bad people. I wanted the young people to tell us a real conflict from today.

Darlene Muschett: I don't qualify for young people.

Pastor Stahlberg: Yes, you are. The youngest at heart that I know.

Darlene Muschett: Bless you. Bless you. Thank you. I'm fresh out of dollars. But how about the conflict between Republicans and Democrats? *[Laughter and a few "ohhhs"]*

Charles Manto (Motioning to divide himself vertically with his hand): Oh, wow. This is interesting.

The right side of me, a Republican, the left side of me, the Democrat. There's conflict within here. So let's do it both ways.

Pastor Stahlberg: Both ways.

Charles Manto (hesitates a moment): Whew.

I'm a Republican, and I'm concerned about all those no-good liberals who are going to destroy the country, and they don't appreciate the Constitution. And because of that, my family may die and my company may die, and all the things we fought for may be out the window. And so I'm looking at it selfishly from my point of view about these people who are threatening if they get into power, and it's done. So what do I pray for?

"The father of me and the people who will may ruin or destroy my country, give us both a safe country. The father of me and the ones who are going to destroy my freedom, give us both freedom. The father of me and the ones who don't want to hear the voices of the oppressed, because we don't want justice anymore, give us both the place where everybody can be listened to."

That's what the Republicans say.

Now the Democrat side.

Pastor Stahlberg: I'm curious.

Charles Manto: Well, the Democrats are going to say these Republicans are just trouncing over the rights of poor people. They're not really caring about the oppressed. They're just caring about the rich people and the friends like themselves. And then when you come up with some, they were saying the friends of mine, the people who are disenfranchised and who don't maybe even a place—

Pastor Stahlberg: The refugees at our borders who are in cages. Come on.

Charles Manto: And some of those refugees might also be my cousins. Not just these people I sort of know about, nice guys and sort of sad. But maybe my cousins, because I'm new here myself as a refugee just a generation ago.

"The father of me and the person who is hurting my cousins and making them homeless, give us both a protected and safe family, and give us both a place—a safe place to live. The father of me and the person who is taking us away from being able to make enough money to make ends meet, give us both enough money to make ends meet."

I'm just starting because in every case and every problem we have, it makes it possible to start at the point of our conflict....

Pastor Stahlberg: Okay. I have a question now. So the father of all will not give those things, but what is do you think the impact of that prayer on yourself as you are praying for your enemies or for those with whom you disagree?

Charles Manto: That's a very good question because people are writing a lot on that topic of empathy. How do you not only stand in someone else's shoes, how do you look through their eyes given everything that you could imagine? It's a very hard thing to do. And what this is saying to another question in this is we create empathy by starting to look at the conflict that we both share.

I and my worst enemy have something hugely intimate together, and that is the thing that may be destroying me or blocking me from the thing I need most. And when I become called into solidarity, not only with the fellow sufferers and oppressed who are cursed by that threatening entity, but I'm called into solidarity with the very one intent even on my destruction, I begin to have the empathy and a concept of unity which is supernaturally far beyond anything else because in our society what we're doing is we're just having unity with people like us.

And when we have the discussion, I basically am debating against the other guy and never winning them. I may win an argument, but I'm never winning them because I started the argument by saying conservatives—and make it religious instead of political.

If I'm religiously conservative, I'll walk up and say, "I don't really know you, but I know what your problem is because the Bible told me what it is. You are evil, you're a sinner, and you're going to hell, and I can prove it right here. And if you don't believe me, I can prove to you that the Bible is the Word of God, and it's absolutely true, and you're really messed up." *(some laughter)*

That may sound laughable, but religious liberals do sort of the same thing. "I really don't know you, but I know exactly what your problem is. And the problem is you're not sufficiently educated. You're not bright enough. You're not logical, and your priorities are in the wrong place."

And either case I try to debate you into the kingdom, and instead all I do is push you off. That's why the "don't throw your pearls before swine" is right there in that next chapter, because that's not how we win people by debating them into the kingdom. We win them by loving them into the kingdom when we become the peacemakers for them.

Pastor Stahlberg: Amen. Hallelujah.

[Applause]

Pastor Stahlberg: Thank you, Charles.

Charles Manto: You're welcome.

Pastor Stahlberg:	I think even as it is hard—and it's hard for me. Maybe you are better than I am. I—this weekend has changed my life as I'm going to pray to the Father of me and all those I disagree with, give us peace. The Lord will give you peace, give us all peace. Amen.
Multiple:	Amen.
Pastor Stahlberg:	Thank you. And now please stand as we sing together, "Blessed Are They."
	[Singing]
Pastor Stahlberg:	Now please be seated, as we would like to share with you how we are a community engaged in conversations and daily peace. After the church in the fellowship hall, Charles will be available if you have even tougher questions, and we just engage in conversation. He was telling his opinion, but you are welcome with your own opinion.
	We would like to invite you also to something new also in the spirit of peace. When I realized that there are issues that I cannot have an impact on, I had the revelation that our church should engage in a healing service, and a healing service can be for mind, body and spirit. We will begin this coming Wednesday at 6:00 PM, and everybody's welcome whether you are a receiver or a giver.
	We will have the traditional healing service with the laying on of hands, with anointing and with intense prayers, again, for healing of the body. If you have an issue of the mind, of the spirit, if you have a conflict, we'll practice healing for peace with oneself, peace with others, peace with God. So please come on Wednesday. Everybody can become leaders sooner or later. We will start Karen, and Lila and Greg are going to be participants. We will have a format—we will demonstrate how this works on Wednesday.
	And, again, read the book and other things. Anybody wants to give an urgent announcement—I don't want to spend time. You can take this insert with you and read what is going on. Now we would like Lila to do the welcoming of the visitors, but quickly and probably first the whole group of Peace Lutheran in Peoria, Arizona.
Lila:	This is the part of our service where we welcome people who might be visiting with us. We know you took trouble to come here, and we want to take the trouble to say a proper hello to you. So I'm going to do it this way. If you're visiting with us, stand up. I'll come to the Peace group first. But everybody stand up. Stand up if you are visiting. Yay. Are you all from the same place? You guys mostly.
Pastor Stahlberg:	They have to stay here. I won't let them go home.
Lila:	So, since you're all from the same place, I don't want to hear—where is it—Peoria 14 times. Tell me the street.
	[Introductions]
Pastor Stahlberg:	Again, take a deep breath and let the spirit fill you as we pray together. I say the words, but your spirit joins with mine into holding all these people in me, dwelling in the presence of God, the Holy Spirit. Let us pray for the church, the world, and all in need. Pray for your church around the world and for our little church here. Bless them, bless us with the peace that surpasses all understanding. We pray for all communities of faith, all the different religious people of goodness who come together to praise you and be good to one another. Lord, in your compassion.
Multiple:	Hear our prayers.

Pastor Stahlberg:	We pray for a thanksgiving, for the beauty of your creation, of our nature here in the Summit County. Bring rain to parched places. Bring sun to drenched places. Help us deal with climate change. Help the poor who live on the coastlines and are encountering different disasters. Help us care for those who are not so privileged. Lord, in your compassion.
Multiple:	Hear our prayers.
Pastor Stahlberg:	We give you thanks for all the visitors today, for the youth of Peace Lutheran Church, for their pastor. Bless them and let them increase in strength and power in faith. Lord, in your compassion.
Multiple:	Hear our prayers.
Pastor Stahlberg:	And now we lift up in our prayers those who suffer in mind, body and spirit. And please there are—there is a list also on the announcement page. Today we lift up especially Creighton Holden, strengthen healing and recovery from sepsis. For Louise, for Scott her caregiver. We pray for Patrick and Elizabeth as he is declining, suffering from ALS. We pray for Lorraine preparing for surgery. For Jenny Miller to be comforted in the death of her husband Bruce. We pray for Barb and her family at the death of Brock. For Barb Hudson. For Amy. For Amy we give thanks because she's back at work after brain injury. We pray for Brian, for Amelia, for Patty, John, Robert, Susie, Jim, family and friends of Arthur Fischer who died. All of these, oh, God, we lift up to you, trusting in your mercy and in your grace, in your care and, Lord, in your compassion.
Multiple:	Hear our prayers.
Pastor Stahlberg:	And now I ask for God's blessing on you, people of God, people of faithfulness, that you are kept healthy. That you will be healed from whatever bothers you. That you, if you are journeying, that you go on safe journeys. May God bless you and keep you and people say—
Multiple:	Amen.
Pastor Stahlberg:	The peace of Christ be with you always.
Multiple:	And also with you. [End of Audio]

LORD'S LYFT PRAYER
June 22, 2019 Cab Ride from Emory University to Atlanta Airport

https://www.dropbox.com/s/gv6t7p586j2atb1/Lord%27s%20Lyft%20Prayer%20Atlanta%20%281%29.mov?dl=0

CHARLES MANTO: Tell me your name and tell me what you just said about the Lord's Prayer, and that you've never heard that. Go ahead, I'm recording you from my cell phone so someone else can hear you.

CHRISTOPHER: Okay. My name is Christopher Okudowah [spelling uncertain] and you have told me a new way at the Lord's Prayer. I have read Luke and Matthew over and over and I've never looked at it like that. As far as our Lord's Prayer, I recite it almost daily. Sometimes I even rush in my head and I never in-depth thought about it or looked at it the way that you have enlightened me about it.

CHARLES MANTO: And how did I enlighten you? What was different about it today when we talked about it? What was different about the Lord's Prayer?

CHRISTOPHER: The most important thing that you told me is how to look at the word "our." Generally, and I never thought about it. Our father who is in Heaven, and I never really thought about who does that "our" includes? Well, when you broke it down, you let me realize that "our" is me and my enemy, then you make the whole prayer have two different meanings.

CHARLES MANTO: Yes.

CHRISTOPHER: And then, it makes you realize that each time you read it, you see the effect of what you're saying for the prayer out to, you know, to you and your enemy. And in there you find out along the way that, guess what? I need forgiveness, too—because I'm about to . . . (laughs)

CHARLES MANTO: I want to kill that guy that hurt me.

CHRISTOPHER: I'm about to do some crazy stuff to this person, and then you realize that God gave you a way out in that prayer. Not only for you to pray for your enemy, but for you along the line to realize you have committed sin doing this. So, this is a chance for you to include yourself in that prayer and beg for that forgiveness.

CHARLES MANTO: Wow.

CHRISTOPHER: And that is very powerful.

CHARLES MANTO: And you're from where? Where are you from?

CHRISTOPHER: I'm from Nigeria, and this is Atlanta, Georgia where I live. And I drive Lyft and I met you, and you have made this period—this one hour—the most important one hour of my life!

CHARLES MANTO: Well, thank you so much.

CHRISTOPHER: Because I'm going to teach this to my son and to other people, and I bet you everybody will be amazed. And I appreciate you giving me this knowledge and then teaching me about just a simple—a simple verse in the Bible. And you have given me a way to think about it that I've never been thinking of it before.

CHARLES MANTO: And I can use this in my Sunday School Classes?

CHRISTOPHER: You can use it anywhere you want!

CHARLES MANTO: Thank you.

CHRISTOPHER: —as long as you have people to understand what it's all about when it comes to Christians, believers, Jesus, your enemy, and the way you live your life and the way you show it to others. Because we wake up all the time thinking that we want to be saved and we want to go to Heaven, and we don't want to associate with the people that don't want to go. But, if we don't enlighten them, then how are we different from them again?

CHARLES MANTO: Yes.

CHRISTOPHER: And I thank you for enlightening me on this, and I appreciate the time that you took up, and I appreciate the moment that you spent with me only.

CHARLES MANTO: Thank you.

CHRISTOPHER: And for that, I have to say thank you from the bottom of my heart.

CHARLES MANTO: Well it was my honor to share that insight with you because we all take turns being the bad guy that needs the forgiveness. And when we receive forgiveness, we want to be able to share it with others. Uh, that's what it is when it's like—the same way when it says "blessed are the pure in heart, because you'll see God. And then when God makes peace for you, based on the sacrifice we want to go out and be peacemakers for others, and give them peace based on the sacrifice we make." And the Lord's Prayer is an example of how we can do that. It's a way to do uh—fishing, it's a way to go fishing.

CHRISTOPHER: That is the best way to fish.

CHARLES MANTO: Yes.

CHRISTOPHER: Because the moment while you're doing it, you are not only just letting that person repent, but you're letting that person know: "I'm in the same boat, I'm a sinner too. And I want you to join me so we can keep on going through this channel, praying and accepting ourselves into the Lord and pray for forgiveness." Because how do you pray for forgiveness if you don't realize that you are a sinner? And even though when you repent, you still continue to sin. So you need to continue repenting and praying, so when you go and witness to a soul and say brother I want you to repent, then when you use our Lord's Prayer you are actually saying: "I'm asking you to repent; and as I'm asking you, I'm begging for my own forgiveness."

CHARLES MANTO: Yeah.

CHRISTOPHER: So every time you go out to preach to somebody about forgiveness and about repenting, you are also doing the same thing to our Lord's Prayer.

CHARLES MANTO: Yeah, yeah.

CHRISTOPHER: Because that is what you just told me a while ago over there. When you were saying all that, I'm like—our Lord's Prayer—I said I say that every day. But I never realized how in-depth it is, especially when you realize that you are using it to fish.

CHARLES MANTO: Right.

CHRISTOPHER: And you are making yourself a fisher or men.

CHARLES MANTO: And what is your name again?

CHRISTOPHER: Christopher, Christopher Okudowah.

CHARLES MANTO: Thank you Christopher Okudowah, it was my joy to talk to you today.

CHRISTOPHER: And I'm grateful that I met you, it was my joy to have met you and for you to have enlightened me the way that you did. Thank you very much.

CHARLES MANTO: Thank you.

Section 3: Appendix

The Lord's Prayer as Preparation for Meditation

(As posted on "Spiritual Ways" website: https://brandonstoneknight.com/spiritualways/the-lords-prayer-as-preparation-for-meditation)

The problem of getting calm when life is anything but calm: I have had the privilege of participating with a number of people in a daily meditative prayer session. As part of that practice, we have read about and briefly discussed multiple meditative and prayer methods and traditions from various faith and meditative practices. What is common to many is the benefit of such meditation but also the struggle many have at doing that when certain life circumstances make it difficult to concentrate and release their minds of all that might be pressuring them at the moment.

The possibility to regain peace: There is a largely overlooked and forgotten prayer practice that might help anyone of any faith or even non-faith tradition seeking to get to that point of calm and silence. This is the conflict prayer recommended by Jesus to the crowds, not just his disciples, in the book of Matthew Chapter 5 and verse 44 when he asks the crowds to "love your enemies and pray for those who persecute you." He is asking to love and pray for the worst-case conflict making it possible to love and pray for all the lesser cases. Scholars have lamented that details on how to do that were not given seeing how important such prayer instructions might be. It appears that at end the of the discussion of love and prayer at the end of Chapter 5, that Jesus changes the subject and starts talking about not giving alms in public in the first four verses of Chapter 6. That is too bad since if it were only possible to have someone in anxiety, fear and loss of peace come to a place of peace, then that would be very practical for conflict situations throughout the day, and in particular for those wishing to calm themselves and enter a period of either silence, meditation or centering prayer.

Discovering the method of the conflict to peace prayer: While searching for embedded memory methods in these ancient texts, hoping to find some to make it easier for me to memorize the material, I discovered those very prayer instructions. It turns out that those four verses in the beginning of Chapter 6 that were thought to have signaled a change of topic were actually a segment that had a number of memory methods that actually tied the section of Chapter 5 with what was to come in Chapter 6 instead of separating them. It turns out that the detailed instructions for such a prayer for conflicts are found in the Lord's Prayer of Matthew Chapter 6 and verses 5-15, immediately following the four verses of memory methods that tie the sections together. These are discussed in an article that is scheduled to be published in an article in *Christian Century* magazine in the summer of 2021 and a resource book for those studying the Lord's Prayer expected to be published in the Fall of 2021.

The instructions: When seen in that light, the entire tone of the prayer changes. Instead of being a worship prayer for a group of disciples, this is a prayer that anyone in the crowd, including those not yet disciples, were asked to pray alone (not in a group) for those causing the conflict. So, now, the "our" in the "our Father," switches from being defined as "the Father of me and the ones praying with me," or "the Father of me and fellow disciples or believers," or "the Father of me and people in general" to "the Father of me and the person I am in conflict in this present moment" and the "daily necessary bread" stands for what is being contested. Each phrase in the prayer becomes a step-by-step approach to relieving anxiety, fear and anger that can bring the person whose peace has been broken to a place where their peace is restored and possibly to a place where they can become the new peace maker instead of a new peace breaker.

The core formula section: The core section where this formula works can be seen in the steps progressing from "give US this day OUR necessary bread and release US from OUR debts as WE release OUR debtors."

"Give us our daily necessary bread": As an example, if the person who is upsetting us and making it difficult to concentrate in peace is someone threatening to take away our housing, we might pray the daily necessary bread for them in this way, "The Father of me and the one who is threatening to take away my housing, give us both a safe place to live." That might seem unusual for one who might merely pray, "protect me from this person threatening to take away my home." Or "give them a taste of their own medicine and have them lose their home." Instead, the crowd member, not even a disciple following this recommendation to love and pray for their worst-case enemy, is being asked to ask that the very thing being taken away from the person praying is the very thing asked to be given to both the one praying AND to the person threatening to take it away in the first place. A typical reaction might be, "why should I pray that way, that housing thief is the last person who deserves that."

"Release (forgive) us": But the surprise does not end there. There might be more reasons to reject this prayer. First, is the notion that there is an "us" whose debts needs releasing or forgiving. Why blame the victim? I worked hard for my housing, certainly need it and deserve it. This guy taking my housing did not work for it. He is the one who has a debt needing releasing, not me. Then after recalling precisely who is to blame for what, then, a doubt may set in about forgiving the one who needs the forgiveness in the first place. Why should I pray that he be forgiven? In fact, the oft spoken phrase, "he should rot in hell forever after what he did to me and my family" might be the very request that aggrieved person might makes of God.

The flip: Then in that moment, the one in the crowd requesting revenge in what should be a prayer of forgiveness might remember what Jesus said just a few minutes before when he said that the one angry at his brother could be brought up on murder charges. Now the one railing against the housing thief before God, has just brought evidence of his own guiltiness of murder before the judge of judges. At that point, the once innocent victim is now guilty of something as big or bigger than the crime he suffered. That is further reinforced when the praying person makes the grand bargain with the Father when asking to be forgiven on the basis of how forgiving he is when asking, "forgive (release) us of our debts AS we release…" No wonder the next phrase is "lead us not into testing" because if the Father were to give the one praying a pop quiz to see how forgiving the one praying person is during the height of his rage, the raging praying person might not fare so well and the consequences would certainly be an evil from which he needs deliverance.

Resulting Peace: Such a prayer brings one to the place where we recognize our greater need for forgiveness. And, if the Father releases us from such a great debt, how much easier for us to release a lesser one? (This is a theme repeated elsewhere in Matthew such as in Chapter 25.) By being brought into a solidarity even with our worst-case enemies, instead of only those who are fellow sufferers, then we may find an amazing love and peace that can bring us calm in our most distressing circumstances. It may even turn us into peacemakers.

Reason for recommending it multiple times each day from second century: For these reasons, it is not surprising to see examples of early church writings like "the Teaching of the Twelve"[5] written around 120 A.D., and the writings of Tertullian[6] where listeners were asked to pray this prayer three or more times each day. Instead of being some kind of worship service, or mindless repetition, this would be an opportunity to address each conflict, one at a time, until a place of peace is reached. Consider taking enough time to reflect on how one conflict may cause another. For example, the one who is threatening me with a loss of my job, might also be threatening my ability to pay for housing, my ability to feed my children, like a Russian nesting doll. Try that for a week and see how it might work in your experience. Such a method might be used by any seeking to get to a place where a calm, meditative time might be achieved.

---

5   *The Ante-Nicene Fathers*, Volume 7, p. 379; "Teaching of the Twelve," Chapter VIII.

6   *The Ante-Nicene Fathers*, Volume 3, p. 68-684, 690, 691; "On Prayer," Chapter XXV, p. 690 including prayer for persecutors.

Section 3: Appendix

Workshop Preparation Material (for Network of Biblical Storytellers Festival Gathering Friday, August 4, 2017, see: http://www.nbsint.org/festival-workshops)

From official NBS program:

F2-4 Lord's Prayer Conflict Skits with Chuck Manto

The presenter proposes Matthew 5-7 as oral teaching facilitating memorizable material, evoking conflict stories of the listener. This session will show how embedded memory devices indicate that the Lord's Prayer is the prayer for persecutors. The workshop will discuss conflict progression within the prayer then map it against age-appropriate conflicts of students. Skits, performable by students, show how their conflict can be processed through the Lord's Prayer in light of community, school and domestic violence.

Chuck Manto presented Matthew 5-7 embedded memory methods in previous NBS Scholars Forums, workshops and adult classes. He is developing material suitable for classes in various conflict contexts and is developing team-teaching activities globally. His small R&D firm develops resilient community infrastructure. He develops conference and publications through the InfraGard National EMP SIG co-sponsored by the FBI and the Policy Studies Organization.

This packet includes the following:

1) Introduction about various skit assumptions and approaches
2) Two skits on the Lord's Prayer
    a. "The Joke," conflict management per Matt 5:44 request to pray for persecutors
    b. "If God Should Speak," general collection of prayer items consistent with traditional views
3) Conflict skit formula
4) Invitation to make your own skit based on conflict skit formula
5) Discussion of psychology of conflict prayer and memorization benefits of conflict prayer method of Matt 5-6
6) Art work basis of "the Joke"
7) Alternate version of The Joke skit
8) Overview of textual setting of conflict prayer (end note iii)
9) Background material on conflict prayer texts and oral criticism (end note iv)

Skit Assumptions and Approach: This exercise compares two different approaches to the Lord's Prayer and the skits that might illustrate them. In the 1977 skit quoted on page 6-8, "If God Should Speak,"[2] the writer Clyde Lee Herring takes the traditional interpretation[7] of the Lord's Prayer of Matthew 6:9 as a general prayer about a number of loosely connected elements. In his resulting skit, the material is a collection of clever dialogue between the person

---

[7] See Hans Dieter Betz's observation in his essay, "Original Purpose of the Lord's Prayer" in his major work, *The Sermon on the Mount*, Fortress Press, 1995, p. 373 (col.2). "What did Jesus intend by the creation of this prayer? **One can only speculate about this question because none of the sources is explicit about this.**" In other words, in the traditional perspective, there is no apparent organizing theme for the prayer.

See also, *Catechism of the Catholic Church*, Libreria Editrice Vaticana, 1994, p. 668-9. "...'our' Father ... his promises of love in the new and eternal covenant in his Christ: we have become 'his' people and he is henceforth 'our' God ... In praying 'our' Father, each of the baptized is praying in this communion: The company of those who believed were of one heart and soul." In this way, both Protestant and Catholic commentators ignore the context which shows that Jesus asked all the crowd to pray for enemies, not just his followers. In effect, he calls the oppressed and hurt into solidarity with the oppressors and those hurting them with this prayer, ultimately creating empathy and greater love.

See also, Ulrich Lutz, *Matthew*, "'Our' connects the praying individual with the community," p. 316. And, earlier commenting on traditional interpretations on p. 313, "The Lord's Prayer was presented to baptized persons as the essence of the new truth in which they live," or "as the prayer of the new covenant," or "a multifunctional text, useful as a model prayer, as a dogmatic compendium, as a catechetical synthesis, as a private and ecclesiastical prayer, and so on." Then on p. 314, "Immediately a difficulty surfaces here: the petitions of the Lord's Prayer are so short and open that seldom is one able to establish their meaning unambiguously." I would suggest that if the community intended was the community or combination of the person praying and the one persecuting him, then the meaning becomes far less ambiguous.

praying and God but does not tightly connect any of the elements of the prayer, even though it has an emphasis on forgiveness. See if you agree with the critical statement: "The dialog is a well-written but thematically disjointed hodge-podge of prayer elements."

The proposed draft skit on bullying by Manto on page 3 -5 is called, "The Joke." This is intended as a draft that the discussion group participants can use as a model to craft their own skits. In the case of this skit on bullying, Manto proposes the Lord's Prayer was intended, according to Matthew 5:44, to be a more tightly woven prayer primarily focused on conflict management as the prayer Jesus requested his listeners say for "their persecutors." When viewed this way, each element of the prayer revolves around the concept of the conflict of greatest concern to the one praying at the time from the beginning of the prayer until the end. It emotionally escalates as the conflict comes to a crescendo and a flip when the person hurt by someone shifts from being the innocent victim to becoming jointly guilty of something equally significant to the offending party and hence, also needing forgiveness. In the Lord's Prayer for Persecutors, the "our" in "our Father" draws the hurting person into solidarity with the very person or organization doing the harm. "Our Father" becomes the "Father of me and the one fighting me" and "our daily bread" becomes "what we are fighting over." See if the skit conveys that message and try to write your own that might better reflect conflicts you experience.

Section 3: Appendix

Lord's Prayer for Persecutor—Sample skit:

"The Joke, by Charles Manto"

Setting: School playground for scene 1; Home for scenes 2-4 with rifle and shells, medicine bottle and pills, Bible respectively.

Characters: Boy, group of kids in playground, bullies, teacher watching from distance.

Scene 1: Middle school boy, Bob, walks into the school's campus (outdoor basketball court nearby) the during start of the school day. Bob walks up to the group apparently talking while at play. Smiling with joyful anticipation, he begins to speak out loud,

"Can I play?" Bob asks them.

Then a few of the kids pivot towards him.

A leader with a couple of sidekicks emerges from the group and answers with a taunt,

"Are you kidding, four-eyes! Boy, your mother dresses you funny."

Another, joins in, "Yeah, wimp. And who gave you that haircut?"

Leader comes closer, and gives the boy (Bob) a back-handed slap in the face and shoves the boy saying, "Why don't you get out of here, you xxx—(whatever derogatory comment the bully might use).

Then the few in the group with the bully point at the bullied boy and laugh, taking turns calling him names and a half dozen others laugh while others look on, including a teacher from the distance who does nothing to intervene.

As Bob leaves the schoolyard and goes into the school, other kids come to him showing their cell phone screen and laughing.

One kid shows screen saying to the boy, "See, you are famous now, 'there is your 'four-eyes' pic.

Another pointing to cell phone screen, "yeah, look at that haircut."

Another, "look at you getting slapped in the face, you wimp."

Another, "Look at all the people who think you are a dork!" —(naming various kids with dozens of "likes" for the screen) ... (All leave stage.)

Scene Two:

Boy at home alone talking to himself, finding his father's rifle and shells,

"I will teach them who's wimpy..." counting rifle shells "one, two, three for the teasers; one, two, three, four, five for the laughers, one for the teacher..."

Light fades...

Scene Three:

Light brightens, (or actor turns pivots in another direction) …

Boy at home alone in front of a medicine cabinet and sets down a glass of water.

Boy takes a medicine bottle from the medicine cabinet. Reads the warning label out loud, "Maximum dosage two."

"They are right. They are better without me. I'll show them. I am better off without anyone.

Pours out pills into his hand and counts. Five, ten, fifteen, … twenty should do it …

Light fades…

Scene Four *(Somewhat Reluctant and Tense Prayer)***:**

Light brightens (or actor pivots in another direction) …

At home, animated, in room alone, boy grabbing Bible, talking out loud to himself …

 "We just talked about what Jesus said to do when we get hit in the face … I wonder how this might work. Glad I underlined these. Here it is, Matthew 5:22. 'He who is angry at his brother is guilty of the same judgment as a murderer.'"

"Uh, not that one."

Scanning down with his finger on the page, he continues to read out loud.

 "Verse 39" — 'If someone slaps you on the right cheek, turn and offer him your left.' And what else can you do? … "And here, in 44, love your enemies and pray for your persecutors." Wonder how you do that. Does not sound normal. Yes, there is that prayer right about here somewhere. Maybe it says it there."

Mumbling a few words as skimming down page…

"when you pray…".

"Ah, 6:9, "here is how you should pray..." his is that prayer. So, if this prayer is the way to do it, how does it work for me now? Maybe the 'our' in 'our Father' means 'me and the person fighting me,' and 'daily bread' means 'what we are fighting over.'" OK, so here goes … "

"Father of me and the bullies who taunted me today and will probably do more again tomorrow, I just want to go to school and find some friends and have a good time, not be teased and hurt."

"So, Father of me and those people who tease me, Who is in heaven, where everybody loves everybody all the time; holy and unique is your name. Your name is special because you can hear me when I call it, strong enough to help me, caring enough to want to help me.

Your kingdom and rule of love come. Your will, your desire for love come. On earth right here and now as it is in heaven. If it were, they wouldn't be teasing and hurting me like this or taking away my fun and friends."

"'Give us this day'—uh, —OK, —Give me and those who are teasing me good times at school this coming day.

Give the bullies and me safety from those who want to hurt us. Give me and the ones who call me bad names that make people laugh at us and make people not like us,—give us good names so the kids at school will like us."

Boy pauses…

"Father, I am not so sure I like this part of the prayer. They are bullies and don't deserve a good time and safety at school; they are the bad guys who take the good times and safety from me. In fact, they don't need good times and safety. They already get good times by teasing me and don't seem to need safety since they are the bullies. Hmmm."

"Forgive us…" —Wait. Father, I don't need any forgiveness here. I am the victim; they are the bullies. They are the ones needing forgiveness, not me. And for that matter, I am not even wanting them to be forgiven. They should be tormented in Hell forever after what they did to me. I am mad and have every right to be."

"Oops. I am mad at them for good reason, but I am mad AT them. Is it true that what Jesus says is true, that my being angry at them makes me a murderer? So, while they are guilty of bullying, am I now guilty of murder? And since I am so mad that I don't want them to ever be forgiven, am I am guilty of multiple murders?"

"Maybe both the bullies and me both need forgiveness."

"I guess now we are at the bargaining part of the prayer […] Forgive me and the bullies based on how well we are forgiving each other."

"Father, I am not sure how that is going to work. Please, don't test us right now to see how well we are doing that because I might fail that test and that would not be a good thing because I would not be forgiven. That would be a bad thing to be delivered from."

Boy seems calm. Lays to rest. Light fades.

If God Should Speak
Clyde Lee Herring, 1977, Broadman Press

"Our Father who art in heaven..."

---Yes?

Don't interrupt me; I'm praying.

---But you called me.

Called you? I didn't call you. I'' praying. "Our Father who art in heaven..."

---There. You did it again.

Did what?

---Called me. You said, "Our Father who art in heaven." Here I am. What's on your mind?

But I didn't mean anything by it. I was, you know, just saying my prayers for the day. I always say the Lord's Prayer. It makes me feel good, kind of like getting a duty done.

---All right. Go on.

"Hallowed be thy name..."

---Hold it. What do you mean by that?

By what?

---By "hallowed be thy name?"

It means . . . it means . . . Good grief, I don't know what it means! How should I know? It's just part of the prayer. By the way, what does it mean?

---It means honored, holy, wonderful.

Hey, that makes sense. I never thought about what "hallowed" meant before. "Thy kingdom come, thy will be done, on earth as it is in heaven."

---Do you really mean that?

Sure! Why not?

---What are you doing about it?

Doing? Nothing, I guess. I just think it would be kind of neat if you got control of everything down here like you have up there.

---Have I got control of you?

Well, I go to church.

---That isn't what I asked you. What about your bad temper? You've really got a problem there, you know. And then there's the way you spend your money--all on yourself. And what about the lies you tell?

Stop picking on me! I'm just as good as some of the rest of those people at church!

---Excuse me. I thought you were praying for my will to be done. If that is to happen, it will have to start with the ones who are praying for it; like you, for example.

Oh, all right! I guess I do have some hang-ups. Now that you mention it, I could probably name some others.

---So could I.

I haven't thought about it very much until now, but I really would like to cut out some of those things. I would like to, you know, be really free!

---Good! Now we're getting somewhere. We'll work together, you and I. Some victories can truly be won. I'm proud of you.

Look, Lord, I need to finish up here. This is taking a lot longer than it usually does. "Give us this day our daily bread."

---You need to cut out the bread. You're overweight as it is.

Hey, wait a minute! What is this, criticize me day? Here I was doing my religious duty, and all of a sudden you break in and remind me of all my hang-ups!

---Praying is a dangerous thing. You could wind up changed, you know. That's what I'm trying to get across to you. You called me, and here I am. It's too late to stop now. Keep praying. I'm interested in the next part of your prayer . . . (pause). Well, go on . . .

I'm scared to.

---Scared? Of what?

I know what you'll say!

---Try Me and see. "Forgive us our sins, as we forgive those who sin against us."

---What about John?

See?! I knew it! I knew you would bring him up! Why, Lord, he's told lies about me, spread stories about my family, he never paid back the debt he owes me. I've sworn to get even with him!

---But your prayer. What about your prayer?

I didn't mean it!

---Well, at least you are honest. But it's not much fun carrying that load of bitterness around inside, is it?

No. But I'll feel better as soon as I get even! Boy, have I got some plans for that neighbor! He'll wish he had never moved into this neighborhood!

---You won't feel any better. You'll feel worse. Revenge isn't sweet! Think how unhappy you already are. But I can change all of that!

You can? How?

---Forgive John. Then I'll forgive you. Then the hate and sin will be John's problem; not yours. You will have settled your heart.

Oh, You're right. You always are! And more than I want revenge on John, I want to be right with You . . . (pause) . . . (sigh). All right. I forgive him. Help him to find the right road in life, Lord. He's bound to be awfully miserable, now that I think about it. Anybody who goes around doing the things he does to others has to be out of it! Someway, somehow, show him the right way.

---There, now. Wonderful! How do you feel?

Hmmm. Well, not bad! Not bad at all! In fact, I feel pretty great!! You know, I don't think I'll have to go to bed uptight tonight for the first time since I can remember. Maybe I won't be so tired from now on because I'm not getting enough rest.

---You're not through with your prayer. Go on.

Oh, all right. "And lead us not into temptation, but deliver us from evil."

---Good! Good! I'll do that! Just don't put yourself in a place where you can be tempted.

What do You mean by that?

---Don't turn on the TV when you know that work needs done around the house. And the time you spend drinking with your friends, if you can't influence the conversation to positive things, perhaps you should re-think the value of those friendships. Another thing, your neighbors and friends shouldn't be your standard for "keeping up." And please don't use Me for an escape hatch!

I don't understand the last part . . .

---Sure you do. You've done it a lot of times. You get caught in a bad situation, or get into trouble, and then you come running to Me! "Lord, help me out of this mess, and I promise You I'll never do it again." Do you remember some of those bargains you tried to make with Me?

Yes, Lord. And I'm ashamed. I really am!

---Which bargain are you remembering?

Well, there was the night that when I was out and I got into that car accident. I remember praying, "Oh God, if you spare me, I'll never miss Mass again."

---I protected you, but you didn't keep your promise, did you?

I'm sorry, Lord, I really am! Up until now, I thought that if I just prayed the Lord's Prayer every day then I could do what I pleased. I didn't expect anything to happen like it did!

---Go ahead, finish your prayer . . .

"For Thine is the kingdom, the power, and the glory forever. Amen."

---Do you know what would bring Me glory? What would really make Me happy?

No, but I'd like to know. I want now to please You. I can see what a mess I've made of my life. And I can see how great it would be to REALLY be one of your followers!

---You just answered the question!

I did?!

---Yes. The thing that would bring me glory is to have people like you truly love Me. And I see that happening between us. Now that some of these old sins are exposed and out of the way, well, there is no telling what we can do together!

Lord, let's see what we can make of me, okay?

---Yes, Let's see!

SECTION 3: APPENDIX

Discussion Questions for Skit Comparisons

Comparing skits: How do the elements of the Lord's Prayer in the conflict skit compare to the elements of the general prayer skit? (In terms of emotional development, connectedness, relevant to stories?)

What might be the trade-offs of doing the skit either way?

Comparison to Lord's Prayer Context: How does each approach make use of the context of the Lord's Prayer in Matthew 5-7?

What kinds of conflicts inherent in the "turn the other cheek" passage in Matthew 5: 38-42 might be relevant for this type of skit?

How might this concept of the conflict prayer be useful in anger management and the development of stronger relationships and communities?

How might this approach be useful in developing empathy and how does empathy develop by the person praying?

What true stories about conflict management and examples of loving enemies have you seen that would be worth sharing either with the group or in writing similar to the website Tom Boomershine is developing?

Tell your conflict story *(use back of pages as needed)*:

Make your own skit: By looking at the suggested conflict prayer skit, it can be relatively easy for the reader to come up with a skit that is based on a conflict more relevant to his or her own conflict where the conflict might be different or the person be of a different age, location, or culture.

You may have other conflicts in mind that would provide a more relevant skit. In the next 5-10 minutes, write out your own example of a conflict and how the peace prayer might be used where "our" in "our Father" is me and the persecuting person or group and the daily bread is what is being contested (food, water, housing, safety, reputation, money, time, jobs, promotions, etc.). Here is the formula proposed in the conflict prayer model. Feel free to use it to develop your own skit.

Prayer skit formula:

The "our" in "our Father" can be a place-holder for any combination of "me" and the "one (or group) I am in conflict." So, that now switches from "the Father of me and people in general or my friends" to "the Father of me and the person I am fighting with now." And "our daily bread" becomes what "we are fighting over." The skit writer can take any conflict and substitute the people in the conflict with the "our" and "us" words and substitute what is being contested with the "daily bread."

Alternate Skit Scenario and Setting:

Skit Characters:

Write out quick four-scene skit:

Scene 1 conflict

Scene 2 resolution 1 (outward violence)

Scene 3 resolution 2 (inward violence)

Scene 4 resolution 3 (peace prayer anger switched to peace)

Psychological and emotional impact: The psychology of the Lord's Prayer as the prayer for the persecutor is interesting because the prayer becomes focused on the conflict that is the most motivating to the listener now. In effect, it (as the section in the beatitudes where it says "blessed are the sorrowful") takes the rough equivalent of their most important current or recent traumatic stress that is difficult to forget and uses it to help remember these key concepts.

The prayer begins with a focus on the conflict between the listener and the persecutor when it says "the Father of me and my persecutor." It provides hope in that the one being persecuted has a common connection with the Father who gives sunshine and rain on both the persecuted and the persecutor. Each phrase then logically builds on the listener's own conflict story. If the Father's rule of love and desire for loving relationships were done on earth as it is in heaven, the listener wouldn't be persecuted in the first place. Then, the persecuted is asked to take his common connection with the Father who sustains the life of the persecutor as an opportunity for blessing instead of a curse. "Give both me and the persecutor what we are fighting over." These are a series of memory enhancing concepts in that the listener is being engaged over their most motivating issue at the moment and applying it to something that comes across as very unusual or difficult, namely, loving an enemy even in prayer.

Psychological escalation: 1) "Give me and my persecutor our daily bread." Then the potential for greater memorable elements may come in. In considering this prayer request, the natural reaction might be, "why should I ask that this persecutor be given this blessing? He is a bad guy and does not deserve it. Furthermore, I might argue, if the persecutor already took my food, housing, money, or reputation for himself, he doesn't even need any of that since he has mine. All these further forces the listener to address his or her cause for understandable anger.

Emotional Judo Flip or Pivot: 2) "Forgive us…" My next objection about the phrase "forgive us" could be at least two-fold. First, I am the innocent victim here. I don't need any forgiveness; only that jerk of a persecutor needs forgiveness. But I don't really want that persecutor to be forgiven. I want that person "to rot in hell forever" after all he did to my family and me. At that moment, I might recall the words of Jesus just before the prayer request where he suggests that when we are angry with our brother (as opposed to angry because of our brother) we are guilty of murder. If I remember that, then Jesus has just accomplished an emotional judo flip on me, which is the most memorable of emotions. At the height of my anger, I realize that while I am internally railing at the evil of the persecutor hurting me, I myself have become liable of murder charges. And, if I am demanding that the persecutor not be forgiven, then I could be guilty of serial murder since I am desiring the repetitive murder or punishment of that person in hell over and over again. Suddenly, I am realizing that I, too, need forgiveness.

Grand Bargain: 3) "As we forgive…" Then, the grand bargain is about to begin. Forgive us both based on how we both forgive … Well, if I ask the omniscient God who knows my every thought and motive to accept me on the basis of how loving I am to this person I'd rather see dead right now, and he gives me a pop quiz right at that moment, how well would I score on that quiz? At the height of my anger, not very well. (The persecutor might not do that well since he started out angry and until seeing my own forgiveness may not realize his own unjust anger and actions against me.) Perhaps, that is why the next phrase is "don't lead me and my persecutor into that test" because if you do, we will fail and that the consequences of that failure would be great evil, namely, not being forgiven. And, I ask that we both be delivered from that.

Skit goals: One goal of this approach of the Sermon on the Mount is to have the audience consider this conflict management approach. The second is to consider conflict management versus debate as one of the ways Jesus is providing fishing lessons to the disciples highlighted in the prayer for the persecutor. If this is true, it provides a great anger management tool both for anyone who might otherwise feel compelled to 'even-the-score' with violence or foster a manic-inducing energy-sapping anger. It also provides a bridge between conflict management and peacemaking actions of followers of Jesus (and churches) and their intentional outreach programs.

A word about the interpretation of the Lord's Prayer—For those who need some justification for this use of the Lord's Prayer, this might be a quick help. Additional material follows at the end-note material, primarily ii-iv.

This approach to the Lord's Prayer is based on exegesis of Matt 5:44 concerning the prayer request of Jesus— "love your enemies … pray for those who persecute you" and proposes that instruction set for the prayer for the persecutors is the "Lord's Prayer" in Matt 6:9 and following. (*In essence, this approach proposes that the written text and its use as an oral teaching framework suggest that the material and its arrangement would make it easier for the listener to remember the material. It also suggests that the audience of Matthew 5-7 was the entire crowd most of whom were not disciples or followers of Jesus. This also suggests that anger and conflict management were not side issues for the early church but the very way in which the early church reached out to others and formed the core of the fishing lessons Jesus gave to his disciples as they experienced Jesus fishing for people among the crowds listening to the sermon on the Mount (Matthew 5-7.)*)[8] See the background material provided as endnotes below.[9] Matthew 5-7 can also be developed in a day-long or multiple session

---

8   **Essence of exegesis:** Immediately after the prayer request (in Matt 5:44) and just before the Lord's Prayer in Matthew 6:9 is a section of text that serves as a memory device (mnemonic) that weaves together two groups of three items to make it easier to remember them. (Two groups of three that are meaningful are easier to remember than 6 items that are less emotionally relevant.) Jesus had just said in Matt 5:16 after the beatitudes that his listeners should "let their light shine so that men might see their good works and glorify their Father..." They do that by being gentle, merciful and peacemaking. Yet in Matthew 6, starting in verse 1, Jesus asks that listeners don't do works of righteousness or justice before men. In Matthew 6 he talks about not giving alms, praying or fasting in public. Well, that sounds like a contradiction. Which way is it? Do works before men or not? First, this apparent contradiction arouses emotion and makes the material more memorable. Secondly, organizing 6 items in two contrasting groups of three makes it even easier to remember. Trying to figure out why do some works before men and not others takes analysis that makes the contrast more interesting and more likely to be remembered. In this instance, being gentle after experiencing harshness, being merciful after experiencing injustice and taking the risk of acting as a peacemaker after receiving peace based on a sacrifice all might be more authentic responses to conflicts not in our control while doing alms, prayer and fasting are altogether under our control as to when and where we do them. Doing good works where the situation is under our control could lead to our doing it for our own benefit and public relations program and not God's. Any kind of analysis like this helps us remember the two groups of three better than mere rote memory.

      As a memory device placed immediately after the request for praying for enemies, the writer of Matthew is in essence showing Jesus to have said, "before I tell how to pray for the persecutor, let me tell you how NOT to pray for the persecutor, namely, not to do it publicly as in alms and fasting. If one were to remove the comments about not doing this in public, the very next words after the prayer request for the persecutor comes the Lord's Prayer.

9   **Background Material on the Lord's Prayer as a Conflict Prayer**

      DRAFT—Update on the Missing Prayers and Guidelines in Matthew 5-6.

      What's missing? In Matthew 5:44, Jesus is recorded as challenging the crowds to love their enemies and pray for their persecutors. (If one loves and prays for the worst-case conflict, then it will be easier to love and pray for the less extreme cases. But, merely loving those who love us might not naturally extend to those we consider enemies.) So, how should those crowds go about loving persecutors—the ones intending to do harm? Commentators are unanimous, if they comment on this part of Matthew 5:44, that it is indeed a noble sentiment to pray for persecutors; however, they do not appear to notice any instructions that might go with such a prayer request. R.T. France is a current example of a leading scholar who claims the prayer for the persecutor and its instructions are missing. See France, *The Gospel of Matthew*, William B. Eerdmans, 2007, p. 226.

      A somewhat similar view is also mentioned by another contemporary scholar, Hans Dieter Betz, when commenting on the Lord's Prayer beginning at Matthew 6:9. (See Betz, *The Sermon on the Mount*, Fortress Press, 1995, p. 373 and related comments.) His observation is that this prayer that covers a range of topics does not appear to have any over-arching purpose or organizing principle in this context. Why do all these elements appear there? What are the connections or their common purpose? He does not find one and, in effect, declares that the Lord's Prayer has lost its way in that it does not appear to have a key purpose.

      So, we are faced with one prayer that is missing altogether along with its instructions in Matthew 5:44 and another in Matthew 6:9 that can't find its way, like a ship without a rudder or destination.

      Retracing our steps to finding the missing prayers: I think both can be found if the text is read with an understanding of how this written material was presented in a way that made it easier to memorize. When originally written, more than 13 centuries before the invention of the printing press, most of those who were literate could not afford to take home scrolls. They had to memorize the material first and then study it at home later from memory.

      Memorization was further enhanced when meaningful material evoked strong emotion, especially when it was applied to the most relevant issues of the listener, namely, their greatest current conflicts.

      Fishing lessons: These conflict prayers and conflict management approaches could be argued to be the very fishing lessons Jesus promised his disciples in Matthew 4 when he asked them to follow him and watch him fish for people. If true, Jesus was not only teaching in memorable ways, he was showing his disciples how to teach in memorable ways. (We may miss this if we are looking for traditional debating or sales methods.) The early Christians who were wishing to evangelize were not in a position to hand out papyrus Bible tracts to the crowds in an urban center nor provide scrolls to those in a catechism class to take home. They, instead, had to speak and teach their message in memorable ways, primarily in the context of their suffering and reaction to unjust treatment. What better way than to discover and connect to the listeners' drama or trauma that they care most about? The implications of the teachings in Matthew 5-7 would be that listeners were encouraged to consider their own stories of suffering and unjust treatment and consider gentle and loving responses instead of harsh or hateful responses. This active conflict management engagement appears to be the fishing lessons even though they do not appear to be debating methods.

set of classes[3] that would provide the time to go into the material in Matthew in greater detail.

Use of stories and skits: These stories can include true stories such as recent examples from victims of the holocaust in Germany, victims of apartheid in South Africa, to genocide in places like Bosnia, Rwanda and Sudan. They might also be examples from literature such as Les Miserable. Dr. Tom Boomershine, founder of the Network of Biblical Storytellers is creating a website showcasing examples of loving enemies.

We might consider collecting stories of conflict from all age groups and cultural settings and turning some of them into skits that youth can act out. The first scene would be the actual conflict event, such as bullying in a schoolyard.

For other examples outside of Matthew, compare the ways Matt 5 requests that those who react with gentleness, mercy and peacemaking are providing light that shows their good works before men who then give glory to the Father, to the request in I Peter 2: 12: "Live such good lives among the pagans that though they accuse you of doing wrong, may see your good deeds and glorify God…" Then, note the examples of suffering provided by Christ further developed in that Chapter, and then in Chapter 3:9: "Do not repay insult with insult but with blessing… " And; 3:15 "… always be ready to give an answer to everyone who asks you to give the reason for the hope that you have." Similar passages can be found in Philippians 2:1-11; Romans 12-13; James 2, 3:17-4:3; and the Didache (Teaching of the Twelve) quoted here for those who may not have ready access to it: Didache Ch.I:3 *"And of these sayings, the teaching is this: 'Bless them that curse you, and pray for your enemies, and fast for them who persecute you.'"* And then citing the Lord's Prayer of Matthew 5:9-13, *"As the Lord commandeth in his Gospel, thus pray…,"* Didache Ch. VIII, then says, *"Thrice in the day thus pray."*

My personal experience: In studying Matthew 5-7, in what has become known as the "Sermon on the Mount," I started to look for embedded memory techniques in my own quest to be able to memorize the material. I am one of the worst at rote-memory. I lack both the skills and patience to do it. In the process of doing pattern recognition to see what I might find, I discovered that the material is filled with a number of them beginning with the beatitudes in Matthew 5 and ending with the story of the crashing waves on a house at the end of Matthew 7.

The memory method inserted between the request to pray for enemies and the prayer itself: One memory method, not requiring mechanical repetition, that is especially relevant to the "lost" prayers and prayer instructions in Matthew 5-6, is a well-known memory method called weaving by some. You might notice that Jesus had previously said in Matthew 5:16 that his listeners should "let your light shine before men so that they might see your good works and honor your Father in heaven." Yet throughout Matthew 6, beginning with 6:1, he asks just the opposite. "Don't do good works before men or you won't get a reward from your Father in heaven."

Why that apparent contradiction? One reason is that it serves as a weaving technique to group three things he just taught in Matthew 5, namely, to be gentle, merciful and peacemaking with the three in Matthew 6, namely to give alms, pray and fast.

Matt 5:16	Do good deeds publicly	VS	Matt 6:1 Don't do good deeds publicly	
Matt 5:5	Gentle		Matt 6:2-4	Alms
Matt 5:7	Merciful		Matt 6: 5-15	Prayer
Matt 5:9	Peacemaking		Matt 6:16-18	Fasting

It is easier to remember two sets of three items than one group of six. That is especially true if you can inject meaning and emotion into the list. In this case, it is by setting up an apparent contradiction of three things to do before people as in Matthew 5 versus the three things one should not do before people as in Matthew 6.

The placement makes it easier to remember both sets of material and keep them in tension. But notice where and how the placement happens. First, Jesus asks that the listeners use their relationship with the Father—who gives sunshine and rain on them and the entity hurting them—as a blessing instead of a curse. "Love your enemies and pray for your persecutors." Then, Jesus sets up a little rabbit trail that serves as a memory device by saying, in effect, "but, before I tell you how to pray for your persecutors, let me tell you how NOT to pray for your persecutors." Don't do it in front of other people."

If the memory device is removed: If one were to take out the memory method injected immediately after the request for the prayer for the persecutors, that shows how not to pray while linking to the prior section of an opposing way to do works before people, then, the immediate material after that request to pray for the persecutors comes the Lord's Prayer in Matthew 6:9.

If that is true, then the instructions for how to do pray for persecutors are not missing. A sample prayer for persecutors is not missing. It is, in fact, the Lord's Prayer of Matthew 6:9. And, as a result, the Lord's Prayer is not a hodge-podge collections of prayer elements without a unifying purpose, but instead a thoroughly integrated prayer for those with whom we are in conflict.

If there is any doubt, one only needs to look at the one comment Jesus gives after the Lord's Prayer in Matthew 6:14 where Jesus, in effect, says, "so, if you forgive those who wrong you, then your Father will forgive you, but, if you don't forgive them, He won't forgive you."

The second and following scenes could be how one goes back home and considers how to react to the bullying. Revenge? Suicide? Prayer? Depending on the time allotted, a given skit could show alternative reactions in lesser or greater detail such as: (1) abused student goes back to school with a weapon to shoot the bully, kids who laughed and the teacher that didn't stop the bully, 2) suicide of the bullied child who will "show them" or seek ultimate peace in his self-destruction, 3) someone remembering the conflict prayer and saying it … possibly, arguing all the way but, ultimately coming into empathy with the bully.

The material about a given conflict might also give rise to a small group discussion, either those contemplating acting in the skit or those discussing it afterwards.

Example of "The Joke"

This is an art assignment given to a class of middle schoolers in Negaunee, MI. They had the full class time to create a drawing of their own on anything that they wished as long as the title would be "the joke." One child drew the following picture.

After looking at the drawing, what do you perceive is "the joke"? Why? What do you notice about the children on the right versus the child on the left? What are their emotions? Why?

The groups who discuss this might either collect examples of art or create artistic depictions of conflict.

Alternate Shorter Scene four

Light brightens (or actor pivots in another direction) ...

At home, sad, in room alone, opened Bible or Catechism item to Lord's Prayer, asking out loud,

"I wonder how this might work."

"Father, I just want to go to school and find some friends and have a good time, not be teased and hurt." So, Father of me and those people who tease me, Who is in heaven where everybody loves everybody all the time, holy and unique is your name. I know you can hear me, strong enough to help me, caring enough to want to help me. Your kingdom and rule of love come. Your will and desire for love come. On earth right here and now as in heaven. If it were, they wouldn't be teasing me like this and taking away my fun and friends."

Give me and those who are teasing me good times at school this coming day. Give me and the bullies safety from those who want to hurt us this day. Give me and the ones who call me bad names where people laugh at us and don't like us, —give us good names so the kids at school like us and are kind to us.

Forgive them for hurting me and forgive me for wanting to hurt them more. And forgive us based on how well we are forgiving each other. But don't give us a pop quiz right now to see how well we are doing because we might fail that test and that would not be a good thing. Deliver us from the result of failing to forgive."

Boy seems calm. Lays to rest. Light fades.

Endnotes

1   See scenario kernel matrix and the similar pattern of discussing third parties in the segments on legal treatment of murder and adultery in Mat 5.

2   "If God Should Speak," by Clyde Lee Herring, 1977, Broadman Press. Used subsequently in a number of publications (including Roman Catholic) that shows up in web searches.

3   **Program elements:** This program includes a set of discussions that could be a full-day seminar or a series of 6-8 classes that cover the biblical material and applies it to relevant conflicts within any given group. It could also be a single 1-2 hour summary session. Preferably there would be enough time given to hear the conflicts of those in the group rather than just listening to presentations of a class leader. (See the example of a video recording of a conflict discussion in Grenada of the Caribbean.) One of the discussions may include the watching or performing of short conflict skits highlighting examples of the Lord's Prayer as the conflict prayer. It might also include interviews of those who experienced considering it that way. The following material includes an overview of the text explaining how and why the Lord's Prayer may be used as a conflict management prayer. There are also examples of a conflict by art, skits and interviews of those in conflict.

Autobiographical Elements

Quick Overview of My Stake in Conflict Resolution
(response to request for personal background on conflict)

Occasion for Personal Conflict Overview

Tom, thanks for asking about an overview of my personal conflict experiences that have, at least indirectly, shaped my perspective on the conflict management passages of Matthew. It might also give me a chance to outline some items that I can pass on to my sons who started the process of asking me to tell them 1-3 minutes stories after which they interview me for additional details.

What I included in *The Lord's Prayer for Persecutors*:

I already shared the story of how I came to terms with the basic ideas of Matthew 5-7 while a secular child in Chicago in 1964-5. As you recall, when I was 12 and in eighth grade, I put together a scenario to try to walk through the various elements of Jesus stories where I imagined being the bully in the playground and discovered the child that I was bullying was God sneaking into the world in disguise as a little boy. I included that story in the preface of my draft resource book on *The Lord's Prayer for Persecutors in Matthew*.

In that book, I also included transcripts of interactive Bible discussions I led on Matthew 5-6 at the Lord of the Mountains Lutheran Church in Dillon, Colorado in June 2019. As we went around the room introducing ourselves on the first night, I disclosed my father's background as a Russian Jewish atheist who had forbidden me to know or meet his family when I first asked about them in 1960 when I was 9 years old at the birth of my youngest brother, Mark. That started me off on a personal quest to discover my father's family. That is a story in and of itself. When I was working in the NYC area in 1986, I was still looking for people with my last name in phone directories and finally came across one by calling directory assistance. There was only one that lived in my father's old Brooklyn neighborhood of Brighton Beach. When I called that number, it was the only time I came across a Manto anywhere in the country that was not Italian or Sicilian. That led to meeting my first cousin and his family, the first time I ever met anyone from my father's family and discovering that my paternal grandmother was still alive at 82. I was able to meet her a few months later in Miami Beach along with her brother and cousin then learned the back-story as to why my father was estranged. I also learned the depths of the holocaust that impacted that side of the family in and from Crimea that resulted in her brother becoming an atheist. She gave me a copy of pictures of herself when she was in her 20s, her mother, and her grandmother along with a copy of the childhood autobiography of her sister who had 13 children and chronicled her family history back into the late 1800s in Crimea and their years in Constantinople until their arrival in the U.S. just prior to 1930. I also got to attend family reunions where I learned about hundreds of relatives I never knew existed. Most importantly, my father was able to become reconciled with his mother after decades. Although they never met again in person, they took turns calling each other every weekend until she died a year later.

High School in Chicago, 1965-1969

Those family discoveries were in 1986-7. I skipped over some years and a lot that was not covered in those two life episodes. I should at least talk about high school starting with my freshman year at Lane Tech in 1965. My mother was happy when I joined high school R.O.T.C. (Neither of my brothers joined high school R.O.T.C., but both enlisted in the Air Force after high school. My brother Sam went on to college R.O.T.C., retired as a full colonel from the Army in special operations, then later retired as a lieutenant from the Chicago Police Department.) I learned later that my mother was glad that we didn't go out for high school football because of her well-kept secret of her family's involvement in extreme sports such as ski jumping that killed one of her cousins from the Bietila family. They are in the U.S. Ski Hall of Fame in part for being in the 1936 Winter Olympics in Germany (just before many of my father's cousins were wiped out in Crimea by the host of that same Olympics).

Moving from a Block North of Fullerton and Clark to a Block South of Belmont and Clark

In the middle of my freshman year (1965), our family moved from their small Lincoln Park neighborhood apartment over Francis's Deli on Arlington and Clark where my father worked as a short-order cook to a slightly larger apartment run by an absentee landlord in a not-so-nice pocket-ghetto at Fletcher and Clark Street (just south of Belmont). It was one of those buildings that was hastily remodeled after a fire and looked nice superficially. But we didn't always get heat in the winter because the building was one of only a handful with very old coal-fire furnaces left in the city. I would smell the smoke of marijuana wafting up to my third story bedroom from the smokers sitting out the front stoop, sometimes doing other drugs or showing off their handguns. There is a lot more to that neighborhood like an occasional drive-by shooting before that name got popular, but you get the idea.

After thinking through my imagined moment bullying God in the playground, I started attending church to learn more. By the end of my sophomore year, I got baptized, joined Belden Avenue Baptist Church at Belden Avenue and Halsted (a block south of Fullerton and across the street from McCormick Theological Seminary) and became the church janitor. I routinely worked my way around a lot of local distress and violence including the riot where McCormick was taken over by local Puerto Rican gangs protesting the shooting death of one of their members in the summer of 1968. I actually walked among the forming protest and gang members who had taken over the seminary preparing to march with loaded sawed-off shot guns that were wrapped by the gang banners they carried on short poles. I opportunistically decided to pass out Bible tracts to the onlookers in the neighborhood. That scared my fellow assistant janitor half to death but likely made for the most thoroughly read Bible tracts in the history of Chicago.

Bible College through Mid Junior Year (January 1972)

After high school graduation in 1969, I worked my first 100-hour week at age 17 by working one full-time 40-hour per week shift as the afternoon janitor at the 1540 North Lake Shore Drive condo building and another 40-hour night per week shift as one of its union elevator operators. My younger brother Sam would occasionally ride his bike to deliver a change of underwear to me at the end of my second shift so that I would not smell too badly when leaving directly from the job on Lake Shore Drive to one of my next of three part time jobs. I did that so I could pay to attend the premier Baptist Bible College of Pennsylvania (GARBC). I started an "Inner City Prayer Band" there and helped groups of these kids to do volunteer ministries in inner city DC and NYC. I spent every college year weekend of my first year or two helping in outreach at First Baptist Church in Manhattan at 79th and Broadway where there is still a painting hanging showing George Washington being baptized by immersion by one of the early pastors who served him as a chaplain. During the summers, I returned to Chicago to work. On the way to Bible College in my sophomore year, I took a train to meet a family in Indiana who offered me a ride there. While on the train I sat next to a pretty young woman who had a book in her hand on love authored by a Christian author named Drummond. She looked more intently into my eyes than any woman I ever met. I thought that she really liked me. We exchanged addresses and wrote that year and met the following summer. By my junior year she switched schools to go to the same school I attended and though I had to drop out in the middle of that year, we got married. Sometime before that summer, I learned that the reason she looked so intently at me was because she had an extreme eye focus disorder and had to stare to see me. It was not love at first sight, but first sight that led to love at some time long after. Such was my life. Just before that third year of college, I was thinking of dropping out to help make money for the family to move because the gun fights in front of the apartment building were getting more intense. But, before I could do that, they moved to an apartment on Sheridan Road near Touhy Avenue, a much nicer neighborhood almost near Evanston. So, I did not have to drop out but could attend school that third year.

U.S. Army, 1972-1974

Bait to Chaplain's Assistant, Switch to Military Police

I stayed in Bible College until the middle of my junior year when my money ran out and my draft number came up. To get in and out as quickly as possible so that I could get back to college, I signed up for a guaranteed two-year job as a chaplain's assistant. But, at the end of basic training at Fort Dix, I was told that the Army rescinded their part of the agreement and was sending me to Military Police and Correctional Specialist Schools at Fort Gordon, Georgia, instead. Apparently, some MPs who hated their stockade guard duty beat up one too many prisoners out west that included a friend of a congressman resulting in the Pentagon agreeing to take the next batch of recruits who scored more than a 100 on the IQ test and send them to these schools.

So, after basic infantry training, I completed MP school with honors, correctional specialist training and was then assigned to put prisoners to work in Ft. Hood, TX. Not being sent to Vietnam gave me confidence to get married then as opposed to waiting after my time in the Army. While there, I was able to take a couple of courses (logic and personnel management) in the early evening at Baylor University in Waco. I also requested and was allowed to hold a Bible study for prisoners in the stockade chapel on Sunday evenings on my own time.

Since I had just gotten married right before arriving at Fort Hood, I lived off-base in Copperas Cove just south of the base. I always drove to work early enough to never be late so I would be certain to avoid an AWOL (absent without leave) charge. So, I would stop by and hang out at the day room of the MP barracks next to the stockade where they had a pool table.

Winning Chaplain's Assistant Job through a High-stakes Pool Game

One morning, I challenged three aggressive fellow MPs (two from New York and one from Ohio who was a Kung Fu expert) to a game of stripes and solids. In a friendly way, I taunted the three of them first to a game if they thought they were good enough to take on high stakes. They asked what those stakes were. I told them that for every point I won over them, I could force them to read any verse in the Bible that I chose. They asked what they would get for every point they gained over me. I told them that they could force me to read any verse in the Bible that they chose. They laughed acknowledging that my bet amounted to "heads I win, tails you lose," but they took me up on it anyway. They had fun arguing with me over God issues during the game then called off the game early since they had to start off for their weekend trip to Dallas. I told them that they wimped out just like I predicted but said the game was not over yet because I was going to pray for them.

Less than two weeks later, a fellow MP asked me if I had heard what happened to the guys who went to Dallas. I said I did not, so here is what he told me. First, not long after the three guys left and started driving, they picked up a long-haired hippie hitchhiker near Waco that turned out to be a "Jesus freak" who continued the God discussion right where I left off. Then, when they returned to base, they learned that there was a drug-sniffing dog inspection of the barracks which turned up drugs in their bunks. So, now the guards became prisoners. The commandant of the stockade was obviously upset and demanded an explanation from them. They said that he had nothing to worry about because Chuck Manto had just converted them to become Christians, didn't do drugs anymore and became pacifists (likely hoping to get out of prison and the Army).

This shocked the commandant who knew he had given me permission to hold the weekly Bible study with the prisoners. Without talking to me, he assumed that I was converting his guards and prisoners to become pacifists or conscientious objectors. We already had at least one or two in prison who claimed to become pacifists and were doing time for being AWOL. He panicked and pulled up my personnel file to discover that I was promised a chaplain's assistant job. He promptly called up the top chaplain at Fort Hood and asked if they needed a really good chaplain's assistant because he had one that he wanted to highly recommend. Before I knew it, I had a two-day notice to begin reporting to Chaplain Major Harlan Confer who received a PhD from SW Seminary in psychology.

Road to Urbana and Psychology

He was a great guy to work with and influenced my decision to continue my college studies at the Psychology Department at the University of IL at Champaign/Urbana after my discharge. The officers liked my work and asked if I would like to get some special commendation. I asked if I might swap that for the use of "Project Transition" normally offered to troops for "on-the-job" training at a factory for a couple of months while on Army pay to attend the university, instead. Then, by doing that side-by-side with a three-month "early out" program for joining the Army Reserves for a year at a medical unit in Chicago, I could get to Urbana the day before the Fall semester. They agreed and I got to start one semester earlier than normal.

Reserve Job Protecting Psychiatrists,

In the Reserves, I was assigned the job of "psychological social worker technician." When I asked what that meant they said that it officially meant that I was an administrative aid for the psychiatrists, but that unofficially my real job was to be the psychiatrists' bodyguard to protect them from the trained killers who returned from Vietnam with anger management issues. In that role I got to work at two hospitals, Hines and Great Lakes. For my two weeks of summer duty, I got to go the hospital to Ft. Sam Houston in San Antonio.

While I attended Urbana for my B.A. in psychology, I tried to make up for lost time by taking extra courses in Russian, Greek, comparative linguistics (in Akkadian, Sumerian and Hebrew), and a couple of philosophy courses. In psychology, I was able to take some graduate courses including some independent research in personality assessment of aggression under Dr. Frank Costin that included some site-specific surveys of prisoners I arranged back in Fort Hood. I also was able to study "Integrity Therapy" under Dr. O. Hobert Mower who did work with Carl Menninger, who wrote "Whatever Became of Sin?"

I lived off-campus in a house I rented from a railroad worker on the North side of Champaign and attended the local Mt. Olive Missionary Baptist Church and sang in the Gospel Choir. I still remember the day when Jesse Jackson came to speak. I learned another aspect of the strife that went on in Champaign while I was in Chicago. That would be another story. Meanwhile, my wife Janis went to school, also, becoming a licensed practical nurse.

Grad School in Wheaton and Church History

After graduation I moved to Wheaton to attend a special year-long program called the Institute of Slavic Studies (ISS) sponsored by the Slavic Gospel Association to learn how to help churches behind the Iron Curtain. There I was able to study early church history and Russian Orthodox theology. I simultaneously signed up for a fulltime load at Wheaton Grad School so I could use some of my GI Bill benefits. I enrolled as a church history major under Dr. Earl Cairns and graded church history papers for Dr. Robert Webber who started off being a Baptist but became an Anglican with strong Orthodox leanings who also taught courses at ISS. My wife and I lived in ISS dormitory apartments. It was during that year in October of 1975 when my first son Jonathan was born. We signed up for natural childbirth classes, so I was able to be there at his birth, as I did for my other two sons.

Grad School at Urbana in Medieval History and Patristics

I was encouraged to go back to the University of IL to pursue a PhD in medieval history and patristics which I did at the end of the year after being accepted into a combined program. I was declared to be too poor for married student housing, so I found a house in a new development that I bought on a contract finance basis where the developer held the note with a balloon payment. That worked out well for us. (When we sold it, we were able to pay off some school loans and still have a down payment for the next house in Bloomington.)

There are many interesting stories to that transition into that first year that I won't go into now. One that I will mention is an initial "problems in medieval history" course where I had to read 20-40 books per week covering a hundred year period of a European country/area, write an annotated bibliography on them and a ten-page paper to show how they all integrated. At the time, I had an office I used as a graduate teaching assistant for Dr. Vernon Robbins who ran the Greek department at the U of IL before leaving to teach New Testament at Emory University. On Fridays of that first semester, I would hire my babysitter to help me sign out the 20-40 books from the 10 million volume university library. Then the following Tuesday, I would go to the office by 4PM and begin an all-night vigil speed reading all the books, writing the annotated bibliography and a draft of the ten-page paper. I would take an alarm clock to set at 1 AM so I would not fall asleep and a hot-water maker for tea. I would drink so much tea that if the caffeine would not keep me up, going to the bathroom would. By 7 AM, I would go home, shower, change and then head back to class with zero sleep. On Wednesday I would get a full night's sleep. On Thursday late afternoon, I would return to the office and work until 1 AM to turn my drafts into final product. In 1976/7, the most advanced technology I could use was a portable typewriter with erasable bond paper. By the middle of the semester, I could feel the fatigue and heaviness in my arms. Later, I would begin to feel tingling sensations in my skin across my chest and face. Three fourths of the way through the semester, I began to lose the ability to feel emotion. I would know when something sad or anxiety producing might happen, but I could not feel the emotion. Near the very end after three months, I started to dream while fully awake and knew that my self-imposed sleep deprivation caused me to begin to hallucinate. Fortunately, we came to the end of the course, and I could get my rest and recover. Ever since, if I get too tired, my body sends those tingling feelings to tell me to get more rest. We started the course with half master's level students and half at the end of their doctoral track. I was the only one at the master's level who did not drop out of the course. At the end I got a B. As I walked from the course with several of my classmates, I asked them how they managed to work through the course. hey laughed and said, "you tell us first." So, I did. Then I asked them to tell me. They said that they have been taking medieval history courses for the past three years, read all those books before and that this was just a refresher course before their comprehensive exams. "Oh, now I get it," I said as we chuckled together.

Interruptions from Family Violence and Conflicts

Near the end of the masters-level program, my parents had divorced, and my mother married a guy who was kicked out of the Chicago Police Department for alcoholism and mental illness of one sort or another. He enjoyed going to bars and picking fights, always packing a handgun in his sock. He would periodically beat my mother and youngest brother Mark who was just starting high school. One day he slammed my brother into a wall so hard that it made a head-sized hole through the plaster board. Mark ran away from home, and I had to go retrieve him from St. Louis and house him for a while until he decided to live with our father.

My mother would call and have me drive up the three hours each way on several different occasions to rescue her from her new husband Carl. On the third occasion, they had moved to his apartment over a bar in the Northwest suburbs. She called saying that it was getting serious, that she got kicked in the head and was bleeding pretty badly. I said that I would come and pick her up but that she would need to pack a bag of important items so that she would not have to go back. I told her that once I picked her up this time that it would be the last time I do it. If she were to go back again, I would leave her to die. She agreed and so I drove up to get her. This was in 1976/7 before the age of cell phones.

After getting off the phone with me, Carl asked who she talked to and the details about the conversation. Being under his control and terrified, she told him the details of our plan. He then proceeded to describe to her precisely how we would murder me when I arrived. He would surprise me when he opened the door, knock me down the straight two flights of stairs, get to the bottom, break my neck and claim that it was an accident.

I knew that he was trying to get a job as a deputy sheriff in that county and did not think he should have that kind of authority. So, I decided to stop by the sheriff's office on the way. I let them know that I was about to intervene to keep my mother from getting beaten further or getting killed but that they were welcome to come with me and learn a little about the guy who was applying for a job with them. They thought that was a good idea and followed me over in their squad car. When Carl opened the door for me, he appeared to be a little surprised to see me with a deputy next to me. My mother grabbed her things and joined me. This and related interventions contributed to my need to take an incomplete for my final semester.

We moved to Bloomington, IL, so that we could be close enough to Urbana to finish my incomplete but find a couple of jobs to help pay off some of the bills. That is where my second son Michael was born in 1978. Meanwhile, I worked selling insurance, retirement plans and securities while working as an interim pastor at a rural American Baptist Church and taking occasional courses at Northern Baptist Theological Seminary or neighboring Bethany Theological Seminary. I fondly remember a church conflict resolution course taught there by David W. Augsburger. So, I did not complete the final semester until 1979.

Starting First High-tech Company in Chicago

Soon afterwards, I moved back to the Chicago area to be closer to my parents. I also took another bi-vocational senior pastor job at Mont Clare Baptist Church in Chicago near Elmwood Park where we took an apartment. As in Bloomington, I worked bi-vocationally in ministry and as an all-lines insurance broker and NASD Series 7 Representative. During that period, my wife became unhappy being a "pastor's wife" and I needed to back off and just make some more money to pay off school bills, so I eased out of that position. I finished my incomplete course and Master's in 1979.

I was frustrated by the lack of tools needed to help consumers offset the information barrage that came from the financial industry but was encouraged by the rise of a personal computer industry. Personal computers were just emerging from Convergent Technologies, Apple and Dell, software from Microsoft, and mass storage devices from Iomega. So, I invented some mass storage subsystems for desktop computers to integrate them together, started Comptech, Inc in 1981 and developed them with the help of some of my clients that were outstanding electrical engineers from the U of IL. That was my first foray into invention, high-tech startups, patents and angel investment. Fortunately, my securities background and certification as an NASD series 7 registered representative provided me with enough securities law to help me raise money without getting into trouble with legal mistakes many make raising money. Eventually, my computer company work took more and more time and I did less and less in the financial arena. It was around that time when my youngest son Jason was born in Chicago.

Multiple Ways to Resolve Conflict

In addition to law enforcement, ministry and conflict interventions, technical and financial innovation are other ways of resolving conflict and meeting needs. It provides the opportunity to take the conflict resolution stories inherent in the story of Jesus and what is going on in the Gospels and apply it to life between Sundays. I often asked from my 20s, how does the view we hold on the person and work of Jesus impact how we work? What difference does it make in how we do technology, whether its finance, science or engineering, applied to communications, power, health care, sanitation or food production? Can we create a theology of anything or everything? I did that in a way by creating a communication model, a capitalization model and a management model based on these core ideas that could be applied to any type of conflict. One would need to review my CV or brief version on LinkedIn to see more of those aspects of my professional life and how I did that, including work with venture capital and investment banking firms (when I discovered my father's family), leading economic development work for Marquette County, MI where my mother grew up and doing work in Industrial Defense Conversion in the former Soviet Union (1993-1996).

Conflict Resolution and the Peace Breaker, Peace Maker, and Peace Faker

All of these experiences likely drew me into being anger-shy and conflict-averse not wishing to hurt the feelings of one I was in conflict and often protecting myself at the same time. It has subsequently made me wonder when in trying to avoid being a peace breaker, whether was I being a peacemaker or a peace-faker. In my studies of the prayer for persecutors and reconciliation, I have revisited the entire process of forgiveness and reconciliation to the point of restoration so that I can more critically view my own willingness to attempt or encourage complete resolution that looks a lot like either Matthew 5:23-26 or Matthew 18:15-17.

Turning Things around In the Next Generation

This rough overview illustrates the complex life of conflict that impacted me within the family, neighborhood or country in my generation and the ones that went before. There are more such stories, but that might be enough for a start. Fortunately, my three boys are doing well. As I write this, I am sitting at a desk of my oldest son Jon's temporary apartment provided him by the State Department as he trains to serve our embassy in Baku, Azerbaijan as a physician's assistant. (He previously served in the Peace Corp in Malawi.) He will be there by mid-September. [*Within less than a week of his arrival, the country went to war on September 27 with Armenia over their border region Nagorno-Karabakh.*] His wife Val, daughter Josie (age 9) and son Will-Tait (age 7) will join him at or just after Christmas break. Fortunately, Azerbaijan issues travel visas so I should be able to visit them if my security clearance does not get in the way. My youngest son Jason, who did a year-long Fulbright in China, several summer stints in Cameroon and China, and six years with an NGO (One Acre Fund) in Rwanda just completed his Nurse Practitioner program at Yale and passed his board exams last month. He did some work on a Covid-19 floor at Yale University Hospital and will start his job a clinic near New Haven by the end of the month. My middle son has likely led the most adventurous and dangerous life but is likely in the safest position of the three now processing Medicare claims for Aetna from his home in Frostburg, MD.

Well, I hope this is enough for a beginning response to your interesting request for my background. Let me know what else I should share that might be of help.

Discussion Questions

Matthew 4

For discussion:

1) What might be the significance of the description of those in the "valley of the shadow of death?" The meaning of "living, sitting or dwelling" there?
2) How might that be a way to describe the "crowds" and the message about to be delivered to them?
3) What is the significance and importance of the challenge to professional fishermen to "fish for people?" and what might "fishing for people" mean?
4) How might "fishing for people" tie into the core message of Matthew and its conclusion at the end of the Gospel where the disciples are asked to make disciples?
5) What evidence do you see in these texts that provide a working definition for key words such as "crowds," "fishermen," and "disciples?"
6) How might disciple making relate to the Gospel of Matthew as a whole?
7) How might disciple making relate to the general concept of persuasion or rhetoric?

Matthew 5

For discussion on the beatitudes:

1) What evidence provides a working hypothesis of who the crowds were, the stresses they endured and the extent they would have lost hope?
2) What evidence indicates the nature of the teaching of Jesus and the setting in which he taught?
3) How do the blessing pairs describe emotionally escalating conflicts?
4) What is the significance of the shift from being "pure" in heart to being "purified" in heart?
5) How does the person find "purification?"
6) How does the purification lead to peace instead of anger or resentment?
7) How does the resulting peace connect to the complimentary blessing of "blessed are the peacemakers?"
8) What are the implications for how someone becomes a peacemaker?
9) What are the implications for making new "peace-making" disciples?
10) What might be the connections between peacemakers and persecutors?
11) What evidence do you see in the text, either in English translations or Greek, for working definitions of "meek" or "gentle," "righteousness" or "justice," "pure" or purified," "persecuted?"

For discussion on the salt and light passage:

Using the material above, including the chart,
1) How might the designation of salt or light apply to the crowds?
2) How might the designation "not losing its saltiness" or "light hidden" apply to the crowds?
3) How might pairs be discussed and taught as memorable units such as "peanut butter and jelly?"
4) How might the application of being salt or being salty tasting, or light seen versus light hidden emphasize the paired nature of the beatitudes and provide insight as to how one becomes salty tasting and light giving?
5) At what point does the member of the crowd transition to becoming a disciple?
6) What implications might there be for the designation of "theirs is the kingdom of heaven?"
7) Later, how might the identification of who "*theirs* is the kingdom" be applied to the Lord's Prayer section in

Matthew 6, the ask, seek and knock prayer in 7, and the "depart from me I never knew you" comment in 7, the house built on the foundation of sand or rock in 7, and the unforgiving servant in 18?
8) How might these passages be applied to current events in the news?
9) How might these passages be applied to conflicts known primarily by the study group?

For discussion:

1) What might be the connections between the various statements of "the kingdom of heaven?"
2) What is the importance of having or entering "the kingdom of heaven?"
3) What might be the connections to the promise of showing the professional fishermen of Matthew 4 to become "fishers of people?" How does this theme continue to grow?
4) What is the significance of having "righteousness (or justice)" exceed that of the scribes and Pharisees? How might that be and how might that be accomplished?
5) How might Jesus be pressing those who feel sufficiently righteous towards a consistency that will show up their inconsistency which might result in their also becoming "poor in spirit" and in need of "purification?"

For discussion:

1) Are the links between actions and thought reasonable to the listeners? And, if so, what might be the ramifications for their sense of being in need of purification or forgiveness?
2) What may be the significance of shifting from being angry to having someone being angry with you? What might be the persuasion of teaching significance of the switch?
3) How serious is the issue of someone being angry with you?
4) What is the significance of being pursued and taken to court?
5) What passages after this section also discuss being taken to court or being pursued?
6) What might have been the consequences of being taken to court according to this passage, the one in Matthew 5:38 discussing "eye for an eye" or 5:40 being sued?
7) What are the objective criteria for succeeding at an out-of-court settlement?
8) How might those criteria inform our attempts at communication in conflicts that might avoid a break in a family, work or community relationship or a need to go to court?
9) What were the consequences of having to answer to the king in 18:23-35?
10) What are contemporary examples of being taken to court or pursued?

For discussion:

1) What is the significance of the range of conflicts in this section compared to the conflicts of the crowd from Chapter 4 until here? To the conflicts after this section until the end of Matthew?
2) What are implications of the legal system for compensatory damages in this era ("eye for an eye") compared to our own?
3) How might the context show how the word "enemies" was used and how does it compare to how we tend to use the word now? What were "persecutors" and how might it have been distinguished from "enemies?" How is that similar or different from use today?
4) What are the relationship dynamics of being pursued for compensatory damages with the use of the word "persecutors?"
5) How is "loving enemies and praying for persecutors" positioned as the climax of the entire sermon (5:1 and following) to this point?

6) What are the range of conflicts, losses and debts under consideration?
7) What are the ramifications for conflict engagement, forgiveness, and reconciliation?

Matthew 6

For discussion:

1) What might be sample conflicts addressed in the Lord' Prayer?
2) How might these examples substitute "our" and "us" with oneself and the person or group causing the conflict and substituting the "necessary bread" with what the conflict is over?
3) How might the initial conflicts reveal related secondary or tertiary problems that result from the primary conflict?
4) Questions that might follow could include: how might these bring a sense of peace, solidarity with the one causing the conflict, and the options for eventual peacemaking attempts suggested in Matthew 18?
5) How might the concept of "forgive (release) us AS we forgive (release)" relate to the extent we forgive and restore relationships?
6) How might the use of this prayer be used as a disciple making tool?
7) How would you compare the conflict progression in the beatitude pairs with the pattern in the Lord's Prayer?

For discussion:

1) How central or important is the concept of conflict, forgiveness and restoration in these passages of Matthew 5-7 and 18?
2) What differences might there be in seeing how we forgive others as either causative or indicative of our own forgiveness and entry into the kingdom of heaven?
3) What do these passages suggest are the objective criteria used to discover whether we fully forgive someone?
4) What implications are there for attempting reconciliation have for the concept of feedback loops in communications that might avert conflict in the first place or resolve it in the second place?
5) What might be examples and ramifications of forgiving partially and not fully?
6) How might the concept of "forgive us AS we forgive" illustrate these ramifications and a working definition of "forgive?"
7) When might there be reason to forgive and attempt restoration but hold back actually restoring a connection when it is not safe to do so?
8) How might the "ask, seek, knock" prayer in Matthew 7 be used to reflect the Lord's Prayer in Chapter 6 and especially in the section on how not to make disciples?
9) What might examples of full or partial forgiveness look like in the circumstances of those in this discussion group, those we know or examples from history?
10) How might a parable of the half-forgiving servant be relevant or not in various conflict scenarios? See the outline of a potential alternative parable for an example.

For discussion:

1) Does the release of the debt constitute half forgiveness when he still fires the servant and does not want his presence on the job?
2) Given reconciliation discussions in Matthew 5 and 18, what objective criteria might be used to establish

due-process, and restoration of the relationhip?
3) How would thorough conversations using that objective criteria make it possible maintain a relationhip in the first place and avoid breaking it?
4) What would Jesus say to us who half-forgives by releasing obligations but keeps us the other at a distance? Would he say, "depart from me?"
5) From the passages here, why or why not?
6) In what ways might the beatitude pairs leading to peacemaking be used as an evangelism or disciple-making method?
7) In what ways might the Lord's Prayer for persecutors be used as an evangelism or disciple-making method?
8) What are the steps or stages of each of these and how might they be used to provide a pathway to that shift to peace, forgiveness, entry to the kingdom of heaven and the encouragement to do the same for others?
9) How might these approaches to disciple-making be successful in an otherwise hostile environment and even with a hostile audience?
10) How might the prayer for the worst-case enemies, the persecutors, work in the worst of times in Matthew 24?
11) How might these methods be empowering as the disciples find themselves dispersed among the nations as in Matthew 28:16-20 even as some wavered in confidence?
12) What other questions come to mind that might be added to the discussion?

Letters from Readers

From: Steve Kramer <stevekrrt@gmail.com>
Subject: The Lord's Prayer in conflict resolution
Date: August 28, 2020 at 11:40:53 AM EDT
To: Chuck <chucklmanto@gmail.com>

Chuck,

I am continuing my "deep dive" into your writings in hopes of gaining a better understanding of Matthew 5-7 and how it relates to your personal struggles as well as to all of our struggles. I hope that what I have written provides you with a better understanding of me personally and my spiritual quest. It is often painful to look back and reflect on the trials and tribulations I have gone through. I can see through sharing your life's experiences that you have had much to overcome and conquer too. Thank you for being transparent and exposing the painful realities you have been through. It makes it easier to understand that we are not alone in our sufferings. Jesus gave the ultimate sacrifice by giving his life and his blood so that we all may be given forgiveness. He suffered more than any of us could ever imagine. So in the end we are going to make it through all of this and live to love another day. Thank you for sharing your knowledge and perspectives and for inviting me to participate in your project.

With much thanks and heartfelt gratitude,
Steve

Chuck,

It was a great surprise for me when I learned of your ongoing perseverance, commitment, and devotion to a life of the gospel after knowing you for years through our common interest in promoting COG. Last summer when I was living in Avon, Colorado you were simultaneously leading classes at The Lord of the Mountains Lutheran Church in Dillon, CO. I was nearing the end of my five-year journey of self-rediscovery that culminated in my retirement from 35 years as a Respiratory Therapist in Los Angeles. During this time, I lived and worked at Sage Memorial Hospital for six months in Ganado, Arizona on the expansive Navajo Indian Reservation. It was a very lonely and oppressive environment but the land and the people intrigued me. I have always been interested in history and lived a short walk away from The Hubble Trading Post. I almost felt as though I had been transported back to a bygone time.

This was an ideal place to reflect on things and come to grips with the realities of what my life had become. It was a mystical and magical place where the spiritual presence was real and powerful. Whether you worshipped one of the many Gods and Goddesses the Navajos believed in or you were saved by Jesus, there was a feeling of intense peace and harmony there. The Native American's are poly-theistic, yet most Navajo families attended one of the half dozen or so churches in Ganado. Still, I elected to do all my praying from home there as I had done for most of my life.

Extreme poverty, desperation, and hopelessness were the norm there. But for me it helped to put things into perspective and to feel less sorry for myself. My misfortunes paled in comparison to the everyday struggles of the Native Americans. If misery loves company, then I was in the right place. But I didn't want to be miserable anymore, so I began to get closer to God and Jesus, again, personally and on a more spiritual level.

I traveled north to Washington and spent my final 3 months of my career in healthcare at Wenatchee Hospital in Central WA. My fingers and toes were beginning to contract involuntarily and I discovered I needed a hip replacement. I had to retire and go on disability as I couldn't physically keep up with the fast pace required to work effectively in a hospital anymore.

I returned to Los Angeles and went through one of the most difficult years of my life. Our 20 year old son Matthew was having drug abuse problems and I spent my time taking him to therapy or to the hospital ER. He ended up in Narcanon, a rehab facility in Ft. Collins, CO. My wife and I had been having marital issues for years before and my return home wasn't the solution to resurrecting our damaged relationship that we had hoped for. The relationship I had with my father deteriorated because I was vocal about expressing my unwillingness to approve of his emotional and psychological abuse of my mother and the wrong signals he was sending to his 3 daughters and the grandchildren with his behavior. He disinherited me from the family trust and made sure my three sisters would never talk to me again before he passed away. I felt as though I had lost everything and felt as though my life had been a waste and there was little reason to continue living. Everything seemed hopeless and that I was helpless to change my destiny. I was alone, desperate, depressed, and at a point in my life that I never imagined I would be.

I felt trapped and thought that leaving California and moving to Colorado close to where my son was in rehab would give me time to sort things out and put my life back in order. It was at a time where I felt a spiritual awakening in me, and I felt a need to get closer to God. I started attending Sunday services at The Calvary Chapel in Edwards, CO. I was welcomed by Pastor Nate and the congregation but I felt somewhat out of place because of my belief in "conspiracy theories" and my lack of faith in the governments ability to see our greater good.

My life could be characterized as bittersweet. I have been more than fortunate to have had the experiences that I've had in too many ways to count. But I have carried around a lot of pain, resentment, and misery throughout my entire life. This has manifested itself in my occasionally losing control and having anger, animosity, and hostility towards total strangers as well as people I love. It has taken a toll on my own personal health and well-being in addition to damaging the feelings of others I never intended to offend or hurt.

For most of my life I would simply blame others for my unhappiness. When I recognized that I had a personal responsibility for my own happiness and that I had choices in the methods of resolving conflict, I had more control over the way I felt. I could choose a spontaneous and hostile response when persecuted or provoked that usually had a less than desirable outcome or I could make a conscious decision to shift and divert the negativity of the experience to a more positive one and to feel better about the outcome.

The end result could still be something other than the outcome I may have been hoping to achieve but the manner in which I feltmentally and physically at the conclusion of an unpleasant experience was still something I could regulate. The consequences of irrational or emotional responses to persecution or provocation can have profound and long-lasting effects on the nature and the course of our life. Impulsive, reactive, decisions made resulting from the antagonistic or threatening behavior into our personal space physically or verbally will generally not serve our best interests.

I have always admired the basic simplicity of the Christian philosophy. The idea that the Son of

God was sent here, to our world and ended up dying on the cross for all of our sins. But we could be redeemed, get salvation and forgiveness, avoid the lake of fire, the depths of hell, and if judged to be fit, earn a place in Heaven with God himself and to live forever without the earthly pain and suffering so common to many of our earthly inhabitants. It sounded like a good deal to me. And all I had to do was to be a good person, ask for forgiveness, be sincere in my beliefs and my actions, and to follow Jesus. I don't take this agreement lightly. I am sincere in my beliefs and convictions. I am trying to be a better father, husband, citizen, human, and person. I am trying to think in terms of Christian values, morals, and interventions, and use what I learn for practical applications in my life. It's a "flying by the seat of my pants" approach but it's been working for me so far throughout my life. Or maybe not so much, but I'm trying to improve on a shaky foundation and incorporate more discipline and tradition with more conventional methods into my regular practices. And besides I still have more to do and contribute before I'm done. If God is willing.

The more of your draft that I read, the less I feel that I know. I'm in awe of the amount of knowledge you have and your unique perspective on things. The manner in which you have crafted such a useful resource manual for anyone of any intellectual level or ability. The way that you have beautifully woven together elements of your own life and struggles with such vivid clarity, depth, and humanity. I have a difficult time putting it down when I pick it up, finding myself reeled into the fishing lesson. But you have dissected, categorized, analyzed, and scrutinized so much information from every possible angle that I am humbled merely by reading your impressions and perspectives. What could I even offer or contribute that could positively impact your readers or to give them any more understanding than the many considerations you have already laid out for our exploration?

The gift that you have given us Chuck is a useful tool to be able to diffuse and derail many confrontational situations we may find ourselves thrust into. If we too can also learn to turn the other cheek by not only forgiving our confronters but to actually pray for them as well then we are following Jesus by being more like him. By visualizing and reciting The Lord's Prayer it serves as a catalyst for me to shift a negative thought or behavior into something divine. It allows us to put love into perspective in a split second and to forgive others as Jesus has forgiven us and to pray for his love to be blessed onto our enemies as we would wish onto our own beloved.

For me this line of thinking serves to help promote my own health and well being by keeping my cauldron on a low simmer and enabling me to mentally and physically de-escalate emotionally charged interactions through something as simple and as truthful as The Lord's Prayer. If more of us utilized this technique in these divisive and turbulent times it could be responsible for helping to lower global warming by a few degrees. We all need to chill out a little more and to exercise real tolerance for our fellow man. With everything so polarized and divisiveness being the norm it's more important now than ever to find more positive and productive methods of resolving conflict and channeling aggression. What could be easier than saying The Lord's Prayer and feeling the love, thankfulness, forgiveness, and gratitude it resonates, and for being a Christian.

I am grateful to have met you Chuck and it's a great privilage to have you ask me to help you with this project of yours. I am honored that you have asked me how I utilize The Lord's Prayer in my personal struggles and in conflict resolution. I'm not sure if I have fulfilled your expectations for that but I have attempted to open myself up to you and give you some insight into how I came to try and get right with God and Jesus and how I am continuing to follow the right path towards living a better life and dying a better death when my time comes. I am truly grateful for everything God provides us with and for the wisdom and comfort I feel when reading the Bible. You are a great inspiration and an encouragement to me and I am thankful that our paths have crossed and that the Lord's light that you shine for him illuminates my path and my life and gives me hope for a brighter and more enlightened future. You are someone who I will always treasure knowing Chuck. Because you are not judgmental and you see the real good in people and that you encourage others in their quest with seeking Jesus and the love of Almighty God. I am enjoying and appreciating your writings. You are helping me to be a better person and motivating me to be a better servant of Christ and The Lord. I pray that I continue to have you in my life and that we can both look forward to better times ahead and to continue to spread the good word of God and Jesus. Thank you for all you do and for having faith and love in me. It means a lot.

With Much Gratitude,
Steve

Time to Abandon the Tower of Maslow?

(See various depictions of the tower of babel in paintings such as the one from Cornelis Anthonisz 1505 – 1553 *The Fall of the Tower of Babel*; https://www.artbible.info/art/large/619.html)

Draft Article Concept—

Our culture continues to be influenced by untested and unscientific assumptions outlined in Maslow's Hierarchy of Needs. This phenomenon is evident in each of eight archived Aeon articles that refer to the "Hierarchy." See: https://aeon.co/search?q=maslow

The proposed article seeks to address the "hierarchy" as false on its face and briefly provides alternatives that prioritize relationships over physical and financial priorities.

"Relationships Come First—Maslow's Hierarchy of Needs Contradicts the Facts of Human Existence"

by Charles Manto

Some of the most capable and caring government leaders gathered this past several years to plan for potential disasters that would impact the safety and well-being of the American public with a particular concern for its essential infrastructure and resources. A leading academic in related planning was brought into an initial discussion through an interactive video connection setting the stage for an unusual discussion of the how the future of infrastructure security might look like over the next 25 years. The academic presented Maslow's Hierarchy of Needs to show the importance of their work since everything else in life, whether relationships or self-actualization of every person depended on the establishment of biological, physiological and physical security that in large measure was provided by the infrastructure and resources the group was attempting to secure.

However, the very meeting that discussed the hierarchy demonstrated the weakness of that model in that the relationships of those attending that meeting and how they communicated was what would produce the safety outcomes. In this case, it appeared that relationships produced biological and physical security and not the other way around.

Despite widespread misgivings, and limitations of "Maslow's Hierarchy of Needs," academic, government and business leaders continue to use it. In this case, it was used to encourage the group, in other cases it might be used to subtly validate new projects in terms of the process they are proposing backed by accepted and indisputable "scientific truths."

The "hierarchy" has taken various forms over the years, even as presented by Abraham Maslow himself. An article by Saul McLeod on the website SimplyPsychology.org. outlines the history of the development and use of Maslow's hierarchy of needs. The portion of the model that focuses on what someone does to become self-actualized to their highest potential has seemed to produce the greatest benefits. But even in his model, self-actualization appears to emerge from relationships though that was based on physical needs first. Yet the model itself could be used to show how relationships may need to be sacrificed for the more necessary need for biological and physical security. The potential negative impact on industry and the workplace has been capably described by Kira Lussier in the *Aeon* article, "The dark shadow in the injunction to 'do what you love,'" https://aeon.co/ideas/the-dark-shadow-in-the-injunction-to-do-what-you-love. Each of the articles appearing in Aeon quoting Maslow's hierarchy of needs assumes its continued broad acceptance despite occasional misgivings or limitations. This is despite articles in 2018 such as, "Why Maslow's Hierarchy of Needs Is Wrong" by Anne Marie Vivienne and the 2014 book it reviews, *Social: Why Our Brains Are Wired to Connect*, Lieberman and *The Village Effect: Why Face-to-face Contact Matters*, by Susan Pinker.

https://www.thehousejournal.org/articles/2018/8/3/why-maslows-hierarchy-of-needs-is-wrong

> "Maslow's famous Hierarchy of Needs tells us that humans, in order to survive, first need food, shelter, and warmth. He claims that these human needs are the foundation of a pyramid that leads to self-actualization. However, UCLA professor and social neuroscience researcher Matthew Lieberman argues that Maslow got it wrong. Food, shelter, and warmth are not the foundation of our human needs."

In his book *Social: Why Our Brains Are Wired to Connect*, Lieberman

Note the "hierarchy" image used in the May 29, 2012 online Forbes article by Steve Denning "What Maslow Missed," reviewing Pamela Rutledge's 2012 article in *Psychology Today* entitled "Social Networks: What Maslow Misses," (November 2011).

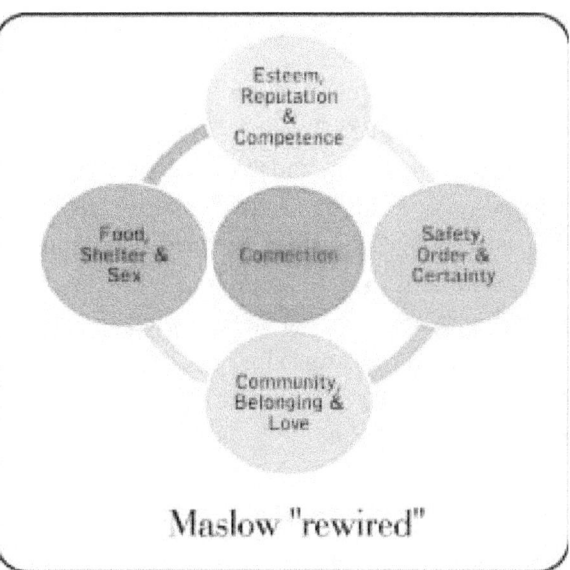

Despite the usefulness of Maslow's hierarchy of needs as a richer model than a mere reductionist version of behaviorist psychology at the time, I get increasingly concerned over its continued use since I have first learned about it in college psychology classes at the University of IL at Urbana in the 1970s.

In his final book published in 1971 by Viking Press, *The Farther Reaches of Human Nature*, underway before his untimely death in 1970, Maslow emphasizes his overarching desire to create "the Good Man" and the "Good Society" (p. 19), quoting scientist Alvin Weinberg for creating those terms. Despite his best intentions and his humble way of presenting his ideas on self-actualization with caveats such as "I plan to discuss ideas that are in midstream rather than ready for formulation into a final version" (p.41), Maslow's model does not seem to help his own cause. Instead, the "hierarchy" appears to be counter-factual, counterproductive, and ultimately self-destructive whether for a team-based project, a company, a community program or a marriage. Maslow's model begins by denying all we know both scientifically and socially about becoming human in the first place or ultimately excelling in our most creative and productive moments. The model starts with physical needs and eventually results in relationship and self-actualization. Aside from the obvious point that we need to exist in order to survive or thrive, I assert that Maslow's model has it inside-out. Both from a scientific and spiritual perspective, that is simply not what being human is in essence. To do otherwise can actually be dehumanizing. Instead, more would say that the core of being human, the beginning of the hierarchy or the pyramid if there is one, is relationship. (I would prefer a hub and spoke where relationships are at the hub like the one in Denning's article. Perhaps, we can come up with a better visual.)

Every human's existence begins with a relationship of a man and a woman whose sperm and egg join together. Up until that moment, there is no human. From the moment the sperm and egg "team up," the joining that springs from a relationship begins forming a new entity from that relationship. From that moment it continues only in the life-support system of the mother's womb which constitutes a relationship between that fertilized egg and the mother throughout the various stages of development, including the fetal development of its own brain. The new human grows until it emerges in birth, not to be discarded and told, "come back in ten years," but nurtured by parents, family and others until such time as that new human can begin the process of interdependent activities that can lead to more independence. But the very existence of the human from the first nanosecond of its existence is grounded in relationship. Then, the ability of that human to make reasonably independent contributions of its own is further grounded in relationship. Even the greatest individual creative achievement can be motivated by the concern for others rather than self-absorbed selfishness. In fact, it may be argued that the most compelling individual creative thoughts may emerge from a creative mind that had its origins and ongoing ability to think, create and be challenged in the context of a human community. It might also be argued that many of the most compelling original thoughts come from a complex system of thinking that results from interacting with that complex human community.

Ultimately, this is not merely a semantic triviality. Whether or not someone values another may drive what happens in a project or a marriage. The willingness to listen and verify that the messages are being communicated may depend on the motivation to value and maintain an interpersonal connection. That can be difficult and requires courage and the motivation of a maintained and growing relationship. Whether that happens may mean the difference between losing a valued customer, employee, friend or spouse. Thinking that relationships and the work it takes to maintain them can wait until after we get physically and financially secure—which could possibly take years—might cause us to miss the relationship potential that could lead to the very physical and financial security for which we may unnecessarily sacrifice our relationships.

Glimpsing at the research:

While there are the proverbial "chicken and egg" discussions regarding correlations between the lack of physical resources and the impact on relationships and social capital, or the impact of the lack of relationships and social capital on physical well-being, the fact that these connections are crucial cannot be denied. It will be interesting to review research to see what might turn up. Meanwhile, ask yourself whether you believe that you and the success of your family, company and community are better served by prioritizing relationships or not.

> (For an example of the impact of communications and relationships on recovery after a disaster, see articles such as: **"Communication, Sense of Community, and Disaster Recovery: A Facebook Case Study"** Douglas Paton* and Melanie Irons,
> School of Psychological and Clinical Sciences, Charles Darwin University, Darwin, NT, Australia; Front. Commun., 25 July 2016 | https://doi.org/10.3389/fcomm.2016.00004
> For an example of the role of relationships and mental distress in an impoverished community, see: Social Capital and Mental Distress in an Impoverished Community by Carey Usher Mitchell and Mark LaGory, first published on 28 June 2008, by "City and Community," https://doi.org/10.1111/1540-6040.00017)

Another way to consider or model the true nature of humanness is even older than these articles. It is through a millennia-old concept of human meaning, as depicted through the model of the development of relationships in the phrase from Deuteronomy 8:3, "man does not live by bread alone but by every word that proceeds from the mouth of God." This suggests at least a parallel need for relationship. The first chapters of Genesis portray humans as created in relationship from and with God in the context of an earthy and cosmic environment. Furthermore, the first dehumanizing event happens when the humans decide to suppress or trade their relationship with God in order to gain God's stuff—the data that could come from partaking of the fruit of God's tree providing knowledge of good and evil (without permission).

The moment we (Adam and Eve) sacrifice our relationship with God in order to acquire the stuff of God, we dehumanize ourselves in the sense that we give up or deny our core of relationship and declare that it is secondary to the stuff. When we in effect tell God that we prefer his stuff to a relationship, we place God's stuff above God. That is known as "idolatry." (In effect, Maslow's Hierarchy of Needs is also "idolatrous.") And from that moment, as we do the same with each other and say in effect, "I don't really want you, I prefer your stuff," we are committing "covetousness." We dehumanize ourselves whenever we value the stuff of another above the relationship. In effect, Maslow's Hierarchy of Needs promotes "covetousness" and its resulting selfishness and narcissism.

In the story of Genesis, it is implied that the worst possible outcome would be to be trapped in an eternal state of getting stuff over relationship and then experiencing absolute and eternal loneliness, alienation and isolation. God, in mercy and love, pushes the humans out of the garden before that can happen into a harsh environment including death that can only be survived when the humans form relationships and teams, and thereby, recover the essential human essence of relationship in order to acquire the stuff and safety needed for survival. So, as in the ancient story, and in the beginning of every human everywhere, we are essentially human because of our relationships. Our physical security and the ability to live at all and grow so that we might contribute to the physical and emotional well-being of others all derive from relationships. That holds true for our most unique contributions. All other paths are dehumanizing. Yet dehumanization is what we do and strive for when we follow the path of Maslow's hierarchy of needs that fails to be grounded in relationships. That dehumanization misses the key components of creativity that can be motivated by love and our relationships with others. In a wealthy and privileged world, we may delude ourselves into thinking how independent we are and how lucky we are compared to those who can barely survive and may not ever hope to achieve "self-actualization." On the other hand, the poorest of the poor are the ones who depend on relationships to make it possible for them to survive at all.

Would you prefer to begin a project with team members who say that the success of the project is more important than the customers that the project serves? Would you prefer a marriage to someone whose ideal concept of a perfect marriage is built on what makes for a great connection financially instead of relationally?

As young people the world over postpone creating families until they finish their education and begin their careers, they may be losing the opportunity to develop their education and careers with their spouses. Many of those lose their most productive childbearing years while trying to establish their physical and financial security first. As practical as that may be on one level, that love might motivate the creative capabilities that conceive a new and productive thought and follow it through with persistence to an amazing success. Each step in the creative process may, in fact, be more capably achieved by embracing relationship first, rather than putting off relationship until we establish physical and financial security. Of course, in establishing a household, project or new company, physical and financial security needs to be considered. But does that physical and financial security lead to relationship or start there? That depends on the kind of marriage, project or company you want—one that is human or dehumanized.

In a time of Covid-19 and the killing of George Floyd, might it be helpful to consider the resilience of relationships alongside if not ahead of our concern for the resilience of our infrastructure? It might just be time to abandon the tower of Maslow and find other ways to honor his productive life and reputation.

Chuck Manto

SCRIPT Reading and Speaking Exercise

Try to read the block text below quickly. Then try to read it out loud. What do you do to help yourself do it comfortably? What implications might there be for how this was conveyed to others either by writing or audibly?

Note how reading a written passage without spaces between words might inadvertently change the meaning of a text. For example, in the last lines of the script above, see the last line: "THATMIGHTMEANTHATAFORGOTTENMESSAGEFROMJESUSONPRAYERAND**LOVEISNOWHERE**. Note the last few words could either be: "love is now here" or "love is nowhere". When copying or translating into another language, it can be seen how such a variation could be made. See the example of an ancient text from the early to mid 300's from Matthew 6.

THISISASAMPLEOFASCRIPTWRITTENWITHOUTPUNCTUATIONORSPACESBETWEENWORDSORSENTENCESITCERTAINLYSAVESSPACEWHENTHEPRICEOFPAPERISHIGHANDABILITYTOPAYFORITISMINIMALIFYOUWEREREADINGTHISSLOWLYOUTLOUDITMIGHTNOTBETOOHARDBUTITWOULDBEDIFFICULTIFYOUWERETRYINGTOSPEEDREADTHISQUICKLYBUTTHATISNOTLIKELYWHATYOUWOULDDOIFYOUWEREHEARINGTHISMATERIALORIFYOUWERETRYINGTOMEMORIZETHEMATERIALINORDERSPEAKITTOOTHERLISTENERSIMAGINEDOINGTHISFORMANYPAGESATATIMEANDTRYINGTOWRITESOMETHINGINTHEFIRSTPLACETHATWOULDCAPTUREATTENTIONANDMAKEITEASEIRTOREMEMBERMEMORIZERECITEORDISCUSSIMPROVISATIONALLYWITHOTHERSYETITCERTAINLYHELPSTOHAVEAWRITTENDOCUMENTTORECALIBRATEWHATISBEINGMEMORIZEDANDSHAREDWITHOTHERSITHELPSIFITSMOREMEMORABLEINTHEFIRSTPLACELIKEKNOWINGWHYWHATYOUARESAYINGISLIKEEATINGAPEANUTBUTTERANDJELLYSANDWICHOUTSIDEWHILEITISRAININGCATSANDDOGSWITHYOURSOCKSANDSHOESSOAKINGWETSOWHATWEREYOUEATINGANDHOWWASITRAININGANDWHATHAPPENEDASARESULTWELLYOULIKELYNOWKNOWTHECOMBINATIONOFWHATYOUWEREEATINGANDTHEANIMALSUSEDTODESCRIBETHEEVENTANDTHRERESULTBECAUSEOFTHEMEMORABLEPAIRSINTHEFIRSTPLACEIFTHERESTOFTHISWASSOPOETICALLYARTICULATEDINAMEMEMORABLEFASSIONITWOULDHAVEMADETHISWHOLEEXERCISESIMPLERANDMORECOMPELLINGPATTERNSTHATWEMIGHTMISSMAYHAVEBEENOBVIOUSTOTHOSELOOKINGFORORALLINKSTHATMIGHTMEANTHATAFORGOTTENMESSAGEFROMJESUSONPRAYERANDLOVEISNOWHERE

OR, TO MAKE IT EASIER IN TWO COLUMNS:

THISISASAMPLEOFASCRIPTWRITTENWITHOUTPUNCTUATIONORSPACESBETWEENWORDSORSENTENCESITCERTAINLYSAVESSPACEWHENTHEPRICEOFPAPERISHIGHANDABILITYTOPAYFORITISMINIMALIFYOUWEREREADINGTHISSLOWLYOUTLOUDITMIGHTNOTBETOOHARDBUTITWOULDBEDIFFICULTIFYOUWERETRYINGTOSPEEDREADTHISQUICKLYBUTTHATISNOTLIKELYWHATYOUWOULDDOIFYOUWEREHEARINGTHISMATERIALORIFYOUWERETRYINGTOMEMORIZETHEMATERIALINORDERSPEAKITTOOTHERLISTENERSIMAGINEDOINGTHISFORMANYPAGESATATIMEANDTRYINGTOWRITESOMETHINGINTHEFIRSTPLACETHATWOULDCAPTUREATTENTIONANDMAKEITEASEIRTOREMEMBERMEMORIZERECITEORDISCUSSIMPROVISATIONALLYWITHOTHERSYETITCERTAINLYHELPSTOHAVEAWRITTENDOCUMENTTORECALIBRATEWHATISBEINGMEMORIZEDANDSHAREDWITHOTHERSITHELPSIFITSMOREMEMORABLEINTHEFIRSTPLACELIKEKNOWINGWHYWHATYOUARESAYINGISLIKEEATINGAPEANUTBUTTERANDJELLYSANDWICHOUTSIDEWHILEITISRAININGCATSANDDOGSWITHYOURSOCKSANDSHOESSOAKINGWETSOWHATWEREYOUEATINGANDHOWWASITRAININGANDWHATHAPPENEDASARESULTWELLYOULIKELYNOWKNOWTHECOMBINATIONOFWHATYOUWEREEATINGANDTHEANIMALSUSEDTODESCRIBETHEEVENTANDTHRERESULTBECAUSEOFTHEMEMORABLEPAIRSINTHEFIRSTPLACEIFTHERESTOFTHISWASSOPOETICALLYARTICULATEDINAMEMEMORABLEFASSIONITWOULDHAVEMADETHISWHOLEEXERCISESIMPLERANDMORECOMPELLINGPATTERNSTHATWEMIGHTMISSMAYHAVEBEENOBVIOUSTOTHOSELOOKINGFORORALLINKSTHATMIGHTMEANTHATAFORGOTTENMESSAGEFROMJESUSONPRAYERANDLOVEISNOWHERE

See this segment of Matthew 6 in book (codex) form from Codex Sinaiticus about 325 -375 A.D. (reproduced with permission from the British Museum Library)

Status of Global Christianity, 2019, in the Context of 1900–2050

Year:	1900	1970	2000	Trend % p.a.	mid-2019	2025	2050
GLOBAL POPULATION							
1. Total population	1,619,625,000	3,700,578,000	6,145,007,000	1.20	7,714,577,000	8,185,614,000	9,771,823,000
2. Adult population (over 15)	1,073,646,000	2,311,829,000	4,295,756,000	1.53	5,734,949,000	6,168,588,000	7,689,005,000
GLOBAL CHRISTIANITY BY TRADITION							
26. Total Christians, % of world	34.4	33.2	32.3	0.07	32.8	33.2	35.5
27. Affiliated Christians	521,307,000	1,117,440,000	1,888,111,000	1.30	2,414,698,000	2,600,912,000	3,342,666,000
28. Roman Catholics	266,263,000	658,556,000	1,025,922,000	1.02	1,243,532,000	1,305,290,000	1,599,608,000
29. Protestants	133,274,000	251,656,000	422,423,000	1.61	571,926,000	616,454,000	861,617,000
30. Independents	8,859,000	95,692,000	297,666,000	2.19	449,424,000	512,411,000	712,435,000
31. African	40,000	17,531,000	76,313,000	2.37	119,019,000	137,263,000	198,476,000
32. Asian	1,906,000	16,265,000	95,054,000	2.79	160,230,000	186,483,000	280,081,000
33. European	185,000	8,222,000	16,275,000	1.99	23,670,000	26,873,000	36,392,000
34. Latin American	33,000	9,129,000	29,301,000	2.29	45,053,000	52,108,000	76,256,000
35. Northern American	6,673,000	44,014,000	79,775,000	1.20	100,084,000	108,125,000	119,089,000
36. Oceanian	22,000	531,000	950,000	1.94	1,369,000	1,559,000	2,142,000
37. Orthodox	115,481,000	142,139,000	256,737,000	0.58	286,395,000	291,745,000	304,139,000
38. Unaffiliated Christians	36,448,000	112,007,000	99,359,000	0.71	113,597,000	117,869,000	124,261,000
39. Evangelicals	80,912,000	105,599,000	234,210,000	2.19	353,677,000	399,950,000	581,065,000
40. Pentecostals/Charismatics	981,000	60,944,000	453,934,000	2.26	693,820,000	794,474,000	1,089,199,000
CHRISTIAN FINANCE (IN US$, PER YEAR)							
61. Personal income of Christians	270 billion	4,100 billion	18,000 billion	6.54	60,000 billion	70,000 billion	190,000 billion
62. Giving to Christian causes	8 billion	70 billion	320 billion	6.24	1,010 billion	1,200 billion	3,400 billion
63. Churches' income	7 billion	50 billion	130 billion	6.09	400 billion	480 billion	1,400 billion
64. Parachurch and institutional income	1 billion	20 billion	190 billion	6.33	610 billion	720 billion	2,000 billion
65. Ecclesiastical crime	300,000	5,000,000	19 billion	6.97	68 billion	80 billion	260 billion
66. Income of global foreign missions	200 million	3 billion	18 billion	6.63	60 billion	70 billion	190 billion

https://www.gordonconwell.edu/center-for-global-christianity/wp-content/uploads/sites/13/2020/12/Status-of-Global-Christianity-2021.pdf

Status of Global Christianity, 2021, in the Context of 1900–2050

Year:	1900	1970	2000	Trend % p.a.	mid-2021	2025	2050
GLOBAL POPULATION							
1. Total population	1,619,625,000	3,700,578,000	6,145,007,000	1.19	7,875,465,000	8,185,614,000	9,771,823,000
2. Adult population (over 15)	1,073,646,000	2,311,829,000	4,295,756,000	1.50	5,878,250,000	6,168,588,000	7,689,005,000
GLOBAL CHRISTIANITY BY TRADITION							
26. Total Christians, % of world	34.5	33.2	32.4	-0.01	32.3	32.5	35.0
27. Affiliated Christians	522,440,000	1,112,655,000	1,889,808,000	1.21	2,432,007,000	2,543,469,000	3,303,112,000
28. Roman Catholics	265,756,000	658,556,000	1,025,102,000	0.95	1,250,319,000	1,286,883,000	1,551,403,000
29. Protestants	134,196,000	251,901,000	429,180,000	1.56	593,660,000	624,924,000	895,056,000
30. Independents	8,859,000	89,480,000	284,439,000	1.60	396,991,000	422,968,000	621,855,000
31. Orthodox	116,199,000	141,930,000	257,741,000	0.62	293,599,000	296,858,000	312,133,000
32. Unaffiliated Christians	35,906,000	116,654,000	99,159,000	0.65	113,572,000	117,105,000	117,996,000
33. Evangelicals	80,912,000	111,809,000	270,635,000	1.80	393,545,000	420,870,000	620,963,000
34. Pentecostals/Charismatics	981,000	57,637,000	442,677,000	1.89	655,557,000	703,639,000	1,031,500,000
CHRISTIAN FINANCE (IN US$, PER YEAR)							
57. Personal income of Christians	270 billion	4,100 billion	18,000 billion	5.08	51,000 billion	54,000 billion	70,000 billion
58. Giving to Christian causes	8 billion	70 billion	320 billion	4.75	848 billion	1,000 billion	2,300 billion
59. Churches' income	7 billion	50 billion	130 billion	4.68	340 billion	400 billion	900 billion
60. Parachurch and institutional income	1 billion	20 billion	190 billion	4.81	510 billion	600 billion	1,400 billion
61. Ecclesiastical crime	300,000	5,000,000	19 billion	5.22	55 billion	70 billion	170 billion
62. Income of global foreign missions	200 million	3 billion	18 billion	4.96	49 billion	60 billion	120 billion

Section 3: Appendix

Bible Manuscript and Greek language resources:

Greek alphabet chart compared to English discussing several different ways to pronounce it: https://web.mit.edu/jmorzins/www/greek-alphabet.html.

Greek alphabet Wikipedia article: https://en.wikipedia.org/wiki/Greek_alphabet

Koine Greek introductory explanation: https://lrc.la.utexas.edu/eieol/ntgol

See the numerous digital resources including Greek and Hebrew classes available in Accordance software: https://www.accordancebible.com

Photo of page of Matthew 6:4 and following from Codex Sinaiticus © and licensed for reproduction to Charles Manto by The British Library Board (Codex Sinaiticus, http://www.bl.uk/manuscripts/Viewer.aspx?ref=add_ms_43725_f202v)

NOTES

NOTES

NOTES

NOTES

NOTES

www.ingramcontent.com/pod-product-compliance
Lightning Source LLC
Chambersburg PA
CBHW082035230426
43670CB00016B/2663